THE VARIETIES OF TEMPERAMENT

A PSYCHOLOGY OF CONSTITUTIONAL DIFFERENCES

by

W. H. SHELDON, Ph.D., M.D.
HARVARD UNIVERSITY

With the collaboration of

S. S. STEVENS, Ph.D.
HARVARD UNIVERSITY

HARPER & BROTHERS PUBLISHERS
NEW YORK AND LONDON

CONTENTS

TABLES

vii

FIGURES

PREFACE

THE hope, or the faith, which lies behind this book is about as follows: If human beings can be described in terms of their *most deep-seated* similarities and differences, it may prove not impossible to differentiate between heredity and the effects of environment. This differentiation, if achieved, would provide the needed leverage for an attack on many social problems, ranging all the way from vocational guidance and military specialization to the isolation and elimination of cancer, and a psychology built around this attack might play that useful rôle in social life which has so long been expected of psychology.

We accept the thesis, therefore, that psychology may rightfully be charged with the task of trying to identify and measure the *elemental or primary components* of human variation. And the series of books in which the present volume is the second may be regarded as one small effort to fulfill this obligation. The first volume (*The Varieties of Human Physique*, Harper & Brothers, 1940) deals mainly with what may be called the statics of the subject —in the sense that physical structure is relatively fixed and static. The present volume deals mainly with behavioral dynamics and with the interrelations between the static and dynamic levels of personality. We had, in fact, originally intended to label this second volume *Physique and Temperament*. Taken together, the two volumes describe the principal tenets of what we have called a constitutional psychology—so named because the primary concern is to describe and interpret the most deep-seated pattern, presumably the constitutional pattern, of the individual personality. Since we have found in most personalities an identifiable pattern of basic components expressed at both static and dynamic (structural and functional) levels, we are led to presume that constitutional analysis may be both feasible and useful.

A third volume will present the results of a recent application of constitutional psychology to the diagnosis, and to some extent to the vocational redirection, of one hundred delinquent or mal-adapted young men. It is hoped that another, less imminent volume will shed light on the problem of constitutional predisposition to disease (constitutional medicine).

Much of the work underlying the two introductory volumes was carried out at the University of Chicago, and some of it at Wisconsin, although both books have been written at Harvard. The project as a whole has now extended over more than a decade, and so many people have contributed to it, in one way or another, that even to list their names would be difficult. Possibly the heaviest debt is owed to those hundreds—even thousands—of young men and women who have submitted patiently to what must have seemed to them an inexhaustible curiosity.

Dr. Stevens has collaborated in the general editing of the manuscript, as well as in the development and formulation of certain of the procedures, and some of the later experimental work has been carried out under his direction. Dr. W. B. Tucker and Dr. C. W. Dupertuis have collaborated in some of the statistical work. We are grateful to Dr. Earnest Hooton not only for critical readings of the manuscript at various stages but for general encouragement and support, and we are similarly indebted to Drs. E. G. Boring and G. W. Allport. Dr. Bryant Moulton has kindly collaborated in some of the experiments.

A portion of the necessary financial aid has come from Mr. and Mrs. Elmhirst of Dartington, England (William C. Whitney Foundation). Miss Geraldine Stone and Miss Margaret Joralemon have assisted materially in the statistical and technical preparation of the present volume.

W. H. S.

Cambridge
December 1, 1941

THE VARIETIES OF
TEMPERAMENT

CHAPTER I

INTRODUCTION AND SUMMARY

TRADITION has it that fat men are jolly and generous, that lean men are dour, that short men are aggressive, and that strong men are silent and confident. But tradition is sometimes wise and sometimes stupid, for seldom does it distinguish between the accumulated wisdom of the ages and the superstitions of ignorance. Especially as regards physique and temperament have the conclusions of careful students been contaminated by the stereotypes of the street and by the dogmatism of the side-show phrenologist. But if we ignore these last and ask only about the opinions of the scholars, the writers, and the artists we find a persistent tradition that the shape of a man promises certain traits in his temperament.

Scholars have sometimes set off physiques and temperaments into *types*. Hippocrates may not have been the first to systematize his observations regarding the dependence of personality on morphology, but he long ago set forth a scheme that has reappeared under various forms in repeated generations. The writers and the artists establish their typologies more by implication than by argument and statistics. They cast their characters by rules mostly unexpressed, but seldom if ever do they put the temperament of a Falstaff into a lean and wiry body, or paint the face of a Scrooge as apple-cheeked and rolypoly.

Now our present concern is not with the traditions of history, except in so far as they suggest that those who have scrutinized people have seen certain resemblances and certain differences, and that various traits of character sometimes pair off with aspects of bodily structure in a way that holds out a hope against chaos and a promise of scientific order. But, since a hope and a promise do not make a science, our present concern is with techniques of inquiry. How shall we observe men, classify them, and measure

1

them? How shall we learn to tell them apart, not as Jim and Joe but as kinds and types of animals? In short, how shall we proceed if we are to ignore superficialities and fasten attention on the basic, first-order variables of a science of individual differences?

WHY INDIVIDUAL DIFFERENCES?

It does not take a science to tell that no two human beings are identically alike, but it does require the discipline of systematic inquiry to give, in terms of scales and categories, a useful description of individual differences. The basic dimensions of human variation are not always obvious. But, granted that there are such things as first-order factors affecting human differences, why should we bother ourselves to discover them? Why, when our usually acknowledged scientific aim is to seek out the generalities contained in the laws of nature, should we be diverted toward the problem of exceptions and differences?

The answer is simple enough. The statement of a scientific law is complete only to the extent that it can account for individual differences. To illustrate, let us consider a simple law of physics. The falling apple gathers speed as it descends. In fact its velocity is very nearly proportional to the time during which it has fallen. The observation that this is true of many different objects leads to a simple generalization relating velocity and time—Galileo's law of falling bodies. But suppose we drop a feather instead of an apple. The feather drifting lazily to earth suggests at least that individual differences among falling bodies are not to be ignored, and we begin to suspect a certain incompleteness in our previous generalization. We have neglected to state for what conditions— for what parameters—the law is true. Here the study of individual differences leads us to correct the equation for falling bodies by a term relating to the size and shape and weight of the object.

We learn from this simple example the importance of parameters —the conditions attached to the operation of a law. In "human engineering," where we can seldom write simple equations for any part of behavior, the importance of parameters is quite as crucial. We learn the laws of a certain disease: bacteria enter the body and multiply at the expense of the host. But in some bodies they do not multiply. Obviously a full understanding of the disease demands an explanation of such individual differences. Emotional upsets, we discover, lead to personality difficulties. But equivalent upsets leave some persons quite as happy and stable as before. How shall we understand the effects of traumatic experiences if we ignore this variability? And so with almost everything from physiological functions to human learning—the *kind* of individual involved enters as a parameter in our laws.

A plea for the study of individual differences, then, becomes a plea for the recognition of parameters.

In this book we present a system for treating the problem of individual differences in terms of what appear to be basic components of temperament. These components in turn are tied back to and interpreted in terms of basic components of morphology. The emphasis is upon constitutional factors, upon the relatively stable qualities of a man which give him his basic individuality. In such an emphasis there is always a danger of creating a wrong impression regarding the relative importance to personality of nature and nurture, or of heredity and environment, those two concepts that have so often split scholars into factions. The study of constitutional differences need in no wise depreciate the effects of environmental influences—nor ought the study of environmental factors to neglect the parameters of individuality. The matter may be resolved by a proper phrasing of the problem. We may ask, "What are the effects of culture (or environment or learning) upon temperament (or personality or attitudes)?" Or we may ask, "What are the effects of different types of 'nurture' upon various aspects of behavior *for persons of differing constitutional endowment?*" The importance of putting the question in this latter form is expressed by the old saying, "What is one man's meat is another man's poison."

STATICS AND DYNAMICS IN PSYCHOLOGY

Constitutional psychology seeks a basic taxonomy of human beings. It asks for a frame of reference against which individuality may be set off and classified and scaled—a frame of reference simple enough to be comprehensible, yet full enough to account for most of the variety of human differences. Since the complexity of human beings makes it advisable to subdivide the problem in such a way that separate attacks can be made at different levels, we have attempted to devise both a taxonomy of structure and a taxonomy of function.

But function itself can be regarded as divisible into levels extending all the way from physiological functions and locomotion to such things as the expression of political beliefs, and it is hopeless to probe all these levels at once. Consequently we have limited the present study to the level called temperament. The level of temperament, like any level of investigation, has no sharp boundaries to mark it off unequivocally from its neighboring regions, but by temperament we shall mean, roughly, the level of personality just above physiological function and below acquired attitudes and beliefs. It is the level where basic patterns of motivation manifest themselves. But for an adequate operational definition of temperament we must refer the reader to the scale of temperament presented below (Chapter III). This scale is the best ostensive definition of what we mean by temperament.

A taxonomy of structure was developed in a previous volume, *The Varieties of Human Physique* (Harper & Brothers, 1940). That study of the size and shape of human beings, expressed in terms of three basic morphological components, constitutes the *statics* of constitutional psychology. Pursuing the analogy further, we may regard the study of temperament as *dynamics*. The study of statics in the field of psychology is the study of the balance among the components comprising the morphology of man at rest. Dynamic psychology, then, is the science of man in motion. When structure takes on function, when man gets up and moves around, expressing his desires and motivations and interacting with his fellows, then he becomes a dynamic organism. And the study of his behavior in its more elemental manifestations is the part of dynamics called the science of temperament.

Viewed in this fashion, physique and temperament are clearly two aspects of the same thing, and we are not surprised if we are led to expect that the dynamics of an individual should be related to the static picture he presents. It is the old notion that structure must somehow determine function. In the face of this expectation it is rather astonishing that in the past so little relation has been discovered between the shape of a man and the way he behaves.

Of course it is possible that there is no such relation. But it is also possible that the relation is definite, although concealed in complexity, and that it is only to be disclosed when we shall have learned to choose the proper variables for our studies. As later chapters will show, there are dynamic and static variables which correlate sufficiently highly to reaffirm our faith in the possibility of a useful science of constitutional differences.

The problem of this volume, and of the earlier work on human physique, is mainly the problem of variables—the search for basic factors. The outcome of the search for basic dynamic components of temperament is told in later chapters, but before proceeding to them let us first indulge in a bird's-eye view of the constitutional project as a whole.

A SUMMARY

Chronologically the studies of temperament, which are here for the first time published, were begun before our morphological investigations were undertaken. The reversal of this order in publication is merely for logical reasons: it has seemed wise to follow the medical precedent of beginning with anatomy, and since the reader may not be familiar with the earlier work (*The Varieties of Human Physique*) we shall first outline the morphological studies.

The Primary Components of Morphology

Having failed in several efforts to arrive at a useful morphological taxonomy through anthropometric techniques alone, we very early came to the conclusion that in order to set up the framework of such a taxonomy *ab initio* it would be desirable to scrutinize a large number of physiques all at one time. Photography not only would make this possible, but also would permit us to see each physique from as many directions at once as might be desirable. Accordingly a procedure was adopted in which the individual is photographed in a standardized posture from the frontal, lateral, and dorsal positions on a single film.

When four thousand photographs were assembled in one place, so that they could be arranged experimentally in series, it was found that a certain orderliness of nature could be made out by the unaided eye. Certainly there were no "types," but there were obvious dimensions of variation.

The first problem, then, was to determine how many dimensions or components of structural variation could be recognized. The criteria we employed in seeking "primary structural components" were two: (1) Could the entire collection of photographs be arranged in an ascending (or a descending) progression of strength in the characteristic under consideration, with agreement between experimenters working independently? (2) In the case of a suspected new component of structural variation, is it, upon examination of the photographs, found to be impossible to define this apparently new component in terms of mixtures, regular or dysplastic, of the other components already accepted? Application of these two criteria revealed the presence of three primary components of structural variation, and we were unable to find a fourth structural variant that was not obviously the result of a mixture of the three.

To arrange the entire series of four thousand along each of the three accepted axes of variation was relatively easy, not only for the body as a whole but also for different regions of the body separately (thus providing a method for the ultimate measurement of dysplasia). The distributions for the body as a whole were then scaled tentatively by the method of equal-appearing intervals, and we had at hand a rough approximation to the general patterning of a continuous tridimensional distribution that was true to life. This was not yet an objectively defined distribution, but the first step toward meaningful objectification had been taken. We now had a fairly good idea of what could most profitably be measured, and were ready to make use of anthropometry.

The second problem was to find such anthropometric measurements as would, (1) most reliably reflect those obvious differences in physique that anthroposcopic inspection had already shown to be present, and (2) refine and objectify these differences so that precise allocations of physiques on the tridimensional distribution could be made. Such measurements were selected by trial and error. It was found that the measurements most valuable for the purpose were certain diameters expressed as ratios to stature, and that most of these diameters could be taken with needle-point dividers from the film more accurately (more reliably) than from the living subjects, provided the photographs were posed in a standardized manner.

The question of how many such diameters to use is simply the question of how precisely accurate an allocation is desired. In dealing with groups statistically, we scale the strength of each of the primary components on a 7-point scale. For this purpose a minimum of seventeen diameter measurements is adequate for determining what is called the *somatotype*. In the detailed analysis of an individual, more precise differentiation may be made by using a greater number of measurements.

In order more readily to determine the somatotype from a series of measurements, a machine was constructed into which the measurements may be entered. The manipulation of switches then discloses the correct somatotype. This machine, as at present constructed, may be used for the somatotyping of any male individual in the age range of 16 to 21.

The somatotype is a series of three numerals, each expressing the approximate strength of one of the primary components in a physique. The first numeral always refers to *endomorphy* (see below), the second to *mesomorphy*, and the third to *ectomorphy*. Thus, when a 7-point scale is used, a 7-1-1 is the most extreme endomorph, a 1-7-1 is the most extreme mesomorph, and a 1-1-7 the most extreme ectomorph. The 4-4-4 falls at the mid point (of the scale, not of the frequency distribution) with respect to all three components.

As these components occur in nature they are single, continuous variables. The designation of the somatotype merely serves the purpose of bracketing a physique within certain defined boundaries. When the somatotype is determined, analysis of the physique is only begun, but the somatotype provides the basis for a morphological taxonomy that is both comprehensive and statistically manipulable. The bugaboo of types disappears in a continuous distribution in which every physique has a place, and the establishment of norms becomes a routine.

Now for a description of the static components:

When *endomorphy* predominates, the digestive viscera are massive and highly developed, while the somatic structures are relatively weak and undeveloped (see Fig. 1). Endomorphs are of low specific gravity. They float high in the water. Nutrition may vary to some degree independently of the primary components. Endomorphs are usually fat but they are sometimes seen emaciated. In the latter event they do not change into mesomorphs or ectomorphs any more than a starved mastiff will change into a spaniel or a collie. They become simply emaciated endomorphs.

When *mesomorphy* predominates, the somatic structures (bone, muscle, and connective tissue) are in the ascendancy (see Fig. 2). The mesomorphic physique is high in specific gravity and is hard, firm, upright, and relatively strong and tough. Blood vessels are large, especially the arteries. The skin is relatively thick, with large pores, and it is heavily reinforced with underlying connective tissue. The hallmark of mesomorphy is uprightness and sturdiness of structure, as the hallmark of endomorphy is softness and sphericity.

Ectomorphy means fragility, linearity, flatness of the chest, and delicacy throughout the body (see Fig. 3). There is relatively slight development of both the visceral and somatic structures. The ectomorph has long, slender, poorly muscled extremities with delicate, pipestem bones, and he has, relative to his mass, the greatest surface area and hence the greatest sensory exposure to the outside world. He is thus in one sense overly exposed and naked to his world. His nervous system and sensory tissue have relatively poor protection. It might be said that the ectomorph is biologically "extraverted," as the endomorph is biologically "introverted." Psychologically, as we shall see later, these characteristics are usually reversed—the ectomorph is the introvert, the endomorph is *one type* of extravert.

The digestive viscera (dominant in endomorphy) are derived principally from the endodermal embryonic layer. The somatic tissues (dominant in mesomorphy) are derived from the mesodermal layer, while the skin and nervous system, which are relatively predominant in ectomorphy, come from the ectodermal embryonic layer.

The anthropometric measurements used to determine the somatotype are standardized for normal or average nutrition within a particular age range. Therefore those measurements

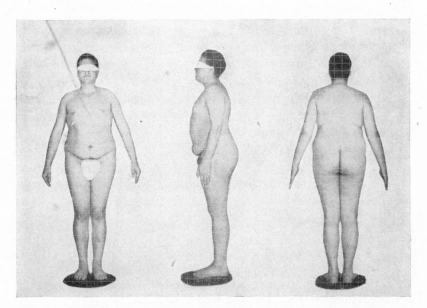

FIG. 1. Predominant endomorphy, with minimal mesomorphy and with a slight secondary strength in ectomorphy. Somatotype: 7-1-1½. Regional somatotypes (see p. 106): 7-1-2, 7-1-1, 7-1-2, 7-1-2, 7-1-1. For comparison with the rare 7-1-1 somatotype, see Fig. 1A, *The Varieties of Human Physique.*

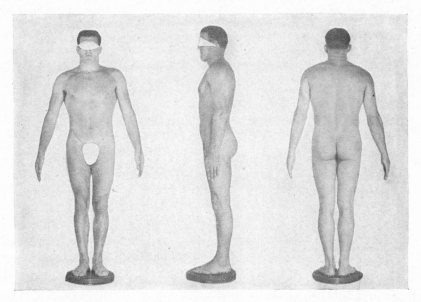

FIG. 2. Predominant mesomorphy, with minimal endomorphy and with a slight secondary strength in ectomorphy. Somatotype: 1-7-1½. Regional somatotypes: 1-7-1, 1-7-2, 1-7-1, 1-7-2, 1-7-2. For the 1-7-1, see Fig. 1B, *ibid.*

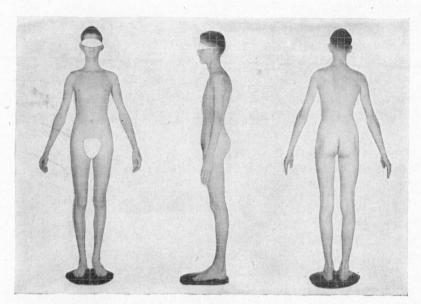

FIG. 3. Predominant ectomorphy, with some slight secondary strength in both mesomorphy and endomorphy. Somatotype: 1½-1½-7. Regional somatotypes: 2-1-7, 1-2-7, 1-1-7, 2-2-6, 1-1-7. For the 1-1-7, see Fig. 1C, *ibid.*

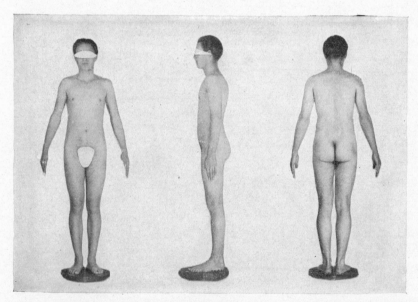

FIG. 4. An average individual. This is a mid-range physique showing almost an even balancing among the three primary components. Somatotype: 4-3½-4. Regional somatotypes: 4-4-4, 4-3-3, 4-3-4, 4-4-4, 4-4-4.

which change with nutritional changes readily detect the under- or over-nourished individual. But apparently no nutritional change can cause the measurements of a person of one somatotype exactly to simulate those of another somatotype. Nutritional changes are recognized as such by the somatotyping process. When an individual's measurements are posted in the somatotyping machine, the machine indicates where the somatotype lies. If a severe nutritional disturbance is present, the machine does not indicate a false somatotype but indicates only an unusual aberration from a normal pattern. We have as yet seen no case in which metabolic or nutritional changes led us to the assignment of two different somatotypes for the same individual, although we have somatotyped people from photographs taken at different periods in their (adult) lives when a weight change of as much as one hundred pounds had taken place.

When the relative strength of the three primary components of morphology has been determined, the physical analysis may be said to be anchored. But identification of the somatotype is only a beginning. So many secondary variables still remain to be described that the horizon of individuality seems only to broaden and to recede to greater distance as the techniques of physical description mature to usefulness.

Some of the important secondary variables are dysplasia (different mixtures of the primary components in differing regions of the body), gynandromorphy (physical bisexuality), texture (fineness or coarseness of tissue, aesthetic harmony of structure), secondary local dysplasias or hereditary local patternings of the primary components often called racial characteristics, pigmentation, distribution of secondary sexual characteristics (gynandromorphic dysplasias and characteristic patterns), hirsutism and hair distribution, and so on. We have tried to standardize the scaling of most of these characteristics just mentioned, but many other important physical variables lie on beyond these. Furthermore the work on secondary factors is for the most part new and incomplete, since none of this work could be done in a meaningful frame of reference until the somatotyping techniques and the norms for the primary components were well established.

The present volume describes the procedures we have employed in the study of temperament and in the analysis of relationships between morphology and temperament. A summary of this work follows.

The Dynamic Components of Temperament

As in the studies of morphology, the first problem at this more complex level of personality was to discover and define criteria for a useful basic taxonomy. It was necessary at the beginning to determine what first-order components are present in temperament. The method which has finally yielded fruitful results is a variation on the technique of factor analysis applied to quantitative ratings on a group of traits.

We have been able to standardize the descriptions of sixty traits —twenty in each of three correlated clusters—which collectively make up a scale for measuring what appear to be three primary components of temperament. Within each of the clusters the traits are positively correlated, while all of the intercorrelations between traits not of the same cluster are negative. The steps by which the clusters were built up are outlined in Chapter II.

Names have been given to the three correlated groups of traits. *Viscerotonia*, the first component, in its extreme manifestation is characterized by general relaxation, love of comfort, sociability, conviviality, gluttony for food, for people, and for affection. The viscerotonic extremes are people who "suck hard at the breast of mother earth" and love physical proximity with others. The motivational organization is dominated by the gut and by the function of anabolism. The personality seems to center around the viscera. The digestive tract is king, and its welfare appears to define the primary purpose of life.

Somatotonia, the second component, is roughly a predominance of muscular activity and of vigorous bodily assertiveness. The motivational organization seems dominated by the soma. These people have vigor and push. The executive department of their internal economy is strongly vested in their somatic muscular systems. Action and power define life's primary purpose.

Cerebrotonia, the third component, is roughly a predominance of the element of restraint, inhibition, and of the desire for concealment. Cerebrotonic people shrink away from sociality as from too strong a light. They "repress" somatic and visceral expression, are hyperattentional, and sedulously avoid attracting attention to themselves. Their behavior seems dominated by the inhibitory and attentional functions of the cerebrum, and their motivational hierarchy appears to define an antithesis to both of the other extremes.

Physique and Temperament

In a study extending through a period of five years we have been able to analyze 200 young men both morphologically and temperamentally, measuring in addition to the primary components a number of apparently secondary temperamental characteristics. Correlations of the order of about +.80 between the two levels of personality (morphological and temperamental) indicate that temperament may be much more closely related to the physical constitution than has usually been supposed.

However, the correlation between the two levels is by no means perfect, and from the point of view of individual analysis it seems to be the disagreements or inconsistencies between the physical and temperamental pattern that throw the most light on behavior. We find, roughly, at least four general factors at work in the development of a personality: (1) the total strength of endowment in each of the three primary components, (2) the quality of such endowment, (3) the mixture of the components, or their order of relative strength, and (4) the incompatibilities between morphology and manifest temperament. Of the latter, several subvarieties can be made out and are often encountered in the analysis of personalities having a history of severe internal conflict.

In later chapters the interrelations among the static components of physique and the dynamic components of temperament will be illustrated both by statistical analyses and by detailed case histories of representative personalities.

CHAPTER II

THE IDENTIFICATION OF THE PRIMARY
COMPONENTS OF TEMPERAMENT

ALWAYS, in the pursuit of science, the first problem is the
choice of variables. What aspects of phenomena shall we attend to, what dimensions shall we measure? Although we may well
understand that the unwise or unfortunate selection of basic
variables may make chaos out of potential order, we know of no
procedure that will guarantee a proper choice. Trial and error
seems to be the rule under most circumstances.

Especially in the study of personality is trial and error the rule
of procedure, and this book is largely a record of repeated trials
and many errors. Temperament has long embarrassed the student
of human behavior by a richness of potential variables. The problem quickly becomes more what not to measure than what to
include. Each of hundreds of adjectives applied to people suggests
a variable, and, since most adjectives have opposites, a kind of
bipolar scale is usually implied: lazy-energetic, bold-cautious, ag-
gressive-submissive, harsh-tender, poised-flustered, optimistic-
pessimistic, extraverted-introverted, etc., etc. There seems no end
to such a list, for the nuances of temperament are practically
inexhaustible. But so are the nuances of the weather. And as men
have learned reasonably well to describe and predict the weather
in terms of certain basic variables, so might it be possible that we
should eventually reduce temperament to order by learning how
to ignore the irrelevant in favor of the basic factors or components
involved. The present chapter tells of our efforts to cut through
the jungle of descriptive adjectives by the use of a technique
basically similar to factor analysis.

We had come to realize that simple dichotomies, simple bipolar
scales, are inadequate. Temperament is more than two-dimensional. Perhaps it is *n*-dimensional, but if so there is still a chance

that some dimensions are basic, first-order variables and need to be studied ahead of the more secondary aspects. This, then, was the question we were asking at the beginning of these studies: what are the primary components of temperament? How are they to be identified and measured? And how much of what we call temperament can they account for?

First a list of 650 alleged traits of temperament was collected. Most of the traits were supposedly related to extraversion or introversion. These were sifted, condensed, and described as systematically as possible. A few contributions from our own observation were added, and the list was finally reduced to 50 traits which seemed to embrace all of the *ideas* represented in the original 650. The 50 traits were then incorporated into a simple 5-point graphic rating scale (later expanded to a 7-point scale). Then began the tedious process of analyzing a series of subjects in order to rate them on these 50 traits. All the ratings in this preliminary study were made by the writer.

A group of 33 male graduate students, young instructors, and other academic people was first selected and a series of 20 analytic interviews extending through an academic year was arranged with each subject. In addition to the interviewing, it was possible to watch these people at their ordinary daily routines throughout most of the year. In the course of the year, all were observed repeatedly in their social relationships. Extensive notes were written after each interview, and sometimes after a casual observation. Notations were frequently made as to the manner in which particular traits would have to be redefined in order to sharpen and point their meaning. The numerous redundancies and obscurities which had escaped the original "armchair" sifting of the traits soon came painfully to light.

In the morphological studies, which were proceeding concurrently with the studies of temperament, we were seeking to find a way of translating patterns of relatively useless specific measurements into meaningful, manipulable concepts which could be used in general scientific research. In the temperament studies we had precisely the same objective, except that the problem was to translate a bewildering mass of quantified ratings on specific traits, rather than metric measurements on specific bodily structures.

The objective kept uppermost in mind was to determine if possible what primary components or elemental factors are present in human temperament. Proceeding under the assumption that whatever general components might exist would probably be represented among our 50 traits, we ran the intercorrelations for the entire series of traits and constructed a correlation table showing the resulting 1,225 correlations. Thurstone's factor analysis technique was not at the time available in its present form, but inspection of the correlation table revealed that some of the traits were positively correlated, while others were negatively correlated. The positive correlations ranged from +.86 to zero, the negative correlations from zero to —.73.

We then proceeded to build up lists of such clusters of traits as showed consistently positive intercorrelations among themselves, much after the manner of building up suits in a game of cards. It shortly became evident that three distinct nuclei of this sort were present. That is to say, we soon found that three groups of traits showed positive intercorrelation among themselves, *and negative correlation with all or nearly all of the other traits*. At the time this was not particularly what we wanted to find, for the writer then entertained a hypothesis that probably at least four primary components existed—both temperamentally and morphologically. Specifically, we rather expected to find a primary component of sexuality which would be statistically independent of other factors.

The fruits of all this work, so far, consisted then in the isolation of three nuclear clusters of correlated traits. We searched in vain for a fourth nucleus of traits which would show (a) consistently positive intracorrelation among themselves, and (b) consistently negative intercorrelation with the traits of each of the other nuclei. There was no such fourth nucleus present in our data.

We did not at first try to name the three nuclear groups of traits, but referred to them simply as factors I, II, and III (later as components I, II, and III, and still later as viscerotonia, somatotonia, and cerebrotonia, respectively). Guided by the nature of our empirical findings, we set up two quite arbitrary criteria for determining the qualification of a trait within one of the nuclear groups. First, the trait must show a positive correlation of at least +.60 with every other trait in its nuclear group. Second, it must show a negative correlation of at least —.30 with every trait in each of the other two nuclear groups. Employing these criteria rigidly, we found that six traits had established themselves in Group I, seven in Group II, and nine in Group III. Twenty-two of the original 50 traits had qualified. These 22 were as follows:

TABLE 1

THE THREE ORIGINAL CLUSTERS OF TRAITS

Group I	*Group II*	*Group III*
V-1 Relaxation	S-1 Assertive Posture	C-1 Restraint in Posture
V-2 Love of Comfort	S-3 Energetic Characteristic	C-3 Overly Fast Reactions
V-6 Pleasure in Digestion	S-4 Need of Exercise	C-8 Sociophobia
V-10 Greed for Affection and Approval	S-7 Directness of Manner	C-9 Inhibited Social Address
V-15 Deep Sleep	S-13 Unrestrained Voice	C-10 Resistance to Habit
V-19 Need of People When Troubled	S-16 Overmaturity of Appearance	C-13 Vocal Restraint
	S-19 Need of Action When Troubled	C-15 Poor Sleep Habits
		C-16 Youthful Intentness
		C-19 Need of Solitude When Troubled

A detailed description of each of these traits will be found in Chapter III. We have here appended the proper identifying symbol of each trait as it occurs in the final form of the Scale for Temperament (p. 26).

Such then was the result of the first effort. Three fairly well-defined clusters of correlated traits presented themselves, and no more such clusters were to be found. The cue at this point seemed to be to accept a tripolar hypothesis as offering a useful lead. We could readily expand the schema if our findings should justify it. The next step was to define more traits. We hoped to expand the original 22 traits to a considerably greater number, thus presumably increasing the statistical reliability and validity of the instrument. Also we proposed to redefine and further sharpen all of the accepted traits. Actually we did not attempt to standardize the instrument until another four years had been spent in preliminary cutting and trying and in the redefining of traits.

During the course of these succeeding years of experimentation the descriptions of the nuclear traits were rewritten many times. Numerous other traits were suggested and were tried out. The problem was always to describe a trait in such manner that the trait must mark a clear antithesis to *two* of the polar concepts. It is not easy to find traits that can be so described, and still less easy to describe them unambiguously after they have been found. Yet only such traits could be used in the projected scale for temperament, for the introduction of a trait not allocating itself sharply to one of the polar clusters would serve only to blunt the instrument.

The tedious element of the job did not lie in hunting and defining traits, however, nor in hunting subjects to be rated. The latter was more like a pleasant game—like what bug hunting is to the entomologist. The pain lay in the statistical analysis of the large masses of data that accumulated. During four years what we now refer to as the Scale for Temperament was revised and rewritten seven or eight times, sometimes with additions, sometimes with deletions.

COMPLETION OF THE SCALE

With 22 statistically acceptable traits serving to define the three polar concepts, it was possible to find other traits which gave promise of fitting into the pattern thus started. As might well be expected the most fruitful source of promising traits lay in the detailed study of persons who fell near one of the polar apices of the distribution, persons fitting clearly one or the other of the groups of traits.

The definition of traits became an interesting task in itself, requiring a good deal of trial and error to determine how broad or how narrow each definition should be made. When the definitions were made so specific as to depend upon a very narrow range of symptoms, or upon symptoms strongly influenced by cultural conditioning, the intercorrelations among the traits fell off markedly. On the other hand, when a trait was defined too broadly, incompatible characteristics would creep in, and these too would lower the correlations. Workable definitions appeared to be those that are neither cut too finely nor expanded too broadly.

On each of eight occasions when we set up a proving experiment to try a new revision of the Scale with a series of subjects, the third cluster of traits returned the greatest number of qualifying correlations and the first cluster of traits the smallest number. The component underlying the third group of traits is apparently the most definitive of the three, and the first is the most concealed of the components. The traits in the third cluster seem to stand out sharply, while traits defining the other components blend more "normally" or inconspicuously with the group mores. Consonant with this finding is the fact that almost everybody overestimates his own third component. In self-rating, the magnification of this component is so pronounced that we have once or twice considered trying to standardize a mathematical correction for the error.

The 20 traits of the third cluster, as finally incorporated in the Scale, had all qualified statistically and were defined about as they now stand at the time of the fourth revision. The 20 second-cluster traits were well in hand by the sixth revision. But a satisfactory definition of 20 first-cluster traits proved amazingly elusive.

The difficulty lay not in the lack of positive correlations among the first-cluster traits themselves, but in the absence of negative correlations with other traits. The first component seems to be less specific, less sharply definable as a contrasting entity, than is the case with the other two components. Against each other the second and third components stand out sharply, but the amorphous first component blends more readily with other aspects of temperament. Nevertheless 20 traits were finally assembled within the first cluster and 20 within each of the others, to make 60 traits in all. There is no magic to this number—it happens merely to be empirically adequate.

The final list of 60 traits was selected only after the completion of another experiment. This time we computed the intercorrelations among the ratings on 78 tentatively selected traits, for a series of 100 male subjects. The age range of this group was 17 to 32, with 96 of the cases falling between 17 and 24. All were college students or graduates. All were of the white race. When the correlations were completed and the results posted in a correlation chart, we were able to select the 20 traits most sharply defining each component. The original correlation charts for the 60 traits thus selected are included in Appendix 4.

THE PROBLEM OF NAMING THE PRIMARY COMPONENTS

Names for the three components presented the interesting problem that names usually present. Suggestive names abound in the literature,[1] but none seemed really adequate—they seemed to bring with them either too little or too much. There is the well-known trio, *affective, conative,* and *cognitive* applied to elements of mind, or the more physiological designations, *digestive, muscular,* and *cerebral.* But temperament, as here conceived, lies somewhere between the two levels implied by these sets of terms.

A suggestive precedent led to the invention of the names finally selected. Eppinger and Hess[2] had published a monograph describing an extensive study of the opposed functions of the two divisions of the autonomic nervous system. They discussed the clinical picture of a condition in which the cranio-sacral element of this system is pathologically dominant over the thoracico-lumbar element. For this condition they coined the term *vagotonia.* The *vagus* nerve constitutes the principal component of the cranial autonomic system. It slows the heart and augments the action of the stomach and intestines, as well as of the auxiliary digestive and assimilative viscera. The vagotonic individual is sluggish, relaxed, vegetative, and has a slow heart. Vagotonia is then a condition of autonomic imbalance in which the visceral functions overwhelmingly predominate. This may not be quite a technically correct use of the suffix *-tonia,* but the usage has now been widely accepted.

Eppinger and Hess also described a condition opposite to vagotonia, which they designated *sympatheticotonia.* In this condition the thoracico-lumbar element[3] predominates. The heart beats rapidly, the body is overly tense, and the whole digestive system

[1] See *The Varieties of Human Physique,* page 22.

[2] Hans Eppinger and Leo Hess. *Vagotonia.* New York: Nervous and Mental Disease Publishing Company, 1915.

[3] In an older terminology, the thoracico-lumbar segment of the autonomic nervous system is called the *sympathetic* segment, or the *sympathetic* system.

is partially paralyzed. The individual is generally apprehensive, hyperattentional, anxious, restrained. Now the thoracico-lumbar or sympathetic system is in one sense an efferent extension through which the forebrain or *cerebrum* exercises inhibitory control over visceral functions. Sympatheticotonia is then indirectly a state of cerebral dominance. In this condition visceral functions are checked and suspended, while the attentional focus of the individual is generally directed upon some external stimulating circumstance. A tense state of the body and a disturbed or emotional state of consciousness usually accompany sympatheticotonia. Normally an individual is "sympatheticotonic" only during some emergency. Pathologically the condition may become chronic. Such was the view advanced by Eppinger and Hess.

These two terms were favorably received and today they are found scattered diffusely through the medical and psychological literature, although they are often used carelessly. There is a tendency to identify the schizoid personality with sympatheticotonia. Similarly the cycloid personality is sometimes called vagotonic. The connection between the two typologies is quite obvious. Vagotonia implies a preponderance of visceral activity, naturally calling to mind Kretschmer's description of his fat, comfortable, cycloid pyknic,[4] although Eppinger and Hess did not use the term in just this way. Sympatheticotonia implies inhibition of the digestive functions and suggests the schizoid picture of fear and anxiety, or great mental intentness, and lean, ascetic qualities.

For our purposes, however, these terms were not quite adequate. They implied a dichotomy where we had found at least a trichotomy, and they were standardized to refer to specific pathological conditions, while we were describing behavior in general. Even more serious, they did not refer to trait clusters which fell at any of the three poles which our own preliminary studies had now begun to define with some clearness. Both sympatheticotonia and vagotonia appeared to represent mixtures of our polar characteristics, a difficulty probably inevitable where a dichotomy is stretched to include behavioral tendencies that are really multidimensional. Nevertheless the names themselves appeared to constitute about the best available terminological precedent, and

[4] Ernst Kretschmer, *Physique and Character*. New York: Harcourt, Brace, 1925.

they had given to the suffix -tonia just the shade of meaning that we wanted. We therefore borrowed this suffix, and used it to refer merely to a relative overresponsiveness or overactivity of one of the hypothetical primary components in the total behavior of the organism. Our three primary components came then to be called *viscerotonia, somatotonia,* and *cerebrotonia.*

Precise definition of these three concepts is the function of Chapter III and of the Scale itself. Viscerotonia, the first component, is so named because the complex of traits to which it refers is closely associated with a functional (and anatomical, we now know) predominance of the digestive viscera. The viscerotonic individual has a relatively long, heavy digestive tube, with large liver, and with other subsidiary organs of digestion showing increased size and development.[5] To use a term popularized by F. H. Allport[6] in another connection, the gut is *prepotent,* and its anabolic function apparently takes precedence over other functions of the organism. The life of a viscerotonic individual seems to be organized primarily to serve the gut.

Somatotonia, the second component, is so named because the complex of traits to which it refers is associated with functional and anatomical predominance of the somatic structures—the moving parts of the bodily frame. In the somatotonic individual, activity of the voluntary muscles appears to be prepotent. Such a person seems to live primarily for muscular expression. He desires more than anything to do something with his muscles, to move about assertively, to conquer, to experience physical adventure and combat.

The third component was not so easy to name, even though the picture presented by this complex of traits is the clearest and most sharply definable one. The prepotent activity seems to be that of conscious attention, which involves an inhibition or "hushing" of other activities of the body. It is presumably a prepotency of the higher centers of the nervous system, yet not quite that alone because these centers are to a degree involved in all conscious activity. In what we have come to call cerebrotonia, those neurophysiological activities which have to do chiefly with attentional

[5] See *The Varieties of Human Physique,* page 32.
[6] In his *Social Psychology.* New York: Houghton Mifflin, 1924.

consciousness are prepotent. But, because we do not understand the nature of these activities, the term cerebrotonia is admittedly a compromise. *Neurotonia* would not do, for it is much too broad a concept. The nervous system is involved in all activity. Sympatheticotonia will not do because it refers specifically to what is really only one element in cerebrotonia, namely inhibition of visceral function and apparent preparation of the organism for emergency (Cannon's theory). Cerebrotonia involves not only visceral and somatic inhibition (tension), but also mental intensity and a substitution of cerebration for direct action.

The overwhelming anatomical predominance of the cerebrum in man, as compared to other animals, *seems* to be associated with his presumably greater development and finer elaboration of attentional consciousness. We know that the cerebrum is primarily a sensory projectional and correlational center, very closely associated with exteroceptive function, and that the motor functions it exercises are mainly inhibitory. The influences exerted by the cerebrum upon the digestive viscera are sharply inhibitory. And the complex of traits to which we desire to refer by a single word involves all of these functions—restraint of both somatic and visceral responses, together with concentration upon exteroception and upon correlational recall or thought.

The term cerebrotonia has been adopted to refer to this complex of functional prepotencies, but we use the term in an analogous rather than a definitive sense. We do not mean to imply that in cerebrotonic people the cerebrum is larger or better than in other sorts of people. Nervous function is too complex and too little understood to be corralled with gross anatomy in so simple a manner. It may be that there are vital histological and chemical differences among different kinds of human nervous systems. Such is indeed probably the case, but we do not yet know what these differences are. Furthermore the physiologically differentiating characteristics of cerebrotonia may be largely peripheral rather than central. These differences may lie mainly in the receptors themselves, in the skin, in the structure of the sensory nerve endings, or even in the general texture of the whole body. The cerebrum itself may play rather a small part in the matter, or perhaps a part only analogous to that of the central switchboard in a telephone conversation. Cerebrotonic people (we now know) are predominantly ectomorphic, which means that peripherally they are relatively delicate and finely elaborated, while centrally they are relatively fragile and weak. The main physical differences may conceivably lie in the peripheral fineness of detail rather than in a cerebral anatomical preponderance.

The term cerebrotonia invites one other possible misunderstanding that needs to be obviated at the start. This concept is not to be confused with intelligence. The latter term always implies some degree of adaptability, and the extreme cerebrotonic is in important respects the least adaptable of human beings. We shall return to this consideration in a later section.

The viscerotonic seems to be glued firmly to the earth, depending for survival or for the fulfillment of his destiny upon his superior absorption of nourishment and upon his social agglutination. The somatotonic has apparently wandered some distance away from the breast of mother earth, but has developed powerful equipment of both offense and defense. He wins what he desires by vigorous muscular effort and in the final analysis depends mainly upon predation. The cerebrotonic appears to have wandered still farther from the maternal source of sustenance, but he seems to have sacrificed *both* visceral mass and somatic strength in achieving a more sensitive exposure and further refinement of receptors. The elaboration of the cerebrum as a center for sensory projection might be regarded as merely incidental in such a process, as the development of the dark room is incidental to photography. It might then be suggested that the term *exteroceptor-tonia*[7] would be more accurately descriptive than cerebrotonia. And so it would, but a man would have to take his pipe out of his mouth to pronounce it.

ANOTHER PROBLEM OF NAMES

When we study the dynamic components of temperament as exhibited by the different individuals we find some persons showing overmanifestations and some showing undermanifestations of various traits. Two suffixes, common in medical terminology,

[7] At one time we used the terms visceral prepotency, somatic prepotency, and exteroceptive prepotency.

suggest themselves as convenient labels: *-osis* for the exaggerated condition and *-penia* for the deficient manifestation of a component. Thus we shall speak of *viscerosis* and *cerebrosis*, and, for the sake of euphony, *somatorosis* (rather than *somatosis*). Behavior that is somatorotic is usually maladaptive because of being overly somatotonic, or ineptly somatotonic, according to circumstances. Similarly, *somatopenia* (literally, poverty of the somatic) refers to behavior that is maladaptive because of insufficient somatotonia.

By this usage we are able, in general, to substitute for the vague term *neurotic* the much more specific and descriptive terms, *viscerotic, somatorotic,* and *cerebrotic.* A viscerotic person is ordinarily one who is overly relaxed, gluttonous, overly socialized and too dependent on people, overly complacent or the like. A somatorotic person may be overly aggressive and assertive, too energetic, too dominating, too fond of risk, too combative, ruthless, loud, manic or hypomanic, overly active, and so on. A cerebrotic person may be overly tense and restrained, too sensitive and overresponsive physiologically, overly secretive, sociophobic and overly inhibited, pathologically intent, emotionally "tied up in a hard knot," and so on.

The conventional "neuroses" may be conveniently described in terms of this frame of reference. For example, such "neurotic" symptoms as tics and the like appear to result from conflict between somatotonia and cerebrotonia. The tic itself seems to constitute an intermittent somatorotic "break through" against an imperfectly sustained cerebrotonic restraint. Furthermore we have observed that persons among whom tics and uncompleted gestures of aggression are common often show peculiar dysplasias between mesomorphy and ectomorphy.

CHAPTER III

THE SCALE FOR TEMPERAMENT

IN THIS chapter the 60 traits making up the Scale for Temperament are defined. The method of definition will be that of describing in each instance an extreme manifestation of the trait, and of pointing out (in the notes which accompany the trait descriptions) some of the principal difficulties of differential diagnosis that are certain to be encountered.

In the later stages of the construction of the Scale the primary problem was to find and define what we call "polar" traits, or traits which fall near one of the three vertices of the triangle VSC.

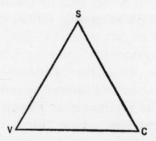

In order to be differentially useful, a trait falling within one of the polar clusters must also, if possible, differentiate *against* both of the other components. A trait which fails to define an antithesis to two of the polar components would for our purposes be worthless. Thus, for example, a trait such as "extraversion" would not be satisfactory, for there can be both viscerotonic (relaxed, sociophilic) extraversion, and somatotonic (aggressive, dominating) extraversion. Similarly, "intelligence" would not be a useful concept, for clearly viscerotonic, somatotonic or cerebrotonic behavior may be equally intelligent, under varying circumstances. Intelligence appears to be an evaluative quality, not a primary component of behavior.

The traits had also to be sufficiently specific and definitive to allow the definition of polar components in terms of relatively concrete criteria. But at the same time, if our conception of temperament were to embrace the constitutional, or relatively fixed and underlying nature of the individual personality, the traits needed to be defined in such manner that their quantitative manifestations would remain relatively constant and independent of cultural influences. Thus traits involving learned skills, relative success or failure and the like, and acquired abilities or adaptations, had to be avoided. Since we were aiming at basic components of temperament, we needed to measure behavioral characteristics, quantitative expression of which would remain relatively uninfluenced by the social and educational history of the individual.

The definition of traits that are both definitive and basic is difficult, but once we had fixed these two criteria in mind so that we knew precisely what we were trying to accomplish, the undertaking proved itself to be far from impossible. The task was to write definitions specific enough to render the traits "polar," yet in another sense, sufficiently general to minimize the influence of the cultural environment.

Figure 5 presents a list of the 60 traits which finally emerged, and also serves as a score sheet for administering the Scale. Note that some of the traits have polar antitheses, while others do not. A trait like *Sociophilia* (V-8), for example, has a polar antithesis in *Sociophobia* (C-8). We sometimes speak of such a trait, together with its antithesis, as a "two-way" trait, meaning by this that light is thrown both on the individual's viscerotonia and on his cerebrotonia.

Likewise, a few "three-way" traits appear in the Scale. The trait *Assertiveness of Posture and Movement* (S-1), for example, has *two* polar antitheses in the traits V-1 and C-1. There are two "opposites" to assertiveness. One is relaxation, the other, restraint. Careful observation of an individual's posture and manner of movement sheds light on the strength of all three of the primary components. Ideally, the Scale should be made up entirely of sets of three-way traits, but unfortunately we have been able to define only five such sets (nos. 1, 17, 18, 19 and 20).

Fig. 5

THE SCALE FOR TEMPERAMENT

Name	*Date*	*Photo No.*	*Scored by*

I VISCEROTONIA....	II SOMATOTONIA....	III CEREBROTONIA....
( ) 1. Relaxation in Posture and Movement	( ) 1. Assertiveness of Posture and Movement	( ) 1. Restraint in Posture and Movement, Tightness
( ) 2. Love of Physical Comfort	(↑) 2. Love of Physical Adventure	— 2. Physiological Over-response
( ) 3. Slow Reaction	(↑) 3. The Energetic Characteristic	( ) 3. Overly Fast Reactions
— 4. Love of Eating	(↑) 4. Need and Enjoyment of Exercise	( ) 4. Love of Privacy
— 5. Socialization of Eating	— 5. Love of Dominating, Lust for Power	( ) 5. Mental Overintensity, Hyperattentionality, Apprehensiveness
— 6. Pleasure in Digestion	(↑) 6. Love of Risk and Chance	( ) 6. Secretiveness of Feeling, Emotional Restraint
( ) 7. Love of Polite Ceremony	(↑) 7. Bold Directness of Manner	( ) 7. Self-Conscious Motility of the Eyes and Face
( ) 8. Sociophilia	( ) 8. Physical Courage for Combat	( ) 8. Sociophobia
— 9. Indiscriminate Amiability	( ) 9. Competitive Aggressiveness	( ) 9. Inhibited Social Address
— 10. Greed for Affection and Approval	— 10. Psychological Callousness	— 10. Resistance to Habit, and Poor Routinizing
— 11. Orientation to People	— 11. Claustrophobia	— 11. Agoraphobia
( ) 12. Evenness of Emotional Flow	— 12. Ruthlessness, Freedom from Squeamishness	— 12. Unpredictability of Attitude
( ) 13. Tolerance	( ) 13. The Unrestrained Voice	( ) 13. Vocal Restraint, and General Restraint of Noise
( ) 14. Complacency	— 14. Spartan Indifference to Pain	— 14. Hypersensitivity to Pain
— 15. Deep Sleep	— 15. General Noisiness	— 15. Poor Sleep Habits, Chronic Fatigue
( ) 16. The Untempered Characteristic	( ) 16. Overmaturity of Appearance	( ) 16. Youthful Intentness of Manner and Appearance
( ) 17. Smooth, Easy Communication of Feeling, Extraversion of Viscerotonia	— 17. Horizontal Mental Cleavage, Extraversion of Somatotonia	— 17. Vertical Mental Cleavage, Introversion
— 18. Relaxation and Sociophilia under Alcohol	— 18. Assertiveness and Aggression under Alcohol	— 18. Resistance to Alcohol, and to Other Depressant Drugs
— 19. Need of People When Troubled	— 19. Need of Action When Troubled	— 19. Need of Solitude When Troubled
— 20. Orientation Toward Childhood and Family Relationships	— 20. Orientation Toward Goals and Activities of Youth	— 20. Orientation Toward the Later Periods of Life

Note: The thirty traits with parentheses constitute collectively the short form of the scale.

THE PROCEDURE FOR USING THE SCALE

The procedure recommended for using the Scale for Temperament is as follows: Observe the subject closely for at least a year in as many different situations as possible. Conduct a series of not less than 20 analytic interviews with him in a manner best suited to 'the situation, and to the temperaments and interests of the two principals. The first two or three interviews are usually devoted to "breaking the ice" and to the medical history, the remaining interviews to the life history and to special topics or special tests as indicated.

After each interview, and after any other satisfactory observation of the subject, turn to the score sheet (p. 26) and assign a rating on as many of the traits as possible, always using erasable pencil marks (for the ratings are to be repeatedly revised). Repeat the observations, interviews, and revisions of ratings until reasonably satisfied that all of the 60 traits have been adequately considered and evaluated.

In the interviews it is necessary to cover rather thoroughly the general physical or health history; the genetic and family history; the economic, social, sexual, educational and aesthetic history; the history of characteristic tastes and habits; and such special clinical matters as the individual case may indicate. A method of guided discussion and systematized questioning is ordinarily employed, although in difficult cases it may sometimes be necessary to resort to the method of free association or even to dream analysis. In such cases the constitutional analysis will require more than the minimal 20 hours of interviewing. In Appendices 2 and 3 are included two special forms which have been found to facilitate the systematizing of some of the guided discussion.

The interview should be conducted in a systematic manner, according to a practiced plan. The interviewer is attempting to take and evaluate a psychological history. This is more difficult and involved than a medical history. In fact the medical history is but one necessary step in a good psychological history. *Training* is necessary before reasonable dependability can be expected in the use of this instrument, for it makes no claim to being foolproof. The *ideal* training necessary for adequate use of the

Scale would be a rigorous one, and would require some degree of both clinical and social maturity, an observant eye, and the long-practiced habit of quantification of judgments. Before attempting to use the Scale, an investigator should himself have the advantage of a constitutional analysis, and if feasible, he should also be acquainted with other systems of analysis. All this may seem too much to ask, but the history of psychology shows that an adequate attack on the problem of psychological analysis is no light undertaking.

An instrument of this sort is almost worthless for self-rating. Most persons tend to overestimate the cerebrotonic component in themselves, and to underestimate the other two components. Men usually underestimate their somatotonia, and women their viscerotonia.

Using a 7-point scale, the various degrees of quantification have approximately the following interpretations. The parenthetical percentages refer to the approximate frequencies of the respective ratings in our own cumulative series of about 600 analyses.

(4%) 1. Extreme antithesis to the trait.

(15%) 2. The trait is weakly represented, although traces are present.

(29%) 3. The trait is distinctly present, but falls a little below the general average.

(29%) 4. The individual falls just about halfway between the two extremes. He is slightly above the general average in the trait.

(15%) 5. The trait is strong, although not outstanding.

(6%) 6. The trait is very strong and conspicuous, approaching the extreme.

(2%) 7. Extreme manifestation of the trait.

It should be noted that while there can be but one kind of "extreme manifestation of a trait," there are two kinds of "extreme antithesis" to each trait. That is to say, a person can be cerebrotonic 7 only by being extremely cerebrotonic, but he can be cerebrotonic 1 by being either viscerotonic or somatotonic. Therefore the rating 1 will be much commoner than the rating 7, possibly about twice as common in a sufficient series of cases. Also note that the means fall below 4, or below the mid-points in the respective scales. (For further discussion of the theoretical problems involved in this kind of scaling, the reader should refer to *The Varieties of Human Physique*, Chapter V.)

Figure 5 serves as a score sheet for the Scale as a whole. Note that half of the traits, or ten representing each component, are marked by parentheses. These 30 traits with parentheses constitute what is called the *Short Form* of the Scale. They refer to relatively objective characteristics which can be judged with a tolerable degree of accuracy upon short acquaintance with an individual. In practice we have used the short form of the Scale for research purposes in a number of instances where only a single interview with the subject was possible (see p. 417).

The Problem of Breaking the Ice

Experience has taught us that when a temperamental analysis is undertaken, a major problem is to find a way to break through as quickly as possible to the "real" person, or to the relatively deep-rooted characteristics which underlie superficial attitudes and verbal stereotypes. This can be accomplished in a number of ways. One good way, we have found, is to ask the subject at the very beginning of an analysis to fill out one or more personality inventories or self-rating scales—and to discuss the results with the investigator. Any of the standardized extraversion-introversion scales or inventories of personality may serve this purpose, and a number of good ones are now on the market. In our practice we employ as "ice-breakers" two such instruments of our own which, through more than a decade of use, have acquired a wealth of interpretative value for us, although we must hasten to add that we do not find much *direct* relationship between expressed verbal attitudes and temperament. Attitudes certainly reflect temperament, but they do not measure it.

The first of our two ice-breaking instruments is a self-administering scale of conservative and radical opinion which was standardized at the University of Wisconsin. This scale will be found in Appendix 2, together with the (1930) norms for a student population of 3000. Most people find the exercise a pleasant one, and they like to compare their own (now usually different and more radical) views with what was conventional only a short time ago. The Wisconsin Scale is our best ice-breaker.

The second instrument is more searching and more revealing. This is a scale which we use for gauging the mental growth, and for evaluating the mental life of an individual who is being analyzed. We find such a scale of great value—indeed a necessity —in guiding the course of a therapeutic or educational analysis, but that is a problem with which we shall not be concerned in the present volume. The Chicago Scale of Mental Growth, as this instrument is called (it was developed at the University of Chicago), can also be used as a self-rating scale, and when so used it is sometimes most revealing with respect to the temperamental pattern. We generally ask a relatively mature or intelligent subject to rate himself on this scale at the beginning of an analysis, and then discuss his ratings with him as an introduction to the study of his mental and temperamental pattern. The Chicago Scale will be found in Appendix 3. Neither the Wisconsin nor the Chicago Scale has been previously published.

We turn now to a description of the 60 traits comprising the Scale of Temperament.

DESCRIPTIONS OF THE TRAITS

1. Traits Defining the First Component (Viscerotonia)

V-1. *Relaxation in Posture and Movement.* Conspicuous relaxation of the body as a whole. Limp relaxation of trunk, legs, feet, arms, hands, fingers, mouth, and all the muscles of facial expression, especially those about the eyes. Movements are slow, smooth and flowing. There is no jerkiness. No assertive (somatotonic) gestures of the head, shoulders or hands are seen. The walk is a smooth amble, with neither hesitation nor vigorous assertiveness. Movement is deliberate, suggesting that of the terrapin, the cow, or elephant. Breathing is slow, deep, abdominal and regular. The pulse is slow and full. All external signs of tension are absent. The voice is even, conspicuously lacking the strident or booming quality of somatotonia, or the constraint of cerebrotonia. Speech is deliberate, effortless, unhurried, and unstrained. There is an essential dislike of bodily exercise. The arms often show a limp relaxation like that of a seal's flipper, and the hands are likely to be soft and flaccid. If basal metabolic rate is taken, it is found to be low.

Note: This trait presents a clear antithesis both to somatotonic assertiveness (S-1) and to cerebrotonic restraint (C-1). The set of traits, V-1, S-1 and C-1 constitutes one of our five three-way or "tripolar" traits. The other four are sets 17, 18, 19 and 20.

The description applies to an individual who would score 7. Normal or average relaxation presents an entirely different picture, details of which must depend on the strength of the other two components. To be well poised or self-possessed, for example, a person must exhibit a modicum, but not the extreme, of the V-1 trait. Poise is perhaps most easily developed in the presence of a blend involving an average degree of V-1 with a little more than average of the trait S-1, and less than average C-1. Similarly, most of the behavioral patterns which psychologists ordinarily call "traits" clearly represent blends or mixtures of what seem to be the primary components. This may still be true to a degree of some of the 60 "traits" which are used in this present attempt to define the primary components. The problem has been to reduce such a factor to the lowest possible minimum.

V-2. *Love of Physical Comfort.* Lassitude. The individual has a primary desire to be comfortable, and to bask in his comfort. He shows relatively great interest in being comfortable, and if he has any ingenuity, a considerable proportion of it is devoted to making himself comfortable. At a level of uncomplicated cultural influence, or at a low economic level, he may exhibit a tendency just to sit lazily in the sun. At a more complicated level, there is likely to be an overwhelming desire for luxuries, and a desire to be surrounded by "nice" things. There is usually a strong preference for soft beds, and for low, deeply upholstered furniture. To be luxuriantly comfortable is a primary goal.

Note: The clearest antithesis would perhaps be asceticism, but this is not a polar characteristic. Asceticism involves a high degree of cerebrotonic restraint, but also some considerable degree of austerity and rigorously enforced (somatotonic) routine, or discipline. The trait asceticism might be defined in motivational language as a 1-3-6 trait, meaning that it involves an antithesis to viscerotonia, but a "3-6 blend" of the other two components. The condition called masochism (love of pain) might be taken as another antithesis. But the motivation of masochism is complex, and so far as we know, masochism is always specific in its manifestation. We have never heard of a case of love of physical pain *in general*, but only of love of *specific* pain, which is usually sexually conditioned. Masochism therefore presents only a partial antithesis and probably involves a specific conditioning history. The trait, love of physical adventure (S-2) also presents a partial antithesis, but V-2 and S-2 are not altogether mutually exclusive. There are many personalities which show alternation between these two predominances. In these two traits an individual might show a 3-5, or a 5-3 relationship. V-2 is not quite synonymous with laziness, for laziness is merely a general antithesis to somatotonia. Cerebrotonic people are often lazy. A person temperamentally 3-2-6 may be as lazy as a 6-2-3.

V-3. *Slow Reaction.* All responses are conspicuously slow. Movement is slow and deliberate. Both verbal and motor reactions are slow, as revealed by the common reaction time experiments of the psychological laboratory. Eye movements are slow, including those involved in reading. The eye wink is observed to be slow, like that of a sleepy child. The facial responses of ordinary social conversation are tardy or absent. The face is therefore bland and relatively expressionless. Pulse and respiration are inclined to be slower than what is given as "normal" by the medical textbooks. Temperature also is about half a degree lower than the 98.6 (Fahrenheit) which is usually called normal. Emotional reactions are slow. Sexual appetite is slow and weak. Hunger comes on slowly but this appetite is strong. If the individual drives an automobile, his reactions are slow and deliberate, often exasperatingly so to an impatient person. If he attempts to take part in athletic sports of any kind, his reactions are found to be too slow for proficiency.

Note: The overly fast reaction time of Cerebrotonia (C-3) presents a clear antithesis. Both the V-3 and the C-3 traits, when exaggerated, represent maladaptation of a sort. The viscerotonic reacts too slowly, and the cerebrotonic too fast, for ordinary adaptation. Somatotonic reactions fall about midway between the two extremes, so far as speed is concerned. Speed of reaction therefore throws no light on the strength of somatotonia. The somatotonic individual may be very slow (secondarily viscerotonic) or very fast (secondarily cerebrotonic).

V-4. *Love of Eating.* Love of food and a warm appreciation of the *process* of eating, for its own sake. Not to be confused with a mere voracious appetite. There is a *deep joy* in eating, and a considerable fuss and ceremony are made over eating. Usually there is a history of having overeaten and of having desired more food than was needed to maintain normal weight or growth. In a true motivational sense the individual lives, partially at least, to eat. Eating is one of the principal pleasures of life, if not indeed the greatest pleasure. Even when not eating, it is very pleasant to be doing something with the mouth—sucking or chewing. (Viscerotonic people are indefatigable kissers). If well educated, or culturally educated, such a person usually has a deep interest in cuisine and a wide knowledge of foods and their preparation. At lower levels he tends merely to become a glutton.

Note: There is no trait presenting a direct antithesis to V-4. There are only rivals to it, such as primary love of physical exercise (S-4), love of dominating (S-5), and love of solitude (C-4). In pathology there is the medical entity sometimes called chronic *anorexia* (absence of appetite), of which two fairly distinguishable varieties may be made out, besides anorexia associated with organic disease. The commonest form is usually seen in a cerebrotonic individual who has developed an ascetic pattern of life as a more or less permanent *persona* (mask) in a world which for one reason or another he does not like very well. The other kind of chronic anorexia appears to be associated with simple constitutional inferiority (see p. 289). In gauging an individual's viscerotonia it is important not to confuse V-4 with the acute voracious appetite often seen in somatotonia (wolf-like devouring of food), or with the sharp craving for proteins usually associated with cerebrotonia. V-4 is love of eating—not need of food. When this trait is low the *process* of eating, especially in company, is neutral or even distasteful in emotional tone.

V-5. *Socialization of Eating.* Eating in company with others, or breaking bread together, is regarded as a kind of social sacrament. Eating together becomes then a process of more importance than the mere biological taking of food (which itself remains also a great pleasure). The greatest of social satisfaction is to be derived from the festive board, and from lingering over a fine, well-served meal. Eating is an occasion of the best in conversation and fellowship. The principal meal of the day—and especially of a holy day—is often regarded as a sacrament of great importance in family life. Eating thus becomes a matter of religious as well as of social and biological significance. There is a deep love of having guests, and sentimentality about the sharing of food. When this trait is predominant, the individual always knows where the best foods are served, and it is a high tribute to be taken, or to take another, to one of the "best places."

Note: None of the traits used in the Scale presents a specific antithesis to V-5. This trait and the preceding (V-4) are closely related, but there are people who are high in one without being correspondingly high in the other. There are lonely gluttons, and there are non-gluttons who make a great fuss and sacrament about eating in sociability. It is important also not to confuse V-5 with a simple, generalized sociophilia (V-8). The hallmark of V-5 is the attachment of an almost specifically religious significance to the social bond which eating together appears to create among people in whom the trait is strong.

V-6. *Good Digestion, and Pleasure in it.* Digestion is excellent, and is a primary pleasure. To sit with a full belly and do nothing but digest, is to experience the fullness of life. Elimination too is pleasant and free from unpleasant psychological complications. It is especially pleasant to sit on the stool with the Sunday paper. If the individual is free from social inhibition, a fine belch is an excellent thing, and often flatus is most agreeable. Peristalsis is slow, pleasant, deliberate and free. In all of these activities the gut "talks," and is heard sympathetically. Cerebrotonia tends to suppress the voice of the gut. Constipation is unimaginable (for that would be deliberate avoidance of a primary pleasure). All sorts of "indigestible" foods can be eaten without embarrassment —such foods as pickles, mince pie, cucumbers and the like. "Roughage" is desired and apparently is handled advantageously, in sharp contrast with the sometimes distressing effect of roughage upon cerebrotonics (see trait C-2). There are no digestive quirks or food idiosyncrasies. Digestion is relatively impervious to emotional upset and to minor environmental changes. The common colics and stomach-aches which harass cerebrotonic ("nervous") people are almost unknown, as are all the so-called functional complaints which are referable to the gastrointestinal tract.

Note: The trait nearest to an antithesis to V-6 is C-2, physiological overresponse. Persons high in C-2 usually show what is known as a sensitive gastrointestinal tract, or one which is thrown off function by many sorts of stimuli. The V-6 people are really endowed with a magnificent gut which, like the muscular system of an athlete, is not easily disabled or distressed. Such a person takes a primary pleasure in his own particular predominant system of organs, as naturally as does the athlete in his predominant muscular system, or the sexualist in his respective superior equipment. Persons high in the V-6 trait are great kissers, chewers and suckers. They are sometimes called "oral-erotic" by the Freudians. They tend to carry their usually heavy, flaccid lips in a permanent sucking position, in sharp contrast with the compressed lips of cerebrotonia.

V-7. *Love of Polite Ceremony.* Among highly viscerotonic people there is a characteristic reliance upon group strength rather than upon individual strength. The individual therefore tends to de-

pend upon the prescribed ritual, or upon the polite and ceremonious manner of approach to what he seeks, rather than upon
his own strength. Such a person usually shows an inordinate love
of doing what is accepted and approved, and is often inclined to
be overpolite, possibly to the point of unctuousness. Propriety
tends to become a good in itself and there is a craving for assurance and reassurance of esteem—and hence of status and security.
The dependence upon the indirect approach generally extends
through all of the major relations of life—economic, social,
sexual, religious and even aesthetic. The proper or expected expressions of gratitude, sympathy, respect, etc., tend to become
more important than the sentiments themselves (although it does
not follow necessarily that there is insincerity). Births, marriages,
deaths and so on are occasions of much sacrament and ceremony.
All emotions and all acts of human intercourse call for some
pattern of vocalization and outward celebration. The outward
manifestations of love and affection are all-important. The viscerotonic individual really participates emotionally in these outward
manifestations or "sharings"—the problem of hypocrisy is another matter altogether.

Note: The trait S-7, bold directness of manner, presents a partial
antithesis, and this latter trait is often simulated overcompensation-
ally by essentially cerebrotonic people who are motivated more
perhaps by hatred of what they may call (viscerotonic) slobber than
by any directly somatotonic desire. Viscerotonic people are extremely agglutinative. They tend to club together and to seek their
satisfactions by supporting the group against the variant individual,
or against individuality. They are Epimethean, as contrasted with
Promethean. This tendency is perhaps a natural outcome of the
combination of strong biological appetite and individual muscular
weakness. Cerebrotonic people, lovers of solitude, represent an
exactly antithetical tendency, and when they have a fairly strong
supporting somatotonia they tend to become individualists, and
haters of viscerotonic propriety. Along this cleavage line, many of
the generalized hostilities seen in human life appear to take their
origin. (See *Psychology and the Promethean Will*, Harper &
Brothers, 1936.)

V-8. *Sociophilia.* Love of company. Appetite for people, in the
general sense. Conviviality, and emotional delight upon being

surrounded and supported by others. There is a deep, persistent craving to have people about, a rich satisfaction is being one among many, and a strong sense of loneliness and weakness when cut off from the fulfillment of this craving. The viscerotonic individual warms up and expands in company. For him social isolation means frustration and inward discomfort, as social over-stimulation means frustration and discomfort for the cerebrotonic. For the viscerotonic, conviviality and love of company are not merely the expression of a mood, but they voice a dominant and a consistently powerful appetite. Such an individual may nourish genuine fondness for people merely *because* they are people.

Note: Sociophobia, C-8, is the direct antithesis. The viscerotonic sociophil is overly dependent upon social support. The cerebrotonic sociophobe is overly free from the mental and moral interdependence which arises from easy social accessibility. Each extreme appears to be offensive to the other. From the standpoint of cerebrotonia, the viscerotonic sociophil is a "waster" and a superficial person who encourages social crowding and overstimulation—two of the "worst ills" in the world. From the standpoint of viscerotonia, the cerebrotonic sociophobe is a dark and suspicious person, a miser at best and a sinister influence at worst.

One hallmark of viscerotonia which seems to be related to V-8 is generosity, both of material goods and of emotion (although sustained generosity involves a degree of somatotonia as well). A hallmark of cerebrotonia is the tendency toward economic and social asceticism, and consequently toward miserliness and poverty. Most cerebrotonics, when fully aware of their own motivation, feel a strong desire for poverty of material goods as well as for poverty of social contact. Cerebrotonics desire but little, but they seem to become inordinately attached to what they have, both in the sense of material goods and in the sense of personal loyalties. Miserliness and jealousy, then, are distinctly cerebrotonic traits. (Jealousy may indeed be a fatal curse of cerebrotonia, and when jealousy becomes associated with fairly good secondary somatotonia, the way is open for the development of the dangerous paranoid personality.)

But the viscerotonic sociophil is well protected from these pitfalls. With his dependence upon a *great number* of others, he is never caught with too many eggs in one basket, and he escapes the horror of jealousy. He is emotionally outgoing or, in Jung's terminology, he is affectively extraverted (the feeling extravert).

V-9. *Indiscriminate Amiability.* General, or promiscuous amiability. The individual is conspicuously demonstrative of good will. There is a constant, effortless emanation of amiable intent, the sincerity of which cannot be, and never is questioned. One high in this trait generates a sense of reassurance as naturally as a fire generates heat. It is as if he were continuously spraying the world with a pot of rose water. There is an externally manifest ingenuous participation in the wishes and desires of others, which no degree of self-conscious solicitude can ever successfully counterfeit. Such a person is armed with a potent gift, for by reflecting an even-tempered and indiscriminate good will, he generally elicits the same good will with equal indiscrimination. The dog who wags his tail is seldom kicked.

Note: With a little practice, this trait can be distinguished very readily from insincerely professed amiability. Perhaps no deceit is so pitifully shallow as that of the bewildered cerebrotonic who, finding himself in a vocation or social situation which seems to call for protestation of amiability, attempts to master a few tricks of speech and gesture and to pass them off for true viscerotonia. A child or dog usually detects the sham without trouble, although it may require a psychiatrist six months or more to reveal it to the (dishonest) individual himself. So badly do people lose their way in a pre-psychological society. Spontaneous demonstrativeness is often a useful gift, but this trait is offensive to many cerebrotonic people, possibly in the way that a wet-mouthed puppy is offensive to a cat. The cerebrotonic hates to be slobbered upon. In sharp contrast with the V-9 trait, one cerebrotonic once wrote of another, "She had not an atom of that amiability which wraps good and evil alike in a mantle of inane praise. She had the awful gift of discernment."

V-10. *Greed for Affection and Approval.* Conspicuous dependence upon reassurance of human affection, and upon the expressed good will and approval of people. Among viscerotonics there is a peculiar inability to tolerate the sense of isolation which is associated with being disapproved of in any respect. The individual is greedy for constant manifestations of approval. He wants to be loved by *everybody* around him, and he is dependent upon frequent reassurance that all is well in this respect. He is therefore inclined to be extremely conventional. This sense of being *persona grata* is almost as important as food, and he feeds upon it emotionally. Such a person is notably greedy for routine outward expression of affection by members of his family, thus in some instances greatly irritating other members of the family who may be of different temperament. Women (who are more viscerotonic than men) frequently irritate their children or husbands in such a manner.

Note: This trait represents a weakness peculiar to viscerotonia. Persons showing the trait often become nuisances with their greed for affection, and suffer chastisement which they cannot understand. Many a marriage or other human adjustment fails through a too vigorous squeezing of a non-viscerotonic personality for the nourishing juices of approval and manifest affection. The trait has a clear antithesis in a quality of militant independence and defiance of convention which is in some quarters cherished as a virtue. But this latter trait does not represent a polar predominance of one component. It is apparently the result of a sometimes uncomfortable mixture of somatotonia and cerebrotonia in the presence of low viscerotonia.

V-11. *Orientation to People.* There is a conspicuous concern to maintain the most accurate orientation with reference to personalities. The individual is profoundly solicitous and is usually well informed about matters of status, prestige and the general standing of people. In general, he knows to whom to go for what —and when—although he may not always possess the somatotonia to act upon this knowledge. He knows who everybody is within his environment, and his relative evaluation of an individual is likely to be a singularly accurate barometer of the general opinion of the community concerning that person. His attitude and opinion about an individual is almost certain to reflect the majority opinion. He is, of course, inclined to be a gossip. Just as a wild creature is rarely at fault with respect to its geographic orientation in the woods, the strongly viscerotonic personality is not often at fault in its orientation to other personalities. Even in extreme mental pathology the patient well endowed with this trait always knows who his doctors and nurses are. He can call them by name. A cerebrotonic under similar circumstances is inclined to lose the memory of his own name. This is one difference between an extensive and an intensive mind. It illustrates in part the difference between what we have called horizontal and vertical dissociation (traits S-17 and C-17).

Note: There is no direct antithesis to the V-11 trait. Somatotonic people, with their agoraphilia (claustrophobia, S-11) tend to develop spatial orientation to a high degree. Possibly it is as difficult to find a somatotonic who is spatially confused and has lost his way geographically, as to find a viscerotonic without friends to turn to for what he wants or needs. The kind of orientation an individual develops seems to depend upon his basic, constitutionally predetermined interests. Viscerotonics depend upon agglutination with the group for the satisfaction of their wants, and they find out about people, remembering what they find out. Somatotonics are stronger and are more independent. They depend more upon their own individual effort and resources, and upon their own moving about. They observe landmarks and they remember directions. This is a manifestation of a general interest, probably, rather than of specific instinct. The extreme cerebrotonic usually has poor orientation both to person and to place. Predominant cerebrotonia may therefore be a sort of biological luxury, supportable for any length of time only by a society which understands its nature and deliberately sets up institutions—such as colleges, monasteries and mental hospitals—for its protection.

V-12. *Evenness of Emotional Flow.* Emotion and general attitudes are well sustained, and are conspicuously even and unchanging. There is a constant outward flow of what transpires within, and there are few mood swings. Affections are steady, dependable, unchanging and manifest. Harmony and evenness of affective outlook prevail. Such people love peace. They are free from emotional depression on the one hand, and on the other hand, from such high peaks of emotionality as lead to megalomania and the lust to conquer. With visceral predominance well established, the outflow of feeling is smooth, and there is conspicuous absence of the tempestuous incident which occurs in the presence of an unhappy mixture of the somatotonic and cerebrotonic components. For recognition of this trait, the diagnostic hallmark is absence of the temper tantrum both in childhood and in the later history of the individual—this in conjunction with a manifest outward flow of feeling.

Note: The trait C-12, unpredictability of attitude, when it occurs without the presence of a complicating secondary somatotonic predominance, presents the most direct antithesis to V-12.

A great deal of lamentable misunderstanding has arisen from Kretschmer's identification of the "manic-depressive" type of temperament with what he called the "pyknic" physique. The difficulty, as usual, lies mainly in terminology. Kretschmer's pyknic is in no sense a pure endomorph, but is a mixture of endomorphy and mesomorphy—usually more of the latter than of the former.[1] Similarly the cyclic or manic-depressive temperament is in no sense predominantly viscerotonic, but is a mixture of viscerotonia and somatotonia (more of the latter than of the former) usually in the presence of a considerable cerebrotonic interference. The manic incident is an incompatible somatotonic (somatorotic) outburst, and the manic-depressive temperament represents a partial antithesis to the trait V-12, but it is brought about by what we may perhaps call incompatible mixing of the primary components, not by anything approaching a polar predominance of one component.

Another nearly direct antithesis is the somatotonic trait S-5, love of dominating, or lust for power. There is no craving for power in the individual who shows the V-12 trait overwhelmingly.

V-13. *Tolerance.* The trait of easygoing toleration of people and of things as they are found. Comfortable acceptance of people, customs, situations, institutions. A fundamental contentment and satisfaction with life is reflected in all that the individual does, and also in his countenance, his expression, and in his manner of speech, which is deliberate and free from controversial statement. There is an easy amicability in all things. Such an individual is well disposed toward life in a most fundamental sense, and he wishes well toward the entire scene. Furthermore he himself is not to be frustrated in his enjoyment of living, by any major or minor irritations. He is singularly insensitive to irritations. His philosophy is "live and let live."

Note: There is no polar antithesis to this trait, for the extremely

[1] See *The Varieties of Human Physique*, p. 238.

intolerant individual shows what may be considered to be an incompatible mixture of somatotonia and cerebrotonia, rather than
an extreme predominance of either. One opposite to the placid,
overly tolerant person, from whose untempered soul no spark of
wrathful fire can be struck, is the reformer, who in spite of the
noblest of motives is generally crucified in one way or another. The
intolerance of the reformer is the profoundest and most cherished
intolerance conceivable, for the latter often stands ready or eager
to give his life for it. The traditional arch reformer or savior of
mankind has been depicted morphologically in Christian times as
falling between the 2-3-5 and 2-3-6.[2]

V-14. *Complacency.* Placidity or Smugness. There is an inclination toward an unshakable complacency which approaches or
reaches smugness. The individual is placidly complacent about
himself and his relations to his world, and about the outer affairs
of life. He sees no hurry or urgency in any situation, however
acute and desperate the matter may appear to others. He is inclined to fiddle while Rome burns, and whether it burns or not
is of little moment to him, so long as it is some distance away.
He goes placidly on in the way which he has found pleasant. He
seems therefore to lack foresight, both for himself and for what
might be called the common good. The idea of "progress" and
the notion of responsibility do not inspire him. His philosophy
is to cross bridges when he comes to them, to let sleeping dogs lie.

Note: There is no specific polar antithesis to this trait, but the
general conceptions of (1) somatotonic energetic expression, and (2)
cerebrotonic (Promethean) foresight and overanxiousness constitute
antitheses. The deep hostility of cerebrotonic people to viscerotonics
who are conspicuous in V-14 has come sharply to the surface in
certain modern semi-intellectual literature. The rather cerebrotonic
magazine, *The New Republic,* has long used as its subtitle, "A
thorn in the side of Complacency." Similarly the incompatibility
between somatotonia and this viscerotonic trait has been made the
subject of a delightful facetiously developed farce depicting the
adventures of Ferdinand, the (viscerotonic) bull, who preferred the
complacent to the somatotonic way of life.

V-15. *The Deep Sleep Characteristic.* Sleep is deep, easy, and
undisturbed. There is complete relaxation in sleep, the individ-

[2] *The Varieties of Human Physique,* p. 155.

ual becoming limp, like a young child. Going to sleep is easy and happens quickly. There is ordinarily no one fixed position in which the person must sleep, but sleep is possible and comfortable in a variety of positions, as is the case with the young child. Snoring is the rule. It is a deep, regular, rhythmic snoring which generally begins shortly after the person has gone to bed, and continues all night without much variation (the deepest relaxation is reached very soon). Respiration is slow and deep during sleep, much slower than is the case with cerebrotonic people, and slower than somatotonic respiration in sleep. There is a great love of sleep, and the individual frequently becomes a sleep glutton, indulging in more of it than he needs. It is difficult to waken such a person during the night. He sometimes can be picked up and carried from one bed to another without being awakened, as is often the case with a young child.

Note: The trait C-15, poor sleep habits, is a direct polar antithesis. The contrast between the two extremes offers an excellent diagnostic criterion when either viscerotonia or cerebrotonia is predominant. In adult life the phenomenon of snoring is of considerable diagnostic use in this respect. Extreme cerebrotonics virtually never snore. When cerebrotonia is moderately predominant cerebrotonic 5) snoring sometimes takes place very lightly in the morning, after the individual has been asleep for several hours and so has reached his deepest relaxation. Somatotonic people fall between the extremes with respect to sleep habits.

V-16. *The Untempered Characteristic.* The individual gives off the general impression of soft metal, which has no temper in it and will not take an edge. There is the strong suggestion of a certain flabbiness or lack of intensity in the mental and moral outlook. It is a personality without fire, and it gives off no sparks. There is a dull, vegetable-like quality, as if the fires of life burned slowly, without concentration of heat. The personality suggests lack of purpose beyond the elementary biological purposes. The relaxed protrusion of the lips (V-1) often brings to mind the picture of infantilism. There is relatively poor circulation in the hands and feet, which tend to be cold, weak, flabby and atonic. In such a personality the biological focus seems to be central, rather than peripheral. Biologically, such a person is "centro-tonic."

Note: There is no direct polar antithesis, but any personality presenting a blend of somatotonia with cerebrotonia in the presence of very low viscerotonia might be taken as a good antithesis. The highly tempered people are low in viscerotonia. This component seems to damp the more volatile fires of the human spirit. The old adage that people with cold hands have warm hearts (in the sense that they are sociophilic) appears to be true. The tense, "periphero-tonic" people with warm extremities tend to be cerebrotonic and to show sociophobic characteristics. Cerebrotonic people nearly always have warm extremities. (Note the high negative correlation between cerebrotonia and central strength—p. 405.)

The general dichotomy of *peripherotonic* versus *centrotonic* predominance is one which the writer used years ago, before a technique for more adequate description was available. The peripherotonic people seemed to have their principal strengths and sensitivities in the skin and in the extremities. They thus seemed "biologically extraverted" and seemed forced to protect themselves from overstimulation by becoming socially introverted. The centro-tonic people appeared to have their principal strength (as well as their concentration of mass) centrally located. They thus seemed relatively insensitive to peripheral stimulation. Being in this sense biologically introverted, they tended to become socially extraverted. This conception, like the extraversion-introversion dichotomy, was in general a useful one, but it did not define any polar manifesta-tions of first order components, and therefore did not open the way to a really meaningful social psychology.

V-17. *Free Communication of Feeling, Extraversion of Viscero-tonia.* The trait of giving way naturally and easily at all times to a free communication of feeling. Nothing is ever choked up or held back. There is no emotional inhibition, no repression of affect. Feeling is smoothly and naturally communicated to whomsoever may be available as recipient. Whether the indi-vidual is pleased, grieved, disappointed or shocked, his feelings are to be read like an open book, or like the feelings of a young child. He conceals nothing. It is as if his very insides (viscera) were laid wide open, so that his innermost feelings are exposed to public appraisal. This is the extraversion of viscerotonia. Such a trait plays an important part in direct social adaptation, for it both guarantees to the individual full credit for his own sympathetic reactions, and directly elicits the sympathies of others at the time when they are needed. Such a person "registers" delight, or sobs and cries convincingly at the time when it will do the most good. His sobs seem to come from the very depths of his abdomen. He is extremely sincere, in the direct, emotional meaning of that term, and he is never misunderstood to his disadvantage. He is always given full credit for sincerity. He "wears his heart on his coat sleeve" in the sense that he exposes his inner feelings to the public gaze.

Note: The trait C-17, vertical mental cleavage or introversion, is a direct polar antithesis, and also S-17, horizontal mental cleavage or extraversion of somatotonia, is an antithesis. That is to say, we are dealing here with our second three-way or tripolar trait. Limiting the descriptions as we have been doing to the extreme polar manifestations of these traits, the two kinds of extraversion, viscerotonic and somatotonic, are mutually incompatible in the same sense (although as Table 14 shows, not quite to the same degree) as each is incompatible with cerebrotonic introversion. There are, then, two entirely different kinds of extraversion. Much of the confusion over the concept of extraversion-introversion appears to have arisen from attempting to use two-way statistical methods in measuring a three-way trait. The trait V-17 when highly developed in an individual often results in his being overcredited in emotional relationships. Sometimes, for example, such persons achieve marriages which from the point of view of the other party are "marriages for sympathy." Many such marriages result disastrously. V-17 has another nearly polar antithesis in the trait C-6, secretiveness of feeling and emotional restraint.

V-18. *Relaxation and Sociophilia under Alcohol.* The response to a moderate quantity of alcohol is simply that of accentuation of the principal viscerotonic traits. There is on the one hand no feeling of internal strain, no sense of confusion or dizziness, no drowsiness or increased fatigue; and on the other hand, no tendency toward becoming assertive, arrogant, or loud. Instead of any of these reactions, the individual becomes more conspicuously relaxed, more ardently sociophilic, more emanative of comfort and tolerance and good will, and more expansive with emotional warmth. The effect of alcohol is thus distinctly pleasant, for it accentuates the tendency already predominant. The increased relaxation and sociophilia remain uncomplicated by any competing motivational tendency. Alcohol appears clearly to agree with people who show this reaction to it.

Note: There seems to be ground for placing some credence in the ancient aphorism, *in vino veritas*. Alcohol is a cerebral depressant. Its physiological effect is essentially that of attacking and weakening cerebral control while not at first greatly affecting the other organic functions. Therefore when cerebrotonia is relatively weak in the motivational hierarchy, alcohol would theoretically depress this component still farther and would thus tend to free the individual from his already weak inhibitory restraint. This in fact is what seems to happen. The result is then a relative accentuation of the dominant characteristic of the noncerebrotonic individual. If he is overwhelmingly viscerotonic, the result of alcohol is simply to bring out viscerotonic traits more conspicuously, without any corresponding amplification of somatotonic characteristics. If he is overwhelmingly somatotonic, it is only this component which seems to be accentuated by the drug. In a predominantly cerebrotonic person, the effect of alcohol is essentially depression and fatigue. If there is a fairly close balancing of components, as is of course often the case, alcohol appears to be a sensitive indicator of the direction in which the motivational beam is tipped.

People showing the V-18 trait are apparently never drunkards. We have not found a "6" in viscerotonia, or a "7," who used this drug for the purpose of getting drunk. The same is largely true of somatotonia. Extreme somatotonics seem rarely to be drunkards, although we have found exceptions. Drunkenness seems to be a response to conflict, and sometimes also to constitutional underendowment, but not to a polar predominance. Extreme cerebrotonics are apparently never drunkards. They have a dislike of alcohol, and to this generalization we have yet to find an exception.

V-19. *Need of People when Troubled.* The trait of regularly seeking social support when confronted with tragedy or trouble, or with the need for making a difficult decision. Stress or calamity appears to exert somewhat the same effect as alcohol upon the human organism. Trouble seems to bring into sharper focus the predominant motivation of the personality, and to throw the individual upon the immediate resources of his strongest component. The highly viscerotonic person seeks people in the face of any stress. He must talk it all over before making a decision. He must pour out the trouble upon the shoulders of others, especially upon other viscerotonic people. He leans upon the sympathy and understanding of these others, and feeds upon their warm protestations of compassion. Often a kind of emotional orgy takes place, and in this process the grief becomes dissipated. It is shared, thrown off, distributed, possibly in something of a literal physiological sense. A highly viscerotonic individual will seek total strangers if he is cut off from acquaintances, in order to share emotional news, of either joyful or tragic nature. He is a great "sharer."

Note: This is another three-way, tripolar trait. Fairly clear antitheses to V-19 are seen in S-19 and C-19. Viscerotonic people must at once share emotional news. Bad news seems thus to be dissipated and to lose its sting. Good news seems thus to take root and to be sustained, as if it were seed to be planted. Somatotonic people feel a strong urge to action in the face of emotional news. They must do something strenuously, either to overwhelm and forget the tragedy, or to celebrate the joyful occasion. If nothing else they must shout and throw their hats in the air, or they must strike out vigorously to leave the scene in disgust. Alcohol facilitates either the viscerotonic or the somatotonic reactions. Cerebrotonic people seek solitude and silence in the face of emotional news, whether good or bad. They must think. The horrible thing must be faced and thought through and made to fit into the picture somehow, or the good news must be contemplated and fully comprehended. Nothing must interfere or disturb the contemplation. In all three instances—in the viscerotonic, the somatotonic and the cerebrotonic instances—the reactions to trouble are more sharply and clearly defined than the reactions to good news. In trouble, as in alcohol, there is truth.

V-20. *Orientation toward Infancy, and toward Family Relationships.* There is deep love of the period of infancy and of the idea of being a child. There is a profound emotional adhesion to the family, to the idea of family, and especially to the mother-concept. The idea of mother-love and of the sacredness of the family induces emotion as easily as turning on a water faucet. True, natural rapport with young children is easy, as if it were second nature. Infancy is regarded as the halcyon period of life, and there is a strong craving to return to that state. This craving is easily brought to consciousness in any simple analytic situation. Usually it comes to the surface in an ordinary discussion. The "maternal instinct" or mothering impulse is strong, even in the male viscerotonic. People in whom this trait is predominant usually do not like to contemplate the idea of death. They have a strong aversion to death, and are nearly always found not to have made peace with it.

Note: This is the fifth three-way trait to be considered. Fairly clear antitheses to V-20 are seen in S-20 and C-20. Somatotonic primary orientation is toward the period of youth with its strife and competition and vigorous assertiveness of the body. Cerebrotonic orientation is toward the contemplative solitude and freedom from either visceral or muscular distraction which is to be associated with the later decades of life, and with intellectual maturity. The "oral-erotic" viscerotonic loves to make a fuss over children, and he loves the intimate physical contact of family life. The pronounced cerebrotonic suggests the Freudian "anal-erotic" type, and the somatotonic has some of the characteristics of the Freudian "urethral-erotic" picture. One further characteristic of viscerotonia worthy of mention is the great rarity of suicide among persons in whom this component is predominant. We have looked as carefully as possible into the records of now over sixty suicides without yet finding a viscerotonic among the lot.

In a very general sense, viscerotonia may be said to look back toward childhood, while somatotonia looks to the present, and the vision of cerebrotonia is fixed upon the distant future.

2. Traits Defining the Second Component (Somatotonia)

S-1. *Assertiveness of Posture and Movement.* The hallmark is bodily readiness for action. Marked assertiveness and muscular readiness of the body as a whole. The trunk is erect, whether in sitting or in standing, the spinal column is held relatively straight, shoulders are back, chest is expanded, abdomen is retracted, the head is high, and the muscles of the face are "set," as if ready for an act of aggression. All this is done without any strain or effort, and without conscious attention. There is no occasion for, or any occurrence of, frequent "correction" of posture, such as throwing back the shoulders, taking a deeper breath, squaring the jaw, etc. When S-1 is a predominant trait, postural assertiveness is effortless, constant and natural. Consequently this trait is easily distinguished from the effects of training. All movement is unhesitant and aggressive. The walk is a brisk, determined, heel-striking one, sometimes stiff and sometimes with springiness in the step. In walking, the body is moved vigorously and there is typically an emphatic rearward and sidelong thrust of the arm, as if the air were a dense medium offering a purchase to movement. There is a tendency to use vigorous gestures of the head and hands in ordinary social conversation, especially when the individual is a little perturbed. When this trait is predominant, blood pressure is inclined to be high.

Note: The three-way polar antithesis between the traits S-1, V-1 and C-1 is so sharply defined and so obvious that it perhaps needs no further emphasis. The S-1 trait is among the easiest of the list to gauge. Yet it offers some perplexity to the beginner, perhaps because we are living in a period marked by something like a somatotonic revolution, not only against the restraints long imposed by the (cerebrotonic) Christian religion, but against all restraint. The modern watchword is liberty, or somatotonic freedom. Many influences are at work which encourage the child or growing youth to simulate somatotonic traits. Among these influences are the now almost universal posture-training exercises offered in the schools and colleges. Such exercises attempt to graft the S-1 trait upon all personalities, regardless of constitutional predisposition, and the teachers of physical education need of course to be S-1 people themselves. The resulting picture is often that of viscerotonic and cerebrotonic

youths attempting for a time to move, stand, or sit in the somatotonic pattern. But this is like teaching ducks and herons the postural habits of fighting cocks. It never really fools anybody, and it
only introduces temporary conflict and confusion into the non-
somatotonic personalities. The resulting artificial imitations of
somatotonic postural aggression suggest random mixtures of comic
strip figures. In a period of motivational confusion we do funny
things to personality. There seems to be no more good reason for
making viscerotonic children stand and sit like somatotonics than
for making the latter stand and sit like cerebrotonics. But this statement should reflect no discredit upon physical education, so far as
the general principle is concerned. We need more, not less physical
education, but we need it constitutionally differentiated.

S-2. *Love of Physical Adventure*. Physical adventure is regularly
sought and enjoyed for its own sake. There is genuine pleasure
in participation in dangerous and strenuous undertakings, not
so much because of the goals involved as because of the nature
of the activity itself. The individual spontaneously and freely
enters upon physical adventure because he likes it. Such activity
expresses itself in a rich variety of fields, like war, exploration,
aviation, racing, horsemanship, hunting, vigorous or dangerous
competitive athletics, mountain climbing, etc. There is generally
a love of speed—fast automobiles, horses, boats, airplanes. The
possessor of this trait in high degree is likely to have a deep love
of horses, for the horse is one incarnation of somatotonia. Similarly there is a predilection for large, muscular dogs, and for
other powerful, destructive animals. There is a sincere love of
physical hardship and a love of danger.

Note: The trait V-2, love of physical comfort, presents a partial
antithesis, although by no means a polar one. Many people love
both comfort and adventure, at different times. The whole concept
of cerebrotonic restraint in general is an antithesis. Table 14 reveals, and the analysis of almost any personality emphasizes, that
the incompatibility between somatotonia and cerebrotonia is more
sharply defined than that between viscerotonia and either of the
other two components. In gauging the trait S-2 it is necessary to
guard against being too strongly impressed by the initial verbal
statement of the subject. Most people will state sincerely enough
that they are fond of the various kinds of physical adventure, and

that they love horses. With a somatotonic outlook predominant in the mores, such attitudes are merely stereotypes. The problem is to determine how real a part these characteristics have actually played in the individual's life. This can be done only by a careful, systematic analysis of his history, carried out according to periods of life and fields of expression (see Appendix 3).

S-3. *The Energetic Characteristic.* Energy is quickly and abundantly available. This trait is the no-sooner-said-than-done trait. There is no impediment to action, no lethargy of overrelaxation, no chronic fatigue or sleepiness, no interfering inhibition or restraint. Hence there is no procrastination. This person seems to think with his muscles, and he is tireless. In general, getting up in the morning is pleasant, and morning is the best time of day. Early rising is the rule, especially in later life. Such a person can endure muscular exertion for long periods without sleep and without food (Simon Kenton, famous Indian fighter, used to say that a man is better off with one meal a day than with two or three, and he considered the optimum amount of sleep to be six hours). These people have a strong pulse and they live by action. The term "bustling" seems to apply excellently to females who are highly endowed with this trait.

Note: There seems to be no direct polar antithesis that is satisfactorily expressible as a single trait. S-3 is however one of the traits which most clearly differentiate the somatotonic from the viscerotonic personality. This trait is an antithesis to laziness, which is perhaps a composite of several viscerotonic characteristics, usually complicated by a generous endowment of cerebrotonia. Laziness is indeed a good example of the sort of trait that cannot be used in a scale of this kind, for it does not define one primary component to the exclusion of both of the others. Laziness was one of the 50 traits with which we experimented in the original effort to develop the scale. We found that its positive correlation with the viscerotonic traits was sufficiently high, but that it did not show a satisfactory negative correlation with the cerebrotonic traits.

S-4. *Need and Enjoyment of Exercise.* There is a strong craving for regular, vigorous muscular exercise, and a manifest zeal for exercise. This is no intermittent or spasmodic craving, with spells of freedom from the desire. The need is a continuous one, and the individual is dependent for his happiness and well-being upon a degree of fulfillment. When cut off from opportunity for regular exercise, he is disturbed, inefficient, churlish or unhappy. There is usually the history of fairly persistent participation in some kind of athletic expression, and a relatively high proportion of time and energy will have gone into the perfection of bodily strength and athletic skills.

Note: S-4 is another trait for which no specific polar antithesis seems to be available. Love of exercise is in general an antithesis both to extreme viscerotonia and to cerebrotonia. Unnecessary muscular exertion is nearly always distasteful to the viscerotonic, but the latter rarely if ever enters upon it to a sufficient degree to do him any harm. He seems to be protected against such a mistake by his great relaxation and inertia. It is cerebrotonics who are most prone to be caught in the monkey trap of falling in with a program of exercise to their own detriment. Cerebrotonic people often become associated with somatotonics who carry the former along into physical exercise which leaves them chronically exhausted and ill able to cope with their programs. Cerebrotonia means low energy and chronic fatigue (see trait C-15). Unnecessary vigorous muscular exercise, instead of building up energy in these people, seems to exhaust the already scanty reserve and to leave them inefficient victims of chronic fatigue. Then instead of successfully grooving their energies in mental channels, they sometimes become confused, unhappy, cerebrotic ("neurotic"). It is possible that there is a cerebrotonic need for *protection from the temptation* to exercise, and such a need may be quite as urgent as the somatotonic need for opportunity to exercise. This is but another specific illustration of the general need for taking cognizance of constitutional differences in education.

S-5. *Love of Dominating, Lust for Power.* There is a deep and constant desire to be important in the world, to wield power over other creatures and over the environment. This trait under various circumstances assumes the garments of ambition, of love of power, of craving for prestige, and of desire to be conspicuous. There is a consummate willingness to assume responsibility. The trait is very closely associated with natural leadership. When present to an exaggerated degree it may lead to what is referred to popularly as the Napoleonic complex, or the ambition to conquer on a large scale. Napoleon serves well to illustrate the trait in this exaggerated form. There is strong desire to conquer and subdue, and to be in a position of such power over others that whatever one does is important and may have life or death significance to others. One must then be taken seriously. This trait represents one of the most dangerous manifestations of somatotonia, for it is the war-making characteristic. Persons with S-5 strongly predominant love to be served and to be waited upon, to have servants about, and to give orders. They love to have other human beings look to them as master. They like to give orders even to Pullman porters, maids, luggage boys, and the like. They are characteristically expansive and are often generous. They fall in easily with a "master race" psychology, in which they are to be the masters.

Note: Possibly the clearest antithesis to S-5 is embodied in what is loosely called humor, or sense of humor. Whatever else may be true of humor, it represents a singular inclination to take life lightly, or whimsically, and a readiness to tolerate (indeed to enjoy) incompatible conceptions. The person with a sense of humor does not put himself in too serious a light, and does not desire to be taken too seriously. He avoids the responsibility of exercising power. People with humor are not directly leaders in the world's affairs. But humor is in no sense a polar trait. It involves both the relaxation of viscerotonia and the restraint of cerebrotonia. What humor *is* is extraordinarily difficult to state, but that it is something of an antithesis to the S-5 trait is clear.

S-6. *Love of Risk and Chance.* The daredevil characteristic. Love of unnecessary danger. Readiness or eagerness to take a chance. Recklessness. Predominance of the "gambling instinct." This person seems deliberately to seek the danger of disaster and to run risks more for love of the risk than for love of the gain involved. He loves to gamble, even when well aware that in the end he can at best only come out even. Games of chance are wholly pleasant, not painfully straining experiences, and the higher the stakes the greater the fun. Recklessness in automobile driving or in other activity is the best of fun. It produces no inner strain, no cringing or "cowardly squeamishness," but only a sense of expansion and of power and happiness. To bluff is pleasant, either in a game of chance or in a social situation, even in a classroom recitation. It is not painful to be caught bluffing. As a boy such a person is a leader in reckless stunts. He will never be outdone, and in his outdoing of others there is frequently a history of accidents and injuries to himself as well as to others. His later accumulation of automobile accidents is often for him more a source of pride than of regret. These are a little like fencing scars among German students.

Note: The entire concept of cerebrotonic restraint presents something of an antithesis to this trait, but the full antithesis is a mixture of viscerotonia and cerebrotonia rather than a polar trait. The people who most abhor unnecessary risk and danger are not only inclined to be full of restraint but also are often persons of strongly compassionate feeling and of sensitive affect. The quality of empathy, or capacity to feel oneself in the situation of another creature appears to arise from a blend of viscerotonia and cerebrotonia in the presence of low somatotonia. What, then, is cowardice? This characteristic seems to have complex and perhaps somewhat variable roots, but certainly it presents a general antithesis to traits S-6 and S-8. In this antithesis lies a singular dilemma. For it is painful to live among people who have traits S-6 and S-8 well developed. They are dangerous and destructive, as well as wasteful, and they exert one kind of demoralizing influence. Yet if these traits were discouraged, and the persons possessing them were to be socially and hence biologically suppressed, we should run the danger of becoming a race of cowards and softies. This is a general dilemma and it always lurks behind any contemplation of the relationship between somatotonia and the other components. Here may possibly lie the roots of the central dilemma of human life which the classical Greeks called the *enantiodroma* of life, or the problem of the opposites. We, like the Greeks, are groping for a social psychology adequate to analyze this conflict into its component elements.

S-7. *Bold Directness of Manner.* Dependence on the direct, bold approach. This trait is reflected especially in the characteristic manner of social address. The individual tends to fix a direct, unchanging stare upon the person addressed. There is no hesitancy of approach, no beating about the bush, no dependence upon overpoliteness or (viscerotonic) unctuousness. And there is no (cerebrotonic) furtiveness. The serious, unsmiling somatotonic face reveals a singular rigidity and immobility of expression which strongly proclaims sincerity and directness. There are no quick changes of attitude or mood. Persons manifesting this trait have a striking frankness about them which is not likely to be discounted. The manner suggests stability, responsibility, trust-worthiness, candor. There is a singularly impersonal objectivity in seeking what is wanted, in sharp contrast with the viscerotonic dependence upon the personal relationship, and in contrast with constrained cerebrotonic subjectivity.

Note: Both V-7, love of polite ceremony, and C-7, motility of the face, present fairly good antitheses to this trait, although neither is quite a direct polar antithesis. The contrast seen here between the three divergent patterns of social address is a conspicuous and re-vealing one. The S-7 trait seems to be closely associated with natural leadership. Persons possessing this characteristic to a conspicuous degree usually stand out in a group as people to be consulted and to be taken seriously. They are never for long outsiders in a situa-tion, but are soon members of the inner circle. When a group or-ganizes, such a person is fairly certain to be elected to office, for stability, objectivity and responsibility seem to be stamped upon his face and manner like the legend on a coin.

S-8. *Physical Courage for Combat.* Courage for actual or poten-tial combat. An essential and unquestionable physical fearless-ness. Confident dependence upon the sturdiness, skill, and mus-cular strength of the body. The individual depends upon his soma as the viscerotonic depends upon social good will, and as the cerebrotonic depends upon the exercise of exteroceptive acuity and wariness. Such a person may be truculently combative. He is often so when slightly under average stature (see Chapter V). But when he is above average stature, and there is no serious dysplasia, the combativeness is generally latent and of slow arousal. Large, powerful men typically present an unruffled composure to the world except when enraged or especially aroused by some cir-cumstance. They are like the great cats when well fed. But the essential fearlessness and sense of physical reliance is easily per-ceived in the most superficial analysis of the social history. In gauging this trait it is necessary to distinguish between the per-son of consistent physical courage, and the irregularly or inconsistently somatotonic individual who often starts what he lacks the physical resources to finish.

Note: The most direct antithesis is cowardice, which is clearly a complex and variable trait involving elements of both viscerotonia and cerebrotonia. There seems to be no approximation of a polar antithesis to S-8. This trait is perhaps the principal somatotonic characteristic for the sake of which somatotonia in general is cherished and tolerated. One of the oldest problems of civilization—and a still unsolved one—is that of devising techniques of conditioning capable of discouraging certain closely associated somatotonic characteristics while retaining this one unweakened. We have had educational philosophies, even religions (such as Christianity), aimed in desperation at the *general* discouragement of somatotonia, but we have as yet found no formula for *differential* conditioning among somatotonic traits. Possibly this is because we have not used a psychology resting on an analysis of primary components.

S-9. *Competitive Aggressiveness.* Enjoyment of competitive strife. Push, drive and enterprise in the struggle to get ahead of others. The individual is one-directional and unhesitant. He is free from restraint, inhibition, or tentativeness. He readily takes the initiative to put himself forward or to secure what he wants. He is not easily abashed and is not afraid to ask. His point of view is essentially a competitive one and he enters into competition with alacrity. He has the "brass" to go after things. In gauging such a trait it is well to remember that aggressiveness is not necessarily an unpleasant characteristic. Aggressive people are not always obnoxious people. Obnoxiousness lies in the manner, not in the fact of aggression. There are people who although extremely aggressive, are likewise tactful and perhaps well endowed with the trait V-7 (ceremoniousness and politeness). To be "taken in" by the aggressiveness of such a person may be a rather pleasant experience, like having one's tonsils removed by a polite and engaging surgeon.

Note: There is no polar trait which is an antithesis to aggressiveness, although the general concept of cerebrotonic restraint is an antithesis. This is perhaps the hardest of the somatotonic traits for the beginner to gauge, because the most successfully aggressive people usually conceal their aggressiveness behind some degree of amiability. Successfully aggressive people often seem modest at first discovery, just as the best athletes seem at first to perform their feats without effort. But upon closer inquiry into the individual's life history it will be found that much practice and training have gone into the present perfection. The unsuccessfully aggressive individual is of the speak-up-in-meeting sort, and is always *regarded* as aggressive. The difficulty of diagnosis just referred to lies only in the study of a small group who have successfully blended their aggressiveness with just the right degree of viscerotonia. For the most part, the S-9 trait sticks out like a sore thumb, and persons conspicuously high in the trait are frequently regarded by their own contemporaries or fellow competitors as obnoxious. The adjective aggressive is often used as an opprobrious epithet. Yet generals like aggressive soldiers, and professors like aggressive satellites. Most parents encourage their own children to be more aggressive, while perhaps considering the neighbors' children to be already too much so. The ethical evaluation of this trait depends upon the point of view.

S-10. *Psychological Callousness.* Lack of inhibitory suggestibility. A singular insensitivity, especially to the less obvious or subtler needs and desires of other personalities in the environment. In sharp contrast to the inhibited mental oversensitivity of the cerebrotonic (trait C-5), this individual is underresponsive to inhibitory suggestion. He does things callously, or without the usual, normal inhibition. Watch him walk. Independently of the strength of trait S-9 (Aggression), of trait S-15 (Noisiness), and of trait S-3 (Energy), there is an insensitive carelessness in his manner of putting down his feet, suggesting the walk of a shod horse on a wooden floor. If the trait aggressiveness (S-9) is also strongly predominant, there is an overbearing callousness in social relationships. If the latter trait is not well developed, the individual may be merely insensitive.

Note: There is no direct polar antithesis, although both the mental overresponsiveness of cerebrotonia (C-5) and the overpoliteness often associated with viscerotonia (V-7) are good partial antitheses. The complete antithesis is clearly a mixture of viscerotonia and cerebrotonia. Persons possessing the S-10 trait predominantly have one distinct advantage. They are inclined to be stable and predictable. There is little variation of social attitude. They are not easily influenced, and therefore are rarely caught out of character, or in a false position. These are the "hardheaded" people, and the term hardheaded has come to carry an essentially favorable social connotation. Men often describe themselves as hardheaded.

Related to the S-10 trait, perhaps, is a certain physiological insensitivity, or physiological underresponsiveness which defines an antithesis to the trait C-2, physiological overresponse. Somatotonic people are peculiarly susceptible to many infections, notably to the chronic sinus infections and to appendicitis. They seem to lack the quick, effective mobilization of physiological defenses (trait C-2) which is so characteristic of cerebrotonia.

S-11. *Claustrophobia.* Or agoraphilia. Love of being out in the open, in conspicuous position. Hatred of being shut in, cramped, or restrained in any way. There is dislike of small, closed-in rooms, of corners, and of places where it is difficult to move about freely. The large, open room is preferred for sleeping, for eating, for working, or for any purpose. The bed or desk is preferred out in the middle of the room rather than in a corner or against the wall. People manifesting this trait like "air." They abhor stuffiness. They dislike things that are "small" and "mean." They love life on the grand scale. They are expansive. They do not wish to be tucked away out of sight. They wish to be out in the open, in both a physical and a psychological sense. They like things to be very open and overt (objective). Such people like doors to be open, not closed. They prefer houses on a hill or in conspicuous, commanding position. They dislike restraining clothing. They like to sleep nude, and to swim nude. In general, they like to be nude. Cerebrotonics sometimes call them exhibitionists. They call cerebrotonics prudes.

Note: The polar antithesis is agoraphobia, or claustrophilia (C-11). One specific gift which seems to accompany the S-11 trait is that of excellent spatial orientation. These people always seem to know where they are in the geographic sense. Both sense of direction and sound localization are often developed to a striking degree.
The hostility and lack of understanding which the extremely claustrophobic person frequently evinces toward agoraphobic people is noteworthy. This problem sometimes becomes especially acute when misguided parents send a cerebrotonic child to a "progressive" school or camp. The progressive educational institution is

frequently one in which a special effort is made to encourage somatotonic traits and to discourage cerebrotonic ones. That is to say, the progressive movement seems for practical purposes to be part of the general somatotonic revolution against an already rapidly disappearing cerebrotonic educational philosophy. In human affairs the pendulum must needs always swing violently.

S-12. *Ruthlessness, Freedom from Squeamishness.* There is marked freedom from "compunctions" of all sorts. The individual is ruthless in the sense that he unhesitatingly will use up things or even people in order to accomplish an objective. He is not bothered by conscience, or by what he perhaps would call overconscientiousness. There is no sentimentality and no inhibition concerning such a matter as perhaps the taking of life. This person does not empathize. He is ruthless in the sense that he is oblivious to purposes or wishes that conflict with his own—not necessarily in the sense of being deliberately cruel. (To be cruel requires a degree of cerebrotonia.) Such people are good executives. They get things done. They are practical. Their friends say they are free from sentimentality. Only their enemies call them ruthless. People of this sort step on ants, but not because they want to "hurt" the ants. Such people enjoy hunting. Killing is easily rationalized and gives them no qualms. Like S-5, this is a trait of importance to the successful military leader.

Note: There is no polar antithesis, for the trait squeamishness obviously includes both viscerotonic and cerebrotonic elements. Squeamishness involves feeling as well as imagination. The S-12 trait is perhaps of all the polar characteristics the nearest approach to what is called practicality. To be practical means to be relatively free from peripheral, outlying considerations of an inhibitory nature, and therefore to be well orientated to the present reality and the immediate need.

The distinction between S-12 and cruelty is worth a word of further emphasis. In the trait S-12 there is no hint of malevolence. If a somatotonic person is also malevolent, as is often enough the case, this appears to be due to some disharmonious (dyscrastic) mixing of the second and third components, not to the primary predominance. To carry out malice and to perpetrate willful harm against another requires both the aggression of somatotonia and the mental intensity of cerebrotonia.

S-13. *The Unrestrained Voice.* The trait of full vocalization. The voice "carries" conspicuously well, and there is no restraint in it. The individual may be habitually quiet-spoken, but nevertheless he can be heard clearly at a surprising distance. His voice has no "brakes." The trait is so conspicuous that it can be readily scaled by a beginner. Sit in a crowded railway carriage and listen. Two or three 6's and perhaps a 7 in S-13 will be heard well above the general hum of the 4's and 5's. In every large office there is sure to be a 6, who can be heard all over the institution when he or she speaks. When a 6 lectures in a college classroom, he can usually be heard distinctly in the corridor or in the next classroom. A woman with this trait well developed can communicate with her children three backyards away, without shouting. Since other somatotonic traits are usually associated with this one, such people frequently appear to employ speech as a form of exercise, and to possess tireless vocal cords. The trait S-7 is often associated with S-13, and when this is the case, the speaker may fix his listener with a direct stare and may bring his mouth as close to the listener's face as he can get it. The listener is then sprayed or vaporized with each hard consonant.   .

Note: A polar antithesis is seen in the vocal restraint of cerebrotonia (trait C-13). Strongly cerebrotonic people typically aim their voices so carefully, and turn their faces away from the listener's face so conscientiously, that it becomes necessary to attend closely to hear what is said. Somatotonic parents impatiently tell cerebrotonic children to speak up. Cerebrotonic parents protest in vain against the vocal assault of somatotonic children.

The close observer will detect two quite distinct kinds of somatotonic speech. There is a heavy, booming, reverberatory variety, rich in sonorous overtones and usually rather deliberate. Such speech is sometimes called pontifical. This kind seems to be characteristic of high somatotonia combined with some viscerotonia but without any very appreciable cerebrotonia. And there is a sharper, strident, more truculently assertive variety, poor in overtones and usually of more rapid delivery. This is the "shrewish tongue" of literary reference, although it is quite as frequently observed in the male as in the female. This kind seems to be characteristic of high somatotonia complicated by an appreciable secondary cerebrotonia. Sometimes highly somatotonic people who also possess a fairly good viscerotonic component are normally very quiet-spoken, becoming loud only when aroused, or alcoholized. But their voices are always free from restraint, and always carry well.

The S-13 trait has a peculiar importance in constitutional analysis, for it is sometimes the only somatotonic trait to be conspicuously present in an individual's behavior—the only clear sign of aggression in a personality which otherwise, upon superficial study, might have passed as very low in the second component.

Clarence Day did not care for the S-13 trait when he wrote:

> The earth is used to bores.
> It heard for ages long
> The Saurians' complacent roars.
>
> . . . .
>
> These restless tongues their lust for action
> Never dies. The noisiness of living dust
> Astonishes the skies.

S-14. *Spartan Indifference to Pain.* The trait of bearing physical injury and pain lightly, sometimes even with manifest indifference. There seems to be a physiological insensitivity or resistance to pain and there is often a true pleasure in the rigor of severe physical strain. The individual appears to remain relatively oblivious to what would be the severest discomfort for a person of low somatotonia. He can stand stitches in an unanaesthetized wound without flinching. Flinching and wincing are rare under any circumstances. There seems to be no advance apprehension of pain, and none of the overreadiness to respond to pain that is so conspicuous in cerebrotonia (trait C-14). Somatotonic people frequently come to the medical clinic with lesions or injuries which would have devastated the composure of a viscerotonic or would have prostrated a cerebrotonic, but they usually make no particular complaint of the pain. Endurance of very cold water appears to be a corollary to this trait. The coldest shower is only stimulating, not painful, and it does not seriously interfere with the respiratory reflex. This latter characteristic presents an especially sharp contrast with trait C-14.

Note: Cerebrotonic hypersensitivity to pain (trait C-14) presents a polar antithesis. The whole concept of viscerotonia, with its love of ease and comfort, constitutes a general antithesis. The physiological mechanism underlying this characteristic is of great interest although little is known about it. Possibly the pain stimulus is less intense when somatotonia is high, but this is speculative. What we see is the response. This certainly is of less magnitude and it is less generalized. Somatotonic people rarely show gastrointestinal upset (nausea) in response to pain, and their respiration and pulse are not much altered by any ordinary pain stimulus. Predominantly somatotonic people rarely faint, even under extreme trauma. Cerebrotonic people are quickly nauseated by pain, faint easily, and their respiration and pulse are subject to profound alteration in response to even moderate pain. The S-14 trait is one which has been highly prized by warlike and somatotonic peoples of all ages. Like the Spartans, the American Indians placed this trait above all others in the scale of virtue, reserving physical torture as a final test of virtue. To wince under torture was unworthy.

S-15. *General Noisiness.* General, hearty noisiness. Noisiness in moving about, and in all personal activities. The shout, the explosive laugh, and the sharp, "pistol-shot" cough are hallmarks of somatotonia. These people are deep, free breathers, and they laugh and cough with the diaphragm. (The pistol-shot cough or laugh is diaphragmatic. Cerebrotonic people nearly always tense the diaphragm, and thereby inhibit it, when they cough or laugh.) There is a general tendency to do things vigorously and thereby to make noise, although not necessarily for the sake of making noise. The noise is incidental to "hearty" somatotonic self-expression in walking and moving, in speaking or laughing, in shutting doors, driving automobiles and in all the routine activity of life. "By laughing under a walnut tree a 6 in S-15 will shake off the ripe nuts in September. A 7 will shake off the green ones in August."

Note: The antithesis to S-15 is not a polar characteristic, for many viscerotonic people are as quiet as the cerebrotonics. Noisiness is polar, but it finds its antithesis wherever somatotonia is conspicuously low. This trait is not quite as easy for the beginner to gauge as are some of the others, for superficially it is sensitive to cultural influence. The extremes are easy enough to recognize and to gauge under any circumstances, but persons near the middle range sometimes show considerable variation in different situations. It is important to observe the individual under a number of different

sets of circumstances before fixing the final rating. When these pre-
cautions are observed, this is one of the easier and more objective
traits to gauge accurately. Somatotonic people do things heartily and
insensitively, that is to say, without inhibitory cerebrotonic control.
They make noise not because they particularly want to do so, but
because through lack of the inhibitory component, they fail to want
not to make noise. Sometimes society, or individuals, attempt to
substitute external restraints for the natural inhibitory component.
A somatotonic person can learn to do *some* things quietly, but these
superficially acquired inhibitions serve but to sharpen the picture
of the true motivational pattern, if the investigator will only look
systematically and persistently.

S-16. *Overmaturity of Appearance.* In general appearance and
deportment, the individual gives the impression of being older
than he is. This is equally true if he is observed as child, boy, or
young man. Young children in whom this trait is predominant
seem a year or two older than they are. There is a striking manliness or womanliness about their appearance, their address, their
manner. Youths seem almost young men. Young men seem older,
maturer, more settled than the average of their age. Men of middle age often seem old. These people come to their maturity early.
They suggest a quick-blossoming flower. They seem to be grown
up at adolescence and to be old at 25. The characteristic does not
appear to lie in outward manner and appearance alone. The individual feels himself to be farther along in life than his chronological age indicates. He seems older not only to others but to
himself as well.

Note: Trait C-16, youthful intentness, is a polar antithesis. A
profound physiological difference appears to lie between these two
extreme trait manifestations. Youngsters showing the S-16 trait have
an early adolescence, sometimes extremely early, and their faces and
bodies take on at once the permanent stamp of their maturity. Youngsters showing the C-16 trait have a late adolescence, and the final set
of the features and mold of the body can be predicted only from a
close knowledge of the course typically followed by the somatotype
which such an individual presents. The S-16 trait is well shown by
many professional athletes so far as external appearance goes. Notice
the faces of baseball players, or of college football players. There is an
overly mature set of the facial muscles and a fixity of expression

which suggests middle age. Take a pair of powerful binoculars to a big league ball game and study the faces of the players. Guess their ages. Then look up the records or call the nearest sports writer for the correct information. This is an instructive exercise.

S-17. *Horizontal Mental Cleavage. Extraversion of Somatotonia.* Dissociation from the "subconscious." Lack of self-awareness. The mind is objective, extensive, extraverted. The mental focus is directed exclusively upon the "outer reality." There is poor rapport with what may be called the latent, remoter, or inward elements of consciousness. This individual is a pronounced extravert in the sense that his attention is turned disproportionately upon the outward scene, and is thus cut off (dissociated) from the inner mind. Reactions to the circumstances in which he finds himself are therefore direct, and are impeded but little by hesitations, misgivings, or considerations of alternatives and reservations, such as flood the subjective (cerebrotonic) mind. Nor is there any viscerotonic interference—any good-natured relaxation, tolerance, or *primary* love of people and of comfort. The viscerotonic reaction is as effectively cut off as is the cerebrotonic reaction. This person does not wear his heart on his coat sleeve any more than does the cerebrotonic.

The diagnostic hallmark of S-17 is freedom from doubt. The individual makes decisions immediately, without insight into himself or into his motivation. He does not, as it were, hear the voices of his own weaker components. There is a relative cleavage, a separative barrier, between immediate awareness and the cumulative body of inhibitive, qualifying awareness which in most minds lies ready to be rearoused and associated with the present perception. Such a cleavage we call horizontal, because the individual seems to be cut off horizontally from his own deeper mental levels and resources. But in being so cut off, he keeps his decks always cleared for action, and is therefore a good natural executive. He avoids the great impediment to decision and action which is in one sense a bane of cerebrotonic existence. He remains in a perpetual state of extraversion of action. Such an individual often shows a history of manic episodes, sudden conversions and the like. Usually he is easily hypnotized. He rarely knows anything of his own dreams or phantasies, and for him dream analysis or any similar delving into the remoter mind is likely to be revelatory, opening a new world.

Note: The three traits, V-17, S-17 and C-17 form one of our most clearly defined tripolar offsets. The two kinds of extraversion, viscerotonic and somatotonic, are as easily distinguishable when the relatively pure or polar forms are encountered, as either is distinguishable from the cerebrotonic extreme. When the V-17 trait is predominant, an observing psychologist senses himself to be in the presence of one kind of nakedness. It is as if the entire intestinal mass, all quivering with compassion, were in plain view before one's eyes. A poet would of course say—it is as if the soul were exposed. When the S-17 trait predominates overwhelmingly, compassion appears to be dissociated. The somatic system seems then to operate almost independently of the visceral system, and to call the latter into play only during episodes of anger or of manic euphoria. The S-17 trait gives the individual a free road to action, with both the affective and the cognitive element of mind relatively cut off.

People who show this trait are cut off from insight into their own internal organic life. They tend not to recognize their own appetites, sometimes not even hunger or internal pain. Fatigue, internal distress, or serious organic pathology may progress to an advanced degree before its presence is recognized. Such people therefore not infrequently break down suddenly, without warning. More accurately, probably, the warnings failed to reach consciousness. The sudden breakdown, either organic or "nervous," is a somatotonic hallmark. In mental pathology, somatotonics tend to become manic, or hysterical.

Cerebrotonic people never have sudden breakdowns, although they not infrequently complain of fatigue and ill health for ninety years. Similarly, whereas somatotonic people experience sudden "conversions" of all sorts, such as religious conversions, cerebrotonic people are not often suddenly converted to anything. They always have reservations, and hence are resistant to suggestion.

S-18. *Assertiveness and Aggression under Alcohol.* The response to a moderate quantity of alcohol is simply that of accentuation of the principal somatotonic traits. The individual reveals his somatotonic motivation more conspicuously and clearly than is normally the case. He becomes more openly, uninhibitedly, and noisily aggressive, more expansive, and full of a sense of power. His postures are more assertive, he envisions vast undertakings and adventures, his energies seem unlimited, the laugh and the voice rise to new achievements in volume, the weak crust of culturally imposed inhibition crumbles away, candor is complete, and the sense of being important holds full sway. Above all, he loves it. That is to say, the cerebral depression or alcoholic intoxication achieves for him a state of organic affairs in which he is at one with his world. He is free from internal tension and conflict. Alcohol attacks and temporarily overwhelms an already weak cerebrotonia, leaving the field clear for expression of the predominant component. In temperament study an ounce of alcohol is sometimes worth hours of the shrewdest inquiry.

Note: The tripolarity of response to alcohol is a sharply defined one. The drug brings out the extremes in motivational predominance more quickly and in sharper relief than any other test or situation of which we have made use. Alcohol often yields a clue when all other observations have failed to establish which of two evenly balanced components is slightly the stronger. The standard dosage of this drug, for our purposes, is two ounces of whisky given one ounce at a time, with a fifteen-minute interval. In a case of marked cerebrotonia, it is unnecessary to offer the second ounce. The individual generally will refuse it anyhow. Sometimes, when the balance between the first two components appears to be a close one, a third or fourth ounce is indicated for accurate diagnosis. Persons accustomed to the use of this drug generally require a larger dosage than those to whom it is a novelty. It is important that at least one or two other persons besides the investigator and the subject be present at this experiment, in order to provide full encouragement to the viscerotonic (sociophilic) component.

S-19. *Need for Action when Troubled or Perplexed.* The trait of turning to action when confronted with tragedy or trouble, or with the need for making a difficult decision. Stress, like alcohol, appears to throw the individual sharply back upon his primary resources, and to cause him to reveal his constitutional motivating pattern. In the face of grief the somatotonic must *do* something. This may take the form of playing hard at a game, of going on a strenuous trip, of undertaking a vast enterprise, or of striving to inflict violent revenge. He may climb a mountain, build something, take up riding or aviation, or he may go on a spree, most often a spending spree. A long automobile trip sometimes answers the need. If of alcoholic inclination, he may simply try to drown the matter out of consciousness. If he has money he will have his physician tell him that he needs a change, perhaps an ocean voyage. In any event the immediate objective is always to get the thing out of mind—to repress it or dissociate it from the conscious focus, or more accurately, to dissociate his own internal reactions. The somatotonic always falls back upon horizontal dissociation.

Sudden good news produces much the same effect, but the reaction is more brief and less intense. When pleased the somatotonic is inclined to shout, to throw his hat in the air, to celebrate, to blow off energy—to have the celebrating festivities then and there. The cerebrotonic takes good news, like bad, down into the inner recesses of his mind and then he contemplates and regales himself in it as a miser with his gold.

Note: The tripolarity of response to trouble and to emotional news is almost as sharply defined as the response to alcohol, and this trait is in one sense even easier to gauge than trait 18. To gauge the latter requires such expenditure of effort as may be necessary to observe the subject under alcohol. To gauge trait 19, only a few casual "watchings," or perhaps a systematic review of the subject's history is necessary. What has this person done in the face of the various exigencies of circumstance to which he has been exposed? How has he reacted to his experiences? The better procedure, of course, is to observe him systematically. Find out (a) what he says he does, and (b) what he actually does, when things happen to him.

S-20. *Orientation toward the Goals and Activities of Youth.* There is a deep love of the activities of the strenuous period of youth. The primary objectives of life are embodied in competitive struggle. Competition for power, for recognition, for money and for status. And there is often a primary desire for power and status *while young*, before it is "too late to enjoy these things." The period of very early manhood or womanhood is regarded as the best time of life, and this feeling is usually fairly strong while the individual is living through that period. There is painful awareness of the fleetingness of youth, and as a rule there is even in the twenties a disturbing presentiment that the best part of life is fleeting rapidly away. Dislike of old age is strong. These people characteristically say, "I *will* not grow old." Yet the painful fear of death so often seen in viscerotonia is conspicuously absent. Somatotonics are not afraid of anything, unless it is the loss of youth. In middle life there is a trenchant nostalgia for the strenuous bodily activities of youth. There is often continual quest of substitutes for these violent exercises and competitions. Many such people turn from sport to sport, only at last to settle pitifully upon tennis, like late butterflies in the autumn alighting upon fallen apples. The weaker ones hunt, now and then experiencing the somatotonic thrill of killing something. The weakest of all who yet remain predominantly somatotonic play golf. Perhaps knocking a little ball about valiantly is to a healthy somatotonia what reading French novels is to a healthy sexuality.

Note: There is a widely held belief among somatotonic people that more emphasis should be placed on youth in all its relationships, and that there should be less repression of youthful vigor educationally. Early marriage should be encouraged. There should be more youthful influence in business, government, and indeed throughout the whole social order. Now and then a group of somatotonic people come together and give impetus to a "youth movement," which is really a kind of crusade on a small scale for the above principles. Enthusiastic subscription to such a point of view is a good diagnostic sign of predominant somatotonia. Another datum of some small diagnostic interest is this: Somatotonics show a tendency to establish their closest friendships during the period of youth, especially during the college period and in the years immediately following. These are chiefly friendships with their own contemporaries or with people of the same generation, and they are usually with other somatotonic people. It is quite rare for a lasting friendship to spring up between a somatotonic and *a contemporary* of cerebrotonic predominance. Viscerotonics are friends with everybody, although there may be insufficient energy for close friendships. Cerebrotonics typically form few but very intense attachments, most often to persons from an older or younger generation.

3. Traits Defining the Third Component (Cerebrotonia)

C-1. *Restraint in Posture and Movement, Tightness.* Painful tenseness and restraint can be seen all over the body. All of the expressive movements are held in check, like horses under close rein. The body as a whole is carried stiffly, and there is the suggestion of a shrinking tendency as if the person were in too strong a light and were trying to pull back into the shadows. The lips are tight, there is strain about the bridge of the nose, and throughout the face an apprehensive tenseness is seen. Hands are often clenched and they are usually kept out of sight as much as possible. Cerebrotonics like to keep their overcoats or topcoats on during an interview, and their hands in the pockets. In the sitting posture, one leg frequently has a tendency to wind tightly about the other. The favorite posture is a kyphotic, round-shouldered one, both in standing and in sitting. In the sitting position the thighs are flexed when possible, as if the individual were trying to fold himself up to become less conspicuous. The walk suggests treading on eggs, or an attempt to move noiselessly in order not to attract attention. If a clinical examination is made, marked sphincter tension is noted. There is continual tension throughout the gastrointestinal tract, often associated with constipation. Respiration is shallow, suppressed, and relatively rapid. There is very little thoracic excursion in respiration. Breathing is silent. The pulse is fast and weak. Blood pressure is usually low.

Note: This trait suggests partially the condition which was described clinically by Eppinger and Hess (p. 18) as *sympatheticotonia*, while the overrelaxation and sluggishness seen in viscerotonia suggest what these clinicians called *vagotonia*. Yet neither of these two clinical entities really defines a polar trait, for the other component, somatotonia, is rather promiscuously mingled in with the descriptions given by Eppinger and Hess.

The C-1 trait presents a clear antithesis both to the flaccid relaxation of viscerotonia and to the erect assertiveness of somatotonia. It would be difficult to mistake any one of the three extremes. However, the mixtures presented by the ordinary run of people sometimes seem confusing to the beginner, for in the average person clear evidence of all three components can be easily made out. The problem is to weigh and balance these various manifestations until it becomes clear which is the predominant component. If after a sufficient series of observations no component emerges either as predominant or as relatively weak, the presumption is that the individual presents an even balance between the three polar tendencies. Such a person would then probably be a 4-4-4 with respect to this particular tripolar characteristic. If generally underendowed and constitutionally weak, he might be a 3-3-3.

C-2. *Physiological Overresponse.* This trait is revealed in a wide variety of manifestations. The digestive tract overreacts to emotional stimulation, or even to the ordinary social situation. The individual is easily nauseated or made sick to his stomach with pain. The vomiting, retching and gagging reflexes are quick and violent. The intense clamping down of sphincters in the digestive tract is frequently painful. Digestion as a result seems to be poor and inefficient. These people appear to require more food per pound of bodily weight than do viscerotonics or somatotonics. They seem especially to need more protein (meat), and they are excessively fond of meat, often to the exclusion of other, bulkier foods. They are frequently distressed by "roughage."

The common head cold produces in cerebrotonic people a peculiarly acute, violent response which seems to be a hallmark of cerebrotonia. Cerebrotonic colds are limited to the head, and very rarely settle in the chest to produce a prolonged cough. The nasal secretions are profuse and there is a sharp elevation of temperature. The colds are usually of fairly regular occurrence and are of rather definitely circumscribed duration. They are periodic, violent head colds, and after the acute period they are generally thrown off completely.

Persons predominant in cerebrotonia often show a history of having been free from almost all other contagious illnesses. If they had the "childhood diseases" at all they as a rule threw them off quickly. There is a conspicuous absence of infections following wounds or injuries. Chronic infections of the sinuses, throat, teeth, appendix, and so on are rare. True appendicitis is probably very rare among these people. (This affliction appears to belong mainly to somatotonia.) There is usually a violent reaction to insect bites, and a large oedematous swelling follows the sting of the mosquito within a few minutes. This may itch for days. Cerebrotonic people itch tremendously. The skin in particular seems to overrespond to irritation. There is general "nervous instability" and a sense of internal jumpiness. Cerebrotonic children are vocally restrained, but they are intent, nervous, inquisitive and jumpy. This trait is often accompanied by a tendency toward constipation. In strongly cerebrotonic people bowel movements sometimes occur regularly on alternate days or even at longer intervals. The necessity for frequent or almost constant clearing of the throat, due apparently to laryngeal oversecretion, is a frequent cerebrotonic accompaniment. In predominant cerebrotonia the normal temperature seems to be about a half degree higher than the 98.6 Fahrenheit which is generally recognized as average. The general factor lying behind all these specific manifestations seems to be a relative physiological hyper-irritability throughout the entire organism.

Note: There seems to be no polar trait presenting an antithesis to C-2, although the general picture of viscerotonic relaxation and slow, deliberate reaction presents an antithesis. Presumably the characteristic of resistance to infection is a direct corollary of physiological oversensitivity and overreaction. There appears to be an extraordinarily fast mobilization of the organism's defenses against invasion by foreign organisms, and quick systemic reaction to the first beginnings of attack. The cerebrotonic organism seems to possess a low threshold of reaction to stimulation of every sort. Persons high in this trait are excellent mortality risks. Many octogenarians show a strongly cerebrotonic history. One peculiar hallmark of a good cerebrotonic representation within the motivational pattern is neurodermatitis, which is an unexplained itching and inflammation of the skin, with a wide range of different manifestations. Persons suffering from this affliction are likely to be well endowed with both cerebrotonia and somatotonia. One other condition presents a striking exception to the general cerebrotonic immunity. This is the acute streptococcal sore throat. The streptococcus seems occasionally to overwhelm these cerebrotonic people who are so resistant to most of the invading pathogens. When infection does get a foothold in a cerebrotonic person, temperature rises with great rapidity to a high peak, as does the concentration of white corpuscles in the blood. These are defensive reactions. Surgical shock, with such people, is violent and is often fatal. Their reaction against the general anaesthetic is acute, and they require surprisingly heavy dosages of anaesthesia. Often they dislike and struggle against anaesthesia violently, as they dislike alcohol.

C-3. *Overly Fast Reactions.* Reaction time is conspicuously fast. Social reactions are so fast that the individual tends to become flustered and tangled up in his own reactions. He responds too rapidly (for effective adaptation) to the average person and to the usual social situation. Verbal stumblings, facial overresponses, and embarrassed false starts at conversation and at gestures of politeness all demonstrate this trait. The individual figuratively trips over himself, especially when attempting to adapt to a slow, complacent, self-sufficient personality. There is quick blushing and blanching, and often there is a peculiar confusion and embarrassment on the occasion of a sudden meeting. The pulse rate increases markedly upon slight provocation. Such a person responds too quickly in crises, becomes too tense and suffers from "buck fever." This is particularly the case in competitive events of all sorts, and in the relations between the sexes. Sexual reactions and hunger reactions are fast and acute, the quick sexual reaction often throwing the individual into difficulties. For an extreme cerebrotonic, the slower, more considerate and leisurely manner of approaching sexual objectives, which is the "normal" and especially the viscerotonic way, is very difficult. It is hard for a cerebrotonic to wait for anything, even his dinner. He becomes hungry with a sudden pang. His internal demands are sudden, acute, and sometimes poorly sustained. When confronted with obstacles he often represses these demands altogether, or if a little somatotonia is present in him, without sufficient balancing viscerotonia, he may present a jagged, irregular, impatient pattern of expression.

Note: This trait is indicated, rather than measured, by the common experiments of the psychological laboratory on reaction time. The so-called "startle response" appears to constitute one of the best indicators. A person with this trait predominant responds with extreme quickness to any sudden disturbance or noise. Also both verbal and motor reactions are fast. The trait is well shown by measurements of speed of eye movements in reading. From the standpoint of effective social adaptation the overly fast reaction is probably a more serious stumbling block than the overly slow reaction of viscerotonia (trait V-3). The quick-reacting cerebrotonic becomes easily confused. People with the C-3 trait predominant are often "misunderstood," and they are sometimes badly bullied, especially by well-meaning friends and relatives who try to normalize them. It is quite possible, for example, that to force a cerebrotonic to sit through a prolonged, deliberate meal may work as much physiological and psychological harm upon him as would be caused by forcing a viscerotonic to eat his meal in five minutes (which is about the tempo for cerebrotonia of degree 6). The fox and stork encountered a comparable difficulty when they attempted to eat together.

C-4. *Love of Privacy*. There is a profound and urgent need of privacy. The individual manifesting this trait predominantly needs to be alone, out of reach of social stimulation during a large proportion of his time, as a storage battery needs periodically to be recharged. For very nearly *all* of the time, the extreme cerebrotonic would like to be alone, or cut off from all save one or two intimate associates. Cerebrotonia communes with itself, and is mentally self-sufficient. It seems to live a mentally intensive (rather than extensive) life. What it experiences needs to be assimilated, to be fitted into what has gone before. Happiness and mental health appear to be dependent upon this assimilative process, which can be carried on only in relative privacy. The love of privacy appears therefore to be as native and as primary in cerebrotonia as love of eating and sociophilia in viscerotonia. In gauging this trait, ignore any superficial statement of verbal attitude. Most people *say* they like to be alone. Study the individual's habits and his history.

Note: No trait presents quite a polar antithesis to the primary love of privacy, although the primary needs and desires seen in viscerotonia and somatotonia are sharply different. It is possible, although rare, for an individual to show a predominant strength of moderate degree (rating of 5) both in C-4 and in one or more of the viscerotonic or somatotonic traits. Even the most vigorously aggressive people often need to return periodically to a brief solitude to gather their strength, as Antaeus returned to the earth during his struggles with Hercules. C-4 is an easy trait to gauge if the investigator has once learned to distinguish between true behavioral data and the superficial stereotypes of verbal attitude. It is "in the language" to think that one likes to be alone, just as it is in the language to think that one is an introvert. But inquire as to how persevering has been the effort to be alone. Unless it has been as persevering as the usual viscerotonic effort to get food, and the somatotonic effort to get exercise, you are not dealing with a person in whom this trait predominates. The trait C-4 illustrates how difficult an obstacle confronts our hope of ultimately substituting short cuts such as paper and pencil tests, questionnaires and the like for the analytic inquiry in the study of so complex a problem as human temperament.

In connection with this trait, one point of interest to the psychological or clinical consultant might be added. Many cerebrotonic people who have begun to show signs of a schizoid cerebrosis and other indications of too great strain, will respond to solitude better than to any other therapy. Try particularly to protect such people from a viscerotonically or somatotonically inclined psychiatrist. It is also worth remembering that parents are not always careful to protect cerebrotonic children from summer camps, progressive schools, and other well-intended institutions of professionalized somatotonia. A child suffering from the result of such misanthropy can often be helped greatly by solitude.

C-5. *Mental Overintensity, Hyperattentionality, Apprehensiveness.* The trait of overawareness. There is a low threshold of attention, and consequently a mental overresponsiveness and often an apprehensiveness concerning everything, including the individual's own organic processes, such as digestion, heart beat, etc. The attentional focus is extremely active and labile. The individual has sharp eyes and ears. He misses nothing. In particular he fails to miss much which, from the standpoint of his immediate adaptation to human society as it is, he might do well to miss. In a psychological sense he is naked to his environment, overexposed, oversensitized. He is therefore singularly vulnerable to overstimulation. He lacks insulation. His case suggests that of a man trying to attend to several conversations simultaneously. Under varying circumstances the trait is expressed as excessive alertness, vexed confusion, strained attentive effort, apprehensiveness. There is sometimes a peculiar apprehensiveness concerning health, although these people often are singularly healthy (trait C-2). The sense of impending disaster often lurks in the mind of such a person throughout a long lifetime. There is an incessant sense of insecurity. The individual usually shows fear and dislike of any kind of risk (antithesis to trait S-6). There is often a suicidal tendency, and there is usually much interest and curiosity concerning death. (Death is a favorite topic of cerebrotonic conversation.)

Note: No trait presents a polar antithesis. Viscerotonic preoccupation with the basic appetites for food and company constitutes a general antithesis, as do somatotonic callousness (S-10), love of risk (S-6) and the general somatotonic preoccupation with physical self-expression. Persons showing the C-5 trait predominantly seem to have been intended for a more thinly populated world than the present one. The recent increase in the physical and psychological proximity of people appears to work a hardship on cerebrotonia. Individuals high in the C-5 trait, with their extreme sensitivity of sensory reception, tend in a crowded world to become overstimulated and confused—sometimes ultimately to become disorientated and schizoid. Possibly we are moving in the direction of suppressing cerebrotonia, or even of eliminating it to a degree. The general movement known as the industrial revolution, with the emergence of electrical appliances and the internal combustion engine, has really been a somatotonic and viscerotonic (extravert) revolution, bringing people closer together, speeding up and extensifying all social relations, and forcing the individual to more and more objective, more superficial social contacts. As human relations thus become more extensive and more superficial, the inevitable tendency is toward suppression, and perhaps in time elimination of the intensive, subjective cerebrotonic temperament.

C-6. *Secretiveness of Feeling, Emotional Restraint.* This is the tight-lipped characteristic. The individual does his mental suffering in silence. He will not "let go" and reveal his emotions or feelings in the presence of others. External expression of feeling is powerfully inhibited, although there may be great intensity of feeling. In high cerebrotonia, to show feeling is like public exposure of the naked body. Signs of emotional weakness are choked back as if subject to great shame. Such an individual stands tearless at a grave, revealing but little sign of feeling to superficial observation, although it may be that his inward grief is more poignant than that of the most demonstrative person. Similarly there is usually a tight checking of outward demonstration of joy and of the pleasant emotions. These people experience intense feeling, but they remain secretive about it. One of them once said, "Overt display of feeling to the vulgar gaze is indecent. It is like doing one's toilet in public, or like making love as dogs do." This kind of cerebrotonic is a "Stoic of the woods, a man without a tear."

Note: This trait is sometimes an inconvenient one to its possessor, for since feeling is not overtly displayed, the individual is frequently not given credit for the sympathy and kindness which he actually entertains. A really painful tragedy resides here, for the cerebrotonic himself usually does not understand why he is misunderstood. He usually thinks that he *does* reveal his feelings, and from his own point of view such is actually the case. That is to say, to another mentally intense, excessively watchful person—to another cerebrotonic showing the C-5 trait—his feelings will have been fully revealed. He gives many signs and subtle indications which he himself would never miss in another person. But he fails to take into account that most people do not possess his habits of acute cerebrotonic observation. They look for what is unmistakable and overt, while for him to be obvious is to be indecent. As observers of human behavior, most people are mere headline readers. The cerebrotonic usually does not think he is secretive of his feelings. He believes that he is merely careful not to be crudely obvious (and hence offensive). Yet in avoiding offense to his own kind he generally succeeds in giving offense to both somatotonics and viscerotonics, who prefer "an open, honest display and plain dealing." Like most other human difficulties, this resolves itself into a language problem. Cerebrotonia speaks an intensive, subtle, subjective language, and the cerebrotonic hates to be obvious, just as he hates to be naked.

C-7. *Self-conscious Motility of the Eyes and Face.* The individual has a singularly intent, sensitive-appearing face. The eyes especially are alert and quick, and they often have a striking brightness of appearance. The eyes usually evade the direct stare of another person, but they are watchful, moving with lightning quickness from point to point. The eyeblink is noticeably fast, and it is usually of frequent occurrence. There is often a characteristic tenseness, and a "slight working" of the lips and mouth. The lips, usually thin and delicately molded, tend to suggest the sensitive "trembling" of a deer's or rabbit's nostrils. All activity of the facial musculature, rapid and alert as it appears to be, is restrained. There are no broad changes of facial set, like those seen in somatotonia. This face presents an antithesis to the open, *specifically* expressive countenance seen in somatotonia and viscerotonia. In the cerebrotonic face all of the fine muscles of expression seem intensely alive, but in a strained, tense manner. It is a highly responsive face, reflecting the world like a mirror, but like a complex, moving, many-faceted mirror, not like a broad, flat one. The cerebrotonic face rarely portrays one specific trait of character well. It is next to impossible to "read" such a face, except to recognize that it is cerebrotonic.

Note: The trait S-7, directness of manner, is almost a polar antithesis, for people showing the C-7 trait are exceedingly hesitant, self-conscious, and indirect of manner. The latter are occasionally accused of furtiveness, although they are not necessarily furtive, in the literal sense. Sometimes these people appear (to noncerebrotonic persons) to overdo their motility of facial expression, as if they were trying too hard to be engaging, or were perhaps hiding real attitudes and reactions, or were sneering. Somatotonics often attack cerebrotonics on this ground, although not always justly, for the difficulty is due principally to self-consciousness. In gauging the C-7 trait, the principal error to guard against is that of confusing the restrained hypermotility and fine movement of cerebrotonic musculature with the broad, slowly executed and stereotyped expressive movements of the athletic (somatotonic) face. Sometimes the latter is an active face, and at a distance it is a more expressive face than that of cerebrotonia. It usually has a definite repertory of characteristic expressions which are relatively unvarying, are deliberate in onset, and appear fairly predictably in response to definite situations. The face of the stage comedian or professional mimic is of course somatotonic, usually blended with a good component of relaxation. The stage professional needs an open, pliable, overtly expressive, somatotonic face, or he becomes too subtle for the average seeker of entertainment. The cerebrotonic face is subtle, variable, poorly controlled, tense. It represents an antithesis to overt pliability. A cerebrotonic can never mimic the expression of another, or for that matter can never assume quite the same expression twice. There probably will never be a successful cerebrotonic actor or actress.

C-8. *Sociophobia.* Dislike of being socially involved. Antithesis to conviviality. The individual avoids and deeply distrusts social gatherings. He is strained, distressed and uncomfortable in the face of any social relationship, especially those of a temporary or superficial nature. The concept of general good fellowship and of a comradeship extending beyond a few intimates is foreign to him. He hates to be recognized and hailed, for he is usually "caught absent-minded." He shrinks away from social contacts, particularly from new ones. In contrast to the insatiable viscerotonic appetite for company and for people, this person retreats from company as from physical pain. He becomes tightened up and confused when thrown into a social situation, and is overwhelmed by self-consciousness. He would rather that people did not know his name, especially his Christian, or intimate, name.

Note: The polar antithesis between this trait and sociophilia (V-8) was one of the first to be observed by social psychologists. Indeed this antithesis has provided one of the cornerstones upon which social psychology has been built, for the contrast between the two extremes afforded the nucleus about which the concepts of extraversion and introversion were developed. It seems remarkable that in the thirty years or so during which these two terms have been used, so little progress has been made toward an educational psychology recognizing the *constitutional* nature of these observed differences. The tacit assumption seems still to be conventional that one or the other of two such polar variations must be "wrong," and should therefore be discouraged. Much effort is just now being spent upon the socialization of cerebrotonic children. Possibly they do not want to be socialized. In other periods the same effort seems to have been directed toward restraint of somatotonic children. Perhaps they did not want to be restrained.

In gauging the C-8 trait, but little reliance is to be placed on the individual's own estimate of his sociophobia. As in the case of trait C-4, we find that it has become virtually a language stereotype for people to regard themselves as sociophobic. In a period when somatotonic extraversion has become an ideal, this is perhaps only a gesture of modesty. Nearly everybody thinks he suffers from sociophobia. A correct diagnosis is made only from careful analysis of the life history and from successive observations of the individual.

C-9. *Inhibited Social Address.* Poor composure when under scrutiny. The trait of not being able to put the best foot forward. Conspicuous lack of poise. Lack of self-possession. Extreme self-consciousness. The unhappy faculty of failing to be at ease when aware of being observed critically or evaluatively. The individual's imagination seems to be too active. Either he will have some nervous habit, possibly some characteristic of pseudo-aggression which makes a bad first impression, or he will be inhibited and tongue-tied on the occasion of any new social contact which he deems important. A third typical pattern of cerebrotonic behavior in such a situation is that of maintaining a watchful, austere silence which suggests hostility or disapproval of the other person. In any event, the cerebrotonic seems to put his worst foot forward and, except when judged by people of unusual insight, makes a poor initial impression. This is not merely the normal reticence and shyness of average people in new situations. There is in addition a painful inner recoiling and a "clamping contraction of my insides as if I were struggling to crawl into a hole." When this trait is predominant the individual never becomes entirely at ease in the presence of a person who for any reason exercises authority over him, that is to say, a person whom he particularly needs to impress favorably.

Note: There is no polar antithesis to C-9. The antithesis to this trait, poise or excellent social address, is not a polar characteristic, but seems to constitute a blending of motivational elements in which the first two components are both well represented and the third is rather low. This is another trait concerning which self-ratings are worthless. Nearly everybody has long established language habits apologizing for his poor social address, his insecurity and lack of poise. And in the end people believe as they speak. The diagnostic hallmark of C-9 lies in the behavior of the individual in the presence of a person whom he needs to please—ideally his employer or a woman who has not yet accepted him. If he has this trait predominantly, he is at his worst in such a circumstance. If the trait is low, he may then seem at his surest and best. Persons with this trait pronounced come sooner or later to feel that their adaptation to people who are below them in authority is excellent, while their adaptation to people above them is poor.

C-10. *Resistance to Habit and Poor Routinizing.* The individual experiences great difficulty in routinizing his life with respect to elementary processes like eating, sleeping and elimination. Everything always has to be decided anew. He must needs entertain the alternative of *whether or not* to go to bed, to get up, or to have a bowel movement. Matters do not reduce readily to routine. Although often brilliant, such a person cannot form regular study habits, and not infrequently he falls by the wayside in academic and similar competition, apparently a victim of the difficulty illustrated by the fable of the hare and the tortoise. Extremely cerebrotonic people are not often found among the leaders in academic scholarship. Cerebrotonia represents an antithesis to the methodical characteristic, some of which seems to be necessary for any kind of consistent competitive achievement. Persons high in this trait do not fall into well-established habits like drinking, smoking, or the use of drugs. These people tend to have great curiosity. They experiment with everything. But they do not become "enslaved by habit." They fight their good habits as well as their bad ones.

Note: The antithesis to this trait, exemplified by the routinized, plodding, smoothly running pattern of life, is perhaps about equally viscerotonic and somatotonic. There is no polar antithesis to C-10. One interesting characteristic of cerebrotonic people which seems to be related to the C-10 trait is a peculiar weakness at learning by rote. Cerebrotonics nearly always do poorly at rote learning. They are weak at memorization of poetry or passages in plays. The element of self-consciousness seems to interfere too strongly with the reproduction of material learned by rote. Cerebrotonics are probably never successful actors, in any role. As students, cerebrotonics appear to study unmethodically, and to depend for their academic success upon their insights and their ability to see relationships, rather than upon the routine mastery of specific assignments. It is conceivable that constitutional characteristics can some day be diagnosed by educators with sufficient accuracy to justify establishment of two or possibly several quite different kinds of academic teaching procedure. There has long been internecine academic warfare between a school advocating a strictly controlled routine recitation of almost a rote nature, and a school advocating a free-ranging type of instruction with little guidance or checkup, but with a very general, comprehensive examination emphasizing relationships more than rote reproduction. Constitutional differences in temperament seem to lie at the bottom of such a controversy.

C-11. *Agoraphobia.* Or claustrophilia. Love of small, snug, closed-in places, which protect the individual from being seen. Distaste for being caught out in the open. Dislike of open, unprotected places. Hatred of being conspicuous. There is a fondness for very small, narrow rooms with low ceilings. Cerebrotonics like attic rooms, and they like small, low, well-hidden houses. They like to be in corners or against a wall, not out in the middle of a room. If the trait is well developed they cannot eat comfortably in restaurants unless they can secure a seat in a corner or along a wall. They like small beds, and want them against the wall. They do not ordinarily sleep well in large beds out in the middle of the room. They like doors closed. These people have excessive physical modesty. They like to hide their (usually sensitive, delicate) bodies as thoroughly as possible. The bathing suit styles of 1890 and the high, stiff collar represent what may perhaps be taken as a hangover from a long period of cerebrotonic predominance. Corresponding styles of 1940 may constitute the culmination of the somatotonic revolution in this respect. Persons with the C-11 trait predominant rarely if ever sleep nude, and they do not like to swim nude. With their associated oversensitivity to cold water (C-14) they usually do not like to swim at all.

Note: The polar antithesis is claustrophobia, or agoraphilia (S-11). Hostility between the two extremes is remarkably intense, and may be of historical importance. The play of styles of dress back and forth from one extreme to the other seems really to constitute a kind of minor skirmishing or guerrilla warfare. The more revealing styles (like the modern bathing suit) constitute somatotonic advances, while the more concealing ones represent cerebrotonic sorties. The same is probably true in general of styles in religion. The intensely subjective wish-fulfilling, otherworldly and claustrophilic rationalization of cerebrotonic imagination which characterized Christianity at its height offers a sharp contrast to the predominantly hardheaded, behavioristic, objective, fact-worshiping point of view of the fully sophisticated exponent of the modern religion of science. The full flowering of scientific method, as we just now interpret and rationalize it, seems to be one product of a somatotonic overwhelming of cerebrotonic subjectivity.

In gauging the strength of the C-11 trait, the investigator does well to compare the subject's behavior with the imagined behavior of a mouse in comparable situations. Mice show the C-11 trait to a remarkable degree. They venture into unfamiliar territory only with the utmost caution. They are terribly lost and disorientated if taken out into the middle of a room or into an unfamiliar place.

C-12. *Unpredictability of Attitude and Feeling.* Lack of uniformity in behavior and outlook. Attitudes are subject to sudden and disconcerting change. The individual tends not to respond to social stimulation in the expected manner. His attitudes seem to be subject more to internal than to external control. He seems to be able to change his mind abruptly, and suddenly to adapt all his feelings and attitudes to the new orientation. Such a change frequently bewilders other, less cerebrotonic people who may have become emotionally entangled with the individual. The trait gives rise to a conspicuous mental and emotional versatility, but so great a changeableness in external attitude often lends an instability or capriciousness to the cerebrotonic personality which may become profoundly disconcerting, and often leads to misunderstanding. Such people have a genius for being "misunderstood." This is the trait of being often called "a mystery."

Note: The trait V-12, evenness of emotional flow, is almost a direct polar antithesis. Yet it should be remembered that the C-12 trait does not indicate *lack* of emotion. Cerebrotonic people are often highly emotional. The phenomenon of emotionality *as such* seems to be a variable nearly independent of what we have called the primary components of temperament. Differences lie in the manner of expressing emotion, and perhaps also in the kind or quality of emotion. Since this last variable refers really to a quality of consciousness itself, we have no way of comparing it in different individuals, except by inference drawn from outward behavior. Cerebrotonic people seem to feel emotion more intensely, or more acutely, than do either viscerotonic or somatotonic people. Their sensory responses in general seem to be sharper and more discriminative. If this is actually the case, then in one sense they have more emotion, or are more emotional. But the problem recedes rapidly to a realm of speculation. Persons showing the C-12 trait tend toward emotional capriciousness. They have quick sympathies and antipathies, and the affective element of consciousness appears to be largely under the control of the cognitive element. Perhaps it is for this reason that such people show remarkable mental versatility, but often fail to find secure emotional anchorage, and frequently develop schizoid tendencies (trait C-17).

C-13. *Vocal Restraint, and General Restraint of Noise.* The trait of characteristically restraining the voice so that it reaches only the persons addressed. One in whom this trait is predominant is rarely heard clearly by persons whom he is not addressing. The voice is under close control, as if the individual were guarding against a danger of attracting the attention of others. Similarly the laugh and cough, or even the hiccough, are always under the closest restraint. The cough is muffled in the throat, and the laugh, however mirthful, never breaks out in an explosion or series of explosions. Likewise bodily movements are executed with meticulous noiselessness, doors are closed as if with thoughtful care, and pieces of furniture are moved as if they were sleeping children. If a radio is played it is played only with sufficient loudness to be heard by those who are directly listening. When such an individual speaks, his voice seems to be consciously aimed, so as to carry just to the listeners and no farther. In all of these manifestations of restraint of noise, there seems to be a conscious effort not to break in upon the attention of others. Attention appears to be of almost sacred significance to the cerebrotonic. He hates to have his own attention broken in upon, and he strives never to intrude upon another's attention needlessly. Cerebrotonic children may join in the fun with other children, but they do not join in the shouting and yelling (see p. 263), and when they speak their voices do not carry far beyond the person addressed. They speak with a restraint which is too constant and too general to be explained in terms of conditioning alone.

Note: This trait defines a polar antithesis to two somatotonic traits, S-13, the unrestrained voice, and S-15, general noisiness. It is of interest to note that while these are clearly distinguishable traits in somatotonia, they become simply one trait in cerebrotonia. That is to say, the exaggerated manifestations of the unrestrained voice and of general noisiness often are observed independently of one another—the one occurring without the other. But when cerebrotonia is predominant and there is conspicuous restraint, both of these manifestations are restrained, not one of them only. If a person is conspicuously restrained, he is so in all respects. If he is conspicuously loud, he may be so only in particular respects. The viscerotonic pattern with respect to this dichotomy is simply that of making no effort to restrain noise. There are none of the signs of cerebrotonic effortful avoidance of creating an attention-distracting disturbance. But likewise there is no conspicuous noisiness, no assertive, strident quality, or booming quality in the voice, and no vigorous, "bumptious" moving about. The somatotonic spends energy in making noise, the cerebrotonic spends energy in restraining noise, and the viscerotonic spends no energy either way. He relaxes, and he is often quiet.

C-13 is an easy trait to gauge if the psychologist will watch his subject with systematic thoroughness. For the beginner, however, confusion often arises from the fact that somatotonic people are usually conditioned to do *some* things with an acquired restraint, which may simulate cerebrotonia. Such a restraint is usually rendered the more conspicuous by its contrast with other behavioral traits of the individual. Note especially the laugh. If somatotonia is predominant it is nearly always revealed by some variation of the explosive laugh, or by a conversational habit of explosive ejaculation. If the C-13 trait is predominant, the individual is restrainedly quiet in *all* respects—his vocal expression, his movements, his contacts with furniture, even in the way he clears his throat.

In the discussion of S-1, attention was called to the general effort just now being made to teach the somatotonic postural habits to school children and college students, regardless of their constitutional endowment. The somatotonic revolution has extended in much the same manner into the realm of speech training. College and school courses in speech are aimed essentially at breaking down cerebrotonic restraint. The youth is encouraged to overcome his vocal inhibitions and to "throw his voice out freely upon the air." If an individual has been exposed to such a course, an excellent diagnostic aid is at hand for gauging the C-13 trait. A 5 in this trait will have been affected but slightly, and will have returned promptly to his normal cerebrotonic pattern. A 6 will not have been affected at all, except perhaps by getting a low grade in the course.

C-14. *Hypersensitivity to Pain.* Conspicuous inability to stand pain without wincing. There appears to be an overresponse to pain, as to other stimuli. The overresponse is shown by such symptoms as wincing, flinching, increased tension, pallor, "cold sweat," suppressed respiration, elevated pulse rate, nausea, and general loss of composure. In situations involving serious injury, such as crushed fingers and the like, there is generally the history of severe nausea, fainting, and physical exhaustion or prostration. There is great difficulty with the dentist and, especially in the case of children, with the doctor. Persons showing this trait tend to be more overwhelmed by the pain of superficial injuries, such as lesions of the skin, burns, stings, injured fingers or toes and the like, than by deeper and graver injuries. There is also a marked inability to tolerate hot foods and drinks. The mouth is easily "burned" by hot coffee, and either hot or cold water at a temperature well tolerated by somatotonic skin is likely to be painful. The cold shower is not only painful but it introduces marked interference with respiration, causing severe gasping or even a degree of asphyxia. A diagnostic hallmark for this trait is a peculiar apprehensiveness of pain, or response-in-advance, before the pain is actually felt. This characteristic is observed especially in the dentist's chair. In these people, salivary secretion is generally profuse while the teeth are being worked on.

Note: The contrast between this trait and the Spartan indifference to pain seen in somatotonia (S-14) is a dramatic one. It is one of the clearest polar antitheses. However, in gauging this trait it is especially important to distinguish between superficial verbal habit and the true organic response to painful stimuli. Many somatotonic people complain loudly or swear vociferously on slight provocation. This is merely part of the general pattern of aggressive noisiness (S-15). Many cerebrotonic people remain tight-lipped (C-6) and verbally restrained even in the face of extreme pain. Vocalization, then, is no criterion for this trait. It is necessary to look more closely into the individual's history, and to observe him carefully. The trait can be tested objectively in the psychological laboratory with little inconvenience, using electrical shock as the pain stimulus.

When this is done, the best objective manifestation of a C-14 predominance appears to be a marked elevation of pulse rate together with suppression of respiration.

Persons showing the antithesis to C-14 (S-14) can usually be hypnotized, and major operations have been performed with hypnosis as the only anaesthetic. Such patients have presumably been somatotonic people who showed the S-14 trait predominantly, although we have no direct proof of this supposition. Cerebrotonic people can rarely be hypnotized at all.

A simple indication of the C-14 trait is the temperature at which a hot drink can be swallowed without discomfort. Persons high in this trait may "burn their tongues" at 55° Centigrade (131° Fahrenheit). Strongly somatotonic people can often drink coffee comfortably at 64° Centigrade (147° Fahrenheit). In a preliminary observation we have found that thirty-two patients suffering from cancer were almost uniformly low in the C-14 trait.

C-15. *Poor Sleep Habits, Chronic Fatigue.* Insomnia of greater or less degree is almost constant in adult life. Even in childhood, habits of going to sleep are irregular and erratic, certainly as early as the second year, probably still earlier. It is hard to get the cerebrotonic child to sleep unless he is close to physical exhaustion. If a hypnotic drug is used, heavy dosage is required. It is often difficult for these people to get up in the morning. They waken very easily, but they tend to lie abed in a half-awake, half-dreaming state. Since the cerebrotonic constitution seems always to resist habit, the problem of *whether or not* to get up has to be faced and decided anew each morning as if it were a new problem. The cerebrotonic is a light sleeper. His relaxation, even in deepest sleep, is incomplete. Typically he has to sleep in one particular position (usually curled up on one side) in contrast to viscerotonics who can sleep in any position. The limpness of viscerotonic sleep is never seen in cerebrotonia after the period of early childhood. Respiration during cerebrotonic sleep is much shallower and faster than is the case with viscerotonia. The cerebrotonic descends into his deepest sleep very slowly. If he snores at all, which is rare, it will be only in the morning, and then very lightly. Associated with such poor habits of sleep, there is almost always a history of chronic fatigue.

Note: Trait V-15, the deep sleep characteristic, is a direct polar antithesis. The contrast between viscerotonic and cerebrotonic sleep is too sharply defined to escape the attention of even a casual observer. Somatotonics generally sleep well. They tend to go to sleep readily, as do viscerotonics, but they do not ordinarily descend into the complete, limp relaxation of viscerotonia. They sleep "vigorously," tossing and moving about a great deal during sleep. They usually like to get up in the morning, and snoring is variable. Perhaps the most conspicuous cerebrotonic characteristic in connection with this trait is the slow onset of sleepiness at night. Viscerotonic and somatotonic people, especially children, tend to become sleepy with relative suddenness. Cerebrotonic people show a peculiar recalcitrancy in this matter. As in other relationships, habit formation is weak. These people who do not become sleepy at night tend to throw off sleep very feebly and inadequately in the morning.

C-16. *Youthful Intentness of Manner and Appearance.* The trait of seeming younger than the chronological age indicates. If a child, the individual tends to lack the assurance and the appearance of manliness or womanliness of the average child of the same age. If an adult, he appears to have bathed in the springs of youth. There is a strong suggestion about him that he will never grow old. The carriage of the body is youthful, as is the general expression of the face. The face lacks the hard, severe lines generally associated with somatotonic maturity. It lacks also the placid, bland relaxation associated with middle age in the more viscerotonic temperaments. There is an alert, intent, childlike or birdlike quality in the facial expression, which defines an antithesis both to the relative overmaturity of somatotonia, and to the overrelaxed, round-cheeked, suckling face of viscerotonia. The walk, the voice, the posture, the general atmosphere of suppressed intent eagerness, all suggest a singular, essential youthfulness. In watching such a person or in talking with him, the impression grows that in some fundamental sense he has carried the outlook and point of view of the child into adult life. Persons showing this trait are uniformly found to have had a late adolescence. We have not yet discovered an exception to this general rule.

Note: S-16, overmaturity of appearance, is a direct polar antithesis. There is little danger of confusion between the alert, birdlike, hatchet-faced intentness of the cerebrotonic child and the placid, baby-faced characteristic which often marks the viscerotonic child. Sometimes this "baby-face" or "suckling-face" quality is retained in adult life. In such instances the individual looks young until he grows fat (the baby-face characteristic is a phenomenon often associated with the PPJ or pyknic-practical-joke pattern of physique), but his appearance is not that of *intent* youthfulness. The intent anxiousness of the cerebrotonic face will never be mistaken, once it has been noted. The C-16 trait is a much distrusted one among somatotonic people. It seems to them that the individual exhibits characteristics of "arrested development," or of mental and emotional immaturity. Such a person should be "psychoanalyzed or something." To the cerebrotonics themselves it may seem rather as if the individual had avoided the main pitfall of life—disillusionment and sophistication.

C-17. *Vertical Mental Cleavage, Introversion.* The characteristic of being mentally intensive, secretive and subjective, in sharp contrast with the broad mental extensiveness and objectivity of somatotonia, and with the open expression of feeling which marks viscerotonia. The cerebrotonic individual is *primarily* orientated toward, and in touch with, his own remoter awareness rather than with the outer scene. Reality to him is essentially and foremost what he dredges up out of his own mental cellars. The outward reality appears to be secondary. The principal business of consciousness is that of fitting or assimilating the incoming stream of external impressions to the *more important* store of what is already accumulated and assimilated. Adaptation or adjustment to the outward scene is therefore secondary, and in the face of the stress of overstimulation and confusion, outward adaptation is the first function to be abandoned.

The individual turns away from "reality," abandoning it somewhat as a captain might first unship the least valuable part of his cargo in a storm. The thing to be saved and protected at all costs is the continuity and integrity of the inner awareness. Such a person dissociates the outer, objective reality but remains in the closest touch with his own inward, subjective reality. Therefore a relatively less sharp separation is observed between his fully conscious attitudes and his dreaming, his phantasy life, and remoter desires. In cerebrotonia the inward illumination is excellent, whatever the outward orientation may be. There is rich phantasy life and the individual is well aware of the trend of his own dreaming. He usually knows what he dreams about and daydreams about, almost as well as what he "thinks" about. For him dream analysis is therefore not often revelatory, although it may be (usually is) amusing or interesting. Dream analysis is only a continuation of the rational analysis of his fully conscious attitude and belief.

Persons showing this trait strongly are difficult if not impossible to hypnotize. They are free from the "horizontal dissociation" of somatotonia, but are prone to develop what we have called vertical dissociation. The mental cleavage seems to be an up and down or vertical one, leaving the manifest, immediate consciousness in close touch with deeper, latent consciousness, but shutting out awareness of some part of the objective scene which is spread out before the individual (figuratively in a horizontal plane). In cerebrotonia the vertical plane of consciousness remains intact, but the horizontal plane is broken (schizoid). Symptoms of this kind of vertical cleavage are absent-mindedness, daydreaming, procrastination, inability to make decisions, poor identifications of people and with people, and in pathology, schizoid manifestations.

Note: The C-17 trait presents a sharp contrast to its two polar antitheses, V-17 and S-17. Broadly considered, this is the trait which provided the most direct basis for Jung's original description of introversion. Descriptions of extraversion have always involved mixtures of V-17 and S-17. Consequently extraversion has been a puzzling and confusing concept. But introversion is more specific.

One of the most striking characteristics of persons showing the C-17 trait predominantly is their acuity and preciseness of intuition. Intuition is of the first order in these people for it is based upon a thorough familiarity with the remote consciousness from which it springs. Such people have excellent insight into their own motivation, within the limits of the relative fineness and precision of their verbal systems. For them the process of psychoanalysis becomes essentially a conducted exercise in semantics, in sharp contrast with the somatotonics, for whom such a procedure may partake of the nature of a religious or conversional experience. Cerebrotonic people rarely experience sudden conversion to anything. By the same token, they do not experience sudden physical breakdown, or "nervous breakdown."

When well educated, cerebrotonic people tend to develop a profound respect for words. This might almost be called a fear of words, in the sense that the term "fear of God" is commonly used. To the educated cerebrotonic mind the word tends to become a fine-edged tool, to be used with great caution and preciseness, if not with reverence. There is sharp differentiation between shades of a word's meaning, hence hesitation and caution with words. For such people it is very difficult to write letters. An "extravert," of either kind (viscerotonic or somatotonic), can usually dash off a dozen letters, while an "introvert" struggles with a single paragraph. Similarly, cerebrotonic people rarely write fiction. When they do, it is generally too involved to be readable. But they often spend their lives "on the verge" of writing fiction.

The ideal fiction writer has a predominant action component (somatotonia) blended with a strong feeling component (viscerotonia) and unhampered by a strong cerebrotonic inhibitory component. Dumas was possibly a 5-5-1 temperamentally. Conan Doyle was[3] about $4\text{-}5^2\text{-}1^2$. H. G. Wells is not far from $4^2\text{-}4^2\text{-}1^2$. The writer has talked at some length with Doyle and Wells. Dumas has to be reconstructed from photographs, anecdotes and biography. No one of these three shows a morphology which seems to vary more than half a degree in any component from the temperamental index tentatively assigned. Such people can get verbal material expressed and out of their systems as fast as it comes into consciousness. Cerebrotonics cannot do so. They become swamped with ramifications and alternatives to every phrase.

The successful writer of fiction, or successful orator, needs to be partially dissociated from his own subconscious awareness (horizontal dissociation). Likewise, only such a person can become sincerely converted to something. Witness Conan Doyle's conversion to spiritualism, and Wells' religious devotion first to socialism and later to such superficial devices as economic and political reforms. To be converted means simply to be able to shut out of consciousness all of the alternatives and inhibitory objections which, in a cerebrotonic mind, immediately well up from the deeper levels of remoter awareness and block single-minded action or single-minded verbalization.

In pathology, when for any reason life becomes too much for the individual, the C-17 trait predisposes to what the psychiatrists call

[3] The superscript 2 should be read as ½. Thus $4\text{-}5^2\text{-}1^2$ is an abbreviation for $4\text{-}5\frac{1}{2}\text{-}1\frac{1}{2}$.

schizoid symptoms. The vertical dissociation becomes more conspicuous, and some part of outer reality may get shut off altogether. Such persons lose personal, spatial and temporal orientation. When somatotonics run into mental pathology their dissociation is horizontal. They maintain their orientation to time and place and to persons, but become disorientated and disconnected from their own inner selves, and hence from inhibition. This seems to be the mechanism underlying manic behavior.

If our argument has been followed up to this juncture, it is perhaps redundant to point out that the term *schizoid*, if used literally, should apply equally to somatorotic as well as to the cerebrotic manifestations. *Schiz-* means cut off. The somatorotic individual is cut off in one plane, the cerebrotic in another.

C-18. *Resistance to Alcohol, and to other Depressant Drugs.* The effect of alcohol is essentially unpleasant. The cerebrotonic sense of strain increases, and after a short time there is a feeling of dizziness and of increased fatigue. The euphoria and sense of expansive freedom which follow moderate alcoholizing in viscerotonia and in somatotonia, are absent in cerebrotonia. Alcohol, a cerebral depressant, produces *general* depression when the third component is predominant. In cerebrotonia, therefore, there appears to be general physiological resistance to the depressive action of this drug, in contrast to the grateful yielding to it that is seen in viscerotonia and somatotonia. The same phenomenon is seen in the reaction of cerebrotonic people both to anaesthesia and to the hypnotic (sleep-producing) drugs commonly used to combat insomnia or restlessness. When cerebrotonia is predominant the common hypnotics in ordinary dosage have little effect except that of rendering the patient more tired the next day, as if he had been through a battle the night before. One of our own earliest clinical observations was the fact that certain patients require from two to three times as large a dosage of general anaesthetic as the normal prescription, to put them to sleep. These patients turned out to be what we have later called the cerebrotonics.

Note: The cerebrotonic reaction to alcohol appears to offer a certain justification for the remarkable differences of opinion which have prevailed regarding the virtues of this drug. Possibly a clue is likewise offered as to the motivation of the prohibitionist. The prohibition fiasco in America (1919-1933) seems to have constituted a sort of *coup de grâce* administered to a rapidly fading cerebrotonic regime by the somatotonic revolutionaries. Successful defeat of the prohibitionist movement paved the way, no doubt, to the supreme somatotonic triumph which is signalized in the modern automobile horn.

In gauging the reaction to alcohol it is especially important to observe the individual directly. Verbal report of an attitude toward the drug is nearly worthless, particularly in the case of cerebrotonia, for in a time of virtual somatotonic dictatorship, only the hardiest or the stupidest of the cerebrotonics are likely to confess openly a distaste for this drug. In the politer and more intellectual circles, such a confession now places an individual in a position similar to that of a czarist in Soviet Russia.

Just as cerebrotonia dislikes and resists alcohol, it resists preaching, and the emotional harangue of public orators. The same mechanism seems to account for both kinds of resistance. Somatotonics and viscerotonics tend simply to become more somatotonic or more viscerotonic under the influence of emotional suggestion, while cerebrotonics become fatigued and depressed, presumably by their own internal resistance.

C-19. *Need of Solitude when Troubled or Perplexed.* The trait of wanting and needing to be alone when faced by trouble or grief. When cerebrotonia predominates strongly, the reaction to bad news or to intense grief is simply that of becoming more cerebrotonic. The individual at once drops all of his superficial "compensatory" viscerotonic and somatotonic characteristics, and he withdraws tightly into his shell. He falls back upon his own resources of consciousness for the way out, or possibly he merely adopts the schizoid formula of vertical dissociation—sometimes called the ostrich solution. In any event, he seeks solitude. The same response is seen when such a person is confronted by a difficult choice, by the need for making a decision, or by a crucial test of any sort. Cerebrotonic students become very silent at examination time, and when they are aware of their own nature they prepare for examinations in solitude. The extremely cerebrotonic individual is inclined to be as secretive about good news as about bad.

Note. The trichotomy of polar antitheses represented by the traits

V-19, S-19, and C-19 possesses a singular virtue for diagnostic purposes, in the fact that these differences can be observed both clearly and objectively in young children. We have found that in using the short form of the Scale (see p. 26) school teachers, cottage masters at boys' schools and camps, and others who have rated children for us nearly always agree remarkably well in their ratings on these three traits. The "19's" have been statistically among the most satisfactory traits in all the studies in which this approach has been used.

C-20. *Orientation toward the Later Periods of Life.* There is a primary longing for a later period of life, and a persistent conviction that greater happiness lies in the later decades, when the individual will be (he believes) relatively free from the inhibitory tenseness and emotional insecurity which seem so fearfully to thwart him in youth. Also, among academic or intellectually ambitious cerebrotonics there is a strong feeling that the best fulfillments of life lie in the intellectual maturation, and in the richer understanding and insight of later years. Among such people the quest for "understanding," and for answers to some of the riddles of life, tends to become the primary quest. There is in any event a deep wish to be older, and an impatience with existence at the present stage of it. The pronounced cerebrotonic typically regards childhood as an essentially painful experience which he would under no circumstances wish to repeat (except for the purpose of doing something differently). Similarly youth, the period of highest physical vigor, is to him mainly a time of distraction and annoyance, of frustration, and of postponement. The idea is singularly persistent in cerebrotonic minds that childhood and youth are but periods of preparation—larval periods—pointing toward something more important which lies on beyond.

Note: In the study of adults who are past 30, this trichotomy of polar antitheses (traits V-20, S-20 and C-20) is the most revealing of all. Adults frequently have their orientational impulses well focused, either back upon childhood (usually upon reliving childhood with children of their own—an equally viscerotonic wish), upon the mental maturation of the future, or frantically upon making the most of the opportunity to do things and experience things or accumulate things in the present. In the study of persons under college age however, this trichotomy of traits is of less utility.

In childhood and during the period of young adult life, the cerebrotonic generally finds his closest companionship with persons much older—at least half a generation older. Later, he may abandon the idea of intimate companionship altogether.

One characteristic of little diagnostic value, but of some interest, lies in the different sorts of attitude toward death that seem to mark the three extreme types of temperament. Cerebrotonics often enjoy anticipation of death, and even death itself. They are frequently observed by the attending intern to die smilingly, as if about to keep a pleasantly anticipated appointment. They always have an active curiosity about death, and presumably many suicides are cerebrotonics (although we have no statistical data on this point). Viscerotonics hate to die. They typically have a devil of a time of it, dying with great protest, as if they were being torn from life untimely by the roots. Somatotonics are fearless people. They are in general no more afraid of death than of other things. A fellow intern, in describing the way in which one somatotonic patient died, once put it thus: "He died sort of careless-like, about the way I putt."

The somatotonic is fearless. The viscerotonic is deeply rooted to his earth. The cerebrotonic suggests a form of life which has wandered a long way from its biological moorings, and has forgotten the way back.

HOW TO CALCULATE THE INDEX OF TEMPERAMENT

In scoring the Scale we simply total the ratings for the 20 traits under each component. We then calculate the Index of Temperament by reducing these scores for each component to a 7-point scale, according to the following table.

TABLE 2

TABLE FOR THE TRANSLATION OF RAW SCORES TO NUMERALS

Score	Numeral	Score	Half Numeral
20– 37 incl.	1	29– 37 incl.	1½
38– 54	2	47– 54	2½
55– 71	3	64– 71	3½
72– 88	4	81– 88	4½
89–105	5	98–105	5½
106–122	6	115–122	6½
123–140	7		

This table is derived by dividing the distribution of possible scores into seven approximately equal intervals. When the Scale is used for an intensive individual analysis, we also make use of half-numerals, thereby expanding the Scale to 13 points. The determinations of these half-numerals are given in the right-hand column of Table 2. Similarly in the morphological studies we use the half-numerals (and thereby a 13-point scale) for purposes of individual comparison and analysis. It is quite possible that in time, after the techniques are better standardized and a more extensive series of cases has been accumulated, a more precise scale may supplant the 7-point scale altogether.

In translating total scores to numerals for the short form of the Scale, all the determining values in Table 2 are halved, as nearly as possible.

CHAPTER IV

CONSTITUTIONAL DIFFERENCES AS SHOWN IN THE LIFE HISTORY

IN THIS chapter the life histories of half a dozen young men of contrasting patterns of temperament are summarized. The summaries are intended (a) to illustrate the use of the Scale in objectifying a description of temperament and in facilitating interpretation of the total personality against the life history as a background; and (b) to help set up in the reader's mind some definite comparative criteria for recognition of at least the extreme temperamental variants.

All of these youths entered college, and came to the attention of the writer through academic channels. All but the first two, Aubrey and Boris, finished college and went on to professional training.

The first three in this group define (by example) and serve as real life illustrations of the rare extremes in temperament. People showing these extreme characteristics so uniformly are hard to find. The fourth and fifth, Eugene and Gabriel, illustrate two different kinds of somatotonic personality. The sixth, Hurleigh, is a cerebrotonic who has found an excellent adaptive pattern.

1. AUBREY: *Extreme Viscerotonia*

SUMMARY

Aubrey at 22 is a fat, round-faced, good-natured young man of medium stature. He derives from old American stock, with some German and Irish admixture, and has lived for nearly all his life in a small midwestern community. Although the family is a fairly well-established and industrious one, Aubrey is far from industrious. He has always been lazy, shiftless and irresponsible. But he is exceedingly good-natured. He is of that sociable, easygoing, placid sort that is never disliked and is usually forgiven for shortcomings. He has never been guilty of serious misdemeanor or delinquency. His IQ, tested at three different times in his school career, has in each instance fallen between 100 and 115. His health has been fairly good.

The boy is the second in a family of four children. Early childhood was essentially normal, although he was slow to learn. The school record was consistently mediocre, but he was never kept back a grade. He went to a Midwestern State University for nearly two years and there also his grades were passing but mediocre. After two years he dropped out of college ostensibly to work in his father's hardware store, but the father states that Aubrey's slovenly and wasteful habits render him a liability rather than an asset.

Aubrey is extremely generous, not only with his own property, but especially with his father's. He assumes no responsibility, overeats and oversleeps, and appears to be altogether unconcerned about his future. The specific trait which most disturbs the father is his tendency to attract loafers. Aubrey is always surrounded by a more or less worthless group of hangers-on. When he is at the store, the "laziest and most worthless young rabble of the town collect there like flies around the sugar barrel."

We shall now consider separately each of the final ratings on Aubrey for the 60 traits making up the Scale for Temperament. In practice these ratings are many times revised throughout the period of observation and analysis, but here they are recorded as they stood at the end of the analysis. In addition a few explanatory notes bearing on each of the ratings have been appended.

TEMPERAMENTAL PATTERN

Viscerotonia:

1. *Relaxation* (7). It is relaxing to look at Aubrey. The trunk is slumped, with the belly projecting well forward. Breathing is easy, with very little movement of the chest. It is the abdomen that expands. The muscles of facial expression are almost completely flaccid. The hands typically hang like a seal's flippers. The legs are rarely crossed. When he sits down he obviously enjoys it, and the effect is not unlike that of resting a loosely filled sack of beans on a chair.

2. *Love of Physical Comfort* (7). He shows ingenuity only in this one respect—he is a genius at making himself comfortable. He loves to sit in the sun, and he loves low, deeply upholstered furniture.

3. *Slow Reaction* (6). Reaction is almost uniformly slow, and deliberate. There are no sudden movements. The face remains bland with little change of expression. Sexual appetite is slow and weak. He shows a trace of alacrity only in seeking comfortable positions and his favorite furniture.

4. *Love of Eating* (7). Eating is for him the primary purpose of life, and it involves the principal pleasure of life. Much of his conversation is centered about it, and his deepest enthusiasms are associated with food. The process of eating is itself a most enjoyable occurrence. He does not eat voraciously like a dog, and then turn quickly to other matters, but he approaches food devoutly, as a sincere lover might approach his mistress. He is, indeed, *enteral-erotic*.

5. *Socialization of Eating* (7). Eating is regarded as the most important ceremony of the day. He is rarely absent or late at mealtime (except breakfast). He loves company at table, and would swamp his mother with his guests if a check were not put on it. The principal seal of friendship, for Aubrey, is an exchange of invitations to dinner. Bread breaking is the main sacrament in response to which he musters sentiment.

6. *Pleasure in Digestion* (7). His digestive equipment appears to function like an incinerator. He finds nothing indigestible, and there is nothing like sitting and resting for a few hours after a

good meal—ideally, until the next meal. Elimination, next to eating, is one of the principal pleasures.

7. *Love of Polite Ceremony* (7). He shows great dependence upon the social amenities. Assurance and reassurance of esteem and of high regard occupy much of his waking thought. He depends upon the virtue of doing the proper thing in the proper way. According to his philosophy, affection or regard is sincere only when it is expressed.

8. *Sociophilia* (7). An extreme manifestation of this trait. He is miserable when alone. He craves constant companionship. Since food has always been provided for him, most of his conscious effort is devoted to seeking people and to holding them about him. He is convivial to the highest degree. His primary ego-support lies in conviviality, that is to say, in superficial contact with numbers of people.

9. *Indiscriminate Amiability* (6). He is indiscriminately demonstrative of his good fellowship. This indeed is his only profession (the one thing he professes). Emanation of good fellowship, within the limits of his motley acquaintanceship, is constant and even. His sincerity is never questioned.

10. *Greed for Affection and Approval* (7). Dependence on approval is abject, and therefore pitiful. He is unable to tolerate any sign of disapproval on the part of his group of associates. Rather than displease one of them, he repeatedly gives away valuable property from the store. His first concern is to be a "good fellow."

11. *Orientation to People* (6). He has excellent orientation to a somewhat limited group. People are his primary conscious interest and concern. He is an indefatigable gossip. His mind is a living barometer of minor social status and prestige within the limits of a narrow outlook.

12. *Evenness of Emotional Flow* (6). There are no pronounced changes of attitude, or apparent reversals of feeling. He is always just about the same. The sociophilia is even and well sustained. His tastes show but little variation.

13. *Tolerance* (6). In general, tolerance is very high. There are no social prejudices, no specific political opinions, and no disapproval of a class of people. He shows a fundamental contentment and

satisfaction with life as it is. He becomes a little sharp now and then, but only in his gossip.

14. *Complacency* (7). This trait is extreme, and is perhaps the trait which most exasperates his parents. He is as placid as the full moon, both concerning himself and concerning the family circumstances. For him there is no urgency in anything, and there is no trace of an ambition extending beyond the day which is at hand.

15. *Deep Sleep* (7). Sleep is superbly deep. He is asleep within a few minutes of going to bed, and becomes as limp and unwakable as a baby. He can be moved (was moved on one occasion in the writer's presence) from a chair to a bed without being wakened. Snoring begins almost at once upon going to sleep. It is heavy, constant, and rhythmic.

16. *The Untempered Characteristic* (7). There is no temper in him, no fire, no intensity. He gives the impression of utter flabbiness of mental and emotional fiber. There appears to be no purpose beyond the elementary purposes of existence and comfort. If people were metals, Aubrey would be lead. At handshake his hand seems as cold and nerveless as a piece of fat pork.

17. *Smooth, Easy Communication of Feeling* (7). He gives way naturally and easily to feelings, and never appears to hold anything back. There is no sign of choking back of feeling. No one could misunderstand Aubrey. He is an extravert in the affective (although not in the conative) sense.

18. *Relaxation and Sociophilia under Alcohol* (7). Alcohol has no effect except to accentuate the viscerotonic predominance. He becomes even more conspicuously relaxed and sociable under alcohol, but shows no aggression or loudness, no somatotonic increment. He likes alcohol, but uses it only moderately.

19. *Need of People when Troubled* (7). The primary need is for people. He never "carries" any perplexity, but at once seeks someone upon whom to pour it out, and this he does without restraint. There is no sign of the somatotonic trait of seeking action when troubled.

20. *Orientation toward Childhood and Family* (7). There is strong emotional tie-up with family, and a great leaning upon the mother. Rapport with very young children is his best rapport. He is liked by babies, for there is no tenseness in him. He believes that early childhood is by far the best time of life.

Somatotonia:

1. *Assertiveness of Posture and Movement* (1). A slumped slouch is the characteristic posture. The general impression is that of a jelly-like softness. This is as true of the body as a whole as of the face. There is no trace of aggression in this physical personality. There is no aggressive side-thrust or back-thrust of the arms in walking.

2. *Love of Physical Adventure* (1). None at all. He does not even like to drive an automobile. He has never taken any interest in games, nor in athletic equipment of any sort. Although he can float in water almost as buoyantly as a piece of butter, and as a child loved to swim, he now rarely goes swimming.

3. *The Energetic Characteristic* (1). He is excessively lazy. There are no bursts of energy in any direction. He never gets up in the morning until forcibly roused. The pulse is weak and slow. Blood pressure is low (100/70).

4. *Need of Exercise* (1). He never feels any need for exercise. As his father puts it, "The only exercise he ever takes voluntarily is swallowing."

5. *Love of Dominating* (1). There is no tendency to dominate anything, not even the cat. Aubrey does not desire power. He desires only identification with others, and reassurance.

6. *Love of Risk* (1). He will not even pitch pennies for keeps. He never jaywalks, and he does not like to speed in automobiles. He has frequently refused an opportunity to go up in an airplane.

7. *Bold Directness of Manner* (1). "Bold like a rabbit." He is weak and apologetic in the face of hostility from any source. He does not go after things directly or impersonally, but depends entirely upon the personal relationship to yield him what he desires.

8. *Courage for Combat* (1). He is a physical coward. There are no incidents of combativeness in his history, except possibly one or two brushes with girls or with much younger boys.

9. *Competitive Aggressiveness* (1). There is no aggressiveness or forcefulness in this personality, and there are no signs of compensatory struggle or resentment for failure of aggression. He is

docile, placid, innocuous. There is none of that testiness of temper toward still weaker people, which those who are only relatively weak in this trait so often show.

10. *Psychological Callousness* (1). He is abjectly dependent upon people, and he is deferent and inoffensive to a high degree. He presents an antithesis to the overbearing insensitivity of extreme somatotonia.

11. *Claustrophobia* (2). There are no evidences of any phobia. He has a slight preference for roominess, but is quite comfortable in corners and in small rooms. On this matter he is almost free from preference or inclination.

12. *Freedom from Squeamishness* (2). He is squeamish about all relations with people. He never steps on anybody's toes, or takes any risk of arousing enmity. But he is insensitive to animals and plants. He carelessly steps on insects without sign of awareness, one way or another.

13. *Unrestrained Voice* (2). Ordinarily there is no vocal aggression. The voice is weak and high. Only when well supported socially is there any vocal overshooting.

14. *Spartan Indifference to Pain* (1). No trace of this trait. If anything he is oversensitive to pain. He has always been a crybaby.

15. *General Noisiness* (2). Ordinarily very quiet. The laugh is a giggle. However, when socially well supported, and especially when slightly alcoholized, he will follow along in the general loudness and vocal aggression of the group.

16. *Overmaturity of Appearance* (1). There is no sign of this somatotonic characteristic. No "maturity lines" in the face. It is a bland, relaxed, baby-like face which lacks the overactivity characteristic as completely as it lacks the youthful intentness of cerebrotonia.

17. *Horizontal Mental Cleavage* (1). There is no suggestion of extraversion of action in this history, and no trace of such a tendency in the present behavior. Aubrey is in no sense a conative, or dynamic person. No temper tantrums in childhood. There is no sign of any particular cleavage between his manifest and latent mental attitudes. He is essentially the same at all times and under all circumstances. No striking new twists of attitude or suppressed

tendencies come to light as the interviews progress or as time goes on.

18. *Assertiveness and Aggression under Alcohol* (1). The effect of alcohol is only that of accentuating the viscerotonic traits a little. There is no tendency toward aggressiveness or assertiveness when this drug is used.

19. *Need of Action when Troubled* (1). There is no tendency toward action, but only an increased need to seek people, when Aubrey is faced with perplexity or trouble.

20. *Orientation toward Goals and Activities of Youth* (1). He has no particular love of the period of youth, and no concern for the primary objectives of youth. He is not interested in competition of any sort, even vicariously, and has no desire for power. Early childhood is the best time of life, and old age is the worst. Youth is merely neutral.

Cerebrotonia:

1. *Postural Restraint, Tightness* (1). No trace of tenseness or tightness. He is loose as a fish net, relaxed in every sense. No suggestion of suppression of breathing. He walks like an elephant.

2. *Physiological Overresponse* (1). Complete absence of these symptoms. There is no disturbance of the gastrointestinal tract under any circumstances. The clamping down of the sphincters is unknown to him, as is constipation. Nothing interferes with the regular and full excursion of respiration. Head colds are never violently acute. There is no reaction to mosquito bites. He believes that these insects do not sting him. There is no nervous irritability or jumpiness. The basal metabolic rate is minus 24 (see p. 279).

3. *Overly Fast Reactions* (1). All reactions are slow. He is never socially confused or flustered. Speech is slow, the pupillary response to light (contraction) is slow, and all reflexes are slow. Eye movements are noticeably slow. There is no blushing or blanching. The sexual reaction is slow and weak.

4. *Love of Privacy* (1). Aubrey rarely if ever experiences the sense of a need of privacy. For him, solitude is torture. He fears solitude more than anything else.

5. *Mental Overintensity, Hyperattentionality* (1). The attentional

response is slow and ponderous, in sharp contrast with cerebro-tonic overquickness of attention. He changes so slowly from one attentional focus to another that one can watch the change. It is like shifting the gears in an old-fashioned automobile. The crowd, far from confusing and repressing him, stimulates him and brings him out.

6. *Secretiveness and Restraint of Feeling* (1). No suggestion of any secretiveness or restraint of the expression of feeling. It is as if there were not even an intervening valve, but only an open channel of communication between Aubrey's inner feelings and external expression.

7. *Self-conscious Motility of the Eyes and Face* (1). The face is as relaxed as the human face can be. It looks like the full moon, and the muscles of expression appear to respond but little.

8. *Sociophobia* (1). The antithesis. He is comfortable only when in a group. He has no secretiveness, no distrust of people in the mass. He is agglutinative to the highest degree.

9. *Inhibited Social Address* (1). There is never a lack of self-possession. He remains as unperturbed and as free from self-consciousness as a bullfrog.

10. *Resistance to Habit and Poor Routinizing* (2). There is no particular resistance to habit. No conscious effort is made to break habits. Very few habits form. The initiative to start habits is lacking. Hence routinizing of life is poor, although the social amenities are well carried out.

11. *Agoraphobia* (1). There is no sign of a phobia in either direction. He has neither a dislike of being conspicuous nor an exhibitionism.

12. *Unpredictability of Attitude* (1). There are no sudden changes of attitude. The direction of feeling seems never to be altered. His wants are direct and biological, and they do not change. Aubrey is easily predicted.

13. *Vocal Restraint and Restraint of Noise* (1). The voice carries no aggression and hence is rarely loud, but there is no trace of the active constraint of cerebrotonia. Aubrey makes no effort to control or aim his voice. The laugh lacks the explosive aggression of somatotonia, but is a free-running unrestrained giggle. He is not noisy, because he is inactive, but there is no trace of conscious restraint of voice.

14. *Hypersensitivity to Pain* (2). He often complains of minor discomforts, but there is rarely any flinching or wincing. The complaint is verbal, not physiological. There is no sign of true organic oversensitivity to pain—no paling, tensing or blanching, no history of syncope. No particular response to minor burns and insect stings. In a laboratory test, the response to mildly painful electrical stimulation involved relatively little change of pulse or respiration (although remonstrance was loud).

15. *Poor Sleep Habits* (1). A perfect antithesis. He is an excellent sleeper. If permitted, he would probably sleep half of the time.

16. *Youthful Intentness of Appearance* (1). This is the viscerotonic "suckling face," one extreme antithesis to the intent cerebrotonic face. This is the baby face, not the intent face.

17. *Vertical Mental Cleavage* (1). There are no schizoid episodes in this history, and no trace of any present tendency of the sort. There is no indication of subjective intentness, but rather of its antithesis. Aubrey has no delusions, no dissociation from reality, no sense of living in another world. He has both feet and his buttocks planted firmly on this earth.

18. *Resistance to Alcohol* (1). No resistance. He likes alcohol, and its effect is pleasant, both at the time of drinking and afterward. There is no evidence of any tension or tightening up in response to the drug, and there is no aftereffect of increased fatigue.

19. *Need of Solitude when Troubled* (1). A sharp antithesis. He needs people, and solitude is precisely what he does not want. Solitary confinement would be cruel punishment for this young man.

20. *Orientation toward the Later Periods* (1). The orientation is very clearly back toward infancy and childhood, toward familial and social dependency.

Totals: Viscerotonia, 135; Somatotonia, 24; Cerebrotonia, 22.
      Index of Temperament, 7-1-1.[1]

[1] For translation of raw scores to the index of temperament, see Table 2, p. 95.

PHYSICAL CONSTITUTION

Note: Below is a condensed summary of Aubrey's basic physical data. In the somatotype, the first numeral refers to total endomorphy, the second to mesomorphy, and the third to ectomorphy. The five partial somatotypes given in the parenthesis refer to the five regions of the body in the following order: Region I, head and neck; Region II, upper trunk (above the diaphragm); Region III, arms; Region IV, lower trunk (below the diaphragm); Region V, legs. Gynandromorphy (bisexuality) is indicated by g, the textural component by t, and total dysplasia by d. Height is in inches, weight in pounds. For definitions of gynandromorphy, the t component and dysplasia, see page 282.

Age 22, Ht. 66.5, Wt. 177. Somatotype 6-2-2 (6-2-2, 5-2-2, 5-2-2, 7-2-1, 6-1-2). g 2.5, t 2.0, d 18.

This is a strongly endomorphic physique, of average stature for the somatotype, and of more than average dysplasia (see p. 282). Total dysplasia is 18 (endomorphy, 10; mesomorphy, 4; ectomorphy, 4). Gynandromorphy is about half of a standard deviation less than average for this somatotype—the 6-2-2 is a somewhat effeminate physique. The *t* component is just slightly above the mean for the general population.

There is a slight increment of endomorphy in Region *I* (head and neck), and a more massive increment of this component in Region *IV* (lower trunk) and Region *V* (legs). This distribution of dysplasia is unusual. When a dysplastic increment of the dominant component occurs in a physique, it usually is seen only at one end of the body, that is to say, either in the head and neck or in the legs, rarely in both. In this physique Region *II* (upper trunk) and Region *III* (arms) present a very different somatotype from what is seen below the diaphragm.

Mesomorphy is low throughout the body, and shows a fairly conspicuous decrement in Region *V*. The rare 6-1-2 somatotype is seen in the legs. These are excessively weak legs, long in proportion to the rather short body, knock-kneed, and the thighs have already become heavy and hamlike. In middle life this man will have trouble in getting around. If he should become as excessively gluttonous as his temperamental picture indicates, and as fat as his somatotype will permit, he may perhaps lose the power of loco-motion entirely. The 6-1-2 is not infrequently chair-ridden in middle life, although this is more common with the female than with the male.

Ectomorphy is low throughout, especially in Region *IV*. In this, the abdominal region—the "boiler room"—there is no sign of fragility or of ectomorphic weakening at all. Here we see only the massive expansion of the 7-2-1, and possibly we here begin to look with some compassion upon the tremendous viscerotonic de-mand which such a gut must levy upon its relatively modest and unaggressive host.

Region *I* shows no characteristics particularly unusual for the 6-2-2 somatotype. The head is slightly brachycephalic, the face is nearly round with an ectomorphic interference in the mandibles, the nose is blunt with a low, weak bridge, and the rather large, coarse mouth shows a prominent viscerotonic protrusion of the lips (suckling lips). The eyes are gray-blue, rather large and widely spaced, and the expressive musculature about the eyes is already largely lost in fat. The neck is a little longer and more slender than the usual 6-2-2. Hair is straight, fine-textured, ash-brown, and rather sparse. The skin over the entire body is distinctly endomorphic, that is to say, white, thin and smooth. Bodily hair is sparse and of slightly feminoid distribution (the usual distribu-tion of 6-2-2 bodily hair).

CLINICAL HISTORY

Aubrey was the second pregnancy and the second child. The father was then 29 and the mother 26. Normal, full-term preg-nancy, and normal, easy birth. Birth weight about 8 pounds. Rapid early weight gain. The baby is said to have weighed well over 30 pounds at 10 months. Breast fed 6 months. Enormous appetite as a baby. He is said to have eaten five bananas on one occasion at age 8 months. (The mother was curious to see how much he could hold.) Very well behaved, quiet baby, distinctly less vigorous or troublesome than his siblings. Talked at 14 months. Walked at 16 months. Dentition began at 8 months. Toilet training com-pleted successfully at 26 months. No history of eneuresis after the third year. He was a very affectionate, dependent child, never had temper tantrums, was somewhat slow to learn, never bit his fingernails, and as a child manifested no noticeable autoeroticism.

During the first four years he had measles (severe), diphtheria, scarlet fever (severe), chickenpox, several heavy, prolonged chest colds, a mastoid infection and mastoidectomy, running ears repeatedly, and pyelitis repeatedly. Later he has had recurrent conjunctivitis, intermittent bronchitis, at least four blood infections from minor injuries (all of which cleared up, however), intermittently enlarged lymph glands (cervical and inguinal), a tonsillectomy and adenoidectomy, and severe trouble with infected gums, together with impacted third molars.

Adolescence was late, beginning near the end of the fifteenth year. The testes are small, with a short, partially hidden penis of very undeveloped corona. This is usual or normal with strongly predominant endomorphy. He has been bothered somewhat with phimosis but has not been circumcised.

The palate is wide and shallow. Teeth are well spaced but rather small. Caries have been moderate. There is a mild degree of myopia. Deep reflexes are present when reinforced. Superficial reflexes are normal. There are no further positive findings at physical examination.

BACKGROUND
Paternal:

The father is a rather stolid, thrifty, intelligent businessman, of old American stock which is predominantly English and Scotch. He is of medium stature and is about a 4-4-3 in somatotype. He is a realistic, matter-of-fact man of good general reputation, and has been moderately successful with his hardware store, which he has now run for about a quarter of a century. He drinks moderately, belongs to the Elks' Club and Masons (in a community where both organizations are strong and include the leading citizens), and although he says he is a Protestant, neither he nor any of his family go to church. On Sundays he usually plays golf or goes hunting.

The paternal grandfather was a stalwart, powerful farmer, and the paternal grandmother was short and fat, growing extremely heavy in later life and dying of diabetes at 55.

The father's attitude toward Aubrey is one of fairly good-natured toleration. "That second boy is lazy as a hog, and gettin' fatter'n one. I don't guess he's quite normal. Doctor says his glands ain't right. He ain't dependable. He'll prob'ly never amount to much. Wish we could send him to market, but seein' we can't, guess we'll just keep on supportin' him."

Among the father's relatives three cases of diabetes are reported. No cancer, tuberculosis or mental illness. There are several instances of high blood pressure.

Maternal:

The mother was a **PPJ** (pyknic practical joke). She was slim-waisted and active when she was married at 20, but after the first pregnancy she came into her full endomorphic blossom. She is of average stature, weighed 115 pounds at 20, and weighs 160 at 48. She is about a 4-4-2 in somatotype, and is of mixed German and old American stock. She has been a good mother, has raised four fairly healthy children, and is generally reputed as a wholesome, conservative, average citizen. She is hearty, eats heavily, and has a rather florid, middle-sized body which is rounded and plump as if under moderate pneumatic pressure. She is healthy-looking. Possibly she is 20 pounds overweight for her somatotype. She gets out of breath easily. The maternal grandfather was short and strong, a farmer all his long life. The maternal grandmother is a large woman, but more tall than fat. As a girl this grandmother was strong and enjoyed doing a man's work on the farm. Now, at nearly 70, she still enjoys working and keeps a boarding house. The mother's attitude toward Aubrey is quite objective. She thinks he is a good enough boy at heart, but that he was born lazy and gluttonous. Neither she nor the father is aware of any favoritism having been shown toward any of the children. "Aubrey's trouble," she says complacently, "is his glands."

Among the mother's relatives there have been four cases of cancer, two of tuberculosis, and two of nephritis. No diabetes, and no mental illness.

Siblings:

1. Brother, now 25. Finished agricultural college after some slight academic difficulty. Now married and farming, apparently with moderate success. About a 4-5-2.
2. Aubrey, 22.
3. Sister, now 20. Rather tall and slender. About a 2-4-4, and pretty. She is in nurses' training, although her academic record is rather poor.
4. Brother, now 17. Not seen. He is in high school and is a substitute on the football team. He has been in some difficulties of a sexual nature, with a high school girl.

GENERAL LIFE STORY

First 6 Years (pre-school period):

Aubrey was slow in learning to talk and walk, but not sufficienty slow to be considered abnormal. His health was rather poor, but he could hardly be called a sickly baby. During the first three years he was ill in one way or another, possibly a third of the time. But there was no outstandingly severe or prolonged illness, and so far as is known there was no specific illness which particularly affected the course of his physical or mental development. He always had an excellent appetite. From age 3 to 6 his health was fairly good but not robust. He was a relatively inactive child.

His associations during this period were chiefly with children even younger than himself, and with girls. He was "no good at games," could not fight or run well, was soft and pudgy, and was easily picked on. Yet he was not considered a crybaby, and he was generally liked. There was no rivalry between Aubrey and his older brother. The brother was well grown for his age, fairly athletic, and strong. He ran with boys older than himself. Aubrey was never taken along, and he rarely if ever tagged along. He could not keep the pace and made no attempt to do so. His brother's world was another world, about which he knew very little. He was on far more intimate terms with his sister, two years younger, but her group teased him and made fun of him. He belonged to no particular group, but was always intimately associated with a sort of motley tag-end assortment of weak, crippled or unusual children, several of whom at this period were girls somewhat older than Aubrey.

This boy was decidedly not unhappy during the period of his early childhood. He was "rejected" certainly by the strongest of his contemporaries, but he did not compete with them, and he hardly knew he was rejected. Actually, his contacts were many and warm. His discrimination was poor. There is no evidence of any particular emotional attitude toward either the father or mother at this time, except one of general overdependence. On the surface, there is no history of hostility to the father or of emotional overattachment to the mother. During this period Aubrey was deeply attached to a small dog belonging to the family. The dog was killed accidently when the boy was 6. The mother stated that for one day Aubrey was prostrated by grief, but that within forty-eight hours he had apparently forgotten all about it, and was as happy as ever with a new puppy.

Aubrey was perhaps slightly on the effeminate side in his early behavior. During this period no overt sexual interests of any kind were shown, so far as is known by the parents or remembered by Aubrey. The mother makes a point of the fact that of the four children Aubrey alone never was known to "masturbate," and that indeed he never took any interest in girls until he was about 17. "Dr. Turner says it's his glands," she always repeats, with a friendly, challenging stare which seems to add, "Therefore the whole matter is settled and everything of importance has been said."

Age 6 to 14 (grammar school period):

Aubrey went to the public school at 6. He was then of average height, and of well over average weight. School was only about four blocks from home. He usually went alone, as he walked so much more slowly than his older brother, but when he came home he generally brought along a collection of the weaker and less gifted children of the neighborhood. (Aubrey has been a "moron-ophile" all his life. He attracts and holds the morons.) These children he desired his mother to feed and tolerate, and apparently she did so to quite an unusual degree. Yet there were moments of recalcitrancy on her part, and consequently of disappointment and frustration on Aubrey's part. Aubrey recalls much bitterness toward his mother on this score, although he is aware of virtually no early bitterness toward his father.

Apparently this boy was generally tolerated by the children of the neighborhood, from the time he entered school. But by boys and girls alike he was regarded as of another kind, possibly as of another sex. He could neither throw a ball nor fight nor run. He had nothing in common with boys of his own age, except swimming. He could swim, and this he liked. From May to October he was continually on the way to and from the local swimming hole, where he was almost an authority. (Indeed, if the human race were still aquatic, or even amphibian instead of terrestial, there can be no doubt that Aubrey and others like him would be in much stronger position. The first component is good at swimming.)

In school, Aubrey did tolerably well, but never better than that. His report cards always placed him in the mediocre group, just out of danger of failing. He had no good subjects, and no especially bad ones. He never became interested in school, and he never learned to compete at anything. Even at swimming he never would race, or enter the life-saving tests. His deportment was always good, except for lapses of attention. He was never involved in any serious pranks and was never disciplined in school.

Aubrey graduated from grammar school (the eighth grade) with the class with which he entered. He was then approaching 15. But the last two years of grammar school were less pleasant than earlier years. The boys and girls were changing. They were like wild birds in the early autumn getting ready to migrate. But Aubrey was not changing, and he did not feel any strange inner urge either to migrate or to do anything else. These others were adolescent, while he was unchanged. They were beginning to talk in a new vocabulary, often a vocabulary without words, and he was entirely left out. He was now more openly than before an object of condescension, and now especially so at the swimming hole. During the last year at grade school he for the most part stayed away from the swimming place.

At this time most of the girls he knew seemed to change from the good-natured toleration and essential fellowship which he had enjoyed for years. They became sharp with him, looked at him with an indifferent stare, or avoided him altogether. This disturbed him, he thinks, even more than the change in his male contemporaries.

After 14:

Aubrey went to high school, still in his home town, and still within easy walking distance from home. The first two years were the worst of his life, he believes. Most of his old grade school companions went to high school with him, and they seemed to carry the old contempt for him, while he, in contrast, pitifully craved warmth and companionability. He now had to find nearly all his happiness in eating and digesting. These others had begun to go about in couples, many of them, and the air was thick with amplified rumors of sexual adventure. But Aubrey, at 15, was only just beginning to feel the first traces of sexual maturation. He was now grossly fat, fatter than he had ever been before or has ever been again, up to the present time.

Several attempts were made during this period to interest Aubrey in hobbies, such as stamp collecting and the like. He took up these interests readily enough but never carried any of them beyond the most superficial beginnings. He appears to have used them only as techniques of socialization. Although given a fairly good stamp collection, he never was known to look at it or work on it when alone. Earlier in his career the same had been true of his toy railways and the like. Aubrey never enjoyed anything alone. He was always a "sharer." From his point of view it is perhaps a serious misfortune that in his community the day of the emotional religious revival and the camp meeting had gone, to be replaced by a sophisticated cynicism which is now almost universal among the rising generations. No channels for religious expression of the viscerotonic sort have ever been open to this young man. That side of life has been a void in his world.

He never learned to read books, and so far as is known has never voluntarily read a book in his life. Reading is to him only something that one has to do in school. He reads nothing, not even newspapers or wild West thrillers. Indeed this youth never learned to do anything which is done alone. He is dependent upon constant social support.

High school was on the whole a strain and a harsh experience. The first two years constituted a period of bewilderment and frustration. His companionship was limited, practically, to younger children and the neighborhood riffraff who for one reason or another were unable to go to high school. During this time he became a great addict to card playing, especially bridge. But he has never gambled, either at cards or in any other manner.

During the third year of high school Aubrey learned spontaneously to masturbate. This was for a time a momentous discovery. He had secretly regarded himself as deficient sexually. There was no particular shame or sense of guilt associated with his masturbation. Indeed he was proud of it, and his first desire was to try to socialize the experience—with some younger boys who, however, were possibly at about his own status in sexual maturation. This friendly effort resulted in misunderstanding and in unhappy recriminations. Aubrey found himself even more cut off socially than had previously been the case. Several of his associates were now forbidden by their parents to associate with (the immoral) Aubrey.

In the meantime masturbation was the first thing he had ever found that was any fun to do alone. For possibly six months he indulged in this practice about once a week, but he noticed that his orgasm now began to take place more easily than at first, and that the effect was less generalized in his body. It was no longer so much fun, and he began to cease to look forward to the experience. He indulged oftener, and the matter became of less consequence. In short, within less than a year, even this pleasant exercise was not any longer much fun to do alone.

During his senior year in high school, at 18, he had his first "date." Although he could not dance, he escorted a freshman girl to the junior prom. She was a fat girl, large, aggressive and noisy. (At the end of the school year she failed, and was removed from school by her parents.) Aubrey did not have a very good time at this dance. He wanted to be very sociable, but even the girl he took to the affair found other company more attractive. He made no sexual advances.

In June he graduated from high school, rather low in his class. All summer he loafed around home and in September entered the State University, more than a hundred miles away. He was approaching 19, was about five feet six, and weighed 160 pounds, which was a little less than he had weighed four years previously, and was perhaps less than he was ever to weigh again. He was sexually virginal, had been masturbating for only about a year and a half, and his masturbation had become rather futile and disappointing to him. He had never taken part in any intimate sexual play with a girl, and was considerably ashamed or embarrassed about that. His anecdotal conversation was desperately impoverished at this facet of universal interest, and he lacked the cerebrotonic imagination either to invent good anecdotal material himself or to evaluate properly the inventive genius of those of his friends who were more expert narrators.

He believed most of what he heard, and so was filled with a great sense of inferiority. His interest, therefore, during the first year of college, was largely sexual. Yet from sex, specifically, Aubrey expected very little. He seemed to know intuitively that for him the sexual side of life had little to offer. It was merely that sexuality was expected of him, and sexuality was the door which barred him from what he really wanted—warm good fellowship. That there were other, and for him better, doors, he had no way of knowing. A mortal fear of prostitutes had been implanted in him and the horror of venereal disease loomed in his mind like the shadow of Satan. He had an allowance to spend, and he had an increasingly desperate desire to spend it on his sexual education, but it was not until May of his freshman year at college, that he achieved sexual intercourse.

In a cheap restaurant he found a high school girl who was a part-time waitress. She was about a year younger than Aubrey, apparently of nearly his own somatotype but with a little more mesomorphy, and presumably she was of wider sexual experience than he. A coarse, loud girl, she was of about his own height and probably of nearly his weight. She was fond of any beverage containing alcohol, and with a little of it inside would become amorously aggressive. Aubrey took her to the movies, and was invited in to meet the family, which he did, lamblike. In the course of a month Aubrey achieved intercourse, on the piano stool. It lasted only a few seconds, and Julia was not pleased.

Yet Aubrey had money to spend on liquor, and Julia liked liquor. Although the two met frequently, even abortive attempts at intercourse were rare, probably not more than three or four altogether. Aubrey left for home late in the following month and when he returned in September, Julia's family had moved away. The incident constituted about 50 per cent of Aubrey's total sexual experience at college. During the succeeding year there was another adventure of a somewhat similar nature, with an even less attractive girl.

This youth passed all his courses in his freshman year, and joined a fraternity. But he did not become interested in anything except sex and, to a lesser degree, liquor. During the sophomore year he became certain of what he had long suspected—that college is a spurious and impractical racket carried on against the public welfare by and for the exploitative professors. He went home for spring vacation, developed an excellent bronchitis, and never returned to college.

During the succeeding year and a half or so, Aubrey has lived at home. College was so unpleasant that he has been relatively happy and comfortable with his parents. He is now the oldest son at home, and he pretends to a considerable wisdom and experience in worldly affairs. He has joined the Elks. He knows about sex and has sage advice to offer (to leave sex alone—it is bad medicine). The same is true of college. He likes alcohol but has never been known to approach drunkenness. He smokes a good deal—says it keeps his weight down. His expressed ambition is to take over his father's hardware store, but this is purely verbal. Actually there is no ambition at all. He rises about eleven unless forcibly ejected from bed, and usually goes to bed rather early.

Aubrey has not been known to have a date for over a year, but when alcoholically confiding he hints mysteriously about a "mistress" whom he meets regularly. This is probably fanciful. At college he learned the conversational role of the sexual anecdote. He is as moronophilic as ever, usually appears at the store shortly after lunch, and his appearance there is regularly followed by the arrival of from two to a dozen loafers and hangers-on whom he has known since childhood. The father is tolerant of everything except this agglutination with loafers, who interfere with his business and pilfer his goods. On the matter of moronophilia there have been stormy scenes recently between Aubrey and his father. A severe strain may come of it.

THE PROBLEM OF TREATMENT

The investigation of this personality was undertaken for research purposes, although with excellent cooperation from relatives and from the subject himself. The question of therapy might be raised for academic reasons, although it is our own feeling that the time is too early to speak with any assurance of therapy in psychology. The problem of therapy is but the aftermath to a solution of the problem of diagnosis. The diagnosis in Aubrey's case is, probably, "simple viscerosis."

Viscerosis in a person of low somatotonia and low cerebrotonia means gluttony, laziness and overdependence upon others. How, then, should it be treated? By disciplining the biological appetites —by dieting? By such a routine as military discipline? By objective and disinterested handling of the child during early formative years? By encouraging and supporting expression of the weaker motivational components? There can be no doubt that all of these suggestions are good under some circumstances, and possibly some of them are good under all circumstances. Yet a human personality is too complex for blanket formulae of treatment.

What could now be done for Aubrey is a matter of speculative interest. Endocrine therapy suggests itself naturally for consideration. Aubrey's BMR was taken several times while he was in high school, at the suggestion of the local physician. It was found to average minus 24, with but little variation. Such a finding suggested treatment with thyroid (thyroxin). This was tried, three different times. On each occasion Aubrey complained of headaches and general discomfort, and the therapy was abandoned. In one instance it was continued for six weeks, but on that occasion, a month after cessation of the treatment, the BMR was found to be minus 28. The physician felt that the thyroxin had only stimulated a counter-reaction.

The same doctor tried two different testicular extracts and at least one pituitary hormone on Aubrey during the period of his postponed puberty. Both the doctor and Aubrey's family state that it was this treatment which brought on the pubertal change. But such an opinion is to be gravely questioned. It suggests too easily the old saw about the Christian Science practitioner causing the kittens to open their eyes. The difficulty is that we do not yet know the *normal* endocrinology for the different constitutional families, or somatotype families, and endocrinology practiced without such norms is a rather blind procedure. Yet endocrine therapy, practiced against a background of insight into constitutional variation, should one day offer a most promising field for experimentation.

Some would suggest psychoanalysis for this youth. This is always a fascinating experiment. Yet in our experience therapeutic psychoanalysis is a specific for that kind of personality which because of some environmental influence is inhibiting and holding back a fairly strong (usually a naturally predominant) somatotonia. Such is certainly not Aubrey's case. It is somatotonic people who easily achieve the "conversion experience," or who find dream analysis and similar indirect approaches to consciousness revelatory. These are the people who show what we have called horizontal mental dissociation. Since Aubrey showed little trace of this phenomenon, we are forced to predict that he probably would not respond to psychoanalysis.

There are students of the problem who would prescribe a "normal" sexual life for such a boy, perhaps marriage, or if not marriage, then if necessary a mistress (a relationship which under our present culture is loaded with difficulties). But Aubrey belongs to a constitutional group which carries little or no sexual appetite, and very inadequate sexual equipment. His sexuality is rudimentary. To try to reorient such a personality around sexuality would be a little like trying to teach a Leghorn hen to take pleasure in a duck pond. It is likely, in our opinion, that the real trauma in Aubrey's sex life was not due to his sexual failure, but to the indiscriminate manner in which his social *milieu* forced sexuality upon him. The problem at this point may be one of social psychiatry, not individual psychiatry. It is possible that this personality never wanted and never should have had sexuality at all, in any form. To irritate the sexual question further with Aubrey might be like reopening an old, poorly healed wound.

Disciplinarians would suggest discipline, and perhaps a strict diet. Get him up in the morning, put him to work, tire him out every day, and feed him sparingly. This might work, even now. It might salvage Aubrey to the extent of changing a lazy sloth into a more or less useful worker. But if that procedure were to be followed, it would seem a cruel pity to begin it so late in life, and also it might seem a bit anomalous to turn to psychology for this the time-honored method of common sense. That would suggest the story of the woman who paid $5000 of her husband's money to be psychoanalyzed, only to discover that what she really wanted was sexual intercourse.

The idea of treating such a problem by stimulating or encouraging somatotonic and cerebrotonic expression sounds attractive on first consideration. But on second thought, this is precisely what society and the whole educational effort has been trying to do ever since the boy first made his appearance. Not only have hundreds of channels of somatotonic and cerebrotonic expression been open to him all his life, but effort has been made almost continually to turn his nose down some of them. Aubrey constitutionally lacks both somatotonia and cerebrotonia. The horse with no thirst will not drink. Get him interested in *doing* something? Get him interested in reading? Get the Leghorn hen interested in swimming.

Somatotonia and cerebrotonia are positive characteristics. They perhaps represent departures from the primeval biological reservoir. In a sense they are different and more or less incompatible efforts to extend human conation and cognition, respectively, into the workings of nature. Somatotonic and cerebrotonic virtues or faults are positive. They can be treated, and can be praised or blamed. In them, the living animal has ventured something and has made an attack on a problem. But viscerotonic traits are essentially negative traits. They represent in one sense a biological reactionism, and it is difficult to treat such characteristics therapeutically. Moreover, it may be well, in the long run, that we cannot get at viscerotonia, for this component may constitute a kind of insurance or reservoir of safety for the species.

In summary, viscerosis is singularly difficult to treat. Just as in medicine there are really only two kinds of drugs—stimulants and depressants—there are in the last analysis only the same two basic kinds of psychological control—reward and punishment. In general, it would appear that cerebrosis indicates a need for encouragement (reward), and somatorosis, a need for discipline (punishment). Then, since viscerotonia is a little nearer to somatotonia than to cerebrotonia (see p. 400), it is possible that such a person as Aubrey would make a better adaptation in a more disciplined society, where he made his way under sterner conditions. If so, then it is Aubrey's environment as a whole that requires treatment, not Aubrey alone. Individual psychiatry divorced from social psychiatry seems, at least in Aubrey's case, to be nearly futile.

2. BORIS: *Extreme Somatotonia*

SUMMARY

Boris is a tall, vigorous youth of 21 who appears slender but actually is muscular and powerful, with very broad shoulders. He looks several years older than he is. The face has a square-jawed, mature set. He laughs easily and explosively, but always aggressively—not humorously. This youth comes from a fairly prosperous Irish family who have lived in Chicago since the marriage of the parents 24 years ago. The family is nominally Roman Catholic but not actively so.

Boris is extremely pugnacious, aggressive, loud, and has dangerous outbursts of temper. Twice he has seriously injured other young men in fights. His IQ, according to early school and high school report, is about 105. His school record is poor, especially so beyond the eighth grade. He has twice been dropped from college for low grades and for refusing to submit to authority. But he is an excellent football player and although at present out of school, is still more than welcome at his choice of several colleges. He has been violently embroiled with one college over the matter of collecting his remuneration for football. He will probably enter his third college as a freshman.

This boy is popular, is regarded as handsome, and is perhaps somewhat spoiled by women, one or two of whom (he boasts) have offered to support him. He plans to be a movie actor or a professional football coach, or both. But he feels that he has grown old, that his powers are declining, and that all that is best in life is hurrying rapidly by him.

TEMPERAMENTAL PATTERN

Viscerotonia:

1. *Relaxation* (1). There appears to be no relaxation at all. Assertiveness both of posture and of movement characterize this physical personality at all times. The face is hard, with a stern set to the muscles which never seems to leave them. The walk is aggressive, with heavy striking of the heels and a lateral fling of the arms. The pulse is strong, and rather fast. Breathing is deep,

regular, and often noisy. The voice is harsh, uneven, and usually strained.

2. *Love of Physical Comfort* (1). He scorns physical comfort. Prefers to sleep on the floor, without a mattress. Often will not wear an overcoat in winter. He never spends any time "being comfortable," and never manifests appreciation of the effort of others to make him comfortable.

3. *Slow Reaction* (1). There is no suggestion of viscerotonic deliberateness. His physical movements are rapid and jerky. In boxing and in other athletic games his reactions are probably faster than average, although he does not show the overly fast reactions of cerebrotonia. His reaction time as measured in the psychological laboratory is about average.

4. *Love of Eating* (1). He is a voracious eater, but he bolts his food like a wolf. There is no love of the *process* of eating. He in no sense lives to eat. He cares nothing for cuisine and is not discriminating about food.

5. *Socialization of Eating* (1). No more sentiment is attached to eating together with people, or to bread breaking, than to riding together in the subway. He never lingers at a table. There is no sentiment in connection with eating.

6. *Pleasure in Digestion* (1). He is not affectively aware of digestion. He never sits placidly after eating. Peristalsis appears to be dissociated from affect. Elimination offers no delights. There are occasional digestive upsets.

7. *Love of Polite Ceremony* (1). He is abrupt, unceremonious. He has in general a scorn of propriety and of the "correct" procedure. There is little politeness in him.

8. *Sociophilia* (2). He is almost completely independent of individual people, boasting that he has no intimates and wants none. Certainly his dislike and suspicion of people is stronger than any gentler emotion. Yet this young man moves freely among many kinds of people, and he is in a superficial sense popular. To him, people are objects to be used, not objects of affection. His attitude is conative, not affective.

9. *Indiscriminate Amiability* (1). There is no warmth of fellowship, and almost no emotional interest in other personalities.

There is no participation in the desires or values of another individual.

10. *Greed for Affection and Approval* (1). He seems as close to complete independence in this respect as it is possible to become in civilized society. He feels no sense of loneliness (possibly because he is widely sought as an athlete), and regards himself as completely self-sufficient.

11. *Orientation to People* (2). He has a fairly wide superficial acquaintanceship with people who are interested in the world of sport, but there is no insight, no discriminative evaluation of people, and no knowledge of what individuals really stand for or want. He repeatedly places his trust or confidence in the wrong quarter, and often "blows off" to the wrong people. But he learns nothing from these experiences.

12. *Evenness of Emotional Flow* (1). One of his most conspicuous characteristics is a violent, hair-trigger temper. This he has manifested all his life, and has on more than one occasion seriously injured people. His mood swings are violent and sudden. His affections are not to be depended upon, and his reactions have no uniformity. He frequently "blows up" without warning.

13. *Tolerance* (1). The extreme antithesis. He is notably intolerant and impatient of people, of institutions and of situations. He expresses no contentment and no satisfaction with anything. His conversation is mainly a violent anathematizing either of individuals or of groups.

14. *Complacency* (1). The extreme antithesis. He is choleric, excitable, critical and dissatisfied under nearly all circumstances, except perhaps for momentary verbalizations of commonplace sentiment.

15. *Deep Sleep* (2). He sleeps fitfully, sometimes soundly, but with no trace of the limp relaxation of viscerotonia. He is easily awakened, says he "always sleeps with one eye open," and rarely snores. He has no trouble in going to sleep, never lies awake, and the concept of insomnia is foreign to him. He thinks that six hours sleep per night is about the right amount. Typically he is up at 5:30 A.M., when he likes to take a very cold shower and to go through his routine of vigorous exercises.

16. *The Untempered Characteristic* (1). He presents an excellent antithesis to this trait. He is the embodiment of temper, and he gives off the general impression of an unyielding hardness or toughness of fiber. The face shows great determination and resolution, or ruthlessness. He is explosive.

17. *Smooth, Easy Communication of Feeling* (1). There is no smoothness to his communication of feeling. He appears unable to express feeling except in a violent outburst. He appears not to inhibit or choke back anything, yet calm, rational communication of any kind seems impossible for him. He is like a pack of firecrackers which, if they go off at all, go off all together. He seems to illustrate the all-or-none principle in affective reaction. Although an extreme extravert in the conative or dynamic sense, he has no extraversion of affect.

18. *Relaxation and Sociophilia under Alcohol* (1). There is no trace of this characteristic. He likes alcohol, but his reaction is simply that of increased aggression. He becomes very violent and noisy with a small amount of this drug. He never gets drunk.

19. *Need of People when Troubled* (1). He does not pour out his troubles, and indeed tends to avoid confidences altogether. The typical reaction to trouble is a marked stepping up of activity. He feels a strong need to meet the situation with his muscles.

20. *Orientation toward Childhood and the Family* (2). In general he despises infants and infancy, and has no interest in that period of life. All of his mental focus seems to be centered on the strenuous competitions and exercises of youth or young manhood. Yet there is a suggestion of sentimental tie-up with the mother-son relationship, and there is some vocalization as to the "sacredness" of the family. But this seems to be principally a religious (Catholic) stereotype.

Somatotonia:

1. *Assertiveness of Posture and Movement* (7). He constantly maintains the most assertive posture. The back is straight and erect, whether sitting or standing. The shoulders are squared and thrown back, the head is carried high, the jaw seems to be protruded, and the firm, muscular lips are drawn tight, as if ready to bare the teeth. Every movement is forceful, particularly the movements of the shoulders and arms in walking. There is no hesitancy or tentativeness about the man.

2. *Love of Physical Adventure* (7). He lives for physical adventure, the more dangerous the better. He is most at home when engaging in vigorous sport like football and fighting. He is excessively fond of "roughing it," and welcomes physical hardship. Aviation is his favorite interest.

3. *The Energetic Characteristic* (7). Energy appears to be inexhaustible. He seems even to think with his muscles. Speech is always accompanied by vigorous gesturing (he talks with his whole body). He is tireless. Getting up in the morning is almost always pleasant, and he fairly springs from his bed to his shower. He has a strong pulse, with blood pressure 130/100 (recumbent).

4. *Need of Exercise* (7). Exercise is carried on regularly as a religious duty, and with almost perfect routine. He has a punching bag which he carries about with him and sets up wherever he goes. When possible he likes a regular gymnasium workout for about three hours each morning, and for perhaps two more hours in the late afternoon. If the program of exercise is interfered with he becomes irritable, uncomfortable, and sometimes depressed.

5. *Love of Dominating* (7). He is certain to be dominant in any relationship which is at all sustained. The desire to conquer and subdue constitutes a primary motivational drive. Boris needs to be important in a situation if he is to tolerate it.

6. *Love of Risk* (7). He is always eager to take a chance. At 13 on a bet he dived off a bridge only a few feet lower than the Brooklyn Bridge. He is fond of stunt flying and automobile racing, and has found opportunities to take part in both. He has a passion for gambling on horse races, and also for other gambling.

7. *Bold Directness of Manner* (7). Under all circumstances he is bold and direct. He comes straight to the point in any matter. There is a striking rigidity and forcefulness of the face, and there is never any quick (or furtive) change of expression. There is no furtiveness, no deceit or tact. He is completely objective and frank.

8. *Courage for Combat* (7). Unexcelled. He is as fearless as a mastiff, and is highly combative at all times. This young man is no cowardly bully who runs from the fight he has started. He would

like nothing better than to fight the heavyweight champion, without gloves. He loves to fight against odds, and he appears to enjoy physical injury.

9. *Competitive Aggressiveness* (7). Extremely aggressive pattern of life in almost every detail. He is in all relationships one-directional and unhesitant. Every movement of the body and every inflection of the voice is aggressive. There is no suggestion of the compensatory factor here.

10. *Psychological Callousness* (7). He is ruthlessly insensitive and overbearing in his relationships with people, although in no sense intentionally or consciously so. This is not generally resented, for his sincerity and the general uniformity of his behavior are obvious. He has no intuition and is perfectly insensitive to inhibitory suggestion.

11. *Claustrophobia* (7). There is a great hatred of closed-in places of any sort, and a love of being unrestrained and out in the open. He loves room, and freedom of movement. He always sleeps nude, and swims nude when he can. He despises what is "small" or "mean" (cerebrotonic). He wants to live life on the grand scale. He loves "fresh air."

12. *Freedom from Squeamishness* (7). There is no trace of squeamishness in anything that Boris does. He has no compunctions, no internal doubts or hesitancies. He is in the most complete sense a practical person. He is as free from inhibition or sentimentality as the general of an army.

13. *Unrestrained Voice* (7). The voice is loaded with aggression. It rises to a strained violence whenever a question is raised, and if there is a suggestion of opposition, he fairly shouts. In normal conversation, there is a sharp, penetrative characteristic in the voice which causes it to carry far beyond the person addressed.

14. *Spartan Indifference to Pain* (7). Extreme manifestation of this trait. He always refuses anaesthesia in the repair of cuts, scalp wounds and the like sustained in athletic competition. He makes a great point of Spartanism. Loves to go swimming in the winter.

15. *General Noisiness* (7). In this trait Boris is supreme. When he walks the room shakes. When he shuts a door it stays shut (as he says). His humorless explosive laugh all but rattles the windowpanes. His breathing is deep and is frequently noisy. His cough is like the sharp explosion of an inflated paper bag. He does not do these things for the sake of noise. It is merely a part of the pattern of routine, unconscious aggression.

16. *Overmaturity of Appearance* (7). The general appearance, especially in the face, is that of a man of 25 to 30. At a little distance he looks even older. The face is weather-beaten and leathery, with long, straight, deeply-marked crease lines in the cheeks. The skin suggests well-tanned and well-creased leather.

17. *Horizontal Mental Cleavage* (7). He has no beginnings of self-insight, and no comparative evaluation of his own motives. His life has been a series of hypomanic episodes. There is no familiarity with his own phantasy or dream life. He seems cut off from the deeper levels of his own mind, and the mental focus is centered upon the outward scene. For Boris there appears to be no valve or check between thought and direct action. He is an extreme extravert in the conative sense, although he is no extravert in the affective sense (see trait V-17).

18. *Assertiveness and Aggression under Alcohol* (7). The effect of alcohol seems to be solely that of exaggeration of the already strong tendency toward assertiveness and aggression. There is no trace of viscerotonic warmth or relaxation, and no cerebrotonic resistance to alcohol.

19. *Need of Action when Troubled* (7). He turns to action entirely, never taking people into his confidence concerning trouble or perplexity. Nor does he ever go off in solitude to try to think things out. What he most desires, in the face of trouble, is a fight, but as substitute behavior he may take it out on the punching bag or in the gymnasium.

20. *Orientation toward Goals and Activities of Youth* (6). The major focus of thought is upon the strenuous and competitive preoccupations of youth. Nearly all of Boris' values lie in the quest for power, money, sex or prestige. He has no craving for understanding or insight—or for an answer to the riddle of life. Old age is a thing of disgust. Yet there is a faint nostalgia for the mother-child relationship, and some trace of sentimentality about the family.

Cerebrotonia:

1. *Physical Restraint, Tightness* (1). He presents the somatotonic antithesis to restraint. There is no suggestion of physical inhibition. All of the bodily movements are free and unchecked. The posture suggests threatened violence, not inhibition.

2. *Physiological Overresponse* (1). No trace of this trait. He is relatively unresponsive to pain, is never affected physiologically by what he sees or hears (never nauseated or horrified, never shocked, etc.). There is no jumpiness or sign of nervousness. He is almost unaware of most minor physical irritations. His basal metabolic rate is plus 5.

3. *Overly Fast Reactions* (2). His mental reactions are slow, and there is no sign of the "confusions of overreaction" which are characteristic of cerebrotonia. Boris is never flustered, never embarrassed. He never blushes or blanches. In physical competitions he never overreacts to the defeat of his own purposes. Yet his muscular responses, as in boxing and in football, are fast enough to render him an efficient athlete.

4. *Love of Privacy* (2). Almost an antithesis to this trait. He is generally found where people congregate, and is a great physical exhibitionist. He has no need or love for privacy, but neither has he any fear of it. Privacy is an irrelevant matter to him. He would tolerate it well in a situation which otherwise met his needs.

5. *Mental Overintensity, Hyperattentionality* (2). He is in most respects grossly unobservant and mentally unresponsive, in sharp contrast with cerebrotonic hyperattentionality. He responds with action, and with his muscles, and is never a victim of (cerebrotonic) overstimulation. He is unaware of most of the subtler stimuli of the social and physical world. Yet there is a certain watchfulness about him, and just the suggestion of an alert predacity. A psychiatrist might say that he has a slightly paranoid look.

6. *Secretive Restraint of Feeling* (1). An antithesis. There is no restraint of any sort, but instead, a direct and free expression of his attitude in any situation. There seems to be no inhibitory restraint in this youth.

7. *Self-conscious Motility of the Eyes and Face* (1). This is a stern, harsh countenance, with rather a glowering stare, a little like that of an Indian (like the mesomorphic Indians of the Eastern woodlands—not the more endomorphic Indians of the Southwest). The expression of Boris' face changes but little, except when he is angry.

8. *Sociophobia* (1). There is no sociophobia. He is highly independent of people, but he is in no sense shy or inclined to avoid people. People are almost irrelevant to him, except insofar as he needs to use them for some specific end. In a superficial way he is popular and well known.

9. *Inhibited Social Address* (1). He has excellent self-possession, and is never confused or at a loss as to what to do or say. His poise is unshakable. There is no sense of inferiority or of embarrassment in him.

10. *Resistance to Habit and Poor Routinizing* (1). Boris is a creature of routines and habit. He is no habit fighter. He has sleeping, eating and elimination reduced to automatic habit. He loves routine, although he has never applied it to any kind of mental effort. He has little curiosity and is not mentally exploratory. He does not readily acquire new habits, but his established muscular routines—his exercising—he follows religiously.

11. *Agoraphobia* (1). The antithesis. He loves the open, and has a strong distaste for closed-in places. He loves to be conspicuous. He is a great exhibitionist, loves to display his body, and often expresses impatience at the restraint of wearing clothes. He loves to parade around in the nude.

12. *Unpredictability of Attitude* (2). There is no general unpredictability. Boris is always much the same—always stormy, loud, violent. His reactions are in general highly predictable. Yet sometimes his attitude toward an individual seems suddenly to change, usually in the direction of a wrathful response.

13. *Vocal Restraint and Restraint of Noise* (1). The voice is supercharged with aggression. It carries far, and can be heard distinctly at an astonishing distance. When he plays baseball he "talks" encouragingly to the pitcher, and people in the stands all over the ball park hear what he says.

14. *Hypersensitivity to Pain* (1). Boris shows the Spartan antithesis to this trait. He has the deepest contempt for anyone who complains of pain, and he boasts that he himself has never been known to utter such complaint. So far as can be ascertained this is true. He once had a broken arm set without an anaesthetic, and it is reported by a witness of the event that he scarcely winced.

15. *Poor Sleep Habits* (1). He never has any trouble with sleep. His sleep requirement appears to be low. There has been no trace of insomnia, and he is never tired in the morning. As is the case with food, he takes his sleep without any psychological complication, and without any overfondness for it.

16. *Youthful Intentness of Appearance* (1). The antithesis. There is a premature "settling" of the face, and a marked overmaturity of appearance. In talking with Boris the impression grows that he is in some fundamental sense old, and that there is no youthful plasticity in his mind. The deep lines and creases in his face are ordinarily associated with middle age. The face makes almost no response at all to ideas. It completely lacks the alert birdlike quality seen in cerebrotonic faces.

17. *Vertical Mental Cleavage* (1). There is no indication of any subjective cleavage of mind at all. He presents a somatotonic antithesis to the schizoid tendency. He is consistently objective, candid, even brazen. There is no trace of dissociation from the overt, immediate reality.

18. *Resistance to Alcohol* (1). None. The reaction appears to be limited to an immediate accentuation of aggression and assertiveness. He never takes this drug in any considerable quantity, and has not been known to be drunk.

19. *Need of Solitude when Troubled* (1). The need is clearly for action, with no trace of a tendency to seek solitude (see trait S-19).

20. *Orientation toward the Later Periods* (1). The somatotonic antithesis. There is suppression of the thought of later life, and the orientation is almost wholly toward the period of strenuous action. Boris has no intellectual curiosity, and little interest in the future

Totals: Viscerotonia, 24; Somatotonia, 139; Cerebrotonia, 24.
Index of Temperament, 1-7-1.

PHYSICAL CONSTITUTION

Age 21, Ht. 72.5, Wt. 178, Somatotype 1-6²-2 (1-7-2, 1-7-2, 1-7-2, 1-6-2, 2-5-3). g 1.1, t 1.8, d 18.

This is a strongly mesomorphic physique of tall stature, with a conspicuous increment of ectomorphy and a decrement of mesomorphy in Region V. The legs appear too slender and brittle for the rest of the body. Region V introduces a considerable dysplasia into a physique which otherwise would show but little dysplasia. The endomorphic dysplasia is 4; mesomorphic dysplasia, 10; and ectomorphic dysplasia, 4. Total dysplasia, 18.

We are dealing with a fairly dysplastic mesomorphic physique of great strength and tall stature. Gynandromorphy is extremely low. The physique totally lacks the leaven or softening, and the smooth subcutaneous finish of a normal gynandromorphy. This youth is far out toward the extreme of masculinity. The textural index, t, is close to the mean for the general population. There is neither any particular refinement nor a conspicuous coarseness here.

The ectomorphic dysplasia and mesomorphic decrement which are so conspicuous in Region V begin to appear in Region IV. This young man has an extremely powerful, massive upper body. His head, neck, chest and arms, while showing some ectomorphic interference, still live up to the extreme mesomorphic development. But Region IV weakens a little in this respect, and Region V introduces a marked dysplasia. These 2-5-3 legs are relatively strong but they cannot stand up consistently to the terrific muscular power of the upper regions of this body.

For purposes of amusement and analogy we sometimes speak of Region I (head and neck) as the control room, Region II (thoracic trunk) as the engine room, Region III (arms) as the fighting equipment, Region IV (abdominal trunk) as the boiler room, and Region V (legs) as the foundational support and driving machinery. Using such an analogy, we see in this case an unusually powerful engine and fighting equipment directed by warlike and single-minded controls, but with a boiler slightly inadequate for such equipment, and with relatively fragile, brittle driving machinery beneath it.

Region *I* presents the typical 1-7-2 picture at its full strength. This is the head and neck of the masculine hero of all time. It can be seen a half-dozen times over in the serial comic strips of any daily newspaper. It is the head of Tarzan, Dick Tracy, Li'l Abner, Superman, Smilin' Jack, and of the Viking kings and Greek gods (except Hercules and Zeus, who are usually 1-7-1).

The face is deep, bony and muscular, with jaws so powerfully developed that facial breadth at the level of the gonial angles is just about equal to facial breadth at the level of the supraorbital ridges. The general outline of Boris' face is almost a rectangle, and the transverse breadth of the neck (which in the 1-7-2 markedly surpasses the anteroposterior depth) very nearly or actually equals the greatest facial breadth. The head, relatively a little small for the massive facial skeleton, is slightly dolichocephalic. The blue eyes are relatively small and of medium spacing. The nose is large, long and cleanly chiseled. The mouth is straight and wide, with firm, rather tight, muscular lips. The jaws are square and very slightly prognathous.

The skin over the entire body is distinctly mesomorphic, and has already become leathery over the face, with deep, long folds and with reddish-brown pigmentation. Bodily hair is of about medium luxuriance, with sharply masculine distribution. The thick, coarse-textured, light-brown hair is short and wavy—almost curly.

CLINICAL HISTORY

Boris was the first pregnancy. The father was 23, the mother 22 at that time. Normal, full-term pregnancy, but the birth was difficult. Birth weight 9 pounds. A very large baby. Normal weight gain during the first year. No breast feeding. The mother, a large-boned, heavy, mesomorphic Irish woman, is said to have had no milk. The baby was normal but extremely active and vigorous. He was an "exceptionally long" baby, but no measurements were taken. Talked at 13 months. Walked at 10 months. Toilet training completed fairly satisfactorily at 30 months, but some enuresis until the age of 6. Violent temper tantrums throughout babyhood. No fingernail biting. Autoeroticism observed frequently, as early as age 3.

During the first four years the youngster had measles, scarlet fever, chicken pox, German measles and bronchial pneumonia (severe). Eardrums were punctured twice for middle ear relief. There were severe colds which seemed to settle in the chest. Whooping cough at age 4. He has repeatedly suffered from acne and boils, although these attacks were severe only during the period immediately following adolescence and the acne has now almost disappeared. A large boil has occurred within the past six months. Tonsillectomy (routine) at age 7. Appendectomy at 20.

Adolescence began in the early part of the fourteenth year, took place rapidly, and the boy was apparently fully mature at 14. The testes are large, with fairly massive penis of moderate length and well-developed corona.

The palate is wide and fairly deep. Teeth are large and excellently developed, with especially strong canines. There has been very little decay. The deep reflexes are exaggerated (as they usually are in this somatotype), and the superficial reflexes (pupillary, abdominal, cremasteric) are weak, as is also usual in extreme mesomorphy.

In general summary, this is an excellent physical specimen of the strongly masculine pattern. There are no sensory or motor handicaps, no neurological or functional handicaps, and no obvious external or internal pathology. There is, however, a fifth region dysplasia which must prevent the youth from achieving the highest success at professional heavyweight athletic competition.

BACKGROUND

Paternal:

The father is an active, alert, rather opportunistic Irish businessman who never finished high school, married young, and has made and lost money several times at various ventures. He is now doing very well with a garage in the outskirts of Chicago. He is of medium stature, rather blocky, and probably a 3-5-2 in somato-type. He is somewhat alcoholic at times, and has been known to go off on brief sprees or vacation trips, but he has never been in any sense a drunkard. He is a Catholic who never goes to church.

The paternal grandfather died young and nothing is known of him. He came from Ireland. The grandmother came from Ireland as a girl, was a housemaid, married young, lost her husband through death, and raised a fine, sturdy family of four children by taking in washing and the like. She is still living and is a "strong, fine-looking woman of medium stature." She goes to church for the whole family. There is no tuberculosis among the known paternal relatives. Three paternal relatives have died of cancer. Two cases of diabetes. Several instances of high blood pressure. Much arthritis. No mental disease.

Maternal:

The mother is a muscular woman, rather tall, with thick, heavy wrists and ankles, and a highly mesomorphic appearance. She has a high *g* component (masculine component) and must weigh 175 pounds. She has been a good wife and mother, outwardly at least, and has raised two boys. A third was killed accidentally as a child. She now has a Negro housemaid who does most of the work. Her interests are principally the two boys (with whom she has no real rapport), the radio, poker, relatives, and the Chicago Cubs. She never misses a National League ball game, and within the limitations of a small purse, she loves to gamble. She is an intense Anglophobe.

The maternal grandfather was a successful Boston Irish saloon-keeper who "knew the great John L. Sullivan well." He died of apoplexy at 58. The maternal grandmother, also of Boston Irish stock, now has a small apartment and three poodle dogs. She raised nine children, nearly all of whom have flourishing families. No tuberculosis is known on this side of the family. One case of cancer. No diabetes. Several cases of painful or crippling arthritis and "rheumatism." At least seven maternal relatives have died comparatively young of apoplexy and high blood pressure. No mental disease.

Siblings:

1. Boris, now 21.
2. Brother, two years younger, died at 5, accident.
3. Brother, now 16, in high school. Resembles Boris in general appearance, although somewhat shorter and possibly even sturdier. His somatotype is probably between 2-6-2 and 1-7-1. He is extremely somatotonic and is already a star on the high school football team. His mother believes that he is the most promising of the entire clan of relatives, even more promising than Boris, of whom she is also proud.

GENERAL LIFE STORY

First 6 Years:

Boris was precocious in learning to walk. He is said to have been a singularly strong baby, and throughout his life he has been unusually proficient at all activities and skills involving bodily strength and muscular coordination. In learning to talk he was slightly, although probably not significantly, retarded. He rode a bicycle at age 4. At 6 he boxed four rounds with a 9-year-old boy at a public exhibition. At 15 he was a freshman star on the high school football team. From babyhood he has been extremely active.

During the early period of life his health was essentially good. Except for an episode of pneumonia at age 15 months there were no severe or prolonged illnesses. He was hospitalized for four weeks at the time of the pneumonia incident, but seemed to recover completely.

His early associations, before the school period, were chiefly with boys older than he. He was reared in a suburb of Chicago twenty miles or more distant from that in which the family now lives. It was a fairly tough neighborhood, but bordered upon relatively open country. Boris was permitted to run almost wild from the beginning. As a child of 4 or 5 he was especially fond of roaming through the countryside with a gang of eight or ten boys ranging from his own age to six or seven years older. The exploration of dumps, Indian fighting, kite flying, and petty thievery appear to have constituted the most popular objectives.

There were few associations with girls during this period, and there is very little memory of contact with the father. There appears to have been relatively little dependence upon the mother, who was busy with the rest of her brood. Skating and winter activities are more prominent in the present recall than are summer adventures. Boris was closely attached to his immediately younger brother, who was killed by an automobile when Boris was 7. This brother was very much like Boris, active and precocious at all athletic adventure. The two are said to have been trustworthy swimmers at ages 7 and 5 respectively.

Boris was rarely if ever punished by his father, although he recalls being whipped repeatedly by his mother. But he believes that there was never very serious resentment on his part. Whipping, he says, in a good honest Irish family, is to be taken for granted. He feels that he should have been whipped a good deal more than he was—should have had his "spirit broken," he says.

Sexuality was taken for granted from his earliest recollection. Autoeroticism was practiced intermittently since the earliest memory, but never with any particular emotionality or sense of sin. He remembers being reproved for it by his mother, but believes that she was not very serious in the reproof. There was a barn, much frequented by some of the older members of his circle, where numerous sexual adventures took place, mostly mutual excitation. But Boris never found this to be much fun. Even now he does not understand why people get so excited about a little sexuality. A sister of one of his companions, a girl possibly three or four years older than Boris, once became sexually aggressive with him in this barn and attempted to masturbate him. But he decided after a reasonable period of open-mindedness that he could do a better job than she could. There were no more heterosexual incidents until he was 14. At age 7 an older boy tried to practice fellatio on him, and he "beat up the guy." During the first six years there were many fights, with Boris usually the winner.

Age 6 to 14. School:

Boris went to public school at 6. He was of about average height, "very slender and wiry." He was already a good athlete, one of the best runners among boys near his age, and was known as a terrific fighter. During this year he boxed at a public exhibition, a feat which brought him undying fame among contemporaries.

He was never a favorite with teachers, for he was troublesome and was generally involved in whatever mischief was afoot. Once when a teacher reproved him for lying or something of the sort, he "nailed her one on the beezer" and gave her a bloody nose. This was at about age 9. The relating of this incident is accompanied by far more pleasure than regret on Boris' part. "The teacher was a bitch, anyway. She had the guts to go to my old woman about it, and she like to've got another bloody nose."

By the time Boris was 8 or 9 he was a well-established leader. It was he who got up the baseball teams and captained them. He melodramatically took up quarrels and fought them out, and when the gang went on a Saturday prowl it was he who determined the when, the where, and the why. The rest came along. His mother never interfered in anything, apparently, except to take his part on the few occasions when matters got out of his hands—such matters as the teacher episode. The father kept out of his affairs entirely.

The death of the brother occurred late in Boris' first school year. He remembers sniffling at the funeral, and starting a fight at the wake, over some alleged slur cast upon the deceased. But he played baseball the day after the funeral, and he remembers that he hit two home runs. "That was what Glenn would have wanted me to do," he philosophized. Boris was proud of his brother, and within the limitations of the affective side of his nature there is no doubt that he was fond of the younger boy, but we think it doubtful that this tragic accident really made much difference in Boris' life.

His marks in school were always low, about as low as possible without retardation. One of his former teachers describes her memory of him as "a vigorous, strapping youth of irrepressible energy and a stunted mind." But his mental tests indicated an innate ability in excess of his scholastic achievement. He graduated from the eighth grade with his class, and went directly into high school as he was approaching 15. By this time he was known as a good athlete and his coming had been heralded at the school ahead of him. He was now entering what has every earmark of being his glorious harvest time of life.

At about the age of 10, Boris had gathered the impression that autoeroticism and indeed all sexual activity and sexual thought reflect more or less unfavorably upon athletic achievement. He therefore became quite puritanical on this subject, and remained so until one late spring afternoon just before graduation from grade school. On this day the older sister of one of his chums, a girl in high school, insisted upon investigating as to whether he was yet "grown up." They both decided that he was. "It was all right," is his comment, "but she seemed to like it better than I did." He states that this girl hounded him thereafter for more and similar attentions, but that he was for the most part indifferent.

After this first experience with sexual intercourse, he looked forward with trepidation to an important ball game scheduled for some days later. He half expected to be unable to give a good account of himself, but was astonished to find that he had never felt better. From that day on, he says, he has been a cynic: "For this stuff about sex hurting you is bunk." That simple statement summarizes Boris' sexual philosophy.

After 14:

Boris went to a high school of some eighteen hundred boys and girls. He was tall, slender and strong. For four years he did badly in school subjects and magnificently in athletics. He played on the football team in his freshman year and received wide newspaper acclaim. By the time he was a senior, at 18, he was six feet tall and had assumed practically his present weight. He was a high school athletic star of the first magnitude, excelling in all of the organized sports, and he was undisputedly the best fighter in the school. He was already fighting as a light heavyweight in amateur boxing tournaments.

He never smoked, and does not now smoke. He has never been drunk, although he is fond of liquors, and he felt even as a high school athlete that a small quantity of whisky tended to "bring his best strength to the surface." This he still believes, and it may be true. Certain it is that a small quantity of alcohol tends temporarily at least to accentuate his somatotonic characteristics.

Boris believes that the high school years were the best years of his life, and that nothing approaching their glory can ever return to him. Now that he is getting old, he says, he realizes that many mistakes were made when he was young, and he would give much to be able to go back and live those years over again.

This youth reached his full stature in high school, and possibly his full physical strength. When did he, or when will he reach his full mental strength? Does he belong to a constitutional pattern which reaches its full mental strength very early, and then strikes a mental ceiling? This is a question of great interest, and perhaps of some educational importance.

Scholarship was almost fair in the freshman year of high school. He failed in no courses, although his grades were minimal passing grades. In the second year he failed two courses but by special tutoring and reexamination was permitted to make them up. In the third year he began to grow openly defiant of school authorities and struck a male teacher. For this he was placed on the ineligibility list and missed one football game, but was reinstated just before the next (important) game. Later he offered to fight the principal for some reason, and was again made ineligible for athletic competition. This time the students threatened to "strike," and he was once more reinstated. It was written into the school records that the school was going to experiment with "generous treatment toward a defiant but unusually gifted boy." That fall Boris helped his school win the district football championship. His publicity was widespread.

During the remainder of the school term he ignored scholastic matters almost entirely, and early in the spring he announced that he was about to leave school. He had been offered a good job by a garage syndicate. But arrangements were made for him to attend a special summer session, and to be paid at the same time for playground supervision. He thus entered his senior year of high school in good scholastic standing and with money in his pocket.

This year was relatively uneventful. The football season ended in a blaze of glory. By Christmas Boris had been offered scholarships of one kind or another at no less than thirty colleges. But he had no mental energy at all now for scholastic studies, and at the end of the school year four teachers refused to pass him. He gathered evidence that these teachers had joined together in collusion against him, threatened to have them all expelled, and persuaded a member of the city council to engage a lawyer to investigate the matter. Arrangements were made for him to take special summer courses, and again to be paid for playground work. He went to school five weeks that summer and his deficiencies were removed.

In September he entered a university of excellent standing, but from the beginning matters went badly. His tuition was paid up ahead by scholarship, and he was to be guaranteed "at least a $2500 job" upon graduation. But the cash he was to receive in the meantime had to be worked for, nominally at least, and the scholarship would automatically terminate if the academic authorities put him on probation, thus making him ineligible for athletics.

After arriving on the campus and considering matters from all angles, Boris decided that he had sold out too cheaply. He wished that he had taken one of the other offers, and wished so out loud. Now some universities are sensitive about their arrangements with football players. The matter is not totally unlike the arrangements of a lady with her clandestine lover. Such a relationship requires to be perfumed delicately with the fragrance of romance, or school spirit.

Boris had no school spirit, and matters went from bad to worse. He was notified at midterm that he was failing in every course. Immediately he went to the dean's office, explained the nature and details of his arrangement, and demanded that his instructors be put in their places. Then he learned something about universities. The dean called in the director of athletics and castigated him with convincing vigor in Boris' presence. The director of athletics promptly disclaimed all knowledge of Boris, and all interest in him. Some muddling alumnus had been at work again, no doubt, making wild promises to this young fool. Boris promptly sought the alumnus in question, demanding a showdown and cash. The alumnus bluntly told him to deliver the goods first on the football field, whereupon Boris in an outburst of temper pounded the young man into insensibility. The alumnus was hospitalized for three weeks and lost the sight of an eye. This matter was hushed up, but was later boasted of freely by Boris' mother.

At the end of the semester Boris was dropped from the university for low grades without having played football, even on the freshman team. He worked in a filling station that spring and loafed all summer. In the following September he appeared on the campus of a smaller college, having accepted a scholarship offer made a year previously. Here almost the same story was repeated, with variation only in details. Boris demanded money, made no pretense of even bluffing the academic side of the picture, and the college passed the blame along to a group of its alumni. But this time Boris was not to be so easily put off. He told his story to an Irish lawyer, who proceeded to try to blackmail the college. There was a promise of a scholarship in writing, signed by a college officer. In the end Boris got $750, a gift by an alumnus, given merely for good will. Of this amount the lawyer received $485. Boris again left college at midyear, but not until after he had broken a student's arm in a brawl over a girl.

While at this second college, Boris played several games of football for a semi-professional team. He played under an assumed name, but at this point it appears that his skill and strength had hardly lived up to the great promise of his high school years. He did not rise in the profession through this channel, and received no regular professional offers. He was now 20, and his height and weight were almost exactly the same as they had been at 17. That fact worried Boris. Could it be that he had reached his full strength and was growing old? Was there now nothing to look forward to but old age and the decline of his great powers? It was concerning this question that he went to a physician during the summer of his twenty-first year. The physician, after some unsuccessful experimentation with a weight-gaining diet, referred him to us for constitutional diagnosis.

We first saw Boris during August of the summer after he had quit college for the second time. He had already arranged a third college scholarship, this time at a university famous for football teams and for little else. He had had a good talk with the director of athletics and a special tutoring course had been arranged for the summer, at the expense of the college. A cash advance had been made, through an alumnus. Boris believed that at last he had found appreciation and honest dealing among the academics. Meanwhile he had made the acquaintance of a successful promoter of boxing, and had appeared in a series of build-up bouts. His circle of admirers among both sexes had been considerably expanded through this advance in his fortunes, but the problem of his lack of weight had thereby become only the more acute. He weighed but 175 pounds, not enough by 30 pounds to get into the big heavyweight money.

He was boxing as a light heavyweight. Could he put 30 pounds of muscle on his (already fully developed and fully muscled) 1-6²-2 frame? If he could, the world was his. If he could not, he was a second rater, and he would rather be a bum than a second rater. This question had begun to assume a somewhat ominous aspect. Boris was going to make an issue of the matter. If he was never to become the powerful giant which early indication had promised him, he had been cheated. He would accept no compromises. Either the gods must deliver what they had promised or Boris would, in some manner not yet decided upon, strike back at the gods with all his terrible somatotonia.

This boy never had any hobbies or intellectual interests, and he never read anything. From the beginning his satisfactions were always direct. No indirection and no substitution or sublimation ever had a part in his scheme of things. Religion to him was possibly what crossing the fingers is to an adolescent who is only slightly superstitious. There was never any emotional dependence upon people, or any viscerotonic agglutination and sharing. Eating had never been an occasion for the expression of feeling, although it was always enjoyable. What should be said about sexuality in such a personality?

Boris was sexually well endowed, in the sense that he had large genitalia, and poorly endowed in the sense that his body was relatively insensitive. Such men can prolong sexual intercourse almost indefinitely. To them the (cerebrotonic) phenomenon of the quick crisis is unknown. They can "satisfy" the most needful of women, insofar as primary genital stimulation is concerned, and they

themselves find relatively complete sexual satisfaction in the intercourse itself. Yet, just as the unfortunate cerebrotonic phenomenon of the quick crisis is unknown in such a personality, so
are such other cerebrotonic phenomena as sensitive appreciation,
insight, lability of mind and adaptation to the varying needs and
moods of even ordinary women.

During the period from age 14 to 21, Boris estimates that he
had sexual intercourse with possibly thirty or forty different
women who were not prostitutes. Whether that is an exaggeration or an underestimate, this boy's sexual life had doubtless been
sufficiently extensive and variegated to protect him from the onus
of being sexually repressed.

By the time he was 18 he had come to know just what he
wanted sexually. He wanted rather large, well-matured, athletic
young women, preferably brunettes and preferably virgins. He
feels that a woman should be "a lot better" than a man, and that
any unmarried woman who is not virginal is a "bitch." Women
are principally what is the matter with society. "Women are
mostly bitches and they let men down."

Sexual intercourse, for Boris, is a realistic, matter-of-fact business. He cannot remember ever having an erection at the *thought*
of a girl, or as a result of reading, or from looking at pictures, or
from being stimulated by meeting a woman. Erection is for the
most part the result of physical intimacy and contact. Intercourse
itself is an exercise requiring from ten minutes to half an hour,
"depending on how much cooperation I get."

Since the age of 16 he has had no spontaneous nocturnal emis-
sions but when no women are available he will masturbate about
once a week, almost always when awakened at night by an erection. He is not aware that dreaming ever has anything to do with
these nocturnal erections.

This boy is relatively in demand sexually. At the moment he
knows many women who are sexually available to him. Of these,
more than one have sought him repeatedly and have given him
presents, in some instances money. He was introduced to his
present fight promoter by a woman who is sexually intimate with
both of them. Boris states that he had a standing offer from her
to support him in return for sexual faithfulness, the latter con-

cept to be defined in terms of two nights of his company per week. That is something like a realistic definition of faithfulness, and Boris approves of realistic definitions.

During the coming fall this youth will enter college for the third time. He blames himself for no part of either of the two previous academic failures, and proposes to bring to the third attempt just about the same point of view. College is essentially a business institution hiring him to play football and other games, undertaking in return to pay his living expenses and to give him certain advantages of a professional or business nature. Specifically he plans to be a college football coach, although he also has a plan for getting into the movies. A woman who is enthusiastic about him knows a man who is said to have connections with one of the successful movie magnates. Beyond these somewhat incomplete plans Boris has no systematic conception of a vocational future.

THE PROBLEM OF TREATMENT

So sharply outlined a case of simple somatorosis as Boris presents is rare. The problem of treatment would be a puzzling one. This is no "compensational" somatorosis arising from a somatotonic effort to overcome a handicap. Such a problem can often be met therapeutically. But Boris seems to be somatorotic by natural right—by divine right. There is neither viscerotonia nor cerebrotonia to build on. To change Boris would be a most radical undertaking. To discipline him constructively would require a disciplined society.

Undisciplined somatotonia is the war-making characteristic. When in some manner a somatorotic impulse becomes dominant, whole nations of people lose both compassion and restraint. They are then ready to make aggressive war and to kill. Probably such a phenomenon can occur only in soil already well prepared, through the predominance for some time past of essentially somatotonic temperaments among the group, and such a probability leads straight back to the question of how to deal in the first place with rampant somatotonia.

The real dilemma lies in the fact that *somatotonia responds only to somatotonia*. The second component is positive and dynamic. The third is in one sense negative, inhibitory, substitutional, *but cerebrotonia is inhibitory only to the individual who is himself cerebrotonic.* A strong component of restraint in A has no inhibitory effect upon B unless B himself has internal strength in the third component. But a strong component of aggression in A does necessarily affect the welfare of B, whatever the latter's components may be. Somatotonia is more or less a matter of public responsibility and liability. Cerebrotonia and viscerotonia, the nonaggressive components, are matters of relatively private concern. No question has been more hotly debated than that of how to treat the (somatotonic) child whose aggression may perchance have led to some inconvenience on the part of controlling adults. Proponents of the school of discipline say, "Spare the rod and spoil the child." But proponents of the school of appeasement say, "Punish a child and reap the harvest of hate." Doubtless both sides are right. In such disputes both sides are usually right.

Somatotonia frustrated, and incompletely frustrated, becomes aggressive hate, the most destructive element in human life. Somatotonia encouraged, guided, and conditioned to constructive enterprise, becomes, theoretically, advancement and ambition. The human ideal is that of guiding and harvesting the energy represented by the second component, rather than suppressing it on the one hand, or permitting it to destroy civilization on the other. Somatotonia is the servant and the strength of the human race, or it is a Frankenstein monster.

But how is somatotonia to be guided and harvested if it knows no language but that of its own expression, and can therefore respond only to somatotonia? The old aphorism that force can be met only with force appears here to hold good.

When dealing with somatotonia the choice seems to lie essentially between a vigorous disciplining or redirecting of it (presumably into more civilized channels), and standing in readiness to yield altogether to its ever-increasing demands. We hold no doubt that in a disciplined society, Boris could have developed into a healthful, useful citizen. We suppose that his crying need was for constant, levelheaded discipline and restraint. Since with his constitutional endowment no discipline or restraint can ever be expected to come from within, it seems logical to suppose that his restraint must then needs come from without.

From the beginning, this boy needed a moral protection and support, as constant and absolute in its application as the physical support needed by one born with a crippled muscular system. When this boy was a very young child, it should have been realized that the elements of compassion and restraint in him were too weak ever to bear any weight on their own account. He should have been educated accordingly. But his own parents, as they were and are, could never have accomplished it.

The lesson here is that psychiatry must be not only individual but social, before it can efficiently be either. That is to say, there can never be adequate treatment of individual problems of adjustment until also there is adequate control of institutions. The idea of the family, for example, doubtless would have to undergo profound modification before a personality like Boris could be educated to constructive citizenship. We have no illusions that by any superficial psychological tricks the biological parents of Boris, constituted as they are, could have reared him very differently from the way they did. He needed an environment, the immediate directors of which understood somatotonia, and also understood cerebrotonia and viscerotonia. This may be only a psychological way of praising the fear of God. For what is God, after all, if not a personification of the extreme manifestation of *all three* basic components? God in three persons—the somatotonic Father, the viscerotonic Son, and the cerebrotonic Holy Ghost.

In summary, we feel that since Boris is a product of both his hereditary constitution and his environment, we need to understand and to learn to diagnose both far better than we now understand either before the problem of therapy is worth very serious consideration. In the meantime we favor a rather close restraint both of somatotonic children and of their parents, lest what civilization now remains should slip away from us.

3. CHRISTOPHER: *Extreme Cerebrotonia*

SUMMARY

Christopher is a fragile, timorous youth of medium stature. Although he is 24, he looks 18. His ordinary social address is hesitant and apologetic, and his voice is so restrained that it is scarcely audible. His anxious, triangular face seems disproportionately small for his high, "intellectual" forehead. The head is not large, but measures just about the general average in length and breadth. In height, the head is above the average. The features are finely chiseled and delicate, the chin is weak, and the small, sensitive mouth looks like a girl's mouth. But the dark eyes are bright and active and they never seem to rest. The teeth are white and strong.

Christopher, like Boris, is Irish, although both parents are several generations removed from immigration. The parents live in their own cottage in a small South Dakota hamlet, where the father has taught school for twenty-two years. The mother taught school before her marriage and now runs the local library. Both parents are quiet, intelligent, rather shy people, fond of reading and of natural history.

Christopher has always been excessively shy. He had a lonely childhood and youth, never took part in any of the usual group activities of children, has had no friends, and has generally been regarded as a "weak sister." His IQ, however, is said to be about 135. He finished grade school at 13, high school at 17, and college at 21, all without distinction or adventure. In high school he was in the fifth tenth (from the top) of his graduating class. In college he was in the fourth tenth. Following graduation from college, after a year of futile effort to get a job, he went to a State University for graduate work. In another year now, he hopes to have a Ph.D. degree, but still feels an acute sense of insecurity.

TEMPERAMENTAL PATTERN

Viscerotonia:

1. *Relaxation* (1). The picture is almost always one of strained tenseness. There is no relaxation. The posture suggests cringing, as if he were expecting violence. The face is tense, and the hands

are typically clenched, with the fingernails pressing the palms. The head is bent sharply forward, and respiration is so suppressed that it is difficult to be certain whether or not any excursive movement of the chest is taking place. The entire body presents an antithesis to relaxation.

2. *Love of Physical Comfort* (1). He generally maintains about the most uncomfortable position possible, and he will protest or even struggle against being made more comfortable. He seems to feel that in some deep sense he doesn't deserve to be comfortable, has not earned the right, and so refuses any comforting of the flesh. There is no religious rationalization of the attitude, however. He does not strive positively to mortify the flesh.

3. *Slow Reaction* (1). Fast reactions, both mental and physical. His verbal reactions are excessively fast. Eye movements are lightning fast. There is none of the slow, relaxed deliberateness of viscerotonia. The superficial reflexes are very fast and exaggerated, although the deep (tendon) reflexes are difficult to elicit.

4. *Love of Eating* (1). He eats rapidly, as if the process were distasteful or shameful in some way, and as if he would like to get it over with as painlessly as possible. He does not look forward with pleasure to eating. "It is like elimination," he says, "something that must be done, and the more efficiently and privately the better."

5. *Socialization of Eating* (1). A clear antithesis to this trait. He much prefers to eat alone, and is indeed emotionally distressed when it is necessary for him to eat socially. He never talks much at meals, and will not linger at the table a moment longer than necessary. He has no sentiment about bread-breaking.

6. *Pleasure in Digestion* (1). He is still, at 24, somewhat disturbed and unhappy about the whole digestive process. Even the "rolling of the stomach" causes him distress or embarrassment. Elimination occurs about three times a week, usually put off as long as possible. That is to say, what in another person would be called constipation is his normal pattern. There are many foods he cannot, or thinks he cannot, digest. In general, digestion is a poor business with Christopher.

7. *Love of Polite Ceremony* (1). He has a general dislike or fear of all ceremony, and a tendency to fail to observe the usual amenities of outward form. He has little sense of propriety, and no "feeling" as to how to go about social matters in the polite or approved manner. He generally says the wrong thing. He cannot attend funerals, weddings, or even routine academic exercises without severe internal discomfort and a strong sense of agoraphobia.

8. *Sociophilia* (2). There is a marked shyness and sociophobia in the general sense, which cuts him off from any easy social contact. He has no appetite for the company of more than one or two persons in any event. Yet there is a certain craving for companionship, and a wistfulness to have a friend or two. Solitude is his customary pattern of life, but he shows a shy gratitude for an act of friendliness.

9. *Indiscriminate Amiability* (2). There is little or no externally manifest social warmth. He has none of the common essence of good fellowship in the social sense. But there is an apologetic gratitude and a little warmth shining through, in return for the compassion and patience which are necessary before anyone can establish rapport with him. He has no capacity for demonstrativeness.

10. *Greed for Affection and Approval* (2). There is very little overt dependence on social approval, perhaps because, in part at least, there has been so little of it. He has not established any habit of expecting, or leaning on, the approval of others. He tolerates his loneliness and isolation very well. But that faint suggestion of wistfulness is always present, and if approval were forthcoming he probably would accept it gratefully—might come to depend on it.

11. *Orientation to People* (2). He has an extremely narrow acquaintanceship, and little real knowledge of people. He never has any idea of where to go for what he wants, or "where his bread is buttered." Yet he has some good insight into the few people whom he does know.

12. *Evenness of Emotional Flow* (1). There is very little outward expression of emotion. The impression is strong that emotional life is poorly sustained. Certainly it is poorly sustained so far as overt manifestations go. The mood of emotional depression is a frequent one with him.

13. *Tolerance* (1). There is a sharp defensive quality to all his attitudes, which amounts to conspicuous absence of tolerance (rather than positive intolerance). He has never developed the trait of tolerance, and he shows no basic contentment or satisfaction, either with himself or with his world. Yet he is not positively antagonistic —he is only negative.

14. *Complacency* (1). A complete antithesis to complacency. He is psychologically "on pins and needles." He does not accept his own role in life, and struggles almost constantly to "see some light in the darkness," as he puts it. But his struggles are feeble.

15. *Deep Sleep* (1). Sleep habits are very poor. He has great difficulty in going to sleep at night, although it is usually easy enough to do so in the daytime. He can sleep in only one position (curled up on his left side), and only on a hard mattress. He usually lies awake for a long time, sometimes all night, and seems to get soundly to sleep only in the morning, when it is about time to get up. He does not relax completely, even in sleep, wakens very easily, and has never been known to snore. Respiration is shallow and completely silent, even in his deepest sleep.

16. *The Untempered Characteristic* (1). A sharp antithesis. He is very intent, although in a fragile, brittle way. There is no soft malleability about him. He is like *over*tempered metal, likely to shatter.

17. *Smooth, Easy Communication of Feeling* (1). Communication of feeling is extremely difficult. He cannot let himself go emotionally under any circumstances. The little feeling that does get expressed comes through jerkily, as if in small driblets. The flood gates are never opened. They remain permanently locked.

18. *Relaxation and Sociophilia under Alcohol* (1). He has a strong dislike for alcohol. It makes him dizzy, fatigued and depressed. There is no trace of the viscerotonic reaction. He becomes less relaxed and less sociable after taking this drug.

19. *Need of People when Troubled* (2). The primary dependence is upon solitude, and upon protection from people when in trouble. He never seeks people when disturbed or perplexed. Yet when sought out by another person and encouraged or coaxed, he will melt and will talk it out a little. When left entirely to his own inclinations and resources, there is almost no trace of the viscerotonic reaction here.

20. *Orientation toward Childhood and the Family* (1). Childhood was an unhappy experience for Christopher, and he regards it as in general a nasty, unhappy time of life. Almost the entire complex of childhood memory is looked upon with aversion. But there is no specific aversion toward either parent. Christopher thinks his parents did the best they could have done. His aversion is toward the whole idea of being a child. There was nothing good in it. He wants to marry but not to have children.

Somatotonia:

1. *Assertiveness of Posture and Movement* (1). The extreme cerebrotonic antithesis. His postural behavior suggests a timid animal trying to keep out of sight. He appears to shrink in upon himself, and there is also a tendency to curl up. The shoulders are rounded, the head is bent forward, and when he sits, the thighs tend to be flexed as far as possible, bringing the knees upward. When he walks he treads with delicacy as if endeavoring not to attract attention, and the arms are kept closely restrained at his side. They do not swing vigorously, as arms do in somatotonia.

2. *Love of Physical Adventure* (1). His primary desire in this respect is to escape from physical adventure or activity, insofar as possible. He despises physical expressiveness of any sort, considers it bestial. He has developed a philosophy that the objective of human life is to remove oneself as far as may be from "the mere physical." This particular cerebrotonic rationalization is not a very new one.

3. *The Energetic Characteristic* (1). His energy is low. He suffers almost continually from chronic fatigue, and has but little strength. He loves to sit almost catatonically and daydream by the hour. Yet this youth is not lazy. He is always willing to undertake his share of a task. He does not shirk. The spirit is willing, but energy is low. He can move around, in his light, ineffectual way, with considerable alacrity.

4. *Need of Exercise* (1). He has an active abhorrence of violent or vigorous muscular activity. "Only horsy people" do that sort of thing. Christopher takes no exercise except walking, and he never does that for its own sake. He has never shown interest in any form of athletics, either as participator or spectator. He would as soon "watch a lot of girls practice their sewing, as watch men exercise their muscles," he says.

5. *Love of Dominating* (1). No desire is shown to dominate over anything. He does not even enjoy dominating over the dog, that last resort of weak people who are frustrated in their somatotonic expression. Christopher is apparently devoid of this almost universal human characteristic.

6. *Love of Risk* (1). Extreme antithesis. He never would do the stunts or run the risks that other boys ran. He never climbed a tree, or jumped off a henhouse, or walked across a railway trestle, or rang a doorbell at Halloween. He finds all gambling distasteful. There is no allure for him in taking chances.

7. *Bold Directness of Manner* (1). All of his behavior is marked by a painful timorousness. His social address is rather more concerned with apology for his intrusion than with the subject under consideration.

8. *Courage for Combat* (1). None at all. He has never in his life reacted combatively to any physical situation. He has never had a fight, so far as is known. He is in every physical sense "cowardly."

9. *Competitive Aggressiveness* (1). Abnormal lack of aggressiveness, in the social sense. He has never been able to speak up in classroom, even when he knows the answer, and this is as true now that he is a graduate student in the University, as it was when he was a boy in grade school. He has no forcefulness at all, and there is not even a trace of compensatory bluff. It is this absence of compensatory bluff (*complete* absence of aggression) that saves him, for he is therefore not disliked or misunderstood.

10. *Psychological Callousness* (1). He is conspicuously sensitive and deferent to even the smallest manifestations of wish or preference on the part of persons within range of his observation. He embarrasses people with his deference and his oversensitiveness, often rendering them, like himself, ill at ease.

11. *Claustrophobia* (1). The antithesis. He has a strong agoraphobia, and is uncomfortable out in the middle of a room. He wants to be in corners, out of sight. He likes clothes which completely cover him up. He would not undertake the experiment of sleeping nude ("just couldn't do it"). He loves to keep his topcoat on, and his hands in its pockets.

12. *Freedom from Squeamishness* (1). He is extremely squeamish. Never steps on an ant or kills a fly, and he abhors the sight of blood. He cannot tolerate being obligated to anybody. A debt would keep him awake all night. He hates to use things up or to get rid of remainders. He is, of course, called stingy.

13. *Unrestrained Voice* (1). The antithesis. There is constant, painful over-restraint of the voice, a trait which is very irritating to somatotonic people. They appear to take it as a personal affront or as a reproach. Several of Christopher's acquaintances are forever admonishing him to "speak up."

14. *Spartan Indifference to Pain* (1). He has extreme sensitivity to pain, presenting an antithesis to Spartanism. He can endure water only of approximately bodily temperature, cold water causing pain and stopping his respiration. To seize him roughly by the arm will cause tears to appear in his eyes, and he will gasp in agony.

15. *General Noisiness* (1). He is so quiet that it is difficult to know when he is around. It is necessary to listen carefully to catch what he says. His laugh and cough are almost completely restrained, as if someone were sleeping near by. He walks virtually on tiptoe. He never whistles or makes any other purely aggressive noise. He shuts doors as if they were cabinet panels.

16. *Overmaturity of Appearance* (1). A good antithesis. He looks much younger than he is. His face and the general outline of his physique suggest a preadolescent fluidity. There is no 'set' to the features. They seem intently alive, motile and immature.

17. *Horizontal Mental Cleavage* (1). There is no free road to action. Christopher presents a sharp antithesis to extraversion of action. He possesses a good deal of insight into his own weaknesses and shortcomings, and he is in close touch with a rich phantasy and dream life. This is a highly subjective, intuitive mind, unusually lacking in horizontal cleavage.

18. *Assertiveness and Aggression under Alcohol* (1). No trace of somatotonic reinforcement after taking this drug. He merely becomes sick and fatigued.

19. *Need of Action when Troubled* (1). He seeks solitude, not action. When trouble or perplexity occurs, he "closes up like a clam and seeks a hole to crawl into." He rarely tells anyone of his disappointments or of his good news, and he never takes action to "celebrate" or to "drown out and forget."

20. *Orientation toward Goals and Activities of Youth* (2). His primary mental focus is clearly toward the later decades, where he expects to find all the fulfillment that there is to be for him. He eschews virtually all of the interests and common practices of youth, except sexuality, which he finds of great interest. Were it not for sexuality, Christopher would already be an old man in mental outlook.

Cerebrotonia:

1. *Physical Restraint, Tightness* (7). He gives the impression of a tense, hunted creature, who scarcely dares to take a full breath. Respiration is shallow and suppressed. All of the expressive or aggressive movements are held in the closest check, especially movements of the hands and arms (as in walking). The hands are kept out of sight as much as possible, as if he were suppressing every trace of aggression. (He practices naturally what is one of the first things an intern in pediatrics must learn: to keep his hands out of sight for a time upon first being introduced to an infant.) The pulse is fast and weak. Low blood pressure (95/65).

2. *Physiological Overresponse* (7) This characteristic is painfully pronounced, especially in the digestive tract. Christopher suffers a good deal from digestive upset in any emotional situation. Diarrhea sometimes occurs under such circumstances. Ordinary academic tests or recitations will at times produce this reaction. Clamping of the anal sphincter is frequently painful. He is sometimes unable to urinate when he "wants" to. He has extreme itching and a violent reaction to insect bites. There is great difficulty with the voice and with clearing of the throat. He has been singularly free from contagious diseases, except for acute head colds. The basal metabolic rate is plus 12.

3. *Overly Fast Reaction* (7). All reactions appear to be fast. He usually manifests a disturbing jumpiness, like that of an adolescent schoolgirl. Verbal reactions and speech are very rapid. Eye movements seem almost lightning fast. Social reactions are so fast that he often becomes confused and flustered. He blushes or turns pale easily. A slight change in the social situation is immediately reflected in his voice and in his whole manner. His sexual reactions are excessively fast, he reports, erection occurring almost simultaneously with a fleeting glimpse, or even a thought.

4. *Love of Privacy* (6). There is a primary need of privacy and solitude. Christopher needs to be alone most of the time, in order to "charge his battery," as he puts it, for the social activities which he cannot escape. Yet this lad intensely enjoys the few friendships that he has been able to make.

5. *Mental Overintensity, Hyperattentionality* (7). He overreacts mentally to everything. He misses nothing that happens in the environment. His attention seems to flit from point to point almost with the rapidity of light. He seems indeed to be naked to his environment, and oversensitized. He is easily confused, embarrassed and flustered by the presence of other people, showing plainly an inability to assimilate so much stimulation at once. He has a profound sense of insecurity, and apprehensiveness of his future. He believes he has bad luck.

6. *Secretiveness and Restraint of Feeling* (7). There is a tight-lipped inhibition of any socially manifest expression of feeling. If he suffers or feels elation, he does so in silence. Christopher "hates people who wear their hearts on their coat sleeves," and he for one will have none of it. To casual observation he seems almost devoid of feeling, but as Kretschmer says of the schizoid temperament, behind the closed blinds there may be festivities within.

7. *Self-conscious Motility of the Eyes and Face* (7). These are unusually active, quick-moving eyes. They are restless and searching, as if their owner were excessively apprehensive, and the face is rarely relaxed. The facial expression changes rapidly, registering many different variations of emotional tone within a brief span, but the changes can be followed only when the closest observation is employed.

8. *Sociophobia* (6). This trait is marked in most situations. He has a strong dislike of crowds or assemblages of any sort, and he becomes painfully tense in any social situation. He is highly secretive. Under ordinary circumstances he will cross the street or make other effort to avoid meeting people, because of the internal strain involved in social greeting. Yet he shows a wistful

craving for friendship, and after a friendship has become firmly established he is jealous of it.

9. *Inhibited Social Address* (7). He shows a painful lack of self-possession. The internal strain in Christopher is so great that it is something of a strain (by empathy) to carry on an interview or even a casual conversation with him. There is in him no trace of the usual intermittent compensatory aggression. His somatotonia is excessively low.

10. *Resistance to Habit and Poor Routinizing* (7). He has difficulty in forming any routine habits at all. He long since gave up all pretense of trying to establish bowel habits or sleep habits. Could never establish study habits, or habits of getting up in the morning. He has never done anything methodically. He could never learn by rote. What success he has had in school has been due to quick insight or momentary brilliance.

11. *Agoraphobia* (7). Extreme. See trait S-12. He has a deep fear and dislike of being conspicuous in any sense.

12. *Unpredictability of Attitude* (6). This trait is marked, although perhaps less manifestly so than in a person of greater energy and hence of more overt demonstrativeness. Christopher can change the whole tenor of his mood and attitude in the midst of a sentence, in response to some subconsciously apprehended sign. He experiences quick sympathies and quick antipathies, before the average person would feel any affective reaction at all. His opinions on people or ideas are most difficult to predict. He is often called "a mystery."

13. *Vocal Restraint, and Restraint of Noise* (7). His voice is so closely restrained that when Christopher speaks, a person a few feet beyond the one addressed would experience difficulty in hearing what is said. His laugh is nearly a silent one, although he at times shows an alert sense of humor and may fairly shake with mirth.

14. *Hypersensitivity to Pain* (7). There is extreme sensitivity to pain. See trait S-5. Twice he has fainted in the dentist's chair while having a tooth drilled for a simple filling. Once in college he became so nauseated from a rough handshake that he vomited.

15. *Poor Sleep Habits* (7). Sleep habits are very poor. See trait

V-15. He seems always in need of sleep, but he will never go to bed in ordinary season. That is the one time, he says, when he *cannot* sleep.

16. *Youthful Intentness of Appearance* (7). The whole physical personality suggests the intentness of a chaffinch or chickadee, or of a sandpiper on a beach. At a little distance, the face resembles that of an eager but somewhat baffled and overintent child.

17. *Vertical Mental Cleavage* (7). This is a highly subjective mind, closely in touch with its own remoter levels but largely dissociated from objective considerations. Christopher knows his own dream life and phantasy intimately, but he tends not to be adaptively responsive to the objective situation and to people. He ordinarily has a poor idea of how he stands toward others, or how they evaluate him.

18. *Resistance to Alcohol* (7). There is strong physiological and psychological resistance to this drug. Alcohol makes him dizzy, fatigued, unhappy, and more tightened up inside than ever. As the effect wears off he is left very tired, and with a sense of eye strain.

19. *Need of Solitude when Troubled* (6). Solitude is clearly the primary need whenever perplexity or bad news disturbs Christopher. He tends to work it out alone, or to "suffer in silence," and he rarely takes anyone into his confidence. Yet that wistful desire of his for comradeship becomes poignant under such circumstances, and with encouragement, that is, with someone else taking all the initiative, he would like to show his feelings—has done so on a few occasions.

20. *Orientation toward the Later Periods* (6). There is a conscious yearning to be older, and to be free from the strife and competition of the youthful period. He has a dislike of childhood and of all that it implies. He believes that "understanding and insight" are the highest human goals, if not the only valid ones. He looks forward to reaching an older period, feeling that in some way the answer to life's riddles lies in greater maturity of mind. But he is perplexed about sexuality, of which he carries an endowment seemingly disproportionate to his physical frailty and mental shyness. He wants sexual fulfillment, although he has little conception of how to achieve it.

Totals: Viscerotonia, 25; Somatotonia, 21; Cerebrotonia, 135.
Index of Temperament, 1-1-7.

PHYSICAL CONSTITUTION

Age 24, Ht. 68.5, Wt. 114, Somatotype 1^2-1^2-6 (1-2-6, 2-2-6, 1-1-7, 2-1-6, 2-1-6). g 2.3, t 3.0, d 16.

This is a strongly ectomorphic physique of medium stature, with a slight increment of mesomorphy in the first two regions of the body (Region *I* and Region *II*), and a distinct decrement of that component in the lower regions. Endomorphy holds the secondary dominance, although it is a very slight secondary dominance. The face (Region *I*) looks more lean and fine-drawn, and a little more mesomorphic, than does the body as a whole. This is an extremely weak, fragile physique, with a slightly stronger secondary tendency toward softness and relaxation than toward strength and energy. The weakest part of the physique is in the arms (Region *III*). There is virtually no fighting equipment at all.

The total dysplasia is 16, which is only slightly above the general average. Dysplasia is distributed almost equally among the three components (endomorphy, 6; mesomorphy, 6; ectomorphy, 4). Gynandromorphy is about average for the somatotype. The textural index, *t,* is more than a standard deviation above the normal. The textural and aesthetic fineness of this physique, while not extreme, is well above the ordinary.

This is a physique which can neither fight nor run, since the arms and legs show almost a maximum of ectomorphy with the human minimum of mesomorphy. The engine room (Region *II*) is a weak, delicate structure, although we have found the 2-2-6 somatotype to be one of the healthiest and longest-lived of the physical patterns. The boiler room (Region *IV*) is still weaker and more delicate. Region *I* (the control room) is the only region of the body showing a secondary mesomorphic predominance. The head is mesocephalic, with a very fragile facial skeleton. The face looks sharply triangular in the frontal view, with a somewhat weak chin in profile. The brown eyes are of medium size and are rather widely spaced. The delicate, thin-lipped mouth is shaped almost exquisitely, like that of a pretty girl. The slender, rather short nose has but little bridge, is finely chiseled, and shows a (dysplastically) wide flaring of the extremely thin nostrils. The skin texture throughout the body is fine, and the skin is strikingly white. The head hair is luxuriant, light brown, fine in texture, and has a long wave. Secondary hair is sparse, showing essentially feminine distribution. The eyelashes are long and silky.

Thus the skin, hair, eyelashes, and the general subcutaneous finish of the whole physique suggest gynandromorphy. But Region *IV* does not show the feminine outline typically seen in a case of high gynandromorphy. The abdominal trunk is long, poorly supported and slightly lordotic. The waist is rather low, and the hips are narrow. In this physique, what we have sometimes called the *secondary* signs of gynandromorphy are prominent, but *primary* gynandromorphy (the general female shape) is absent.

The legs are long, poorly muscled and loose jointed. The arches are high. This youth walks with a springy, up and down movement, making very little use of his heels but walking chiefly on his toes.

CLINICAL HISTORY

Christopher is the second of two children, the other being a brother five years older who in many respects resembles Christopher, both as to physique and as to behavior. The pregnancy was full term and the birth comparatively easy. (The first birth had been difficult for the fragile, ectomorphic mother.) Birth weight, about 6 pounds. Breast fed for 10 months, as the mother (like most ectomorphic women) had an excellent milk supply. Weight gain was rather slow, however, and there was much concern about Christopher's puny appearance and his inability to catch up to "normal." Yet he had a good appetite and was exceptionally free from illness of any kind. At the end of the first year he was "far underweight," but he had talked at 9 months, and was a bright, very watchful baby. Christopher was an "angelic child." He rarely cried, never had a temper tantrum, never got into mischief, and caused no trouble of any sort. He never even fell ill. He walked at 12 months and toilet training was completed at 28 months. Autoeroticism was observed frequently, even in babyhood, but the mother had been educated up to the idea that this might be considered normal. However, there seemed to be an unusual amount of such activity.

Christopher escaped all of the so-called childhood diseases, except one instance of severe earache and middle ear infection. On this occasion, at the age of 3, he was seriously ill, was hospitalized for one week, and is said to have run a temperature of 107. But recovery was complete and he has not been sick since, except for acute head colds, which occur two or three times a year, are severe for about three days, and clear up completely thereafter. There have never been any complications accompanying these head colds. Christopher has never had a protracted cough. His appetite has always been excellent, but there are many foods he will not eat. He has a strong preference for proteins.

Teeth erupted rather late, but they are excellent, hard teeth and well spaced except for some slight crowding in the lower jaw. At age 24, he has had but three fillings and no extractions. The palate is high and rather narrow, but this is a normal ectomorphic characteristic. The deep reflexes (especially the patellar) require reinforcement to be elicited, but this also is normal where cerebrotonia predominates strongly. (The strong knee jerk is a somatotonic characteristic.) The superficial reflexes are extremely active (they are nearly always so when cerebrotonia is predominant). He suffers from painful constipation at times.

Adolescence began during the fifteenth year, and was rather an acute event. Christopher's discovery of the phenomenon of ejaculation, in his sixteenth year, rather swept him off his feet for a time. There had been no "homosexual period" in his life, or at least no period of overt manifestation of this sort, and there had been no physical contact of any kind with either boys or girls. His sexual pressures and their demands for release were suddenly imperative. Masturbation, his only outlet, became the main business of life, and he developed the technique to a considerable degree of refinement. Christopher has highly developed genitalia, as is frequently the case with his somatotype.

In general summary, this is a fragile, sensitive, ectomorphic young man, with a weak, effeminate manner, with a history of excellent health and almost "perfect" general behavior, and with a heavy endowment of sexuality.

BACKGROUND
Paternal:

The father is a quiet, rather kindly and shy teacher of history and civics in the local high school. Like Christopher he is a pronounced ectomorph who has never been a source of trouble to anybody and has, within his somewhat anemic limits, enjoyed excellent health. He married at 32 and is now 62. He is about Christopher's height and weighs 128 pounds. He appears to have the same extreme weakness and fragility of the arms that is seen in Christopher. From a little distance he looks like a youth of 20, but upon close inspection he looks as if he might be 50. The hair is just beginning to turn a little gray. There is no baldness. He walks with the same egg-treading up and down movement that Christopher employs. There is an eagerness or ingenuousness about his social manner, and an alertness in his face which suggest perpetual youth. He feels that only within the past ten or twenty years has he begun really to enjoy life, and he wishes he "could have been born at 30."

Always extremely thrifty, Christopher's father has saved enough money to own a respectable little cottage and lot, has sent both his boys through college and graduate school, and has ten thousand dollars besides. He worships his wife. They seem to be just beginning to get acquainted with each other, and they give the impression of being newlyweds. They have never owned an automobile, but all four of the family have bicycles. The father is quite a local authority on natural history, and this is the central interest of the family.

The paternal grandfather was a Civil War veteran who settled in Ohio on a small farm, and married late in life. He was tall and slender, although probably of a stronger build than the present generation. He died at 97, killed by an automobile. The grandmother died at childbirth and little is known of her. She was the only one of the four grandparents not of Irish extraction. Her racial roots were "Ohio."

There is no tuberculosis among the paternal relatives, so far as is known, and no cancer. No diabetes and no kidney disease or high blood pressure. No arthritis. No mental disease. Unfortunately, but few of these relatives are known. It appears to be a singularly healthy stock.

Maternal:

The mother is very much like the father, although ten years younger. She is probably an intellectually more brilliant and capable person than her achievement shows. At 52 she has almost exactly the same figure that she had at 22, when she married. She is five feet three, and weighs about 100 pounds. Her face is rather plain and pinched, with a singularly (dysplastically) weak chin. The light brown eyes are as alert and bright as are those of the rest of the family. She has what all the other members of the family lack, a quick sense of humor and a manifest playfulness of mind. The impression grows from talking with her that she could have adapted to almost any pattern of life and could have made a success of her marriage at nearly any level.

The maternal grandfather was a schoolteacher in this same little hamlet, and his father had been an early circuit rider in that part of the state. This grandfather died at 65 of coronary thrombosis. The grandmother died at 76, presumably of the same cause. Both of these grandparents were slender, healthy people, although among other maternal relatives there are numerous individuals of heavy and corpulent build.

No tuberculosis is known among the maternal relatives, but cancer is common. At least eight persons within three degrees of relationship have died of this cause. All of these have descended from a common maternal grandparent of the mother, and none of them has been an ectomorph. (We have found cancer to be rare among ectomorphs whose cerebrotonia matches their ectomorphy.) There are two cases of diabetes among maternal relatives (both of these people being of pronouncedly mesomorphic physique). No extreme high blood pressure is known. There are several minor complaints of arthritis. No mental disease, but there is one case of chronic alcoholism, in a first cousin.

Siblings:

1. Brother, now 29, still unmarried and practicing law in a small city of the State, some hundred or more miles from the family home. This brother's career resembles Christopher's in many ways. He too was a frail, shy youth, late developing, quiet, well behaved, and for the most part serious, worried and humorless. He is said to be a little heavier or stronger than Christopher, but not more than 10 pounds heavier, and of about the same height. The two played together more or less as children, although both were essentially lonely creatures and they did not find much in common. They quarreled very little. Neither had enough somatotonia to quarrel, apparently. The older boy appears to have been slightly the father's favorite, but the mother believes that Christopher always had a little the better mind and disposition. "Christopher has some humor," the mother says.

   Both boys have always been on excellent terms with the parents, and with each other, in a passive sort of way. Christopher pities his brother for practicing law, "because it is a stupid, vulgar thing to have to do." The brother has been engaged for six or seven years to a girl three years older, who is teaching school. The mother believes that in another year or two they will reach the kissing stage. Christopher and the mother agree that the brother is "unimaginative."

2. Christopher.

GENERAL LIFE STORY
First 6 Years:

Christopher was precocious in learning to talk although he was not quite so quick in learning to walk. He never had very good muscular coordination, and was always rather awkward ("all legs and arms"). Throughout childhood as well as later, he remained far below the weight level prescribed by the medical chart which hung in the doctor's office. He was never very much "picked on" by other boys for the reason, apparently, that there was no fight whatsoever in him. He never made any pretense of defending himself against attack, and seems to have been accepted by the boys of his generation as a harmless nonentity who enjoyed a license to be let alone. He never tried to play baseball, football, or any other group game, and never attempted to learn to swim. His parents encouraged him sporadically in the direction of group participation of one kind or another, but generally desisted upon observing the pain and frustration with which any such effort seemed to be accompanied.

He spent much of his early childhood wandering around alone, or staying home with his mother. His older brother, likewise a lonely youngster, generally went off upon some errand of his own. Sometimes Christopher went along, but his enthusiasm never seemed to hold out, and there was little close association or common interest between the two boys.

Parental discipline was rarely needed and was never severe. No episodes of serious resentment against either parent are recalled by Christopher or by the parents. Furthermore there was no very strong wish on the part of either parent for the boys to be essentially different from what they were. The mother was if anything rather pleased that these youngsters were not of the more normal and active stamp. She placed "intellectual achievement ahead of mere normality." If she was seriously disappointed, the disappointment came later, when the boys both failed to distinguish themselves mentally.

Christopher never played much with girls. Girls called him a sissy and he let them alone. Until adolescence he disliked girls. After adolescence he suddenly became dependent upon his rapport with girls, and he had none. His early childhood must have been unusually rich in phantasy life. He was an avid reader, first of the usual childhood books and later of everything.

At age 4 he was fond of sitting in a favorite little chair in the kitchen, where he would apparently daydream for half a day at a time, almost without moving. Another of his favorite occupations was to walk about the yard, apparently aimlessly but actually he was living out a complete romantic drama in imagination. The principal theme, so far as can be recalled, was that of being grown up. In phantasy he was an adult, and in these phantasies he was surrounded by the finest of equipments of every nature. He seemed to be a prince or king of some sort, and there seemed to be an arrangement whereby through some power of magic he could change himself back and forth between the two estates, the phantasy reality and the Christopher reality. The two estates were of about the same order of reality, and even today Christopher believes that his objective existence is hardly more real than is his dream existence. On this point he will argue with more spirit than on any other.

Childhood was a period of yearning to be something other than a child—presumably to be an adult. Christopher thinks it was a most unhappy period, and that the repeated shock of awaking from dreams of untrammeled beauty to the squalid reality of being a miserable child with bowels and a weak body, was more painful than any later experience can be. He could stand it, he says, to be forced to go back to the frustration and painful disappointment of having to waste his splendid adolescent sexuality with no outlet but the despised masturbation. This he could stand again if he had to, but the bitter grief of always awakening from those childhood dreams of extraphysical beauty, only to find his awful physical limitations "stifling his soul"—that he could not do again.

Christopher's sexuality was a source of possibly his greatest reality interest during his early childhood. In some way he had gathered the notion (perhaps from his mother) that it was something good rather than sinful, and that it contained the promise of much of his best future happiness. He had frequent, "terrific" erections, and was astonished at the size and strength of his erect penis. Christopher did not know, as a child, that the penis was sinful. He played with his penis frequently, and sometimes personified it, regarding it as a companion, and often in some manner identified it with the other, nobler self of his dreams. He did not masturbate, in the technical sense, until adolescence. He only practiced autoeroticism. At no time during this period was there any contact of an erotic nature with another boy or with a girl, and he never had any erotic associations, either mental or physical, with his mother.

Age 6 to 14. School:

Christopher entered the grade school at 6. He was mentally somewhat advanced for his age. It is said that he could already read with some facility. He was physically weak and extremely shy, however, and during the first three years of school he suffered from a sort of vocal inhibition which may be akin to stage fright. When asked to talk or speak up in class, he was unable to do so. It was discovered that although he could do very well on written spelling tests, he could not spell aloud. Furthermore, when for any reason attention was called to him in school, he sometimes would have diarrhea. Also he experienced great difficulty in making himself heard, when he did speak aloud, and this contributed to his distress. All of these cerebrotic experiences were of great intensity.

In the early spring of Christopher's third year of school he appears to have broken down for a time, and to have lost his voice altogether for some ten days. He was taken out of school for the remainder of that spring, and was tutored by his mother. Under this treatment he blossomed astonishingly, and appears to have made progress which put him well ahead of his class, for in the following autumn, after starting the fourth grade, he was jumped ahead a year to the fifth grade.

This jump of a year may have been a mistake. Christopher now thinks it was. The educational philosophy of the move was based on a supposition that his shyness might be due to a sense of inferiority or insecurity arising from lack of achievement, and that if he were to be identified with the mentally brilliant, then he might begin to think of himself as in one sense strong. Actually he did do better in the fifth grade that year than he had done in the third grade during the previous year, but his shyness and the strain of competing with children who in social maturity were years ahead of him rendered his life difficult. (We might ask here, what would have been the result if instead of being advanced to a group who were at his own mental level, he had been put back among a group nearer to his level in social maturation? Would he have "found himself" socially, and would he then have developed some slight strength in viscerotonia and somatotonia—possibly a strength corresponding to or slightly exceeding his morphological endowment in these components?)

Christopher continued on through school with the class in which he was now placed. Although it was suspected by several of his teachers that he was actually more gifted mentally than his achievement indicated—and this suspicion was supported by mental test results—he finished grade school with a poor record. His marks placed him in the third quarter of his graduating class. At this time he hated and feared school, and looked with dread upon the prospect of going to high school. His mother considered the plan of keeping him out for a year, but for some reason decided against it.

He entered high school at 13, a frail boy who had never learned to do anything but study, and that not very well. He was now slightly above average stature, and some 30 pounds below average weight for his age and stature, although he was probably of normal weight for his somatotype. During the second week of school, the children were routinely vaccinated. Christopher fainted, falling and injuring his head so severely that he was out of school a week. But he went on, and finally graduated from high school with his class, although with a mediocre record.

During the period of grade school Christopher made no friends. He was generally tired in the afternoon, and usually came straight home from school to take a nap. Often he would read. Sometimes he slept till supper time. He loved the evening. Once in a while he was allowed to go to the movies—Friday evening. But he almost always went alone or with his brother. He took up stamp collecting, and also penny collecting. Sometimes he would pore over these treasures for hours, but he lacked the aggressiveness to beg or trade for additions, and had no money with which to purchase them. He never had any ability at tinkering, and would as soon have tried to take a locomotive apart as pry into the mysteries of a clock. He learned to ride a bicycle only later, when in high school. He disappointed his father by never taking very enthusiastically to natural history. His father is one of the most enthusiastic ornithologists in town, and also an interested entomologist, but Christopher's interest never would quite hold up, and he was generally left home when the father and older brother went on a Saturday jaunt to discover whether those brown thrasher eggs had yet hatched.

Sexuality had not yet burst upon this boy. He still entertained what might possibly be called a Narcissistic admiration for his penis, and was secretly proud of what he supposed was its unusual length. But there were no heterosexual or homosexual adventures.

He had learned to respond to the sexual theme in literature, however, and frequently experienced what he now terms "delightful Priapism," both from directly sexual descriptions and from descriptions of violence, torture, or physical mutilation. His threshold of erection remained a very low one, the response taking place at a passing thought. His sexual imagery during this period was wholly feminine in nature, but was very vague. It was never specifically that of intercourse, but seems to have been related particularly to a conception of the partially mature female breast. Masturbation was yet to be discovered.

After 14:

In high school as in grade school, Christopher found life essentially painful. He suffered through the loneliness and emptiness of month after month, buoyed up only by the thought that in later years when he would be a grown man most of the present discomforts would be gone. There would no longer be the painful shyness, he thought, and the internal clamping down in the face of every social situation. In the freedom of fully adult life all that would surely vanish, as would the embarrassment arising from his inability to compete in the physical rivalries of his contemporaries. He looked forward to the day when all these then mountainous tragedies would recede to the proportions of child's play. In the meantime he found virtually all of his satisfaction and delight in the world of phantasy. He did not quite have the energy, or the resolution, or whatever else it is that is required, to turn to indirect *achievement* for his fulfillment. He did not do his school work faithfully, or try to excel in any study, and it seems never to have occurred to him during this period that any weapons of compensational fulfillment were *now* available to his hand.

The idea of intellectual growth and achievement *sometime in the future*, in adult life, was always present in his mind, but there was no suggestion that he already had the power to enter upon any such achievement. For the present, it seemed to him, he must just keep alive, struggle through the painful days as best he could, and recreate his soul at the end of every day in the land of his phantasy.

Saturdays he generally stayed home all day, sleeping most of the forenoon, or rather, lying in bed and indulging in a kind of phantasy which appears to be intermediate between the daydream and the night dream. In the afternoon he usually would read, but never anything touching on school work. He read mostly the so-called light novels, or "psychological" novels, as he calls them. Stories of adventure had no fascination for him. He read almost none of the popular boys' books of his day. He loved Sherlock Holmes and often dreamed about him (still does). The Fenimore Cooper tales were stodgy, stupid. D'Artagnan and the three musketeers were "ineffably tiresome." Galsworthy, a little later, became one of his favorite authors. He has read all of Dickens, twice. He waded through nearly all of Thackeray. George Eliot was a favorite.

There were many efforts to "bring him out," by encouraging him to take part in plays, to go to parties, to learn to dance, to develop hobbies of a social nature. All of these efforts failed. His mother, during the high school period, had a strong intuition that the boy was in some fundamental sense younger than his years and that he should not be so far along in school. But relatives, and for some reason the father, overruled her half-resolve to take him out of school for a year or two.

Christopher never showed any particular ability in one high school subject as compared with another. He did just enough work in all subjects to pass, and no more. Beyond that, he was too tired to be interested. He was, during these years, and to a lesser degree is even now, obsessed with an idea that he was not a true participant in life. He felt that he was only a visitor, and somehow a visitor let into the wrong house. Therefore his failure to distinguish himself was not really a reflection upon him. He was only a detached watcher of the scene. He never entered into any kind of competition, and has never recognized the existence of a competitive relationship in which he himself was a part.

This youth never became interested in religion. Although not church members themselves, his mother and father conceived the idea during Christopher's high school career that young people's social life at the most popular local Protestant church might constitute an excellent tonic for him. The result was that "for nearly a whole year Sunday evenings were ruined by my having to dress up and go sit with a lot of stuffy, social-minded fools to be up-lifted."

In about the middle of the junior year of high school, when he was 15, while looking at a more or less nude female picture in a magazine and manipulating his penis, he had an ejaculation. This was possibly the first really somatotonic physical event in which he had ever participated. The momentarily untrammeled, con-centrated somatotonic ecstasy was an entirely new experience to Christopher (in sharp contrast with Boris, to whom the first sexual orgasm had appeared as a rather natural, or almost routine event. Boris was used to violent, ecstatic, sudden exertion of his body, in one way or another. For Christopher it was a bolt out of the blue). He tried it again, that same night. He had been reading in bed at the time of the first occurrence. This second time, the violent opisthotonic stretching of his muscles left him exhausted. He thinks he went to sleep immediately, a very rare event for him.

Masturbation set in in earnest, almost at once. It was the first thing he had ever found of a physical nature that he could do well. He experimented and developed many subsidiary techniques of excitation, discovering that almost his whole body was more or less sensitive to erotic stimulation. One Saturday night, after resting up all day, he succeeded in producing so violent an orgasm that he strained some small muscle in his thigh, and then had a bad limp for a week or so. His father called it a "Charley horse." Christopher did not explain how he got it, but after that he called masturbation "Charleying."

Although most of the boy's energy now went into this new ac-tivity he believes that no one ever knew of his discovery, and that no changes in his external behavior were noticeable. There was no effect on his school work, a fact which possibly demonstrates what a small part of his real interest ever had been centered there. From childhood he had been taciturn and secretive. To have con-fided in anyone now concerning his marvelous discovery would have been comparable to a gross betrayal of his nature. This was a secret between him and his world of subjective construction.

High school was uneventful and graduation was routine. After graduation the question was again raised as to whether Christopher should be kept out a year or two before going to college, but this idea was overruled. He went to a small coeducational college in his own State, coming home for vacations and summers. He lived on a very small allowance, partaking only of the cheapest of everything, and entering into no activities of any kind. He earned no part of his own way. College was taken with almost complete passivity. During the college years he developed the custom of indulging his fondness for the movies. Most of that part of his allowance which was not used for food went to the cinema houses. Christopher has never smoked, and of course he never drank. He lived for three years in one rooming house, paying $2.00 a week for his attic room. At the beginning of the fourth year he moved into one of the college dormitories, but moved out again at Christmas to another rooming house. It was quieter. He was never asked to visit a fraternity house, and he never did visit one.

During the entire four years of college his mind was preoccupied with sex. He had a tremendous desire for sexual intimacy with a girl. He had never kissed a girl, however, and had never actually escorted a girl anywhere. He had only wanted to, very intently, and the more intently he wanted to, the more difficult it was to find an opportunity to do it. He was now continually resolving not to masturbate, but nevertheless was continuing to masturbate, at irregular intervals. If he would go two nights without masturbating, on the third night he would go out and prowl. That is to say, he would walk the streets in a forlorn hope of "picking up" a female. There was no open prostitution in this college town. To find a prostitute it was necessary to be "in on the know," and to do that it was necessary to "belong" somewhere. Christopher did not belong, and during his four years of college he found no prostitute, although he had long since laid aside the three dollars which he had been told was the necessary fee, and this three dollars he always carried with him on his lonely night prowls.

Nor could he find a girl with whom there seemed to be a possibility of developing any intimacy. He found one or two "hefty, vulgar females" who appeared to be willing, but that would be worse than nothing, he thought. The girl must be delicate and slender. "Otherwise a horse or cow would be better." He had nothing to offer an attractive girl, externally, and in reality he had nothing to offer but his great desire and an extreme sensitivity.

These were not very marketable. He altogether lacked the address and assurance to make an initial contact, and in four years he made no such contact. He graduated from college as virginal as when he entered. But in the meantime he had masturbated excessively, and he had read somewhere that such a practice leads to impotency. His ejaculations had become noticeably easier to produce, and the orgasm was less intense than formerly. All this he interpreted as a sign of approaching impotency and he was well on the way to developing a masturbational cerebrosis.

Christopher never became interested in any of his college studies. Some of them looked promising, he now recalls, but he postponed all serious consideration of such matters, pending the solution of his major sex problem. He "concentrated" in education, having at this time some vague idea that he might ultimately teach school.

After college Christopher returned home, where he virtually went on a sitdown strike, refusing to try anything on his own behalf for about a year, although there were some futile, abortive efforts to get a job. But in September of the following year he appeared at one of the Midwestern state universities and enrolled for graduate work in the School of Education. There he came to the writer's attention, being referred for psychological consultation.

That fall he found sexual experience, apparently in quite a satisfactory manner. I never inquired into the details, for on that point he manifested great reticence. I know only that he established a liaison with a sensitive young woman some two or three years his senior, who was herself in academic work. His comment eighteen months later was that had he found such a relationship some years earlier, he believes he could have focused his effort upon academic achievement. Whether or not this is actually the case must remain a speculation.

Christopher has done fairly well in graduate work. After two years he is rather well regarded in the Departments of Sociology and Education. He is now working on a thesis in Sociology, which bears on the problem of prostitution. He has been out in the field "investigating," and although he is considered a little slow and lacking in initiative, he certainly has developed an interest. He probably will receive the Ph.D. degree.

THE PROBLEM OF TREATMENT

The practical question of treatment of such a cerebrosis as Christopher's is an interesting one to raise, but the answer, as in the previous instances, must for a long time await the further development of a constitutional psychology. Cerebrosis is relatively common, in its different degrees. It is easy to recognize, has long been described in various terminological systems, and there are numerous hypotheses bearing on the problem of its therapy.

Many psychologists advise attempting to socialize the overly inhibited child, and this is actually the predominant practice of the day. Yet we are not sure that this is not a bad practice when carried out blindly. In Christopher's case there was so little native somatotonia upon which to build that to have forced the socializing process would possibly have been very unwise. Such an effort might throw a child of this kind into schizoid mental pathology, possibly into psychosis. What would have been the result if such a child were thrown into the water to teach him to swim? Possibly he would then have learned to swim. But we would not have advised it. Not with 1^2-1^2-6 morphology.

With endomorphy showing a slight secondary predominance at the morphological level (Christopher's endomorphy is 1.6, his mesomorphy 1.4), the primary indication would probably be to try to build up viscerotonia rather than somatotonia, as the cushion against which to buttress such an overwhelming cerebrotonia. That is to say, with such a child we should prefer to concentrate on affection, security and a slowed-up program rather than on activities, and in selecting a companion or companions for him, we should seek viscerotonic rather than somatotonic personalities, whether as childhood playmates or as guiding adults. His own parents lacked both viscerotonia and somatotonia. This was probably true of his entire immediate environment, as well as of his constitutional endowment.

Presumably the constitutional endowment as revealed by morphology predetermines only within rather broad limits the patterning of the temperament. Very likely a 1^2-1^2-6 is necessarily going to be extremely cerebrotonic, but perhaps the nature of the early (and late) conditioning will within limits determine *how* cerebrotonic, as well as whether the secondary temperamental components will exceed or fall short of their respective morphological indications, ,and in what manner. This postulates a reasonable latitude of play for environmental influences. It may be that Christopher could have developed into, let us say a 2-2-6 pattern temperamentally, under different influences, instead of the 1-1-7 pattern which he did develop. As a temperamental 2-2-6 he might well have been happy, efficient and full of achievement.

If this hypothesis is countenanced, then it is permissible to speculate as to what specific influences might have brought about results different from those which did emerge. We do not now propose to wander very far into this attractive field of speculation, but will content ourselves with one or two simple observations.

To begin with, excessive cerebrotonia presents a problem very different from that of excessive somatotonia. Cerebrotonia can be 'contacted' in a number of ways. It responds to all languages. For one thing it can often be considerably mellowed, softened, or 'snowed under' by viscerotonic influences. Sometimes the simple expedient of overfeeding a person, or feeding him cream to raise his weight, will alleviate cerebrotonic symptoms. (This also works the other way. It is sometimes possible by dieting and weight reduction to accentuate cerebrotonic symptoms. The theoretical question as to whether such procedures actually change the temperamental components, or merely change the manifest-latent relationship among them, we shall not attempt to answer here.) Cerebrotonic people change more, superficially at least, in response to a changing environment than do viscerotonic or somatotonik people. They are mentally more labile, less secure in their anchorage, and more easily influenced, although they are less demonstrative.

Had Christopher's parents been more viscerotonic, especially the mother, it is possible that Christopher would have reflected this component to a considerably greater degree, and his way would then have been appreciably smoothed. Very possibly his early achievement would have been greater. But we feel that if more pressure had been put upon him to develop somatotonic characteristics, the result would probably have been disastrous. He was sufficiently fragile to have been destroyed rather easily, had any attempt been made to force the second component upon him.

We have learned from experience one psychological generalization which seems to be important. That is: *Never try to reverse a morphological predominance in the educational development of a personality.* In the working out of this generalization, the secondary predominance (that of the second strongest over the weakest component) is of more practical importance than the primary predominance (that of the strongest over the second strongest component). The primary predominance is usually obvious, and the temperamental pattern ordinarily follows it quite naturally. But the two weaker components are likely to be of nearly the same strength. The predominance of one of them may be slight, and may be (morphologically) dysplastic, or (temperamentally) dyscrastic. When this is the case the competition for secondary predominance at the temperamental level is likely to be held in close balance, and environmental influences may then turn the scales either way.

We feel that much of the *avoidable* human frustration and misery takes its origin from misanthropic reversal of the secondary predominance. For example, a child who is morphologically 3-2-5 may have a father or brother in whom the second component holds either a primary or a secondary predominance. There is then a strong tendency on the part of the latter to influence the child in a somatotonic direction, thus inadvertently attempting to reverse the child's natural personality pattern. The 3-2-5 child then may try to live out a 2-3-5 pattern. It seldom works. It is always obvious that something is radically wrong.

A large number of the "neurotic" or maladapted people whom we have studied have shown this kind of reversal of what their morphology indicated (see Chapter VI). This is why it seems important that somatotyping be done with the utmost care. A careless approach to somatotyping is possibly as dangerous as a careless approach to surgery.

In Christopher's case, the above danger was avoided. Instead, *both* the assertive component and the viscerotonic component remained for a long time almost vestigial, and a high degree of cerebrosis developed. Whether or not this could have been prevented by a more viscerotonic influence is something we should like to know. In any event this boy was later rescued by his (rather heavy endowment of) sexuality, which now appears to have opened the way for him to live something like a normal life and possibly to make an achievement.

There is one other thing we should like to know. Christopher is bitter about the long frustration of his sexuality. He thinks now that he could have made a good college record if he could have had a normal sexual contact. Could he have done so? What would have been the outcome had he lived during his 'teens in a sexually more healthful environment?

4. EUGENE: *A Disturbing Somatotonic Personality*

SUMMARY

Eugene is a short, chunky, powerfully built Rumanian Jewish youth of 22, who as a member of the first year class in the medical school has shown such extremely aggressive characteristics that the dean of the school has become concerned about his personality. His IQ is about 120, he has a good academic record, and there is no question about his continuance. The question is how best to handle him and to advise him. This is his fourth year on the campus at the State University. He will graduate in June and will also have completed one year of medical school, since admission to the medical school is possible here with only three years of college work.

This young man was born in a suburb of Boston, but at the age of five moved to Newark, New Jersey, where his father has been successful in the department store business as the partner of a relative. There are seven other children, two of them (sisters) older than Eugene. The family is orthodox Jewish in religion, but is only nominally so.

Eugene has always been short, as are his father and mother and sisters. He has heavy, coarse features, and curly black hair of conspicuously coarse texture. He is extremely hirsute. He has a long body, with short, thick arms and legs. His voice is high, and it generally has a strident quality which immediately catches the attention.

At the university he has worked prodigiously in all of his courses and has earned fairly high grades consistently. He has taken no part in campus activities of any kind, but is a member of one of the Jewish fraternities. Wherever he is known he is considered aggressive and obnoxious, but his professional outlook is probably favorable.

TEMPERAMENTAL PATTERN

Viscerotonia:

1. *Relaxation* (4). The body as a whole is assertively erect. He is always ready for action, so far as the central bodily regions are

concerned. When he sits, the back is straight and the head is far back. But there is peripheral relaxation in the hands, feet and face. The face looks almost bland.

2. *Love of Physical Comfort* (4). The primary motivation lies clearly in the competition for status. Yet there is a strong secondary desire for physical comfort. He always wears the most comfortable clothes possible, seeks and usually gets the most comfortable chair, loosens his tie and shirtband, never stands up when it is possible to sit down, is concerned about the proper softness of his mattress and pillows, etc.

3. *Slow Reaction* (4). Peripheral reaction is slow. The hands are rather clumsy. The walk is a clumsy, deliberate, heel-pounding one. On the reaction-time experiments in the psychological laboratory, he is a trifle slower than average. But the *general* reaction is fast. In classroom he is always among the first to speak up, and usually has the right answer.

4. *Love of Eating* (5). This is probably his greatest indulgence. He will eat gluttonously when the opportunity offers, and at times will go to great pains to secure and prepare his favorite foods. Yet the love of eating does not interfere with the vigorous prosecution of his main endeavor, which is now centered upon competition for academic grades.

5. *Socialization of Eating* (4). On occasion, principally on Jewish holidays, he loves to make a great fuss over the principal meal of the day, and the proper serving of it is important. The wine must be just right and served in the correct manner. Company is of primary importance on these occasions. Yet on ordinary days the second component takes over, and he eats like a wolf, without ceremony, in the nearest cheap restaurant, hurrying immediately back to his studies or laboratory work.

6. *Pleasure in Digestion* (4). Digestion is excellent. There are never any disturbances of digestion. Peristalsis is slow and regular and is never subject to emotional upset. He has an essential pleasure in elimination, and no more shame over it than over eating. Yet he rarely "sits and digests." His drive toward the main competition is always predominant in his economy of energy.

7. *Love of Polite Ceremony* (4). He follows the proper ritual in essential matters. He has a deep love of order and a profound

personal respect for vested authority. He is politely obeisant toward professors. Yet he is a political anarchist, is usually dirty in his appearance, is a chain cigarette smoker (often where smoking is theoretically prohibited), and he takes advantage of people ruthlessly if the opportunity is presented.

8. *Sociophilia* (4). There is a fondness for small gatherings. He likes to study with two or three others, and the noisier and more jolly the gathering the better. In general, it is unpleasant for him to be alone. Yet his sociophilia is more superficial and external than profound. He always avoids large gatherings, and he is highly clannish.

9. *Indiscriminate Amiability* (2). He is expressive and demonstrative, but is singularly free from personal sentiment, and while his good fellowship is genuine, it is far from warm. He is in no sense emotionally involved with other personalities, even with those who know him best. His relationship to others is like that of a professional salesman.

10. *Greed for Affection and Approval* (2). There is essentially an austere independence of social approval. His primary attitude toward the majority of his fellow students is one of contempt and of almost warlike rivalry. Even among his Jewish friends in his fraternity, this essentially competitive attitude is predominant. Yet he is watchful for disapproval on the part of a professor, and is energetic in mending the situation.

11. *Orientation to People* (4). He knows where his bread is buttered, all the time, and he also has the somatotonia to act on his knowledge. Within the limitations of his rather narrow interests he has accurate orientation to people. He is more deeply interested in status and in the outward manifestations of authority and recognition, than in people as people.

12. *Evenness of Emotional Flow* (2). Emotional expression is uneven and tempestuous. At times warm emotion is expressed. At times there is an austere harshness which suggests a cold universal hate.

13. *Tolerance* (1). He expresses intolerance in almost all of his relationships. Politically he is intolerant of Republicans; sexually, of those who preach "prudery"; aesthetically, of anything but a certain crass sophistication; religiously, of everything, including

the religion of his own people. In his immediate, personal relationships he is harshly intolerant of disagreement or contradiction, and when he is with two or three of his comrades, the noise and the gesticulations of impatience suggest imminent mortal combat.

14. *Complacency* (3). In general, he is not complacent about human society or about life at large. But when well fed and resting, he is complacent about himself. He then becomes boastful and likes to review his achievements.

15. *Deep Sleep* (5). He goes to sleep easily and quickly, and snores loudly, usually beginning to snore after he has been asleep for a couple of hours or so, never immediately. Also he talks and thrashes about in sleep. He is a noisy sleeper.

16. *The Untempered Characteristic* (2). Almost an antithesis. At long range the face looks bland. But upon close contact this personality emanates a rigid fixity of purpose. There is a centralized unyielding quality, in contrast with the peripheral intensity seen in cerebrotonia. The set of the body suggests watchfulness for the main chance, and disregard of details.

17. *Smooth, Easy Communication of Feeling* (3). Communication of feeling seems on the surface fairly unimpeded. But the violent, explosive nature of his social address constitutes an impediment. It is difficult to know where feeling begins and where somatotonic assertiveness leaves off.

18. *Relaxation and Sociophilia under Alcohol* (3). The reaction to alcohol is partly viscerotonic, but mainly somatotonic. He is fond of alcohol in moderate quantities. He becomes appreciably warmer and more expansive, but the main reaction is a loud aggressiveness and an expression of the sense of power.

19. *Need of People when Troubled* (5). One primary need seems to be for people when trouble occurs. He can pour it out to a listener without inhibition. There has also been strong indication of the somatotonic response to trouble, especially to the kind of trouble which he frequently brings upon himself (social hostility).

20. *Orientation toward Childhood and the Family* (5). The tie-up with family is very strong. He is anxious to have children and a family of his own as soon as possible. There is perhaps a still stronger urge toward somatotonic fulfillments, however.

Somatotonia:

1. *Assertiveness of Posture and Movement* (6). The primary assertive set of the body is a conspicuous characteristic, although there is peripheral relaxation. See trait V-1.

2. *Love of Physical Adventure* (6). He loves fast automobiles, and will drive at 80 miles an hour. He has twice had bad smashups, once killing a young woman in another car. Also he is passionately fond of horses and of (German) police dogs. Yet he scornfully dislikes athletics of all sorts. He plays no athletic games.

3. *The Energetic Characteristic* (7). His energy is limitless, and he has it well harnessed to his primary purpose. There is never hesitation or procrastination. He goes straight at his work on all occasions. He seems to think with his body as a whole.

4. *Need of Exercise* (5). There is almost constant activity. He is never still for long. The body needs to be doing something all of the time. Yet formal or prescribed exercise is not indulged in. There appears to be no call for it. He combines business with pleasure, exercising the body continually, but harnessing this energy to the achievement of his primary competitive purpose. As a fixed policy he always does about twice the laboratory work assigned in a course.

5. *Love of Dominating* (7). This is his religion. He lives, he says, to become powerful in his world, and he rationalizes that this is the mainspring behind *all* human motivation. Man strives in order to rule others. All else is humbug. The strong accept this challenge, he thinks, and the weak rationalize. Capitalism is a rotten arrangement through which the weak get the best of the strong or falsely maintain an advantage won by strong ancestors.

6. *Love of Risk* (6). He loves danger, and loves gambling. His passion is poker for good stakes, although he now rarely has time to indulge, for he studies nearly every evening. After he qualifies as a physician he proposes to "live up to the standard of the profession" and become a great poker player. He keeps a weather eye on the stock market, against the day when he will have money with which to gamble.

7. *Bold Directness of Manner* (6). His manner is always bold and direct. There is no beating about the bush with Eugene. He fixes everybody with a direct, unblinking stare, and goes straight to the point.

8. *Courage for Combat* (4). He has never been known to fight, and he has more than once been called a coward by pugnacious contemporaries. Yet he is fearless of physical injury in his notoriously reckless automobile driving, and readily accepts a bet on a race from one city to another. He is aggressively courageous in trying to sell a pint of blood (for transfusion purposes) more often than the rules of the hospital permit.

9. *Competitive Aggressiveness* (7). So strongly marked that the trait has attracted the attention of university authorities, and Eugene is in some quarters considered pathologically aggressive.

10. *Psychological Callousness* (7). This trait seems pathologically accentuated. He not only is insensitive to the desires of people in his immediate environment, but he seems driven by an overwhelming impulse to bend people to his will. He browbeats and bullies wherever it can be done.

11. *Claustrophobia* (6). There is a dislike of small places and of corners. He wants to be out in the open. A closed door is a great irritation to him.

12. *Freedom from Squeamishness* (7). Eugene is often depended upon by other students, as the official killer of frogs, cats, dogs, turtles and other animals used for experimental purposes in the laboratories. He seems to experience no particular emotion from killing. There certainly is no sadism. He is merely free from squeamishness. He is calloused in this respect. He likes to use things up and get things done.

13. *Unrestrained Voice* (7). This trait is so marked that he carries the nickname "Foghorn" on the campus. His high, strident voice rises far above competition.

14. *Spartan Indifference to Pain* (6). While he complains loudly of all discomforts, there can be little question of his relative insensitivity to deep pain. In his last automobile accident he broke his jaw and his arm, and cut a deep gash in his face. He missed just one meeting of one class, and made that up during the same week. For some reason he was dissatisfied with the stitches taken in his face, and had them taken out and done over again.

15. *General Noisiness* (7). He is supremely noisy. He whistles incessantly. If a radio is available he will turn on the noisiest program, and settle down comfortably to study. When he moves, something usually slams.

16. *Overmaturity of Appearance* (6). He gives the impression of being older than he is. The heavy features are rigidly set. The skin of his face shows heavy creases. There is a pronounced early frontal (mesomorphic) baldness.

17. *Horizontal Mental Cleavage* (6). Eugene is not unaware of the *primary* trend of his own innermost cravings. He grasps the main drift of his inner nature fairly well, probably accurately. He is, however, quite cut off from the inner expression of his secondary and tertiary (weakest) components. He does not hear the minority voice within himself. There is almost complete suppression of the component of restraint. This is the common and the main symptom of horizontal mental cleavage.

18. *Assertiveness and Aggression under Alcohol* (5). The reaction is essentially somatotonic. Under alcohol he expresses principally the sense of power and vaunting ambition. There is also a secondary note of viscerotonic good fellowship and good will.

19. *Need of Action when Troubled* (5). There is a strong viscerotonic reaction, but also there is a strong somatotonic reaction. He is prone to take long, fast automobile trips when he is distressed or disappointed, and in the face of social frustration or attempted chastening (of which he has had a good deal), he accepts no blame but throws his energy the harder into the competition for grades and thereby for status. With respect to the set of traits to which we refer as "the 19's," Eugene shows the rare 5-5-1 pattern.

20. *Orientation toward Goals and Activities of Youth* (5). There is a strong inclination toward the viscerotonic affiliations of family, but there is an even stronger urge to compete for power, money, and similar goals of youth. It is in this latter direction that the primary orientation lies. 5-5-1 is also the pattern for "the 20's."

Cerebrotonia:

1. *Physical Restraint, Tightness* (1). He presents a good antithesis to this trait. There is no external or internal inhibition. He "lets himself go" at all times.

2. *Physiological Overresponse* (1). No trace. No digestive disturb-

ance under any circumstances. (He has what is called "guts," or "good kidney.") Colds are not acute, and are inclined to settle in the chest. He has had several infections and all the common contagious diseases. Mosquitoes do not bite him. He believes that the sting of the mosquito is "mostly imagination." There is no trace of constipation in his history. The BMR is minus 2.

3. *Overly Fast Reactions* (2). Specific bodily reactions are slightly on the slow side. His social adaptation is effective. There are none of the overly fast (cerebrotonic) reactions which result in confusion. Eye movements are rather slow and deliberate. There is never any suggestion of blushing or blanching. The face remains impassive. The only suggestion of the overfast reaction is his tendency to speak out too quickly.

4. *Love of Privacy* (1). Eugene does not like privacy. He feels that man was never intended to be a lonely animal. He is unhappy and restive when alone. He feels that he cannot concentrate on his studies when alone, or when it is "too quiet, like a graveyard." If no people are about, he must have the radio.

5. *Mental Overintensity, Hyperattentionality* (2). He is in certain fundamental respects watchful. He is aware of just what is going on all the time. In baseball language, he knows exactly where the ball is, and he pretty well anticipates the play. But he is not *hyper*attentional. He is not attentional to the point of interference with efficiency of general adaptation. He is alert in the somatotonic sense, but not *over*alert in the cerebrotonic sense. There is no overawareness of the internal organic processes. He is never confused by overstimulation, but loves overstimulation.

6. *Secretive Restraint of Feeling* (1). There is no inhibition of the expression of feeling. On the contrary he seems to express more feeling externally than exists internally. This is especially true in argument, of which he is very fond. Eugene has no secrets.

7. *Self-conscious Motility of the Eyes and Face* (3). The face is essentially impassive, immobile. But there is a disconcertingly sharp watchfulness about the eyes, which are restless. Eugene does not miss much. He has been called self-conscious, although he is in no sense inhibitively self-conscious.

8. *Sociophobia* (1). No trace of a phobia here, although he rarely

seeks large crowds. He is highly agglutinative, in the small-group sense. See trait V-8.

9. *Inhibited Social Address* (1). He presents an excellent antithesis to this trait. His composure is so unassailable that he is in some quarters hated on that account. In all situations he maintains the social initiative.

10. *Resistance to Habit and Poor Routinizing* (1). He has his life almost perfectly routinized, with respect to sleep, eating and elimination, getting up in the morning, and work. There is not even momentary hesitancy about getting down to work, and he almost always does what he plans.

11. *Agoraphobia* (1). None. He loves large rooms, large houses, likes to be out in the most conspicuous position possible, and avoids corners. He is an exhibitionist of the deepest dye.

12. *Unpredictability of Attitude* (2). There is little suggestion of cerebrotonic unpredictability. His basic attitude remains constant. But there is at times almost a hypomanic violence in his social address, and he has been accused by superficial observers of "emotional instability." He has been called "emotionally labile."

13. *Vocal Restraint and Restraint of Noise* (1). He presents the antithesis to this trait (see S-13 and S-15).

14. *Hypersensitivity to Pain* (2). The trait of Spartanism (S-14) is predominant. But he complains loudly of small pains, inconveniences, and discomforts.

15. *Poor Sleep Habits* (1). Never any trouble of this kind. He sleeps well, although noisily. See V-15.

16. *Youthful Intentness of Appearance* (2). The general appearance of the face suggests overmaturity, and at a distance, lack of intentness. But when the face is looked at closely, a certain watchful intentness is seen in the eye.

17. *Vertical Mental Cleavage* (1). A clear antithesis. This is a highly objective mind. The dissociation is horizontal. There is no schizoid tendency, and there is strong indication of a manic tendency.

18. *Resistance to Alcohol* (2). Very little. He is fond of alcohol, and he uses this drug (moderately) to accentuate his strongest component. There is no conflict and no reversal of a primary or

secondary morphological predominance under the influence of alcohol.

19. *Need of Solitude when Troubled* (1). No indication of ever turning to solitude under stress. He turns to people, and to action.

20. *Orientation toward the Later Periods* (1). He is not concerned about intellectual maturity, or about religion or philosophy, and he has no love for old age. He shows a strong primary predisposition both toward somatotonic goals (competition for power, money and status) and toward viscerotonic goals (family and children)

Totals: Viscerotonia, 70; Somatotonia, 121; Cerebrotonia, 28.
Index of Temperament, 3^2-6^2-1.

PHYSICAL CONSTITUTION

Age 22, Ht. 63.5, Wt. 142, Somatotype 3^2-6-1 (3-6-1, 3-6-1, 3-6-1, 4-6-1, 4-6-1). g 1.7, t 1.2, d 6.

This is a powerful, sturdy, mesomorphic physique of short stature. Mesomorphy is overwhelmingly the primary component, and endomorphy shows an equally overwhelming secondary predominance over ectomorphy, which is at the extreme minimum. There is no particular dysplasia, although the concentration of endomorphy below the diaphragm (Regions *IV* and *V*) is notably greater than that above the diaphragm. Total dysplasia is 6 (endomorphy, 6; mesomorphy, 0; ectomorphy, 0). This is a very low dysplasia, and physical constitutions showing only two different somatotypes in the five regions of the body are less common than those which show three or more somatotypes. Gynandromorphy is about average for this somatotype, and t is very low. This is a coarse-textured physique.

There is massive strength throughout all regions, most notably in the two lower regions. The legs are especially powerful. The thighs are really mesomorphic 7, but the legs below the knee show a certain spindling or weakening which is seen so frequently in Jewish men (and women) that we have come to regard it as a racial characteristic. There is a peculiar knottiness or loss of shape in the singularly short lower legs. (The extensor muscles of the foot are weak.)

This somatotype is likely to take on weight enormously in

later life. With its powerful, sturdy frame and the heavy musculature, a 361-461 can put on fat almost unlimitedly. These people,
when not controlled by external or internal restraint, are likely
to double their weight in the middle decades. But a mesomorphic
6 cannot become flabby, and will never lose its general shape.
There will never be a sagging bay window. The whole trunk
seems to inflate and expand, just about as much above the waist
as below it.

The forehead is fairly high and sloping. The extremely hairy
eyebrows are high-arched so that the face has a singularly open,
frank expression. The dark brown eyes are large and widely
spaced. The coarse, black hair has begun to thin out frontally,
and it has a short curl which starts close to the scalp. The nose,
which has only a moderate Semitic hump, is broad at the base,
large as a whole, and high at the bridge. The mouth is large, with
very thick, heavily muscled lips. The lips show a moderate viscerotonic protrusion when the face is relaxed, but this characteristic is not pronounced. The beard is so heavy that even immediately after shaving there is a deep blue-black hue over the
face. The head as a whole is large, and slightly brachycephalic.
The face is long, broad and deep—a very large face. The neck
is short and extremely massive. Even at 22, it is already difficult
to distinguish between head and neck posteriorly.

The trunk seems very long, in contrast with the short legs
and the short neck and arms. The shoulders are broad, and sloping. The chest and abdomen are very heavily muscled. The
front of the body and the arms and legs are thickly covered with
black hair. The testicles are large but the penis is small and short,
with poorly developed corona. The hips are fairly wide, but there
is little suggestion of any feminoid flaring. The waist is a little
high for the somatotype (this somatotype is likely to have a very
low waist). The distribution of the luxuriant pubic hair is
markedly masculine.

The hands and feet are relatively small and weak-appearing
for a physique which as a whole is mesomorphic 6, but this is a
common characteristic among Jewish people. They are "centrip-
etal," in the sense that their concentration of strength and mass
tends to lie close to the center of the body. Nordics are frequently
"centrifugal" in the sense that they often show relatively great

strength in the forearms and lower legs, as compared with regions nearer the center of the body.

CLINICAL HISTORY

Eugene is the third of eight living children. The two oldest are sisters, six and five years older, respectively, than Eugene. There are two younger sisters and three younger brothers.

Pregnancy was full term, and birth weight normal. The baby appears to have been vigorous. He gained weight rapidly. At 1 and also at 2 years of age he was well over average weight. Since the family was on public charity at the time of Eugene's birth, he was born at a good Boston maternity hospital, and his early development was watched by the Welfare Department of one of the best pediatric clinics in the city. He is described as a "normal, active, vigorous infant."

During the first three years he had measles, mumps, chickenpox, whooping cough and diphtheria, the last two severely. At 13 months there was a severe exudative, generalized eruption of the skin which was undiagnosed. This never recurred. Three times within the first two years the baby was hospitalized for acute or chronic upper respiratory infections. There were several middle ear infections. Tonsils and adenoids were removed at age 5. Severe pyelitis was recorded four times between age 2 and age 6. Blood poisoning (septicaemia) followed twice from infected minor injuries, once at age 7, once at 14. Acute appendicitis and appendectomy at 19. Boils intermittently since age 12.

Teeth are small, well spaced, and show only moderate caries. The palate is very broad and shallow. The deep reflexes are exaggerated and the superficial reflexes are almost absent, except the cremasteric, which is very active.

Adolescence began at 12. Ejaculation discovered at 12. First intercourse at 13. Sexuality has never been an overwhelming, or perhaps even a predominant interest with this youth. He has taken sexuality as a matter of course.

BACKGROUND
Paternal:

The father came to this country from Rumania as a youth in 1895. He was one of fifteen children, most of whom are now in the United States. He worked for a relative in New York for several years, then ran a small clothing business in a suburb of Boston for a few years, and finally established himself successfully in Newark as a partner in a department store, which has since became a chain of department stores. He has made money. Physically he is described by Eugene as a short man of great muscular strength, who has never grown very fat. He has short, thick legs and like Eugene is excessively hairy. He might be anything from a 2-7-1 to a 3-6-2. Nothing is known of his predecessors. The scourge of this family is said to be diabetes, with several cases of gall bladder disease also on record. Three of the father's sisters have been operated upon for gall bladder disorders. One of the paternal uncles (father's younger brother) died of cancer. Another died of apoplexy. Eugene believes that all fourteen of his father's brothers and sisters were short and stocky.

Maternal:

The mother came over from Rumania in 1898 to marry. She is said to have been the prettiest of a family of eleven children, nine of whom eventually came to this country. This woman is four feet eleven inches tall and now weighs about 160 pounds. She looks merely short and fat to the casual observer, but she is predominantly mesomorphic, not endomorphic. She has the same sort of long, muscular trunk, and the short, thick arms and legs that Eugene shows. At sixteen, when she married, she was called "slender." She is probably a 4-6-1 in somatotype.

This woman has worked tremendously, and has been an excellent wife. Her principal sorrow is that she has only eight children (now that there is lots of money). Two of her sisters and also two of her brothers beat her in the number of children. She estimates that altogether Eugene has between 110 and 120 first cousins. Her people have done well, she reminisces, but if only the times had not been so hard, they would have done much better.

Both of the mother's parents have been brought to this country. The maternal grandfather died of "gall bladder and kidney trouble" at 62, and the grandmother, now 67, has for some years been confined to the house by "bad feet and obesity." Both of these grandparents were short and heavy. On this side of the family, kidney disease and high blood pressure have been the predominant causes of death. There have been several cases of gall bladder disease. No diabetes, no cancer, no arthritis, no tuberculosis.

Siblings:

1. Sister, now 28. Married and has five children. She is about five feet tall, is said to have been "slender" at marriage. Now weighs 140.
2. Sister, now 27. Married, has four children. About the same physique. Slightly taller.
3. Eugene.
4. Brother, 21. In college in New York. Said to be doing well, and plans to study law. Close to Eugene's physique, but possibly an inch taller.
5. Sister, 20. Married, and has three children. She, too, is short and since marriage has broadened out remarkably. The mother thinks that this girl is the star of the family, and that she may ultimately have twenty children. Her husband, a second cousin, has already made half a million dollars in the wholesale drug business, and is still under 30.
6. Brother, 18. In college in New York. The tallest of the family. Said to be about five feet six inches, and muscular.
7. Brother, 16. In high school. Short and stocky.
8. Sister, 14. In high school. Short and stocky.

GENERAL LIFE STORY

First 6 Years:

Eugene's mother believes that he was the most vigorous and demanding of her eight children, a characteristic which she thinks was manifest almost immediately after birth. She remembers him as having a more powerful voice than her two older children, but at the time she attributed this to his being a boy. However, the later boys did not as babies show this characteristic, but were, if anything, less demanding than the girls. Eugene walked and talked at about the same time, presumably at about 1 year of age.

When Eugene was a baby, the family lived in a suburban tenement apartment of four rooms which the mother says was poorly furnished and badly heated. During most of Eugene's babyhood the family received support from a public welfare agency. This included fuel and medical service. The father in the meantime was working for a relative but was not being paid in cash. However, the father received a "cash present" from this relative after six years of such employment, and with this he started his partnership in Newark.

Eugene played in the city streets as a little boy, mostly with other Jewish children. But little is recalled concerning this period. The mother thinks that Eugene was large for his age, and that he was "the boss" in most of his relationships. He never did any fighting, so far as is known, but his voice was overwhelming. His excessive fondness for bananas is one of her clearest memories. It was apparently only after this boy had entered public school, and had reached perhaps age 10, that he seemed appreciably shorter than his companions of like age. He himself remembers "suddenly observing" at about that age, that he was shorter than several other boys whom he had hitherto considered smaller than himself.

Eugene remembers numerous associations with other children which occurred before he moved to Newark. There was one family of five or six children at whose home he spent much of his time. These were second or third cousins. They lived well, and he always was given choice food there. They were musically inclined. Their parents often tried to interest Eugene in the piano and in dancing, but he was not to be interested. His interest was in cakes and tarts, and bananas. He remarks now, "All that foolish stuff, that dancing and art and piano playing must have ruined those kids. None of them has amounted to much."

As a child Eugene was taught to manifest (and to feel) great respect for older relatives, including the two older sisters, whom he regarded as persons of authority rather than as rivals. The parents seemed closer, and more nearly on a level with him than these sisters. Even now he looks upon these two as merely older relatives, rather than sisters. He never had any fear of his father, so far as he knows, or any jealous aspirations regarding his mother. Nothing is known of his early autoerotic life. Sexuality did not become of any overt importance to him until after adolescence. No sexual incidents of early childhood are recalled.

Religion was essentially family worship, or the worship of procreation and "racial purity." The father and mother have both called themselves "atheists," as long as Eugene can remember, but they always observed the Jewish holidays, and the principal tenet of their faith appears to have centered around the primary duty to marry within the Jewish race and to produce a large number of children. Both Eugene and his father are singularly fond of roast pork, although the mother, due to what Eugene calls a "religious hangover," has always abstained from pork.

Age 6 to 14. School:

Eugene entered a synagogue school at 6 and transferred a year later to the Newark public school system. He disliked the former but appears to have greatly enjoyed the latter. At the time of starting public school this boy was 7 years old, was of at least average stature, and was much heavier and stronger than average. The family now had more money, and Eugene considers that he was really one of the aristocracy in his new environment. About half of the children in his first public school were Jewish. The sisters continued in some sort of private school, and we hear little more about them from Eugene.

He was apparently well liked by both teachers and school companions. He remembers no fights, and does not believe that he was ever bullied or particularly picked on by older boys. He brought home excellent report cards, and the mother has a letter written by the principal of the school at the time when Eugene finished the second grade, in which the principal congratulates her on the excellent school showing of the boy. At home, both mother and father constantly impressed upon this youngster's mind the importance of excelling at school. The gratification of his special appetites of the moment, mostly for pastries and the like, depended usually upon getting "hundreds" in his spelling or arithmetic. And doing so apparently was quite natural for him, for although his mental tests never revealed him as possessing a particularly high intelligence quotient, he was extraordinarily industrious.

All through the grades, school went along well for Eugene, and he graduated at 15 with an excellent record. During this time he never manifested interest in any kind of athletics, or in any kind of exercise for its own sake. His mind was intensely practical. He did not see anything to be gained from playing games, he says, and so he invested his time where it would pay dividends. In the summer he went frequently to a beach resort, sometimes with his mother and father, sometimes with older relatives. There were at least a hundred fairly close relatives now living within a short radius of his locality, and they constituted what amounted virtually to a nation within a nation. They went to the beach in force, taking possession twenty or thirty strong. In a short time they usually had the space all to themselves. Most of them talked German or Yiddish on these occasions, and this seemed to help drive out the "foreigners" from the area selected.

Eugene found that swimming was as natural to him as walking, and swimming is still what he calls his "greatest carnal pleasure." He and the army of relatives would swim and lie in the sand possibly half of the time through the summer. All of them would darken up almost to Negro color. His mother, by this time, was "nearly an oval" in general outline, but he recalls that she was regarded among the relatives as one of the more slender, petite women.

Sexuality happened to Eugene quite suddenly, at 12. His pubic hair sprouted, and a fine down began to appear all over his body. One summer afternoon, after he had been disturbed for several days by a singularly persistent erection, his manipulations produced an ejaculation. He masturbated a few times, for it was a pleasant experience, but upon discussing the matter at some length with both his mother and father, he decided that masturbation was a bad thing, and should be done but rarely. He feels that he has never had any very intense urge to masturbate, but that masturbation has always been a question comparable to that of whether or not to go to the movies. The matter is usually decided quite rationally and objectively in his mind.

Both his mother and father recommended that he should seek sexual intercourse, and several prospective partners were mentioned, all of them relatives or close friends. His father gave him a box of condoms and explained their use. Several months later he experienced his first intercourse, with a second cousin three years his senior, her mother tacitly approving.

In discussing these matters with him, his father urged that he never have intercourse with other than Jewish girls, and that he maintain the most strict hygienic protection, both of himself and of his partner. He feels that he has always followed these suggestions. During the past six years Eugene believes that he has had intercourse with about a dozen different girls. He has never contracted venereal disease or caused a pregnancy. His sexual endowment is not high. He has never needed or craved sexual indulgence, he feels, oftener than once in two weeks. He masturbates at infrequent intervals. He has never had any homosexual relations, and knows nothing of any abnormal sexual techniques. He is extremely fond of kissing, but has no other bodily sexual sensitivity except primary genital sensitivity. He derives no particular satisfaction from touching or fondling any part of a girl's body. His sexual pleasures are practically confined to kissing and intercourse (and to close, sweaty, prolonged contact with another body). This has been the case since his first sexual experience.

Eugene's school life appears to have been a happy one, especially before the age of about 10, when he seems rather suddenly to have become aware of a deficit in stature. At about this time some of the boys whom he had regarded as of his own size or smaller, began to lengthen out and to leave him behind, so far as height is concerned. This disturbed him no little. He recalls lying in bed thinking about it, and resolving nevertheless to excel over these taller ones in some manner and thus to put them in their places. The mother believes that it was during this period, when he was in the fourth grade, that he began to show marked impatience and to talk more loudly than he previously had talked. Certainly his sense of rivalry increased at about this period. For one thing he determined to "take no lip" from any of these now taller boys. He became quarrelsome and hostile, more keenly conscious that he was a Jew, and therefore better, and he expressed bitter scorn for the non-Jewish element in the school (the Gentiles were now in the minority in Eugene's district). He never came to blows with anyone, so far as he can remember, but he found that he could shout other boys down, and this was his principal weapon. Many of the boys who were taller were non-Jewish, and these he particularly hated. All of his friends were of his own stature or shorter. He would have nothing to do with anyone over whom he could not dominate, and this characteristic has become more prominent in his nature as time has gone on. Today he counts as enemies or rivals all contemporaries who do not listen deferentially to him. He is ruthless and harsh with weaker people who cross his path, and freely expresses a general contempt for the college population as a whole. His contempt extends indeed to nearly the entire population except the medical profession, all of whom he regards with something like religious deference.

After 14:

Eugene graduated from grammar school at 15, standing high in his class. He was by now generally disliked by all but those over whom he dominated. He was considered disagreeably aggressive, a loud mouth, and a "cocky Jew." He had little in common with his classmates and contemporaries, and he defiantly despised most of them. He found a pattern of life in which he had the utmost confidence, and he "knew in his bones" that he would win out in the end—knew that he would become important and would win status while most of these others would be nobodies. For Eugene there were, and are, no distractions. Nothing can distract him or draw his interest away from the main business at hand. He never forgets what he is primarily after. That has been the central characteristic of his nature. As a baby he always knew where the bananas were. He never pointed sparrows. His eye has always been glued upon the main chance. He has never been sidetracked by incompatible desires, by hobbies, or by aesthetic distractions.

In high school for four years he attended strictly to business. He had made up his mind that he was going to study medicine, and he concerned himself avidly with the high school courses in science. He was interested only in science. The rest was done passably well because that was the way to play the game in which he participated.

He was now a runt in stature, but his body was tireless. There was prodigious strength in his compact trunk, and his massive, short legs had the sustained driving force of a couple of steel pistons. His ambition was high and personal. He would in the end put them all in their places. If he was ever tired, he never knew it. Somewhere back in the early years of high school, at the suggestion of his father, he adopted the fixed principle of always turning in exactly twice as much schoolwork as was assigned. He had learned that quantity counted more than quality. This policy he followed to the letter. It won the hatred of his classmates and it won him consistently high standing in his classes. Best of all, it cost nothing.

Sexuality was of little moment to Eugene. He feels that he was never seriously distracted by it. When the need was upon him he knew where to go. Always there were girls in his snug world of relatives who were only too glad to accommodate him. And he was never particular. Indeed he rather liked the sturdier, fat ones best—and these were the ones who were most amenable, for nobody else wanted them. The problem of competition for sex was sidestepped. He could use a commodity which was constantly on a buyer's market.

His family was prospering. His father was making money fast, in a society which as a whole was bewildered and confused. Most of his relatives were prospering, and they were year by year becoming more strongly intrenched. Their numbers were increasing by leaps and bounds. His sisters were being married off amid much celebration and rejoicing. The two fortunate young husbands were well on the way toward making money. The family had moved into a fine house, and now had two "Christian" servants. Eugene was to have an automobile when he went to college, and a liberal allowance. All this distracted him none at all. He continued to turn in his doubled assignments and to express his defiance.

He graduated from high school in the second tenth of his class, and in September entered a Midwestern university at which about eight hundred Jews were already enrolled in the undergraduate body. Nearly half of these came from the vicinity of New York, and Eugene knew several of them before entering college.

College has been essentially a repetition of high school. He found that his formula of depending upon quantity production worked as well in college as in high school. Eugene made no pretense of being brilliant. He was sound, not brilliant. He had a formula, a plan, and the capacity to live out a routine. He was a general, not a genius. Assigned a ten-page theme to write, he turned in twenty pages, typed by the typing bureau at so much a page. Assigned three laboratory experiments to turn in on a specific day, he did exactly six, and they went in on time, fully written up. It is in laboratory work that he really excels, for there his physical energy, his drive and aggressiveness, and his freedom from distractibility give him a great advantage. With Eugene every day is a strenuous competition, and he proposes never to be beaten if he can help it. He set his whole energy to the task of getting high grades, and for the most part he has got his high grades. One of his professors once said of him, "I personally despise that young man. In fact, I hate his guts, and I suspect that they are made of brass. I would have flunked him if he had given me half an excuse. But the fact is, he got an 'A' in my course. He did so much more work than anybody else, and did it so voluntarily, that I was forced to grade him in the highest group. I could not have avoided it except by cheating against him."

Eugene feels that he made one mistake in college. That was when he joined a fraternity, in his sophomore year. He complains that much of his energy has thereby been wasted in "arguing with fools," and that the total effect of all that the fraternity does and stands for is essentially a stupid distraction. His appearance at the fraternity house always results in violent altercation, he says, and now that he is no longer young, he has little time or energy for that sort of thing. During the past year he has visited his fraternity only rarely.

The sexual problem has offered no more difficulty at the university than in high school. He likes short, thickset, uninhibited Jewish girls (he calls them slender), and fortunately the supply of these on the campus well exceeds the demand. All told, there are no less than nine of Eugene's known relatives now attending the university. Five of these are women. Eugene has had a new automobile each year at college. During his sophomore year he killed a young woman in a smashup on the highway, but he was not prosecuted, and the incident appears to have had no effect on him. He did not at the time miss a single full day of college. He has been in one other accident in which his car was a total wreck, and also he has had minor crashes. He must get full value from his insurance money somehow, he says. It would be poor business to pay for insurance and not have any accidents.

At the end of the third year he started medical school, where we now find him. Since the medical courses emphasize laboratory work heavily, he is very much in his element. The early indication is that he will do excellently in his professional training. He plans to go into surgery, "where the big money is."

THE PROBLEM OF TREATMENT

This is not a case for therapy. This young man is securely in-trenched in his world, and in a sense he represents the aristocracy of one type of the new order in America. He is destined almost certainly to succeed in his profession, and by hard, honest work rather than by any short cut. He is sincere, he is sound in his methods, and he is shrewd. Without much doubt he will be rich, and he will probably procreate extensively. Numerous and power-ful is his clan already.

He has a somatorosis, in the sense that he is exceedingly ag-gressive, ruthless, and selfish. To many he is personally offensive. He has little internal restraint. He can be imagined as ordering the destruction of a million people or of a nation without qualm of conscience, if he should get the power. According to some of the (cerebrotonic) standards of the past, he is essentially uncivilized, and there are families in which he would not be a welcome son-in-law.

Yet Eugene's star is in the ascendancy. If he is pathological, then the society which produced him is pathological. For he has been true to his own nature. His somatotonic predominance is natural and in keeping with his structural make-up. Under any circumstances he must needs have been somatotonic, although under other circumstances the manifestations would have been different. Probably the ratio between manifest and latent somato-tonia would have been a very different one a few generations ago.

Shortness of stature, in a person predominantly somatotonic, seems often to precipitate a more or less vigorous striving in the direction of manifest overexpression of that component. The most loudly overaggressive people are usually short, and they are of course somatotonic. But shortness of stature alone produces no such reaction if the individual is not constitutionally somatotonic.

What would such a person as Eugene have been like in a society which vigorously restrained him through externally applied controls? Doubtless a study of the personalities of many of Eugene's ancestors for centuries past would answer this question. Some of these people have probably seethed with hate and with forcibly suppressed fury for most of their lives. But they did not, in all probability, become thereby the less somatotonic. Their somatotonia may have been more latent, and less manifest. Among a people who have inbred as closely as have the Jews, we should scarcely expect that a few score of generations would greatly alter the primary components.

We fall back once more to the extremely perplexing question of how to treat somatotonia, the component of aggression. The answer tacitly postulated in the still incomplete experiment of democracy is to encourage it, let it blossom, and hope that in some manner which is not yet understood, in the process of blossoming it will mature and mellow, and will gradually become civilized. Some of us are willing to fight for democracy just because we don't want our experiment interrupted.

In the meantime we know well enough that we shall never understand how to control war or any other socially disintegrative process until we understand the constitutional roots of somatorosis. Social psychiatry and individual psychiatry must become essentially a single concept before cogency or effectiveness can adhere in either. The postulation of a descriptive frame of reference common to social and individual psychology is the central problem of modern life. In the meantime there seems to be nothing in particular to do about Eugene.

5. GABRIEL: *A Comfortable Somatotonic Personality*

SUMMARY

Gabriel at 30 is a vigorous, healthy young man who stands a little over six feet tall and weighs 240 pounds. He is well proportioned, with broad shoulders and a deep, tremendous chest. Although he has recently put on about 30 pounds, the fat is well distributed. There is no conspicuous deposit in any one place. He looks sleek, shapely, and well fed. The head is large and the face is both broad and long, with level, widely spaced gray-blue eyes. The large mouth is straight and firmly molded. There is the beginning of a double chin.

Born on a small farm not far from Philadelphia, Gabriel was the second of six children. There was a brother two years older, and four younger ones. The father deserted at about the time the last child was born, and the maternal grandfather then came to live with the family and help on the farm, which had belonged in the maternal family.

From earliest days Gabriel appears to have had a good time. He has always been vigorous and jolly. Both he and his older brother were strong for their ages. Between them it is said that they did a man's work almost as soon as they could walk. Each of the six children has grown up and has so far done well in life. Gabriel went to a rural school, worked on a neighbor's farm all through high school, earned hs way through college, got married, taught school for two years, and then went to a seminary for three years. Mental tests show his IQ to be about 108. He is now a minister in a rural Pennsylvania community where his influence is both extensive and healthful. He has a farm of his own, four children, and "the best small herd of Holsteins in the county." He is not just a preacher, it is said, but is the best and most popular young pastor that the community has known within the memory of its oldest inhabitants.

TEMPERAMENTAL PATTERN
Viscerotonia:

1. *Relaxation* (5). He is both relaxed and relaxing to other people. There is no suggestion of flaccidity, but he enjoys his relaxation.

He sits down and stretches out as if he liked it. There is never a sign of strain in his face, and there is no tenseness in his body. It is a body which in a muscular and postural sense is always ready for action.

2. *Love of Physical Comfort* (4). There is a great love of comfort, and a remarkable capacity to enjoy comfort. Yet this trait does not interfere with routines. Gabriel is a hard worker. He gets things done. The love of comfort is strong within him, but does not disarrange his order of values.

3. *Slow Reaction* (4). Speech and movement are deliberate. There is no jerkiness. He has a drawl which is irritating to cerebrotonic people. But the general reaction to physical circumstance is adequately fast. He is a good driver of automobiles, and a fairly good (lumbering) boxer and tennis player. Respiration and heart rate are about average. Sexual appetite is probably a little slower than average.

4. *Love of Eating* (5). This trait is marked. He eats enormously, and with the gusto of a deep appreciation of food. His wife says, "He all but wags his tail when he eats." Much of his conversation bears on eating. He loves to cook, especially outdoors. There is a strong tendency to overeat. He eats fast, however. There is no prolonging of the eating process, or lingering at table.

5. *Socialization of Eating* (5). He is sentimental about eating with people, and loves to have company at table. It is of great importance to him to have his family all together at mealtime. The business of saying grace is more than a perfunctory habit. But the sacrament of eating does not interfere much with his other routines.

6. *Pleasure in Digestion* (5). He loves to sit and digest. Elimination is a pleasure, especially with the Sunday paper. A few good belches after a rich meal are among the good things of life. He knows nothing of constipation, and thinks that the indigestibility of mince pie and the like is all imagination.

7. *Love of Polite Ceremony* (4). Gabriel follows the social amenities with singular faithfulness. He loves to do things in the gracious and orderly manner. Yet he is a direct person, and over-politeness is offensive to him. He follows the ceremonies and

rituals of the church at least with tolerance, and he is a conservative in politics.

8. *Sociophilia* (5). Wherever he is, he is a center of social life.
His tremendous energy and buoyancy and physical exuberance
make him one kind of natural leader. He loves to be surrounded
by friends, especially by women and children. Yet he dislikes
cities, and frequently insists upon an evening or a whole day of
isolation in his study. His sociophilia does not divert him from his
work.

9. *Indiscriminate Amiability* (4). Sincere general amiability and
natural warmth are unquestioned. He is at his best in the face to
face relationship with people. Yet he never slobbers on people.
His warmth is not offensive (not viscerotic).

10. *Greed for Affection and Approval* (4). He likes to have social
approval, and obviously warms up to affection like a cat to having his fur rubbed. Social approval is one of the good things in
life. Yet there is also independent strength in this man, and below
the surface of fellowship are reservoirs of energy which under
sufficient provocation might well find expression even in the face
of disapproval. Somatotonia is in the end stronger than viscerotonia.

11. *Orientation to People* (4). He knows everybody, and what
everybody stands for. His insight into people is good. In a minor
sense, he knows where his bread is buttered. Yet there is in him
a deep independence of individuals. He does not seek to adapt
himself to the will or desire of influential persons with whom he is
not in essential agreement. He is in the final analysis the kind of
man who puts "principles" first and personalities second.

12. *Evenness of Emotional Flow* (5). Emotional life is well sustained and is on the whole even. There are few periods of emotional depression. There is an essential evenness of affective outlook. But on rare occasions the storm does break. He has been
known to lose his temper.

13. *Tolerance* (4). Superficially there is an easygoing toleration
both of people and of circumstances. Gabriel rarely finds it necessary to express irritation. Indeed, few of the common irritations
of life reach him. Yet he is far from tolerant of what he calls

"evil," or of human weakness at large. With respect to institutions he is at times almost a crusader.

14. *Complacency* (3). He has a healthy optimism but there is little real complacency, either about his own life or about affairs in general. There is dissatisfaction with his own achievement, and a deep disquietude concerning the general human picture.

15. *Deep Sleep* (4). Sleep is deep and going to sleep is easy. There has never been any insomnia. He tosses about, however, and "sleeps vigorously," as he does most other things. There is no sign of the limp relaxation of a predominantly viscerotonic person. Snoring is loud but irregular. There are times when he does not snore at all—just enough of these times to hold out the alluring hope to his wife that the habit might be overcome.

16. *The Untempered Characteristic* (3). There is no flabbiness. This is a purposeful man. He is determined upon a course of life, and has the drive and resolution to carry out his purposes. However, at times he becomes a little slobbery and pointless in his personal relationships.

17. *Smooth, Easy Communication of Feeling* (5). This man expresses feeling easily. He does not often give way to overt emotionality, and in crises he remains practical, effective and calm. His feelings are not always easy to read. He can be inscrutable. But he is rarely misunderstood to his disadvantage, and by everyone he is credited with being warmhearted.

18. *Relaxation and Sociophilia under Alcohol* (5). There is a singular fondness for hard cider, and there has been some conflict over other alcoholic beverages. He has now compromised on wine, of which he is very fond. With a little alcohol he warms up remarkably. All sign of consciousness of being a minister vanishes, and he becomes a hale and hearty fellow, full of eloquence and full of energy, perhaps a little more of the latter than of the former.

19. *Need of People when Troubled* (4). The primary reaction is probably somatotonic, but he does depend heavily upon talking over problems with those whose judgment he respects. When perplexed or in doubt he never makes a major decision without discussing it fully with somebody.

20. *Orientation toward Childhood and the Family* (5). The tie-up with family is strong. There is much sentimentality, superficially at least, over the mother-child relationship. Rapport with young children is easy and natural. The "mothering impulse" toward people is strong. But there is also strong orientation toward the activities of youth.

Somatotonia:

1. *Assertiveness of Posture and Movement* (5). The trunk is nearly always held upright, and the head is erect. The arms are flung vigorously about in walking. This is a body which, although well relaxed, is always ready for action.

2. *Love of Physical Adventure* (5). This trait is probably stronger than the history of its manifest expression reveals. Gabriel loves to hunt, to explore, and to climb mountains. Also he loves horses and automobiles, and he would like to have an airplane if he could afford it. He has a passion for getting out week ends and "roughing it" with a tent and campfire. But as a youth he was never able to do many of these things, for he was too busy earning his way.

3. *The Energetic Characteristic* (6). Energy is tremendous, except for brief periods of laziness and overeating. This man can keep at his farm work from dawn until dark, and then spend a long evening on his sermons without any apparent fatigue. He likes facetiously to quote a parishioner who once said of him, "That young preacher is the best manure-spreader we ever had in our pulpit."

4. *Need of Exercise* (6). Gabriel loves exercise, but his inclinations turn more toward work and "doing things around the place" than toward exercise as such. He likes to saw up a cord of wood or plow a field. In college, and particularly in seminary, the long periods of physical idleness irritated him. He likes to be up at dawn and "get half a day's work done before breakfast."

5. *Love of Dominating* (5). He will not for long remain in a social situation without dominating it. But he is not particularly aware of any desire to be important. The burden of most of his sermons is humility and appreciation of what is common and lowly, but he preaches in as unhumble a manner as may be.

Preaching is one of his main avenues for expressing the desire to dominate. Yet he is in no sense domineering. He dominates his home, but there is no straining in the role.

6. *Love of Risk* (4). This trait is manifested in Gabriel's moments of somatotonic abandon. He loves to ski on steep hills, and he likes to drive a car at its fastest speed. He would like dangerous mountain climbing. His recreational reading has been almost limited to stories of adventure. But in his routine life he is conservative. He does no petty gambling, although the stock market is his principal interest in the newspaper. He manipulates his few hundred dollars' worth of stocks with a zest which does not spring entirely from love of money.

7. *Bold Directness of Manner* (6). His manner is boldly direct. He goes straight to the heart of a matter. There is no hemming and hawing about funerals, weddings and the like. When Gabriel takes hold of the situation, any embarrassment or uncertainty which may have been in the atmosphere vanishes.

8. *Courage for Combat* (5). Courage is unquestioned. But it is not a reckless courage, and the combativeness is chiefly potential (latent), not actual. This man has not been much of a fighter, perhaps because he has rarely had to fight. He is seldom bluffed, and he usually gets what he wants without fighting.

9. *Competitive Aggressiveness* (6). Although Gabriel is good-natured, and although his social contact is usually tactful, he is a notably determined man when in pursuit of what he wants. He is on the whole successfully aggressive. There is no sign of the strained aspect of compensatory aggression.

10. *Psychological Callousness* (4). At times this trait is conspicuous. When off-guard, Gabriel sometimes becomes boorishly insensitive to other people. At such times no hint will break through to his awareness, and he then causes his wife considerable distress. But he has learned to guard against this characteristic and under ordinary circumstances he manifests lavish verbal solicitude toward all.

11. *Claustrophobia* (6). Marked. He loves to be in the open, whether indoors or out. Windows and doors are made, he says, to let in air, not to shut it out. He dislikes restraining clothing,

would prefer never to wear a collar or tie, and loves to swim nude. He always sleeps nude.

12. *Freedom from Squeamishness* (5). Gabriel was always the official pig killer around the farm, and he has been known to undertake similar chores during his present incumbency. The vocabulary of his profession might mislead one to underestimate him in this trait, but he is a good executive. Also he is no modernist when it comes to the routine spanking of his own children.

13. *Unrestrained Voice* (5). This trait is still pronounced, although in response to pressure from his wife, some effort has been made to modulate his unusually resonant, eloquent voice. He hates to prepare sermons, but he loves to preach, and once launched on his favorite theme (the rights of "labor"), his voice booms forth like the new church organ.

14. *Spartan Indifference to Pain* (5). He has always taken minor injuries lightly, although he has never had a serious one. He can stand in the coldest shower without flinching. But he does not like the dentist's drill.

15. *General Noisiness* (5). This is a noisy person. When he comes into the house, everybody knows it. His laugh is like a mild clap of thunder. A friend says of him that he has the noisy clatter of an honest man. He breathes deeply and belches with gusty appreciation. One of his few vanities concerns his unsurpassed flatulative power.

16. *Overmaturity of Appearance* (5). He appears to be about 35. The face already shows the inflexible set of early mesomorphic middle age.

17. *Horizontal Mental Cleavage* (6). This is a conspicuously objective, externally focused mind. Gabriel does not inquire into the roots of his own motivation, and if he dreams, he is hardly aware of it. In an experiment in psychology, he was one of the best subjects for hypnosis. His rationalization is virtually always based on objective data, rarely on subjective statement.

18. *Assertiveness and Aggression under Alcohol* (5). He becomes both more sociable and more aggressive with alcohol, although he often preaches against "the saloon." He loves to drink hard cider or wine when there is farm work to be done—says it makes the hay lighter to pitch. He will not touch "hard liquor," but once

when Mexican whisky was substituted for the hard cider in his jug, he thought it was pretty good cider. This sort of trick has been played on him so many times that he has been suspected of not being always fooled.

19. *Need of Action when Troubled* (5). A primary reaction to perplexity or to a knotty problem is to tackle the woodpile. Sometimes he goes on a trip. Usually he sooner or later talks it over with somebody. He rarely goes off alone to think.

20. *Orientation toward Goals and Attitudes of Youth* (5). He loves to talk about keeping young with the youth of the community. Recently he has taken up tennis strenuously. He is jealous of his prowess as a long-distance swimmer. One of his favorite sermons is on the youth movement. He thinks that youth is by far the best time of life.

Cerebrotonia:

1. *Physical Restraint, Tightness* (2). There is usually complete freedom from cerebrotonic tension in the face and in the body as a whole. But when theological matters come up for discussion, the mouth tightens up a little, and a slightly anxious look appears in the eyes. Gabriel is not fond of theological discussion. He thinks there should be a sharp separation between theology and the ministry.

2. *Physiological Overresponse* (2). There is no clamping down of sphincters, and no serious interference with digestion in the face of any emotional situation. He retains his composure, externally at least, at all times. He is not at all bothered by mosquitoes. He has hay fever, however, and every year makes quite a fuss about it. His vocal resonance is unimpaired by any emotional situation. He has had most of the contagious diseases, as well as several infections. Basal metabolic rate, plus 4.

3. *Overly Fast Reactions* (2). Reaction is in general a little on the slow side. There are no signs of the overfast reactions of cerebrotonia. Social adaptation is entirely free from cerebrotonic fluster or confusion.

4. *Love of Privacy* (1). Gabriel does not like solitude. He becomes truly unhappy only when he is forced to be alone. He has never

felt the need of a room of his own (or a bed of his own). His sociability is well sustained.

5. *Mental Overintensity, Hyperattentionality* (2). Traces of this trait can be seen only on those rather rare occasions when he is caught in an intellectual discussion. Usually the tide of conversation can readily be turned, but there are two or three people in the parish (intellectuals) who mercilessly snipe at him in this respect. On such occasions he manifests signs of jumpiness and of confusion.

6. *Secretive Restraint of Feeling* (1). Gabriel's *persona*, which is for him a successful one, is founded upon living out an antithesis to this trait. He holds nothing back. There is no secretiveness in him. His life is an open book.

7. *Self-conscious Motility of the Eyes and Face* (2). In the main his face is impassive, but he has a characteristic set smile, and there is a responsive twinkle about the eyes. The smile breaks slowly and involves a drawing back of the whole lower facial musculature. The eyebrows lift with the smile, and the whole effect is that of open candor and sincerity, traits which Gabriel indeed possesses.

8. *Sociophobia* (2). He loves the small social gathering, which he dominates. Here he finds unquestionably his best fulfillment. But the very large group, with its impersonal agglutination, repels him a little. His sociophilia is highly personal. It is warm and direct.

9. *Inhibited Social Address* (2). He is ordinarily a paragon of social composure. But he is secretly somewhat sensitive about what he regards as his intellectual shortcomings for the ministry, and he squirms in his collar a little at meetings of his board of deacons and the like. His characteristic social address is almost completely free from inhibitory interference.

10. *Resistance to Habit and Poor Routinizing* (1). He lives a remarkably well-routinized life, with respect to all of the essential biological processes, and when in college succeeded in so organizing his program that he not only carried a full-time job most of the time but made a good record as well. All this in spite of the fact that he is far from brilliant in the academic sense.

11. *Agoraphobia* (1). A clear antithesis to this trait. He has a highly developed claustrophobia (trait S-11).

12. *Unpredictability of Attitude* (2). Almost an antithesis to this trait. Gabriel clings to his established pattern with tenacious and trustworthy predictability. Yet he does succeed in fitting and rationalizing his attitudes to his own needs (witness his attitude toward alcohol).

13. *Vocal Restraint and Restraint of Noise* (2). Gabriel always overshoots vocally. When slightly stimulated by a social gathering, he unleashes his voice and it ranges out beyond all bounds, like a headstrong bird dog. But he has learned the trick of modulating the voice for emotional effect in praying or saying grace, in describing mother love or the like, and this lends him a powerful weapon.

14. *Hypersensitivity to Pain* (2). The antithetical trait of Spartanism is well manifested except for one or two minor inconsistencies. He is peculiarly sensitive to irritation within his mouth (gums, tongue, teeth) and experiences a good deal of difficulty with the dentist.

15. *Poor Sleep Habits* (2). His sleep habits are excellent, but he does not quite present an antithesis to this trait. He sleeps soundly in the early part of the night and becomes wakeful toward morning. He loves to be up early, and cannot understand others who do not.

16. *Youthful Intentness of Appearance* (2). Almost an antithesis. He looks mature, and older than he is. Only in the twinkling eye, when seen from close up, is there anything suggesting this cerebrotonic trait.

17. *Vertical Mental Cleavage* (1). Gabriel presents an antithesis to the overly subjective tendency. He has his feet planted firmly on the ground, and he knows the direction in which he wants to move. He is highly objective in his thinking. He has poor rapport with his own remoter consciousness and therefore his intuition and subjective evaluations show poverty of insight.

18. *Resistance to Alcohol* (2). He has a superficially active conscience about alcohol which causes him to use it restrainedly. When he does use it, the reaction shows little trace of cerebrotonic influence, but is both viscerotonic and somatotonic.

19. *Need of Solitude when Troubled* (2). The predominant re-action is somatotonic, with a viscerotonic secondary tendency. His verbal response to the direct query is simply that he always consults God. This might imply a cerebrotonic reaction, and the point well illustrates the necessity of looking deeper than the verbal response. In this instance, Gabriel "consults God" by do-ing something actively, or through the minds of other people, not through solitary communion.

20. *Orientation toward the Later Periods* (1). There is a painful shrinking away from the idea of growing (inactively) old, and there is beginning to be a somewhat frantic clutching at youth. Gabriel does not look forward to anything like intellectual mat-uration. He altogether dissociates from consciousness what Freud called the death instinct (horizontal dissociation).

Totals: Viscerotonia, 87; Somatotonia, 104; Cerebrotonia, 34.
Index of Temperament, $4^2\text{-}5^2\text{-}1^2$.

PHYSICAL CONSTITUTION (at age 21)
Age 21, Ht. 72.0, Wt. 202, Somatotype $4^2\text{-}5^2\text{-}1$ (4-6-1, 4-6-1, 5-5-1, 5-5-1, 5-5-1). g 2.6, t 2.0, d 12.

This is a massive, powerful physique, of tall stature. Meso-morphy is the primary component, with endomorphy a fairly close second, and ectomorphy is at a minimum. The primary pre-dominance (mesomorphy over endomorphy) is a relatively narrow one, but the secondary predominance (endomorphy over ecto-morphy) is overwhelming. There is but one dysplasia, an increase of mesomorphy in Regions *I* and *II*, together with a decrease of endomorphy in these regions. The arms, and the body below the diaphragm, present an unusual extreme in massiveness.

Total dysplasia is 12 (endomorphy, 6; mesomorphy, 6; ecto-morphy, 0). Gynandromorphy is high for this somatotype, and it is almost entirely primary. The hips are wide. The general out-line of the lower body is rather feminoid, and the waist is a little high. But there are no secondary characteristics of gynandromorphy. The features of the face, structure of the extremities, cutaneous texture, and the abundant secondary hair are all strongly masculine. The *t* component is slightly above the general average.

The entire body is strong, although in comparison with the huge massiveness of the other regions, Regions *I* and *II* appear relatively slender. Such a physique will take on weight tremendously in middle life unless held under a strict dietary regime, but the expansion of the trunk will be almost uniform. There will be no pot belly or bay window. Already Gabriel has put on 40 pounds since the somatotype photograph was taken nine years ago. He could easily put on another 50 within the next few years. Indeed there is some likelihood that he will do so. He is strong enough to carry it. This is the kind of physique which could readily be fattened up to 400 pounds or more if the individual were to lose all desire to control his weight. (Many of the excessively heavy Negro and Jewish women who may be seen on the streets of Harlem and Manhattan are 5-5-1's or 4-6-1's. Endomorphic physiques with a low mesomorphy grow excessively fat very early in life, before adolescence, and they stay that way, but with their weak musculature only a certain amount of weight can be carried. Therefore their "ceiling" is a rather well-defined one. But when the total strength of the first two components reaches 10, as against a minimum of ectomorphy, there is almost no limit to the potentialities for fattening.)

Gabriel's head is large and slightly dolichocephalic. The face is extremely large, both long and broad. All of the features are of generous proportions. The nose is long and straight, with a high, broad bridge. The forehead is high. The big ears lie well back against the head (they show no ectomorphic flaring out at the pinnae). The gray-blue eyes are widely spaced and they seem a little small, in so massive a head. The mouth is broad, the jaw well developed and rounded, rather than square, and the thick, sturdy neck seems short. The medium brown hair is of relatively fine texture for this somatotype. It is straight and thick. Bodily hair is rather sparse.

The trunk as a whole is long, but not disproportionately so, for the legs are also long. Posture is very upright and straight.

The general curve of the back is distinctly mesomorphic (low, sharp lumbar angle). The hands and feet are large, being both broad and long. The genitalia are rather small, although normal.

CLINICAL HISTORY

Birth was normal and comparatively easy, although this was a large baby, weighing a little over 9 pounds. He was the second pregnancy and the second living child. The mother states that he was a most satisfactory infant, vigorous and demanding, but of excellent general health, and his early weight gain was rapid. He was 10 pounds over average weight at 1 year of age. The most notable thing about him at this early period was the tremendous power of his voice. He could "roar like a lion in full cry," his mother says. But he cried only when he wanted something. He was never a fretful baby. He was breast fed for only two weeks and was then put on a formula.

During the first three years Gabriel had the usual run of children's diseases. The mother thinks that he had "them all," although none very seriously. The worst was whooping cough. There has never been a serious illness since childhood, excepting appendicitis and appendectomy at 18. He has, however, suffered somewhat from chronic sinusitis, and he occasionally has protracted "chest colds" which leave him with a cough for a time. He does not have the acute, cerebrotonic head cold which rages violently for a few days and then subsides. The sinusitis bothers him most in the summer, seems to be associated in some way with an allergy, and especially inconveniences him with respect to swimming. He is extraordinarily fond of swimming, but this appears to stir up his sinusitis. He has had a number of minor injuries, but never a serious infection from any of them. During the past ten years there has been almost perfect health, except for sinusitis.

Teeth are rather soft. There have been many fillings, and two extractions of third molars. The teeth are well spaced and of average size. There has always been a moderately unpleasant breath odor (his wife says).

Adolescence began at 13 and proceeded rather uneventfully. He became aware of ejaculation at 15, but was not greatly concerned about it. Sexual intercourse did not occur until after marriage, at 22.

BACKGROUND
Paternal:

The father, who has not been heard from during the past fifteen years, was a native of upper New York state and had been to college and studied accounting. He had moved into the Pennsylvania community where Gabriel's mother lived, only a year or two before meeting the latter. He had a job as adjuster of some sort for the railroad. This man is described as of medium height and of rather "stocky," probably endomorphic, physique. He was quiet, kindly, and apparently of a weak or retiring disposition. He left the family when Gabriel was about 6, although he made financial contributions for several years afterward. Gabriel does not remember him very well, and thinks that the mother (who was physically the more powerful of the two) probably made life pretty hard for him.

Nothing is known of the paternal grandparents except that they were "good American stock," the grandfather being a storekeeper in a small city. Whether or not either is living is not known, and nothing is known of their medical history.

The father had few interests. He seems to have been decidedly unhappy in his marriage, and probably also in his work. The mother is not communicative about him, although she is highly cooperative in every other respect. The pair met at church, at a time when the mother, a large, muscular young woman, had been teaching school for several years. She was a few years the older of the two. Gabriel, who has had a smattering of Freudian psychology, is now very sympathetic toward both parents. He suggests that this father, seeking a mother substitute, "put his neck into a monkey trap," and after some years of fruitless struggle fled, leaving the neck behind.

Maternal:

The mother is now a tremendous woman. She has less endomorphy than Gabriel, but may possibly be a 3-7-1. She is about five feet nine inches tall, weighs 210, and has the same broad,

mesomorphic features that Gabriel shows. She had a happy childhood, being the third child among five on a small, fairly prosperous farm a few miles out of Philadelphia. Her stock is Pennsylvania Dutch on both sides, with a considerable infiltration of
other old American stock. She was active, and was rated as useful
as a boy on the farm. At about 12 she became fat, although she
had previously been slender (mesomorphs who have any endomorphy at all seem always to go through this early endomorphic
preview just before adolescence—girls especially). After adolescence, her slim figure returned for a time. She went to the local
high school, where she was a leader and did well enough to win
a scholarship to a state normal school. After graduating from
Normal School, she returned to her own community, taught school
for six years, and lived at home. Gabriel's father was probably
the first knight to spur his white horse into tournament for her
hand. He was 23 and she was 27 when the two were married.
They lived for a year in the city, but after the birth of the first
child returned to the maternal ancestral farm, where she has
lived ever since. She virtually runs the farm, and she does it well.

The maternal grandmother died at 71 of "high blood pressure,"
but the grandfather, at 86, still gets around. He is slender and
wiry. His wife was heavy and sturdy, as she is remembered. Among
the immediate relatives no constitutional diseases are known
unless apoplexy and arthritis should be so classified. There is no
cancer, tuberculosis, diabetes or mental disease.

Siblings:

1. Brother, now 32. A man of medium height, mesomorphic,
   probably between a 2-6-2 and a 3-5-3. The brother and
   Gabriel were close companions all through childhood and
   youth, the older boy apparently being slightly the stronger
   and more athletic of the two. When in high school Gabriel
   was the regular catcher on the baseball team, and his brother
   was the star pitcher. The two virtually ran the farm, between
   them, after the father left, and up to the time when both
   went away to college. This brother now has a state job as
   stock inspector. He went to an agricultural college, married
   young, and has a home in a suburb. It is said that he is con-

templating moving back to the old family farm and "fixing it up."

2. Gabriel.

3. Sister, now 28. She has almost her mother's physique, is a practical nurse, and is highly regarded in the community. She makes her home at the old farm, goes to church every Sunday, and keeps a weather eye peeled for what may turn up.

4. Sister, now 27. About a 4-4-3, and a good PPJ. She married at 20, has three children, a substantial young farmer for a husband, and has gained 40 pounds since marriage. Both of these sisters look up to their brothers with pride.

5. Brother, now 25. He is a lawyer, having graduated from the State University and attended an Eastern law school. He is about a 3-6-2, tall and full of energy. Great achievement is expected of him. He is going to run for State legislature next year.

6. Brother, now 24. This youth appears to be an ectomorph, possibly a 3-3-4. He is relatively frail, and shorter than Gabriel by two or three inches. But he has excellent health. He is a graduate student in a Midwestern university, with a good record but very perplexed as to what to do with himself.

GENERAL LIFE STORY

First 6 Years:

Gabriel had a happy childhood. He talked and walked at about 12 months. The older brother was his companion in all things. Both were vigorous and healthy, and learned easily to do things with their hands. They had air rifles at 5 years of age, and won renown for prowess at sparrow hunting and rat hunting. The family farm abounded in both of these varieties of game, as well as in rabbits, skunks, woodchucks, chipmunks and other wild animals. Gabriel had a .22 rifle at 7.

The two boys were doing regular chores by the time Gabriel was 5, he says. He was milking two cows at 6. Also it was his special function to feed the hens and collect the eggs. Yet there was time for adventure. Meanwhile the father is a very indistinct figure. He was often away throughout the week, and the maternal grandfather appears to have usurped the place of the real father. Many were the long tramps and fishing excursions on which the grandfather took the two boys. There seems to have been virtually no quarreling between the youngsters. Gabriel was rather fat and good-natured. The brother was stronger, and was on the way to becoming a good athlete. The two have never had a serious quarrel, so far as either can remember. "Who could ever quarrel with that fat, good-natured horse," is the modern comment of the brother.

The mother appears to have been a most practical, realistic person who kept the boys healthy and well fed, and washed them on Saturday night. Sunday morning they were marched to church, as soon as they were old enough to walk that far. Sunday afternoon the grandfather usually took over. Gabriel recalls that when the second sister and the later brothers were born, the mother's routines were interrupted "only for a few days at the most."

Sexuality appears to have been taken for granted from the earliest memory. Gabriel always observed this phenomenon with humorous interest. The grandfather chuckled about it, especially about the roosters and the hens. Gabriel thinks now that much wisdom is to be acquired from the barnyard, and much good humor. His own sexuality does not seem to have played any particular role in his life during this early period.

Age 6 to 14. School:

By the time Gabriel was old enough to go to school, the first sister (then 4) was old enough to relieve him of some of his duties with the hens, so he graduated to the pigs. School was a full mile away, reached by a path through the woods, and then a little distance along a country road, crossing two brooks. Only about sixty children attended this school, which included the first four grades. Nearly all of the families represented were well known to one another, and the beginning of school was far from a traumatic experience. Probably two-thirds of the children who met at school had already met at Sunday school, and both of the teachers also taught Sunday school.

From all that can be gathered, Gabriel had an excellent time at school, from the first day to the last, four years later, when he transferred to a larger school three miles away. At the age of 8 he rode a bicycle to school, as did his brother.

When a number of boys come together to be associated for some time, certain ones always stand out immediately—the leaders, the weaklings, the braggarts, and so on. Others remain for a while in the background, revealing their true *personae* gradually as time goes on. Still others remain enigmas to the end, perhaps to the end of time. A few are seen to be perplexed, confused, self-contradictory. From Gabriel's present story, and that of three others who knew him at the time, he was a round-faced, good-natured, apple-cheeked, oversized and energetic youngster who was a sort of general favorite. He was not pugnacious, was never much of a fighter, and seems not to have had much occasion to fight. Yet he was aggressive, was always in the midst of what was going on, and was usually among the first volunteers in any enterprise, from supplying popcorn balls for the Christmas festival to fishing Percy Joesting's tomcat out of Miss Bromsen's well. He had the happy gift of being aggressive without being disliked. Gabriel believes that in all his life he has never had an enemy, and he does not recall the experience of having another person wish him ill.

It was never reported that this boy was brilliant, but he always did his school work faithfully and satisfactorily. At the end of four years in his first school he was advanced to the larger county school. There appears to have been no regret at the transfer, and no particular nostalgia for what was now past, pleasant as Gabriel believes the latter to have been. He carried the same abounding energy and overwhelming optimism to the new school, and was soon as well adapted in that atmosphere as in the previous one. Four years later he did the same thing again. High school was as much fun as grade school. And college was not essentially different. Graduate school and the seminary were met in the same manner, and still later, his parish work. He had a pattern of personality which, always the same, opened for him all the doors he tried to open, and, perhaps better than that, protected him from wanting to open any which he could not. Gabriel has what might truly be called a healthy personality.

At 6 this boy had been chubby. Thereafter, he had lengthened out considerably, and although he must have remained chunky, he was considered rather slim until about age 12, when he suddenly grew fat. During the greater part of his attendance at the county school (grades 5 through 8), he was called by the nickname "Fat." This never displeased him. He didn't mind being fat. But after adolescence, by the time he was 14, the fat seemed to disappear. He was now shooting up again, and he grew rapidly between 14 and 16, then soon filling out to the massive proportions seen in his somatotype photograph, which was taken at 21.

Gabriel was well aware of sexuality in himself long before adolescence. Many times he and his brother had discussed these problems, often comparing their own relative Priapic achievements, and there had been similar comparisons at the swimming hole. Gabriel did not like these experiences very well. For one thing, his was among the lesser endowments. This did not really interfere much with his enjoyment of the swimming hole, for he was an excellent natural swimmer (he could float for an indefinite period, which was something few others could do). But he was singularly receptive at an early age to the idea that sex was sinful, or at least was something to be ignored. No one ever molested him sexually, and no older boy ever took any particular liberty with him in that respect. He was not the kind. As for girls, he never became aware that there were girls in his environment who might be interested in sexual play, and he does not yet altogether believe that such was the case.

After 14:

Gabriel entered high school at 14, just getting over being fat, not yet acquainted with ejaculation, rather religious, and perfectly secure in his own strength and good will toward everybody. He was considered a normal, healthy boy, of the "cleaner, more moral sort." His family was prospering in a way. They had no money in particular, but they had a fine little farm. Some small financial settlement had been made by the father, who had now dropped out of the picture entirely. The grandmother was dead, but the grandfather was as active and beloved a companion as ever (still is). The mother was much happier, now that matters were all straightened out, and she was settled in as the real boss and manager of the farm. She once said, "I have had a perfect divorce, the happiest and most model divorce that anybody could desire." All six of the children were of excellent health, and they got along together. There was very little quarreling. The mother punished them soundly now and then, but only routinely—she never lost her temper. She was never really disobeyed. One look at her massive jaw and stern eye, and disobedience is out of the question. Her wrists and arms are as powerful as a man's. But she was impartial with her children, and today their loyalty to her is almost fanatical.

Gabriel was soon one of the big boys of the school, and although he was never quick enough to be a really good athlete, he was on the football team as a sophomore, and was regular catcher on the baseball team as a junior. He was president of his senior class, and upon graduation had saved $200, which he had earned by working half time on a neighboring farm. With this as a nucleus he went to college, graduating four years later with over a thousand dollars in the bank. He saved that amount from several sorts of odd jobs and summer jobs, in addition to paying his own way. The combination of a pleasing, optimistic personality, good health, and a tremendous somatotonic energy had worked out well. In college he did not try for athletics, but he was something of a social leader among what might be called the "YMCA crowd" of a decade ago.

His scholarship both in high school and college was good but not excellent. He was in about the middle of the second quarter in his college graduating class, having specialized in history and in religious education.

Gabriel had no sexual life in high school or college. In high school he "never went with girls," although he was popular and (except for the sophisticated and the intellectual ones—both less common then than now) he probably could have had his choice. He feels that he always had strong sexual interests, although from a comparative point of view this is to be doubted. At 15 the discovery of ejaculation stirred him up considerably, and he was for some time bothered with a strong desire to masturbate. He did masturbate a few times, but after earnest communion with Mr. G. he decided that this practice was sinful, and he "conquered" it. He believes that he has masturbated not more than a dozen times in his life. Once, after a high school dance, the girl he walked home with propositioned him, "or practically did." It was a warm moonlight night, and they sat on the brow of a little ridge, among new-mown hay, at the edge of an orchard. He pulled himself together, held a hurried consultation with Mr. G. and preached the girl a sermon. He is glad he resisted that temptation, for she was a pretty girl. Having resisted her, it was easy, later, to resist lesser temptation.

In college, Gabriel developed a close attachment to a very spiritual-minded young lady who was active in YWCA work. In spite of his remarkably heavy program he succeeded in seeing her nearly every day for the better part of two years. She was the first girl he kissed. He remembers now that because of her "buck teeth" and widely gaping lips, "she wasn't much to kiss." In the end tragedy stalked this romance. The girl took some courses in psychology and lost her faith. She decided not to marry Gabriel. They broke up in the spring of his senior year. But Gabriel was not one to cry for long over spilt milk. Within three months he got himself married to a more buxom, "finer, truer-hearted girl" than his old love had ever thought of being. Such is the power of recovery in the noncerebrotonic mind.

Gabriel then taught in a country high school for two years, after which he was offered a scholarship for three years in one of the leading seminaries. The seminary treated him so well that during the three years he accumulated not only the degree, Bachelor of Divinity, but also three children. A fourth has since arrived.

At 27 this young man returned as an ordained minister to be pastor in the community immediately adjoining that in which he grew up. Within the past three years his influence and good reputation have grown steadily. He has bought one of the most attractive little farms in that section, and the farm gives every promise of future prosperity. His home has become a social center in which a large part of the fun and civic enterprise of the entire community is planned. His wife is about a 4-5-2, almost as healthy and energetic as Gabriel. Doubtless the four children are only a beginning. Gabriel puts very little theology into his sermons. He is a full-throated champion of "the working man," with whom he identifies himself. He preaches democracy, he says.

As for treatment, the problem appears rather to be one of emulation.

6. Hurleigh: *A Well Adapted Cerebrotonic Personality*

SUMMARY

Hurleigh at 29 is a lean, sensitive-faced young man of average stature, who walks with a stoop to his shoulders and a peculiar spring in his step. He might easily be mistaken for 22. His exceedingly fine-textured hair is almost blond. It is just lighter than light brown, and his eyes are as blue as the sky. His features are delicately chiseled, like the features in a cameo. There is a long wave in his hair. His grandfather was a famous Protestant Irish nobleman who fled to this country for political refuge.

This young man was born in Evanston, Illinois, where his father was an instructor in the university which is located there. Hurleigh was the second of three children. When he was 8 years old his father was taken off by a streptococcal throat infection, and the burden of the family was thrown upon the mother, who at once opened a small restaurant. This enterprise she has now kept running for twenty years, living and raising her family in a small frame house back of the restaurant.

Hurleigh's older sister is delicate and lives at home. The younger brother, a brilliant student, is now an intern in a hospital. Hurleigh was a frail child and boy. It was at one time thought that he lacked the strength to make his way in the normal competition of life. But when he went to school it was discovered that he was mentally bright to an unusual degree. He finished both grade school and high school at the head of his class and went to the State University where he likewise distinguished himself scholastically. Although frail, sensitive and squeamish by nature, he then put himself through medical school and turned to the specialty of endocrinology, where he gives promise of an important scientific career.

TEMPERAMENTAL PATTERN

Viscerotonia:

1. *Relaxation* (2). Externally he seems tense and under strain. He never appears to relax comfortably in the presence of others. The face is fine-drawn, the fingers are nervous, and respiration ap-

pears to be suppressed. The voice is constrained and it lacks resonance when strangers are present. Yet he can relax when alone or with intimates. He loves to sit on the end of his spine and to permit the entire body to droop, as if in lassitude.

2. *Love of Physical Comfort* (2). He likes to be comfortable, but this desire is relatively far down the list in his hierarchy of values. Comfort is always a secondary consideration. His natural choice is toward rather stern simplicity in furniture and in clothes, as in food. He dislikes luxuries. Yet within his simplicity of taste there is something of an eye for what is comfortable.

3. *Slow Reaction* (1). The reactions are lightning fast. He speaks so rapidly that he is hard to follow. He has fine coordination of movement, and his manipulations, as in adjusting laboratory apparatus, are exceedingly rapid. His intellectual reactions are perhaps relatively even faster.

4. *Love of Eating* (3). His ordinary custom is to spend five minutes at lunch, three minutes at breakfast and about ten minutes at supper. He will not as a rule eat where it is necessary to sit patiently and be waited upon. Yet he enjoys food greatly. He becomes excessively hungry, usually suddenly, and he has a voracious appetite, often astonishing others with the speed at which he can put away food. There are many foods he will not eat. In general, he loves only meat and protein.

5. *Socialization of Eating* (2). Almost an antithesis. He has a strong distaste for all ceremony, and for outward expression of "sentimentality." He prefers to eat alone or only with intimate friends. He says, "Eating in public is like doing one's toilet in public." Yet he has a good time when eating with friends.

6. *Pleasure in Digestion* (2). Digestion is on the whole fairly good, but he gives little attention to it. He never sits after a meal to enjoy digestive relaxation, and to him the feeling of a full stomach is more unpleasant than pleasant. "Elimination is of about the same order as shaving." There is mild constipation but this has never been a serious problem. Like nearly all medical people he has long since learned to avoid purgatives and to fit his routine to the normal cycle of his peristalsis rather than attempting the converse.

7. *Love of Polite Ceremony* (2). He has a strong dislike of propriety, and can generally be depended upon to offend respectability to some degree. His rationalization is that many of the primary shortcomings of society lie in lack of humor and imagination, and that these deficiencies in turn derive from overemphasis upon outward form in the social relationship. Yet Hurleigh is not personally discourteous.

8. *Sociophilia* (4). He has a wealth of Irish warmth to express, and in the face to face relationship, or with one or two intimate friends he becomes wholeheartedly convivial. He avoids total isolation, and although he frequently "retreats to refreshing solitude," he wants and needs to have a few people about. He has an inexhaustible supply of spicy, sexy or satirical stories, adaptable to any occasion and told with an offhand, rapid, dry flow of language which is highly effective among intellectual people.

9. *Indiscriminate Amiability* (2). His warmth of fellowship is conspicuous in the small group, but is sharply limited. He is not tolerant, and has little warmth for people who fall outside his circumscribed area of approval. Those who do not know him well often believe him to be harsh and ruthless.

10. *Greed for Affection and Approval* (2). He likes social approval, warms to it, and bathes in it when it is showered upon him. But there is little dependence upon it. Behind the expressed gratitude for appreciation and approval lies a primary defiance and a fine-tempered scorn for the opinions or plaudits of people. His mind is set upon a distant, and what he considers a better, objective than the approbation of contemporaries. Present approval is like the whipped cream on his pie. He likes it, but should he miss it he scarcely would stop to inquire the reason for its absence.

11. *Orientation to People* (3). He has a keen, accurate sense of evaluation of people in his environment. He knows where to go for what he wants, but he does not always get what he wants. He so manifestly scorns the fabric of social status and prestige that he inevitably offends many whose good will is interwoven within this fabric. He has many critics whom he has never met. Personalities who do not hold his primary respect mean little more to him than furniture.

12. *Evenness of Emotional Flow* (2). Nearly an antithesis. At times he shows an almost schizoid austerity of manner. At times there are violent outbursts of impatience, but these are rare. With the two or three people who are his most intimate friends, he maintains an essentially even emotional rapport.

13. *Tolerance* (2). On the face of the matter he seems to present an antithesis to this trait. He has no tolerance of weakness, and since he believes that human life is degenerate beyond recall, he is not essentially tolerant of it. Yet he is intellectually tolerant, and is searchingly critical of his own hypotheses.

14. *Complacency* (1). An extreme antithesis. There is no complacency in him, either concerning his own achievement or concerning life at large.

15. *Deep Sleep* (2). He has trouble in relaxing and going to sleep at night. Hates to go to bed. Often sleeps poorly. He has never been known to snore. Yet insomnia has not been an acute problem.

16. *The Untempered Characteristic* (1). The antithesis. The temper of Hurleigh's metal is extremely high. His purposes are clearly formed and they lie far remote from immediate biological purposes. He suggests steel which is overtempered, and therefore approaching brittleness.

17. *Smooth, Easy Communication of Feeling* (2). Superficially there is easy communication. His words flow freely in the ordinary situation, and feeling seems to flow with the words. But the communication of his real feeling is difficult. Concerning matters close to his heart, where he thinks important future relationships are at stake, he becomes as apprehensively tense and choked up as only an intelligent cerebrotonic can be.

18. *Relaxation and Sociophilia under Alcohol* (2). He is not fond of alcohol. Secretly he believes he dislikes it. But he pretends a liking for certain wines and he will join in a little with the noisiness and oxerexpressiveness which usually follow drinking. He always has a good racy story for the occasion.

19. *Need of People when Troubled* (1). When faced with trouble or perplexity he keeps it strictly to himself. In adversity he confides in no one, but seeks solitude for the answer to the difficulty.

20. *Orientation toward Childhood and the Family* (2). There is a deep affection for his father, whom he remembers as the noblest of men, and also for his mother. But there is no nostalgia for childhood. He believes that the family as an institution is "on the way out," and he himself expresses the intention of rearing no children.

Somatotonia:

1. *Assertiveness of Posture and Movement* (3). The posture of the body as a whole is not assertive. The shoulders are usually slumped and the head is forward, often as if "buried in thought." He rarely stands up to his full height. But his detailed movements are quick, direct, and sometimes truculently assertive. His eyes are sharp and penetrating. He has a way of looking directly and searchingly for an instant into people's faces, which often embarrasses or startles them.

2. *Love of Physical Adventure* (3). As a youth Hurleigh entered deeply into the spirit of athletic competition, and regarded himself as an outdoorsman. He has a secret ambition to fight a real duel with rapiers. He often fought bitterly as a boy. Yet physical adventure never was put high in his order of values. He never neglected intellectual pursuits for physical activities.

3. *The Energetic Characteristic* (4). In an impulsive sense he is energetic. He frequently undertakes tasks with intense energy, and he sometimes finishes what he starts. He has had the energy to make a first-rate academic record, both in the university and in medical school, the latter requiring persistent application to laboratory work of various kinds. Yet he lacks sustained physical energy. He tires rather easily, and frequently appears to be "worn out." He makes excellent use of just about all the energy that is physiologically available.

4. *Need of Exercise* (3). He likes to play tennis at times, and he loves to go off alone or with one or two companions on a brisk walk. Surprisingly enough, he is a fairly good boxer and fencer. All of these things he enjoys. He loves to skate. But he has never made a routine of exercise. He never goes to the gymnasium or swimming pool, merely for exercise. Sometimes he feels no need for muscular activity for weeks.

5. *Love of Dominating* (3). For the most part there seems to be little desire to dominate. Certainly he has no social ambition, and

no desire to be recognized as important. He has no craving for power in general. He would prefer to remain incognito. Yet he will not ordinarily maintain a friendship in which he is not dominant. There is little compromise in him. His social relationships are of the all-or-none nature.

6. *Love of Risk* (4). This trait is not dominant. He does not live recklessly, and he has never gambled. Yet in certain moods he loves danger. He is a great "jay walker," constantly walking among fast traffic. He loves guns, and is an expert shot, although he kills no game. Fencing is his favorite sport. On a whim he has been known to risk a fatal misunderstanding with one whom he loves.

7. *Bold Directness of Manner* (3). Under most circumstances he presents somewhat of an antithesis to this trait. Yet to some people he seems overbold. He is intellectually bold to a degree of ruthlessness, and may become disconcertingly curt and direct in social conversation or argument. In the presence of a person whom he particularly respects he is shy, almost furtive. With women whom he regards as desirable he is diffident, sometimes to an extreme.

8. *Courage for Combat* (5). Seen under ordinary circumstances he might appear low in this trait, but when fully aroused he can fight with a fierceness surpassed by few. He is sensitive to fear, in the sense that heart rate, respiration and voice are markedly affected even by slight emotion. In this physiological sense he is a coward. Yet when past a certain threshold of anger the agitation disappears and he becomes a cold fury. In the face of severe stress, Hurleigh seems able to fall back upon something like an emotional "second wind."

9. *Competitive Aggressiveness* (4). He sometimes appears more aggressive than he is, for in his manner he often overcompensates for inner sensitivity. He is aggressive with his intimate friends, and he is intellectually aggressive. Under some circumstances he is sexually aggressive. Yet on the whole he shrinks from social contacts, and those who know him well consider him shy.

10. *Psychological Callousness* (2). For the most part he presents an extreme antithesis to this trait, revealing the utmost sensitivity to people and to their respective needs. Yet his intolerance or impatience gets the better of him sometimes and he deliberately "prods" persons whom he considers tedious. In these latter moods he not infrequently makes bitter enemies.

11. *Claustrophobia* (3). He is variable in this respect. Generally he is more agoraphobic than claustrophobic. He likes to work in a small, closed study. He never sleeps or swims nude, and he is in no sense exhibitionistic. Yet at times he becomes expansive, he says, and then he has a strong desire to be out in the open, on the top of a hill, or out in the middle of a lake, away from stuffiness and the cramped life.

12. *Freedom from Squeamishness* (2). His lack of this trait constituted a hardship in medical work. He has fine sensibilities, and found the killing of experimental animals in the laboratory almost impossible for him. Yet he feels that he could kill a man with coolness and deliberation, if once he should make up his mind to do so.

13. *Unrestrained Voice* (2). In general, he suggests the antithesis. However, in the presence of a loud person whom he dislikes (and he nearly always dislikes loud people), he sometimes raises his voice in competitive altercation.

14. *Spartan Indifference to Pain* (4). He is probably more sensitive to pain, in the physiological sense, than the average person. But all his life he has lived up to the *persona* of a degree of Spartanism. He plunges into cold water and although he gasps and his body turns blue, he pretends to like it. The same is true of minor hurts sustained in fighting or in athletic competition. In high school he tried to play football, but was repeatedly injured or knocked out. He flinches violently under slight pain, but does not complain.

15. *General Noisiness* (2). He is ordinarily very quiet. Voice and the laugh are excellently controlled. He rarely closes doors insensitively or moves about noisily. He dislikes radios. Breathing is well suppressed as a rule. His cough is a suppressed one—never explosive. Only at rare intervals does he release the brakes and join in the normal noisiness of a group.

16. *Overmaturity of Appearance* (2). He looks distinctly younger than he is, especially at a little distance or in a photograph. As one looks at his face closely, however, a certain firmness of the mouth is seen, and there is almost a fierce set about the eyes.

17. *Horizontal Mental Cleavage* (2). In spite of remarkable intellectual attainment, and considerable external achievement, his is a singularly subjective, intensive mind. Hurleigh lives out almost a romantic phantasy of life, the essential difference between him and the schizophrene being perhaps that he makes real some of his dreams, and he has the intensity of energy to force his will upon his surroundings to a degree. He is an extreme romanticist, constantly analyzing his motives and interpreting his experience against a background of mythology and folklore.

18. *Assertiveness and Aggression under Alcohol* (2). The reaction to alcohol is essentially cerebrotonic, and he uses the drug sparingly. In a small slightly alcoholized group he shows about equal degrees of sociophilic and aggressive accentuation. He finds alcohol most fatiguing in aftereffect.

19. *Need of Action when Troubled* (2). Principally, he turns to solitude, never, apparently, to people. Sometimes he seeks the solitude of the outdoors or of the deep woods if he can reach the woods. This may perhaps involve a degree of need for action.

20. *Orientation toward Goals and Activities of Youth* (2). Primary orientation is strongly toward the achievement and affiliations of intellectual maturation. He lives for the future, not for the present. Yet he participates with what seems to be a secondary pleasure in some of the games of youth. He has little interest in money, social status, power, recognition or the like. He considers ordinary marriage a preoccupation of "morons."

Cerebrotonia:

1. *Physical Restraint, Tightness* (5). He is a rather tense person. Restraint is the predominant note in his makeup. The face shows tension, as do the hands especially, and breathing is closely restrained. The walk is generally restrained as if he were being careful not to wake someone.

2. *Physiological Overresponse* (5). He feels emotion strongly in the digestive tract. He becomes quickly nauseated with pain. Sphincter contraction (anal) is sometimes painful (often in the presence of complacent people—they give him anal pain, he says).

3. *Overly Fast Reactions* (5). The reaction time is very fast, in some respects extremely fast. His intellectual and verbal reactions are disconcertingly quick. The eye blink and superficial reflexes are almost abnormally fast. Yet he is not readily confused. He usually maintains his presence of mind fairly well, except when with superiors or women whom he admires. This trait is manifest but not sufficiently so to cause chronic confusion.

4. *Love of Privacy* (5). Hurleigh works best alone. He is a better loneworker than teamworker. He loves solitude and has found it difficult to room happily with anybody. He rarely seeks people out, but he maintains a few friendships which he appears to enjoy. Loneliness is rarely unpleasant for him.

5. *Mental Overintensity, Hyperattentionality* (5). He seems over-alert, and (from the ordinary point of view) too narrowly observant. He misses but little that goes on. Yet he is not hyper-attentional to the extent of being jumpy and ineffective in his response. He is apprehensive, but never to the point of stampede.

6. *Secretive Restraint of Feeling* (5). This trait is well developed. He feels that only "weak" people reveal their deepest feelings readily. (He is intolerant of viscerotonia.) Except for occasional bursts of wrath or anger, he virtually never "lets go" emotionally. Yet his stoicism is in one respect a concealed one, for he generally hides it beneath a superficial flow of language which to uncritical inspection often passes for affective participation.

7. *Self-conscious Motility of the Eyes and Face* (5). It is a singu-larly expressive face, especially in the fine play of the muscles about the eyes and mouth. This motility is never gross. The play of expression is delicate, like the faint rippling of a body of water in response to varying air currents. Much of this muscular play would be unnoticed unless one were watching for it. The face is tense, but not to the point of self-conscious confusion.

8. *Sociophobia* (4). This trait seems strongly manifest at times, but at other times Hurleigh appears to crave company. In certain moods he shrinks from any human contact at all. In other moods he hunts up his friends and behaves in a sociable manner. The two moods seem fairly well balanced.

9. *Inhibited Social Address* (5). He is restlessly ill at ease with life in general, with superiors, and with the women he admires. He sometimes seems to be very much at ease with ordinary people

and with his friends. Yet even with close friends, composure is not usually long sustained.

10. *Resistance to Habit and Poor Routinizing* (4). He expresses more verbal resistance to routine than he shows in his behavior. Actually he has organized his life fairly efficiently, and he turns out work dependably, although he rails against routine and regards himself as one who cannot form habits. He has more difficulty with the basic biological habits (eating, sleeping and elimination) than with work habits. He works in spurts, but the spurts are of frequent occurrence. He has never been able to memorize poetry, and probably has only fair rote learning.

11. *Agoraphobia* (4). In general, he has a manifest agoraphobia, but it is not constantly sustained. During intermittent periods he shows claustrophobic traits (see S-11). He loves to get out on open water and on open ground, although this may be merely one way of hiding away from people.

12. *Unpredictability of Attitude* (5). Sometimes his attitudes seem to change with inexplicable rapidity. He is excessively responsive to other personalities, but his response is generally corrective rather than adaptional. That is to say, he usually reacts compensationally to the prejudices of others, taking up the weak or suppressed side of an argument. With Republicans he is a Democrat, and with Democrats a Socialist. With rakes he is a reformer, and with Christians (whom he dislikes), he is a rake.

13. *Vocal Restraint and Restraint of Noise* (6). The voice is closely controlled. He speaks characteristically in a rapid monotone which seems aimed with precision at the point where the listener is located. A person across the aisle from him in a railway carriage would rarely catch a syllable of his conversation—indeed might not know he was talking. He can raise his voice in wrath, and sometimes in a group, but these occasions are infrequent.

14. *Hypersensitivity to Pain* (5). He believes that he is of only average sensitivity to pain, and has lived up well to that *persona* (see S-14), but the superficial reflexes, the blink reflex, and the "start" in response to electrical stimulation are all accentuated. He becomes quickly nauseated in the dentist's chair, and is extremely sensitive to insect stings or nettles. We believe that he is far more sensitive to pain than the average person, but that he has to a degree steeled himself by internal discipline to the Spartanism which he professes.

15. *Poor Sleep Habits* (5). He sleeps poorly, usually resisting going to bed until a late hour. If anything is on his mind he cannot sleep at all, but may work at the problem feverishly for half the night, becoming more and more awake, until sometimes he gets up and turns on the light. But after two or three such nights in a row he sleeps well. He has never worried about insomnia.

16. *Youthful Intentness of Appearance* (6). The face looks young, even strikingly immature, to casual observation. It suggests intent alertness, like that of certain species of small, insectivorous birds (warblers, flycatchers, chaffinches).

17. *Vertical Mental Cleavage* (5). This mind is primarily subjective and it is well aware of its own deeper levels. Intuition is as sharp as objective perception. Words are handled with a workman's precise care for his fine-edged tools. Hurleigh is intolerant of persons who lack feeling for words. The subjective inner reality is the primary reality for him. The outer, objective picture is a secondary reality (although it is real enough for him to be a good scientist).

18. *Resistance to Alcohol* (6). Physiologically the resistance is probably extreme. The preliminary somatotonic effects of the drug are followed almost immediately by a general tightening and sense of strain, especially about the eyes. He limits his alcoholic intake to a single ounce of wine (about .2 oz. of alcohol). Even this amount produces an unpleasant aftereffect within ten or fifteen minutes.

19. *Need of Solitude when Troubled* (6). When disturbed by any perplexity he immediately shuts out the world of other human beings and becomes "schizzy as hell," he says. He feels that the only possible solution to perplexity must come from within, and must be harmonized to the complexity of what is already within. Therefore (he says) any social intrusion or suggestion from another person in the face of difficulty is like "throwing mud into the waters you are trying to clear." This is a good cerebrotonic ratiocination.

20. *Orientation toward the Later Periods* (6). There is a primary wish to be older, and a conviction that the wisdom and understanding of the later periods are worth more than the vigor and strength of youth. His most intimate associations are with much older people. He is a romanticist in the sexual realm of thought. He hopes to marry, but only with an ideal woman of a rare and gifted sort (whom he scarcely expects to meet).

Totals: Viscerotonia, 40; Somatotonia, 57; Cerebrotonia, 102.
Index of Temperament, 2-3-5².

PHYSICAL CONSTITUTION (at age 20)

Age 20, Ht. 69.5, Wt. 129, Somatotype 2-3-5 (2-3-6, 2-3-5, 2-3-5, 2-3-5, 2-4-5). g 3.0, t 3.8 d 8.

This is a fragile, slender, fine-textured (high *t* component) physique, a little above the average stature. Ectomorphy is strongly the primary component, with mesomorphy showing a clear secondary predominance over endomorphy. It is what we call a meso-ectomorphic physique. The 2-3-5 is the traditional physique of the Christ as portrayed by artists.

Total dysplasia is 8 (endomorphy, o; mesomorphy, 4; ectomorphy, 4). This is low, and each of the two dysplasias seen here is a slight one. However, the increment of ectomorphy in Region *I* exerts quite an effect upon the general physical appearance, for it lends an accentuation of fragility and delicacy which somewhat belies the relatively stronger structure of the rest of the body. Region *V*, the foundational support, shows a tendency opposite to that of Region *I*. Here is increased strength and mass. This youth is physically more powerful and durable than his face indicates.

Gynandromorphy is high for this somatotype, and is both primary and secondary. There is a slightly feminoid curve of the hips, and a slight feminine fullness of the groins. The waist is a little high and the hips are rather wide. In the dorsal photograph there is in Region *IV* a distinct suggestion of femininity. The features are a little small. They are of almost sufficient delicacy to be those of a handsome young woman. The subcutaneous finish of the whole body is soft, without the harshness of bony and muscular detail sometimes seen in the 2-3-5. No secondary hair is seen except the pubic hair, which is a sharply defined tuft, like that of the female. Gynandromorphy is at 3 (which would be about normal for the 3-2-5, but is dysplastically high for the 2-3-5).

The high t component is the most striking characteristic. This is about as high a t as is usually seen outside of a group which tends to show gynandroid psychopathology (often either a variant of homosexuality, or schizophrenic characteristics). The entire body appears almost as a work of fine sculpture. The features of the face, neck, arms, hands and fingers, trunk, legs, feet and toes, are so perfect in their symmetry and fineness of molding that they suggest the handiwork of an artist. The face appears to have been chiseled in marble, the balance and perfection of detail in the features are so fine. There are no inconsistencies or aesthetic disharmonies in the face. The t is at 3.8, but this physique does not even suggest the bloodless, Dresden china effect or excessive overrefinement of t 6 or t 7. There is vigorous, healthy resiliency, and a certain slender athletic quality here, especially in the legs and in the somewhat dysplastically broad shoulders. This youth can fight. His physique shows no *over*refinement. A male of t 5 could not fight.

Such a physique will remain slender, taking on perhaps 10 pounds altogether in the thirties and forties, under normal dietary conditions. With a relatively high gynandromorphy the 2-3-5 may in the late thirties develop a certain feminoid roundness below the waist.

Hurleigh's head is dolichocephalic. It is both long and high, but rather narrow. The forehead is high and broad. The blue eyes are of medium spacing, with moderately arched brows. Hair is of fine texture, of almost golden color, and of luxuriant growth, with a long wave. The long narrow nose has no trace of a hump, but the nostrils flare a little, and the bridge, although of moderate breadth, is a little high. The face is narrower at the level of the gonial angles than at the level of the eyes, but the triangularity which thus results is not pronounced. The mouth is neither large nor small, is perfectly level, and there is a trace of fullness of the lower lip. The well-developed jaw shows just a slight tendency in the direction of disproportionate strength, or massiveness. The teeth are large and white, well spaced, with strongly developed canines.

The trunk as a whole is well proportioned to the long arms and legs, with the shoulders a little broad for this somatotype, and the waist appearing correspondingly narrow. Except for the feminoid flare at the hips this physique would do as a model of masculine aesthetic proportions for the somatotype. The genitalia are large. The penis is long and well developed, with large corona.

CLINICAL HISTORY

Hurleigh was the third pregnancy, the first child having died shortly after birth. The living sister is three years his senior. Birth was somewhat difficult, although pregnancy was full term. Delivery was instrumental. Birth weight was about 6 pounds. Both parents were pronounced ectomorphs. He was breast fed for 10 months, the mother's supply of milk being great (as is frequently the case with ectomorphic mothers). The baby was very active and always had an excellent appetite, but greatly to the mother's distress (she did not then know about ectomorphy), the doctor's charts of normal weight showed consistently that the baby was underweight. Although every effort was made to correct the "defect," nothing availed. Hurleigh has remained "underweight" all his life.

This baby was singularly well behaved and quiet most of the time, but had a temper. Occasionally he put on a fearful rumpus, especially on one occasion when the mother discovered after a while that she had pinned up a little of Hurleigh with the diaper. (A viscerotonic mother would have never done so.) One of the striking features of his early history was that he had none of the children's diseases, not even measles. The only illnesses of his childhood were severe, acute colds, and a recurrent attack of middle ear infection. The ear trouble disappeared completely after the age of 4. Eruption of teeth was uneventful, although apparently painful, for it produced violent protest. The baby talked at 9 or 10 months, and walked at 11 months. (Cerebrotonic children seem often to talk before they walk—somatotonics seem to walk before they talk.) He developed into a very active child, with a tremendous endowment of curiosity. Between the ages of 2 and

5 his mother estimates that he asked questions at an average rate of thirty a minute. His only other serious divagation from normal was his unwillingness to take afternoon naps.

At the age of 29 there have been only two fillings in his teeth, and no extractions. He has had no illnesses except acute head colds, which occur slightly oftener than once a year and last about a week. At 13 he broke his arm tobogganing, but this healed normally. Otherwise he has never had occasion on his own account to seek medical help. All through childhood he remained below average weight, grew tall rather rapidly between 8 and 12, and at 12 and 13, just before adolescence, seemed to be a little fatter than he had been before, or ever has been again. He was adolescent at 14 and discovered ejaculation at 15. He is strongly sexed, and feels that he has had a "devil of a time" with sexuality. First intercourse at 18, as a college sophomore. His weight is just about the same at 29 as it was at 21.

BACKGROUND
Paternal:

The father was descended from old American and Irish stock, mostly from people who for several generations had lived in North Carolina. He was the third and youngest son in a formerly aristocratic North Carolina family which had been ruined by the Civil War. Physically he must have been very similar to Hurleigh, but taller, and perhaps even more ectomorphic. He turned early to intellectual pursuits, made a brilliant academic record, taught history for a time in high school, then returned to graduate school and became an instructor in a Midwestern university. At 30 he married the daughter of a Protestant Irish gentleman who had come to this country and settled in the South. Hurleigh was born five years afterward, and the father, who had been singularly free from illness all his life, died suddenly at 43 of an acute throat infection which apparently blocked his respiration. He died while on a camping trip. The mother was at the time told that he could have been saved by prompt medical attention (intubation).

Hurleigh's father had been a lover of the woods. He taught the boy a good deal of the rudiments of nature lore, and made him at home in the outdoors. Also he imparted to his son a love of books, and a primary regard for simplicity and truth. But he was a shy person who had few friends. Hurleigh is apparently made of somewhat tougher fiber than was his father. Possibly the father's central passion was atheism. He lived in a period, and had been reared in an environment, in which religious controversy was taken seriously. Hurleigh's earliest god was Robert Ingersoll.

Both of the paternal grandparents were slender people. The grandfather lost his life in some kind of accident, long ago, but the grandmother still lives. Tuberculosis, diabetes, cancer, circulatory and kidney ailment, and arthritis are all unknown among the immediate paternal relatives. They are a delicate, healthy stock.

Maternal:

The mother was an only child. Her father, after the tragic early death of his wife through some kind of mob violence, left Ireland and came to a North Carolina city to make his home. Hurleigh's mother is a slender, ectomorphic woman of medium height who at 55 weighs about 115 pounds. She thinks she weighed 105 when she married, at 20. She is probably a 2-3-5 in somatotype. Her coloring is about the same as Hurleigh's and she has the same finely chiseled features (high *t* component). She still runs her little restaurant, and this, together with the house and a small insurance fund left by her husband, provides a certain security. She no longer works regularly in the restaurant herself. Her health has been excellent. She has an eager mind and is a tremendous reader. The daughter, who is also an ectomorph, lives with her. All three of her children are so good to her, she says, that she is spoiled. Her father still lives. She says she is planning to promote a romance between him and her husband's mother, both of whom are coming to visit her this coming summer. She is bright, witty, and looks with a shrewd kindness into the human face.

Her relatives are known in Ireland, she believes, as a singularly healthy group of people, although two cousins have died of cancer, and there has been at least one instance of death from tuberculosis —a maternal aunt.

Siblings:

1. Sister, now 32. She is an excessively fragile, tall girl, probably on the 1-1-7 side of 2-2-6 in somatotype. She is above

medium height for women, and weighs but 95 pounds. She shows the same high t component seen in the rest of the family, the features suggesting those of a pretty, small-faced child. She is said to have a congenital heart murmur and low blood pressure. Throughout childhood she was regarded as sickly, although she did not have much specific illness. She speaks in a low, scarcely audible voice, and has a kindly, wistful smile. She has always lived at home, although she would probably have gone to college had not the family finances been in such low condition when she finished high school. She was kept out of school two years as a child because of her weak heart, yet made up most of this time and finished high school at 18. The mother thinks that a bad mistake was made in not sending her to college. She helps in the business of running the restaurant, reads a lot, and sometimes attempts to write short stories. She dreams of writing a novel, featuring the triumphs of her two brothers (but 2-2-6's do not write novels—they only dream of it). Apparently she has little social, and no sexual life. Hurleigh went to school with his sister throughout grammar and high school, but was never in the same class with her. He is fond of her but treats her as a child. She never entered into his scheme of things.

2. Hurleigh.

3. Brother, now 26. Not far from Hurleigh's somatotype. A little shorter, and a little more mesomorphic. Very likely a 2-4-5, or 2-4-4^2. This boy has more energy, more somatotonia, and far more personal ambition than his older brother. During early childhood he was closely devoted to Hurleigh. They had many interests in common, chiefly outdoor interests. At one time they were in a boy scout troop together. But by the time Hurleigh went away to college, a rift had grown up between the two. Their tastes had come to differ markedly. The older boy was socially retiring. The younger one was relatively aggressive and ambitious. The latter was academically as brilliant and successful as his brother. He won a scholarship which sent him to a famous university, and after distinguishing himself as an undergraduate went on to medical school. He is now an intern, with plans to "make a lot of money."

GENERAL LIFE STORY
First 6 Years:

Hurleigh is described by his mother as having been an excellently behaved baby, except for infrequent but violent temper outbursts. His own earliest memories are of his father reading to him and of his mother answering his questions. He believes that his childhood was among the happiest possible. Yet he does not love childhood, and considers it an "evil, nasty, messy time of life." He wishes that children could be hatched full grown from eggs (as in one of Bernard Shaw's plays). His father and mother were as kind, wise, and farseeing as human parents can be, he thinks, but he is convinced that there must be a better way to raise children than for two adult people to let it "interfere fatally with their lives and achievement just to raise two or three paltry brats like the ones my parents brought forth." He feels that his father was worth something to the world, and that "he threw away his life at the monkey business of child-raising. That sort of thing should be done by people delegated and paid to make a profession of it— probably stable but mentally inferior people who aren't good for much else—viscerotonic people, I suppose you would call them." This is a classic statement of one cerebrotonic outlook, worthy of Plato who must also have had some cerebrotonia.

The family lived in a modest cottage which at first they rented but later bought. The small yard had a few shrubs and three or four trees. Hurleigh stayed in his yard much of the time as a little boy, or tended to play with the few polite and proper children who were his sister's companions. He never mixed much with other boys until he went to school. He remembers none of the children well whom he knew in this early period. The clear early memories are all centered around the outdoor life of the family during the long summer vacations at a place on Lake Michigan which has since become a summer resort. They had the use of a small cabin built on the edge of the woods on the lake shore. The spot was almost isolated, the nearest other cottages being perhaps a quarter of a mile up the lake. The woods immediately surrounding the house were mostly young pine. In them many wonderful creatures lived. Both the father and the mother were fairly good amateur naturalists. Hurleigh remembers the personalities of skunks and rabbits, of birds and fishes, and even of the insects of his early acquaintance, better than the personalities of children who were his contemporaries.

There was a boy about a year older than Hurleigh, who spent his summers just up the lake. These two eventually became friends, although it was with this lad that Hurleigh had his first memorable fight. The fight followed an attempt by the older boy to appropriate a piece of fishing net which Hurleigh had found. Hurleigh describes the incident in this manner.

"When my new acquaintance started to walk off truculently with the possession which I then prized above all earthly goods, there was suddenly a terrible transformation inside me. I cannot of course remember just how I felt, but I have had what I think is the same feeling several times since that day. For one thing there is a tingling and tightening in the jaw, and a prickly feeling up and down my spine. My nostrils seem to open wider, and the focus of attention narrows to just one objective. I am aware of nothing but the object of this great hate—of Herbert, that first time. In that moment of concentration, I do not suppose I could have felt anything, not even a jab with a knife. I can remember that I went for him, and that there was a struggle. He told me afterward that I shouted over and over, 'I'll kill you.' And I almost did. I am ashamed to say that in some manner I seized a piece of iron, a heavy timber bolt, and with this I laid his head open. Then there was blood all over him and he was down in the sand. In a moment my rage had turned to fear, and I ran to call my father, who fortunately was at home. My father brought him into the house and fixed him up a little. The relations between the two families must have been strained at the time, but afterward Herbert and I became close friends, and we never fought again. He was and is much stronger than I am—at least he is stronger in cold blood."

At this time Hurleigh was approaching his seventh birthday and was in his first year of school. Except for violent outbursts of rare occurrence, he was apparently a quiet, shy, intent, sharp-eyed little boy of about average stature and well under average weight for his age. There was a good deal of autoeroticism during this early period. His mother recalls that he manipulated his penis so much that once she took him to the doctor about it.

Age 6 to 14. School:

At 6 he went to a school controlled by the university. Most of the other children were from families associated with the university and from the more well-to-do element of the neighborhood. The first year is remembered as a period of fear and anxiety. He felt smaller, weaker than the others, was essentially lonely, left out of things, and his chief memory is that of watching the big clock on the side wall as it ticked off the minutes. Yet at the end of the year the teacher reported that this boy was unusually bright. It was late in that spring that he had his fight with Herbert. During this period the closest associations were with his father, who read to him nearly every evening, mostly on natural history. They read *Swiss Family Robinson* together that year.

In the spring of Hurleigh's second year of school, his father suddenly became ill and died, up at the cabin on the lake. Late on a Friday afternoon the father and the son hunted Ladies' Slippers (orchids) in the woods. Within twelve hours the father was dead, and the event constituted a shock from which Hurleigh believes he never recovered. Although he was back at school within two weeks to finish up the year, he was no longer interested in what the clock on the wall said. His present philosophy of the family rests on the proposition that society could do better than place so heavy a burden of emotional responsibility upon the individual parent. He thinks that children could and should be protected from the emotional dangers and traumata which the small individual family necessitate. Such a point of view raises questions of great interest.

Hurleigh feels that he never quite forgave his mother for not possessing "a certain spiritual warmth" which he believes his father had. He never became emotionally dependent upon his mother, and he believes that he never really took her into his confidence at all after his father's death. During the years following that event he would often lie awake at night, not crying much or feeling sorry for himself, but planning his future with a "steely cold" detachment. For two or three years afterward he would go and sit by his father's grave alone at night, especially by moonlight. He seemed then to think most clearly. But at about 12 it suddenly occurred to him that this was weakness, and that his responsibility now lay in the direction of strength and self-sufficiency. He would carry no mental graveyard through life but would be like his father in intellect. But he would be sterner, colder, and he would make a deeper, more enduring contribution, one of which his father might be proud. Then he stopped visiting his father's grave.

It is said that Hurleigh did rather poorly in school during the first year after his father's death. But except for this brief relapse, his school achievement was brilliant. He was valedictorian of a large class in graduating from the eighth grade, and also he led his high school class, four years later.

During the late years of grade school he found that he possessed a certain speed of movement and a coordination of his muscles which made him a fairly good athlete, in spite of his fragile, slender build. It has occurred to him that had anyone strongly encouraged him in athletic participation and competition, he probably would have become "deeply embroiled" in ambitions of this nature, and perhaps would thereby have been turned aside from his more important objectives. As it was he ran on the school track team, played on the baseball team, and became quite fond of tennis.

Following an early interest implanted by his father, he spent much of his time in the summer practicing with his rifle, or in hunting hawks. Later, an older boy whom he met in high school taught him to box, and he found that he liked it. In college he was fond of fencing. Yet none of these things ever became a major interest, even for a short time. He seems to have formed a clear resolution, at about 12 or 13, to distinguish himself academically, and he never departed from it.

Two or three hobbies intruded themselves upon his interests. More than once he revived interest in natural history—insects, old birds' nests, botanical specimens, and sea fauna at different times. These interests always died away as soon as they began seriously to conflict with school work. Occasionally Hurleigh's violent temper flared. There were possibly half a dozen fights during the grade school period. Once he was badly beaten. On one occasion he had an altercation with a teacher who had accused him (falsely, Hurleigh says) of some minor misconduct. He acquired the general reputation of possessing a violent temper, but it is not to be supposed that his fighting ability was taken very seriously among the more powerful boys who were his contemporaries. When Hurleigh fought he fought in deadly earnest, but he was not strong.

The real threat to a successful fulfillment of his early resolution did not come from athletics, or hobbies, or from his dangerous temper, but from sexuality. As far back as the first year of school Hurleigh was "in love." There was a slender, blue-eyed, light-haired girl in his class. She was about a year older than Hurleigh, and was full of spirit. Once at a party at her house she kissed him and said that when he grew up she wanted to be his wife. Hurleigh took to the idea. Sometimes the thought of her kept him awake for a long time at night, and there was a strange feeling inside when he thought of her. He developed a very romantic imagination. There was never any thought of specific sexual contact, but when he had that strange tingling which she seemed to engender, a throbbing erection of his penis was part of it. This romance lasted for four years, although physically it never went beyond that first kiss at age seven, and nobody but Hurleigh and Irma themselves ever knew of it. Irma went away to a private school and out of Hurleigh's life when she was 12.

There was no period of homosexual play in this boy's career, but the intensity of his erections all through boyhood (and later) was so great that they are remembered as painful. His masochistic impulse was distinctly delineated. At 13 he frequently experienced a "burning desire" to slash himself with a knife. He at about this time developed the habit of driving (with a quick stab) a heated needle into his flesh, particularly the pectoral muscles. This was always accompanied by excessive and painful Priapism, which would last for hours afterward. He never at the time confided in anyone about these things.

By the time he was 14, he had developed a great sexual curiosity and interest, and it was about a year later that he first had an opportunity to satisfy any of his curiosities. His mother rented spare rooms at this time to two girls who were students in the university. Hurleigh had apparently been quite a favorite with one of them for some time. He describes her as a quiet, shy, pretty girl. A physical intimacy developed in some manner, and before the year was out it became a passionate one on the girl's part as well as on his. She would sometimes permit him to come to her room on a Friday night, after everyone had gone to bed. On these occasions he would "nearly burst" with prolonged sexual excitement, and she apparently would respond in much the same manner. But she explained to him that she was virginal, and she never permitted him to try to have intercourse with her. "She would kiss me and hug me all over, and would go into exquisite rapture over mutual manipulation—it would last for hours. Finally she would masturbate me, sometimes by kissing. I think that her body was a more lovely experience to me than anything can ever be again."

Intercourse was unknown to Hurleigh for nearly another four years. No one ever knew of these nocturnal visits, and even in June, when the girl graduated from college and left the house never to return, there was no external sign of emotional disturbance. So well had this youth learned to hide his feelings. This is cerebrotonia. The episode extended through about the second half of Hurleigh's sophomore year in high school.

Eleven years later he hunted her up, and found her a happily married mother of several children. "She only laughed at my stupid efforts at seduction, kissed me and gave me her picture. This time I think she did as much for me spiritually as once she had done for me physically." Hurleigh believes that his experiences with that girl played a large part in helping him toward what achievements he has accomplished. He thinks that by "showering a superb sexuality" upon him at a time when he most needed just that, she gave him an insight and a sexual ideal which saved him from smashing up later on the rocks of his own (too strong) sexuality.

After 14:

Hurleigh did better than well in high school. He learned to control his temper, rode out his flood of sexuality, led his class in scholarship, and established the general reputation of being something more than a "grind." He was not popular in the sense of being a leader, for his way of life is an intent, subjective, introverted way, but he played on two athletic teams, and one year was vice president of his class. Furthermore he won a scholarship which paid a large part of his expenses at the State University for four years. He did not have any particular girl friend in high school. During most of the last two years he constantly fought a nearly overwhelming desire to masturbate. The battle was about even, he says. "One day I would and the next day I wouldn't." Once he went seventeen days without a slip. That was during the baseball season. He believes that he masturbated an average of three times a week during the two years of this period. Usually the image before him was some scene with the college girl of his sophomore year. Sometimes it was another girl. Several times during this period he came close to intercourse, but always he drew back at the last moment. He wanted something fiercely, but could not quite decide what it was. In the meantime he would not compromise, and at night he took it out on himself. After a time he began to visualize the female ideal he sought. Meanwhile it was borne home to him that he was attractive to women.

Hurleigh had a fairly good time in college. The sexual problem still seemed to be his major interest. Yet he did his work and did it well. He decided early that he would be a scientist. First chemistry was his chosen field, but by the time he was a junior and had won the approval and encouragement of some of the faculty, he had set his heart on medicine. He made no attempt to enter athletics or any kind of "activities" in college, and he stayed away from fraternities. His social contacts were therefore limited. For a year he lived in a dormitory, then moved to a rooming house. His academic record was so good that in his senior year he was offered an assistantship to continue in the graduate study of chemistry. But a few months later he was given a scholarship which would materially help to send him through one of the best medical schools. He graduated from college at 21 and from medical school at 25. For the past four years he has been doing research in a branch of endocrinology, where he is considered an unusually promising young man. His professional future seems secure.

Late in his sophomore year of college Hurleigh indulged in his first sexual intercourse. He didn't like it. "The girl was coarse, crude and loudmouthed. She stunk of beer and cigarettes," he reminisces. Yet she was what passed as a fairly pretty girl. Some months later, he tried again. This time it was a prostitute whom he had picked up in a dance hall. "She was trim and slender, at least, but she chewed gum and at the crisis she didn't even change the rhythm." He didn't like that either. He next attached himself to a girl he had met on the campus—a classmate. After several evenings spent in this girl's intimate company he found that he grew critical of her intellect, and that his sexual desire waned correspondingly. This happened repeatedly, with variation of detail. "Far better," he decided, "to stick to morons than to try to mix intellectual and sexual companionship." Yet after a time he decided that even morons demand too much time for cultivation. Then the best bet must be prostitutes. But where are there some good ones?

With the problem still unsolved, Hurleigh went away to medical school. Almost immediately he met a girl with whom he fell in love, but unfortunately she was engaged. He raised a fuss and wrote her ardent letters but to no avail. For the succeeding two years he lived a fairly dissolute life, devoting more and more time to the sexual pursuit. He had learned how to be successful in this endeavor, but he found imperfect satisfaction in it. His sexual appetite was now such that it seemed to demand increasing attention. He found a pretty nurse whom he really liked, and for nearly a year saw her twice a week. She was sexually satisfying, but she was in love with him, and that was almost more painful than abstinence. For she fell far short of the now painfully clear ideal picture that lived in Hurleigh's head. He was not yet ready to compromise.

Now and then he would see Her, or an approximation of Her, on a city street or in some similarly inaccessible stretch of wilderness. He could not compromise his ideal by offering his whole affection at any other sexual shrine. Yet sexuality was all but overwhelming him. He had so much to offer, and seemed cut off from expressing it.

Hurleigh is now 29, handsome, slender and boyish, with a brilliant record and a good professional future. He has ridden out the crest of his tidal wave of sexuality, and has now so composed his mind on this subject that he is good-humored about it. Yet what he thinks he most wants is marriage with his ideal, whom he cannot find. This is what he believes he lives for. He thinks that all his intellect and his technical skills are secondary or incidental to his great marriage to be. What will be the outcome?

THE PROBLEM OF TREATMENT

For us, the problem is but to watch, and to record what happens. For Hurleigh, it may be that breakers lie ahead. He is resting his house on a foundation not yet made secure. If fortunate in his marriage-to-be, he may go on to make a rare contribution. Such a personality comes into its full strength and development late. Probably the 2-3-5 at its best does well to postpone final determinative decisions, including marriage, until the thirties, perhaps until the mid-thirties. For indivduals who reach the full human mental stature, something like a crisis appears to occur at about the age of 35—an event perhaps roughly analogous to adolescence. We have sometimes referred to it as mental adolescence.

Hurleigh, with his great sensitivity of feeling (he is high in both gynandromorphy and cerebrotonia), is peculiarly dependent upon a good marriage. With it he may flower to the best human achievement. Without it, he may find the strain too severe, and then his secondary somatotonic predominance might render him dangerous. When a strongly endowed 2-3-5 is frustrated, he is likely to cause trouble. There is no compromise in him. (Consider the lesson of the Christ, and the much older legend of Prometheus. These seem to be only projections of the 2-3-5 temperament.)

Hurleigh is counting heavily on his marriage. He has six more years before he is 35. During these years he presumably must find and successfully woo his ideal. But with each passing year now he grows more critically exacting, and he is already a shrewd critic of women. Also he is growing worse at wooing, for youth possesses the advantage in this art.

This man needs marriage. He is carrying all his eggs in that basket. If he should miss, there may be the devil to pay. His ideal may be too high for probable fulfillment, he is too normal and realistic for any perversional substitute, such as homosexuality, and the 2-3-5 temperament not infrequently fails to arrive at the decision to compromise until too late.

CHAPTER V

ADDITIONAL NOTES ON THE PRIMARY COMPONENTS OF TEMPERAMENT

WITH the foregoing sketches illustrating temperamental extremes now in mind, together with an acquaintanceship with some of the intermediate variations, we are in position to try to summarize general definitions of the primary dynamic components at the level of temperament. In the summaries which follow, it has seemed desirable in a few instances to anticipate the correlational findings which are presented in later chapters, but these anticipations will be indicated as they occur.

The student of medicine may find the case sketches, and also the summaries which follow, grievously lacking in reference to physiological and endocrine correlates. As yet we know but little concerning the relation of endocrinology either to temperament or to general physical constitution. We should like to know the physiology, the differential chemistry, and the predispositions to organic pathology which may underlie the various patterns of temperament. Indeed, without such data, the life portraits we have just presented seem almost fatally incomplete in vitally important regions. That is one reason why we are loth to attempt much explanatory interpretation or to recommend therapy.

The constitutional description of an individual, divorced from a thorough physiological workup, is probably in the long run of little value. On the other hand, medical and physiological diagnosis alone, divorced from the constitutional workup, is also a more or less ineffectual procedure. The problem of basic individual differences is beginning to loom as the most important *general* problem in medicine. The specific task of bringing cancer under control, for example, can hardly be attacked until we know—in terms of a meaningful taxonomy—*who* are the people susceptible to that malady. The big job is to combine the two attacks—clinical and constitutional—in well-planned correlational studies, and this must be done through cooperative research. But first we must bend a vigorous effort to the further clarification of some of the variables that are to be correlated.

1. VISCEROTONIA

Given a measure of poetic license, we might describe the first dynamic component as a manifest desire to embrace the environment and to make its substance one with the substance of the individual's own person. At the most unsublimated level this is the drive to ingest and to assimilate food, which is then transmuted into the flesh of the self. The predominantly viscerotonic personality generally remains close to the earth. Viscerotonia means earthiness. Such a person seems to express a dominant mood not far from the mood of the nourishing soil: he is unhurried, deliberate, and predictable. At high levels of culture he radiates warmth, stability, and (if cerebrotonia is low) indiscriminate amiability. At low levels he is gross, gluttonous, and possessive. In any event he knows what he wants, and his wants are tangible.

In contrast to viscerotonic motivation, the somatotonic desire is centered upon action and somatic expression, and in cerebrotonia the whole visceral and somatic organism seems to be held in a state of subjugation to the inhibitory, attentional function.

The viscerotonic's craving is for food, for comfort, and for the mental and somatic relaxation which accompanies the digestive process at its full best, when the main blood supply is withdrawn from the brain and from the peripheral somatic structures, and is vested in the digestive viscera. For cultured viscerotonics, the food-taking time is the high spot of the day, and the principal focus of feeling-awareness is in the assimilative business. The soul has its seat in the splendid gut.

Such a personality rarely can understand the cerebrotonic, who wants to eat quickly and have it over with, who prefers to eat in private, and cares little for service and ceremony or for fancy dishes. The viscerotonic is likely to devote a tremendous interest to *cuisine*, and he achieves ecstasy in the imagination and anticipation of fine food. Furthermore, he is prone to carry into adult life his natural early childhood interest in faeces and in the eliminative functions,[1] for viscerotonia loves all digestive activity, including the peristalsis of defecation.

At lower cultural levels the viscerotonic becomes simply the glutton, growing heavier and more hoglike in his obesity if the food supply holds out, and less so when kept on a limited diet or on a rigid schedule of work and exercise. Peasant stock from all lands appears to carry a heavy viscerotonic component. The great majority of the overly fat, full-gutted personalities so conspicuous in American urban and political life, have presumably sprung from stock which for many generations had lived on limited diet under sterner conditions. Rioting now in the rich spoils of a newly exploited continent, some of these men and women of strong first component fail to maintain the balance, and they go to gut and fat.

The viscerotonic may of course express his temperamental predominance in a wide variety of ways. He may be culturally polished and urbane, or crude and uneducated. He may be bishop or bumpkin, scholar or butcher, aggressive or meek, energetic or lazy, courageous or cowardly, ruthless or squeamish, loud or quiet —in short he may live out *any* role in life which permits the expression of a predominant viscerotonia. The predominant component is but one of the variables determining the personality. How that component is to be expressed must depend upon the relative endowment in the other two primary components and upon many other factors, including the cultural influences to which the man has been exposed. We see that to know the strength of one of the primary components *and that alone* is to take but one short step toward describing or predicting a personality.

Viscerotonic people tend to be hypoattentional and to remain overrelaxed. The viscerotonic gives the impression of being slow. Yet although his conscious response may seem sluggish to the faster reacting cerebrotonic, the basic conscious orientation of the viscerotonic is surer and in some respects more accurate. Viscerotonics can always be trusted to maintain a close grip upon imme-

[1] There can be no doubt that many persons with a strong viscerotonic component which has been suppressed by an unperceiving social environment or by a cultural emphasis, derive a certain benefit from a kind of psychoanalysis which simply encourages the patient freely to talk out and to meditate upon these long sequestered visceral interests.

diate, practical reality. They are certain to know where they are at all times, in relation to their jobs, to their marriage, to their social status, to their basic likes and dislikes. Attitudes toward these things do not change readily or suddenly in the viscerotonic personality, and for some reason, both viscerotonic and somatotonic people possess a better sense of spatial orientation than do cerebrotonics.

The cerebrotonic is also concerned with the problem of orientation, but his worry usually concerns orientation in time. He lies awake nights thinking of distant plans, of the general course and objectives of his life as a whole, of the state of his religion, of the ethics of some projected undertaking, or of the future of his progeny, of mankind, and of the universe. In both kinds of mind the problem of *orientation* is vital and urgently important, but the reference of the orientation in the two cases is different. For the somatotonic and viscerotonic components, orientation is essentially a spatial, earthly, immediate need. For cerebrotonia the orientational need seems to take the form primarily of a craving for a sense of direction in time, and for some hierarchy of values transcending the apparent value hierarchy of present experience. This is a relative difference. There seems to be no necessity for calling one kind of orientation religious, and the other nonreligious.

The viscerotonic digests his food with the highest efficiency. All of it is utilized, and made the most of. Food is eagerly absorbed into the organism. The organism consequently tends to expand, and in a realistic sense to glue itself more closely to the earth. If given full sway, the viscerotonic component seems to lead the organism back to the earth and insidiously to bring about a reunion with the basic earth stuff. The cerebrotonic is always in danger of flying too far from the earth and suffering an Icarian fall. The viscerotonic runs the danger of growing back and becoming attached to his earth like a Siamese twin, losing his conscious individuation and remerging prematurely with the maternal stuff from which he was molded. He must watch his diet with great care, or he grows heavy of body. If then he fails to master the desire to absorb, he degenerates, spreads out in a clod of flesh, and the mental and somatic functions are drowned in a rising tide of biological surfeit.

In well-developed viscerotonia the actual food requirement is less per unit of bodily weight than that in cerebrotonia. Furthermore the digestive apparatus in viscerotonia is equipped to accommodate larger quantities of food at more infrequent intervals. Two meals a day are therefore probably ample for any predominantly viscerotonic person, and we have seen viscerotic symptoms clear up in persons of this pattern through the simple expedient of changing temporarily to a program of *one* meal a day. Similarly, a pronounced viscerotonic probably requires less sleep than a cerebrotonic, but here as in the matter of food, the viscerotonic is prone to take more than is good for him, or perhaps we should say, more than is conducive to his best mental development. The viscerotonic *loves to sleep*, in marked contrast with the somatotonic, who loves to wake up and be active, and in contrast with the cerebrotonic who hates to *go to sleep*, but who, when once asleep, also hates to wake up and be severed from his dreams.

Viscerotonics are remarkably susceptible to habit formation. Food taking and sleeping in overdoses become habitual, and if drugs once are taken, especially sedative drugs, there is danger of the development of a drug habit. The habit of constant dependence upon tobacco is very common among viscerotonic people, who often tend to use this drug to hold down their weight, thus substituting a habit for internal (cerebrotonic) discipline.

The mechanism of viscerotonic susceptibility to habit is a matter of speculation. The same phenomenon is seen in somatotonia, at times even more conspicuously. It is possible that this phenomenon is related directly to the relative degree of cerebral dominance in the personality. Where cerebral dominance is pronounced, there is marked resistance to habit formation. Where the cerebrotonic component is low, the organism appears readily and willingly to fall into all sorts of habits which obviate the recurrent necessity of making choices and decisions. Habit is a psychological antithesis to hyperattentionality, which is perhaps associated with an innately determined taste for mental conflict, and is certainly a cerebrotonic trait. It may be that the common habit addictions of mankind are simply manifestations of relative failure of the cerebrotonic component.

Viscerotonic people like alcohol. They are frequently connoisseurs of alcoholic beverages. But they are rarely drunkards. The overuse of alcohol is almost certainly a response to conflict, not to a temperamental predominance. The common picture of the alcoholic personality is one in which is seen an intense struggle for dominance between the cerebrotonic and the somatotonic components, *usually with the third component slightly the weaker*. The chronic excessive use of any depressant drug seems psychologically to constitute an attempt to achieve internal peace by putting down the cerebrotonic component. Alcohol attacks this component selectively, depressing the higher centers of the forebrain first, then the intermediate brain centers, and if in sufficient concentration, finally paralyzing the lower nerve centers.

In moderate quantities alcohol appears to be good food for the viscerotonic and seems to agree with him, as tobacco seems to agree with him. These two relatively mild depressants appear to balance the internal economy of the biologically overefficient viscerotonic organism in an ordinarily pleasant and innocuous manner. At any rate there is no convincing evidence that either of them in moderate quantity is injurious to one who possesses a good viscerotonic component, and for such a person alcohol and tobacco seem to add materially to the comfort and enjoyment of life.

Sir Arthur Conan Doyle pictured his immortal Sherlock Holmes as an indefatigable smoker, capable of smoking half a pound of strong tobacco in a single night. Yet the Holmes of Doyle's fertile imagination was *also* a cerebrotonic ectomorph who in most respects conspicuously lacked the viscerotonic component. Holmes, as Doyle *generally* pictured him, could no more have smoked a strong pipe in such a manner than the late Calvin Coolidge could have put away a case of 6 per cent beer at a sitting. But Doyle himself had a flourishing viscerotonic component, and he loved his tobacco. The Holmes he created, like many legendary heroes, was a composite ideal, but not quite psychologically probable. Holmes was partly Doyle, and partly what Doyle dreamed of being. Viscerotonics and somatotonics dream of being *also* cerebrotonic. We all dream of being *also* what we are not.

Viscerotonia means realism. Viscerotonic ecstasy lies in the achievement of a "real" surrounding made up of nice things that taste good, smell good, look good, sound good, feel good. The viscerotonic wants to dig in, to establish himself in a good place on his earth, and to feel the warming and nourishing earth juices flowing in his veins. In the face of trouble and dismay, this personality does not go off into solitude and think it through alone, but seeks social support at once, and finds respite in outward lamentation. Sorrow and grief are inhibiting things. They are foreign to the inner organic economy of the viscerotonic personality. Sorrow is not to be cherished and reflected upon, but must be expressed and thrown off and got rid of. After a little time of dismay and lamentation, the viscerotonic component asserts itself like the returning tide, again takes over the management of affairs, and demands the satiation of appetites. Then there may be feasting, drinking, and spending. The viscerotonic bruises easily but recovers rapidly. A cerebrotonic, however, may carry his deep emotional hurts close to the conscious focus for a lifetime.

The viscerotonic youth does not get "buck fever" in the face of crises and opportunities. He does not lose his nerve and go to pieces at the time when it is most vital that he should be normal and relaxed. His mind is not so vulnerable to distraction as is that of the cerebrotonic, whose attention can be reached in an instant by almost every distracting stimulus. The viscerotonic controls are deeper, harder to reach, and slower to respond. This individual is thus insulated against the danger of hasty, confused, rattle-brained action. He is not likely to flinch or to lose his head in an emergency. He has good kidney, good intestinal fortitude, a strong stomach. He has guts, bowels. Indeed, it is remarkable that so much of our common language descriptive of stability in the face of emergency should point so consistently to the digestive tract. The somatotonic has courage (a strong heart). He is the one who goes out to meet danger. The cerebrotonic sees too much, too many alternatives and consequences, and he is frightened.

Neurodermatitis, nervous disorders, functional bowel distress and the like are not often found in predominant viscerotonia.

nor do we often encounter sexual hypereroticism (quick, intense sexual excitability). This is a cerebrotonic characteristic.

With the viscerotonic component high, there is excellent thermal adaptability. Such people typically enjoy both cold weather and hot weather, although hot weather may be uncomfortable in cases where the physique has been permitted to degenerate to obesity. The heavy layer of subcutaneous fat prevents the normal irradiation of heat in hot weather, but this same fat layer acts as an insulation against cold. Viscerotonia loves the water, loves to swim.

Viscerotonic emotional expression is direct and sincere, in the sense that the outward response tends to reveal what the individual feels within. Since the restraining cerebral controls are relatively inactive and weak, outward expression of feeling in viscerotonia is a more accurate barometer of the true state of inner feeling than is the case in cerebrotonia. Viscerotonics are relatively predictable, and therefore in a superficial sense more trustworthy, and more trusted. They are open. There is relatively little about them that is mysterious. To live with them is to know them, to understand them, and therefore to sympathize with them.

It is far different with the cerebrotonic, whose sharp, watchful countenance and overly responsive eyes advertise that something is going on among the inner workings which is not revealed to the light of day. There is no predicting what such men are thinking. They work, as it were, behind an intervening screen, and the screen may cover the darkest morass or the brightest garden of thought. It is possible to live for years with a cerebrotonic and be totally mistaken as to what manner of man he really is. People like that make life interesting, but they also make life complicated. In viscerotonia there is surety, although perhaps also boredom.

Persons with a good viscerotonic component can *cry*. They can pour out their souls. It is *real* crying, sobbed up wholebelliedly from the depths of the abdomen. The entire abdominal musculature joins in with a will and a rhythm. The cerebrotonic cries through clenched teeth, usually in silence. His crying is not so convincing to the uninstructed listener. This viscerotonic ability to cry convincingly is at times a remarkably potent weapon. Many a resistant heart has been melted by it, and many a marital fortress taken, which could never otherwise have been scaled. When a viscerotonic male sets his heart upon a woman whose quality lies a little beyond his reach, he is apt sooner or later to resort to this weapon, and in such a beginning many unfortunate marriages take shape. Men as a rule may be fairly well disciplined in resisting feminine tears, but against good viscerotonic masculine tears the female is at a serious disadvantage, for her own weapons are then turned against her.

The cerebrotonic who has not been embittered and beaten back by a relatively unsympathetic outer world tends frequently toward anthropomorphism. He becomes affectionately attached to *things*, reads human qualities and feelings into them, and often focuses deep affection upon things that are not human. In predominant viscerotonia this anthropomorphism is not found. The viscerotonic has in the beginning better natural rapport with other human beings, and the main targets of his affection usually remain through life essentially direct human objectives.

In our own Christian history cerebrotonic virtues of restraint and the viscerotonic virtue of brotherly love have defined the cornerstones for religious thought and for a theological rationalization of life. (We have, however, for the most part *practiced* an aggressively somatotonic way of life, and perhaps in this incompatibility lies some of the reason for present-day orientational confusion.) Our Christ has been portrayed, historically, as an ectomorph (see p. 268), and much of the teaching attributed to him has centered around cerebrotonic self-effacement and inhibition of the somatotonic impulse. Up to the time of the "somatotonic revolution," which became so readily apparent at about the period of the first World War, we were attempting, so far as the common conscious rationalization was concerned, to live out a religious ideal based essentially on cerebrotonia, although complicated by an undercurrent of sublimated viscerotonia (love of man). But for some time now, as is especially obvious in Germany, a vigorous religious movement has been afoot which is based squarely on unsublimated somatotonia.

As another alternative, it is possible to rationalize a general orientational schema for life on essentially viscerotonic grounds. Buddhism has done so, and Buddha is rarely pictured as less than 5 in the first component, both morphologically and motivationally. In Buddhist doctrines we find a fairly consistent exposition of viscerotonia. We find relaxation, deliberateness, love of comfort, pleasure in digestion, ceremoniousness, tolerance, complacency, love of sleep, orientation toward family, in short, viscerotonia. And for an honest *rationalization* of viscerotonia, read Lin Yutang's book, *The Importance of Living*.

It is quite appropriate that we should speak of viscerotonia as the *first component*. The elemental business of digestion may probably be taken as the first and oldest biological function. In the beginnings of life, among the simplest animals and throughout the plant kingdom, this function appears to constitute, together with reproduction, both the end and the means of existence. The entire body of a tree may be described as a specialized digestive, respiratory, reproductive and circulatory apparatus. The body of an ameba may be in some ways less differentiated and specialized than that of a tree, but the ameba's sun of life appears so clearly to rise and set in the pursuit of basic viscerotonic activities, that motivationally an ameba would probably have to be described as a 7-1-1.

If we may be permitted to speculate about the origin of things, it appears that in the beginning all life is predominantly viscerotonic. When the text of evolution is finally written, it may well turn out that even in point of time, viscerotonia was the first component. The other components may conceivably be regarded as evolutionary developments which came into being as specializations designed to support the first organic function, but which in the course of time have become to a degree autonomous in themselves.

In the ontogeny of human life the picture is complicated by the activity of the huge forebrain, with its consequent third component, but even in human beings the visceral need appears first and so long as the first component remains ascendant, it seems to constitute a sort of reserve or buffer against and about which the storms of conscious life play harmlessly. The first is the component of biological security and insurance. It is only in its conscious elaborations that it appears as the principle of love, or affect. And in the same sense somatotonia becomes the principle of conation, and cerebrotonia the principle of cognition.

The viscera are the *insides* of the human being. They fill the great central bodily cavity. From one point of view they are the most valuable and the most-to-be-protected things in the body, and they are given the safest internal position. The soma is in effect a fortified carriage built around the viscera. If the viscera are relatively large and predominant, they press outward to give the body the spheroid or endomorphic shape, causing the antero-posterior diameter to approach and even to exceed the breadth diameter, as it does in the newly born infant. Then the individual tends to maintain in adult life the overwhelming viscerotonia of infancy.

In summary, viscerotonia refers to a motivational organization dominated by the gut and hence by the function of anabolism. The primary desire seems to be to assimilate the earth and to merge with it. Viscerotonia means warmth, earthiness, and in general, *indiscriminate* good will.

Predominance of this component generally means a slowness of reaction, but it means also a tenacious grip on reality, especially upon social reality, and a sure orientation in the spatial and personal sense. Viscerotonia means practicality. It provides the central *thema* for a group of religions older than Christianity, and, in terms of total number of sincere adherents, probably more influential.

2. SOMATOTONIA

The second component is the 'motional' element in life. Somatotonia is the craving for vigorous action and (when fully admitted to consciousness) the resolution to subdue the environment to one's own will. Successful somatotonics are conquerors. They conquer mountains, oceans, forests, wild beasts, Chinese, and other less somatotonic or less strongly united peoples. Somatotonic ecstasy is that of vigorously overcoming obstacles, and somatotonic hell is inaction.

A constant characteristic of predominant somatotonia is physical endurance, accompanied by a low sleep requirement and a relatively infrequent food requirement. When the second component is predominant, without the complication of a strong first or third, we find typically a person who requires from a fifth to a third less sleep than the average individual of his age. These are the voluntary early risers of youth and middle age, and sometimes in the later decades of life they give the impression of being almost independent of the need for sleep. It is not uncommon to find a somatotonic 6 with the established habit of sleeping only five or six hours nightly, while retaining seemingly boundless energy and evidencing no signs of fatigue.

Extremes in the second component have solid, compact bodies, ruddy complexions, large blood vessels, and usually they have high blood pressure. They are rarely very long lived, but are prone to go out suddenly with a "coronary or cerebral accident," not infrequently in the sixth decade of life. The somatotonic mesomorph is certainly closer to the *habitus apoplecticus* of Hippocrates than is the viscerotonic endomorph. In our own studies we have found that it is principally mesomorphs and not endomorphs who tend to develop manic-depressive psychoses. (We suspect that many of Kretschmer's manic-depressive "pyknics" were really fat mesomorphs.)

Somatotonics do not require frequent feeding, but often they are voracious, eat too much, and grow fat. For the full-fledged somatotonic, two meals a day probably constitute a better feeding schedule than three. These people like to "wolf" a large quantity of food at a sitting, and if permitted, are inclined to gorge themselves. In middle life, somatotonics almost invariably eat too much. In several instances when confronted with the picture of a somatotonic complaining in middle life of boredom, loss of interest, and of disturbing somatic symptoms, we have recommended a change to two meals a day instead of three. This recommendation has in certain cases been followed by remarkable improvement.

Both viscerotonic and somatotonic people can often be benefited by a stern dietary regime. (But this is not a safe generalization to give the public, for cerebrotonics often need the opposite, or an increase in both frequency and quantity of intake, especially protein intake.) Somatotonics love a vigorous life and are at their best when meeting physical hardship. Under such conditions they reach their peak of energy output and when in the best of training are capable of enduring great exertion for long periods without food, eating enormously when the opportunity is presented.

Somatotonics feel good in the morning. They love to jump out of bed, take a shower, make a lot of noise, and greet the sun. Normally they become sleepy or tired rather suddenly at about their usual bedtime, and typically drop off to deep sleep at once upon retiring. A person in whom either the first or second component predominates strongly over the third is not likely to have chronic difficulty in going to sleep.

Somatotonic sleep is deep and seems to be relatively dreamless. Such sleep is refreshing and it may be that an explanation of the lower sleep requirement of people high in the second component lies partly in the fact that they sleep *better*, or more thoroughly than do cerebrotonics. Whoever has attempted to use a dream analysis technique in the therapeutic or diagnostic study of somatotonic people is aware of the peculiar early difficulty which they present. Most somatotonics will state that they rarely dream and never remember their dreams upon awaking (see trait S-17).

Cerebrotonics nearly always, and viscerotonics usually, are more or less aware of the trend of their own dreaming, and can without practice recite their recurrent dreams in some detail. But for individuals of predominant somatotonia an introduction to their own dream world often amounts to revelation, and the event not infrequently constitutes a religious (conversional) experience. These people then tend to become converts in quite a religious sense to the analytic procedure which has introduced them to their "other side," and if wealthy they make very satisfactory patients or communicants. The somatotonic mind offers an admirable target for exploitation by conversion because by its nature such a mind is cut off from its own subconscious levels. But that people who are successfully analyzed or suddenly converted to a religion are generally somatotonic reflects no discredit on the devices through which the conversion experience has historically been exploited. If there is to be criticism, it should be directed at commercial exploitation, not at the priestly function itself.

Somatotonic people tend to lack introspective insight. They are like loaded guns and they want to be pointed somewhere and set off. Their function is action. Hence it is that the clever medicine men of all time have made a good living by pointing and exploiting the action-loving somatotonic component in their contemporaries.

In general, somatotonia lives for the present, cerebrotonia for the future. The cerebrotonic often feels as if the present were a sort of valley or depression between a better yesterday and a potentially brighter tomorrow. The somatotonic tends to feel that the present is like a high and sunny ridge between the dead valley of the past and the misty nothingness of the future.

Somatotonics typically like high or mountainous country and sunny weather. Cerebrotonics show a predilection for low country, and for rainy weather. However, this trait is so obscured by the individual history that it is hard to get at, and its diagnostic value is questionable. Ectomorphs are usually more comfortable in wet weather, possibly due in part to their peculiar susceptibility to dehydration (relatively greater surface exposure). They tend to be uncomfortable in strong sunlight, probably because of visual and general cutaneous oversensitivity. Cerebrotonics love the twilight, and if the preliminary evidence of general observation is to be trusted, they often see better at night than do either somatotonics or viscerotonics.

Somatotonic people are generally tolerant of noise and are frequently noise makers. The cerebrotonic hates noise. His hyperattentional responsive mechanism is especially sensitive to noise and renders him at the mercy of his environment. He is physiologically unable to prevent responding to what is going on, especially to what is making a noise. He is like a delicate instrument which records a slight disturbance in its environment, but can be ruined or destroyed by heavier, more violent disturbances. Noise therefore exhausts and frustrates cerebrotonic people.

Cerebrotonics seem to have suffered a misfortune in the invention of the radio, for this is a weapon against which, in full-fledged cerebrotonics, no dissociative effort can prevail. Somatotonics, however, *like* the noise bombardment. To them the radio is mild stimulation, comparable perhaps to what the distant voice of wildfowl is to a nature lover. Their threshold of attention is high, and relatively little really breaks through. Rhythmic noise lulls and only gently stimulates the somatotonic mind when the same noise may distract and disrupt a cerebrotonic mind. Automobile horns often constitute a pleasant sound to somatotonia. Such sounds mean fellowship, action and high health. The cerebrotonic, with his more labile attentional focus has to attend to every noise as though it were a meaningful stimulus. But for the somatotonic, the noise may constitute merely an encouraging and reassuring background item in the total complex of stimulation, like the distant voices of children. These two kinds of people are different inside.

To highly cerebrotonic people the experience of attempting to converse with the deaf is a traumatic one. The cerebrotonic is not able to raise his voice well, and the effort to do so in order to make himself heard sometimes constitutes a severe strain. Some time ago the writer was asked to consult a young woman who had been suffering from a number of cerebrotic manifestations, among them neurodermatitis, insomnia, return of a childhood habit of fingernail biting, and a peculiar sense of impending disaster. She was morphologically 2-2-6, very shy and quiet, and her motivational components seemed to be also about 2-2-6. She had unusual beauty, of her delicate type, and was engaged to marry a young man of excellent standing. This girl had been to a psychiatrist and had been encouraged to proceed with her marriage. The young man to whom she was engaged turned out to be a hearty, athletic 3-5-2 in his early thirties. He had been successful in a business job, was aggressive and popular, fond of somatotonic activities, and as innocent of cerebrotonia as a Chicago congressman. But he was partially deaf. To one who has noted the pain of the cerebrotonic who is forced to raise the voice, it may not be surprising to learn that today the girl is institutionalized. Diagnosis, "schizophrenia, type undetermined."

Could this girl have been saved from a fatal breakdown? That we do not know, but at least her departure could have been made more pleasant. A cerebrotonic 2-2-6 should not have been forced to make her final struggle against such odds as the combination of somatotonia and deafness. (Incidentally, is there a genuine correlation between somatotonia and deafness—do vulnerable ears go with the second component—or is it merely that somatotonic deaf people are the most conspicuous?)

It is excessively rare to find a cerebrotonic who snores, even in deep sleep. Snoring is probably due to relatively complete relaxation, especially of the structures in the upper respiratory path. The cerebrotonic goes to sleep very slowly, and his body relaxes incompletely. This is probably why he does not snore. Somatotonics seem to snore only when a fairly good viscerotonic component is also present. They then are inclined to snore noisily. The heavy, rafter-shaking snoring that is sometimes heard in army barracks or Pullman cars will usually be found upon investigation to emanate from a viscerotonic-somatotonic throat. But the more frequent, regular, musical snoring which is nearly always heard in such places comes from the softer, shallower-breathing viscerotonics.

Psychologically the most important thing about snoring is doubtless its devastating effect upon cerebrotonic morale. Cerebrotonics typically cannot sleep within range of the sound of snoring, particularly somatotonic snoring, But snoring is a habit almost impossible to break because it takes place when the organism is so completely relaxed that the cerebral inhibitory (habit-breaking) functions are entirely cut off. When a snorer and a cerebrotonic are married there is often little to do except sleep in different parts of the house, or better, in different parts of the city.

In this same connection a minor diagnostic difference between the three dynamic components lies in the habitual posture of sleep. Viscerotonics sleep limp and sprawled in any posture, like infants. They often sleep on their backs. Adult cerebrotonics seem almost always to assume a characteristic flexed or curled position lying on one side, with one or both thighs drawn up. They sleep quietly. Somatotonics thrash about vigorously in sleep. They seem to dream with their muscles, as dogs sometimes seem to do.

It is commonly supposed that children in general are somatotonic, at least in the sense of being noisy. This may not be the case, however. Watch 50 boys pour out of a schoolhouse at letting-out time in the afternoon. To a cerebrotonic ear it may sound as if all 50 are shouting at once. But move up closer and really ob-serve these children. Get acquainted with them as individuals and watch them over a period of many days at letting-out time, at recess, and at coming-in time. Construct a rough rating scale, and through a period of ten days or more carefully gauge the quantity of noise that each one habitually makes. Put the rating down in black and white, until you have a fairly accurate measure of the noisiness of each of the 50 youngsters. You may be surprised by what you find.

The writer once carried out exactly this experiment and found to his astonishment that only about 20 per cent of 80 boys observed were really noisy. Nearly 40 per cent were virtually noiseless, and there was an intermediate group of about 40 per cent. On the basis of these observations it was estimated at the time that 90 per cent of the noise was being made by 10 per cent of the youngsters. This was so revealing that with the help of a colleague I undertook to make a somewhat similar observation of adult somatotonia. We went to several big league baseball games, picked out 10 adult men to watch at a time, and rated the amount of noise each made, until we had ratings on one hun-dred men, each of whom had been watched and listened to for at least an hour. Again, we were astonished. It is not quite true that American baseball *crowds* are noisy. Only 15 to 20 per cent of these people yell or shout or talk loudly even at exciting moments. Sixteen of the 100 men were rated "noisiness 5" or higher (on a 7-point scale).

This was so interesting that we carried it further. I was at the time associated with the University of Chicago nursery school. We had about 50 youngsters between the ages of 20 months and 4 years coming daily to the school. Over a period of fifteen days 40 of these children were watched carefully, and close records were kept of the amount of noise each child made. Finally each was rated for noisiness on a 7-point scale. Once more about the same curve held. Nine of the 40 were noisiness 5 or higher. Seven-teen were noisiness 2 or lower, and 14 were 3's and 4's.

Boys, middle-aged men and nursery school children all show approximately the same distribution curve for at least one as-

pect of somatotonia, noisiness. About one individual in five may
be called predominantly somatotonic in this respect.

Somatotonia is characterized by vigorous muscular expressiveness. In infants, the second component can probably be gauged
by the relative vigor of kicking and squirming which takes place.
Somatotonic infants squirm and cry with great vehemence and
when picked up by the arms will frequently strike out powerfully
and repeatedly with the hind quarters. When a scaling technique
was applied to the squirming vigor of 50 infants less than one year
of age in the children's hospital at the University of Chicago,
essentially the same distribution curve resulted as that which had
been found in the study of noisiness. We have noted also that
mothers who have reared several children can frequently identify
the comparatively somatotonic ones by recalling their bodily vig-
orousness as infants. Some mothers insist that they can gauge the
vigor of a child by its prenatal movements.

In older children somatotonia gives rise to rough and dynamic
play, to self-assertiveness, and to pugnacity and dominational qualities. As the child grows on toward maturity these somatotonic
manifestations either yield to sufficient sublimation and "socialization" to render the emerging personality socially acceptable,
and to lend it the quality of leadership, or they settle it at relatively unsublimated levels and the individual takes on the nature
of incorrigibility.

Most people in our present crowded world become gradually
discouraged in the twenties and early thirties, and after the discouragement has well set in they typically fall back upon some
simple and usually innocuous routine expression of the inherently
dominant motive. Somatotonics tend to enter upon the most
tragic of all human quests, the quest of lost youth. One of the
cardinal indicators of somatotonia is a horror of growing old.
Somatotonics want their bodies to stay young, and they want to
continue to do the things of youth. Athletic games, gadgets of
locomotion, competitions, money, status, power, success—these
are the things that preoccupy somatotonia growing older against
its will. Somatotonics love to keep up with the tennis, the football, the hunting, the races. Professional athletics and gambling
are so highly commercialized and so vulgarized that their follow-

ing is a variegated one. You see more than vicarious somatotonia at the horse races, ball parks and gambling places. You see also the backwash of human life. But when you see a man in the fifth or sixth decade of life faithfully practicing his tennis or religiously following the hunts, you are looking upon gentlemanly somatotonia. So gentlemanly that sportsmanship means more than victory, and so somatotonic that the mind has long since surrendered to the muscles.

Alcohol depresses the cerebrotonic component selectively, and therefore acts as a relative stimulant, especially to the somatotonic component. This drug seems to release hidden springs of action in people whose motivation reveals the stress of conflict between the second and third components. Such people seem to be natural candidates for chronic alcoholism (possibly because of the peculiar incompatibility between these two components. See p. 400). They are frequently and, so far as anyone knows, are rightly fond of alcohol. If cerebrotonia predominates, it presumably protects them from being entirely mastered by the habit. If somatotonia predominates in a close struggle with cerebrotonia, alcohol may offer an easy way out of a difficult situation.

Somatotonic people who are free from cerebrotonic interference are singularly open, guileless people. (The open face is the somatotonic passport, the amiable face is the viscerotonic passport, and the cerebrotonic face has no passport, but wears a lean danger sign which arouses universal suspicion.)

Somatotonia means susceptibility to habit. The even regulation of habitual overt behavior in somatotonics is striking, but is perhaps relatively unimportant in comparison with the same habitual ordering of mental activities. Somatotonic people who have more viscerotonia than cerebrotonia think in orderly, habitual patterns, and they rarely change their minds or their internal attitudes. They are prone to wear the same mental clothes through life, and whatever cerebrotonia may be present is readily bent to the role of rationalization or self-justification.

In adult cerebrotonics, on the contrary, an astounding capacity for changing the mind is encountered. To live with a cerebrotonic is to walk in a forest thickly planted with surprises. Yet the other side of the story may also be a painful one. The deep habit formation and mental inflexibility of somatotonia often spells ineducability, and many a bright cerebrotonic-somatotonic marriage, after dawning with a brave reeducation program has sobered into the gray drizzle of sullen conflict.

Predominant somatotonia carries relative immunity to the common nervous or functional disorders, but somatotonics frequently have high blood pressure and are susceptible to cardiac, vascular and renal ailments associated with hypertension. Somatotonic people are also peculiarly susceptible to staphylococcic infections, particularly to acne and boils. But the most characteristic of all somatotonic afflictions is acute, fulminating appendicitis. There is ground for believing that this condition is rare where somatotonia is low.

Bodily coordination is one of the most conspicuous of somatotonic characteristics. Where somatotonia is predominant the body appears to function as a unit. Legs, arms, head and trunk are never in each other's way. Somatotonics move with grace, swim, skate and climb easily, and adapt readily to athletic games. They seem to think with the body as a whole, so perfectly does the physical self hang together.

The varying postural preferences of people of different motivational components are distinctive. When the second component is dominant people stand up straight and sit up straight. They have long, erect bodies and hence prefer rather low chairs with level seats. The viscerotonic endomorph often has short legs, and hence he too wants his chair low. But the cerebrotonic ectomorph is made differently. His long shanks indicate the need of a chair with a high seat. His typically short body with its innate need to flex the neck and thighs indicates the need of a chair seat which slopes backward (the seat should follow the plane of the flexed thighs if support is to be distributed—and ectomorphs need their support distributed because their padding is scanty).

Ectomorphs sometimes make the best of a bad furniture situation by tipping their chairs backward and getting their feet as far off the floor as possible. Yet many of them find calling on people with their conventional somatotonic and viscerotonic chairs an ordeal. Possibly there is nothing more unkind in education than the custom of making all children sit in the same sort of (somatotonic) chair and in the same (somatotonic) posture. Postural preferences are unquestionably innate, and it is probably as natural and desirable for a cerebrotonic to sit round-shouldered on the middle of his back as for a somatotonic to sit square-shouldered on the end of his back. The ectomorphic round shoulder is perhaps as normal as the endomorphic round belly.

There is little to be said for the perfectly upright posture except that it is the somatotonic preference, and that it is often associated with high blood pressure. Persons with high blood pressure seem naturally to maintain a posture as upright as possible. Those with low blood pressure naturally seek a position tending toward the horizontal, which eases the strain upon the circulatory system. This is simple mechanics. The tire with the highest pressure stands up the straightest. The practice of trying to make people of low blood pressure stand and sit erect seems to rest on about the same rational foundation as did the prohibition movement. In the one case somatotonia has the upper hand. In the other case, cerebrotonia made an abortive effort to hold it.

The essential characteristic of the period of Christian dominance in human affairs seems to have been an attempted suppression of the somatotonic component. Under Christian influence it was wrong to express somatotonia vigorously, wrong to be ruthless, wrong to lust for power, wrong to worship the muscular body, wrong even to kill people, except heretics, heathens, and enemies of the crown. Probably some of these tabus were good and some bad, but they were in general tabus on somatotonia. With the relatively recent weakening of this (cerebrotonic) influence, the general tabu on somatotonia was so suddenly lifted that a countersuppression of the inhibitory component appears to have resulted. In some quarters children now are as strongly impelled by adults toward somatotonia as they were formerly restrained from it. Yet this vigorous "progressive education" is actually as suppressive as was Christian education at its darkest. It suppresses the third instead of the second component. It is as suppressive to a young cerebrotonic to press him to join in the dance or in the swim, and to make noise and mix and socialize, as it is suppressive to a young somatotonic to make him sit still.

Christianity may in time come to be viewed as a unique anti-somatotonic revolution in human affairs. In a study of one hundred twenty-four different historical paintings of the central figure of Christianity made available to a class in psychology through the Art Institute of Chicago, we found that the Christ had been depicted with a mean morphological first component of about 2.2, second component about 2.6, and third component about 5.4. These were paintings which had been made prior to 1900. The psychohistorical picture of the Christ, then, is approximately that of a 2-3-5 (2-2^2-5^2). Here we have an emphasis upon the third component and a depreciation of somatotonia. It is interesting to note, however, that of seven paintings of the Christ produced since 1915, four depict him as mesomorphic 5 or higher! The counterrevolution has set in. The ban on somatotonia is lifted, and if our grandchildren go to Sunday school they may be shown pictures not of a Christ suffering in cerebrotonic tight-lipped silence on a cross, but of a Christ performing heroic feats of athletic prowess.

The somatotonic component is called the *second* component. This seems biologically appropriate, for somatic development certainly precedes cerebral development. The evolutionary elaboration of the soma doubtless progressed a long way before the cerebrum appeared and complicated matters. So far as our scanty knowledge goes, the first beginnings of an animal skeleton are simply a hardening or toughening of swimming appendages which by vibration assist protozoa in locomotion and hence in the pursuit of food. As the ladder of animal complexity is ascended the chief changes encountered at precerebrate levels are changes in the direction of greater complexity and efficiency of bodily movement. The skeleton with its muscular attachments develops into many experimental forms, serving both as an aid to locomotion and prehension, and as a defense against predatory attack. In crustaceans the skeleton becomes purely external, is wholly a means of defense, and constitutes a fatal hindrance to locomotion. Higher in the animal scale the turtle is found with both an internal and an external skeleton. The turtle has tried to carry on two somewhat incompatible somatic specializations at once. He is well protected against many enemies, but his locomotion and pursuit of prey are hampered. He has made relatively little recent evolutionary progress. Likewise many other animal species have bogged down at some point, apparently through overspecialization of somatic structure.

In some instances the cessation of adaptive change seems to have been brought about through development of sheer mass, as in the case of the mammoths and saurians. In these animals the soma became so enormous and required such huge energy supplies for maintenance that life was overwhelmed. Among the primates there has probably been less somatic overspecialization than among some of the other vertebrates, yet enough of it so that the more somatotonic members of the human race derive their primary ecstasies from aggressive bodily expression, and are able occasionally to stir up a good war.

In young civilizations the second motivational component is at a premium. In old ones it sometimes is regarded as a disturbing inconvenience. Often the same cycle of changing values can be observed in the course of an individual life. Different components sometimes seem to determine friendships and tastes in different periods of life. This is a fact against which sociologists occasionally stumble in their studies of marriage.

Somatotonia is generally the most difficult of the components to gauge. Since it is a dynamic concept, referring to somatic expression, there is conspicuously present in it a gradient which extends from a latent to a manifest extreme. Depending on the predominant environmental pressures, somatotonia may be largely latent and potential, or largely a manifest, surface expression. To gauge this component accurately, it is necessary to know how the individual behaves under *all* circumstances, including those which fully challenge or fully test somatotonia (crucial athletic competition, physical attack, apparent discrimination against the individual, insulting offense, the challenge to competition, etc.). Also it is necessary to study in detail the breathing habits, the cough, laugh, manner of movement and the like. In short it is necessary to look beneath the veneer of civilization.

One of the major skills to be developed by the student of constitution is the ability accurately to detect latent somatotonia. Were it not for this factor, the diagnosis of temperament might

be almost child's play. When not immediately needed, somatotonia exhibits a tendency to disappear from sight, like a cat's
claws. This is especially the case with the more intelligent and
more successfully adapted somatotonics. In a superficial sense
they simulate viscerotonia when not excited (as do the cats). Yet
when subjected to appropriate stimulation the somatotonia makes
itself clearly enough manifest. People showing this characteristic
are frequently quiet-spoken, although the cough, the laugh, and
especially the vigorous breathing are fairly certain to reveal signs
of the latent second component. (Trait S-13, *Unrestrained Voice*,
is thus not always a loud voice. It may be loud only in the cough
or laugh, and under conditions which bring the somatotonia to
the front.)

For a long time we were confused and puzzled by this phenomenon of latent somatotonia. At one time we attempted to score
latent and manifest somatotonia separately, thus introducing a
most disconcerting statistical complication. The difficulty with
such a procedure, of course, is that the manifest-latent factor is a
continuum, not a dichotomy. We now try to meet this problem
by making sure that the ratings are based upon a relatively adequate and complete observation of the individual. In studies in
which the Scale has been used by beginners in this work (see p.
416), we have noted a consistent tendency to underrate the second
component, particularly in the temperamental analysis of women.

The manifest-latent factor operates less conspicuously in the
study of viscerotonic and cerebrotonic traits. In rating cerebrotonia, perhaps because of its contrast in this respect with somatotonia, there is a general tendency for beginners to overrate many
of the traits. Beginners also tend to overgauge the viscerotonia
of the somatotonics, and undergauge that of the cerebrotonics.
In self-ratings nearly everybody grossly overestimates his cerebrotonia and underestimates both of the other components. (Similarly, in self-ratings, most people exaggerate their introversion
and underestimate their extraversion.)

In summary, somatotonia means dynamic expression of the
soma. This component is closely associated with physical drive
and endurance, with a relatively low sleep requirement, with infrequent food requirement, with high blood pressure and the

danger of apoplexy, and with a youthfully athletic body which tends to become solid and heavy as life advances. Somatotonia needs exercise and loves a vigorous life. Dreaming is very remote from waking consciousness and dream analysis is often suddenly revealing to somatotonic people. Somatotonics love noise and the strong voice and the strong walk. They snore irregularly but loudly.

There is about the same proportion of somatotonia in young children as in adults, if noisiness is a good criterion. Somatotonics are likely to enter upon the pathetic quest of the springs of youth. Alcoholism seems typically to be associated with a motivational conflict in which somatotonia and cerebrotonia are at war within a personality, with the former barely holding the upper hand. Somatotonia implies habit susceptibility. The functional or nervous disorders are rare when this component is predominant, but acute appendicitis is common (and dangerous) with somatotonia. People high in the second component love rhythm, the dance, and martial music.

Christianity has been in some sense a religious suppression of somatotonia, but we seem now to have come into a counterrevolution, with a tendency to hoot automobile horns and to amplify every kind of noise in general celebration. We have been on a somatotonic joy ride. Possibly we were a degenerating race, gone too far to brain: the long period of cerebrotonic ratiocination which we call the Christian period might indicate as much. From such a point of view the recent somatotonic revolution, if such it really is, may be a sign of health, even though it be a regression to barbarism. From another point of view somatotonia in the ascendant may be a catastrophe. In any case, we may be sure of one thing: the appraisal put upon history will always depend upon which component pronounces the judgment.

3. CEREBROTONIA

The third component is the element of restraint, inhibition and attentionality. The forebrain holds in check both visceral and somatic functions, apparently to maintain a closer and more sensitive attentional focus. The cardinal symptom of cerebrotonia is tense hyperattentionality. The physical foundation for it seems to lie in relative predominance of exposed surface over mass.

The cerebrotonic is tense, incapable of peripheral relaxation, and chronically aware of his internal tension, although not necessarily disturbed by it. Cardiac distress or heart consciousness, and temporary digestive distress of all sorts are normal manifestations of cerebrotonia, a fact which if generally known might save the public millions of clinical dollars, and the medical profession many headaches. Cerebrotonics are often called nervous or neurotic when they are quite normal, just as viscerotonics are sometimes accused of gluttony and lethargy when they are behaving normally.

The cerebrotonic uses up a great amount of "nervous energy" and flirts with the danger of "nervous exhaustion." He needs more sleep than a person high in one of the other dynamic components. His basal metabolic rate is usually high and he tends to become chronically fatigued in the normal routines of life. The history of fatigability, poor sleep habits, inability to get up in the morning, abnormal caloric requirement, and a chronic sense of internal tension are good clinical indicators of cerebrotonia. These people sleep lightly. The forebrain seems never to let go its dominance completely even in sleep. Dreaming is constant. The dreaming is relatively close to the threshold of clear consciousness, and the process of going to sleep is invariably a slow one. All relaxation is slow. The sphincters "let go" slowly and incompletely. In cerebrotonia the urinary stream is small, and the length of time required for urination is relatively great.

Cerebrotonia is accompanied by resistance to depressant drugs, and nothing is gained by attempting to use the violence of drug depression against the stubbornly resistant forebrain, except possibly in acute pathological conditions. Many cerebrotonics learn in middle life to go to sleep by a routine of "relaxational" exercises. But along with the remarkable resistance to drug depression there is usually a similar resistance to habit. The cerebrotonic avoids enslavement by habit, but often fails to form the routine habits which play so important a part in a normal and comfortable life.

Cerebrotonia gives rise to many manifestations of chronic fatigue in an overstimulated and hurried world. Among these the commonest are the various skin conditions called neurodermatitis, and the symptoms collectively called functional bowel distress. Such conditions are best treated, except for immediate palliation, by the simple procedure of explaining to the patient what is really the matter with him, and inducing him by one means or another to rest and relax, *particularly in the morning* if possible.

For a person high in the third component, the process of getting up in the morning is often an exceedingly painful business. It is only after several hours in bed that this individual descends to really refreshing and recuperative sleep. His deepest sleep is his latest sleep. It may be that for cerebrotonics we should revise the old proverb to read, *an hour of sleep in the morning is worth two before midnight.* Cerebrotonics often become most alert and do their best work in the evening of the day. They are usually most wide awake at about bedtime, and they are often worthless in the early part of the morning.

These people perhaps need to eat four times a day instead of three. They need more food than they have usually been taught to believe. They particularly need protein and the easily digested carbohydrates. Their digestive tracts are under predominantly thoracico-lumbar control, which is really forebrain control. Normally this means tension. Under emotional circumstances it means virtual intestinal paralysis. Absorption is relatively poor, hunger is quick in onset, poorly sustained, and promptly relieved. In cerebrotonia the stomach is ordinarily small, of low capacity, and best adapted to taking frequent small amounts of food rather than infrequent large amounts. The cerebrotonic should never go without breakfast, for to do so is to draw heavily upon his slender store of reserve energy, and this means flirting with the danger of chronic fatigue. It seems to be best for him to space his meals so that he eats about every three and a half or four hours during the waking day.

Cerebrotonic hunger is quick in onset and sharp in quality. But it is poorly sustained. Cerebrotonics do not for long *suffer* from hunger. In them hunger tends soon to give way to a (sometimes rather pleasant) sense of exhaustion and dissociation from physical reality. For viscerotonics, prolonged hunger is extremely painful and death by starvation presents a terrifying prospect. Hunger and solitary confinement are potent weapons of punishment against viscerotonia but not against cerebrotonia. Viscerotonics do not enter upon hunger strikes.

Alcohol is a selective depressant, acting first on the higher cerebral centers, and theoretically releasing the rest of the organism from the inhibition which the cerebrum exerts. This produces a transient exhilaration or feeling of well-being in somatotonic and viscerotonic personalities. There is nothing imaginary about the exhilaration. In persons whose basic motivation is for some reason caught in a state of poorly tolerated conflict, alcoholic removal of cerebral control sometimes comes to be the main ecstasy of life. These people may become as incurably alcoholic as a dementia praecox patient is incurably schizoid. There is little medical or psychological apparatus for reaching such personalities, for as yet there has been no systematically planned therapy based on insight into the relationships among the primary components.

Cerebrotonics can often resist the depressant effect of alcohol with remarkable fortitude, and sometimes they acquire the social custom of drinking, perhaps following the path of least resistance, but they pay well for it. Instead of yielding graciously to the effect of the drug, the cerebrotonic constitution resists violently, using up its reserve energies in its resistance, and a cerebrotonic bout with alcohol tends to be followed by fatigue and low energy for days afterward. For the individual of cerebrotonic motivation, alcohol is a poison. For viscerotonics and for some somatotonics the drug is without doubt beneficent. For all temperaments, alcohol possesses diagnostic value.

It is to be observed that stress or emotional crisis of any sort appears to exert nearly the same effect as alcohol, so far as revealing the relative strength of the primary temperamental components is concerned. Upon this general principle the logic of the "third degree" is perhaps grounded. If a suspected person is badgered long enough, or deprived of sleep for a sufficient length of time, he falls back at last upon his true character and tends to reveal his true nature.

The concept of *intelligence*, or of intellectuality, must not be confused with cerebrotonia. No one seems to have any very definitive conception of what he means by intelligence. The term is too general. There are as many kinds of intelligence as there are kinds of behavior situations. There is symbolic and intellectual intelligence, imaginative intelligence, affectional intelligence, somatic and manipulative intelligence, social and sexual intelligence, economic intelligence, aesthetic intelligence, time orientational or religious intelligence, topographic or spatial intelligence, and many other sorts. Some of these are intimately related and some vary more independently. Spearman and his followers believe that there is more dependence than independence of variability among these several factors. This we also believe to be true, but whether it is true or not, cerebrotonia is a very different and (we believe) a more primary concept.

If there is a factor which can meaningfully be called general intelligence, its definitive principle may lie partly in the way the primary components blend with and integrate with one another. It may be that the most *generally* intelligent person is he who most successfully carries and integrates a heavy endowment in more than one component, possibly in all three. The most supremely intelligent person in the world may then be temperamentally something like a well-integrated 4^2-4^2-4^2. (God is usually pictured as about a 7-7-7: all-loving, omnipotent, and omniscient.)

The cerebrotonic may be literate or illiterate, may be trained or untrained in the conventional intellectual exercises of his *milieu*, may be an avid reader or may never have read a book, may be a scholastic genius or may have failed in every sort of schooling. He may be a dreamer, a poet, philosopher, recluse, or builder of utopias and of abstract psychologies. He may be a schizoid personality, a religious fanatic, an ascetic, a patient martyr, or a contentious crusader. All these things depend upon the intermixture of other components, upon other variables in the symphony, and also upon the environmental pressures to which the personality has been exposed. The essential characteristic of the cerebrotonic is his acuteness of attention. The other two major functions, the direct visceral and the direct somatic functions, are subjugated, held in check, and rendered secondary. The cerebrotonic eats and exercises to attend, the viscerotonic

attends and exercises to eat, the somatotonic eats and attends in
order to exercise. Loss of one of the major exteroceptive media—
eyesight for example—would be more tragic for the cerebrotonic
than for one in whom the first or second component predominates.

The cerebrotonic component finds its primary ecstasy and its
freedom not in eating or drinking, not in fellowship or for long
in sexual companionship, not in physical adventure or in the
power of social domination, but in a certain intensification of
consciousness which appears to arise from *inhibition* of all of
these (somatotonic and viscerotonic) "freedoms." Freedom is perhaps only a general name for the ultimate objective of all striving, and our historical difficulty in defining it possibly takes origin
from the polydimensionality of the first order components of
motivation. For cerebrotonia, freedom seems to be activity of attention relatively unhampered by objective "reality." Even in
schizophrenia, which whatever else it may be, is one condition
closely associated with cerebrotonia, the dissociated mind achieves
a freedom to suppress the objective reality and to range in its
own delusional system, or within its own chaos. For somatotonia,
freedom is freedom of direct action, and for viscerotonia it is freedom to be comfortable, to have a full belly, and to feel possessive
toward the world. Cerebrotonic freedom appears to arise as a
direct function of inhibition—inhibition of viscerotonic and somatotonic freedom.

The major cerebrotonic danger is dissociation from reality.
The freedom of the forebrain is likely to be purchased at the price
of a biological losing of the way, and hence at an apparent end-
cost of suicide. Those who leave the earth and fly too close to the
sun may melt their wings. Those who taste the fruit of forbidden
knowledge run the Promethean danger of divine wrath. Those
who walk in deep thought sometimes fall from the precipice. But
the cerebrotonic can become suicidally schizoid and can thereby
escape all these dangers at once. He throws the baby overboard
to keep it from falling out of the boat.

The nature of the basic motivation in a personality can easily
be determined if an observer can discover what has been the
typical behavior in the face of trouble and stress. The cerebrotonic

in trouble may lose appetite and all desire for action, exercise, travel or companionship. He may resent intrusion and may resist any attempt on the part of others either to cheer him up or to distract him. Intense contemplation of the thing may leave him sleepless for many days and nights, may finally exhaust him altogether, but if the cerebrotonic temperament is predominant, this is his way out.

Much harm is done to cerebrotonics by persons who do not comprehend the nature of this process. Cerebrotonia means that the function of thought is the naturally dominant one, and that in the face of crisis it is this function which must take over the responsibility to find the way out. This may be why cerebrotonics can rarely act effectively in crises. The cerebrotonic finds both his delights and his defenses in the system and detail of his own consciousness. He is internally self-sufficient. He may be kind and affectionate, according to the strength and quality of his first component, and he may be fond of action, according to the strength of the second component, but he is not in the final analysis dependent upon affection or action. In the face of trouble the cerebrotonic must always fall back upon the system and organization which is in his own head, even though the resulting delay may be fatal.

Cerebrotonia is probably the major characteristic of what Jung originally called *introversion*. The principal difficulty with this term is that it sometimes implies pathology and in its common use indicates something undesirable or unhealthy. In the popular conception introversion is a thing which, like ectomorphic posture, ought to be "corrected."

Cerebrotonic skin is typically dry and finely lined, with notable sensitivity to insect bites and to itching. The outer layer of the skin is rapidly shed and replaced. In this sense cerebrotonic skin is highly active. Such people produce large crops of dandruff, but they hold their hair. The baldheaded cerebrotonic is relatively rare.

In cerebrotonia the basal metabolic rate (thyroid function) is typically high. Appendicitis, furunculosis (boils), gall bladder infections, nephritis, and indeed nearly all of the common overwhelming infections except those of the upper respiratory tract are distinctly rarer among people with predominant third component than among the general population. Cancer also appears to be rare among cerebrotonics. The swallowing and gagging reflexes are overly sensitive, and rapid edematous swelling of the laryngeal region presents a peculiar danger in cerebrotonia. Many cerebrotonics appear to have been killed by acute streptococcal infections of the throat, accompanied by edema and strangulation.

Cerebrotonics show remarkable resistance to general anaesthetics. Recovery from a general anaesthetic is slow, however, for the cerebrotonic appears to use up his energy resources in fighting the depressant effect. There is often marked sensitivity to tobacco, and the cerebrotonic constitution cannot as a rule stand up to regular pipe smoking. Tobacco produces a rapid heart, dizziness, and if persisted in, loss of weight.

Cerebrotonics, for some reason, can rarely sing. The difficulty is probably associated with their inability to relax, and with what is called self-consciousness. There is so much internal restraint that it is very difficult for a cerebrotonic to "throw out" his voice. If he succeeds in overcoming this difficulty at all, there is still so much strain that the overtones are lost, and the voice under forced effort so lacks lability that accurate tonality is next to impossible.

In summary, cerebrotonia is related to what has been called introversion but it has more specific meaning than that term has carried, and it has no normal-abnormal connotation. It carries its own norms, as do the other basic dynamic components.

There are a number of distinctive, although not necessarily diagnostic clinical correlates of cerebrotonia. The more conspicuous of these are (1) tenseness, unrelaxability and apprehensiveness, associated with a low, labile blood pressure, (2) neurodermatitis, dry skin, sensitivity to insect bites, and a history of itching, (3) functional digestive disturbances, (4) high sexual eroticism with intense crisis in both sexes, (5) poor voice control and "the paralysis of overawareness" in crucial or emotional situations, (6) thermal instability and poor toleration of both heat and cold— especially of cold water, (7) resistance to contagious diseases except colds, (8) oversensitive upper respiratory tract, with consequent laryngeal irritation and overly active gagging reflexes, (9) resistance to alcohol and to all general depressants, (10) sensitivity to tobacco, (11) suppression (paralysis) of visceral activity in the face of emotion, (12) increased food requirement with inability to gain weight, (13) increased sleep requirement, light sleeping, and resistance to hypnotic drugs, (14) easy or chronic fatigability but with quick recovery, (15) overawareness of or overresponse to pain and to normal organic processes, and (16) a moderately elevated basal metabolic rate which is permanently sustained and therefore not due to intercurrent thyroid pathology.

CHAPTER VI

RELATION OF CONSTITUTION TO ACHIEVEMENT AND ADJUSTMENT

WITH the completion of the investigations giving final form to the Scale for Temperament (p. 26), we were in possession of instruments for measuring personality against a frame of reference applicable simultaneously at both the static and the dynamic levels of personality. It was then possible to describe a personality in such manner that structure and function became meaningful *each in terms of the other*. The six cases presented in Chapter IV illustrate a general truth which we had been forced to accept—that when human structure and human behavior are described in semantically defensible concepts, they turn out to be far from unrelated.

The question of practical application now arises. How might this approach to a dynamic psychology best be applied? What fields of research most need such an approach, and which are most likely to yield returns of direct value to society? At least two fields suggest themselves as equally promising—the field of clinical medicine, and the field of the achievement and adjustment of the individual. A research project may some day be set up which will follow a group of human beings from birth to death—or even through several generations—in a manner so well planned and systematic that these two areas of investigation will become one. But since the practical machinery for this utopian enterprise has not yet been made available, what, in the meantime, should we do?

Our answer has been to carry out as best we could a series of preliminary investigations which extend into both fields. Specifically, three studies have been undertaken, as follows: (1) Two hundred young men, all active members of a university community, have been analyzed both morphologically and tempera-

280

mentally, in a study which extended over a five-year period. The statistical results of that study are presented in Chapter VII. In the present chapter is included a brief descriptive portrait, or psychosocial profile, of each of the 200 cases, and, in order to probe certain of the more sociological aspects of the constitutional problem we have subjected each case to another type of classification—really a common-sense classification of achievement and adjustment. Our interpretations of achievement are made against the background of the constitutional analysis.

(2) In a second, parallel study, we have carried out a three-year analysis of 100 delinquent, homeless, or maladjusted youths (age range 16 to 25) who have been referred (to the writer's vocational guidance clinic) by a Boston social agency. This study, although completed, must for the present be reserved for a separate volume.

(3) We have for a number of years collected constitutional data on clinical entities as they have presented themselves at several hospitals. That measurable constitutional factors are of importance both in clinical diagnosis and prognosis, and in the determination of differential treatment, grows more clear as these studies progress. The constitutional picture appears to play a particularly important role in cancer, tuberculosis, hypertension, peptic ulcer, appendicitis, and disorders of metabolism. Also many of the conditions which have been described as psychiatric entities—such as the schizophrenias, the manic-depressive psychoses, and even chronic alcoholism—appear to be closely related to dyscrasias or irregularities among the primary temperamental components. But at present our observations in this field must be regarded as preliminary and tentative, although in a later volume we hope to be able to present an adequate statistical analysis of these clinical findings.

Here we shall confine our attention to the achievement and the adjustment of 200 men, as they relate to the morphological and temperamental aspects of constitutional analysis.

BASIC DATA FOR A STUDY OF 200 YOUNG MEN

The 200 individuals were all white college students or college graduates, most of the latter associated with academic or professional pursuits. Nineteen of the 200 were either doctors or medical students. The subjects of the original standardizing experiment (p. 13) were excluded from this study. The age range was from 17 to 31, and all but 9 of the 200 were between 18 and 27. In Appendix I (p. 441) the basic data for these 200 cases are presented on a summary form blank which in this study was used for permanent record. Since the record form requires a little preliminary explanation, a copy of it appears below.

No.	Age	Race	Ht	Wt	Somato- type		Regions	1 2 3 4 5	d- g- t-

IT	V	S	C	Health	Strength	C	P	PI	IQ	AI	S	Gp

Comment:

Age, race, height and weight are self-explanatory. **Height** is in inches, **weight** in pounds. The indication of race is only an approximate grouping, following Hooton,[1] according to the four principal variants of the white race. With respect to race, the following abbreviations are used:

     N = Predominantly "Nordic."
     A = Predominantly "Alpine."
     M = Predominantly "Mediterranean."
     J = Jewish, with "Armenoid" characteristics predominant.

The somatotype is given to the nearest half numeral for each component. The somatotypes of the five regions of the body are given only to the nearest whole numerals. d (total dysplasia) is the sum of the differences in somatotype among the five regions of the body. These differences are totaled for the three components separately, after which the three sums are combined (see *The Varieties of Human Physique*, p. 68). Once the five regional somatotypes have been posted, the calculation of dysplasia requires but a few seconds.

g (gynandromorphy or bisexuality) is gauged on a 7-point scale in the manner described on p. 74, *ibid.* The distribution of gynandromorphy, for the male or female population, is a skewed one, the mean for males falling at 2.24 (for 4000 college students). This skewness means simply that the rare extremely effeminate men vary more from the common average than do the extremely masculine men.

As a first step in setting up a scale for gynandromorphy, we followed the same procedure as that used in devising a scale for somatotyping. That is to say, we rank-ordered a series of (in this case 2000) somatotype photographs and then divided the whole series into seven groups which represented equal-appearing intervals of progression from the most extremely masculine to the most extremely effeminate physiques. The former were the 1's in gynandromorphy, the latter, the 7's. But when this was done, it was seen that many more cases fell at the low end of the distribution than at the high end. In fact, the extreme gynandromorphs —the males who most closely resemble women—were found to be very rare, whereas those extremely lacking in gynandromorphy —the highly masculine men—are common. Thus while the total physical difference between gynandromorphy 1 and 2 is about equal to that between gynandromorphy 6 and 7, we found only two or three cases falling in the latter category, and hundreds of cases in the former category.

Upon examining further the large number of photographs which fell at 1, 2 and 3 on this scale, we found that *within each degree of gynandromorphy*—at least at the lower range of the scale—there was sufficient variation to render a further refinement of rating practicable. We therefore adopted the practice of rating gynandromorphy to the decimal within each of its seven degrees, and in constitutional analysis, where detailed comparisons become important, we have found the resulting scale to be adequate and useful. Actually we find it necessary in practice to make use of the decimal ratings only at the lower end of the scale.

The textural component, *t,* is measured by a rating on the physical refinement or aesthetic quality of the individual, taking an average for the five regions of the body as a whole. For practiced eyes, the aesthetic judging of human bodies is quite as easy, and may be as accurate, as any other rating. The textural component, like gynandromorphy, is gauged to the decimal on a 7-point scale, and the curve for its distribution is even more sharply skewed than that for gynandromorphy. The mean *t* index for 4000 college students was found to be 1.96. In a study not yet published we have found the mean t index for 2000 men of the general population to be 1.81. So far as the first region of the body (head and neck) is concerned, it is easy to set your sights to match our scale for t. Sit in a public place like a railway station, and carefully grade each adult who passes a selected point. When your mean for a few hundred cases is about 1.8, your scale matches ours. For the other regions of the body, try a public beach in summer. It will be found that both the t component and gynandromorphy are easier to learn to scale than are the primary morphological components, for the former are simple linear variables—not multidimensional concepts.

IT is the index of temperament, following Table 2. V, S and C are the raw scores for the three components of temperament.

In addition to the above basic data, supplementary observations were made on each individual's health, strength, physical, mental and aesthetic intelligence, and on manifest sexuality and gynandrophrenia.

For the purposes of this research **health** is graded on a 7-point scale as follows: extremely good (7), very good (6), good (5), fair (4), poor (3), very poor (2) and extremely poor (1). The ratings are based on an analysis of the medical history.

What we call central strength (**strength C**) was measured by an adaptation of the "back and leg lift" or total lifting strength of the individual, as standardized by Dr. Sargent at Harvard. The scaling was done by plotting the raw scores for the 200 cases, and dividing the range into seven equal intervals. The 1's are the extremely weak people, the 7's the extremely strong.

Peripheral strength (**strength P**) is measured by the hand dynamometer (also standardized by Dr. Sargent) and is scaled in the same manner as central strength.

PI is a rating on "physical intelligence," gauged on a 7-point scale. The mean of the distribution for the 200 cases was 3.07. In gauging this characteristic the problem is simply to observe and estimate how well the individual handles himself in a physical sense—that is to say, how well he handles his particular physique, and how effectively he uses his muscles. In considering a 2-2-6, we would of course not look for ability at fighting or at competitive athletics, and would not expect the individual to stand, sit or

walk in the somatotonic posture. The 2-2-6 appears to be legiti-
mately entitled to his ectomorphic stoop, his round shoulders, his
slightly projecting belly, and his need when sitting to have his
point of support well forward (in contrast to the mesomorph, who
likes to sit erect, with his point of support well back). But the
2-2-6 may be a tireless long-distance walker and an excellent
dancer, and he may show grace of movement and dexterity in
whatever he undertakes. Or he may be clumsy and awkward in
all things—a physical moron. The 1-7-1 with his erect mesomorphic body and straight back may be blundering and oafish, or
he may function as a superb physical machine in both gross and
fine dexterity. The 7-1-1 may vary in physical intelligence from
an almost helpless mass of shimmying fat to a fairly active and
industrious physical personality. Persons who are 7 in endomorphy
are usually good swimmers, and they frequently possess fine
dexterities.

IQ is simply the conventional intelligence quotient. We did not
administer any intelligence tests ourselves but made every effort
to obtain old records of **IQ** wherever such records were available.
Four or five different tests of **IQ** are represented. We have made
no attempt to correct these to a common standard except that they
have all been corrected to the 16-year age basis. Where more than
one **IQ** report was available, the average was taken. **IQ** records
were secured on 110 of the 200 cases.

AI is aesthetic intelligence, a factor doubtless of interest in any
study of personality, but one which is generally disregarded because there are no objective standards for its measurement. As
we use the concept, **AI** measures the degree to which an individual
reveals fine discernment and sensitive appreciation of his environment. It is the extent to which he shows a discriminative insight
into, and a participating empathy with the surrounding world,
human and non-human, living and non-living. For a time we
attempted to scale this trait on a curve approaching the "normal"
distribution, but we were forced at last, as in the case of the *g*
and *t* components, to recognize that the distribution is a skewed
one, with the median close to the low end. Using a 7-point scale,
the mean **AI** for the 200 cases was 2.34. For a better grasp of our
procedure in scaling **AI**, see Appendix 3.

S is manifest sexuality, or the relative importance and prominence of the sexual impulse in the individual's history. We are attempting here to measure, through analysis of the medical history and the life history, how prominent a part sex has played in the individual's consciousness and in his general adjustment to life. **S** is not to be confused with sexual potency or with any such concept as sexual strength—we have no way of estimating that. We are concerned here with *manifest* sexuality, or with the question of how much of a stir sexuality has made in the individual's life, and how much of his attention and energy go into this channel.

We find enormous differences in **S**. In the matter of frequency of masturbation, for example, there are three youths in this series who have presumably never induced the sexual orgasm auto-erotically. There are two others whose masturbation rate exceeds fifty times per month. Three who have long established habits of regular intercourse find that they are able to keep up a rate of thirty (in one case forty) times per month. There are others who consider that once a month is about the right cycle. One married man estimates once in four months as his normal gait.

Some individuals who for one reason or another have fought and restrained both masturbation and intercourse are nevertheless subject to frequent or chronic Priapism, and to almost unceasing sexual desire. Others find that life proceeds in placid freedom from any such intrusion upon consciousness. We hoped to find out who these different kinds of people are, in constitutional terms.

A rating of 7 in **S** indicates an individual in whom the sexual impulse is so strong and so sustained as to set him apart as an extremely erotic person. A rating of 1 means that the individual is almost entirely free of sexual impulse. The intermediate steps represent "equal-appearing" intervals of progression from the low to the high extreme. The mean rating on sexuality for the 200 cases is 3.10.

Gp is gynandrophrenia, which is presumably the dynamic counterpart or temperamental counterpart of gynandromorphy. Gynandrophrenia represents the strength of the element of mental femininity in the male. At the behavior level, gynandrophrenia is the strength of the "sissy" element in the male, and of masculinity in the female. At the mental level it is (to use Jung's terms), the strength of the *Anima* in the male and of the *Animus* in the female. Using a 7-point scale, the mean strength of the *gp* characteristic for the 200 cases was found to be 2.55.

The order of presentation of the cases in Appendix 1 is the same as that to be followed in the present chapter. The cases are presented in order of ascending strength of the first morphological component (endomorphy). Within each of the seven degrees of endomorphy they are arranged according to ascending strength of mesomorphy.

A CLASSIFICATION ACCORDING TO ACHIEVEMENT AND ADJUSTMENT

The 200 young men whom we are about to introduce as individuals have been classified according to somatotype and index of temperament, and also according to the other, presumably secondary variables which have just been described. But all of these data have to do with the description of the individual himself—supposedly with his constitutional endowment. Also of interest is the question of what the individual has done, what he has accomplished with his endowment, and how he has adjusted to life. Constitutional analysis, in and of itself, may not be particularly interesting, but it may be of value insofar as it can throw light on such a matter as achievement and adjustment. We need, therefore, some sort of sociologically meaningful classification against which to review and assess the constitutional variables.

As we review the social histories of the entire series of 200 youths, with this problem of classification in mind, it seems evident that all of the cases can be included reasonably within four general categories—plus six subcategories—of achievement. There will be a good deal of overlapping, of course, and many of the cases will appear to fall between two such classificational groups, but a rough distributive device of this kind may nevertheless serve a useful purpose. Our sociological categories, or achievement-groups, are to be described as follows:

1. *The Superior Group.* People of superior achievement, who not only show well-integrated personalities but give promise of making a contribution, and seem to have the psychological wherewithal needed to make good the promise.

2. *The Normal Group.* Adequately integrated personalities of ordinary achievement. People who have found a *persona* through which comfortable or acceptable adaptation is achieved.

    2a. Those who appear to have fallen naturally, or without the effort and struggle of readjustment, into a normal and acceptable pattern. Strictly speaking, these are the only "normal" people and to them we refer as "normal-without-effort."

    2b. Those who by dint of struggle and readaptive effort have achieved a socially acceptable adaptive pattern, usually in the face of difficult constitutional endowment. These are "normal-through-effort."

3. *The Unadapted or Poorly Integrated Group.* Persons of sufficient endowment who yet are caught in such conflict or internal difficulty that socially acceptable adaptation has not been achieved.

    3a. The temperaments that appear to be swamped with too much competing strength in two or more of the primary components. The "overloaded temperaments." In most instances the index of temperament (**IT**) falls outside the normal occurrence of somatotypes, in the direction of over-endowment. Roughly speaking, these are the people who are overwhelmed by too many gifts. They are the "overly endowed."

    3b. The overcompensational somatoroses. Personalities showing such excessive aggression (presumably in the face of some degree of environmental suppression) that an acceptable adaptation has not been achieved. So far as our observation extends, such people are always mesomorphs, and are usually (but not always) of short stature. We call them the "soma-torotics."

    3c. The dyscrasias (bad mixtures) associated with temperamental reversal of a morphological dominance. Most of these contradictions occur in the mid-range, or rather evenly balanced somatotypes. It is most often the second order dominance rather than the first order dominance that is reversed (e.g., a 3-2-5 in somatotype becomes a 2-3-5 in temperament). We refer to these cases simply as "reversals."

3d. Miscellaneous maladjustments. Normally endowed but badly integrated personalities caught in difficulties not accounted for in one of the three preceding subgroups. Many of these people show an unresolved conflict between the second and third components. Some are heavily endowed both with sexuality and with one or more of the primary components. Some appear to be victims of purely environmental or vocational maladjustment. In some instances the difficulty may lie mainly in a low intelligence. A few cases are encountered (none in this series of 200) in which the individual seems simply to be endowed with too much of one component, while both of the other components are held at the minimum. These are the simple visceroses, simple somatoroses, and simple cerebroses. All are rare, but an example of each was presented in Chapter IV (Aubrey, Boris and Christopher, respectively). This miscellaneous group sometimes gets called "sexual-environmental misfits."

4. *The Constitutional Inferiors.* Weakly endowed temperaments. Insufficiency of primary component strength, especially insufficiency of the second component (somatopenia). In most instances the index of temperament falls outside the normal occurrence of somatotypes, in the direction of underendowment.

TWO HUNDRED CASES PRESENTED INDIVIDUALLY ACCORDING
TO SOMATOTYPE

The four general groups of behavioral patterning just described seem to suffice as a frame of reference for indicating the major variations of achievement commonly encountered on a university campus. The sample of 200 personalities which we shall now present individually is too few to establish more than the most general tendencies among the individual somatotypes, but with such a frame of reference in the background, it will be worth while to look at the series in some detail. Comparison of physique with temperament within the different somatotypes offers a rich soil for speculation. In making these comparisons it would repay those not already familiar with the various somatotypes to turn to Chapter VI of *The Varieties of Human Physique* and read the

morphological description of each somatotype as it occurs in the
series.

In the section to follow, the 200 cases are presented according
to somatotype, as indicated by the center headings. (Following
each somatotype is a page reference to *The Varieties of Human
Physique* [VHP] which the reader may consult for a description
of the somatotype and, when available, a photograph of an illus-
trative case. For the basic data on each of the 200 cases the reader
may refer to Appendix I.) The cases that follow are arranged (as
in Appendix I) according to ascending strength in endomorphy,
and within each degree of endomorphy, according to ascending
strength in mesomorphy. The classification according to "achieve-
ment-group" (appended at the end of each description) represents our best effort to fit the individual into the foregoing classification as to basic achievement.

The 1-1-7
(VHP 143—Fig. 1C)

A single example is encountered in this series. Case 1, temperamentally 2-1-6, is a weak, inconspicuous youth who has succeeded
in making an acceptable integration in the face of what must perhaps be regarded as poor constitutional endowment. He is inoffensive, quiet, defenseless, extremely low in physical strength and
somewhat below average in mental endowment. He has no special
gifts of a productive or creative nature, although he is said to
possess unusually sensitive appreciation of art. He has a fairly
strong endowment of sexuality, which has been expressed mainly
in excessive masturbation. He is markedly dependent on people,
and since he has little access to women, he cleaves to men. He is
what might perhaps be called an "intellectual homosexual," but
he is not a true homosexual. His masturbational imagery is entirely feminine. His vocational outlook is fairly good. He will
never offend anyone, and he thus offers one of the essential prerequisites for success in many endeavors. He stands at the borderline of constitutional inferiority but escapes into normality. By

taking up a position behind the *persona* of the arty way of life
and speech (Wagner becomes for him a reverential "Vaahgner"),
he has achieved a modicum of personal distinction and a degree
of successful adaptation. Fortunately some of the most desirable
women experience a peculiar attraction to this fragile, arty pattern of male personality which seems to be poised on the brink
of both constitutional inferiority and homosexuality. Classification, *group 2b*.

The 1-2-6's
(VHP 148—Fig. 22)

Two examples, the first a gifted representative of group 1, the
second an illustration of group 3a.

Case 2, temperamentally 2-3-6, combines the extreme sensitivity
and mental intensity of a high cerebrotonia at its best with sufficient somatotonic drive to aim high and to keep the course, and
he has enough viscerotonia to give him a modicum of relaxation
and sociophilia. This youth is highly intelligent, and ambitious. He has a secondary social aggressiveness which makes
enemies, and sufficient sexual drive to assure him of entangle-
ment in monkey traps of diverse sorts. Trouble he will find in
plenty. He is already strongly disliked in some quarters. But his
chance for first-rate achievement appears to be uncommonly good.
Group 1.

Case 3, temperamentally 1-3-7, is swamped under a total temperamental strength of 10 in the second and third components
against the minimal 1 in the relaxing viscerotonia. He is bright
and has excellent health, but the storm he has to ride out during
the first three or four decades of life is a severe one, and his physical craft is frail. The situation is complicated by that intense
manifestation of sexuality (S) which seems to be the rule with
this somatotype. The temperamental index (1-3-7) falls outside
the range of occurrence of somatotypes. That is to say, in his temperamental manifestation this youth ventures out beyond the
boundary of what nature suffers to occur morphologically. In this

sense he appears to defy natural law, although we do not know what significance is to be attached to such an aberration. Any case which does so depart from the morphological distribution must necessarily deviate in one of two directions, i.e., either in the direction of overendowment, such as the present instance, or in the direction of underendowment. Instances of the latter deviation seem to be always constitutional inferiors (group 4). Instances of the former sort appear always to encounter serious trouble and conflict, but a few are apparently able to ride out the storm and to achieve an integration of personality at a high level, often comparatively late in life. Possibly many of our geniuses are drawn from this group. In one sense these people are constitutional superiors, although many of them fail to find an adequate adjustment, and are destroyed.

Case 3 is involved in a Laocoön-like struggle between his cerebrotonia and an interfering somatotonia. Possibly he will win out and come in the end to a good integration of his impulses, but the law of averages is very much against him. He is more likely to become confused, frustrated and cerebrotic. This is one "schizoid type" of personality. *Group 3a,* but with a chance for group 1 or 2.

The 1-2-7
(VHP 144—Fig. 18)

A single example. Case 4, temperamentally 2-3-6, is a highly intelligent, rather bewildered youth who is immature for his age and seems more like a high school student than the college senior that he is. Like many of the ectomorphs he is overloaded both with sexuality and with (cerebrotonic) restraint of it. He has not yet begun to reveal his full mental strength in overt achievement. He is a good example of the kind of personality which may well develop toward successful integration at a high level (group 1), or may fall back upon normality (group 2), or may in the face of badly resolved conflict fail to make an acceptable integration (group 3). He is too young for any final classification. People of his pattern mature late. Since he has not shown evidence of any special gifts, and since his index of temperament falls safely within the normal range, the chances are strongly in favor of a normal adjustment. We place him tentatively, therefore, in *group 2b*.

Note: It might be helpful to remember that from the point of view of total component strength there are four subfamilies of somatotypes, each having its own distribution within the general distribution of physiques. These four are what we call the 9-totals, 10-totals, 11-totals, and 12-totals. The 9-totals are comprised of the various permutations of 1, 1 and 7; of 1, 2 and 6; and of 2, 2 and 5. The total strength of the three components adds up to 9. All of the 9-totals are scarce, most of them rare. Altogether there are twelve of these somatotypes. Hunt them up in Figure 6, p. 375, and it will be seen that they form a symmetrical pattern by themselves (as does each of the four subfamilies). If temperament were to follow physique exactly, all of the 9-totals would border upon under-endowment in basic component strength. Possibly, as a group, they do so border. Certainly when the total temperament endowment falls below 9, the individual appears to fall short of adaptive potentiality and is then to be classed among the constitutional inferiors (group 4).

The somatotypes 1-1-7 and 1-2-6 fall among the 9-totals. The 1-2-7 introduces the second subgroup, the 10-totals. This group, which includes 33 somatotypes in all, is made up of the permutations of 1, 2 and 7; 1, 3 and 6; 1, 4 and 5; 2, 2 and 6; 2, 3 and 5; 2, 4 and 4; and 3, 3 and 4. Some of these somatotypes are of frequent occurrence, although as an average they are less often encountered than are the representatives of the 11-total subfamily. (For the frequency of occurrence of the various somatotypes see Table 23A, p. 268, *The Varieties of Human Physique*.)

The 1-5-4's
(VHP 164—Fig. 36)

Two examples, one showing normal integration of personality, the other presenting a severe somatorosis with many of Adler's now classical symptoms of overcompensational striving.

Case 5, temperamentally 2-5-4, presents a serious countenance to the world. He is intelligent, hard-working, and successful in his profession, but he gives the impression of being one who finds life neither pleasant nor funny. He has a conspicuous twitch of the mouth (tic), and suffers from a painful gastric ulcer. He seems always to be under internal strain, as if he were working too hard. Actually he drives himself hard, and manifests a remarkable degree of energy. He appears to have achieved an acceptable integration of a difficult temperamental endowment. According to our observation, the 5-4 combination in the second and third components is a difficult one to handle, especially when gynandromorphy is unusually low. *Group 2b.*

Case 6, temperamentally 1-6-4, is a short, wiry mesomorph with a painfully well-developed somatorosis. Aggression pours out of him like steam from a teakettle. He would like to conquer the world and to feel it groveling under his heel. If only he were a Jew he would be a good example of the stereotype "the aggressive Jew." However, we have not found it to be the "Jew" who is aggressive, but the somatotype, particularly the short mesomorph. We have indeed found that a singularly high proportion of Jews are short mesomorphs, and somatorotic, but this is equally true of some other groups. For case 6 the temperamental index 1-6-4 falls outside the range of the distribution of somatotypes, in that sense defying nature. Such an individual needs to be highly gifted to make his position good, or needs the advantage of some unusual social circumstance, and where one such person finds successful integration out at this level of motivational overloading, it is apparent that many fail. A total strength of 10 in the second and third components against the minimal 1 in viscerotonia constitutes too great a strain. We have yet to see a personality carry that combination without encountering serious trouble. This youth has several times been referred to the university psychiatrist. He periodically boils over with hatred and frustrated aggression, but also he suffers from cerebrotic symptoms, especially insomnia and intense itching (neurodermatitis). He seems to have no academic future. The university psychiatrist gives him a poor prognosis. *Group 3b.*

The 1-6-2
(VHP 188—Fig. 54)

A single example, Case 7, temperamentally 2-7-2, is perhaps an even better illustration of somatorotic overcompensation. His index of temperament likewise falls outside the morphological distribution, and does so at one of the polar corners of the distribution. This young man, now 29, has a long history of pugnacity and physical violence, but he never fell into trouble with the law until about a year ago when he killed a man with an automobile. At that time he was given a suspended sentence for manslaughter. Although overwhelmingly somatotonic, he yet manifests enough viscerotonia and cerebrotonia to introduce a singular unpredictability of behavior. He is quick to violent anger, and his moods cannot be trusted. They almost invariably give way after a little time to some violent somatorotic outburst. During the past seven years he has had numerous jobs but has always quarreled with his superiors. For a year now he has been unemployed and has been drinking heavily. *Group 3b.*

The 1-7-1's
(VHP 203—Fig. 1B)

Two examples, both illustrating comfortable integration of personality. Case 8, temperamentally 3-6-2, is a short, powerful youth who is popular and highly regarded in all quarters. He is considered modest. He is highly somatotonic but shows no trace of somatorosis. That is to say, there is nothing socially maladaptive or unacceptable about his manifestations of somatotonia. He is relaxed, good-natured, sociable. In a physical sense he is aggressive and highly competitive, but he is free from hostility. *Group 2a.*

Such a case demonstrates that short stature and mesomorphy alone are not enough to account for somatorosis. There is more to the matter than merely these two variables. Alfred Adler used to postulate that behind the overcompensational (somatorotic) manifestations there is always the problem of some kind of felt inferiority, usually an organic inadequacy. Perhaps Adler's conception was a sound one. Possibly the basic elements lying behind somatorosis are (1) mesomorphy and a somatotonic temperament, and (2) some essential physical incompetence of which short stature is a common but by no means a constant example. Needless to say, if such a conception is to be accepted, the idea of a physical incompetence must be considered in relation to the social situation in which the individual is placed, as Adler pointed out.

Case 9, temperamentally 2-6-1, is a youngster of 17 who presents a picture remarkably similar to the last. He is an open-faced, sociable, candid youth with an extremely active body and a quiet manner of speech. His central interests are almost entirely in athletics and in hunting and similar outdoor adventures. He is mentally slow (mentally muscle-bound, he himself says), but sound, dependable, and thoroughly honest. *Group 2a.*

According to our observation, the 7's in mesomorphy who are of normal stature tend as a rule to fall back to 6 in somatotonia, and are less likely to be somatorotic than are the 6's in mesomorphy, who often become 7 in somatotonia. Possibly the mesomorphic 7's are more internally secure, and less prone to feel the organic inferiority and incompetence which Adler described. In any event, the 1-7-1 as we have observed him (possibly two dozen examples all told) is typically "well adjusted." He seems to be very secure in his world, and seems rarely to experience the motivation which disturbs men sufficiently to spur them to unusual mental achievement. We never quite escape from the suspicion that mental achievement is at bottom something of a pathological phenomenon, perhaps usually of a substitutional nature, substituting for such physical certainty and security as is felt throughout life by the 1-7-1.

The 1-7-2
(VHP 190—Fig. 56)

A single example, Case 10, temperamentally 2-6-3, is in at least a physical sense a highly gifted young man, for he has the physique which is almost the universal masculine ideal (see *The Varieties of Human Physique*, p. 190). Furthermore he has a high t component. That is to say, his physique presents a relatively high degree of aesthetic perfection, and his features are finely chiseled. His somatotonia drops back to the more comfortable 6, while a 2 in viscerotonia gives him a degree of relaxation and poise. But the picture is a little complicated by an intruding 3 in cerebrotonia, which in the face of the 6 in somatotonia necessarily introduces strain and some inconsistencies. This youth is aggressively ambitious, but he suffers from an internal friction which at times becomes severe. He has had intermittent spells of insomnia, and suffers mildly from a recurrent ulcer of the duodenum. When tired, he is irritable and shows signs of tension. But outwardly he is a hard-driving, extremely energetic young man who is successful and popular. Intellectually, he is only mediocre. *Group 2a.*

Note: The gauging of somatotonia in the extreme mesomorph requires comprehensive observation. One must not be misled by the general characteristic of security and composure. Sevens in mesomorphy do not usually display their somatotonia quite so conspicuously as do many of the mesomorphic fives and sixes. With them the somatotonia tends to fall back away from the surface a little, lending them a social composure and a modesty or quietness of personal manner which may falsely suggest viscerotonia to the unguarded observer. Before gauging a trait it is necessary to analyze the individual's entire history and if possible to observe him in crucial and arousing situations as well as in routine adjustments. The extreme mesomorphs are singularly secure in their world and when not under any particular stimulation they tend often to behave in what may be called a pseudo-viscerotonic manner. They are composed and comfortable, like well-fed great cats. It is necessary to know how one of them behaves when fully aroused before his true somatotonic endowment can be gauged accurately. To jump to the conclusion that, because of an habitually calm exterior, a mesomorph's somatotonia is low, is like supposing that a purring tiger or tomcat lacks his normal lust for the kill. Watch the cat in the presence of what he considers game or danger before deciding about his somatotonia. The felines with their supremely efficient musculature are extreme mesomorphs. Except when coddled by the human race, they live exclusively by the kill, which is somatotonia rampant. Yet a superficial observer of a fat tomcat purring in Aunt Agatha's lap might miss the somatotonia and might overestimate the viscerotonia. We suspect that the great mesomorphs of human society are somewhat similarly coddled, and quite rightly, for else they might be dangerously knight-erranting about the country. As a result of soft and easy living the somatotonia drops back away from surface manifestation. This is one reason why rating scales superficially applied are of such doubtful value in psychology.

The 2-1-7
(VHP 145—Fig. 19)

A single example. Case 11, temperamentally 3-1-6, has achieved a good integration with a difficult constitution—if an adaptation involving homosexuality can be called good. It is really a source of wonder how this weak, fragile young man can belong to the same species of animal as the 1-7-1. He has virtually no physical resistance or aggression at all. He is almost as defenseless physically as an oyster out of its shell. Such a personality could thrive only in a highly organized, protective society. But *in* such a society this youth has made an acceptable adjustment. He lives in a world of meticulous discrimination of form, color, sound and speech, and he lives only for the minute discriminations. He has no interest in general social theory, and none in scientific fact. He has been an overt passive homosexual since the age of 16, always playing the feminine role in the relationship. He has what is in some respects an excellent mind, and appears to be a good instructor in the field of romance languages. *Group 2b.*

Note: The extreme ectomorphs appear to have a most difficult adaptation to make. They are in a physiological sense the most exposed, or most highly sensitized of people. They are therefore, theoretically at least, especially subject to overstimulation and confusion. Because of this excessive biological overexposure they need to make an adaptation largely of a protective nature, to cut down the overstimulation. The biological overexposure of the ectomorphic organism may represent an extreme evolutionary departure from an original, safer, more endomorphic condition. The ectomorphs may in one sense be hyperevolute, as has been repeatedly suggested in speculative anthropological literature, especially by the Italian anthropologists, Viola and di Giovanni.

If such a notion is sound, then the cerebrotonic phenomenon of "introversion" is perhaps a natural compensation for the *biological* extraversion of the ectomorphs. Introversion would then be an adaptive turning away from an overstimulation which, as the world becomes crowded with human beings, tends to overwhelm the ectomorph. Conversely, extraversion, which is perhaps only a manifestation of a relatively strong need and appetite for more stimulation, may be a natural adaptive response of the relatively underexposed (biologically introverted) organism.

Case 11 is a well-adapted extreme introvert. His salvation appears to lie in complete absence of somatotonic aggression. He has accepted that wholly passive role in life which men have traditionally prescribed for women, thus avoiding external conflict and protecting himself from confusion and stress. The homosexuality is possibly an unfortunate but natural by-product of such a complete abandonment of "normal" aggression. It is doubtful that homoeroticism is in itself ever a first choice adjustment, but in such a circumstance as this it may perhaps be the only available adjustment outside of pure autoeroticism. The competitive sexual arrangements and conventional sexual stereotypes being what they are, it is possible that society offers case 11 no hope of finding a heterosexual outlet which can meet his peculiar needs. The homoeroticism might then represent for him an intermediate step between isolative cerebrosis and a generally acceptable social adaptation.

The 2-2-5's
(VHP 159—Fig. 30)

Three examples. The first is a confused, homosexual theological student who has made a poor adjustment. The second, in spite of strong distraction by sexuality has made a brilliant record. The third is a hebephrenic schizophrene.

Case 12, temperamentally 3-2-6, after making a mediocre undergraduate record, entered the theological seminary, where he has done poorly. He seems always to have been confused and morally weak. He has a way of seeking people out and enlisting their sympathies through his very bewilderment, and through his viscerotonic dependence on others. There have been intermittent spells of viscerotonic expression of piety. For about five years he has been a passive homosexual, at times somewhat promiscuously. He is something of a *poseur* in several aesthetic fields, but is accurately informed in none. Twice he has been in trouble on account of petty thievery, and has been tricky and dishonest in a petty way concerning money. Yet he is in a sense personable, and has been given a supporting scholarship at the theological seminary. He himself does not believe that he will ever become a minister. Classification, *group 3d.*

Case 13, temperamentally 2-3-6, has made a good integration in spite of the combination of high sexuality and high cerebrotonia. He is shy and restrained, and makes poor rapport with women, although his sexual need is great. Outstandingly brilliant in high school, he entered the university at 16, at just about the time when adolescence was fully bursting upon him (adolescence seems nearly always to be late in the ectomorphic somatotypes). Sexuality hit him like a tidal wave. He became an excessive masturbator, often masturbating five times a day. In the freshman year he did poorly, and dropped out of college during the second year with a "nervous breakdown," losing that whole year. During the following year he established for the first time a sexual liaison. From this time on he has achieved brilliant academic success, although a considerable portion of his energies has been lost in an incessant struggle with sexuality. He is now regarded as one of the promising young men of the academic community. Although, as he puts it, he had to "masturbate his way furiously" through college, and sexuality has severely staggered him, it has not quite stopped him, and he now shows signs of steadily increasing intellectual strength and efficiency. Classification, *group 1*.

Case 14, temperamentally 3-1-5, seems to present a clear case of somatopenia and constitutional inferiority. Always an excessively weak, effeminate person, he graduated from high school with his class, but in college he very soon showed schizophrenic symptoms and became altogether disoriented at about Christmas time of the first year. Hospital diagnosis, hebephrenic schizophrenia. After six months in the hospital he was sent home temporarily, but has not greatly improved. As a child he avoided other boys, and girls too for the most part, although he played a little with his sister. He seemed to learn easily in school, but never took part in any of the usual activities of other children. He is hypogenital, and in fact had virtually no adolescence. He has never shown any interest in sexuality. *Group 4*.

The 2-2-6's
(VHP 151—Fig. 24)

Five examples, two poor adjustments, two fairly good adjustments, and one excellent personality.

Case 15, temperamentally 3-2-6, has been a weak, flaccid kind of individual since childhood. He is what is known as a "sissy." Avoiding all of the usual interests of boys, he was something of a dilettante aesthete in high school and in college, becoming mildly interested in art and music, but he never found the energy to become accurately informed in either field. He has never become accurately informed in anything. He is physically weak and mentally mediocre. Unfortunately he has a strong sexual endowment. This keeps him frustrated and unhappy, for he has little to offer women. He has never turned to homosexuality, but has built up a complicated routine of autoeroticism. He has a collection of imported etchings and also a collection of symphony records, but experiences poor success in showing them to young women. As a schoolteacher he has been a failure, and although still associated with the School of Education he is actually drifting. *Group 3d.*

Case 16, temperamentally 3-2-6, presents a picture remarkably similar to the last. He too is weak, with a difficult combination of 6 in cerebrotonia with 3 in viscerotonia. He is of rather low intelligence and is without any special gifts, but is swamped with frustrated sexuality. Like case 15 he has turned to an arty, effeminate *persona* and this is but a thin mask with which to cover a pitiful mental and spiritual poverty. He is a great symphony listener and art gazer. After graduating from college in five years, this youth is now living at home and loafing. He has no plans and has made no serious effort to get a job. *Group 3d.*

Case 17, temperamentally 3-1-7, appears to have been thrown by nature into a still thicker constitutional briar patch, but he has crawled out of it to make a good integration of a difficult personality. The total of 10 in the first and third components against 1 in the second component does not occur morphologically, save in the rare 5-1-5 somatotype which, so far as we now know, is always Froehlich. This youth has a Froehlich or eunuchoid suggestion morphologically, and temperamentally he is almost totally lacking in sexual drive or interest. He is hypogenital. Possibly he owes his successful adaptation in part to his freedom from sexuality. He has selected the highly protected vocation of library work and appears to have effected a permanent escape from the frustration and perplexity of a viscerotonic-cerebrotonic overendowment. *Group 2b.*

Note: It is interesting to observe that the highest manifest sexuality appears to occur in those males whose physiques approach, but do not too closely approach, the feminine pattern. Cases 15 and 16, for example, have weak, feminoid physiques. They show rather high gynandromorphy and also very high sexuality. But case 17, with a still weaker physique, and a *very* high gynandromorphy, has almost no sexuality at all. These three cases but illustrate a principle which seems to be general throughout the series. Especially in the presence of a predominant ectomorphy, sexuality appears to rise with gynandromorphy up to a certain critical threshold, beyond which it drops off steeply or perhaps disappears altogether.

Case 18, temperamentally 2-3-5, is one of the brilliant and effective people of the series. A tall, conspicuously frail but unusually healthy and boyish-appearing young man, he seems to have met with universal acceptance. He appears never to excite hostility in any quarter. Yet he has a distinct undercurrent of ambitious drive and has entered into academic competition with much of the zest and eagerness with which a 2-6-2 might enter into athletic competition. In the academic field, which he has now made professionally his own, he is looked upon with great favor, and may perhaps be considered a champion. There is a touch of the Messiah about him. In his best moments he plans world reform. Yet in this youth's private life there is the problem of a disturbingly strong sexual appetite. So far, he has confined his Messianic inclinations mainly to the disciplining of his own life, and up to the present he has been fortunate in his sexual adventures. *Group 1.*

Case 19, temperamentally 2-2-5, is a bedraggled Jewish youth who is really a sort of refugee from the world at large. He is weak, both physically and mentally, but he knows it, and by adopting the *persona* of excessive humility has solved his problem of adaptation. He entered college at 20, struggled through five years of undergraduate poverty, and graduated at 25 with mediocre standing. He has been taken under the wing of the Sociology Department, and is now working on a survey. *Group 2b.*

Note: As a general observation, it is worth noting that none of the 2-2-5's or 2-2-6's, of which we have just considered eight examples, seem to experience the common difficulty of socially resented aggression. People of these two somatotypes sometimes show traits of aggression, but so far as we have observed, their aggression very rarely brings trouble upon them. Nobody seems to mind the aggression of a 2-2-6. Possibly this is because the 2-2-6 does not present a serious physical threat. In contrast, 2-3-5's are frequently involved in bitter turmoil, and are often badly beaten. Indeed, we sometimes refer to the 2-3-5, 2-3-6 and 2-4-5 as "Promethean" somatotypes.

The 2-3-5's
(VHP 160—Fig. 32)

Nine examples, presenting a wide diversity of personality patterns. Case 20, temperamentally 1-3-6, is one of those harsh, sharp-faced and sharp-tongued little men by whom nearly everybody is irritated, but he seems to thrive on the concerted effort of his acquaintances to put him down. He has a vocal somatorosis. His high, piercing voice lifted in strident argument is one of the familiar sounds of his environment. He has not yet been known to be pleased by anything except Russian politics, and among those who know him best the suspicion is strong that the true charm of Russian politics lies in its remoteness from his own real circumstance. The aggression of this youth is mainly vocal and mental. He lacks the somatotonia necessary for physical aggression. To the best of our knowledge, and of his, he has never been in a physical combat, and very rarely has anyone used violence upon him. *Group 2b*.

Note: To classify such a personality in terms of achievement is a matter of predicting events which may still be well in the future. Such a youth is likely not to "find himself" for many years. He might in the end become identified with group 1, 2, or 3. Whatever else may be true of the 2-3-5, he usually matures late, remains flexible and relatively unpredictable well into adult life, and is likely to contradict the overt rationalization of his *persona* many times in the course of his development. There is fairly good indirect evidence for associating the 2-3-5 somatotype with the traditional Messiah or Christ (see *The Varieties of Human Physique*, p. 155). The Christ picture is in some respects at least a personification of one human ideal. Possibly one of the "ideal" male *personae* tends to invest its morphological anchorage in the 2-3-5 somatotype. But if so, the temperamental expression of such an ideal *persona* would probably not very closely resemble the harsh, uncompromising, unsympathetic 1-3-6 pattern seen in Case 20.

Case 21, temperamentally 1-3-7, presents a further exaggeration of the preceding temperamental pattern, and this personality borders upon psychiatric pathology. The 10 to 1 ratio against the first component appears to represent an overendowment which nature cannot tolerate. The university psychiatrist diagnoses this youth as: psychoneurotic personality with a chronic anxiety neurosis. The prognosis is considered poor. *Group 3a.*

What treatment might be suggested? The successful adjustment of case 17 recommends for one thing the advisability of a highly protected vocation, and complete freedom from competition of any sort. Our own experience with cases of this kind suggests two other expedients which have in some circumstances appeared to bear fruit: (1) protect the individual completely from physical exercise, especially from group exercises, gymnastics or postural exercises (the objective here is to relieve the strain of the conflict through de-emphasis of somatotonia); (2) fatten him by cream feeding, and keep him in a condition of physical rest as much as possible (the objective here is to support and if possible to stimulate and develop the weak component, which is viscerotonia).

Case 22, temperamentally 2-4-4, has developed his personality in a direction opposite to that of the last two cases, and has achieved a remarkably effective harmonizing of the second and third components. This is one of the most promising young men to have been associated with the university in some years. It is worth noting that he has a very high dysplasia. Yet his personality as a whole is splendidly integrated and harmonized. Conflict and frustration are certainly not to be blamed in any simple, direct way upon dysplasia. The dysplastic physical weakness of case 22 is in his lower trunk (region 4), while both his arms and legs (regions 3 and 5) are relatively strong. Classification, *group 1.*

Case 23, temperamentally 1-5-4, presents for the first time in this series an index of temperament which reverses a morphological predominance. The third component predominates over the second morphologically, but in the temperamental index, the second component is stronger than the third. This is a highly aggressive, almost a somatorotic youth, who is violently disliked and who in turn expresses bitter hatred and scorn toward most of his environment. He is pugnacious, although he lacks the physical strength to make good his pugnacity, and is generally regarded as a physical coward. There is no relaxation or humor in him. He is always under a strain, always quarrelsome. In an uncivilized society this kind of person would probably be destroyed very early, for his aggression far outruns his physical resources as to either offense or defense. But in society as it is the prognosis for Case 23 may be good. His academic standing is good, and his ambition is rigidly fixed. He will probably become a successful doctor, and may eventually make an important contribution. On the other hand he may "crack up." He illustrates an apparently successful integration of a most difficult pattern of personality. *Group 2b.*

Case 24, temperamentally 1-4-5, is a youth showered with the best gifts of both nature and man, who is yet at the moment essentially unattractive and repellent. He has what might be called a cold, austere outlook. He is trying to be an aristocrat in the worst sense. Handsome, well-bred, intelligent, wealthy and secure, he is aggressively intolerant and gives every indication of wasting his life. But the present indication may be misleading. With the temperamental index of 1-4-5, and good intelligence, he ought theoretically to develop mental drive and intellectual curiosity. He may be a late developer. His adolescence was in fact very late. Classification, *group 2a.*

> Note: This may be a "pure" motivational problem, in the sense that a different manipulation of environmental influences might even now greatly alter this youth's achievement and the expression of his personality.

Case 25, temperamentally 2-3-6, lives under an almost cerebrotic strain. He carries the weight of *Weltschmerz* on his slender shoulders. In a society built upon a theological certainty he would probably be quite happy, for he is tender-minded and a born savior, but he is sufficiently intelligent to have realized the difficulty of determining in just what direction society can best be saved, and so he is caught in the position of a hen with an egg to lay but with no nest in which to lay it. He has made the common last-ditch effort of turning to psychologists, psychiatrists, "personnel people" and "guidance experts" for help. All of these have turned him away not with empty hands but with empty words. In the end he will probably become disillusioned and "twice born" or will be an embittered radical. The 2-3-6 temperament is not likely to turn to orthodox preaching. This youth closely resembles what has been called the Promethean personality, but probably falls just short of it through insufficient strength, and perhaps also through insufficient intelligence. The great weakness of Prometheus is an inability to compromise. Case 25's present classification must be *group 2b*, but this is likely to change either to group 3 or to group 1.

Case 26, temperamentally 3-4-4, has developed his personality in the direction of strengthening both of the first two components against the third. This young man is secure and solid in his world, well relaxed, intelligent, attractive, good humored. Except for numerous episodes of a sexual nature his life proceeds smoothly and successfully. He must needs poke his nose into every possible sexual adventure, like a setter dog into bumble bees' nests. Classification, *group 2a*.

Case 27, temperamentally 3-3-6, illustrates psychopathology arising both from overendowment in primary component strength and sexual overendowment. The temperamental index 3-3-6 is another of those which fall out beyond nature's morphological limits. As a freshman in college and as a senior in high school this youth "found it necessary" to masturbate at least twice daily. As a college sophomore he established a homosexual relationship, but later went over to completely heterosexual adjustment. Sexuality has become, at least for the present, the dominant factor in his life. His chief intellectual interest is now the collection and reading of *erotica*. Yet his mental endowment is excellent. He is said to have an IQ of 145. Classification, *group 3a*, but he may later achieve either group 1 or group 2b.

Case 28, temperamentally 3-3-5, is still another highly sexed 2-3-5, but one who has made an excellent adjustment. He is considered a promising young biologist, who next year will be made an instructor in that field. He admits a "slight trace" of emotional ecstasy associated with cutting into living tissue, and this sometimes has a specific sexual reference. In the sexual act he experiences a strong desire to bite, or to destroy. Active flagellation has given him excitement, and a young woman who enjoys this art exercises considerable power over him. Yet in this case the sexuality has not interfered with the main line of achievement. He states that he lives for sexuality, but maintains that he "lives well" for it. Classification, *group 1*. Probably there is danger of a later relapse into group 3d.

The 2-3-6
(VHP 154—Fig. 26)

One example, Case 29. The 2-3-6 somatotype introduces the relatively populous subfamily of the 11-totals. This subfamily, which includes 24 somatotypes, is made up of the permutations of 2, 3 and 6; 2, 4 and 5; 3, 3 and 5; and 3, 4 and 4, in addition to the six rare somatotypes, 3-7-1, 4-6-1, 5-1-5, 5-5-1, 6-4-1 and 7-3-1. These comprise, as a group, the most commonly occurring of the four subfamilies, although the 2-3-6 is not common. No somatotype containing a 6 in a component is common.

Case 29, temperamentally 2-3-6, is a young theologian in whom a strong cerebrotonia and a strong sexuality have combined in such singular manner as to give rise to a remarkably flourishing variety of prudery. He is a great crusader about short skirts and similar encroachments upon decency. Meanwhile he is married to a voluptuous little creature whose general atmosphere is so sexy that she might be called rakish. It seems to be a very happy marriage. The young man announces without a smile that one of his primary duties to God is to keep his wife sexually happy. Classification, *group 2b*.

The 2-4-4's
(VHP 166—Fig. 38)

Six examples, illustrating a variety of what for the most part are rather normal adaptations. Case 30, temperamentally 2-5-4, is a somewhat aggressive, but well-integrated young Jewish medical student of average standing. His index of temperament does not depart from his somatotype except for an increment in the second component. He has a singularly low *t* component, and is intolerant of anything "impractical." He shows a number of minor cerebrotic interferences with the major somatotonic theme. He bites his fingernails, has a peculiar eye-blinking tic, and had irregular eneuresis up to age 10. He is an incessant cigarette smoker and has a mild peptic ulcer. Classification, *group 2b*.

Case 31, temperamentally 3-3-4, is well relaxed, docile, weak and colorless. This is a good, average citizen, undistinguished and morally dependable. Temperamentally, there is almost an even balancing of the three primary components, but with a slight predominance of the component of restraint. His boyhood, school and college history, marriage, and his later high school teaching are all perhaps best described as uneventful. Nothing very good or very bad has happened. *Group 2a*.

Case 32, temperamentally 1-5-4, is possibly a good example of "the aggressive Nordic." This lad is strained, pugnacious, impatient, unrelaxable, and he is called excessively aggressive. He has a number of (what we presume are) minor cerebrotic symptoms. These include a marked insomnia, severe migraine headaches and a most disturbing neurodermatitis centering about the anal region. He must be considered to be achieving a normal adjustment, however, since at 19 he is fully self-supporting and is doing acceptable work in college as well. Classification, *group 2b*.

Case 33, temperamentally 3-5-4, appears to be carrying a heavy load, but it is a well-balanced load and except for sexual complications he carries it well. This is a rather deliberate, sound and cautious, but singularly determined and stubborn individual. It is a temperamental pattern that is common with the 3-5-3 somatotype, but is not often seen with the 2-4-4 somatotype. This youth has a peculiarly strong sexual drive which he refuses to curb. He speaks jokingly of retaining an abortionist on a year-to-year basis. Possibly the combination of high sexuality with a strong somatotonia is a little dangerous. Fortunately, this combination appears to be fairly rare. Classification, *group 2b*.

Case 34 is a 2-4-4 both morphologically and temperamentally. He is low in dysplasia, and is about at the mean in both *g* and *t*. He is indeed about average in everything. This is about as average a youth as is often seen. His social adaptation is above reproach. He is a rather protected young man who mainly does and says the right things, and except for his rather insistent sexual desire (which irritates and disturbs him), he would be perfectly serene and happy in his world. His principal sin is masturbation. Classification, *group 2a.*

Case 35, temperamentally 2-4-5, shows the insecurity and tenseness of a predominant cerebrotonia complicated by fairly strong somatotonia. He is a sort of intellectual crusader. He is personally modest to the point of shyness, but he is intellectually aggressive and messianic. Such personalities, to be happy, seem to have to express a religious devotion to some cause. Case 35 shows a religious devotion to one of his professors. Classification, *group 2b,* although he may well achieve group 1 later on.

The 2-4-5's
(VHP 162)

Four examples, two with brilliant records. Case 36, whose temperamental index remains constant to his somatotype, is an outstanding academic success. Yet during the past year he has been experiencing difficulty because of his sexuality. He is sexually aggressive but tactless and impatient. Of late he has been on the prowl much of the time, attracting unfavorable attention from academic authorities. He would abolish marriage, having worked out a detailed plan for the extra-marital scientific rearing of children. Our prediction is that he will run into increasing difficulties for some time to come but that he will keep his head and will fulfill his early promise. Classification, *group 1.*

Case 37, temperamentally 3-4-4, is relatively easygoing and relaxed as compared with other ectomorphs. He seems contentedly complacent about his world, mixing sociably in a young married set to whom intellectual ambitions or interests are as foreign as full dress at a ball game. Among this group he is considered quite a model husband. He does not let it be known that he is a college graduate. Classification, *group 2a.*

Case 38, temperamentally 1-3-7, is so pitifully cerebrotic, so tense and apprehensive, so schizoid and overwhelmed with restraint that interviewing him is a painful experience. No vocational adjustment seems possible for him except one of the most protected nature. Library work has been suggested, but this involves graduation from college, which seems nearly impossible. We believe that such a situation as this can sometimes be met successfully by keeping the boy out of college until he is two or three years older than the average of his class, then sending him to a small college where girls predominate numerically. Classification, *group 3a*.

Case 39 is temperamentally and morphologically a 2-4-5. He has an enviable academic record and is looked upon with great favor by his faculty, but like case 36 he struggles with a sexuality which threatens him with confusion. What *ideally* might be done for these brilliant, overly sexed ectomorphs? Certainly not early marriage, in the conventional sense, for with a predominant cerebrotonia and a good somatotonia they are too exploratory and too full of curiosity for early acceptance of monogamy, except perhaps at the expense of a general settling back and stifling of their best potentialities. A more open and better controlled prostitution? Another kind of marriage, more experimental or noncommittal in nature? These have been and still are interesting questions. Case 39, like many 2-4-5's, is a religious fanatic. He preaches atheism and the "religion of scientific method" upon all occasions. Classification, *group 1*.

The 2-5-2
(VHP 193)

One example. Case 40, temperamentally 1-7-3, illustrates what might be termed a successfully defiant somatorosis. With this combination of components an individual usually leads a stormy life. Case 40 is an "aggressive Nordic-Alpine" of short stature who openly defies his entire environment, but strangely enough he appears to be making good his defiance. Concerning him the Dean of the Medical School says, "I'd enjoy shooting him, but he is one of our good students and I believe he may in time become a good doctor." Classification, *group 2b*, with a possibility of reaching group 1 or of falling back into group 3b.

The 2-5-3's
(VHP 177)

Ten examples, showing a remarkable variety of adjustments. Case 41, temperamentally 2-6-3, is a young physical educator who has a little too much ectomorphy for comfortable success in this field. He is somewhat brittle and fragile in the distal segments of his extremities. Having made a poor academic record, he has nothing else to which to turn, unless he drops out of academic life altogether. This is a case of fairly serious vocational maladjustment, and the situation is complicated by a tactless over-aggressiveness as well as by a certain personal crudity (note the low t component). The prognosis in his present vocational field is poor. Classification, *group 3d.*

Case 42, temperamentally 2-6-3, shows the same temperamental and morphological components as the last, but is a size larger and is making an excellent adjustment. His excessive somatotonia goes mainly into exercise and athletics, at which he excels. His social bearing is pleasant and essentially modest, although he shows several minor evidences of cerebrotic interference and is easily embarrassed. Occasionally he loses his temper badly. He has a peculiar love of privacy, and a pronounced sociophobia. He has no intellectual ambition and makes no intellectual pretense, but wants to be a good farmer and will probably succeed. Classification, *group 2b.*

Case 43, temperamentally 2-7-2, illustrates a somatorosis which appears to be out of bounds so far as nature is concerned. This youth has displayed sufficient aggression to fall several times into the toils of the law. Recently, upon pleading self-defense, he was acquitted of a homicide charge. Possibly the short, overly somatotonic mesomorph of low t component comes as close to a *general* criminal type as we are likely to find. Among a group of 170 Massachusetts criminals recently examined by the writer, about 40 per cent were found to fit this general description. Only about 3 per cent of the general population fit it. Classification, *group 3b.*

Case 44 is a tall 2-5-3 with a temperamental index of 3-4-4.

This is a normal, well-adapted, rather popular youth who lays no claim to brilliance or to humor, but aspires to become a successful doctor and to take over his father's practice. He is about average in nearly everything except tennis, at which he excels. He has got himself engaged to a most desirable young woman. Classification, *group 2a.*

Case 45, temperamentally 2-5-4, is a confirmed alcoholic who at 22 appears to have given himself over entirely to that escape pattern. This youth's earlier history shows an unhappy struggle between somatotonia and cerebrotonia. He has always been intermittently somatorotic and arrogant, but likewise he has been hyperattentional, tense, and unable to routinize his life. The 5-4 combination in somatotonia-cerebrotonia seems peculiarly difficult to harmonize, although we have observed that the temperamental 3-5-4's appear to be better integrated than the 2-5-4's or 1-5-4's. In one group of sixty institutionalized chronic alcoholics we have found no less than eleven apparent examples of the 2-5-4 temperamental pattern. Among this same group there are thirteen examples of the 2-5-3 physique, although the overlap between the eleven 2-5-4 temperaments and the thirteen 2-5-3 physiques is only four cases. No. 45 seems to be caught in an almost hopeless conflict between the second and third components. Classification, *group 3d.*

Case 46 shows the "unnatural" 1-6-4 in temperamental index, and the strain under which he lives is painful to watch. He has a terrific drive which keeps him feverishly at something or other. He seems scarcely to sleep at all. He believes that he sleeps only four hours a night, but that is probably not strictly true. The cerebrotic interference is manifest almost constantly. He has spells of extreme sociophobia, insomnia, periods of exhaustion, intermittent bouts with alcoholism and with excessive cigarette smoking, and he suffers recurrently from a severe peptic ulcer. It is perhaps this last difficulty which makes his surprisingly good adjustment possible. For the ulcer places him in medical hands two or three times a year, when he is forcibly put to rest and has his life routinized for him. It also frightens him away from alcoholism, which otherwise might destroy him. In the face of this background, case 46 has made a rather brilliant academic record, although his social adjustment is jagged and paranoid. He is harshly intolerant, and suspicious. Now a graduate student in psychology and also a medical student, he plans to become a psychiatrist. Classification, *group 2b,* with perhaps a chance for group 1 in the end.

Case 47, temperamentally 2-6-2, is an aggressive, go-getting young man who yet is rather comfortable and good-natured in his general adjustment to life. He is restless, unhappy unless doing something with his muscles, and he must always be going somewhere. But there is little sign of tension. He remains mentally relaxed and intellectually undeveloped. He is regarded as a good real estate salesman. His health is perfect. He likes to drink but never drinks too much. Classification, *group 2a.*

Case 48, temperamentally 2-6-3, is a somewhat somatorotic, noisy youth who has been a nuisance both to himself and to others. He periodically besieges the university psychiatrist about his problems. On such occasions he becomes loquacious and is difficult to be rid of. He envisions himself as organizer of a new movement in psychiatry calculated to revolutionize social life by applying Freudian philosophy to education. He knows almost nothing of Freudian theory, however, and is in danger of failing out of college. During the past year he has developed signs of a duodenal ulcer, although no confirming diagnosis has been made. Classification, *group 2b.*

Case 49 is another example of the interesting 2-5-4 temperament, this time accompanied by first-rate intelligence. This is a ruthless, aggressive, but clearheaded and efficient person, who has an excellent academic record and permits no grass to grow under his feet. He hates the world, essentially, but he intends to make it give him what he wants, which is principally money and sexual surfeit. During the past two years he has complained of pain and discomfort which suggest peptic ulcer, but no confirming diagnosis has been made. Classification, *group 2b.*

Case 50, temperamentally 3-6-2, reverses the secondary predominance between the first and third components, yet the resulting personality appears to be a well-adapted and a flourishing one. We have in our records only a few cases of this particular reversal of a dominance—a reversal in favor of the first component against the third. So far as we can see, such a reversal puts little strain on the adjustment, but perhaps in some instances rather favors a comfortable integration. However, the converse of such a reversal, where the third component rises at the expense of the first, places a heavy strain on the personality. Case 50 illustrates another principle which will grow increasingly evident as the series progresses, namely that the incompatibility between the first and second components is less sharp than that between the second and third. A temperamental index of 3-6-2 usually produces (as in this case) a happily integrated personality. This young medical student has a good time living, and on the practical, hard-working side will probably become a good doctor. Classification, *group 2a.*

The 2-5-4
(VHP 168—Fig. 46)

A single example, case 51, with temperamental index remaining constant to the somatotype. This is a vigorous, hearty, but internally insecure young student preacher, who expresses his insecurity by crushing people's bones in the "warm" handclasp of enthusiastic fellowship. The internal tension from which he suffers is great. He seethes with energy, and with the wish to go out and save the world. But when he is alone, fatal doubts assail him. Relief is generally to be found only in masturbation. He does not drink, and normal overt sexuality seems to him still far out of reach. He has symptoms of duodenal ulcer. Classification, *group 2b.*

The 2-6-2's
(VHP 194—Fig. 62)

Six examples, all athletic and all showing for the most part excellent integration of personality. If all the world were made up of 2-6-2's, most of the mental perplexities which vex human society might soon disappear.

Case 52, temperamentally 3-5-2, is ordinarily calm and composed, but he becomes transformed into a raging fury when fully aroused, as in the last quarter of a football game after somebody has kicked him in the face. He then generally rises to superhuman feats. This is a truly happy young man. Intellectually he has climbed only to the lowest fork of the apple tree and will very soon hop down from even that perch, for he likes to have the ground under his feet. But he will become a good citizen. Vocational plan: athletic coaching. Classification, *group 2a.*

Case 53 holds temperamentally to the 2-6-2. He has an ectomorphic dysplasia in his legs and is too easily injured for great success on the football field, but he is on the team. This lad carries his somatotonia closer to the surface than does the last. He is more overtly or more obviously aggressive. He is rather loud of speech and reckless or breezy in manner. After a serious automobile accident last year, he was out and about within a day or so, as carefree and extraverted as ever, rather pleased with his exploit. He is called happy-go-lucky, and is generally well liked or at least tolerated. Vocational plan: athletic coaching. Classification, *group 2a.*

Case 54 is a very short 2-6-2 who has a temperamental index of 2-7-1. This little mesomorph bounces about like a bull terrier. He is one of those not very rare cases who establish a popular and rather widely accepted *persona* founded upon aggression and cockiness, blended with tolerance and generous good nature. The combination of 2 in viscerotonia with 7 in somatotonia against the minimal 1 in cerebrotonia seems to work out better than any of the other five permutations of 1, 2 and 7 in temperament. This boy is on the wrestling team and hopes to find a vocational niche somewhere in the field of physical education. Classification, *group 2a.*

Case 55, who drops back from the 2-6-2 somatotype to the more comfortable 3-5-2 temperament, has too much gynandromorphy (2.8) for football success, but is a star swimmer. Swimming profits from, or even requires, an increased buoyancy of the hindermost part of the body—hence the gynandromorphic mesomorphs are usually excellent swimmers. Case 55 is also an excellent student, and is a leading candidate this year for a Rhodes Scholarship. He is celebrated as one of the most approved all around personalities in the university. Classification, *group 1*.

Case 56 is a short 2-6-2 who is a 3-6-1 in temperament and has achieved an excellent integration of his personality. He has inexhaustible energy, together with a good natural buoyancy and excellent physical and mental health. Doubt and conflict are concepts almost entirely foreign to him. He will probably never have insomnia. Note the low *t* component and the fact that he is excessively hirsute. He springs from "menial" stock, but he is not worried about it. Indeed, in his present social *milieu* he finds this an asset. He will probably make a good doctor. Classification, *group 2a*.

Case 57, temperamentally 2-7-2, is a somatorotic mesomorph who shows an index of temperament falling outside the natural boundary. He rises to the extreme 7 in somatotonia without falling back correspondingly in either of the other components. This is an "aggressive Jew," with a vengeance, who makes life uncomfortable both for himself and for others. If he were king, or even an outstandingly good student, he could perhaps successfully live out his *persona*, haughtily overriding his environment. As matters are, his resentment and aggression continually boil over, like a kettle of stew. He has one gift, however, which possibly leavens the picture sufficiently to help him make a normal adjustment. He is an excellent swimmer, and an intercollegiate champion in this sport. Note that we find two champion swimmers in the 2-6-2 somatotype, both with relatively high gynandromorphy. (We have observed that the swimming sprinters are nearly always mesomorph 6's or 7's. The longer distance swimmers are higher in endomorphy.) Classification, *group 3a*, with a good chance to settle into group 2b later in life.

The 2-6-3's
(VHP 179—Fig. 6B)

Two examples. Case 58 is a 2-6-3 with a temperamental index of 3-5-3. He has what for a 6 in mesomorphy is an extremely high gynandromorphy, and this apparently has made his adjustment difficult. He has always been a physical coward, regarding himself as abnormally weak. Among his undergraduate classmates he was known as a sissy, and was considered queer, but he has never been homosexually inclined. He is an excellent swimmer, although he never competed for the college swimming team. Fortunately he has a first-rate academic record, and has now moved into a period of life when the disappointments and frustrations of the younger period have begun to be replaced by the satisfactions of solid achievement along intellectual lines. He is now relaxed, good-natured and humorous, as well as energetic. Classification, *group 1*.

Case 59 is a 2-6-3 temperamentally as well as morphologically, and it is without doubt a difficult pattern of temperament. This youth might be described as an unsuccessfully aggressive mesomorph, with a good deal of cerebrotonic interference. He stutters badly. (While we have not yet observed many stutterers, those we have observed have been most often persons showing conflict between the second and third components with the second generally the strongest component.) He has poor sleep habits and complains of much internal sense of tension and strain, associated with emotion. He has done poorly in college after entering on a football scholarship, which he lost during the second year, without ever making the team. He has no plans. Classification, *group 3d*.

The 2-7-1
(VHP 207—Fig. 67)

One example of this rare, powerful physique. Case 60, temperamentally 3-6-1, is a big Polish-Italian who has cashed his fame as a football player and has already been hailed as a businessman although still an undergraduate. He has become an associate in one of the lucrative Chicago rackets, and is riding high on the wave of fortune. Last spring his girl was runner-up for the title, "Miss America." He boasts that this honor cost him $1500. He is generous, expansive, and as innocent of morality as of Greek philosophy. Classification, *group 2a*.

The 3-2-5's
(VHP 160—Fig. 33)

Five examples, all of them rather weak and gynandrophrenic personalities. All of them are bewildered and troubled in one way or another about sexuality. Case 61, temperamentally 4-3-5, is lazy and overly fond of good living, while at the same time overly apprehensive and restrained. He has intermittent periods of energetic effort and of good resolution, but these spurts never last long. He is neither a man's man nor a woman's man, and life for him is perpetual confusion. He has no sexual life except auto-eroticism, which he practices to excess. Endowed with a good natural intelligence, he appears to be swamped and checkmated by conflicting impulses. The 4-3-5 temperament seems in this case to be a little too much for the 3-2-5 somatotype. Classification, *group 3a.*

Case 62 shows the temperamental index 4-1-5, which index, at the level of morphology, corresponds to a very rare and extremely effeminate somatotype. This youth should have been a girl. He is almost an example of the Froehlich syndrome, and has been under extensive medical treatment, first for an undescended testicle and later for his borderline Froehlich condition. Also he has been hospitalized for tuberculosis. In spite of these handicaps he has made a fairly good adjustment in his work at the School of Music. He is hypogenital and is almost entirely lacking in sexuality. Classification, *group 2b.* He probably falls very close to the threshold of group 4.

Case 63 has the difficult temperamental pattern of 3-2-6. He is mentally gifted but is overwhelmed with sexuality and cerebrotonia. He is driven by so strong a sexual desire that sexuality is a constant obsession, while he yet altogether lacks the courage and address to achieve any sexual fulfillment. He "abhors" homosexuality, and this perhaps gives him a good prognosis. During the teens he masturbated excessively and was badly frightened by a (probably misguided) physician who told him he would ruin himself by his daily practices of this nature. He has never had sexual intercourse except with two or three apparently repulsive prostitutes, who seemingly but made matters worse. In spite of his difficulties he is considered by his faculty to be a good risk. Classification, *group 2b*. If he can avoid being totally ruined during the next few years, it is to be supposed that the sexuality may recede, and he may then achieve group 1.

Case 64 is a 3-2-5 who holds to the same pattern temperamentally. He is probably a good example of simple vocational maladjustment. Of better than normal intelligence, he has done poorly in medical courses and is in imminent danger of being dropped from the medical school. His father, a 3-5-2, is a successful doctor, and the son turned willy-nilly to that profession. No pressure was put upon him to do so, but nobody ever discouraged him from it. Actually he dislikes medical work, and probably could never become a good physician. He wastes much of his time in a chiefly unsuccessful pursuit of sexual satisfaction. Classification, *group 3d*. He may change this classification after a vocational readjustment.

Case 65, temperamentally 3-2-4, is a constitutional inferior with a temperamental index which falls outside the morphological distribution in the direction of underendowment. This boy is hopelessly weak in every sense. He has been so since childhood, probably since birth. A son of moderately wealthy parents, he was placed in private schools because of failure in the public schools. Entered college as a special student at 19. His personality is a pleasing one. He is shy, modest, well relaxed, with a faint, wistful smile which misleadingly suggests insight and intelligence. Classification, *group 4*.

The 3-3-4's
(VHP 167)

Eight examples of this common somatotype, which closely approaches the "balanced" group. As a group the 3-3-4's seem to be a rather well-integrated and academically successful lot.

Case 66, temperamentally 3-3-5, has a good academic record which probably would have been a brilliant one but for interference from his imperative sexuality. This has brought him embarrassment in several respects. At 27, he has twice been married; and twice divorced. He considers himself a connoisseur of women, and perhaps rightly. He is very attractive to women. Note the high *t* component. The dean of the graduate school considers him one of the most promising young men in the natural science field. He has already done important and original work in chemistry. Classification, *group 1*.

Case 67, temperamentally 2-4-4, is another graduate student of high standing in the university. He is a harder, more intent, and more ruthless person than case 66. He seems to know just where he is going, and has little time for foolishness. He is not pugnacious, but is sharp and curt with people. He is in general disliked but respected. He is overly fond of sex, but few know it. In sexual matters he is shrewd and discreet, as well as ruthless. His professional future appears to be bright. Classification, *group 1*.

Case 68 rises to a 4 in viscerotonia while the other components are equal to those of the physique. He is overly sociable, complacent, and at loose ends. In four years he has found nothing to hold his interest for more than a few months, although there have been numerous abortive beginnings of interest. He has much superficial curiosity. He has made many friends and antagonizes nobody. His only plan is the very general one of depending on his friends. He thinks somebody will give him a job, and indeed he has several vague promises. Classification, *group 2a*, but he may in time come to grief and join group 3d.

Case 69, temperamentally 2-4-5, probably illustrates vocational misplacement. He has a pretty high cerebrotonia for engineering. He has complained frequently of migraine headaches during the past year, has had a good deal of trouble getting his glasses adjusted properly, and has been subject to insomnia. The vocational problem has been discussed with him, and he proposes to continue stubbornly with engineering, even in the face of strong discouragement from his dean. The dean calls him headstrong. The 4 in somatotonia against a 5 in cerebrotonia makes a difficult personality to handle. It is our own prediction that this youth will some day make his mark, although probably not in engineering. He has both perseverance and intelligence, but has not yet harnessed the two together. Classification, *group 2b,* with a chance for group 1 later on.

Case 70, temperamentally 3-4-4, appears to have an almost perfectly integrated personality for academic success. He is too fragile to suffer much distraction from intrusion of athletic activities or interests, yet he is physically strong enough and healthy enough to carry a heavy work load comfortably. He is in every sense normal, and is without distracting outside interests or even hobbies. He is near the top of his class in scholarship. Classification, *group 2a.*

Case 71, temperamentally 3-3-4, appears to be a victim of prosperity. He says, "I didn't ask to be born. Why should I get serious about it?" His principal interest is in sexuality, a game which he plays with the poise and skill of an expert tennis player on the practice courts. He is mentally alert and watchful, but he is also physically relaxed and is always well poised. He leaves an excellent taste in the mouth, for he is simple, candid and intelligent. Women go for him like trout for a fly. He seems to offer just what sexy, attractive women, in at least one of their common moods, most desire. In interviewing this youth we at first were inclined to pity, but in the end were inclined to envy him. What mental development he may undergo later is an interesting speculation. He is now drinking a good deal. Classification, *group 2a.*

Case 72, temperamentally 3-3-4, is constitutionally very similar to the last, except that he lacks the background of wealth. He too is strongly interested in sexuality, and is attractive to the more sensitive and discerning women. Women seem to know intuitively that only these moderate ectomorphs possess both the physical sensitivity and the sexual vigor that they crave. Women who feel secure in their world appear to seek 3-3-4's, even 3-3-5's and 2-3-5's, with singular frequency. We believe that women who feel less secure tend to desire the more massive and reassuring strength of the male mesomorph. In one sense ectomorphy is a luxury in this world. Case 72 has given excellent promise of a fruitful career in biological science. Classification, *group 1,* but he may well fall back to group 2a.

Case 73, temperamentally 3-3-3, is a constitutional inferior whose graduation from college reflects the gravest of doubt upon the integrity of American higher education. This weak creature has only one strength. That is his very helplessness and dependency. He has an effective way of expressing gratitude, and of making people feel responsible for him. With an IQ of 83 and with no compensatory special ability of any sort, he graduated from a university, majoring in art appreciation. His passive homosexuality is well known about the campus. Classification, *group 4.*

The 3-3-5's
(VHP 161)

Five examples, showing a wide diversity of adjustment. Case 74, temperamentally 2-4-5, is perhaps as good an illustration of the "typical Messianic" personality as an individual can be. He is intent, strong-willed, overly watchful and suspicious, yet highly intelligent and competent. At whatever period he might be born, he would surely save the world with something or other. In this particular incarnation he has already employed two salvational media: first atheism, then communism and "rights of labor." Note the great strength in his hands (peripheral strength). Such a personality is socially uncomfortable, but it may be that these are the really important people. They are sometimes dangerous. Many of them become paranoid and implacably revengeful. They are sometimes heroic idealists. Unfortunately, they come usually from a somatotype heavily charged with sexuality. Sometimes they tend to mix their sexuality with heroic idealism, and then they put a great strain on women. Now and then this terminates tragically. Classification for case 74, *group 1.*

Case 75, temperamentally 4-3-5, illustrates a heavy loading in temperamental components which in this instance has not swamped the boat. Here the total strength of 12 has been carried in good balance. This youth appears to have developed for the most part only the positive or useful traits contributing to his viscerotonia and cerebrotonia, and to have avoided most of the impedimentary characteristics—such as laziness and complacency on the one hand, and sociophobia and apprehensiveness on the other. Such a happy solution is unusual when the component strength rises to 12. Classification, *group 1.*

Case 76, temperamentally 3-3-5, seems on the face of things to be merely a normal, well-adapted, pleasant young man. He is rather sociophobic, spends much of his time alone in the woods and fields, and is an expert amateur naturalist. He seems singularly immature and socially undeveloped for his age. One is surprised to discover that he carries internally a very disturbing sexuality, the chief outlet of which has been through vivid autoerotic phantasy. Like most persons of his somatotype and of the neighboring ectomorphic somatotypes, he shows a relative genital hypertrophy (relative to his total physical mass) and an overendowment of sexuality. He does not seem yet to have found himself in an adult sense, although his academic record is good. We suspect that he may later develop unusual mental strength. Classification, *group 2a,* with perhaps a chance for group 1 later.

Case 77, temperamentally 3-2-5, drops back away from his somatotype on the somatotonic side. He is effeminate and weak, without a compensating intellectual strength. Such a picture is not a bright one from the point of view of future achievement, although this boy is happy enough in his world. It is a world of limited horizons, to which he himself has adapted admirably. His highest ambition is to be a teacher in the secondary schools. Prognosis, therefore, excellent. Classification, *group 2a.*

Case 78, temperamentally 3-3-4, drops away from his somatotype on the cerebrotonic side. He lacks the quick sensitivities and the fast reactions of a 5 in cerebrotonia, without any compensating increment in the other components. He seems to have settled into a rather passive, colorless role. He is an insignificant, rabbity looking little man, with a weak chin and a sparse red mustache. In the field of social service administration, competing almost entirely with women, he seems to be doing well. *Group 2a.*

The 3-4-3's
(VHP 181—Fig. 50)

Eight examples of this common somatotype, most of them rather normal, average people. Case 79, temperamentally 3-5-4, is another illustration of heavy temperamental loading without serious maladaptation. It is often said of this youth that he is his own worst enemy. He is at times unnecessarily aggressive and overriding. He makes many enemies among classmates, but his adjustment as a whole is a satisfactory and successful one, at least within the limits of narrow intellectual horizons. He has symptoms of abdominal distress suggesting peptic ulcer. Classification, *group 2b*.

Case 80, temperamentally 2-5-3, has as unpleasant a disposition as is often met. He suggests a partly tamed native gray rat among a generally well-behaved colony of white ones. He continually bares his teeth, although he rarely bites. Actually he seems to show a compensatory somatorosis, but the interference with his adaptation is not sufficiently serious to render him an unassimilable personality. Many adopt the tolerant attitude toward him that is often shown toward a noisy terrier. Classification, *group 2b*, with some likelihood of dropping back into group 3b.

Case 81, temperamentally 4-5-2, when compared with the preceding case illustrates how widely persons of the same somatotype may differ. This young man, now 30, has settled into a groove of life in which his livelihood depends principally upon making himself pleasantly acceptable to people. He has simply adapted his own mind to the tastes and superficial attitudes of the average person, thus vulgarizing himself (in a literal sense). Fortunately, he has a low *t* component and has been able to adapt to this role with good success and with some degree of self-satisfaction. Classification, *group 2a*.

Case 82, temperamentally 3-4-4, has advanced a degree beyond his somatotype in cerebrotonia without dropping back in somatotonia. He is a normal, "hardheaded," practical young man at a higher level of intellectual awareness than average. He has his impulses well integrated, having drawn in the boundaries of his intellectual and orientational horizons until they lie within comfortably easy access. He knows just how he stands with his world. He will soon write editorials which ring with sophisticated conviction. Classification, *group 2a*.

Case 83, temperamentally 3-4-3, has achieved an excellent integration and has started a probably successful academic (research) career, although possessing only mediocre intellectual endowment. He has succeeded by narrowing his interests, or perhaps merely by letting them remain narrow, and by developing no offensive traits. He is almost entirely free from the interference of sexuality, and is physically unattractive. He "goes with a girl" now, a droopy young woman of about his own somatotype and of about his own degree of sexual marketability. The outlook is very good. Classification, *group 2a.*

Case 84, temperamentally 3-5-3, is one who has advanced the second component without any compensatory recession, but the somatotonic increment expresses itself in his case more through an unusual industriousness and perseverance than in social aggression. This is a youth of lower than average intellectual endowment who is making good in a professional field. He is eventempered, hearty, self-sufficient, and he enjoys life. Sexuality is of little consequence to him, although being a medical student he takes it in stride. Classification, *group 2a.*

Case 85, temperamentally 4-4-4, is loaded to the limit in the primary components, and he appears to stagger under the load. A transfer record from another university gives his IQ as 139, which is high. He has shown ability in several directions but cannot focus his energies. The main trouble seems to be an interfering sociophilia. He spends most of his time seeking people out and wasting their time as well as his own. He seems to need to lean on people constantly. He is well tolerated. Nobody dislikes him. But he has only superficial interests, and appears to fit in nowhere. Classification, *group 2a,* with a strong likelihood of ending in group 3a.

Case 86, temperamentally 2-6-3, is an example of serious maladjustment. He is sufficiently somatorotic to be offensive, and sufficiently small to be mercilessly punished by even the ordinary run of irritable people. When the mesomorphs, even the 5's in that component, become somatorotic, they are generally able to take care of themselves against much of the enmity they arouse, but when a little 3-4-3 shows excessive aggression, many essentially weak people save up their wrath for him. Case 86 "catches it" from all sides, and the situation is not helped by the fact that the first region of his body (head and neck) lends him an altogether misleading appearance of toughness and strength. He is almost constantly involved in fights and quarrels, usually getting the worst of things. Classification, *group 3b.*

The 3-4-4's
(VHP 169—Fig. 41)

Thirteen examples of this, the commonest somatotype among the male college population. Most of them show good, normal adjustments.

Case 87, temperamentally 2-4-5, is brilliant and gifted, with a strong undercurrent of the Promethean idealism which so often characterizes persons of this temperamental pattern. His particular plan for saving the world is to do it through the field of international relations. He is the sort of youth who would have made a splendid ecclesiast in the days when ecclesiasticism was intellectually respectable, but now, in a time when emotional uplift is (at least academically) unpopular, he is at a great disadvantage to achieve what are perhaps his deserved laurels. He has turned first to a field in which he, with a sensitive, idealistic nature, is doomed to disillusionment. But presumably he will continue to attack the problem, perhaps in the end at a deeper level. Classification, *group 1.*

Case 88, temperamentally 3-4-5, illustrates a degree of staggering under the heaviest load of component endowment that nature seems to tolerate. Gifted both mentally and physically, he has found it difficult to concentrate his effort long enough to produce tangible or negotiable results. Like case 87, he is something of a Promethean, and he tends to become dissatisfied with a conventional attack on the problems of life and science. He wants to do something grand, and is still too young to have quite discovered that there is no short cut. More intelligent, and more emotionally resourceful or buoyant than case 87, he has already explored and rejected several fields. This youth would never sell out to so superficial a mental monkey trap as that of an emotional or unimplemented attack on "international relations." He knows that men must cut deeper than that. But he has not found out where or how to cut deeper. He will continue to try. Classification, *group 1.*

Case 89, temperamentally 2-5-4, advances from his somatotype in the second component while retreating in the first. To carry the 5-4 combination in the last two components seems to be a little like walking a tightrope. But this youth appears to have solved it fairly well. His plan, idealistic to a degree, but also direct and practical, is to save the world not by theory and research but by social legislation. He has already released great energy on the problem of lifting up the lower economic levels of society by the bootstraps. He proposes to clear up all the slums in America, and also to increase the birthrate no end. He lacks humor. Classification, *group 1.*

Case 90, temperamentally 2-4-4, seems to be a clear case of vocational maladjustment. There was a time when the combination of the 2-4-4 temperament and a high IQ could be successfully integrated in the profession of the Protestant ministry. But that time has passed. The 2-4-4 lacks the viscerotonia for "emoting" convincingly, or for being expansive and relaxed among "folks," and the day of successful preaching at a relatively high intellectual level *without* the viscerotonia is gone. In the meantime, since the church has not yet learned to divert its energy into a research program to any considerable degree, the plight of case 90 appears to be an unhappy one until he changes his vocational identification. Classification, *group 3d,* with a good chance for group 2b or even group 1, after he becomes a sociologist (if he does).

Case 91, temperamentally 3-5-4, presents a heavily loaded temperament and has made an excellent integration of this personality. With no interference from intellectual or sexual overendowment, and with excellent physique and health, this young man participates well in the life around him. He is a schoolteacher who is called a good influence in his community. Married four years ago, he has two healthy, happy children, and his average-looking wife reflects the best of mental and physical health. Classification, *group 2a.*

Case 92, temperamentally 3-4-4, is a youth who has behaved only in the most normal and expected manner throughout his life. He is moderately intelligent, self-centered, respectable, proper-minded in virtually every respect. So perfectly normal a personality is rare. Even his somatotype is the most conventional one. Classification, *group 2a*.

Case 93, temperamentally 3-4-5, has a heavily loaded temperament with which he is struggling valiantly for balance and integration. The present indication is favorable, although he has not yet found his *persona*, and his vocational plan is still uncertain. He is a Promethean at heart. What he really wants to do is write books that will save the world. At first he contemplated the medium of the drama and fiction. As a junior in college he experienced a great revulsion from that "superficial and arty" plan, and decided to be a philosopher like Plato and like one of his instructors. Now he has progressed to psychology, and is already finding psychologists a little lacking in Promethean fire. He expects next year to begin a career in biological science. He has had a perplexing time with his sexuality, but has recently acquired a "mistress," and his world is very bright just now. Classification, *group 1*, with a good chance to lose momentum and to fall like Icarus into *group 3a*.

Case 94, temperamentally, 2-5-3, has fallen back upon a relatively low level of adjustment, and has there found what appears to be a satisfactory integration. He was impatiently unsympathetic with everything academic while at college. He has made a verbal fetish of the word "practical." During high school he fell into some trouble with the police over stolen bicycles, and he has always been regarded as possessing a dangerously violent temper. Classification, *group 2b*.

Case 95, temperamentally 4-4-3, shows the reversal of a dominance. The temperamental index reverses the morphological dominance between the first and third components. Whether or not such a reversal is an etiological factor in the picture, this youth has failed signally to achieve any satisfactory integration of his personality. He is sociophilic almost to the point of viscerosis. That is to say, he shows a peculiar gluttony for attention and companionship, but has nothing to offer in return except his indiscriminate amiability. He is aggressively amiable, but has never focused his energy either upon academic or "practical" achievement. He has seemed unable to understand that sincere human affection must be earned indirectly, through work. He forever seeks a short cut to the viscerotonic goal. Classification, *group 3c.*

Note: We do not, of course, mean to imply that this classification "explains" anything. It is merely a way of recording a datum. Why the reversal of a component dominance, between the levels of morphology and what we are calling temperament, should be related to poor integration of personality, we cannot say. But such a relationship does in many cases appear to exist.

Case 96, temperamentally 3-5-3, is a most satisfactory and dependable person. He is energetic and industrious, but rarely shows any trace of offensive aggression. He is even tempered and good-natured, stubborn when pushed, but obliging and adaptable to a high degree. His speech is modest, quiet. He is completely free from intellectual pretense, as well as from intellectual ambition. Classification, *group 2a.*

Case 97, temperamentally 3-3-5, appears to have been cheated when intellectual endowment was apportioned out. He has an "intellectual temperament," in the sense that he lacks the gifts for anything else. He is physically sensitive and ineffectual. He *ought* to be intelligent, it would seem, and ought to rest his case on mental achievement. But instead, he is intellectually weak, emotionally unstable, and mentally at loose ends. We have no "explanation" of this case, in constitutional terms. This may be simply an instance of inadequate IQ. *Group 3d.*

Case 98, temperamentally 4-4-4, has achieved a remarkably good balancing and a pleasant integration of nature's heaviest normal loading of components. This young man really has a good time in life. He is a sort of combination of beau brummel, sheik, politician and intellectual, although he is not actually very intellectual. He claims to have "initiated more virgins than there are in South Dakota," for whatever that is worth. He is genial enough, and plausible enough to make his way, almost anywhere. But he is now living out a *persona* of intellectual bluff, and will doubtless settle back in the end into a somewhat unambitious routine. Classification, *group 2a.*

Case 99, temperamentally 4-3-4, reverses the morphological

dominance between the first and second components. This youth appears to have a well-integrated personality in his own way, but he leaves a sickish taste in the mouth, like lukewarm coffee with too much sugar. He is overly polite without being really overly shy, and his thinking is conventional and personal, with no trace of humor or of healthy vulgarity. Ideas and facts presented to him academically are returned unscathed, as if they had been encapsulated against the fermentative juices of mental digestion. We fear that he may realize his ambition to become a successful psychologist. Classification, *group 2a.*

The 3-4-5's
(VHP 163—Fig. 32)

This somatotype introduces for the first time in the present series the 12-total subfamily, in which there are seven somatotypes. These are the six permutations of 3, 4 and 5, and the 4-4-4. All except the latter are scarce, although none is really rare. Of the 3-4-5 we have two examples. One is a complex, confused personality, the other an efficient and gifted young man.

Case 100, temperamentally 3-3-6, falls outside nature's boundary on the side of overendowment. He has shown signs of brilliance but the signs seem to point in several different directions. Homosexuality has been a stumbling block, although he is now also heterosexual. His personal habits point strongly in the direction of aesthetic and literary interests, but intellectually he wants to be a scientist. He entertains little respect, indeed an essential dislike, for the people whom his own personality attracts. He respects only vigorous scientific thinking, but has been unable to face the rigor of a scientific discipline. Even within his homosexuality, he has a severe internal conflict, for he has been what he calls a "bivalent" homosexual, playing both the active (male) and the passive (female) role at different times. The present vocational compromise is journalism, which he "detests." Classification, *group 3a.*

Case 101, temperamentally 3-4-4, has dropped back a degree in cerebrotonia with no corresponding advance in either of the other

components, and has found a pattern of personality which promises to carry him well up the scale of human achievement. He is
wise, shrewd, efficient and tolerant, with a supporting humor and
a little touch of vulgarity which seasons everything he does. His
future seems bright and secure. Classification, *group 1*.

Note: What *essential* differentiating characteristics lie behind
this attractive personality? The answer is almost certainly complex,
and probably still lies beyond our reach. But we can at least define
some of its ingredients by meaningfully describing *him*. The answer
does not lie in being temperamentally a 3-4-4, but does it lie partly
in being a temperamental 3-4-4 which has come into being by way
of the 3-4-5 physique? Possibly that helps us a little. We then must
include all of the other variables that can be described, such as
IQ, *t* component, sexuality and the like. But it is quite evident that
any of these *in vacuo*, out of their context or apart from a frame
of reference which quantitatively describes the *first order* variables,
would throw no light on our question. Having once described a
person as he is, we may perhaps then be in position to make a
fruitful attack on that other complex of variables, his environmental history, but to do this without putting first things first
(establishing first order variables) seems but to lead to statistical
chaos.

The 3-5-2's
(VHP 196)

Five examples. We return now to the general family of mesomorphs. Case 102, temperamentally 4-5-2, is a Jewish youth who
has achieved excellent integration of his personality, is well relaxed and good-natured, and is likewise active and efficient, with
a good weather eye peeled for the main chance. There is nothing
brilliant about him. His outlook seems altogether good. Classification, *group 2a*.

Case 103, temperamentally 2-7-1, is a little chunky Jewish mesomorph whose somatorosis can be seen, or heard, a mile away. He
is one of the noisiest, most aggressive individuals we have ever
seen. During the present year he has virtually moved into and
taken over the Psychology Department. He is so excessively soma-

totonic that in a sense he has made that *persona* good, and has built an integration around it. People tend to accept him in the way that a noisy, ugly little Boston bulldog is accepted and played with. He himself, however, is very serious about his aggression. He means it, as the bulldog does. This may perhaps be a case of normal integration of a pathological personality, the integration possibly depending upon an unusual condition of society. This youth seems to have an excellent chance to achieve a happy position in his world without changing from his (somatotoric) *persona*. We can imagine him successfully operating an advertising agency, or something of the sort. *Group 2b.*

Case 104, temperamentally 3-5-3, has what according to our observations is usually a well-adapted temperamental pattern. Certainly most of the 3-5-3's get along happily and successfully. But this youth is trying to be a physical educator and seems to have chosen the wrong vocation. He has drifted into the vocational niche of a 2-6-2, and the strain of trying to be an exemplary mesomorph has begun to tell on him. The profession of athletics and physical education has quite naturally been preempted by the extreme mesomorphs. When someone not a 6 in that component drifts into this professional group, such a person is sure to have a difficult adjustment on his hands. Quite a few succeed in making the adjustment (because of extra size or some other factor), but case 104 has not done so. He has been experiencing severe cerebrotic symptoms, especially neurodermatitis and insomnia, and has developed a peptic ulcer. We think that this is a simple case of vocational maladjustment. Classification, *group 3d*, with an excellent chance for group 2a, or 2b in another vocation.

Case 105, temperamentally 4-4-3, is a mesomorph with (for mesomorphy) a high *g* component. He is soft-spoken, quiet, composed, and almost effeminate in manner. But this is most misleading, for he is as strong as a bull and is a member of the university wrestling team. He is possibly a good prototype for Dumas' famous Aramis of the Three Musketeers. He shares with the latter a high sexuality, and substituting philosophy for theology, has perhaps adopted somewhat the same general *persona*. Philosophy appears to serve him more as a sexual hunting ground than as a potential vocation. We expect him to turn to one of the natural or physical sciences before many years have passed. Classification, *group 2a,* with a good chance for group 1, the latter possibility perhaps being accentuated by the high sexuality. This youth will not become complacent.

Case 106, temperamentally 3-6-2, is almost a well-integrated personality. He has great energy and enthusiasm for his work and does it well. He pleases his faculty, but is frequently in trouble with his own contemporaries because of over aggression. He seems to "press" a little too much. He is the butt of some of the most biting wit that emanates from his Department. This is possibly a case of overendowment in somatotonia without quite the necessary intelligence to sustain the offensive. We think, however, that the prognosis is good, and that as he grows older (and fatter) the somatotonia will be sufficiently "blanketed" to render possible an excellent integration of the personality. Classification, *group 2b.*

The 3-5-3's
(VHP 184)

Six examples of this, the commonest of the mesomorphic somatotypes, excepting the 3-4-3. Case 107, temperamentally 4-5-3, presents a heavily loaded temperament which also has become happily integrated. The 4-5 combination in the first two components appears to function better, so far as social integration is concerned, than this combination in either the second and third or the first and third components (see p. 399). This young man turned to the barnyard in his youth, and he has there found the happiness which many of his contemporaries will seek vainly in more distant places. Classification, *group 2a.*

Case 108, temperamentally 3-5-4, illustrates a well-integrated temperament carrying the 5-4 combination in the second and third components. Here a man heavily endowed in somatotonia and cerebrotonia has turned his predominant somatotonia to outdoor life and forestry, and has there found the solitude and protection from overstimulation which his cerebrotonia demands. Classification, *group 2a.*

Case 109, temperamentally 3-5-4, is constitutionally very similar to the last, but has chosen a pattern of adjustment which
throws him into urban life and into continual close contact with
people. He is doing badly in his environment, and is suffering
from a number of (cerebrotic) symptoms of internal strain. Possibly these last two cases represent the difference which good
vocational guidance might bring about in human affairs, but it
should be remembered that however important diagnostic insight
may be in such a picture, more than that is needed. It is necessary
also to be able to provide young people with opportunities for
taking advantage of the diagnostic insight. Vocational guidance
needs to be planned as a large-scale project if it is undertaken at
all. Classification, *group 3d*.

Case 110, temperamentally 4-5-3, is another illustration of excellent integration with a heavily loaded temperament. This is
one of the most mentally surefooted young men we have encountered. He knows exactly what his bearings are at all times.
But he has no trace of humor, no mental playfulness at all. He
has an odd unilateral eye blink, or tic, and strangers sometimes
think he is winking at them. It is to be noted that the 12-total
temperaments that are founded on the massive 3-5-3 physiques
appear for the most part to be well integrated. The 3-5-3 appears
to be a "good" somatotype, from the point of view of integration
of personality. Classification, *group 2a*.

Case 111, temperamentally 3-6-2, is perhaps on the borderline
of somatorotic maladjustment, but he remains on the safe side of
the border. He is ruthless, mercenary and materialistic, but he
has both the energy and the intelligence to make good most of
his impulses. His plan is to use law as a means of making money,
and to use money as a means of expressing his hatreds and his
craving to be conspicuous. Classification, *group 2b*. From the
individualistic point of view this is group 2. From a social point
of view this kind of personality may be more harmful than the
most cunning criminal.

Case 112, temperamentally 4-4-4, presents still another example
of a good, acceptable integration at the level of the 12-total in
temperament. He has a high gynandromorphy for the somatotype,
and there is a faint suggestion of effeminacy about him. He has no

mental playfulness, or humor, and is regarded generally as a bore. He has become a satellite of one of the Sociology professors, who himself is well integrated but humorless. The two turn out work steadily, very much as a meat grinder turns out hamburg. Classification, *group 2a.*

The 3-5-4's
(VHP 172—Fig. 42)

Four examples of this fairly scarce somatotype, one showing excellent and three showing poor integration. Case 113, temperamentally 4-5-3, reverses the morphological dominance between the first and third components. This youth has made a failure all along the line and has finally been expelled from college for low grades. He has made many abortive efforts to reform. For two years he held off expulsion from college by tearful conferences with college authorities. But he has never done his work faithfully for more than a week at a stretch, and in spite of tremendous energy and activity, he seems never to have been able to harness his impulses to any adequate degree. With an examination coming up he will spend his days in sociophilia and his nights at the beer gardens. Classification, *group 3c.*

Case 114, temperamentally 2-6-3, is a highly intelligent and able young man whose virtues have already been widely acclaimed. In our experience the 2-6-3 temperament has often proved a difficult one to integrate successfully, but here is an instance where one of the most effective personalities in a university community has been built on that foundation. We have encountered a number of cases of this general sort where a distinctly superior personality has come into being through the medium of an apparently difficult temperamental pattern. Indeed there are so many such cases that we are inclined to hypothesize that a large proportion of the unusually able people, as well as many of the total wrecks, will upon inquiry show patterns of temperament which nature places out near the periphery of her distribution. Classification of case 114, *group 1.*

Case 115, temperamentally 3-6-3, shows a pattern of temperament so overloaded as to fall outside the morphological distribution. This youth has shown academic as well as general ability in numerous little false starts that he has made. But always an acute somatotonic restlessness seems to get the better of him, and then he is soon off on a new tangent. Last summer he built a boat in which he and two companions made a thirty-day cruise. He is quite active as an amateur aviator, and was manager of an athletic team while an undergraduate. In spite of having twice left college in the midst of semesters he made a respectably passing record. At present he is studying chemistry, but unsuccessfully and unhappily. He wants to be more active. The most recent plan is to go seek his fortune in Texas oil fields. This case probably represents a remarkably persistent effort to harness incompatible impulses, and to achieve an integrity of general orientation in the face of great internal strain. Classification, *group 2b*.

Case 116, temperamentally 4-4-4, has a high gynandromorphy for this somatotype, and also a high *t* component. This youth was president of the sophomore class, after distinguishing himself as a freshman both in scholarship and in "activities" (the college daily, debating, etc.). It is only within the past year or so that he has frankly identified himself with the arty group, and has also become an overt homosexual. He has a stupendous collection of symphony records. His scholarship has fallen off, and he now has no sustained interest in any pattern of achievement. He has become tricky in his relations with people. The prognosis may be poor. Classification, *group 2b*, with danger of falling back to 3a.

The 3-6-1's
(VHP 209—Fig. 69)

Three examples of this, one of the most powerful and massive of somatotypes. Two of them show excellent adjustment, and the other is sufficiently tough to survive anyhow.

Case 117, temperamentally 3-7-1 and a big man physically, is supreme in his athletic world, an all-American football player. This boy is natural and true to himself at all times. Wherever his two hundred odd pounds of bulk goes, and whatever it does, the world comes to attention, at least the little college world does.

He is perhaps the nearest thing possible to a king in his own right. Classification, *group 2a.*

Case 118, temperamentally 4-5-2, presents an almost equally successful adjustment, although the temperamental pattern has developed in a direction opposite to that of the last, dropping away from instead of accentuating the powerfully dominant morphological component. This hard-working, popular and good-natured youth could have almost anything he might ask for at the medical school. Although he is a slow thinker he made a good undergraduate record, and is making a still better record in professional school. Intellectually he is limited and his horizons are low, but his professional future is almost certainly good. Classification, *group 2a.*

Case 119, temperamentally 4-7-1, is a rare specimen. Such a pattern of temperament falls outside the "normal" limits at one of the corners of the distribution. This is a short, stubby Jewish youth who in a few years will be nearly as thick as he is tall. He looks like something out of the jungle (especially in his somatotype picture because of his hirsutism), and oddly enough he behaves very much as he looks. He is so outstandingly aggressive, greedy, and disregardful of others that his medical school faculty look upon him as an interesting phenomenon, and in a way are rather fond of him, possibly in the way that some people are fond of aggressive dogs. He is altogether himself, without pretense. All of his energy is focused upon getting ahead, or upon the competition for grades. Although obnoxious to fellow students, he probably will do well in his profession. Classification, *group 2b.*

The 3-6-2's
(VHP 199—Fig. 91)

Three examples, two good adjustments and one poor one. Case 120, temperamentally 4-5-2, has one of the best formulas in the world for success. He is aggressive but politely and genially so, thus wearing the *persona* of modesty. He is a systematic and a perfectly oriented person who always knows just about what he wants and has abundant energy to carry out his plans for getting it. His vocational objective, in his own words, is "to get money without having to work for it." He wants to be a business executive. Classification, *group 2a.*

Case 121, temperamentally 2-7-1, is one of those vigorous little fellows (short stature) who make up for lack of size by boiling over with energy. He wears hard heels and makes the house shake when he walks. A star basketball player, his short legs move so fast when he runs that they can hardly be seen. His posture is so straight and upright, and his chest is typically thrown so aggressively forward that he suggests a pigeon in mating season. He is aggressive, but for some reason which is not altogether clear to us, he is not offensively aggressive. Almost everybody knows him, and likes him. He is often called Napoleon, but always good-naturedly. If we could analyze a series of personalities with sufficient cogency to bring out just why aggressiveness is sometimes offensive, and sometimes not offensive, we should perhaps have discovered a psychological principle of importance. Classification, *group 2a.*

Case 122, temperamentally 2-6-3, reverses the morphological dominance between the first and third components. This boy has visited the student health clinic repeatedly with complaints for which the doctors have discovered no organic foundation. At one time he suffers from severe bowel pains, at another from the fear that he has syphilis. He has repeatedly convinced himself that he has ulcers of the stomach. He always suffers more or less from itching (neurodermatitis). He is frequently told to relax and rest, but he can no more rest than can a tumbling weed in the wind. He is under an irresistible compulsion to do something. He has a high gynandromorphy and is a fine swimmer. Classification, *group 2b,* with danger of falling into 3c.

The 4-2-4's
(VHP 166—Fig. 38)

Three examples of this weak, endomorphic-ectomorphic somatotype. All three are poorly integrated personalities. Case 123, temperamentally 3-2-5, is an excessively shy, apprehensive youth who, finding the real world of human beings, very different from his far more beautiful romantic imaginings, tends to dissociate the former from his consciousness as much as possible. He is swamped with autoeroticism. His particular horror is the required gym class, where he feels punished (ridiculed) for not being a meso-morph. We have the notion that if he were taken out of college and returned when he is about four years older, he might make an excellent adjustment. Classification, *group 2b.*

Case 124, temperamentally 5-1-4, presents the picture of a youth who can regurgitate fairly well what is in books, but can do prac-tically nothing else. He is swamped with viscerotonia and cere-brotonia, and the great weight of 9 in these two components sits upon the puny 1 in somatotonia like the fat lady of the circus on a sickly pony. He is physically almost as helpless and somatopenic as could be imagined. He masturbates with homosexual imagery, and probably is protected from passive homosexuality only by his excessively low somatotonia. Classification, *group 4* (insufficiency of the second component).

Case 125, temperamentally 4-2-5, is a physically and morally weak individual, who is swamped with sexuality and has found it too much for him. His academic record is good, and he is a fairly able young botanist, but he is in trouble with the univer-sity because of his sexuality, and his professional future is in doubt. He has practiced excessive autoeroticism since the age of 15, thereby perhaps keeping his energy at a low point. More recently he has been involved in both homosexual and hetero-sexual misunderstandings and recriminations. Classification, *group 3d,* with a good chance for group 2 later, when sexuality ebbs a little.

The 4-2-5's
(VHP 162—Fig. 34)

Three examples, two showing excellent integration, the other a constitutional defective. Case 126, temperamentally 3-1-5, was always weak and effeminate but did well enough scholastically to pass until he came to college. As a little boy he played only with girls, and was a flaccid, physically incompetent child with very low energy. He is markedly hypogenital. He never could learn to do anything with his hands. During the fifth month of college he became completely disoriented, and has now been in a mental hospital for two years. Hebephrenic schizophrenia is the diagnosis. Classification, *group 4*.

Case 127, temperamentally 4-2-4, is physically frail and he is soft and awkward. He associated very little with other boys, never played any of the common games of boyhood, and today he knows nothing about baseball or football, or indeed about any of the competitive games of physical prowess. Such matters are as foreign to his mind as the religious practices of Australian bushmen. He is free from any distraction in that quarter, and he has applied a good learning mind to academic work so successfully that now he is in strategic position as a young scientist. Classification, *group 1*. There are, it seems, numerous roads to group 1.

Case 128, temperamentally 4-3-4, shows much the same picture as the last, but he is of slightly tougher, more "normal" fiber. He is a success in the medical field, and the secret of his success seems to lie principally in freedom from competing interests. He pays no more attention to the world of sports, or politics, or social gossip, or economics, than he would to the distant barking of dogs. For a long time he had no sexual life but masturbation. More recently he has made successful heterosexual arrangements. This he finds pleasant and satisfying, but not seriously disturbing. He seems to have *one* of the excellent constitutional patterns, from the standpoint of adaptation at a high mental level. Classification. *group 1*.

The 4-3-3's
(VHP 182)

Three examples, all of them rather poorly integrated personalities. Case 129, temperamentally 5-2-4, is both viscerotic and cerebrotic, in a mild sense. He seems to be in need of constant social support and reassurance. Most of his rather weak supply of energy goes into seeking people out and "telling them all about it." He is considered a nuisance, for he himself has but little to offer. Even his output of social slobber is imperfectly sustained, and he lacks the aggression necessary to maintain contacts. The result is that most of his time is spent with new acquaintances. Classification, *group 2b*. He falls just about at the borderline of group 3d.

Case 130, temperamentally 3-3-4, reverses the morphological dominance between the first and third components. He always seems to suggest a whipped but viscerotonic puppy, who wants to fawn about people and lick their faces, but instead, slinks about in a sidelong way with his tail between his legs. In short, this boy suggests a conflict between viscerotonia and cerebrotonia, in which the latter has got the upper hand. Physically he is unattractive, with an unhealthy-looking fat face and a weak chin. He has a silly, self-conscious giggle. Yet, notwithstanding these weaknesses and the discouragement they engender, there is a certain pertinacity about him. He will probably succeed in getting a Ph.D. in Education, and will then "mold America's youth." Classification, *group 2b,* bordering on 3c.

Case 131, temperamentally 4-4-4, is a youth of good health and good native intelligence, who seems temperamentally overloaded and finds life a sea of many strange winds and cross currents. He has enough somatotonic aggression to make a real nuisance of himself under the guise of seeking counsel and guidance. He seeks it in all quarters, and after making the rounds he starts over again. He has at different times started to specialize in half a dozen of the departments of the university, but still remains vocationally confused and at loose ends. Classification, *group 2b,* perhaps bordering on 3a.

The 4-3-4's
(VHP 170—Fig. 38)

Five examples, showing for the most part rather poor integration. This is the commonest somatotype among college women (according to a study of 2500 cases), and if our preliminary observation is sound, women of this somatotype are generally well-integrated and rather happy people.

Case 132, temperamentally 3-4-4, reverses the morphological predominance between the first and second components. This is a most insecure, baffled and unhappy young man whose chief external difficulty seems to lie in unprovoked, tactless, poorly sustained fits of aggressive hostility. The people whom he attacks are usually his best friends, and after one of his outbursts he is generally filled with remorse. He suffers a good deal from a persistent feeling that he ought to be more successful and more happy than he is—that somehow what he wants lies tantalizingly just beyond his reach. He is rather heavily endowed with sexuality but his sexual advances, like his general social life, are hasty, impatient, poorly sustained and hampered by emotional instability. Classification, *group 2b*, bordering on 3c.

Case 133, temperamentally 5-3-3, presents what is perhaps a fairly good viscerotonic adjustment at a low level of desire. The striking characteristic here is the hypogenitalism and freedom from sexual interest or sexual desire of any sort. He is not particularly gluttonous, but is lazy, overly relaxed and almost completely complacent. He goes to college because his father pays him to do so. In a passive way he is genial and cooperative. Classification, *group 2a*.

Case 134, temperamentally 3-2-5, appears to be almost a constitutionally deficient weakling, but he escapes into normality and has successfully established the *persona* of a thoroughly "nice" young man. He is weak in every sense, including sexuality, but he always does and says about the right thing. His pastor at the Methodist church has been preaching blood and thunder pacifism (which is popular in the churches just at the moment as these notes are being written), and this youth has taken up the pacifistic stereotype. But he would be no pacifist in wartime. Classification, *group 2a*.

Case 135, temperamentally 4-4-3, reverses the morphological dominance between the second and third components. This, we believe, is the most dangerous of the reversals. The incompatibility (as measured by the negative correlation, see p. 400) between these two components is the sharpest incompatibility to be found between the three sets of pairs. When such a reversal occurs, it is probably a safe assumption that a severe strain has been thrown on the personality. This youth seems to be a good illustration of profound maladjustment associated with such a reversal. Already showing signs of chronic alcoholism and possessing a history of minor episodes of criminal delinquency, he presents a poor prognosis. Classification, *group 3c*.

Case 136, temperamentally 3-3-5, is a youth who has almost gone over to an arty escape pattern but has for some reason stopped just short of it. He seems to fall in between such a pattern and that of the practical, urbane young man. Although he loves symphonic music, the theater, art galleries and all institutionalized sophistications, he tends to seek these things alone, and to draw away from the group whom he finds sharing such interests. He has a weak sexuality, and has never felt any identification with homosexuality. He has little aesthetic sensitivity to people, to nature, or indeed to anything but human artifacts. In the nonsophisticated sense he is aesthetically undeveloped. He is almost entirely unaware of the natural world. His vocational plan is that of becoming a businessman of some sort. Classification, *group 2b*.

The 4-3-5's
(VHP 163—Fig. 34)

Three examples, two of them showing reversal of a dominance. Although it is our impression that integration of a personality around this 12-total somatotype presents an unusual complexity of alternatives, and unusual opportunity for disorientation, the present examples have achieved good adaptation.

Case 137, temperamentally 3-2-5, has dropped back in both of the first two components, and has found at least an innocuous integration in a weak, polite, colorless personality. This young professor bores his students and reads them only the most conventional lectures. He loves an afternoon of bridge. Classification, *group 2a*.

Case 138, temperamentally 3-4-4, shows a reversal of the dominance between the first two components, together with a decrement in the third component. He is unquestionably brilliant but he is unsuccessful in his social relations and cannot control his compulsive impulses to irritate or deflate complacent people. He has quick humor and a sharp tongue but rather poor physical poise. It is obvious to a close observer that his mental aggression lacks the backing of a true physical pugnacity. Possibly this is one reason why so many people become "furiously enangered" by him. He cannot fight. Physical attack on him, or the threat of it, is perfectly safe and is not uncommon. Considering cases 137 and 138, note how diametrically different the personality integrations of two individuals of the same somatotype can be. Classification, *group 2b*.

Case 139, temperamentally 3-4-4, shows a pattern remarkably similar to the last. He too is brilliant, humorous, physically awkward, and poorly poised. He offends many, but for some reason he has been accepted by people in power and is generally looked upon as a bright and important young man. Those who dislike him call him a "Smart Aleck," or a cocky Jew. Those who like him call him a genius, "one of the most civilized," etc. Classification, *group 1*.

The 4-4-2's
(VHP 198—Fig. 58)

Five examples, all but one of them rather well-integrated people. Case 140, temperamentally 3-5-2, has taken up a highly stable and rather impregnable position as a practical-minded, aggressive young businessman. He entertains no uncertainties about life and has no questions, except how best to make money. He is sophisticated and free from romantic or intellectual ideals or from religious loyalties. He has given over no hostages to disillusionment, and he is amenable to no argument or persuasion except force and money power. Classification, *group 2a*.

Case 141, temperamentally 3-5-3, is near to the same pattern as the last, both in physique and in temperament. The principal physical differences are that he is taller, has a higher t component, and is Alpine-Mediterranean rather than Jewish. This youth is confused and vocationally uncertain of himself. His somatotonia is rather ineffectively and unevenly expressed. He tends to be harsh, impatient and unhappy, although the 3-5-3 temperament is often conspicuously well integrated. Possibly he represents simple vocational maladjustment. Classification, *group 3d.*

Case 142, temperamentally 5-4-3, shows a pattern of temperament loaded to approach the extreme limits, yet well integrated in one way of life. This young preacher overwhelms people both with his energy and with his viscerotonia. He has great power at the emotional harangue. When he preaches his voice is one of those inescapable voices in which an emotional crescendo throbs like steam in a hotel water faucet. He perspires profusely when he preaches. This is the PPJ (pyknic practical joke) physique, and he has already begun to grow portly through the middle. Classification, *group 2a.*

Case 143, temperamentally 4-4-3, is a successful, well-regarded young man who has done well in aviation but plans to return to academic work in the biological sciences. His essential strength lies in his general good sense and evenness of mental balance, rather than in brilliance. He is regarded favorably by nearly everyone who knows him. If he has a weakness, it lies in a certain easygoing quality, or complacency of outlook. He will probably be a successful, but not an original scientist. Classification, *group 2a.*

Case 144, temperamentally 5-3-2, is a good example of a fairly recognizable group who depend for their success and welfare almost entirely upon viscerotonia. This man is weak and soft, both mentally and physically. He knows it, however, and makes no pretense of competing in either somatotonic or cerebrotonic patterns. He maintains social contacts, offers many extra courtesies to people, teaches Sunday school, speaks with the utmost tolerance and consideration on all occasions, sends hundreds of Christmas cards, and so on. People like him and support him. He has enough somatotonia to live up to routines. Classification, *group 2a.*

The 4-4-3's
(VHP 183—Fig. 58)

Eleven examples of this common somatotype. This is the somatotype which we have found to be of most frequent occurrence in the general (nonacademic) population. The 3-4-4 is commonest in the colleges. This particular group of 4-4-3's seems rather unusual. Among it are a number of cases of serious maladjustment, and possibly not one of the eleven could be considered a very good academic investment. Six of the eleven cases show reversal of a dominance. That is a singularly high proportion, even when we remember that most of the reversals of dominance are seen in the mid-range somatotypes.

Case 145, temperamentally 4-3-4, shows reversal of the dominance between the second and third components. This boy appears to be moving in the direction of alcoholism, although he could hardly be called a chronic alcoholic. His outstanding psychological characteristic is an inability to face anything. He is an abject coward, both physically and mentally. He seems to realize vaguely that he has no place in an academic setting, but he has made no alternative plans. He responds to all efforts at "vocational guidance" by getting drunk. Classification, *group 3c.*

Case 146, temperamentally 3-3-3, is constitutionally a defective. The IQ ranges between 73 and 98, according to different reports. He is pleasant, polite, unselfish, but mentally and physically flaccid. He does even more poorly on tests of motor aptitude than on mental tests. He is like a dog who continually tries to please, but lacks the equipment necessary for the job in hand. We have watched this boy for more than a year, and believe that when protected entirely from competition he is essentially a happy person. In this sense he has an excellent integration of personality, although at too low an activity level from the point of view of social adaptation. Classification, *group 4.*

Case 147, temperamentally 3-5-2, has made a good integration in a narrow sense. He has no humor, and he sees life mainly as a sort of disagreeable duty which needs to be done. He seems to go about his relations with the world much as a hangman might go about his work. He is physically well relaxed, deliberate, very formal and judgmental of mien. He has an unsmiling, big-bodied wife, and three children. Business associates consider him sound and dependable. Classification, *group 2a.*

Case 148, temperamentally 3-5-4, reverses the dominance between the first and third components. He is a rather futile person who is always busy but never seems to get anything done. In medical school he appeared to be one of the faithful workers in the laboratories, yet rarely succeeded in getting reports in on time. Carrying a heavily loaded temperamental pattern, he seems to have ample somatotonia, but suffers from such excessive cerebrotonic interference that little headway is made. As one of his friends puts it, he seems always to be walking uphill on pine needles. Great energy is expended, but the retrogression is almost as great as the progression. Classification, *group 2b,* perhaps bordering on 3c.

Case 149, temperamentally 3-5-2, resembles case 147, but at a lower mental level. This youth has made a good adjustment within the limits of his own narrow outlook. After graduating from college, he returned to the small Midwestern town where he was born and has fitted into life quite happily as real estate salesman for a cousin, automobile salesman for an uncle, and general frequenter of the local beer gardens and poolrooms for himself. He knows everybody in town but has severed all connections with matters academic. Classification, *group 2a.*

Case 150, temperamentally 4-5-3, has achieved successful integration of a heavily loaded temperament, although at a low mental level. He is a "hustler" in his department store work but he also likes good living and has expensive tastes, notably in women and automobiles. He reads detective stories voraciously, and explains that they are a better "sharpener of the mind" than any college course. When excited, he stutters. He has a conspicuous tic-like twitch of the mouth. Classification, *group 2b.*

Case 151, temperamentally 4-3-3, presents still another example of a good adjustment at a low intellectual level, that is to say, low for a university graduate. This young man has gone well over toward the "softer" side, possibly as a reflection of his vocational setting as clerk in a bookstore. In his speech he is overly polite and invariably trite. His manner suggests that of a butler about to extract a tip from a tedious guest. Life itself seems to be tedious to this young man, but he has resolved to be a good citizen and to drown his irritation in bridge and in moral respectability. Classification, *group 2a.*

Case 152, temperamentally 4-4-4, has made a good integration as a graduate student of education, although his success rests upon social acceptability, not on intellectual strength. He offends nobody, and lives up to routine requirements. He is sociophilic, generous with his time and energy, and plays an excellent part at social gatherings. He is especially good at charades. Classification, *group 2a.*

Case 153, temperamentally 3-5-4, reverses the dominance between the first and third components, and carries a heavily loaded temperament, but nevertheless has achieved a good integration. He has a high component of sexuality for this somatotype, and has at times masturbated excessively, but has become involved in no serious sexual difficulties. He is tall and strikingly handsome. He stutters badly and suffers from gastrointestinal distress which he calls "ulcer" although no medical diagnosis has been made. His future in engineering appears to be good. Classification, *group 2b.*

Case 154, temperamentally 5-3-4, reverses the dominance between the second and third components, as well as advancing to a 5 in viscerotonia. He is distinctly viscerotic. Most of his energy appears to go into the quest for sympathy and social support. He is insecure and dependent. Either pity or censure will bring tears to his eyes. He has no buffer of humor or playfulness. He is very self-conscious about his posterior broadening tendency (*g* component). No plans of any sort. He has only the pitiful desire to adapt and to be in the sun with the others. Yet he is on the verge of being dropped from college for low grades. Classification, *group 3c.*

Case 155, temperamentally 3-5-4, presents nearly the same constitutional picture as case 153, but has failed to achieve as good an integration. He has an IQ of 129, eleven points higher than case 153, but his excessive energy and intermittent outbursts of conflicting ambition lead him into almost continual difficulty. He complains of painful internal insecurity, and of the recurrent sense of impending disaster, alternating with periods of excessive euphoria and of sense of power. During the latter moods he makes decisions and dramatic reversals of direction which keep him in trouble. Classification, *group 3c*. If this youth should become psychotic, he would probably present a good example of the manic-depressive condition.

The 4-4-4's
(VHP 171—Fig. 43)

Four examples, all showing good integration of their complex and well-loaded temperaments. Case 156, temperamentally 3-4-5, has an IQ of 150, and a comparably brilliant academic record. Very tall and of strikingly good appearance, he shows the physical poise of a professional actor, in addition to possessing an alert, well-trained mind. Although his features are boyish and youthful, his conversation is that of a college president, earnest, to the point, and well annotated. Yet he lacks humor. During more than a year we have seen him possibly fifty times, under various circumstances, and have not yet seen a sign of mental playfulness. Classification, *group 1*.

Case 157, temperamentally 3-5-4, tried for years to live up to the *persona* of athletic prowess and somatotonic mesomorphy. All through high school he struggled to be a football player, a fighter, a ballplayer. Eventually he won a place on the baseball team. In college he did much the same thing, and suffered severely from frustration. Finally, after being somatotyped and learning that 4-4-4's are not mesomorphs, he gave over the ambition to excel at competitive athletics and has contented himself with "roughing it" out of doors. He is doing well in geology. Classification, *group 2b*.

Case 158, temperamentally 4-4-4, has adopted the *persona* of a nice, respectable young man, a little on the effeminate side. He has made a success of this, and now seems to be one of the happiest, most self-satisfied people in the whole series. He has no intellectual strength, and no real interest in science. He is arty, almost an aesthete, and perhaps almost a homosexual, but there is no overt homosexuality in his history. He has found a pattern for living and a vocational outlook which seem perfectly to fit his temperament. Classification, *group 2a.*

Case 159, temperamentally 5-4-3, carries the effeminate *persona* almost to an extreme, yet achieves a happy integration. This young instructor in music talks like a girl, and minces like a literary young matron when he walks. When he swears, he says "darn." There is the gravest of suspicion that he wears corsets. His affectation of speech and manner is so complete and so constant that it is genuine. No overt homosexuality is known in his history, and he is perennially engaged. Classification, *group 2a.*

The 4-5-1's
(VHP 212—Fig. 76)

Three examples of this massive, chunky, usually short-statured somatotype. Two of them show excellent integration.

Case 160, temperamentally 3-5-3, shows a fairly wide departure from the somatotype, but this is an effective and well-adapted personality. It is said that he works an average of twelve hours a day in the laboratories, besides assisting in some of the elementary chemistry courses. Away from his work, he shows many signs of tension and strain. In ordinary social relations he is pugnacious, overbearing and irritable. But from the point of view of his potential contribution, and his basic usefulness, he is a first-rate person. Classification, *group 1.*

Case 161, temperamentally 5-4-2, reverses the dominance between the first and second components. He has achieved no adequate integration of his rather abundant energies, but at 21 is spending most of his time in the direct pursuit of viscerotonic fulfillment at unsublimated levels. He has been having a long series of conferences with a psychiatrist whose point of view places great weight and importance on the early intrafamilial relationships. This has turned the youth's attention more than ever toward his parents and toward internal familial entanglements, rendering him perhaps still more viscerotic. He has learned to blame his mother and father for his every disappointment. Classification, *group 3c.*

Case 162, temperamentally 3-6-2, has achieved a splendid integration at a high level of somatotonia. His *persona* is defined essentially by simplicity, energetic good nature and openness. He has a genuine love for the barnyard, and at an intellectual level well above the college average. As a sophomore in college he for a time wanted to study medicine, but appears to have resolved the conflict by adopting a plan to study veterinary medicine later on. Classification, *group 2a.*

The 4-5-2's
(VHP 201—Fig. 63)

Five examples of this rather common somatotype. In our experience the 4-5-2 is usually well integrated and secure in his world. The combination of 4 and 5 in the first two components seems to present a much easier problem of adjustment than does this combination in the second and third components.

Case 163, temperamentally 4-4-3, is a large, heavy, good-natured man who as a high school principal is comfortable and happy, and consistently makes others so. People spontaneously seek him out and entrust him with their emotional burdens. He always listens patiently and sympathetically, and never suggests anything radical. Classification, *group 2a.*

Case 164, temperamentally 4-5-3, is a brilliant young rabbi who with a heavily loaded temperament has made a first-rate integration. He seems to have developed the quality of manifesting principally positive or virtuous aspects of all three components, while avoiding negative or malintegrative characteristics. So far as outward expression goes, he is viscerotonic principally in the warm, sociophilic sense, somatotonic principally in the energetic sense, and cerebrotonic principally in the sense of alert hyper-attentionality. In short, he seems to have made the best of all three components. Classification, *group 1*.

Case 165, temperamentally 4-4-4, strongly suggests temperamental overloading. He seems always to be pulled in different directions, and never quite arrives at a harmonizing of his energies. His somatotonia is expressed in spurts. He has abundant energy but it is unevenly sustained. He is aggressively solicitous, or perhaps aggressively both viscerotonic and cerebrotonic at the same time. The 4-4-4 temperament is not uncommon, perhaps because so many different patterns add up toward 4-4-4, but integration of such a temperament is unquestionably difficult. Classification, *group 2b*.

Case 166, temperamentally 4-6-1, has made an excellent integration of a presumably difficult endowment. This Jewish medical student is one-directional to the highest degree, and although disliked by his contemporaries, he knows where he is going and has the necessary steam pressure to maintain his one-directionality. His opinion of his fellow students is singularly unflattering, and his intellectual outlook is a narrowly limited one. Note the excessively low *t* component. He is often called "the gorilla." Classification, *group 2b*.

Case 167, temperamentally 3-6-1, shows a pattern of integration remarkably similar to the last. In both of these cases the second component has been advanced to the extreme 6, while the third has dropped back to the minimum. Both young men have achieved excellent adaptation, at least from their own point of view. Yet both are rather hated by their classmates, that is to say, by their competitors. Both are considered "aggressive, undesirable Jews." Why so? Is that part of the picture inevitable because of a constitutional heredity which is common among Jews? Is the difficulty due, on the other hand, simply to unprovoked persecution and unfair treatment of Jews in the past? Is it more the result of an inadequate grasp of constitutional differences on the part of our own educational institutions of the present day? Are there some other factors at work? Classification, *group 2b*.

The 4-5-3's
(VHP 186)

Four examples of this, the last of the 12-total somatotypes. Three have achieved passably good integration of personality. One has failed to do so.

Case 168, temperamentally 4-4-4, presents a rather unusual picture. Actually he has done well and has made a good integration. He has a good record and promises well in his field. But he takes little pleasure in this. He is devoid of humor or perspective, believes himself to be a weakling, and suffers acutely from imaginary illnesses of many sorts. He has normal but small genitals, and has on occasion carried out intercourse, although without much pleasure. He never masturbates and rarely feels sexual desire. He is well liked and generally trusted by both sexes, and both by his own contemporaries and by older people. He dances well. Women like him and lay plans to capture him. Although he works hard and faithfully, he is always genuinely surprised at any success or recognition. Classification, *group 2b*.

Case 169, temperamentally 3-4-4, reverses the dominance between the first and third components. This is an apprehensive, "jumpy," dyscrastically cerebrotic person who has intermittent spells of intense resolution and ambition, but never succeeds in focusing his energy upon any goal for a long enough time to show appreciable achievement. He has a fairly strong sexual drive, masturbates excessively (by spells), and is often obsessed by a desire for sexual perversional experimentation. He has tried two or three different variations of homosexual perversion but has not become addicted to any of them. He is more strongly attracted by women than by men. The university psychiatrist calls him a psychopath, explaining the difficulty as due to early weaning and rejection by his mother. Classification, *group 3c*.

Case 170, temperamentally 3-6-2, is a hard-driving, singularly one-directional young man who is sophisticated and knows just what he wants. His religion, he says, is "one hundred per cent materialistic," and his interpretation of human history is "purely economic." He does his work well and has the energy to attract favorable attention by overdoing academic assignments. He will be well recommended by his dean. Classification, *group 2a*.

Case 171, temperamentally 4-4-4, although of the same somatotype as the last, illustrates a *persona* of singularly different nature. This man is a sentimentalist and a romanticist. He loves to preach, especially to boys. His first duty (and pleasure), he feels, is to set a high moral example by living "spiritually and unselfishly." He is mentally soft, intellectually flabby, and many of his mannerisms suggest effeminacy. As a child he was often called a "sissy." But there is no overt homosexuality in his history. In his own way he has made a good integration around his "Scoutmaster persona." Classification, *group 2b*.

The 4-6-1's
(VHP 214—Fig. 70)

Two examples of this rare, extremely massive and powerful physique. Both are Jewish and both are graduates of medical school. One is a successful psychoanalyst, the other an institutionalized manic-depressive.

Case 172, temperamentally 5-5-1, has achieved a successful integration in the face of a difficult pattern of temperament. As a medical student he showed signs of serious internal difficulty. At times he was almost manic, showing extreme aggression and euphorial expansiveness which brought him into a number of minor embarrassments. At times he suffered severe depression of his spirits, accompanied by excessive emotionality and by a tendency to pour out his grief promiscuously. His psychoanalysis started when he was a senior medical student. As it progressed, he became much better integrated, showed the traditional symptoms of the "conversion experience," and during the succeeding four years he has been a happy and an excessively vigorous person. He had a didactic, "teaching" analysis, conducted by an experienced analyst. He is now a passionate proselyter to psychoanalysis as the true pattern for universal salvation, and he himself is doing well as a young analyst. It can hardly be doubted that psychoanalysis has in this case filled, at least temporarily, a religious need. We are greatly interested to observe whether or not he will in later years again show manic-depressive symptoms. Classification, *group 2b*.

Case 173, temperamentally 3-7-2, showed an early history remarkably similar to the last, except that there was a weaker viscerotonia and apparently a more violent somatorosis. During the early periods of depression, he kept more to himself and did not pour out his grief so easily. He went over into a frank manic-depressive psychosis at age 30, and a year later has shown but little sign of improvement. There is a good deal of paranoid symptomatology. During the past eight years he has suffered from a chronic duodenal ulcer. This young man has had no contact with psychoanalysis. It would be of interest to observe, even now, what psychoanalysis might do for him. Classification, *group 3b*, perhaps bordering on 3a.

The 5-2-2
(VHP 194—Fig. 59)

A single example of this very scarce somatotype.

Case 174, temperamentally 6-1-2, seems to be hopelessly bogged in the marshes of viscerosis. He has clung to people, and to the simple pleasures of the gut, as a weak, grateful puppy might cling to its mistress in the wilderness. This youth does not look out upon the world at all. He has never accepted any responsibility or formulated any ambition. He is a baby at heart and he wants only to remain a baby. In almost every sense he preserves the innocence of an infant. He is hypogenital and has no sexuality, no malice, no cunning, no resentment. Superficially he is effeminate. His general physical outline is feminoid. Psychologically he is not effeminate, but infantile. Classification, *group 4*.

The 5-2-4's
(VHP 169—Fig. 44)

Two examples, one illustrating the Froehlich syndrome, the other an excellently integrated personality.

Case 175, temperamentally 4-1-5, presents the unhappy combination of a predominant cerebrotonia resting upon an excessively weak and sexually deficient physique. He is apprehensive, shy, overly sensitive to pain. Yet he has an overwhelming craving for attention and affection, and an abject dependency on people. Such a combination of traits, existing in what is somatotonically almost a vacuum, renders this boy unhappy, frightened and insecure. A long history of experimentation with endocrine therapy seems to have intensified the unhappiness without improving the situation. Classification, *group 4*.

Case 176, temperamentally 4-4-4, shows an excellent integration. He has adopted the *persona* of the somewhat arty, intellectual young man, and has made a success of it. His academic record is consistently brilliant, and he is a productive young scientist. Most people like him, although he is considered effeminate by the "intolerant normals." Like most males in whom mesomorphy is low, he has been accused vaguely of homosexuality, but he is in fact strongly heterosexual, and now that his academic career is securely under way he devotes perhaps a disproportionately great amount of time to the sexual pursuit. He has no etchings but his collection of symphonies has begun to grow a bit notorious. He seems young for his age, and did not mature sexually until he was 16. His first sexual intercourse occurred at 23. Classification, *group 1*.

The 5-3-2's
(VHP 197—Fig. 53)

Three examples, all of them showing normal integration of personality. Case 177, temperamentally 6-3-2, is a youngster who has not as yet developed any serious inclinations except those of self-indulgence. But his indulgences are so honest and so normal, and his sociophilia and human good will are so manifest and hearty that he is everywhere well received, even in the dean's office. Such a youth is almost certain not to develop critical intellectuality, but he is likewise nearly certain never to have need of it. His *persona* is that of the good-natured, tolerant fat man. He lives out his pattern consistently, and thereby he has in his hands one solution of most of the problems of human life. Classification, *group 2a.*

Case 178, temperamentally 6-4-1, is a youth remarkably similar to the last, except that he has more energy and drive. His popularity is more widespread. Porky, as he is called, is one of the most dynamic personalities on the campus. He is virtually a social clearing house in his own right. Whenever a party or dance is planned in the School of Business, the event is centered around Porky. He does his academic work fairly well too. For him, business success appears virtually assured. Classification, *group 2a.*

Case 179, temperamentally 4-4-3, presents a different kind of personality from the last two, but shows an equally good integration to his own pattern. This young man has fallen back away from the 5 in viscerotonia and has set up the *persona* of simply an average or "normal" person. He is content to be a good pharmacist, to mind his own business faithfully and to allow the rest of the world to go its way. No ill is spoken of him. Everybody who knows him considers him a dependable fixture. Classification, *group 2a.*

The 5-3-3's
(VHP 185)

Six examples of this the commonest of the endomorphic somatotypes (except the 4-3-3). Five of them show at least passably good integration of personality. One is among the most brilliant men of the university. One of the six is a weakling.

Case 180, temperamentally 5-2-4, is one of those seemingly inexplicable young men who appear languid, lazy, overly viscerotonic and disconcertingly relaxed of body, yet maintain a high academic standing and are unquestionably brilliant of mind. His round, myopic face is so relaxed that he almost drools. His hands are soft, tiny, weak and seem nerveless (like the hands often seen in hebephrenic schizophrenia). His intimate friends are men exclusively and he is sexually virginal, although he has a strong sexual drive and masturbates excessively. There has been no overt homosexuality. He carries a strong sexual conflict, and also severe conflict between the first and third components, but he has so far carried them well, and seems to have a good academic future. It is to be supposed that he will ultimately find his best vocational adaptation somewhere in the field of the arts. Classification, *group 2a.*

Case 181, temperamentally 6-2-3, although an overt homosexual, appears to have achieved a fairly well-integrated pattern of personality with an unusually difficult constitutional endowment. With so high a gynandromorphy (5), complicated by a strong sexual drive, he has been hard put to it to find an acceptable adaptive pattern. Except for his homosexuality, which he has so far managed with discretion, his general adaptation is good. As a preacher he is successful, for he talks well and has an inexhaustible flow of sincere viscerotonia. It wells up out of him like spring water. At funerals he sheds sincere, copious tears. At social gossip and small talk he is ardently in character. Classification, *group 2b.*

Case 182, temperamentally 5-1-4, is a weakling in almost every sense. He has poor physical coordination, cannot run, fight, or throw, and has no compensatory mental strength. He is distinctly hypogenital and is nearly sexless in desire, although he masturbates occasionally and likes to pretend that he has dates with girls. He has never faced or accepted his situation. His *persona* is merely a muddled picture of himself as he is not, i.e., a successful, normal young man who in professional social work would help others to "normality." His recent psychoanalysis appears to have been a waste of effort. Classification, *group 4.*

Case 183, temperamentally 6-3-2, has integrated his life around the supposedly popular *persona* of joviality, gluttony and expansive complacency. He is known as a bluff, or as a "bag of wind," but as a good-natured, well-meaning, and tolerable person in his role. He plans a journalistic career. He reads widely but super-ficially, and blandly reveals an astonishing ignorance in complex fields at every opportunity. He knows he is a bluff, but feels that journalism has lots of room for a good bluff. Classification, *group 2a.*

Case 184, temperamentally 4-3-4, has developed in a direction opposite to that of case 183. He falls away from the 5 in viscero-tonia and advances to a 4 in cerebrotonia. This young medical student has the highest IQ in the entire series, and is regarded as one of the most promising people associated with the university. As his dean puts it, he "has everything." He is modest and per-sonally serene, well relaxed. The impression he makes is always good. Instructors and superiors seem to expect him to do well, but he surprises by doing superbly well. He has a quiet, friendly smile, and a disconcerting mental alertness is seen in his face when his myopic eyes are observed closely. He does not seem ever to be pressed in his work, or to be behind in his schedule. He likes women and boasts of a "mistress." Classification, *group 1.*

Case 185, temperamentally 4-4-4, seems to be caught in the per-plexing entanglements of overendowment. He is gifted in several different directions, hence finds the greatest difficulty in making a vocational adjustment. He is, in different moods, a poet, art critic, scientist, libertine and ascetic. At times he is sociophilic, at times painfully sociophobic. He found sociologists "but a step re-moved from YMCA secretaries," and he now finds biologists "crude and unimaginative." Yet he has done fairly well in both fields and has an excellent general record. He will grow much heavier in a few years and in all probability will then settle into a more comfortable outlook. He may then make a better adjust-ment. This is often the way with endomorphs. The 5-3-3 is a rare somatotype in the mental hospitals. Classification, *group 2b.*

The 5-3-4
(VHP 173—Fig. 45)

One example. Case 186, temperamentally 4-2-5, has made a good integration in his own way by falling back in the second component and taking up virtually a feminine *persona*. He is not only a young lady, but a "nice" one. Soft, meticulous language and the teacup are his weapons both for breadwinning and for ego fulfillment. They serve him admirably, for he is fortunately low in sexuality. For him there is no disturbance from that often disquieting quarter, and his life alternates serenely between Mary Baker Eddy and counterpoint. His symphony collection cloaks no hidden pitfalls, either for man or for woman. Classification, *group 2a.*

The 5-4-1's
(VHP 213—Fig. 71)

Two examples, each making a good adjustment. Case 187, temperamentally 6-4-1, is a vigorous, healthy, well-groomed young Irishman with high color in his cheeks and a goodly paunch under his belt. He is ambitious, expansive, romantic in an extraverted way. He has two gifts, swimming and singing. His outlook seems very bright in a material sense, although no intellectual ambitions have taken root during his educational exposure. At 22, this young man has a blood pressure of 142/110. He is a likely candidate for trouble from this source in middle life. Note that in this instance the total strength of 10 in the first two components against 1 in the third appears to be associated with excellent social adjustment. A similar strength in the second and third against the first, or in the first and third against the second is usually associated with serious difficulty. Classification, *group 2a.*

Case 188, temperamentally 4-5-2, shows reversal of a dominance between the first and second components. There is an increment of aggression here which belies the essential physical softness and weakness of the man. In physical strength and prowess he cannot support the truculent *persona* behind which he lives. When his bluff is called he is lost. Yet he has made a fairly good adjustment. Although his bluff is often called he is not as a rule severely punished. Possibly this is due to the "softness and looseness" of the times. Perhaps this kind of "false aggression" can be integrated in a successful adjustment where natural penalties are peculiarly relaxed. Classification, *group 2b*.

The 5-4-2's
(VHP 202—Fig. 64)

Two examples, both of whom have made good adjustments in very different ways. Case 189, temperamentally 4-3-3, has found integration behind a *persona* which is essentially effeminate and self-effacing. He loves food, comfort, music and masturbation. He does not love strife and competition. Although well endowed with sexuality he is also well endowed with viscerotonia, and the latter appears to blanket or dampen the manifestations of the former. He has not yet achieved a good heterosexual relationship, but neither has he turned to homosexuality. He is quite happy in his vocational adjustment as a pianist. If of lower sexuality his outlook would be singularly serene. As matters are he has made a good adaptation in the face of a rather difficult internal conflict (between viscerotonia and sexuality). Classification, *group 2b*.

Case 190, temperamentally 6-3-1, has made an excellent integration in a direction just opposite to that taken by case 189. Instead of retreating from the massed strength of the first two components against the third, he has advanced still further out toward that peripheral segment of the distribution. Case 189, temperamentally 4-3-3, has moved in almost to the center of the distribution (see Fig. 6). Case 190, temperamentally 6-3-1, masses a total strength of 9 in the first two components against 1 in the third and takes a position out at the periphery. His *persona* is that of the jolly, expansive, a-moral extravert. He lives up to this without any sign of internal conflict, and has a wife who has made almost exactly the same integration. She is morphologically as well as temperamentally about a 6-3-1. Classification, *group 2a*.

The 5-4-3's
(VHP 187)

Two examples. Both show reversal of the dominance between the second and third components, yet both have made reasonably good adjustments. Where the first component is strong, general social acceptability seems to be relatively easy to obtain. Persons well buffered with viscerotonia often seem able to adapt comfortably, even in the face of a reversal of dominance between the other two components.

Case 191, temperamentally 4-3-4, is shy, sentimental, and rather weak. He is a plaintive young man who craves attention and affection but rarely gets either, except perhaps from home. To show him kindness is to be rewarded at once with viscerotic manifestations of gratitude, but also to be followed about and haunted for some time to come by a shy, inhibited, uninteresting youth whose principal motive is to plead for more attention. Actually this young man has little to offer. He is weak and flabby in mind as well as in body, and is personal and slobbery in his emotion. But he never offends and therefore he will probably become a successful educator. He is low enough in sexuality to be protected in that quarter. Classification, *group 2a.*

Case 192, temperamentally 5-3-4, presents a personality remarkably similar to the last, except that he is more conspicuously viscerotonic. This youth is considered very "sincere," and most of those who have contact with him adopt a protective attitude toward him. He is like a bather who cannot swim but whose flounderings are so sincerely and pitifully helpless that he receives support from all who are contiguous to him. In short, his adaptive *persona* rests almost entirely upon strength in the first component. His prognosis is probably good for he will never give offense, and human society in its present phase is prepared to tolerate great weakness so long as mental conformity is shown. Classification, *group 2a.*

The 6-1-3
(VHP 176—Fig. 47)

One example of this rare somatotype. Case 193, temperamentally 5-2-4, borders closely upon the Froehlich syndrome. His family has money and possibly a thousand dollars or more has been spent on endocrine therapy for him. A little tuft of pubic hair has sprouted and it is said that his voice has deepened, but he remains hypogenital, and his somatotype is still the same. His social adaptation is a very good one. He is always pleasant and cooperative. While affectionate and overly dependent upon social support, he is not aggressively so, but on the contrary his modesty and shyness attract much friendly notice. Within the limits of his almost complete lack of sexuality, his outlook seems to be excellent. Classification, *group 2a.*

The 6-2-2's
(VHP 195—Fig. 60)

Two examples, both showing a strong temperamental increment in the second component and both achieving excellent integration.

Case 194, temperamentally 6-3-2, is perhaps a good example of the traditionally jolly fat boy. He has always been a playboy, oversupplied with money and as devoid of moral responsibility as is humanly possible. Indeed, freedom from inhibition and good fellowship constitute the theme song of his *persona,* and he has consistently lived up to his pattern. Like many endomorphs who have found happy integration in this pattern, he makes a great bluff of sexuality, but in common with nearly all who reach a 6 in endomorphy he has small genitalia and is actually low in sexuality. He drinks a good deal, but has never been known to be drunk or to show somatorotic symptoms under alcohol. This drug seems only to enhance his viscerotonic propensities. It is almost impossible to avoid the conclusion that alcohol "agrees with" and is in a sense "good for" such a person. Classification, *group 2a.*

Case 195, temperamentally 5-4-2, shows a pattern somewhat similar to the last although he is more active and more energetic. He has the same buoyant good humor and optimism, the same freedom from restraint or doubt, and the same general popularity and acceptability. He is a bustling "go-getter" and although in some respects rude and overbearing, he seldom encounters serious resentment. He is never pugnacious. His aggression takes the form of perseverance and good-natured insistence, of energetic sociability and omnipresence, never the form of somatic threat or hostility. He is the kind with whom nobody becomes angry. He seems to be living out his pattern successfully, but the jump from 2½ in mesomorphy to 4 in somatotonia is a wide one. Such a person is under a continuous strain. He is carrying a five-ton load with a two-ton truck. Sooner or later the strain is certain to tell in one way or another. This young man's physical health has so far been excellent. As he grows older and runs into organic pathology of some sort, there is likely to be a decided change of personality, but with so low a mesomorphy he is not likely to become manic. Classification, *group 2a.*

The 6-3-1
(VHP 210—Fig. 72)

A single example. Case 196, temperamentally 6-4-1, presents a personality still further out in the direction taken by the last two. Combining a total of 10 in the first two components against 1 in the third, and possessing a massive, heavy body with no ectomorphic dysplasia, this young man rings as true to himself as a ripe pumpkin. He knows exactly what he wants, has the energy to work hard for it, and the viscerotonia to buffer his contacts. He is as crude and insensitive as men can be, and so gluttonous that the woman who runs his boarding house threatens to feed him on the kitchen floor. His snore is so loud and famous that two of his classmates once made a recording of it "for posterity." But he reflects warmth and he is well liked. Should he leave the medical school a distinct loss would be felt by all who know him, and that is nearly everybody. Classification, *group 2a.*

The 6-3-2
(VHP 200—Fig. 61)

One example. Case 197, temperamentally 5-4-3, is an "aristocratic" Jewish youth. He comes from good stock, shows fine quality both in physique and personal deportment, and has made a brilliant record, particularly in mathematics. He is relaxed and sociophilic, likes alcohol, and under its influence tends to become somewhat offensively viscerotonic. He is highly sexed for his somatotype, both morphologically and functionally, and is popular with women. He is passionately devoted to classical music, and especially Bach. A heavily loaded temperament, we see, does not always lead to frustration. Classification, *group 1.*

The 7-1-1's
(VHP 204—Fig. 1A)

Two examples of this scarce somatotype. One is gluttonous and viscerotic. The other has made a fairly good adjustment.

Case 198, temperamentally 6-1-1, presents what appears to be a hopeless picture. He has a low IQ, is uncontrollably greedy, and remains nearly as dependent upon others as a baby. No effort has been successful in awakening in him any sense of purpose, or shame, or self-discipline. He is one of eleven children in a family which has long been on public charity, although several of the other children have now set up independent existences. This index of temperament, 6-1-1, falls outside the morphological distribution in the direction of underendowment. Classification, *group 4.*

Case 199, temperamentally 6-2-3, has succeeded in making a fairly good integration. He does passably good work in his classes, maintains a friendly outlook most of the time, and is known as a likable and obliging young man. He suffers from intermittent periods of melancholy depression, however, and during these periods he is peculiarly emotional, sometimes crying alone in his room for hours. He never shows any corresponding "manic" tendency. There are no periods of euphorial expansion or intensified aggression. His sexuality is very low. During and immediately following his periods of melancholy he tends to be pious. His present plan is to accept a scholarship to a theological seminary and to enter the ministry. Classification, *group 2b.*

The 7-3-1
(VHP 212—Fig. 75)

One example. Case 200, temperamentally 6-4-1, is a prominent figure on the campus. Few important events transpire without his having a hand in them. A regular on the football team for three years, he is also prominent in dramatics, in campus politics, and in the interfraternity council. He has inexhaustible energy and good nature, knows everybody "worth knowing" by his first name, and is conspicuously present at whatever is going on. Withal, he has found time to make a fairly good college record and has been admitted to the medical school. Although hypogenital, he lays claim to a goodly interest in sexuality, and has a lewd eye for feminine beauty. He is at his best when slightly alcoholized. Classification, *group 2a.*

A NOTE ON NATURE VERSUS NURTURE

Although these studies were carried out mainly to develop and standardize a technique for diagnosing temperament, they have also yielded a degree of clarification of the general statistical interrelationships among the morphological and temperamental variables. An analysis of these relationships is presented in the chapter which follows.

If anything is demonstrated conclusively by the study as a

whole, it is this: that neither the somatotype alone, nor any other single factor, will suffice to "explain" a personality. Persons of the same somatotype frequently develop into singularly different kinds of people. Note especially the diverging personalities developing from the somatotype 2-3-5, and study the contrasts of personality seen in the following pairs of cases—each pair falling within a single somatotype: cases 80 and 81, 137 and 138, 170 and 171, 175 and 176, 183 and 184, 189 and 190. Furthermore, although the correlation between somatotype and temperament, taken at large, is of about the order + .80 (see p. 400), so many (apparently secondary) variables are at work that the *specific manifestations* of temperament can be predicted from the somatotype only within very wide limits.

That a person who is 5 in mesomorphy will express a fair amount of aggression can be predicted, almost with certainty. But *how* he will express it, and through what traits of aggression, cannot be predicted without a knowledge of many secondary factors, among which the environmental history unquestionably plays an important role.

On the other hand, unless the technique of analysis we have used is grossly misleading, it is equally clear that the somatotype and other constitutionally determined characteristics need to be taken into account in any successful effort to interpret a personality. Those who are 2-3-5's are not found to behave like 7-1-1's, however they may have been "conditioned," and mesomorphs do not ordinarily develop cerebrotonic characteristics. Two major sets of variables appear to be at work in the determination of a human personality—the original endowment, and the molding or directing influences.

Psychologists have long shown a cyclic tendency to try to deemphasize first one of these sets of variables and then the other. Each generation seems suddenly to discover that thought has been leaning too far in the one direction, and a violent overcorrection follows. Thirty years ago it was not uncommon in psychology to hear that all a man could hope to become was largely predetermined by his (instinctive) constitutional endowment. Today we often encounter the equally fanatical view that the genetic and constitutional side of the picture is no more than an irrelevant constant—that personality arises almost wholly from what happens after birth.

That such diametrically opposed dogmas should have become successively fashionable within half the span of a century is remarkable. How could it happen?

One seemingly unavoidable conclusion is that we have been very much confused as to what is to be meant by personality. The term can be defined in such a manner as to include (1) only learned attributes, or (2) only genetically determined attributes. Or it can be defined willy-nilly to support one's own hypotheses. For our own part we propose no intolerance as to the definition of personality, and especially we desire to avoid taking sides in the ancient warfare between schools of nurture and schools of nature. The studies which have been summarized in the present chapter seem only too poignantly to drive home the lesson that a psychology of personality must rest upon techniques of both constitutional and environmental analysis.

CHAPTER VII

STATISTICAL RELATIONS AMONG
TEMPERAMENTAL AND MORPHOLOGICAL
VARIABLES

IN THIS chapter we turn to statistical data and to correlations among the different variables which have been described. Here we shall see that achievement, as defined in the previous chapter, is found to be somewhat related to the manner in which temperament reflects the somatotype. When the series of 200 cases is arranged according to achievement groups, morphological and temperamental factors appear to have played a differentiating role in determining achievement, and a study of the means and standard deviations of the primary components within the respective achievement groups points toward the same conclusion.

We shall also consider the important matter of the correlations found to exist between the static components of morphology on the one hand and the dynamic components of temperament on the other. Analysis of the intercorrelations among these different variables indicates a closer relation between the morphological and temperamental levels than has previously been supposed to exist. In addition there are several instructive connections to be noted between the primary components (both physical and temperamental) and various second-order aspects of physique and behavior.

ACHIEVEMENT AMONG VARIOUS PATTERNS OF PERSONALITY

1. *Where There is Perfect Agreement between Temperament and Somatotype.*

Table 3 gives the somatotypes, the indices of temperament, and the achievement groups for the 200 cases. Perfect agreement between somatotype and temperament is seen to be uncommon. There are but 14 instances of it in the series. Seven of these 14

TABLE 3

SHOWING THE SOMATOTYPE, THE INDEX OF TEMPERAMENT AND THE ADJUSTMENT GROUP FOR THE 200 CASES

No.	Som.	IT	Group	No.	Som.	IT	Group	No.	Som.	IT	Group
1.	117	216	2b	50.	253	362	2a	99.	344	434	2a
2.	.126	236	1	51.	254	254	2b	100.	345	336	3a
3.	126	137	3a	52.	262	352	2a	101.	345	344	1
4.	127	236	2b	53.	262	262	2a	102.	352	452	2a
5.	154	254	2b	54.	262	271	2a	103.	352	271	2b
6.	154	164	3b	55.	262	352	1	104.	352	353	3d
7.	162	272	3b	56.	262	361	2a	105.	352	443	2a
8.	171	362	2a	57.	262	272	3a	106.	352	362	2b
9.	171	261	2a	58.	263	353	1	107.	353	453	2a
10.	172	263	2a	59.	263	263	3d	108.	353	354	2a
11.	217	316	2b	60.	271	361	2a	109.	353	354	3d
12.	225	326	3d	61.	325	435	3a	110.	353	453	2a
13.	225	236	1	62.	325	415	2b	111.	353	362	2b
14.	225	315	4	63.	325	326	2b	112.	353	444	2a
15.	226	326	3d	64.	325	325	3d	113.	354	453	3c
16.	226	326	3d	65.	325	324	4	114.	354	263	1
17.	226	317	2b	66.	334	335	1	115.	354	363	2b
18.	226	235	1	67.	334	244	1	116.	354	444	2b
19.	226	225	2b	68.	334	434	2a	117.	361	371	2a
20.	235	136	2b	69.	334	245	2b	118.	361	452	2a
21.	235	137	3a	70.	334	344	2a	119.	361	471	2b
22.	235	244	1	71.	334	334	2a	120.	362	452	2a
23.	235	154	2b	72.	334	334	1	121.	362	271	2a
24.	235	145	2a	73.	334	333	4	122.	362	263	2b
25.	235	236	2b	74.	335	245	1	123.	424	325	2b
26.	235	344	2a	75.	335	435	1	124.	424	514	4
27.	235	336	3a	76.	335	335	2a	125.	424	425	3d
28.	235	335	1	77.	335	325	2a	126.	425	315	4
29.	236	236	2b	78.	335	334	2a	127.	425	424	1
30.	244	254	2b	79.	343	354	2b	128.	425	434	1
31.	244	334	2a	80.	343	253	2b	129.	433	524	2b
32.	244	154	2b	81.	343	452	2a	130.	433	334	2b
33.	244	354	2b	82.	343	344	2a	131.	433	444	2b
34.	244	244	2a	83.	343	343	2a	132.	434	344	2b
35.	244	245	2b	84.	343	353	2a	133.	434	533	2a
36.	245	245	1	85.	343	444	2a	134.	434	325	2a
37.	245	344	2a	86.	343	263	3b	135.	434	443	3c
38.	245	137	3a	87.	344	245	1	136.	434	335	2b
39.	245	245	1	88.	344	345	1	137.	435	325	2a
40.	252	173	2b	89.	344	254	1	138.	435	344	2b
41.	253	263	3d	90.	344	244	3d	139.	435	344	1
42.	253	263	2b	91.	344	354	2a	140.	442	352	2a
43.	253	272	3b	92.	344	344	2a	141.	442	353	3d
44.	253	344	2a	93.	344	345	1	142.	442	543	2a
45.	253	254	3d	94.	344	253	2b	143.	442	443	2a
46.	253	164	2b	95.	344	443	3c	144.	442	532	2a
47.	253	262	2a	96.	344	353	2a	145.	443	434	3c
48.	253	263	3d	97.	344	335	3d	146.	443	333	4
49.	253	254	2b	98.	344	444	2a	147.	443	352	2a

TABLE 3—(Continued)

No.	Som.	IT	Group	No.	Som.	IT	Group	No.	Som.	IT	Group
148.	443	354	2b	166.	452	461	2b	184.	533	434	1
149.	443	352	2a	167.	452	361	2b	185.	533	444	2b
150.	443	453	2b	168.	453	444	2b	186.	534	425	2a
151.	443	433	2a	169.	453	344	3c	187.	541	641	2a
152.	443	444	2a	170.	453	362	2a	188.	541	452	2b
153.	443	354	2b	171.	453	444	2b	189.	542	433	2b
154.	443	534	3c	172.	461	551	2b	190.	542	631	2a
155.	443	354	3c	173.	461	372	3b	191.	543	434	2a
156.	444	345	1	174.	522	612	4	192.	543	534	2a
157.	444	354	2b	175.	524	415	4	193.	613	524	2a
158.	444	444	2a	176.	524	444	1	194.	622	632	2a
159.	444	543	2a	177.	532	632	2a	195.	622	543	2a
160.	451	353	1	178.	532	641	2a	196.	631	641	2a
161.	451	542	3c	179.	532	443	2a	197.	632	543	1
162.	451	362	2a	180.	533	524	2a	198.	711	611	4
163.	452	443	2a	181.	533	623	2b	199.	711	623	2b
164.	452	453	1	182.	533	514	4	200.	731	641	2a
165.	452	444	2b	183.	533	632	2a				

fall in achievement group 2a—the group called normal-without-effort. Two are in group 2b, the group called normal-through-effort. Three fall in achievement group 1 (superior achievement), and two are in group 3d (miscellaneous maladaptation). All the perfect agreements except one fall among the 2's and 3's in endomorphy. Table 4 presents the cases showing perfect agreement.

All the somatotypes in Table 4 are fairly common and an odd thing about them is this: in no instance is the first component predominant, and in every case but one (case 64, a 3-2-5) the first is exceeded or tied by both of the other components. Taken as a whole, this is a normal, excellently adapted group of people.

TABLE 4

FOURTEEN CASES SHOWING PERFECT AGREEMENT BETWEEN SOMATO-TYPE AND TEMPERAMENT

No.	Som.	IT	Group	No.	Som.	IT	Group	No.	Som.	IT	Group
29.	236	236	2b	53.	262	262	2a	76.	335	335	2a
34.	244	244	2a	59.	263	263	3d	83.	343	343	2a
36.	245	245	1	64.	325	325	3d	92.	344	344	2a
39.	245	245	1	71.	334	334	2a	158.	444	444	2a
51.	254	254	2b	72.	334	334	1				

2. *Where There is Radical Disagreement between Temperament and Somatotype.*

In contrast with those showing perfect agreement between the two levels, 11 cases reveal a disagreement as large as two degrees between temperament and somatotype in one of the components. These are the following.

TABLE 5

ELEVEN CASES SHOWING RADICAL DISAGREEMENT BETWEEN SOMATO-
TYPE AND TEMPERAMENT

No.	Som.	IT	Group	No.	Som.	IT	Group	No.	Som.	IT	Group
21.	235	137	3a	*43.*	253	272	3b	*176.*	524	444	1
23.	235	154	2b	*103.*	352	271	2b	*182.*	533	514	4
38.	245	137	3a	*160.*	451	353	1	*199.*	711	623	2b
40.	252	173	2b	*165.*	452	444	2b				

The first of these, case 21, jumps from 5 in ectomorphy to the extreme 7 in cerebrotonia and presents a personality so cerebrotic that the prognosis must be considered poor.

Case 23, also a 2-3-5 in somatotype, jumps from 3 in mesomorphy to 5 in somatotonia to establish a somatotonic predominance which reverses the morphological predominance between the second and third components. This youth has fallen into bitter somatorotic hostility toward his environment and even toward his species as a whole. But he has thrown unusual mental and volitional resources into the struggle and he appears to stand a good chance to survive. His resistance to disintegration should sound a warning for any who may need it, against the misconception that a personality can be explained or a career predicted from constitutional data interpreted independently of their social setting. To try to explain a personality from the constitutional pattern alone is as futile as to attempt such an explanation solely from the life history of the individual.

Case 38 is a personality remarkably similar to case 21, although morphologically a 2-4-5 instead of 2-3-5. He, like case 21, jumps all the way from 5 in ectomorphy to 7 in cerebrotonia, and the cerebrotic strain under which he lives is a painful thing to watch.

Case 40 jumps from 5 in mesomorphy to 7 in somatotonia. He is perhaps a classic illustration of overcompensational somatorosis, but like case 23 he appears to be making good under great pressure. Case 43 shows nearly the same pattern as case 40, but unlike the latter has failed to achieve satisfactory social adjustment and will probably commit repeated acts of violence until he is destroyed. Case 103 is a third example of the long jump from 5 in mesomorphy to 7 in somatotonia. This is one of the most "objectionably aggressive" youths we have seen in an academic environment, but he is apparently happy and physically healthy.

Case 160 advances from the minimal 1 in ectomorphy to 3 in cerebrotonia, while case 165 advances from 2 to 4 in this same third component. The first of these two, temperamentally 3-5-3, is well embarked on a brilliant career. The second, temperamentally 4-4-4, seems to be a victim of some degree of temperamental overloading but is making a good adjustment.

Case 176 advances from the weak 2 in mesomorphy to 4 in somatotonia and is making an academic success without the physique to back up his 4 in somatotonia. Probably this particular kind of success is possible only in an artificially protective environment such as academic life offers.

Case 182 presents the only example in our series of a person falling back two degrees in a component. He falls back from 3 in mesomorphy to the minimum of 1 in somatotonia. He is classed as a constitutional defective.

Case 199, like case 160, advances from 1 in ectomorphy to 3 in cerebrotonia, achieving a fairly good integration of his difficult 6-2-3 temperament and 7-1-1 physique.

The fact that we do not in any instance find the first component involved in the radical two-degree discrepancy between somatotype and temperament is highly suggestive. Somatotonia and cerebrotonia are possibly to be regarded as biological adventurings away from a more primeval viscerotonia. (That they are extensions in two very different directions is indicated by the high negative correlation between them. See Table 14.) It may be that these two components tend, under unusual circumstances, to depart more radically from the hereditary morphology than does viscerotonia. However, the correlation between morphology and temperament in general, for the 200 cases, is nearly the same for all three components (Table 14). The dramatic extremes of disagreement between morphology and temperament are apparently confined to the second and third components, but the *average* disagreement is about the same for the three components. There was no case in this series which showed a disagreement as great as three degrees, in any component.

Among the 11 cases making up Table 5 are 2 examples of

achievement group 1; 5 of group 2b; 2 of group 3a; 1 of group 3b; and 1 of group 4. The conspicuous absence of any representatives of group 2a (the "normals") from this list indicates that a severe strain on the personality is associated with so wide a disparity between morphology and temperament. But it does not follow

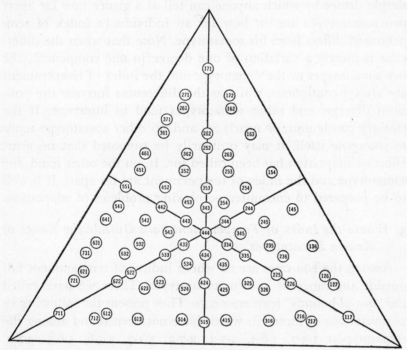

FIG. 6. A Schematic Two-dimensional Projection of the Theoretical Spatial Relationships among the Known Somatotypes.

that such a strain *per se* leads necessarily to maladaptation. Indeed, more than half of these people have made good adjustments to their social world, and there is food for thought in the fact that two representatives of group 1 are found here. That is 18 per cent. If 18 per cent of the whole population could be classed as group 1, the future might perhaps be faced with equanimity.

Figure 6 will perhaps assist a reader not familiar with the theory of somatotyping to visualize what is meant by a radical disagreement between temperament and the somatotype. Contained within the triangle is a schematic two-dimensional projection of the theoretical spatial relationships among the 76 known somatotypes.

In looking at this figure it must be borne in mind that the third dimension (depth) has been telescoped or collapsed into a flat surface. A more adequate three-dimensional scheme representing the geometrical distribution of the somatotypes is to be found on p. 117 of *The Varieties of Human Physique*. Figure 6 offers a simple device by which anyone can tell at a glance how far apart two somatotypes are, or how far an individual's index of temperament differs from his somatotype. Note that when the difference is merely a variation of one degree in one component, the two somatotypes or the somatotype and the index of temperament are always contiguous, while as the differences increase the positions diverge, and other somatotypes tend to intervene. If the two are contiguous, or nearly so, and no other somatotype tends to interpose itself, it may ordinarily be supposed that no great effort of adaptation has been called for. If, on the other hand, the somatotype and the index of temperament are far apart, it is well to be prepared to encounter perplexing problems of adaptation.

3. *Where the Index of Temperament Falls Outside the Range of Known Somatotypes.*

Among the 200 cases are 21 whose indices of temperament fall outside the range of known somatotypes. These we have called the "out-of-bounds" temperaments. They present the following 13 permutations of numerals which have not been found among the somatotypes: 1-3-7, 1-6-4, 1-7-3, 2-7-2, 3-1-7, 3-3-6, 3-6-3, 3-7-2, 4-7-1, 3-1-5, 3-2-4, 3-3-3 and 6-1-1. Of these new permutations, the first 9 depart from morphological occurrence in the direction of overendowment, toward the hypothetical or imaginary 7-7-7 (see Fig. 9B, p. 117, *The Varieties of Human Physique*). The last 4 fall back, in the direction of underendowment, toward the hypothetical 1-1-1. The presence of new permutations among the indices of temperament raises some questions of theoretical interest. In the first place, we of course have no way of knowing whether these new indices represent actual departures outside the boundaries set by nature for morphological variation, or whether they indicate only the relative imperfection of our administration of the instrument for measuring temperament. In any event it will be noted that none of the new permutations varies more than one degree in one component from some known somatotype.

Our observations on psychotic patients indicate that indices of temperament occur (pathologically) which fall further outside the morphological distribution than do any of the above list. We think that among manics such temperaments as the 4-7-2, and the 5-6-2 occur. These are two degrees removed from anything that occurs morphologically. Similarly, among constitutional defectives, and among patients labeled *schizophrenia simplex* we have made out what seem to be such indices as 3-1-4 and 4-1-3. These also are two degrees removed from the nearest known somatotype. And in a recent study of a group labeled *paranoid schizophrenia*, we found what looks astonishingly like a 2-5-6 and also a 2-6-5.

But in these studies of psychopathology we are severely handicapped by the difficulty in adequately reconstructing the patient's history, and also by the fact that we are observing him only under conditions of artificial restraint. Such difficulties can perhaps be met, but they have not yet been met, and we cite these indications only as directional pointings.

The 21 cases who depart temperamentally from nature's schoolyard of somatotypes make up a striking group. Table 6 lists them, together with their somatotypes and their classifications according to achievement of social adjustment.

TABLE 6

LISTING TWENTY-ONE CASES WHOSE INDICES OF TEMPERAMENT FALL OUTSIDE THE RANGE OF KNOWN SOMATOTYPES

No.	Som.	IT	Group	No.	Som.	IT	Group	No.	Som.	IT	Group
3.	126	137	3a	38.	245	137	3a	100.	345	336	3a
6.	154	164	3b	40.	252	173	2b	115.	354	363	2b
7.	162	272	3b	43.	253	272	3b	119.	361	471	2b
14.	225	315	4	46.	253	164	2b	126.	425	315	4
17.	226	317	2b	57.	262	272	3a	146.	443	333	4
21.	235	137	3a	65.	325	324	4	173.	461	372	3a
27.	235	336	3a	73.	334	333	4	198.	711	611	4

This table would seem to reflect the implacability with which nature punishes those who deviate too far from her conventions. Note that only 5 of the 21 have been able to escape an apparently hopeless social maladjustment (groups 3 and 4). Of the 5 who achieve group 2b, 4 are "out-of-bounds somatotonics" (cases 40, 46, 114 and 119). Only one of the "out-of-bounds cerebrotonics" (case 17) has found a *persona* which meets his problem.

Still more striking is the absence of viscerotonia from this company. In only 2 of the 21 cases does this component exceed a strength of 3, and in only one instance is it the dominant component. That instance is one of temperamental underendowment (case 198). Just as the first component is rarely involved in a radical discrepancy between somatotype and temperament, it seems likewise to be rarely involved in a temperamental departure from the boundaries set by morphology.

The 6 examples of group 4 (constitutional inferiority) among these 21 cases fall outside nature's distribution on the side of insufficient total strength in the primary components, especially as regards somatotonia. The other 15 cases are examples of temperamental overendowment, and these are somewhat unequally divided between somatotonic and cerebrotonic predominance. There are 9 of the former and 6 of the latter. But nearly half of the somatotonics have achieved an acceptable pattern of life, while only one of the cerebrotonics has been so fortunate.

The number of cases here is too small for generalization but the presence of four "adapted" or accepted somatotonics among such a group may indicate that nature (or man) is more tolerant of an excess of this component than of an excess of cerebrotonia. To be overly aggressive is perhaps not quite so severe a handicap as to be overly restrained, at least at the present point in American civilization. Possibly we shall some day know enough about measuring the strength of these two components to make use of their respective thresholds for maladjustment as an indication of the state of the civilization. It may be that because of the value of somatotonia in war and in the struggle for individual power and status, a relatively militaristic or predatory culture tends to place a premium on that component and to tolerate exaggerations of its expression. Perhaps as a culture departs from predation as its central objective, the balance between somatotonia and the other components tends to swing back, and to de-emphasize somatotonia.

4. *Where the Index of Temperament Reverses a Morphological Predominance.*

There are in the series 19 instances in which the index of temperament reverses one of the morphological dominances. These are the following:

TABLE 7

LISTING NINETEEN CASES WHOSE INDICES OF TEMPERAMENT REVERSE
ONE OF THE MORPHOLOGICAL DOMINANCES

No.	Som.	IT	Group	No.	Som.	IT	Group	No.	Som.	IT	Group
23.	235	154	2b	132.	434	344	2b	155.	443	354	3c
50.	253	362	2a	135.	434	443	3c	161.	451	542	3c
95.	344	443	3c	139.	435	344	1	169.	453	344	3c
99.	344	434	2a	145.	443	434	3c	186.	534	425	2a
113.	354	453	3c	153.	443	354	2b	191.	543	434	2a
122.	362	263	2b	154.	443	534	3c	192.	543	534	2a
130.	433	334	2b								

Eight of these young men, or 42 per cent of all the reversals, are caught in serious maladjustments (group 3c). Note that we refer to group 3c as made up of the dyscrasias *associated with* (we do not say caused by) temperamental reversal of a morphological dominance. We have no way of knowing whether the reversal is a causative factor here, or merely a correlate. In all probability the cause, if there is one, lies deeper than anyone has yet penetrated.

In this series there are but three reversals of the first-order morphological dominance, that is to say, of the dominance between the strongest and the second strongest components. One of these, case 23, we have encountered before (p. 373). He not only reverses a first-order dominance but jumps two degrees in the second component and still makes an acceptable social adjustment. He is the exception who defies the rules. Case 161 reverses the first-order predominance between the first and second components. He falls into difficulties which are a little too much for him. Case 186 reverses his first-order endomorphic-ectomorphic predominance to become a cerebrotonic and a happy, well relaxed one, with (temperamentally) decreased second component. Note, incidentally, that all three of the reversals who are endomorphs (the last three in the table) have made comfortable social adjustments without effort (group 2a). It may be that when endomorphy predominates, the temperamental reversal of a dominance becomes unimportant. Perhaps the relaxing effect of a predominant first component is sufficient to override whatever disturbance may ordinarily be involved in a reversal.

Of the 8 unadapted reversals who are classed in group 3c, 4 reverse the first and third components (cases 95, 113, 155, and

169), while 3 reverse the second and third (cases 135, 145, and 154). The third component is involved in 7 of the 8 cases. There is but one instance of serious trouble associated with reversal of dominance between the first and second components, although there are 4 instances in which this reversal occurs (cases 99, 132, 139 and 161). In the whole series case 139 is the only example of a reversed dominance who has achieved group 1.

Note that nearly all of the reversals occur among what we call the mid-range somatotypes, or those limited to the permutations of the numerals 3, 4 and 5. Only 4 exceptions are seen in Table 7 (cases 23, 50, 122 and 161).

It must remain a possibility, of course, that the whole concept of reversal of a dominance is a spurious one arising from inadequacy in our technique for measuring temperament. Perhaps the dominance is in reality never reversed. We may be placing too much weight on some of the traits and thereby deriving spurious indices of temperament. Supporting such a possibility is the fact that most of the reversals have been found among the mid-range people, whose temperaments are the most difficult to gauge. It is among this group that we are most likely to make mistakes. But contrary to such a likelihood is the fact that our reversals have been fairly evenly distributed among the components. We are not, apparently, overgauging one component at the expense of the others.

One interesting observation to be made from Table 7 is the excellent representation of endomorphy there. Thirteen of the 19 cases are at 4 or 5 in this component. Endomorphy is scarce among the people whose temperaments fall out of bounds or contradict morphology by two degrees. But the first component seems to constitute no impediment to the reversal of a dominance.

ARRANGEMENT OF THE SERIES AS A WHOLE
ACCORDING TO ACHIEVEMENT GROUPS

Table 8 shows the distribution of the 200 cases arranged according to the categories of adaptational adjustment. There are many ways in which this material can be broken down for statistical analysis. The difficulty is that nearly all of our conventional statistical devices are adapted only to describing the variations of one component at a time. In constitutional analysis, averages and means taken on one component at a time are often of little meaning because components do not vary *in vacuo*. It is the person as a whole that lives and reacts, not mesomorphy or ectomorphy as such. The 3 in mesomorphy in a 2-3-5 is psychologically a very different thing from the 3 in mesomorphy in a 4-3-5. In the one case mesomorphy holds a second-order dominance, in the other it is the weakest component.

If we deal with averages and product-moment correlations, a 1-3-6 and a 3-1-6 are lumped in together as if they were nearly alike. But nothing could be further from the truth. They are alike in possessing a 6 in ectomorphy, but in other respects they point in opposite directions. Taking what we believe to be a justifiable analogy from chemistry (which, as we know it, is far

TABLE 8

LISTING THE 200 CASES ARRANGED ACCORDING TO ADAPTATIONAL ADJUSTMENT

Group *1*		*2a*		*2b*		*3a*		*3b*		*3c*		*3d*		*4*	
Som.	*IT*	*Som.*	*IT*	*Som.*	*IT*	*Som.*	*IT*	*Som.*	*IT*	*Som.*	*IT*	*Som.*	*IT*	*Som.*	*IT*
126	236	171	362	117	216	126	137	154	164	344	443	225	326	225	315
225	236	171	261	127	236	235	137	162	272	354	453	226	326	325	324
226	235	172	263	154	254	235	336	253	272	434	443	226	326	334	333
235	244	235	145	217	316	245	137	343	263	443	434	253	263	424	514
235	335	235	344	226	317	262	272	461	372	443	534	253	254	425	315
245	245	244	334	226	225	325	435			443	354	253	263	443	333
245	245	244	244	235	136	345	336			451	542	263	263	522	612
262	352	245	344	235	154					453	344	325	325	524	415
263	353	253	344	235	236							344	244	533	514
334	335	253	262	236	236							344	335	711	611
334	244	253	362	244	254							352	353		
334	334	262	352	244	154							353	354		
335	245	262	262	244	354							424	425		
335	435	262	271	244	245							442	353		
344	245	262	361	252	173										
344	345	271	361	253	263										
344	254	334	434	253	164										
344	345	334	344	253	254										
345	344	334	334	254	254										
354	263	335	335	325	415										
425	424	335	325	325	326										
425	434	335	334	334	245										
435	344	343	452	343	354										
444	345	343	344	343	253										
451	353	343	343	344	253										

TABLE 8—(*Continued*)

Group 1	2a	2b	Group 1
Som.IT	Som.IT	Som.IT	
452 453	343 353	352 271	
524 444	343 444	352 362	
533 434	344 354	353 362	
632 543	344 344	354 363	
	344 353	354 444	
	344 444	361 471	
	344 434	362 263	
	352 452	424 325	
	352 443	433 524	
	353 453	433 334	
	353 354	433 444	
	353 453	434 344	
	353 444	434 335	
	361 371	435 344	
	361 452	443 354	
	362 452	443 453	
	362 271	443 354	
	434 533	444 354	
	434 325	452 444	
	435 325	452 461	
	442 352	452 361	
	442 543	453 444	
	442 443	453 444	
	442 532	461 551	
	443 352	533 623	
	443 352	533 444	
	443 433	541 452	
	443 444	542 433	
	444 444	711 623	
	444 543		
	451 362		
	452 443		
	453 362		
	532 632		
	532 641		
	532 443		
	533 524		
	533 632		
	534 425		
	541 641		
	542 631		
	543 434		
	543 534		
	613 524		
	622 632		
	622 543		
	631 641		
	731 641		

simpler than human physiology and psychology), to average in the social reactions of a 1-3-6 with those of a 3-1-6 is like averaging in the chemical reactions of NaCl with HCl. One of these chemical compounds is a highly active acid, the other a neutral, inactive salt. The 1-3-6 has a secondary somatotonic predominance and is often a troublesome, aggressive character. Savonarola and the Shakespearian Cassius are perhaps classic 1-3-6's. The 3-1-6 is an excessively weak, soft, effeminate, harmless person with the muscular strength of a girl and the resolution of a rabbit.

In the field of constitutional analysis, statistical tables based on component averages can be at best hardly more than a sop to statistical convention. Although they are sometimes helpful, often they are nearly meaningless. The problem in this field is to interpret an individual in terms of his *combination* of components, not to interpret components apart from individuals. We therefore present the material of Table 8 as individual data to be studied in their complexity before classification and analysis is attempted.

Examination of this table reveals that 14.5 per cent of the 200 cases fall into group 1 (superior achievement). This is doubtless too high a figure for the general university population. A reasonable effort was made to keep the series "representative," but the selection was on a voluntary basis, and perhaps the more brilliant and gifted people were more willing to volunteer for such a study. Further, many of the people who were encouraged to participate were doubtless for one reason or another conspicuous. We suspect therefore that this distribution is too heavily weighted at the upper end.

Five per cent of the series are constitutional inferiors (group 4), and 17 per cent are classed as socially unadaptable (group 3). These figures are perhaps about twice too high for the general university population. We were aware of this weighting of the study at the lower end of the distribution, for 18 of the subjects were referred through university administrative offices or through the Department of Student Health.

Sixty-three and a half per cent are classed as "normal or well adapted, but undistinguished" (group 2). Possibly as many as 80 per cent of the average university population should be so classed.

ACHIEVEMENT AS RELATED TO THE MORPHOLOGICAL COMPONENTS

Tables 9 and 10 give an indication of how much can be predicted in the way of adaptational success from the somatotype alone.

TABLE 9

SHOWING THE INCIDENCE BY ADAPTATIONAL GROUP OF 200 CASES LISTED ACCORDING TO SOMATOTYPE

Group	1	2a	2b	3a	3b	3c	3d	4
Somatotype								
117			1					
126	1			1				
127			1					
154			1			1		
162						1		
171		2						
172		1						
217			1					
225	1						1	1
226	1		2				2	
235	2	2	3	2				
236			1					
244		2	4					
245	2	1		1				
252		1						
253		3	3		1		3	
254			1					
262	1	4						
263	1						1	
271		1						
325		2	1				1	1
334	3	3	1					1
335	2	3						
343		5	2		1			
344	4	5	1			1	2	
345	1			1				
352		2	2				1	
353		4	1				1	
354	1		2			1		
361		2	1					
362		2	1					
424			1				1	1
425	2							1
433			3					
434		2	2			1		
435	1	1	1					
442		4					1	
443		4	3			3		1
444	1	2	1					
451	1	1				1		
452	1	1	3					

TABLE 9—(Continued)

Group	1	2a	2b	3a	3b	3c	3d	4
Somatotype								
453		1	2			1		
461			1		1			
522								1
524	1							1
532		3						
533	1	2	2					1
534		1						
541		1	1					
542		1	1					
543		2						
613		1						
622		2						
631			1					
632	1							
711			1					1
731		1						

It is clear from a glance at Table 9 that each of the adaptational groups is recruited from a wide range of somatotypes. Group 1, for example, is drawn from practically the whole range of somatotypes in the sense that every general region of the somatotype distribution is represented. Endomorphs, mesomorphs and ectomorphs are all present. Yet Table 10 shows that they are not all present in the same proportion.

TABLE 10

SHOWING THE INCIDENCES BY ADAPTATIONAL GROUP OF 200 CASES LISTED ACCORDING TO THE PREDOMINANT COMPONENT IN THE SOMATOTYPE

Group	1		2a		2b		3a		3b		3c		3d		4		Total	
	Incidence	%	Incidence	%	Incidence	%	Incidence	%	Incidence	%	Incidence	%	Incidence	%	Incidence	%	Incidence	%
Endomorphs	3	10	15	50	8	27	1	1.5			3	4			4	13	30	15
Mesomorphs	5	7	29	41.5	21	30	1	1.5	5	7	3	4	6	9			70	35
Ectomorphs	16	30	10	19	13	25	6	11					4	7.5	4	7.5	53	26.5
Balanced	5	11	19	40	12	25					5	11	4	9	2	4	47	23.5
Total	29		73		54		7		5		8		14		10		200	100

Sixteen of the group 1 people are predominantly ectomorphic, while but 5 are mesomorphs and only 3 are endomorphs. Thirty per cent of all the ectomorphs in the total series are classed in group 1, as against 10 per cent of the endomorphs and only 7 per cent of the mesomorphs.

Group 2a (the naturally adapted group) shows a sharp contrast with group 1. Here 50 per cent of the endomorphs are found, and 41.5 per cent of the mesomorphs, as against only 19 per cent of the ectomorphs. The ectomorphs do not appear to fit into society as readily or as comfortably as do endomorphs and mesomorphs. Yet in the consequent *effort* to adapt, a considerably larger number of the ectomorphs achieve the highest level of success (group 1). A number of interesting questions arise.

First of all, are there more ectomorphs in group 1 because ectomorphs are more gifted in some fundamental sense, or is their achievement mainly an illustration of the compensatory principle? Have these people grown to the full human *mental* stature because they were born to do so, or have they done it only because, being physically weak, they had to in order to adapt? If we take the latter view, then is group 2a to be regarded as a sort of reservoir of good stock which did not and probably will not (within this lifetime) develop to its full mental possibilities, presumably because it does not have to do so?

There is, of course, another possibility to consider. Ectomorphy may have nothing to do with the mental development of people of group 1, but may be an irrelevant concomitant. It may quite easily be that while no causal relation exists between ectomorphy and the full use of consciousness, both are by-products of biological degeneration due to specialization. The deficient digestive and muscular systems found in ectomorphy may, for example, be a product of specialization, and the (over)development of consciousness may be a concomitant not merely of ectomorphy but of something like a general process of biological degeneration.

We cannot answer such questions directly, but in one sense this whole study is an attempt toward an answer. It is unfortunate that we have only 200 cases in the series. It would be of great interest to know whether or not such a clearly defined morphological disparity between groups 1 and 2a would hold for the whole university population. The sample we used was not quite a random one, although it may have been essentially representative. At any rate it was not deliberately weighted either with ectomorphs or with gifted people, and a comparison of Table 3 with Table 23a (p. 268, *The Varieties of Human Physique*) will show that the morphological distribution for our 200 cases runs just about parallel with that for the general university population.

Assuming for the moment that some such general relationship as the one we found does hold for the university population, would it also hold for the population outside the universities? Probably not. It seems reasonable to suppose that the universities represent a kind of protected sanctuary where the usual (normal) criteria of competitive existence and priority are to a degree replaced by criteria favoring the more delicate, sensitive, and perhaps more intellectually inclined ectomorphs. There are of course other refuges, notably the church, the clerical and pedagogical occupations, and the mental hospitals. But these are for the most part refuges *only*. They do not offer much opportunity for mental advancement. Perhaps the universities alone offer to ectomorphy both physical protection and an opportunity to achieve distinction through the exercise of mainly cerebrotonic qualities.

Group 2b (those who have successfully struggled to adapt in the face of difficulties) is composed of 30 per cent of the mesomorphs, 27 per cent of the endomorphs, and 25 per cent of the ectomorphs, as well as 25 per cent of the balanced somatotypes. Note that group 2 as a whole accounts for 77 per cent of the endomorphs and for more than 70 per cent of the mesomorphs, as compared with 44 per cent of the ectomorphs. It is certainly clear that the "normal" people about a university are mainly endomorphs and mesomorphs. A youth born in the endomorph-mesomorph morphological range appears to have about an even chance of being "normal" without effort (group 2a), and about a three-to-one chance if he makes an effort (group 2a *or* 2b). An ectomorphic youth, according to these data, has about a one-in-five (19 per cent) chance of adaptation without effort, and about a two-in-five (44 per cent) chance of being "normal" if he makes an effort. The balanced somatotypes follow along in just about the same pattern as the endomorphs and mesomorphs in this respect. It is the ectomorphs who stand out as different. The rest of the population seems to set the norm.

Group 3a (the people who appear to be embarrassed with the riches of overendowment) is almost exclusively ectomorphic. Six of the 7 "temperamentally overloaded misfits" are ectomorphs. The seventh is a mesomorph. Group 3b on the other hand (the overcompensational somatoroses) is exclusively mesomorphic, and is nearly so by definition, since we now know that the correlation between mesomorphy and somatotonia is about + .80 (p. 400). For practical purposes we can almost call group 3a the ectomorphic misfits, and group 3b the mesomorphic misfits.

Group 3c (the dyscrasias associated with reversal of a dominance) is recruited principally from the balanced somatotypes. Five of its population of 8 are balanced. The other 3 are mesomorphs who are almost balanced (a 3-5-4, a 4-5-3 and a 4-5-1). Since most of the reversals occur in connection with the mid-range somatotypes (see Table 7), we are probably safe in referring to group 3c roughly as the "mid-range misfits."

The group 3d (normally endowed miscellaneous misfits) has 6 mesomorphs, 4 ectomorphs, and 4 balanced. This for the present is our wastebasket group of misfits. We shall let these 14 cases present themselves to the reader on their own merits, lest we fall into the common error of explanatory overrefinement. Possibly all 14 could be squeezed into the other three categories of group 3, but it may be that when larger populations are adequately studied, additional categories of maladjustment will define themselves clearly.

We sometimes refer to group 3d as the sexual-environmental-vocational misfits, or the S-E-V misfits. We suspect that representatives of some schools of psychological thought would be able to make out a case for including more than 7 per cent of the total series in this general category. Nor do we mean to imply that such an approach would be "wrong." What we desire to indicate again, even at the risk of growing tiresome, is that constitutional factors as well as environmental factors are at work, and that *either* set of variables *can* be used in building up a fairly plausible explanation of individual differences. But a one-sided explanatory philosophy cannot in the long run be a healthy one. We are writing at a time when the recent wave of "environmental" overenthusiasm has not yet subsided, and are therefore in this book pointing mainly to the constitutional side of the picture. However, we cannot too often warn the reader that *if this book had to stand alone,* apart from the mass of other contemporary work on personality, its emphasis on constitutional factors would be disproportionate. The current trend of psychological literature to environmentalistic hypotheses shows that it is quite as easy, and perhaps just as logical, to explain the (group 3) population in terms of environmental misanthropy as in terms of constitutional concepts. Either extreme view is bound to provoke a counter-emphasis.

Perhaps the most striking thing about group 3 as a whole is its singular dearth of endomorphy. There is not an endomorph to be found among these 34 normally endowed but poorly integrated personalities. About a fifth of the mesomorphs (21.5 per cent) and almost a fifth of the ectomorphs (18.5 per cent) are found in group 3, but no endomorphs. Endomorphs seem to be born for normality.

Group 4 (the constitutional inferiors or the underendowed) has too small a population to warrant much speculation, but probably the absence of mesomorphs from among these ten weaklings is significant. Group 4 is composed of four endomorphs, four ectomorphs and two balanced. One of the latter is a 4-4-3 (temperamentally 3-3-3). The other is a 4-2-4 (temperamentally 5-1-4). Strictly speaking, this last should not be classed among the balanced somatotypes, but should be described as a member of an intermediate group, the endomorph-ectomorphs.

Note: For the purposes of this book we are including 5 somatotypes in the balanced group which really belong in small separate classifications of their own. These 5 are the 4-4-2 and the 5-5-1 (intermediate group, endomorph-mesomorph); the 4-2-4 and the 5-1-5 (intermediate group, endomorph-ectomorph); and the 2-4-4 (intermediate group, mesomorph-ectomorph). Collectively, these somatotypes constitute about 8 per cent of the male university population. They make up 7 per cent of our group of 200, and to avoid confusion we have here carried them simply as 14 additional members of the balanced group. Their distribution according to achievement is as follows: group 2a, (6), group 2b, (5), group 3d, (2) and group 4, (1). It will be seen that these somatotypes follow very closely the distribution of the balanced group as a whole. The justification for including them in the balanced group is that each of them is "balanced" in two of the three components.

In summary, so far as these data are indicative, an endomorph in the universities appears to enjoy better than a three-to-one (a 77 per cent) chance of being a normal, adapted but undistinguished person. If he departs from this general category he has a slightly better chance of being a constitutional inferior than of rating a distinguished achievement. He is extremely unlikely to become a troublesome misfit, or a victim of conflict and frustration arising from what may loosely be termed "maladjustment."

A mesomorph in the universities has a little better than a seven-to-three (a 71.5 per cent) chance for the normal but undistinguished category, and if he departs from the majority in this respect he has a fairly good (21.5 per cent) chance of becoming a troublesome misfit of one kind or another. He appears to be more or less immune to what we have termed constitutional inferiority, but on the other hand he has only a 7 per cent chance for distinguished achievement as that concept has been defined in this book.

The university ectomorph seems to enjoy the widest range of possibilities, both for better and for worse. He has only a 44 per cent chance for the normal-undistinguished category, but under the protection of the academic sanctuary he has a 30 per cent chance for distinguished achievement. Failing in both of these possibilities, he has an 18.5 per cent chance of becoming a troublesome misfit, and a 7.5 chance for constitutional degeneracy.

ACHIEVEMENT AS RELATED TO THE TEMPERAMENTAL COMPONENTS

Table 11 shows the adaptational distribution of the 200 cases when arranged according to temperament instead of somatotype. There are no striking variations from Table 10, although somatotonics are found to be of slightly more frequent occurrence than mesomorphs. This might be interpreted as indicating a certain popularity of the temperamental manifestations of the second component. Perhaps young men tend to strive to develop more somatotonia than their physiques provide for. It might be possible to strain this point just a notch further and to find here a partial "explanation" of the relatively large number (20 per cent) of troublesome somatotonic misfits. It is a fact that of the 13 somatotonics who fall into groups 3a, 3b, and 3d, 10 show an increase in somatotonia over mesomorphy and not one falls back in this component. However, it does not necessarily follow that these troublesome ones have become so because of social stereotypes urging them on toward increased manifestations of somatotonia. For if we adopt that explanation, we might then find difficulty in explaining the fact that of the 12 cerebrotonics who fall into groups 3a and 3d, 8 show an increase in cerebrotonia over ectomorphy, while 4 remain at the same level in this component. It might more cogently be argued that our social influences tend to hold out *both* somatotonic and cerebrotonic goals as objectives toward which to strive, so that some are pulled too strongly in one direction and some in the other. All of these speculations may point in the general direction of truth, but more vigorous studies than our present one will be needed to settle the issues.

One more interesting indication from Table 11 is the singular piling up of viscerotonics in group 2a. Sixty-one per cent of all the viscerotonics fall among these "comfortable normals," while only one viscerotonic remains in group 1, and but four are found in group 2b. Two viscerotonics are found in group 3c (reversal of a dominance) but both are synthetic. That is to say, neither is an endomorph.

TABLE 11

SHOWING THE DISTRIBUTION BY ADAPTATIONAL GROUP OF 200 CASES ARRANGED ACCORDING TO TEMPERAMENTAL PREDOMINANCE

Group	1		2a		2b		3a		3b		3c		3d		4		Total	
	Incidence	%	Incidence	%	Incidence	%	Incidence	%	Incidence	%	Incidence	%	Incidence	%	Incidence	%	Incidence	%
Viscerotonics	1	4	17	61	4	14					2	7			4	14	28	14
Somatotonics	6	8	28	37	26	35	1	1	5	7	2	3	7	9			75	37.5
Cerebrotonics	14	26	9	17	15	28	6	11					6	11	4	7	54	27
Balanced	8	19	19	44	9	21					4	9	1	2	2	5	43	21.5
Total	29		73		54		7		5		8		14		10		200	100

The cerebrotonics show nearly the same distribution as the ectomorphs, and the balanced temperaments are distributed in nearly the same manner as the balanced somatotypes. This last observation is of peculiar interest, for the *individuals* found among the balanced temperaments are a very different lot from those who constitute the balanced somatotypes. Of the 47 individuals who have balanced somatotypes (Table 10) only 12 are found among the balanced temperaments. The other 35 have developed some primary temperamental predominance and have moved over into another classification. Seventeen of them reappear as somatotonics, 11 as cerebrotonics and 7 as viscerotonics. Meanwhile the 35 have been replaced by 31 recruits to the balanced temperament group, all of whom have of course fallen away from a morphological primary predominance. Yet in the face of this 74 per cent change in personnel, the balanced temperaments show very nearly the same distribution of social adjustments as do the balanced somatotypes.

ON THE DIFFICULTY OF INTERPRETATION

It is difficult to interpret this singular agreement between the distributions of two series of individuals who have only 26 per cent of common identity. Perhaps our most dangerous pitfall in this kind of study lies in what psychologists have called the "halo error." It is impossible altogether to exclude this danger in the assignment of temperamental ratings, for the investigator cannot make the ratings without seeing the subject, and if the investigator is well trained in constitutional methods of analysis he cannot look at a subject without somatotyping him, approximately at least. To ask a constitutional psychologist to look at a jiggly 6-2-2, or a stalwart 2-6-2 without "realizing" what they are is like asking an ornithologist to observe geese and crows without being aware of which is which. An ornithologist usually finds that crows behave like crows and geese like geese. His "mental set" expects crow-behavior among crows, and the mental set of a constitutional psychologist expects 2-6-2 behavior among 2-6-2's. In either event—ornithology or psychology—it is the exception or the unexpected which is startling and is almost certain to be noted. In this fact lies what is possibly our best defense against the halo error. The more experienced the psychologist becomes, the more likely he is to be startled by and to note any true deviations from the expected pattern. The defense against the halo appears to lie in the very nature of the difficulty itself. We believe that in constitutional psychology, as in any other branch of natural history, the halo error is in the long run self-correcting, and that the more experienced the naturalist becomes in his field the *less* likely he is to generalize his identifications from isolated factors of resemblance.

The singular resemblance between the distributions of the balanced temperaments of Table 11 and the balanced somatotypes of Table 10 seems to constitute some indirect support for our belief that the halo factor is at any rate not entirely responsible for the apparent relationship between temperament and physique. The common element in these two distributions is "balance," not somatotype, and not temperament. If we were judging temperament from physique we would presumably find the *individuals* distributed in about the same manner in the two series. It is of course possible that some other error-causing factor is at work here, and if so we must some day learn what it is.

It is not only among the balanced temperaments and somatotypes that changes of personnel occur in these distributions. Ten of the 30 endomorphs of Table 10 are missing from the viscerotonics of Table 11, to be replaced by 8 new recruits to a first component predominance. Similarly 12 mesomorphs lose their second component predominance at the temperamental level, but these are replaced by 17 non-mesomorphs who become somatotonics. And 11 ectomorphs are lost, to be replaced by 12 cerebrotonics who are not ectomorphs.

The turnover is thus 74 per cent among the balanced people, 33 per cent for the endomorphs, 21 per cent for the ectomorphs, and only 17 per cent for the mesomorphs. Here is further evidence of the essential popularity or "normality" of the second component, in the human male. Only one mesomorph in six abandons his second component predominance in his expression of temperament.

1. *For the Primary Components*

Table 12 gives the means and standard deviations for the primary components, distributed according to the achievement groups. This table contains many indications, some of which may be significant, but from a statistical point of view the number of cases is distressingly small.

Considering the series as a whole, the means for endomorphy and viscerotonia remain practically constant, but somatotonia shows a notable increment over mesomorphy, and cerebrotonia increases over ectomorphy to about the same degree. Our studies indicate, then, that the total strength of the primary components tends to be a little greater at the temperamental level than at the morphological level. In progressing from morphology to temperament, about twice as many individuals advance as fall back. The standard deviations for the second and third motivational components are likewise higher than the standard deviations for these two morphological components.

In group 1 (superior group), endomorphy falls a little below its general average, while viscerotonia drops more sharply. In this group mesomorphy drops sharply below its average and somatotonia also falls short but less markedly. Ectomorphy rises very sharply above its general average, and cerebrotonia does the same to an almost equal degree. The third component presides at the table of genius. In group 1 all three of the standard deviations for the motivational components are low. They are indeed singularly low, but with so small a group (29 cases), an interpretation would be unsafe.

In group 2a (normal-without-effort) the relationships seen in group 1 are almost exactly reversed. Here endomorphy rises moderately above its general mean, while viscerotonia shows a more marked increment. Mesomorphy is increased sharply, and somatotonia is likewise increased, although more moderately. Ectomorphy is sharply reduced from its general mean, and cerebrotonia is still more reduced. The third component is but a poor relative at the table of normality.

TABLE 12

MEANS AND STANDARD DEVIATIONS FOR THE
PRIMARY COMPONENTS

Group	*1*	*2a*	*2b*	*3a*	*3b*	*3c*	*3d*	*4*	*Whole Series*
	N = 29	N = 73	N = 54	N = 7	N = 5	N = 8	N = 14	N = 10	N = 200
Endomorphy									
Mean	3.10	3.45	3.13	2.14	2.20	3.75	2.64	4.20	3.23
S. D.	1.10	1.27	1.19	.64	1.17	.43	.72	1.33	1.23
Mesomorphy									
Mean	3.48	4.19	3.78	3.43	5.20	4.25	3.79	2.30	3.86
S. D.	1.13	1.25	1.29	1.29	.75	.66	1.42	.78	1.31
Ectomorphy									
Mean	4.14	2.88	3.57	4.71	2.60	3.13	3.79	3.60	3.42
S. D.	1.20	1.16	1.49	1.16	1.02	.93	1.26	1.29	1.35
Viscerotonia									
Mean	2.90	3.70	2.93	2.14	2.00	4.00	2.71	4.10	3.24
S. D.	.84	1.25	1.17	1.13	.63	.71	.59	1.22	1.19
Somatotonia									
Mean	3.86	4.22	4.19	3.57	6.60	4.00	3.93	1.50	4.03
S. D.	.86	1.26	1.61	1.40	.49	.71	1.62	.81	1.49
Cerebrotonia									
Mean	4.28	2.93	3.85	5.71	2.60	3.38	4.29	3.60	3.60
S. D.	.94	1.22	1.42	1.67	.80	.70	1.16	1.28	1.41

Group 2b (normal-through-effort) shows a slightly decreased endomorphy with a more conspicuously decreased viscerotonia. Mesomorphy also is slightly decreased but somatotonia, on the contrary, is somewhat increased. Here is an interesting phenomenon. The young men in this group, although a little less rugged than the general average, have at the motivational level more than made up the second component decrement. There is fight in these people. Both ectomorphy and cerebrotonia are slightly above the general mean, thus establishing a striking contrast with group 2a.

Group 4 (the constitutional inferiors) and the four subdivisions of group 3 (the maladapted group) are so small in numbers that only the most general indications seem to be worthy of comment. The *overly endowed* misfits (group 3a) appear to be principally ectomorphs who show a pronounced increment in cerebrotonia. They are weak in the first component at both levels, but have enough somatotonia (3.57) to constitute an apparently incompatible interference with the overwhelmingly predominant cerebrotonia (5.71). The difficulty seems to lie in the struggle between the second and third components. It will be remembered that there is no somatotype which carries a total strength of more than 9 in these two components, although five rare somatotypes show a total strength of 10 in the first and second components, and one somatotype—the extremely rare 5-1-5—has a total of 10 in the first and third.

The *somatorotic* misfits (group 3b) appear to illustrate another variation of this same basic difficulty. Here too the first component is consistently weak at both levels, while in this case the temperamental level shows an overwhelming increment of the second component (6.60). In group 3b cerebrotonia remains at a comparatively low level (2.60), but the total of somatotonia and cerebrotonia (9.20) is nevertheless higher than nature seems easily to tolerate, and the adaptational difficulties encountered by these individuals may arise largely from this circumstance.

The misfits showing *reversal of a dominance* (group 3c) are drawn from mid-range somatotypes, and as a group they also show mid-range temperamental indices. Averages reveal nothing here. The standard deviations are very low, but the number of cases is only 8.

The averages for the *miscellaneous* or "sexual and environmental" misfits (group 3d) likewise are not particularly revealing. Here the first component is relatively weak at both levels and the third is relatively strong, more particularly at the temperamental level. The second component remains just slightly below the general mean at both levels. This is a "slightly cerebrotic" group, apparently made up in the large of many so-called borderline psychopathic personalities. Oddly enough, the cerebrotonia here (4.29) has almost exactly the same mean as the cerebrotonia in group 1. Consider, then, the danger in generalizing from means.

The *constitutional inferiors* (group 4) appear to be a rather distinctive lot of people. They are characterized by a relatively high first component at both levels (physique and temperament), by about average third component at both levels (slightly higher than average ectomorphy), and by a singular decrement in the second component, particularly at the temperamental level (soma-totonia = 1.50).

2. *For the Secondary Variables*

Table 13 gives the means and standard deviations for 11 secondary variables, also distributed according to the eight classificational groups. In this table IQ has been reduced to a 7-point scale with the following equivalents.

I	86– 98
2	99–110
3	111–122
4	123–134
5	135–146
6	147–158
7	159–170

Group 1 is singularly high in *t component, health, peripheral strength, IQ, aesthetic intelligence* and *sexuality.* It is low in *dysplasia, central strength* and *physical intelligence,* although in none of these three does it deviate from the mean by more than about one-third of the standard deviation.

Group 2a shows deviations above the mean in *central strength* and *physical intelligence;* below the mean in *dysplasia, IQ, aesthetic intelligence, sexuality* and *gynandrophrenia.* However, in none of these characteristics is the discrepancy greater than half of the standard deviation. The most marked weaknesses in group 2a lie in aesthetic intelligence and sexuality.

The peculiarity of group 2b is its lack of any noteworthy deviations in either direction. There are no departures above the mean worthy of mention. *Health, peripheral strength* and *physical intelligence* fall about one-fifth of their respective standard deviations below their general means. The averages within group 2b run parallel with the general averages to a remarkable degree. However, the standard deviations within this group are rather high.

Group 3a (7 cases), in sharp contrast with the last, shows noteworthy deviation in nearly everything. These people are relatively high in *dysplasia, t component, health, IQ, aesthetic intelligence, sexuality* and *gynandrophrenia.* They are low in *central strength, peripheral strength* and *physical intelligence.* In all ex-

TABLE 13

MEANS AND STANDARD DEVIATIONS FOR ELEVEN
SECONDARY VARIABLES

Group	1	2a	2b	3a	3b	3c	3d	4	Whole Series
	N = 29	N = 73	N = 54	N = 7	N = 5	N = 8	N = 14	N = 10	N = 200
Dysplasia									
Mean	10.8	10.1	11.5	15.7	17.6	11.0	11.9	14.6	11.35
S. D.	5.39	4.57	5.64	7.39	3.44	6.48	5.28	6.64	5.59
Gynandromorphy									
Mean	2.41	2.34	2.36	2.54	1.68	2.28	2.43	3.98	2.43
S. D.	.71	.71	.98	1.14	.61	.48	.74	1.43	.93
t **Component**									
Mean	2.65	2.07	2.05	2.29	1.68	1.97	1.89	1.70	2.11
S. D.	.60	.53	.72	.64	.45	.39	.51	.52	.64
Health									
Mean	6.45	5.79	5.48	6.14	6.40	5.63	5.57	3.20	5.68
S. D.	.61	.99	1.26	.66	.49	.42	.92	1.25	1.19
Central Strength									
Mean	3.52	4.30	3.74	2.71	5.0	4.13	3.43	1.7	3.81
S. D.	1.24	1.47	1.30	1.40	.89	.75	1.59	.90	1.49
Peripheral Strength									
Mean	4.31	3.79	3.59	3.29	4.60	3.88	3.93	1.40	3.76
S. D.	1.23	1.06	1.33	.69	.80	1.16	1.28	.49	1.12
Physical Intelligence									
Mean	2.79	3.54	2.83	2.14	5.0	2.75	2.93	1.40	3.11
S. D.	.86	1.76	1.32	1.56	1.10	.83	1.28	.66	1.51
IQ	(N = 14)	(N = 36)	(N = 27)	(N = 5)	(N = 4)	(N = 8)	(N = 6)	(N = 10)	(N = 110)
Mean	5.79	3.41	3.78	4.20	3.75	3.13	2.83	1.80	3.66
S. D.	.83	.95	.98	1.17	.83	1.04	.91	.87	1.37
Aesthetic Intelligence									
Mean	3.45	1.83	2.31	3.71	1.0	1.69	2.67	2.30	2.34
S. D.	1.22	.89	1.37	1.68	0	.58	1.29	1.33	1.34
Sexuality									
Mean	4.38	2.73	3.39	4.43	2.60	3.0	4.29	1.60	3.27
S. D.	1.19	1.13	1.31	1.50	.49	.50	1.80	1.02	1.39
Gynandrophrenia									
Mean	2.55	2.26	2.56	2.86	1.60	2.38	2.86	4.90	2.56
S. D.	.82	1.05	1.49	1.35	.80	.46	1.59	1.87	1.37

cept strength and coordination they seem to be truly over-
endowed.

Group 3b (5 cases) also shows many deviations, but in a very
different general direction. This group is high in *dysplasia, health,
central* and *peripheral strength,* and *physical intelligence.* It is

low in *gynandromorphy, t component, aesthetic intelligence, sexuality* and *gynandrophrenia.*

The 3c group is not significantly high in anything, although *central strength* is slightly above average. This group is a little low in all three of the intelligence ratings, *physical intelligence, IQ,* and *aesthetic intelligence.*

The sexual and environmental misfits (group 3d) are somewhat high in *aesthetic intelligence, sexuality* and *gynandrophrenia,* but low in *t component, central strength* and *IQ.*

The constitutional inferiors (group 4) are high in *gynandro-morphy* and extremely high in *gynandrophrenia.* In *aesthetic intelligence* they fall at about the general average. In everything else they are low, and for the most part extremely low.

CORRELATIONS

1. *Among the Primary Components*

Table 14 includes the intercorrelations between the primary components at the two levels (of physique and temperament), and the intracorrelations among these components at both levels. Note that the negative correlation between mesomorphy and ecto-morphy (—.63) is higher than that between endomorphy and ecto-morphy (—.41), and that the latter is in turn higher than that between endomorphy and mesomorphy (—.29). Similarly, the nega-tive correlation between somatotonia and cerebrotonia (—.62) ex-ceeds that between viscerotonia and cerebrotonia (—.37), while the latter exceeds that between viscerotonia and somatotonia (—.34).

At both levels, it is between the second and third components that the greatest incompatibility exists, whereas the least incom-patibility is found between the first and second components. The relationship between the first and third components more nearly approximates that between the first and second, at both levels, than that between the second and third. If, then, we were to repre-sent these relationships with a two-dimensional drawing, the equilateral triangle which has conventionally been used (p. 24) would be inaccurate. An irregular triangle somewhat like Figure 7 would be more representative.

TABLE 14

INTERCORRELATIONS AND INTRACORRELATIONS AMONG THE
PRIMARY COMPONENTS

N = 200

	Viscero-tonia	Meso-morphy	Somato-tonia	Ecto-morphy	Cerebro-tonia
Endomorphy	+.79	−.29	−.29	−.41	−.32
Viscerotonia		−.23	−.34	−.40	−.37
Mesomorphy			+.82	−.63	−.58
Somatotonia				−.53	−.62
Ectomorphy					+.83

According to these correlations, endomorphs become cerebrotonic more easily, or at any rate a little more frequently, than

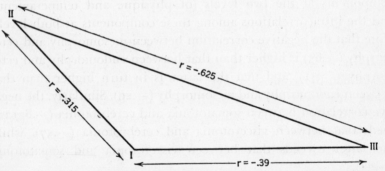

Fig. 7. A Triangle Representing the Apparent Relationships among the Primary
Components.

ectomorphs become viscerotonic (r, endomorphy-cerebrotonia =
−.32; r, ectomorphy-viscerotonia = −.40). Mesomorphs, on the
other hand, tend to manifest viscerotonia a little more readily
than endomorphs manifest somatotonia (r, mesomorphy-viscero-
tonia = −.23; r, endomorphy-somatotonia = −.29). And ectomorphs do a little better in somatotonia than mesomorphs do in
cerebrotonia (r, ectomorphy-somatotonia = −.53; mesomorphy-
cerebrotonia = −.58). However, these slight differences may re-

flect only the peculiarities of a relatively small sample of the population.

The correlations between morphology and temperament are +.79 for the first component, +.82 for the second component, and +.83 for the third. These are higher correlations than we expected to find, and they raise some questions of great interest. If we were to regard the product-moment correlation as a measure of the degree to which two variables are made up of common elements, correlations of the order of +.8 would suggest that morphology and temperament, as we measure them, may constitute expressions at their respective levels of essentially common components. The question as to whether, with the simple techniques used, we have penetrated to "basic" components, or to what we might like to suppose are first-order components, can be answered only in terms of the results of further effort to define still more basic factors. If we *have* already reached basic factors in personality, the correlations are not higher than should be expected, for then with the two techniques we are but measuring the same thing at different levels of its expression.

We have approached the problem from two quite different angles, and the two approaches have led, through the application of quite different techniques to different types of material, to very much the same hypothetically basic structure of personality. Using this hypothetical structure as a purchase against which to differentiate among individuals, we find that a meaningful method for individual analysis emerges. This in itself is useful, but the high correlations between morphology and temperament seem to hold out hope that perhaps there is something more important here than merely a method of analysis or an approach to a therapy.

If indeed it can be demonstrated, through the work of other investigators, that measurable primary components are present in personality, the way will be open to a psychology which offers a general frame of reference for all fields of study where individual differences are measured. Such a psychology would serve a useful purpose in the coordination of biological and sociological research. It should lead also to a uniting of research energies in medical and social fields of investigation.

One further point might well be raised in connection with the correlations appearing in Table 14. Aware as we are of the scientific importance of any demonstration of the presence of primary components in the structure of personality, we are not unaware of the possibility that these correlations might be in some degree misleading. The Scale for Temperament, after the preliminary correlational analyses had indicated the presence of three nuclear clusters of temperamental characteristics, was built up expressly to reflect and to focus attention upon these three primary components. The further selection of definitive traits was based upon the correlation of such traits with the (by now preconceived) pattern of a polydimensional structure of personality.

In a sense, then, after the early steps, we deliberately put the three components into the Scale, and the skeptic may conceivably be justified in pointing out that it is not surprising that we get them out again in the analysis of individuals. Psychologists tend notoriously to extract from their analyses about what they put into them at the beginning, and nobody knows this better than psychologists themselves. Now we are far from denying that some cogency may attach to such a criticism in the present instance. Indeed, we suspect that this factor must be present. But the question is, to what degree is it present? Before answering too dogmatically, one should weigh the following considerations:

(1) We did not *start* with the three components. These were arrived at empirically. Indeed they in the first place forced themselves upon us, and we believe that anyone who will follow our procedure in detail will be confronted by the same three components. We merely *accepted* these three components, building around them only in later stages of the construction of the Scale.

(2) The Scale for Temperament was not constructed to fit a preconceived conception of morphological variation. The work on morphology was not begun until after the work on temperament was well under way. We turned to morphology in seeking a field for validating and corroborating the work on temperament, not vice versa.[1]

---

[1] In the publication of the material it has seemed wise to bring out the work on morphology first because this is the more "objective" and in one sense the more foundational. It is easier to develop the general argument of constitutional analysis against the background of a widely understood morphological technique, than

(3) Even in the field of morphology we did not start with a tripolar hypothesis. We merely collected some thousands of physiques in such a manner that they could be compared one against another (a) *as whole entities,* and (b) *all at one time.* We were looking for primary components, but not necessarily for three of them. Three primary components were finally selected because physiques were present which could not be described as mixtures of two components, and no physiques were present which could not be described as mixtures of three components. The tripolar frame of reference was as empirical a development in the field of morphology as in the field of temperament.

(4) If a constant error of judgment is present in the study, the error must reside in the ratings on temperament, for somatotyping is an objective procedure in which the results are practically automatic. On the other hand, it should be remembered that the ratings on temperament were made before the somatotyping was done. If the investigator was influenced by the somatotype, it was by some vague intuitional and subjective knowledge of the somatotype, not by the objective records.

(5) It might be added that we did not at the beginning expect positive findings in this field. The writer's earlier publications in the field (see bibliography accompanying *The Varieties of Human Physique*), were pessimistic in that the findings were mainly negative and the conclusions discouraging.

For all these reasons it seems probable that the correlations between temperament and morphology are not due entirely to the "error of the bias," or the error of overenthusiasm for a point of view. It is true that just as Freudians usually find some misanthropy of the parent-child relationship associated with "neuroses," and Marxians generally find economic "causes" for war, we have observed in ourselves a noticeable inclination to discover physical and constitutional factors in close association with many manifestations of individuality. Possibly this should be named the "error of human nature." We do not see how it can be entirely escaped without running into the danger of an overly complete

---

against the background of a more specialized and necessarily more difficult psychological technique. But for us the morphological studies were in the nature of an afterthought. They did not shape the study of temperament.

detachment, which leads by way of *blind* measurement to the "error of futilitarianism."

The study has at least escaped the error of futilitarianism. Possibly the error of the bias remains an unknown factor. Against it we have no particular defense to offer except the fact that we are aware of the cunning with which it hides in such a study as this. For our own part we are satisfied that the correlations between temperament and physique are not entirely spurious.

2. *Between the Primary Components and Secondary Variables*

Table 15 gives the correlations between each of the three primary components, at both levels, and nine secondary variables.

Note that endomorphy and gynandromorphy are positively, but not too closely, related, and that endomorphs are less gynandrophrenic than gynandromorphic. Viscerotonia is more closely related to gynandromorphy and to gynandrophrenia, than is endomorphy. Mesomorphy shows a high negative correlation with gynandromorphy and a higher one with gynandrophrenia, while somatotonia shows these same relationships to a still more marked degree. There is a low positive correlation between ectomorphy and gynandromorphy, and a somewhat higher one between ectomorphy and gynandrophrenia. Cerebrotonia also shows a positive correlation with gynandromorphy, but the correlation between cerebrotonia and gynandrophrenia falls to $+.13$.

These correlations indicate that while both the first and third morphological components predispose somewhat toward a gynandroid pattern of personality, the male gynandrophrene is more ectomorphic than endomorphic, and more viscerotonic than cerebrotonic. The gynandrophrene is typically a viscerotonic ectomorph, although neither viscerotonia nor ectomorphy is, in itself, very closely related to gynandrophrenia.

The second component is negatively correlated with the gynandroid characteristic, and more markedly so at the temperamental than at the morphological level.

There is a negative relationship between the t component and both the first and second components, at each level, but these negative correlations are very low. The textural component, which is really the factor of "physical aristocracy," is correlated

TABLE 15

CORRELATIONS BETWEEN THE PRIMARY COMPONENTS AND SEC-
ONDARY VARIABLES

	Gynandromorphy	t Component	Central Strength	Peripheral Strength	Physical Intelligence	IQ	Aesthetic Intelligence	Sexuality	Gynandrophrenia
Endomorphy	+.31	−.19	−.11	−.33	−.29	+.07	−.16	−.43	+.21
Mesomorphy	−.48	−.16	+.86	+.64	+.70	−.07	−.48	−.16	−.56
Ectomorphy	+.23	+.31	−.69	−.19	−.49	+.19	+.61	+.54	+.34
Viscerotonia	+.39	−.12	−.08	−.35	−.24	−.10	−.13	−.39	+.31
Somatotonia	−.63	−.17	+.81	+.62	+.75	+.05	−.50	−.10	−.69
Cerebrotonia	+.28	+.36	−.66	−.16	−.55	+.31	+.67	+.55	+.13

positively with ectomorphy, but the correlation is low. An ectomorph is somewhat more likely to be physically "fine" than is an
endomorph or a mesomorph, and the likelihood is increased a
little by the presence of an increment of cerebrotonia over the
ectomorphy.

Central strength and peripheral strength offer an interesting
comparison. Both correlate negatively with the first and third components, at both levels. But peripheral strength shows a much
higher negative correlation with the first component than does
central strength, and the converse is true of the correlations with
the third component. Peripherally, endomorphs are weak. Centrally, ectomorphs are very weak, and these relationships hold for
both components to about the same degree at the temperamental
level. Mesomorphs are strong, of course, but they are stronger
centrally than peripherally, according to the correlations, and
those who manifest the highest somatotonia are a little less strong
than the less manifestly somatotonic mesomorphs.

The three varieties of "intelligence," physical, aesthetic, and
"IQ," also offer good material for comparison. Endomorphy is
correlated negatively with both physical and aesthetic intelligence, and viscerotonia shows the same relationship, although to
a less degree. The correlation between endomorphy and IQ is

very low and positive, while that between viscerotonia and IQ is similarly low but negative. According to this, endomorphs whose viscerotonia is relatively low are a little more likely to have high IQ's than those whose viscerotonia keeps up with their morphology.

Mesomorphy shows a high positive correlation with physical intelligence and a high negative one with aesthetic intelligence, while somatotonia shows both of these relationships to a slightly accentuated degree. The correlation between mesomorphy and IQ is just barely on the negative side, while that between somatotonia and IQ is similarly a little on the positive side. Somatotonia in a mesomorph seems to raise IQ to about the same slight degree that viscerotonia in an endomorph lowers it.

The third component here presents an excellent contrast with the second. Ectomorphy shows a high negative correlation with physical intelligence and a high positive one with aesthetic intelligence, both of these correlations rising a little when cerebrotonia is increased over ectomorphy. The correlation between ectomorphy and IQ is $+.19$, that between cerebrotonia and IQ, $+.31$. The third component is positively correlated with the conventional IQ, but a correlation of so low a degree has only the slightest predictive value. Perhaps the only conclusion we would be justified in drawing from these correlations with IQ would be this: that the conventional IQ slightly favors the third component and may be to that degree unfair to the other two components. The fact that IQ shows no significant negative correlations with any of our three primary components seems to indicate that, whatever intelligence may be, it is probably not another primary component of personality.

The phenomenon of manifest sexuality shows a high positive correlation with the third component at both levels, and a rather high negative correlation with the first component at both levels. Endomorphs are low in sexuality. Ectomorphs are high, with mesomorphs a little on the negative side but singularly variable. However, in considering this characteristic it should be remembered that we are gauging *manifest* sexuality, not sexual potency, or procreative ability. It is the third component people who are sexually most sensitive, who express sexuality most imperatively,

are most conscious of it, and in general find it most disturbing
or exciting. The genitalia of endomorphs are relatively small,
while those of ectomorphs often seem conspicuously large, but
the genitalia of ectomorphs are probably not absolutely larger
than those of mesomorphs. Third component people seem to be
more influenced by their sexual drives than are second component
people, perhaps in somewhat the same way that they are more
influenced by cerebral activities. Both phenomena may be related
to the presumable relative weakness of competing somatic impulses.

3. Among the Secondary Variables

Table 16 includes the correlations among nine secondary variables.

The correlation between gynandromorphy and gynandrophrenia ($+.82$) suggests that these two factors may be related in
the same way, and to about the same degree, that the morphological and temperamental expressions of the primary components
are related.

The low correlation between gynandromorphy and t ($+.09$)
indicates that whatever it may be which gives rise to aesthetic
excellence in the male body, this phenomenon is not derived to
any appreciable extent from the bisexuality factor. Beauty in the
female and t component in the male may be comparable or
parallel concepts, but it is clear that the latter is not to be explained as a resultant of gynandromorphic linkage. The t concept
is not merely a manifestation of femininity. This is a point of some
interest since we have found in another (unpublished) study a
rather high negative correlation between gynandromorphy (masculinity) and t component in the female.

Physically effeminate men are weak, but not quite as weak
peripherally as centrally. They are of low physical intelligence
and of rather high aesthetic intelligence, but there is virtually
no correlation ($-.02$) between IQ and gynandromorphy. Similarly, there is almost a zero correlation ($-.05$) between sexuality
and gynandromorphy, and this is of interest, for the regression
of sexuality on gynandromorphy is somewhat curvilinear. Among
the series of 200 there are a dozen individuals who are high in

TABLE 16

INTRACORRELATIONS AMONG SECONDARY VARIABLES

	Gynandrophrenia	t Component	Central Strength	Peripheral Strength	Physical Intelligence	IQ	Aesthetic Intelligence	Sexuality
Gynandromorphy	+.82	+.09	−.53	−.46	−.52	−.02	+.38	−.05
Gynandrophrenia		+.06	−.63	−.53	−.58	−.07	+.43	+.04
t Component			−.12	+.17	+.02	+.39	+.58	+.40
Central Strength				+.65	+.75	−.01	−.50	−.18
Peripheral Strength					+.55	+.26	−.14	+.24
Physical Intelligence						−.13	−.39	−.11
IQ							+.47	+.42
Aesthetic Intelligence								+.57

gynandromorphy but very low in sexuality. These young men as a group border upon the Froelich syndrome. Their presence in the series destroys what otherwise would be a positive correlation between sexuality and gynandromorphy.

Gynandrophrenia, like gynandromorphy, seems to be unrelated to the t component. Mentally effeminate men are even weaker than physically effeminate men, and like the latter, they are weaker centrally than peripherally. Gynandrophrenia shows the same relationships as gynandromorphy with the three kinds of intelligence, but all three of the correlations are a little higher. Gynandrophrenes are physically incompetent but aesthetically they are both alert and adaptive. The correlation with IQ (−.07) is too low for significance, as is that with sexuality (+.04), but here we see the same curvilinear relationship to sexuality that is seen in the case of gynandromorphy.

The t component shows a low negative correlation with central strength (−.12), and a low positive correlation with peripheral strength (+.17). Although t is positively correlated with ectomorphy (+.31), it does not appear to be a characteristic associated with physical weakness. The t component is the only variable we have found which correlates positively with *all three* kinds of intelligence. The correlation between sexuality and t is surprisingly high (+.40), and this seems to contradict the once popular notion that sexuality is vulgar.

Central and peripheral strength are positively correlated (+.65), but they appear to be far from identical phenomena. The former is more closely related than the latter to the general characteristic which we have called physical intelligence. The correlations indicate that people whose strength is central handle themselves more effectively, in the physical sense, than people whose strength is more peripherally distributed. However, peripheral strength shows a positive correlation with IQ (+.26), while central strength shows a zero correlation (—.01) with this variable. The differentiation between the two kinds of strength becomes more manifest in the correlations with aesthetic intelligence (—.50 in the case of central strength, and —.14 in the case of peripheral strength), and still more manifest in the correlations with sexuality (—.18 for central strength, and +.24 for peripheral strength). Sexuality seems to recede where the concentration of strength is central, and to rise where strength is peripheral.

IQ is correlated negatively with physical intelligence (—.13), but positively with aesthetic intelligence (+.47). Physical and aesthetic intelligence are correlated negatively (—.39). While these three kinds of intelligence are in no sense antitheses, they do unquestionably involve incompatible abilities, and since what we have called physical intelligence is related negatively to both of the other variables, it appears to follow that if such a concept as *general* intelligence is to be statistically meaningful, it must be so defined as to exclude the physical factor. This seems to be equivalent to saying that general intelligence, to be meaningful, must be so defined that it is *not* general.

Sexuality is correlated negatively with physical intelligence (—.11) but positively with IQ and aesthetic intelligence, and both of these positive correlations are high (+.42 and +.57 respectively).

We find then that the correlational matrix which constitutes Table 16 yields a cluster of four variables among which a strong positive relationship exists. These are *t* component, IQ, aesthetic intelligence and sexuality. The average of the six intracorrelations among these variables is +.47. This average is lower than that among the traits defining the respective primary components of temperament (p. 400), but it is high enough to be interesting. If a project were set up with the primary objective of defining intelligence, here would be a beginning. This nucleus of traits would not lead to a completely *general* definition of intelligence, for at least one important element would be omitted, namely that which involves physical skills, but the clearer definition of such a nucleus might contribute to a clarification of what begins to loom as a vital human problem.

CHAPTER VIII

SOME THEORETICAL CONSIDERATIONS

$\mathbf{M}$ANY problems can be raised in connection with the theory and practice of constitutional analysis. For some of them we can attempt no answers, but some are of such persistently controversial interest that they can hardly be evaded. The question of reliability of the ratings, the problem of rendering the technique practicable, the role of the "halo," the question of objectivity, the notion that the constitutional approach is pessimistic or fatalistic, and the question of the stability of the primary components—all of these raise inescapable issues which need to be met. In this final chapter we shall explore briefly some of these issues.

THE QUESTION OF RELIABILITY OF RATINGS

One encouraging fact in human psychology is the singular accuracy of observation and fineness of discrimination we are able to muster when our interest and training are adequate. If a young man becomes interested in automobiles, he may soon find that he can astonish his less observant friends by telling them not only the make and model but many other distinguishing features of a car seen for only a few seconds as it speeds along the highway. I have a young friend, age 12, who shows this skill with airplanes. From almost as far as he can see it, he can accurately diagnose every common variety of ship. Apparently he can give details of construction pertaining to more than 60 different designs, and can recognize most of these varieties when he sees them. His Aunt Geralda cannot understand how he does it. But neither has she been able to tell the difference—at a glance across the street—between the somatotypes 6-3-2 and 6-2-3. However, there are some who can, and with a high degree of reliability, for the differences in design between a 6-3-2 and a 6-2-3 are as conspicuous, for those

411

who are interested, as is the difference between a pursuit plane and a trainer.

It is difficult to escape the belief that in our struggles with the complex data of psychology we have neglected unduly the technique of ordering, classifying and scaling our materials through ratings by trained judges. This neglect probably derives from our willingness to make a fetish of objectivity. Of course, objectivity is safe. Exclude "subjective" procedures and agreement follows more readily. But objective methods are sometimes blind—especially where so many parameters affect a phenomenon that its adequate description would entail an almost limitless number of objective measures, each entering the final formula according to a different weighting. Certainly in some cases these complex phenomena can best be evaluated by a complex instrument properly "tuned." The human observer is a complex instrument, and one that for certain purposes can be "tuned" through training.

The intensive training of judges and raters is actually more common in certain commercial enterprises than in psychology. The prices set on various kinds of leather, silk, wine, coffee and many other items often depend directly upon the "subjective" judgments of expert graders. The judgment of trained observers is relied upon because the aspect graded can in many cases be reduced to measurement by no finite set of objective tests. Minor disagreements among judges must certainly occur, but agreement is at least sufficient to keep the processors in business. Could the business of psychology be expedited by the training of judges who would practice controlled observation and who would check and double check their ratings, both with objective criteria (when available), and with those of other raters? Somehow we believe such training would be a good investment. Actually, we have been impressed more by the ease than by the difficulty with which people learn to agree regarding qualitative and semi-quantitative ratings on the complex aspects of temperament and physique.

Learning to use the Scale for Temperament with reliability is more difficult, certainly, than learning to somatotype. But the two procedures are related in that both involve the development of efficiency in observing people. They are different in that one of them, somatotyping, is backed by an objective anthropometric technique by which the estimated somatotype can be checked or corrected. Despite the availability of objective anthropometry, we do not always use it in somatotyping, for we have found that the trained eye can do the job many times faster and in some respects more adequately than can the calipers and the millimeter scale. But we have found that training in the anthropometric procedure is of great value in *learning* to somatotype, and that a knowledge of this procedure lends a sense of confidence to somatotyping by the eye alone. In somatotyping, the anthropometric technique is like the gold reserve behind a paper currency. Upon request the reliability of the somatotype can be guaranteed and proved by anthropometry, but for purposes of practicability and general usefulness somatotyping can be made far more facile and available than can a purely anthropometric procedure.

An experiment to investigate the reliability of somatotype ratings was set up at Harvard in 1940. The reliability of a series of judgments of somatotype made by the eye alone was tested against the results obtained from the somatotyping machine (see *The Varieties of Human Physique*, p. 103). Fifty somatotype photographs of young men between 17 and 20 were selected more or less at random from a larger series of about 200 cases and were presented to 20 graduate students and instructors from the Departments of Psychology and Anthropology. Although some of them had read *The Varieties of Human Physique*, none had had previous experience at somatotyping, or had seen any of the photographs. The instructions for the experiment were as follows:

> The problem is to somatotype each of these 50 photographs. Please try to rate the amount of each of the three components—endomorphy, mesomorphy, and ectomorphy— exhibited by each photograph. For gauging each component use a scale from 1 to 7, and use the half-values whenever they seem appropriate. Assign the numeral 1 when the component is at a minimum and the numeral 7 when the component is at a maximum.

> To aid you in somatotyping you will have available a copy of "The Varieties of Human Physique" together with three photographs showing examples of physiques extreme in each

of the three components and three illustrations of the somatotype 4-4-4. Please examine carefully these extreme somatotypes and read the check lists of their characteristics (pp.
37-45).

Proceed then to assign the appropriate numeral for each
component to each of the 50 photographs.

Table 17 shows the correlations between the somatotypes assigned by each of these inexperienced volunteers, and the anthropometric somatotypes for the 50 cases as returned by the
somatotyping machine.

TABLE 17

CORRELATIONS BETWEEN ANTHROPOMETRIC SOMATOTYPES AND
SOMATOTYPES-BY-UNAIDED-EYE AS ASSIGNED BY TWENTY INEX-
PERIENCED VOLUNTEERS. N = 50. ALL CORRELATIONS ARE POSITIVE

Rater	First Component	Second Component	Third Component
GS	.91	.90	.96
FS	.94	.90	.93
DM	.89	.92	.96
MJ	.89	.92	.94
BF	.91	.90	.93
EH	.89	.89	.95
JV	.92	.92	.91
CH	.91	.85	.95
OM	.90	.91	.92
JM	.88	.83	.95
BV	.84	.85	.96
RM	.87	.86	.93
DF	.88	.89	.91
DH	.88	.83	.88
AB	.84	.83	.92
AT	.83	.90	.90
RR	.85	.90	.83
EB	.83	.70	.90
CM	.76	.76	.89
HO	.83	.70	.82
Total	.87	.86	.92

Four experienced students of somatotyping also assigned
somatotype ratings to these 50 photographs before the anthropometric measurements were taken and entered into the somatotyping machine. They followed the same procedure as did the
inexperienced people, except that they made use of the single

additional datum, height over the cube root of weight. The correlations between their ratings and the somatotypes returned by
the machine were as shown in Table 18.

TABLE 18

CORRELATIONS BETWEEN ANTHROPOMETRIC SOMATOTYPES AND
SOMATOTYPES-BY-UNAIDED-EYE FOR FOUR EXPERIENCED STUDENTS
OF THE METHOD

Rater	First Component	Second Component	Third Component
CWD	.98	.98	.97
HSD	.96	.97	.98
SSS	.97	.95	.98
WHS	.98	.98	.99
Averages	.97	.97	.98

This experiment demonstrates that by experienced judges ratings at one of the levels at which we work—the morphological
level—can be made with a reliability that approaches machine
precision. Even untrained raters give ratings that are generally
as reliable as the scores obtained by many "objective" psychological tests.

But what of the more complex, temperamental levels? The Scale
for Temperament is *presumably* an instrument whose administration requires considerable practice. On a gradient of objectivity it lies perhaps midway between conventional clinical diagnosis and the more exact kind of measurement which can be
practiced in somatotyping. It is difficult to test the reliability of
such an instrument experimentally, but we have been able in a
number of studies to throw certain indirect light on the problem.
Three of these studies may be worthy of mention.

1. When the analysis of the 200 cases presented in Chapter V
was carried out, one series of 83 cases was reinterviewed and re-
rated by the writer a full year after the first completion of all the
ratings for this series. The product-moment correlation between
the two series of ratings for these 83 cases was +.96. The subjects
were not somatotyped until all of the second ratings had been
completed.

It is not held that such a finding proves much, for most of the subjects were of course well remembered by the experimenter. However, the detailed ratings were not remembered, and the high correlation proves at least that the experimenter was on the two occasions rating variables which lie deeper than the super-ficial manifestations of day-to-day attitudes—variables which do not change appreciably from one year to the next. We are per-haps justified in the assumption that ratings on variables that can be measured with such close agreement on different occasions are more likely to be reliable than ratings on more superficial aspects of personality. Our evidence here supports the claim of reliability, but it is only presumptive evidence.

2. Using the short form of the Scale (see p. 419), and the tech-nique of the one-hour interview, we have carried out one specific study to measure the agreement between ratings made by the writer and those made by other persons less trained in the use of the Scale.

A class of 21 graduate students rated one another in this man-ner, each individual observing the others for a period of three months and then spending one hour interviewing each of the others (these interviews were doubled up, so that when A inter-viewed B, B was also interviewing A). The writer likewise inter-viewed each member of this group, rating him or her on the 30 traits making up the short form. Table 19 gives the correlations between the ratings made by the writer and those made by the 11 men and 10 women who composed the group.

This table reveals remarkable differences between the best and the poorest raters, among both men and women. Since all of these people had been exposed to nearly the same training, the con-clusion seems inescapable that great differences in natural apti-tude for this kind of work exist. But among persons who possess both an observant eye and the habit of quantification, the pros-pect of establishing high reliability for the instrument appears to be rather brightened by such a study as this. The two best men and the two best women, that is to say, about 20 per cent of the class, show a mean correlation of $+.90$ with the writer's ratings. The mean of the intercorrelations for these four raters among themselves was $+.86$.

3. In 1940, Dr. Bryant Moulton of Boston and the writer,

TABLE 19

SHOWING THE CORRELATIONS BETWEEN THE WRITER'S RATINGS OF
A CLASS OF GRADUATE STUDENTS, AND EACH INDIVIDUAL'S RATINGS
OF THE OTHER MEMBERS OF THE CLASS. SHORT FORM OF SCALE.
ALL CORRELATIONS POSITIVE. N = 20 THROUGHOUT

Men	First Component	Second Component	Third Component
JK	.92	.94	.88
LA	.83	.91	.87
BC	.77	.74	.79
YH	.73	.59	.57
WA	.61	.63	.63
LK	.51	.69	.64
RR	.44	.62	.46
MB	.48	.55	.47
BD	.52	.41	.38
AS	.31	.26	.42
TT	.17	.19	.24

Women	First Component	Second Component	Third Component
LB	.94	.92	.91
MC	.86	.93	.87
SS	.68	.78	.76
BB	.50	.66	.52
SA	.52	.61	.54
OF	.46	.49	.49
MN	.41	.53	.50
NH	.41	.40	.33
PT	.31	.23	.27
PA	.24	.30	.24

using the same short form of the Scale, interviewed independently
a group of 50 delinquent boys at one of the Massachusetts institutions. These boys ranged in age from 11 to 16. The writer spent
about one hour with each boy, while Dr. Moulton, who as a psychiatrist was working with them in another connection, spent a
somewhat longer time with each. Somatotyping was not done
until after the studies of temperament were completed. The
product-moment correlations between the two series of ratings
were, for the first component, +.81; for the second component,
+.89; for the third component, +.87. Agreement of this degree
on the short form seems to indicate a high potential reliability,
although it does not necessarily follow that still closer agreement
would have been found if the entire Scale had been used.

Such substantiation of the reliability of the instrument as these studies have indicated is far from a guarantee that the technique can be made equally effective in the hands of two different investigators. We do not even hope that an instrument of psychological analysis can be made altogether foolproof and yet retain diagnostic value. Administration of the Scale will remain a complex and difficult undertaking—as difficult and exacting, possibly, as surgery—but nevertheless it is by no means an impossible undertaking. Dr. Harvey Cushing used to say that doubtless a certain proportion of young surgeons possess the native aptitude to become good brain surgeons. He always added that in order to do so it is necessary to give over everything else and to *live* brain surgery under close supervision for a long term of years. That may be about how matters stand in the field of temperamental study.

In the beginning, the writer entertained little expectation of developing a scale which even in simplified form might be made generally available. The initial hope was merely to objectify and validate to a degree his own researches, and to attempt to make a contribution to the technique of what might be called constitutional medicine. But it appears now to be a reasonable hope that by using this Scale in close association with other physicians and psychologists, with an opportunity for frequent checking of ratings, the steps of quantification for each of the various defining traits may in time become well enough standardized to lend the instrument a high degree of *general* reliability.

CAN THE TECHNIQUE BE MADE PRACTICABLE?

In the experiment described in Chapter IV, 20 hours of interviewing time were spent with each subject, and in addition to this, each subject was observed for at least an academic year. In this study, four distinguishable procedures contributed to the temperamental analysis. These were (1) a standardized medical history, (2) a standardized life history, (3) systematized general observation of each individual, and (4) a number of special tests of a laboratory and clinical nature. Often the question has been asked whether some shorter technique cannot be substituted for so laborious a procedure—now that the basic experiment has been completed.

Since it is obviously impracticable to employ so time-consuming a method for purposes of general research, we have considered a number of shortening devices—two in particular. The first of these consists of an attempt to arrive at a specific rating on 30 of the more objective of the 60 traits, in the course of a short acquaintance with the subject, usually in a single interview. Thirty of the traits—10 from each of the 3 clusters—make up what we have called the short form of the Scale. These are indicated by brackets on the score sheet (p. 26).

An experiment to test the validity of the short form was carried out as part of the main study presented in Chapter VI. At the first interview with each of the 200 subjects, the writer tentatively made the 30 ratings which constitute the short form. These first interviews were devoted mainly to medical histories, and were not conducted with the short form especially in mind. The correlations between these early (short form) ratings and the final (long form) ratings are given in Table 20B.

TABLE 20 A

CORRELATIONS BETWEEN MORPHOLOGY AND TEMPERAMENT FOR THE THREE COMPONENTS

	Viscerotonia		Somatotonia		Cerebrotonia	
	Short Scale	Long Scale	Short Scale	Long Scale	Short Scale	Long Scale
Endomorphy	+.60	+.79				
Mesomorphy			+.54	+.82		
Ectomorphy					+.59	+.83

TABLE 20 B

CORRELATIONS BETWEEN RATINGS ON THE SHORT FORM OF THE SCALE AND THE LONG FORM, FOR THE THREE COMPONENTS

	Viscerotonia	Somatotonia	Cerebrotonia
$r =$	+.73	+.61	+.68

Note that the first component, viscerotonia, was apparently the easiest component to estimate quickly, on short acquaintance. Somatotonia, in this case at least, was the most difficult to estimate. We believe that this is true in general—that people tend to conceal their aggression and to reveal their full complement of sociophilia and relaxation on very short acquaintance.

The correlations in Table 20B do not necessarily represent the present validity of the short form of the Scale. Effective use of this scale is certainly to some degree dependent upon experience, and upon practice with the scale, as a clinician's efficiency is dependent upon his practice. These ratings were made rather early in the writer's experience, before he had used the Scale extensively in its present form. It is possible that he could now do better. The small experiment mentioned on p. 417 points to such a likelihood. In that study two different raters found an agreement of about +.85, using the short form of the Scale. However, in the absence of more satisfactory evidence, we have been content to assume (following Table 20B) that in the writer's hands the correlations between the short form and the long form of the Scale are at least about +.70 for viscerotonia and cerebrotonia, and about +.60 for somatotonia.

The second shortening device aimed at practicality is one of which we have made only recent use. This consists in a 20-minute interview during which the subject is asked to participate in certain standardized activities. At the beginning and end of the interview the subject must walk the length of a long anteroom within view of the experimenter. The interview itself consists mainly in a condensed medical history, but during the course of it (1) the subject has to sit in a very low, heavily upholstered (viscerotonic) chair, from which he must several times rise in order to meet the requests of the experimenter; (2) the subject is requested to try to twist a broom handle in the experimenter's hands; (3) his strength is tested with a hand dynamometer, and at another time, by an assortment of weights to be lifted; (4) at the five-minute point the subject is offered an ounce of whisky, which he may refuse, and at the end of the interview, his choice between a Hershey bar and a cigar.

After each interview (before starting the next one), the experimenter takes ten minutes in which to rate the subject *on as many of the 60 traits as he may see fit.* He rates all the traits on which a definite indication seems to have been given. In the writer's hands, about two-thirds of the traits are generally rated after such an interview. The final step (which can be taken afterward by an assistant) consists in computing the arithmetical means of the ratings for each of the three components, and in assigning a final score for each component.

This technique has been developed as a partial answer to a growing demand for a procedure of practical value in military selection. It has not yet been used in that connection, but during 1940 and 1941 it was tried by the writer in a study in which 100 young men of age range 16 to 23 were subjected to a two-year study as to physique, temperament, medical history, social background and life history. For the first 50 of these youths, the work has been completed and the final ratings on temperament are available. The correlations between the final ratings and the writer's initial ratings based on the 20-minute interview follow.

TABLE 21

CORRELATIONS BETWEEN FINAL RATINGS ON TEMPERAMENT AND "TWENTY-MINUTE" RATINGS

$N = 50$

	Viscerotonia	Somatotonia	Cerebrotonia
$r =$	+.82	+.84	+.91

These correlations show a marked improvement over the earlier work with the short form of the scale, especially in the rating of somatotonia. It is difficult to say whether the improvement is due more to a normal increase in the writer's diagnostic skill, or to the introduction at the first interview of activities which may tend to bring out the subject's personality more clearly. Because of the relatively high degree of statistical interdependence among the components, it is quite possible that the improvement in the rating of viscerotonia and cerebrotonia is only a reflection of an improved diagnosis of somatotonia. Accuracy or inaccuracy in the rating of one component is necessarily reflected to some degree in the ratings of the other two components. By introducing a few simple tests of somatotonia—or challenges to somatotonia—in the first interview, we may have succeeded in correcting the most glaring weakness of the earlier practice. It is possible, also, that an advantage may have been derived by permitting the experimenter a free choice of the traits about which he felt most sure, in place of the more rigid insistence upon the 30 traits making up the short form of the Scale. Unfortunately, the short form was not used as such in the experiment described above.

These correlations encourage us to believe that the approach to temperament can be made highly practical. If one investigator can condense his observations to such a degree that in a 20-minute interview he can arrive at quantitative measurements of the primary components which show an average correlation of $+.85$ with the results of a two-year study, it is more than likely that with adequate training others can do as well. The diagnosis of temperament is probably not intrinsically more difficult than ordinary clinical diagnosis, once the point of view is acquired. The original "finding studies" to set up a multidimensional scale (Chapter II), and the "proving experiment" to standardize its use (Chapter VI) were necessarily laborious. Similar laboriousness is encountered in the history of clinical diagnosis. But once the diagnostic sights are set by a course of suitable training, it seems logical to suppose that judgments on temperament can be made with a precision and confidence comparable to that with which an experienced clinician makes his judgments.

It is clear that in 20 minutes a diagnosis of temperament can be made which agrees fairly well with the diagnosis arrived at in the course of the full constitutional analysis. It may be that this particular skill can be acquired only with long practice, and the experiment mentioned on p. 416 raises a question as to whether more than a relatively small proportion of a population of graduate students possess the qualifications necessary to do this kind of work. But the fact that it *can be done at all* is encouraging. A start has been made. A few decades of the practice of describing human beings in a frame of reference having roots in first-order components might lead to a psychology which can coordinate its efforts with those of the medical clinics.

A psychology which *works* would be worth mastering, even if mastery is slow. A good clinician may require five years of training to make his first diagnosis, but in the end he can diagnose the principal entities "almost by the patient's knock on the door." Perhaps it will be the same in psychology.

THE PROBLEM OF THE HALO IN RATING

Much has been written concerning the "halo effect," although the halo in psychological ratings is perhaps at bottom only a special instance of the general problem of bias and rationalization. Human beings that we are, we tend to jump to conclusions on but slight provocation, and to note what supports, while overlooking what contradicts an impression once established. A single outstanding characteristic in an individual may lead an unwary observer to assign the individual falsely to a class, and then deduce (rather than independently observe) other characteristics supposedly associated with that class. This is what happens under the influence of the halo.

It has been pointed out, quite rightly, that a constitutional approach to psychology is peculiarly open to the bias of the halo. At an earlier period in this work, before the term *Gestalt* had acquired so technical a set of connotations as is now the case, we used to think of constitutional studies as an aspect of *Gestalt* psychology. We were seeking to identify the fundamental pattern (*Gestalt*) which we supposed underlay and to a degree determined the overt behavioral reactions of the individual. Now, this concept of a pattern or *Gestalt* (of any kind) lying behind the observed behavior of an individual is both a fascinating and a dangerous plaything. Fascinating because it lets meaning and prediction into psychology, and dangerous precisely because prediction is always dangerous. (Prediction is the Latin-derived name for the sin of Prometheus—the Christ of the Greeks.) The step from *Gestalt* to halo is but a short, and sometimes a slippery one.

In attempting to define an individual in terms of so general a concept as a patterning of his static and dynamic components, we of course expose ourselves more or less recklessly to the danger of the halo error. Having once set up criteria for the measurement of ectomorphy, for example, and having established (or even suspected) the existence of a relationship between cerebrotonia and ectomorphy, it is admittedly difficult *not* to see cerebrotonic characteristics wherever ectomorphy is observed. Moreover, there is no way of removing the influence of the morphological patterning totally from the picture, for any investigator who has learned to think in constitutional terms observes the general morphological pattern of individuals as inevitably (and as subconsciously) as a trained ornithologist notes the identity of birds he meets. It cannot be denied that whenever the writer talks with an individual, he becomes as aware of the fellow's somatotype as of the general state of his physical and mental health. Also a preliminary estimate of the relative strength of the various temperamental components is inevitably formed. The early estimate is not always correct, but it is always present.

Perhaps the strongest defense we can offer against the halo is simply the fact that we are well aware of its nature. We look for it suspiciously behind every bush in the psychological garden. Darwin, too, was aware of this danger. Concerned as he was with tracing out the broad outlines of a basic taxonomy according to an hypothesis which ran against the conventional academic stereotypes of his day, he sensed a particular danger from that "inward emotional glee" which he found to accompany observations diametrically refuting his ("smugly complacent") critics. He noticed too that observations supporting his hypotheses stood out in consciousness and were well remembered, while apparent exceptions tended to slip lightly by. He therefore took to writing down the latter, for emphasis and preservation.

We have done the same, with a zeal which we hope (but do not altogether assume) has been adequate. The series of 200 cases presented in Chapter VI contains at least a dozen cases which were worked up in detail because of the preliminary impression that an unusually wide disparity between morphology and temperament existed. In most of these cases the apparently great disparity melted away as we went more deeply into the life history and into the detail of present behavior.

There is one apparent disparity, however, which is peculiarly persistent and is often encountered. It arises from the presence of the manifest-latent gradient in the expression of somatotonia (see p. 297). In the case of the commonly reported disparity (high mesomorphy—low somatotonia), the halo seems to operate in reverse. It tends to *obscure* the correlation between the morphological and temperamental levels—a correlation which emerges clearly only when the details of the life history and of the behavior are examined. The large mesomorphs often show a superficial serenity —and the student is off on a false lead. Upon closer analysis, however, the apparent lack of somatotonia is found to be only civilination-deep. We have sometimes referred to this phenomenon as the obscuring halo of somatotonia.

The halo, then, is a general phenomenon and one which works both ways—toward obscuring as well as toward exaggerating relationships. Furthermore, it is a concept not unrelated to the idea of pattern in general, which is both a useful and a dangerous idea. Halo is a vague, general concept which refers really to the shortcomings and to the *general* susceptibility to error inherent in the dullness and inadequacy of our tools of description. The only defense we have to offer against the halo is the sum of what efforts can be made to render the procedures thorough and the tools of description sharp.

THE PROBLEM OF OBJECTIVITY

It cannot be denied that in constitutional analysis the objectivity of some procedures is greater than that of others. Completely objective is somatotyping by anthropometry—almost wholly subjective is the rating of gynandrophrenia. We do not hold with those proponents of absolutism who would rule out of scientific respectability all procedures except those which are reducible to meter readings. Such an intolerance (or such an idealism!) would throw into discard not only much of psychology but most of clinical medicine. If medicine were completely objective there would be no doctors, but only technicians. The same would be true of psychology and psychologists (indeed there are some who would say that this *is* true—that there are no psychologists). The difficulty is that a literal objectivity would rule out our looking at people. Such an approach is shortsighted in that it fails to make use of the synthesizing intelligence that a man may possess, while seemingly investing a great faith in some *ultimate* synthesizing intelligence which may never exist. As for objectivity, we can be almost perfectly objective so long as we do not much care what we measure, but we must then be prepared to face the implications of the cryptic modernism, "so what?"

The truth is that the need for objectivity is but one facet of a still more vital need. It is necessary, if truth is to be kept within hailing distance, to maintain the highest possible degree of objectivity—to render every procedure as nearly foolproof as it can be rendered. But since we no longer entrust *everything* to divine guidance, it is equally necessary to maintain a degree of *relevancy* —to keep an eye open to where we are going. Scientific investigation might be compared (for our present purpose) to driving an automobile. The relations between the driving machinery and the controls partake of the nature of pure objectivity, thanks to good engineering. But the driver must maintain a relation of relevancy to the road, at least until all roads are so mechanized that driving can be reduced to the objective automaticity of pushing a button labeled Schenectady.

Instrumental objectivity and carefully documented observation from life are not really opposed concepts, but are rather like the two slopes of a roof. When harmoniously combined they function as a more efficient watershed than either alone. In the studies reported in this book we have tried to keep a balance between these two procedures. The morphological work rests solidly upon instrumental objectivity (after a suitably long period of elastic growth through an adolescence of subjectification). The work on temperament and motivation rests mainly upon what might be called clinical documentation. The 60 defining traits were arrived at and rendered discriminative by subjecting a large number of observations to a statistical procedure. The procedure as a whole was both subjective and objective. The later use of the traits, considering the traits individually, is perhaps about as objective and systematic as medical diagnosis. That is to say, we admit freely that a subjective element is present—that no machine has been built which can make a diagnosis of temperament.

Yet each of these traits we measure rests upon a fairly specific system of related symptoms and quantifiable behavioral reactions. Such symptoms and reactions *when watched for* are as plain and objective as cows and horses. When not watched for they may be as unrecognized as migrating warblers. With a degree of practice and training comparable only perhaps to the training of experienced clinicians, we believe that naturally observant psychologists can diagnose the key traits defining the temperamental components with trustworthy precision. We do not claim that an untrained person can do so, even with the help of the detailed instructions contained in this book. Who would attempt to perform, let us say, a simple appendectomy merely because he had read a book? Constitutional analysis is unquestionably a job calling for a high degree of specialization.

THE QUALIFICATIONS OF A CONSTITUTIONAL PSYCHOLOGIST

The question is frequently asked, "Can I become a constitutional psychologist? What natural qualities are needed? What training is desirable?" To these questions we shall here attempt such answer as seems indicated by our limited experience at training others in constitutional methods.

As we have already indicated, at the morphological level somatotyping can be accomplished with almost foolproof objectivity, although, of course, somatotyping is only one step in physical analysis. Training in this part of the procedure is about comparable to training in cattle judging. To start with, it is necessary to be interested in cattle, and observant of them. In perhaps a year's time an observant person who has a true interest in human stock, and some background in anatomy or physical anthropology, can be taught to carry out a physical analysis with dependable accuracy. The two first prerequisites are then (1) the quality of being interestedly observant of human stock, and (2) an accurate anatomical knowledge of the human body.

Measurement at the more complex dynamic levels also requires that the student be full of curiosity. If this characteristic is not well represented, nothing can make up for the deficit. Beyond this, the ideal step in training is doubtless that of general clinical medicine. The constitutional analyst needs to know how to take a thorough medical history and must be well practiced in the art of interpreting symptoms. To try to build psychological understanding without a solid purchase in medicine may be comparable to trying to build airplanes without a knowledge of aerodynamics. Medicine may not be essential from the factual point of view, but such training constitutes good insurance against half-baked diagnosing.

What then shall we say of training in *psychology*, as that term is conventionally interpreted? Academic psychology is just now hard to define. However, nearly all advanced courses in psychology drill the student in the idea of a fairly rigorous, quantitative measurement of something. Psychology may be rather confused as to its subject matter, but psychologists are, perhaps for that reason, all the more zealous that their procedures shall be rigidly quantitative and therefore scientific.

This is good training. The constitutional psychologist must somewhere acquire the habit of systematic quantification, which is precisely the habit that many of the best clinicians lack. However, in constitutional psychology it is necessary to learn to apply this habit to the observation of people—*whole* people, not merely behavioral fragments of people—and at this point our present training in psychology sometimes falls short of the mark. The notorious hesitancy of psychologists to look at the physical reality of a human being is due perhaps to the fact that there have been no good tools available by which a psychologist could grapple with the subject. The physiological, anatomical and anthropological sciences have failed to provide the psychologist with a physical taxonomy useful to him. Hence he has often had to content himself with eclectic inquiry into isolated and therefore lifeless fragments of his subject matter.

Psychiatry has little to offer in the way of *specific* training, for this study is relatively new, and it has yet to formulate an adequate taxonomy of its own. Its classificational system is still a loose one, resting for the most part on a mixture of two vague and shifting adjectival typologies (Freudian and Kraepelinian). The conception of continuously variable components has not yet taken hold in this field. Yet psychiatry has much to offer in the way of general maturational experience. It is in its pathology that the mind best shows its predominant motivational undercurrents. No better background for constitutional psychology can be found than a few years of work in a psychiatric clinic. In this respect, psychiatry offers an excellent finishing school for psychology.

Psychoanalysis is a good experience for anybody, especially if carried out in the spirit of whimsical good humor and sympathetic objectivity—as one would watch the courting of sparrows. Such an experience enriches consciousness and tends to bring tolerance and perspective. A rich background of sexual experience appears to exert about the same effect, *in those who can assimilate it*. But the latter seem to be in the minority. Both psychoanalysis and overt sexuality are seen sometimes to coarsen the ordinary person, to render him more obnoxiously aggressive (if his second component predominates), and more crassly sophisticated.

Psychoanalysis, in some instances, appears to effect a kind of artificial speeding up of the natural tempering of character which life generally affords in more leisurely tempo. Coarse minds when psychoanalyzed lose their superficial veneer of civilization and become more manifestly coarse. Fine minds add a deeper and more securely humorous perspective. We have felt that what psychoanalysis actually accomplishes is a sort of mental undressing of the individual, and a rendering of his true character more manifest. People who have been analyzed usually show their temperamental components more clearly (more manifestly) than before analysis. The *therapeutic* value of the technique appears to lie in rendering naturally somatotonic people more manifestly somatotonic (giving them a sense of expressive freedom).

We should like to see every prospective constitutional psychologist analyzed. It separates the sheep from the goats. If analysis "takes" in the sense that the individual thereby finds a theology and becomes a "convert," he is not of the stuff of which constitutional psychologists ought to be made. If on the other hand he only becomes wiser, quieter, and more humorously observant, a good experience has been assimilated.

In summary, the constitutional psychologist needs to be (1) interestedly and humorously observant of human stock. Such a characteristic may be largely innate in its origins, but is probably brought out and made manifest by early example. Perhaps the best early training is therefore that of natural history, coupled with living much among the people of the barnyard.

(2) Clinical training is, we fear, an almost unavoidable prerequisite. In no other way is the necessary intimate familiarity with basic physical and physiological problems of life to be achieved. This raises the consideration that a special kind of clinical training needs to be made available for psychologists, one which for example omits surgery, obstetrics, and much of the didactics of general therapy, as well as the treatment specialities. But no such course of training is yet available. *Faute de mieux,*

therefore, we feel that the regular medical training is a distinct asset in constitutional psychology.

(3) Academic psychology offers training in the methodological techniques of rigorous and systematic quantification. That is about all it offers to constitutional psychology at the present time. Such training is of the utmost importance, but it can be had in other places. Advanced training in psychology is therefore desirable, but not a prerequisite. A background of supervised research in almost any well-controlled scientific field might serve as a substitute.

(4) A background of experience in judging and diagnosing human beings constitutes what is perhaps a necessary internship. Psychiatry offers a splendid opportunity for acquiring such experience, but does not offer much that is useful in the way of theoretical constructs.

(5) Psychoanalysis at its best appears to bring about a kind of artificial maturation, not unlike artificial ripening of fruit. Those of fine fiber assimilate it as an experience which adds perspective and understanding. Those of coarser fiber tend also to reveal their nature more clearly, and it is these who often emerge from analysis with an experience of conversion. We urge analysis. (For one thing it may be well to be psychoanalyzed in order to discover whether or not one *really wants* to attack a subject like constitutional psychology.)

CONSTITUTIONAL ANALYSIS AND PSYCHOANALYSIS

The primary objective of our project has been that of standardizing a procedure through which relatively fixed, basic individual differences can be recognized, identified and measured. The resulting procedure as a whole has sometimes been referred to as constitutional analysis. Constitutional analysis and Freudian analysis, although employing different methods and terminologies, are not totally unrelated procedures. The two approaches have been described as the upward and downward extensions, respectively, of a continuum. The Freudians start with consciousness and go as far (down) as they can. We start with the solid bone and flesh of the individual and go as far (up) as we can. Ideally, the two procedures need to be carried on conjointly, and indeed in certain cases where the two analyses have been so conducted, excellent results have obtained.

It is from psychoanalysis that one of the principal modern supports for the constitutional approach has been derived. Freudians speak sometimes of "psychogenic factors affecting the organism," and sometimes of "somatogenic factors affecting the mind." In either case a step is taken toward recognition of the need for substituting a conception of a continuum for the rudimentary dichotomy of mind and body.

Among the psychoanalysts, Alexander of Chicago has particularly emphasized the proposition that any system of analysis aimed at comprehension of a fragment of behavior must in the end deal with the personality as a whole, including both mental and physical processes, or fail in its purpose. Alexander and some others have felt that when once a systematic description of physical and physiological variation becomes available, couched in terms of concepts which have common roots (common components, possibly) with a similarly systematic description of psychological variables, the way will be open to a more effective attack on the general problem of analysis. Analysis would then become, not merely *psycho*analysis, but general, constitutional analysis, or total analysis. The descriptive adjective is unimportant, so long as it refers to a process by which the analyst directs his attack upon more than a single level of personality. By approaching an individual simultaneously from the directions of both statics and dynamics the analyst is able to effect a kind of "pincers movement," and the efficiency of the analytic attack should be enhanced.

CAN THE COMPONENTS BE CHANGED?

This is a question of great practical and theoretical importance, for it involves the fate both of individuals and of nations, but to answer it, or even to begin to answer it, will require generations of research. There are two phases of the problem: (1) To what extent can group changes be brought about, through generalized influences? (2) To what extent can individuals be changed by educational, clinical and other procedures?

There is some evidence that stature in the United States has increased within the past few decades. According to an Associated Press report, the first 100,000 drafted soldiers examined in 1940-1941 are about 1.4 inches taller (when age is held constant) than the general average for men drafted in 1917-18. College students at Harvard are nearly two inches taller than they were in 1900. However, in both instances weight has also increased. We have no way of knowing whether there has been any shift in the distribution of somatotypes. Possibly America has been growing a little more ectomorphic.

If physique has changed within the past half century, then have the motivational components also changed? As we grow taller do we tend to become more cerebrotonic—and more cerebrotic?

According to a sample of 186 Chinese students in American colleges, the South Chinese are at the present time among the least mesomorphic (and presumably among the least somatotonic) of the peoples of the earth. Were they once more mesomorphic? Have they degenerated (or perhaps evolved) from a more mesomorphic and somatotonic stock, like that of the present-day Japanese? Would it be possible through selective breeding to speed up or reverse the present trend—whatever it may be?

Is it possible that the problem of war need not carry the fatal germ of inevitability? Only a little while ago men thought that the black death was inevitable. The development of a single diagnostic idea led to its abolishment. Today the general pessimism is abroad that war and the cyclic rise and fall of peoples are inevitable. There may be an alternative to such a pessimism. Possibly these costly tidal waves of somatorosis among geographic groups can be predicted (and therefore controlled), once their symptoms are diagnosed in terms of a psychology rooted in an understanding of human constitutions and freed from irrational sentiment.

Men knew that the second World War was brewing almost before the echoes of the first had quieted. But they did not know *why*. What might have been the story had they sought causes in the differential constitutional endowments of groups of men? No diagnosis ordinarily was made except in terms of economics. Hence no treatment followed except a kind of halfhearted gesture toward the economic and political appeasement of an essentially impenitent, historically somatorotic group of people. The policy seems to have been sound only in the sense that one way to stop a fire is to encourage it quickly to burn up everything combustible. We of the English-speaking world are repeatedly scolded because we faced a grave responsibility in 1919, and flunked the test. Had we been able to define somatotonia, is it possible that we might have saved Germany from herself and ourselves from Germany?

It is the diagnostic side of the business that needs attention. There has been much discussion of the question as to whether children should be punished, and how, but there is no blanket answer to such a question. The first problem is to diagnose the child. What to *do* about a somatorotic child will then depend upon circumstances. Whether or not the second component at what we have called the temperamental level can be changed within a single lifetime, we have as yet no way of knowing, but we do know that the *manner of expression* of the somatotonia can be modified, even though the change may be only in such variables as the manifest-latent and the "sublimational" dimensions. The "civilization" of an individual may then in large part consist in rendering his somatotonia more sublimated and more latent. Contrariwise, the militarization of the individual (or sometimes the therapeutic resolution of his conflicts) seems to consist in rendering his somatotonia more direct and manifest. At any rate, with reasonably dependable techniques of constitutional analysis available, the problem of discipline, both as it affects individual control (crime and punishment) and group control (group arrogance and war), ought to move in long strides toward scientific enlightenment.

As to the problem of change in the individual somatotype, the reader may wish to refer to *The Varieties of Human Physique* (pp. 221-226). Actually we have found no instance of change in the somatotype, although we have seen dramatic enough changes in nutrition and metabolism. The question as to whether or not the somatotype changes is merely the question of how basic is the level at which the somatotype is identified. It is our impression that the level of the somatotype is below that at which environmental influences operate after birth, and that the question of changing the somatotype is comparable (although not equivalent) to that of changing the race of an individual. We believe that the somatotype designation offers a basic and reasonably stable taxonomy of individuals.

Nevertheless, marked changes sometimes take place in the internal physiological balance of an individual, due either to uncontrolled or to such controlled causes as endocrine therapy and surgery. Can such interferences change the balance of the temperamental components? We presume that changes of this nature do take place, although we have no direct supporting evidence, and most of what evidence we do have seems to be on the other side. We have found that some individuals, shortly after thyroid therapy (administration of thyroxin) show more manifest symptoms of cerebrotonia, and to a lesser degree, of somatotonia. But they always appear to return shortly to about their previous pattern of temperamental manifestation. The effect seems to be temporary, like the effect of alcohol. (We have used thyroxin, like alcohol, for diagnostic purposes. When cerebrotonia is above 4, the effect of this drug is unpleasant. The patient usually develops a headache and a sense of fatigue.) The problem of change in temperament associated with endocrine pathology or with permanent endocrine change is of great interest but it is one upon which we are not yet prepared to throw light.

Certain testicular and pituitary extracts seem temporarily to elicit a display of somatotonic manifestations even in young males of low mesomorphy and extremely high gynandromorphy (Froehlich syndrome cases). In these cases such administrations sometimes appear to hasten the sprouting of pubic hair, deepening of the voice, and (a limited degree of) genital development. But it is probable that therapy of such a sort *merely* hastens these developments. We have never seen it change the somatotype or influence the motivational components permanently. Presumably it only brings on a quicker blossoming of a development which would normally have occurred more slowly. Yet this is a fascinating field for experimentation. When constitutional methods of study are more closely integrated with clinical diagnosis and treatment, it may be possible to pick up a trail in the field of endocrinology which will lead to rapid advance in the constitutional field.

We need a constitutional endocrinology. Endocrinology itself is a complex field, still ruled largely by the kind of pre-constitutional thinking which would (in the heat of an enthusiasm) try to explain the whole personality in terms of the effect of endocrine variables. Perhaps the endocrines function a little like the various instruments of an orchestra in playing out a symphonic theme. More fundamental than the individual instruments is the theme of the symphony, the components of which will remain recognizable even in the face of great distortion of specific instrumentation.

There is probably some association between thyroid function and cerebrotonia. At any rate cerebrotonic people seem uniformly to show an elevated basal metabolic rate. Yet it is possible that interference with the thyroid will not change cerebrotonia any more radically than the symphony would be changed by amplification or muffling of the French horns. The constitutional picture is not "merely endocrinology." But the importance of carrying on endocrine and constitutional studies concurrently and in the light of one another ought to be obvious enough.

IS THE CONSTITUTIONAL APPROACH FATALISTIC?

It is often said that the constitutional approach is fatalistic. The general notion has seeped into the philosophy of the hour that the only hopeful and therefore tolerable social outlook must be one which regards men as potentially all alike, except for environmental conditioning. This point of view has not always been in favor, rather it comes and goes like a swinging pendulum. Just at present, it seems the pendulum has swung violently from the extremist position of the endogenists, some of whom have held that human personality is determined almost entirely from within, to the extremist position of the present-day exogenists or environmentalists, holding that personality is determined almost entirely from without.

The first view rationalizes what may be named an individual pessimism but a racial and evolutionary optimism. According to such an outlook, not much can be accomplished in one generation, but through controlled reproduction and through discriminative education, an almost unlimited evolutionary future may lie ahead for the race. The optimism of the present is sacrificed for an optimism extending into time. Under this view, salvation would lie in constitutional and genetic research and in critical discrimination applied to human beings by human beings.

The second view rationalizes an evolutionary futilitarianism but an immediate and individual optimism. If the proposition that all men are to be considered equal is taken literally, it follows that under an indiscriminately uniform environment all should achieve the same mental and spiritual stature. Indeed it follows that the *central* problem before us is not that of heredity and the measurement of constitutional endowment; it is rather that of the production and distribution of goods, the standardization of education, the elevation of rates of consumption and the like. In short, the central problem of life becomes the very concrete and (somatotonically) acceptable one of creating and distributing material goods. It is as though all our problems could be solved by *doing something* with our hands and bodies—by industry. Salvation, then, lies not in critical discrimination among human beings (that indeed is heresy), but in numerical growth, expansion, and in expressive "freedom."

Now this is quite an old controversy, and its life history is to be traced in our basic literature through many guises. A good university course in philosophy lays this central conflict before the sophomore in perhaps a dozen different settings. It is the conflict within that ancient misunderstanding between the (cerebrotonic) stoics and the (viscero-somatotonic) epicureans, and between idealists and materialists of all time. There is always a smoldering warfare between the (materialistic) *expressivist,* and what we might perhaps call the (idealistic) *inhibitivist.* The former rationalizes his basic tenet as love of freedom and liberty; the latter, as love of personal effacement, self-discipline, and understanding. The basic conflict is well brought to the surface in the incompatibility between the Freudian (expressivistic) and the Christian (inhibitivistic) religions, or between the educational philosophy of the modern (progressive) school and that of the old New England Latin School.

Between one extremist position and the other the pendulum has swung violently, and on the most recent swing the somatotonic component has for the time being taken the upper hand. Liberty and self-expression are in the saddle. But can they stay there for long? Or must a somatotonic blowout so wholehearted as our present one lead soon, like an alcoholic orgy, to a reaction that is severe—and painful?

Now, the point in the above digression is simply this: from the immediate, materialistic, or purely somatotonic point of view, it may be true that the constitutional outlook is fatalistic and pessimistic. But the pessimism which is sounded here is only that of the short term. It is long-term optimism. From the standpoint of rampant somatotonia we are indeed pessimistic: temporary palliation seems hardly worth the effort. Nor is the problem to be solved by a swing to the other extreme where somatotonia and its devices would be in turn suppressed, for there is naught to be gained from a cerebrotonic tyranny as opposed to a somatotonic tyranny. Instead, the way of escape would seem to be the extension of a general understanding of the elements, both static and dynamic, whose patterning constitutes the individual. We need first to understand the internal relations among these elements before there can be much hope of adequately adjusting external appliances. If constitutional studies can lead to the establishment of a rational foundation for a science of heredity and eugenics, we may then hope, for example, to eliminate the principal constitutional and degenerative *physical* scourges of the race (like cancer, tuberculosis and low t component). But of greater importance than that, it might then also be possible by discriminate breeding to strengthen the mental and spiritual fiber of the race. This is optimistic enough.

But these are *remote* optimisms, not immediate ones. To reach them, it may be necessary to tolerate an *immediate* pessimism, such as might lie in an emotional acceptance of the possibility that the predominant social philosophy of the moment may reflect only wishful thinking. It may be in one sense fatalistic to suppose that Christopher (p. 147) cannot become a heavyweight champion, or that Boris (p. 121) will never read cuneiform. Yet to try to fit Christopher and Boris to an indiscriminate behavioral or mental mold would seem a cruel misanthropy. This would be to pretend psychological alchemy.

The aim of constitutional psychology, so far as individuals are concerned, is actually a direct antithesis to what should fairly be called fatalism. The aim is to develop every individual *according to the best potentialities of his own nature*, while protecting him from the fatal frustration of a false *persona* and false ambitions. This is not fatalism, but naturalism. Its end result is to increase, not decrease the individual's opportunities for accomplished living.

The accusation of fatalism is an accusation of narrowness of outlook. If we seem to overemphasize the constitutional factor throughout this book by largely omitting the factor of environmental influence, it does not mean that we consider the latter unimportant. It means only that we are presenting here the neglected side of the picture, without which a general psychology seems fatuous or anomalous. The problem of synthesis lies on beyond. In these two volumes (*The Varieties of Human Physique* and the present one) we have attempted to do no more than write in the foundation for the constitutional side of the structure as a whole. That, in itself, has been sufficiently difficult.

Constitutional psychology we regard as only a contribution to general psychology, not a substitute. Its place in the total scheme is possibly comparable to the description of the skeleton in anatomy. If such a point of view does not seem to have been maintained dispassionately in all of the sections of the present book, let the shortcoming be charged (in the reader's generosity) to counteremphasis.

APPENDICES

APPENDICES

BASIC DATA FOR 200 CASES

(See p. 290)

	1—117	
	2—117	d-10
No. 1 Age 23 Race N-M Ht 71 Wt 116 Somato 1²-1-7	3—217	g-2.8
type	4—217	t-1.8
	5—216	

IT 2-1-6   V 45   S 29   C 110   Health 5   Strength C 1
Strength P 2   PI 1   IQ 117   AI 3   S 3   Gp 4

Comment: A weak, rather helpless and dependent youth. Some homosexual inclination but no overt homosexuality. A senior in the Art Department. Academic standing, fourth decile (fourth tenth from the bottom). He wants to teach art appreciation.

	1—136	
	2—136	d-10
No. 2 Age 23 Race J Ht 69 Wt 114 Somato 1-2²-6	3—126	g-1.6
type	4—226	t-2.5
	5—126	

IT 2-3-6   V 47   S 65   C 108   Health 7   Strength C 2
Strength P 3   PI 3   IQ 141   AI 4   S 5   Gp 2

Comment: An unusually brilliant Jewish youth of great academic promise. Graduate student, social sciences. Deep bass voice and a vocal somatorosis (vocally aggressive). He lectures to his admiring associates on political and economic theory. Plans to be an expert on taxation. Undergraduate record, tenth (top) decile.

	1—127	
	2—127	d-12
No. 3 Age 21 Race N Ht 71 Wt 123 Somato 1-2²-6²	3—136	g-1.1
type	4—136	t-3.5
	5—136	

IT 1-3-7   V 28   S 63   C 124   Health 7   Strength C 2
Strength P 3   PI 2   IQ   AI 6   S 5   Gp 2

Comment: Excessively apprehensive and insecure but naturally very bright. Frightened of life, but irregularly and inadequately aggressive. Mediocre student of history. Academic standing, third decile. He has a most disturbing sexual need. Only present outlet, autoeroticism. Note that this IT falls outside the normal occurrence of somatotypes.

[1] For definitions of these abbreviations, see p. 282.

1—236
2—127   d-12
No. 4   Age 19   **Race** N   **Ht** 70   **Wt** 113   **Somato** 1-2-7   3—127   g-2.6
                                                              type   4—127   t-5
                                                                                  5—127

IT 2-3-6   **V** 44   **S** 61   **C** 118   **Health** 6   **Strength C** 2
Strength P 4   **PI** 3   **IQ** 142   **AI** 6   **S** 6   **Gp** 3
Comment: A quiet, fragile young man, outwardly very shy, but he has almost a serene inward determination. Although still virginal he is struggling with a strong sexual drive. He seems about 17. Undergraduate, not yet able to find a major field of study. Academic standing, eighth decile.

1—254
2—145   d-14
No. 5   Age 26   **Race** N   **Ht** 68   **Wt** 129   **Somato** 1²-5-4   3—154   g-1.3
                                                              type   4—254   t-2.0
                                                                                  5—154

IT 2-5-4   **V** 47   **S** 97   **C** 82   **Health** 6   **Strength C** 5
Strength P 5   **PI** 4   **IQ**   **AI** 2   **S** 3   **Gp** 1
Comment: A well-adapted, severe young man. Excellent academic record. Married. Practicing law. He is a serious, humorless fellow who has no time for foolishness but cuts straight to the heart of a problem and is certain to collect his fee. Undergraduate record, tenth decile.

1—154
2—254   d-12
No. 6   Age 22   **Race** N   **Ht** 66   **Wt** 120   **Somato** 1-5-4   3—154   g-1.0
                                                              type   4—154   t-2.5
                                                                                  5—163

IT 1-6-4   **V** 34   **S** 109   **C** 75   **Health** 7   **Strength C** 4
Strength P 5   **PI** 4   **IQ** 121   **AI** 1   **S** 3   **Gp** 1
Comment: Short stature, with an overly aggressive manner. Called a psychopathic personality by the university psychiatrist. He is extremely loud, and strained. An undergraduate student of psychology. Academic record, second decile.

1—262
2—171   d-18
No. 7   Age 29   **Race** N-A   **Ht** 65   **Wt** 130   **Somato** 1-6-2   3—162   g-1.4
                                                               type   4—163   t-1.5
                                                                                   5—163

IT 2-7-2   **V** 41   **S** 125   **C** 43   **Health** 7   **Strength C** 6
Strength P 5   **PI** 7   **IQ**   **AI** 1   **S** 3   **Gp** 1
Comment: Short stature and very powerful physique. Formerly a star basketball player and college wrestler. Entered the engineering course but never finished. He has always been uncontrollably quarrelsome. Under suspended sentence (manslaughter). Academic record, second decile.

1—271	
2—271	d-14
3—171	g-1.6
4—262	t-1.6
5—171	

No. 8   Age 20   **Race** N-A   **Ht** 66   **Wt** 151   **Somato** 1²-7-1   **type**

IT 3-6-2   **V** 59   **S** 115   **C** 46   **Health** 6   **Strength C** 7
Strength P 4   **PI** 6   **IQ** 112   **AI** 1   **S** 2   **Gp** 1
Comment: Popular, likable youth. College sophomore on a football scholarship. Great physical strength and energy, but also good relaxation and control. Academic standing, fourth decile. Studying physical education and considered to have excellent prospects in that field.

1—171	
2—171	d-4
3—171	g-1.4
4—171	t-2.8
5—271	

No. 9   Age 17   **Race** N   **Ht** 68   **Wt** 162   **Somato** 1-7-1   **type**

IT 2-6-1   **V** 48   **S** 117   **C** 35   **Health** 6   **Strength C** 7
Strength P 6   **PI** 7   **IQ** 106   **AI** 1   **S** 2   **Gp** 1
Comment: College freshman. Football scholarship. Considered a most promising athlete. Note the rather high *t* component. This youth is pleasant, relaxed, generally modest, although he can readily become aggressive when sufficiently aroused. Such a temperament is ideally adapted to the "heavy-contact" sports. Academic standing, third decile.

1—172	
2—172	d-8
3—172	g-1.8
4—172	t-3.0
5—262	

No. 10   Age 24   **Race** N   **Ht** 70   **Wt** 169   **Somato** 1-7-2   **type**

IT 2-6-3   **V** 45   **S** 109   **C** 64   **Health** 6   **Strength C** 6
Strength P 6   **PI** 6   **IQ** 116   **AI** 2   **S** 5   **Gp** 1
Comment: Law student. Considered a leader. Excellent athletic and social record. Fair academic record. Much sought after by women. This youth is mentally limited and is conservative or righteous in social outlook, but he has his world just about as he wants it. Undergraduate record, sixth decile.

1—217	
2—217	d-0
3—217	g-3.5
4—217	t-3.0
5—217	

No. 11   Age 26   **Race** M-N   **Ht** 69   **Wt** 114   **Somato** 2-1-7   **type**

IT 3-1-6   **V** 60   **S** 34   **C** 107   **Health** 6   **Strength C** 1
Strength P 1   **PI** 1   **IQ**   **AI** 7   **S** 5   **Gp** 7
Comment: Instructor in languages. High academic honors. A complete aesthete. Overt passive homosexual. He is physically as weak and defenseless as a sick rabbit, but by being completely so has made a good adaptation.

                                                          1—216
                                                          2—225   d-24
No. 12   Age 23   Race N   **Ht** 68   **Wt** 123   **Somato** 2²-2-5   3—334   g-3.0
                                              type   4—226   t-1.4
                                                          5—325

IT 3-2-6   **V** 63   **S** 45   **C** 110   **Health** 4   **Strength C** 2
Strength P 3   **PI** 2   **IQ**   **AI** 4   **S** 5   **Gp** 6
Comment: Theological student. Confused and uncertain of his faith. An amateur art and music critic. Overt homosexual. He is really a professional aesthete, with little interest in religion. Undergraduate record, fifth decile.

                                                          1—235
                                                          2—136   d-16
No. 13   Age 25   Race M-A   **Ht** 69   **Wt** 122   **Somato** 2-2²-5²   3—225   g-2.5
                                              type   4—225   t-2.5
                                                          5—226

IT 2-3-6   **V** 48   **S** 58   **C** 111   **Health** 6   **Strength C** 2
Strength P 4   **PI** 3   **IQ**   **AI** 5   **S** 7   **Gp** 2
Comment: A quiet, shy, hard-working graduate student of social science, struggling with a strong and usually frustrated sexual drive. He is a "sex-fighter" in the sense that some people are booze-fighters. His mind is keen and original. Undergraduate record, ninth decile.

                                                          1—225
                                                          2—216   d-24
No. 14   Age 17   Race M-N   **Ht** 66   **Wt** 107   **Somato** 2-2-5   3—216   g-3.6
                                              type   4—334   t-1.5
                                                          5—225

IT 3-1-5   **V** 64   **S** 28   **C** 95   **Health** 3   **Strength C** 1
Strength P 1   **PI** 1   **IQ** 128   **AI** 3   **S** 1   **Gp** 6
Comment: An exceedingly quiet, effeminate youth who entered college at 17 with a fairly good high school record, but spent all but four months of his freshman year in a mental hospital. Tentative diagnosis: hebephrenic schizophrenia.

                                                          1—226
                                                          2—226   d-8
No. 15   Age 28   Race N-M   **Ht** 72   **Wt** 137   **Somato** 2-2-6   3—226   g-3.0
                                              type   4—226   t-3.0
                                                          5—325

IT 3-2-6   **V** 56   **S** 42   **C** 109   **Health** 5   **Strength C** 2
Strength P 2   **PI** 2   **IQ**   **AI** 4   **S** 5   **Gp** 5
Comment: A highly effeminate, arty young man with a strong sexual drive. Mediocre (fifth decile) academic history. An unsuccessful schoolteacher. No happy sexual outlet. Unhappy, dependent personality. Almost cut off from desirable women because of his general weakness and effeminacy.

No. 16 Age 24 Race M-N Ht 71 Wt 134 Somato 2^2-2-6
type

1—235	
2—226	d-14
3—326	g-3.2
4—226	t-1.5
5—326	

IT 3-2-6 V 59 S 44 C 113 Health 6 Strength C 1
Strength P 2 PI 2 IQ 105 AI 2 S 5 Gp 5

Comment: Effeminate and arty. Narrow range of interests. Rather poor stock and rather low intelligence. Conspicuous sexual frustration. Academic standing, about the third decile. Another weak, overly sexed individual who is not homosexual but is caught in between.

No. 17 Age 23 Race N-M Ht 68 Wt 118 Somato 2^2-2-6
type

1—226	
2—217	d-18
3—326	g-5.5
4—225	t-2.2
5—326	

IT 3-1-7 V 57 S 31 C 124 Health 4 Strength C 1
Strength P 2 PI 1 IQ AI 4 S 1 Gp 7

Comment: Almost a girl. Excessively shy and apprehensive. Mediocre record (fourth decile) but a faithful worker. Student of library work. He is free from the disturbing sexual need so often observed in this somatotype.

No. 18 Age 24 Race M Ht 73 Wt 141 Somato 2-2-6
type

1—245	
2—226	d-16
3—226	g-2.2
4—226	t-3.5
5—216	

IT 2-3-5 V 46 S 67 C 102 Health 7 Strength C 2
Strength P 3 PI 3 IQ AI 5 S 5 Gp 2

Comment: An intent, brilliant, academically successful young man who has achieved the distinction of being an instructor in a first-rate university at 24. He is idealistic, with a touch of the reformer or Messiah about him. Academic record, tenth decile.

No. 19 Age 28 Race J Ht 70 Wt 130 Somato 2-2^2-6
type

1—225	
2—236	d-10
3—226	g-3.5
4—236	t-1.7
5—226	

IT 2-2-5 V 44 S 54 C 95 Health 2 Strength C 2
Strength P 1 PI 1 IQ AI 2 S 3 Gp 3

Comment: A rather frustrated, physically incompetent Jewish youth who is attempting to become a sociologist. He is handicapped by poor eyesight and poor general health. But he is a good person in a passive sense and is fairly well regarded. He has the good will of his faculty. Academic standing, sixth decile.

1—245
2—235 d-18

No. 20 Age 22 **Race** N-M **Ht** 67 **Wt** 116 **Somato** 2-3-5² 3—235 g-1.4
                                                    type   4—136 t-2.6
                                                                  5—226

IT 1-3-6 **V** 35 **S** 65 **C** 111 **Health** 7 **Strength C** 3
Strength P 4 **PI** 3 **IQ** 139 **AI** 3 **S** 4 **Gp** 1
Comment: A somewhat harsh, sharp-tongued little ectomorph who is highly intolerant of Republicans. He is a communist and is being psychoanalyzed. Plans to enter medicine and become a psychiatrist. He is frequently "taken down a peg" by all sorts of people, but he has a sharp mind and outrides the suppression buoyantly. Academic standing, ninth decile.

1—236
2—225 d-22

No. 21 Age 22 **Race** N **Ht** 68 **Wt** 120 **Somato** 2-3-5² 3—136 g-1.6
                                                    type   4—236 t-2.2
                                                                  5—244

IT 1-3-7 **V** 28 **S** 61 **C** 124 **Health** 6 **Strength C** 2
Strength P 4 **PI** 2 **IQ** 126 **AI** 3 **S** 3 **Gp** 1
Comment: A worried, apprehensive youth with a cerebrotic history and with a persistent sense of impending general disaster. He repeatedly threatens suicide. Once swallowed fifty aspirin tablets. Undergraduate major in psychology. Academic standing, fifth decile.

1—235
2—235 d-24

No. 22 Age 21 **Race** N **Ht** 69 **Wt** 125 **Somato** 2-3-5 3—244 g-2.0
                                                    type   4—126 t-2.8
                                                                  5—244

IT 2-4-4 **V** 48 **S** 77 **C** 86 **Health** 7 **Strength C** 3
Strength P 4 **PI** 4 **IQ** 151 **AI** 3 **S** 3 **Gp** 2
Comment: Graduate student in social science at 21. Undergraduate record almost perfect. Considered a genius. Already the recipient of many honors. He seems to have no distractions or hobbies to divert him from direct, main line achievement.

1—244
2—235 d-10

No. 23 Age 20 **Race** J **Ht** 71 **Wt** 139 **Somato** 2-3²-5 3—235 g-1.3
                                                    type   4—235 t-2.2
                                                                  5—245

IT 1-5-4 **V** 32 **S** 96 **C** 85 **Health** 7 **Strength C** 4
Strength P 5 **PI** 4 **IQ** **AI** 2 **S** 4 **Gp** 1
Comment: A pre-medical student who works hard and seems to entertain no doubts or uncertainties as to his ultimate success. He has an inflexible, intolerant mental outlook. Considers himself a communist. Good (eighth decile) academic record.

1—235
2—235 d-16
No. 24 Age 22 Race N Ht 73 Wt 151 Somato 2-3²-5 3—235 g-1.7
type 4—235 t-2.8
5—145

IT 1-4-5 V 34 S 77 C 100 Health 7 Strength C 3
Strength P 4 PI 3 IQ 130 AI 3 S 3 Gp 2

Comment: An undergraduate fraternity boy who is something of the beau brummell of his group. He has found nothing as yet that interests him. He is intolerant, cold, aloof. Academic record, seventh decile.

1—235
2—335 d-4
No. 25 Age 22 Race N Ht 68 Wt 122 Somato 2-3-5 3—235 g-1.4
type 4—235 t-3.0
5—235

IT 2-3-6 V 46 S 66 C 112 Health 5 Strength C 2
Strength P 3 PI 2 IQ AI 4 S 4 Gp 2

Comment: A tense, anxious young man who takes life and himself very seriously. He is a senior. Expects to enter a theological seminary and to study vocational guidance and counseling. He rarely smiles. No humor. Academic standing, eighth decile.

1—345
2—235 d-16
No. 26 Age 28 Race N-M Ht 69 Wt 132 Somato 2²-3²-5 3—345 g-2.5
type 4—235 t-2.0
5—344

IT 3-3-6 V 65 S 60 C 109 Health 5 Strength C 2
Strength P 3 PI 2 IQ AI 2 S 5 Gp 2

Comment: An intern in medicine, and a good one. He has a good record in professional school, although his undergraduate record was mediocre (fourth decile). Excellent sense of humor, a little on the vulgar side.

1—335
2—335 d-6
No. 27 Age 23 Race M Ht 70 Wt 134 Somato 2²-3-5 3—235 g-2.5
type 4—235 t-2.5
5—235

IT 3-3-6 V 65 S 60 C 109 Health 5 Strength C 2
Strength P 2 PI 2 IQ 145 AI 4 S 7 Gp 4

Comment: Left college in the third year, after doing well in the first two years. Now working in a department store. Apparently swamped by sexuality. Lives in a cheap tenement among a group of prostitutes.

1—236
2—335 d-14
No. 28 Age 24 Race M-N Ht 68 Wt 123 Somato 2²-3-5 3—235 g-2.8
type 4—334 t-1.8
5—235

IT 3-3-5 V 59 S 64 C 99 Health 6 Strength C 3
Strength P 4 PI 3 IQ AI 3 S 6 Gp 3

Comment: A promising graduate student in the biological sciences. Has a somewhat sadistic tendency. Loves to practice experimental animal surgery. Has practiced flagellation as a sexual stimulant. Undergraduate record, tenth decile.

                                                        1—236
                                                        2—236   d-0
No. 29   Age 25   Race N   Ht 72   Wt 137   Somato 2-3-6   3—236   g-2.2
                                            type   4—236   t-3.2
                                                        5—236

IT 2-3-6   V 41   S 60   C 113   Health 7   Strength C 2
Strength P 4   PI 3   IQ 119   AI 4   S 6   Gp 2

Comment: A shy, overly anxious and overly serious, but highly intelligent theological student. He is obsessed with the idea of sin, especially in sexuality. At 23 he married an attractive, sexy girl. Undergraduate record, eighth decile.

                                                        1—154
                                                        2—244   d-14
No. 30   Age 23   Race J   Ht 66   Wt 120   Somato 2-4²-4   3—253   g-1.6
                                            type   4—244   t-1.3
                                                        5—254

IT 2-5-4   V 47   S 92   C 83   Health 7   Strength C 4
Strength P 4   PI 3   IQ   AI 1   S 4   Gp 1

Comment: A run-of-the-mill medical student. Academic standing about average. Markedly hirsute. Smokes two packages of cigarettes daily. Works hard. Practical, tough-minded, realistic.

                                                        1—244
                                                        2—244   d-8
No. 31   Age 30   Race N-A   Ht 70   Wt 144   Somato 2-4-4   3—334   g-2.2
                                              type   4—244   t-2.6
                                                        5—244

IT 3-3-4   V 61   S 66   C 82   Health 5   Strength C 3
Strength P 4   PI 2   IQ   AI 2   S 4   Gp 2

Comment: Teaches sciences in high school. Seventh decile academic record. Well liked by his superiors. Rather colorless and undistinguished. Married. Plays bridge. Tinkers ineffectually and meticulously.

                                                        1—244
                                                        2—244   d-12
No. 32   Age 19   Race N   Ht 68   Wt 127   Somato 2-4-4   3—244   g-1.7
                                            type   4—145   t-1.7
                                                        5—254

IT 1-5-4   V 34   S 93   C 83   Health 7   Strength C 4
Strength P 4   PI 3   IQ 128   AI 2   S 4   Gp 1

Comment: A harsh, striving youth who is considered loud and aggressive. A student in journalism, he works for a daily paper. Highly ambitious. Sophisticated. Insincere. Academic record, sixth decile.

                                                        1—344
                                                        2—244   d-14
No. 33   Age 23   Race N   Ht 69   Wt 139   Somato 2²-4-4   3—244   g-1.8
                                            type   4—343   t-2.0
                                                        5—354

IT 3-5-4   V 56   S 94   C 79   Health 6   Strength C 5
Strength P 4   PI 3   IQ 118   AI 1   S 5   Gp 2

Comment: A medical student. Well regarded. Has planned his life in detail and gives some promise of being able to carry out his rather ambitious plans. But frequently involved in trouble with girls. Has three times sought abortionists. Undergraduate record, fifth decile.

No. 34 Age 23 Race N-M Ht 69 Wt 141 Somato 2-4-4
type

1—244
2—244 d-8
3—345 g-2.0
4—244 t-2.2
5—244

IT 2-4-4 V 48 S 80 C 85 Health 6 Strength C 3
Strength P 4 PI 3 IQ 124 AI 2 S 4 Gp 2

Comment: Above the average graduate student in the social sciences. Popular with young women. Considered safe and desirable, although not brilliant. The son of a professor in the university. Undergraduate record, sixth decile.

No. 35 Age 20 Race N Ht 70 Wt 138 Somato 2-4-4²
type

1—235
2—244 d-14
3—145 g-1.8
4—244 t-2.6
5—244

IT 2-4-5 V 41 S 80 C 94 Health 6 Strength C 3
Strength P 4 PI 2 IQ AI 4 S 4 Gp 2

Comment: A brilliant and industrious college senior. Plans to do graduate work in social science. He is already something of a "man Friday" for one of the "intellectuals" among the younger faculty group. Somewhat insecure and apologetic about himself but a passionate crusader for his preceptor. Academic standing, ninth decile.

No. 36 Age 21 Race N Ht 71 Wt 144 Somato 2-4-5
type

1—245
2—244 d-4
3—245 g-2.6
4—245 t-3.6
5—245

IT 2-4-5 V 44 S 77 C 90 Health 7 Strength C 4
Strength P 5 PI 3 IQ AI 5 S 6 Gp 3

Comment: An academic success. Now an assistant in one of the natural sciences, having graduated at 20 with high honors. Since graduating, however, he has been on the sexual prowl almost constantly.

No. 37 Age 24 Race N-M Ht 69 Wt 134 Somato 2²-4-5
type

1—345
2—345 d-10
3—245 g-2.2
4—235 t-1.8
5—345

IT 3-4-4 V 62 S 79 C 85 Health 6 Strength C 4
Strength P 3 PI 2 IQ AI 1 S 3 Gp 2

Comment: Graduated from college at 23 with a fairly good (sixth decile) record. Has a job with a retail merchandising house where he seems to be taking hold successfully. Happily married. No intellectual ambition. Complacent.

No. 38 Age 24 Race N Ht 66 Wt 115 Somato 2-4-5
type

1—254
2—254 d-28
3—236 g-1.5
4—136 t-1.9
5—245

IT 1-3-7 V 36 S 58 C 129 Health 6 Strength C 2
Strength P 3 PI 1 IQ AI 5 S 3 Gp 2

Comment: Painfully cerebrotic. Never shows any mental or physical relaxation. Unable to carry out routines. Failed out of college as a sophomore. Has tried half a dozen jobs but always "breaks down."

1—244	
2—245	d-4

No. 39   **Age** 23   **Race** N   **Ht** 69   **Wt** 130   **Somato** 2-4-5   3—245   g-2.1
                                                       type   4—245   t-3.2
                                                                  5—245

IT 2-4-5   **V** 39   **S** 78   **C** 101   **Health** 7   **Strength C** 3
Strength P 5   **PI** 2   **IQ** 142   **AI** 3   **S** 6   **Gp** 2

Comment: A graduate student of psychology. Excellent (tenth decile) academic record. Highly regarded by the departmental faculty. Attractive to women. He has a religious devotion to atheism.

1—263	
2—252	d-16

No. 40   **Age** 25   **Race** N-A   **Ht** 64   **Wt** 134   **Somato** 2-5²-2²   3—253   g-1.3
                                                        type   4—252   t-1.4
                                                                   5—163

IT 1-7-3   **V** 31   **S** 127   **C** 55   **Health** 7   **Strength C** 5
Strength P 6   **PI** 4   **IQ**   **AI** 1   **S** 3   **Gp** 1

Comment: Apparently a case of somatorotic overcompensation. This young man is hated and has at times been cruelly beaten down by his contemporaries. But he does good work in medical school and may succeed eminently. He is insufferably loud and aggressive. Undergraduate record, eighth decile.

1—253	
2—253	d-8

No. 41   **Age** 26   **Race** N   **Ht** 67   **Wt** 135   **Somato** 2-5-3   3—253   g-2.0
                                                       type   4—252   t-1.3
                                                                  5—263

IT 2-6-3   **V** 51   **S** 108   **C** 59   **Health** 6   **Strength C** 5
Strength P 6   **PI** 4   **IQ**   **AI** 1.5   **S** 4   **Gp** 1

Comment: A tough, wiry individual, somewhat overly aggressive and generally disliked. Graduate student in physical education, with perhaps not quite enough of either the first or second components, and too much third, for this work. He is unhappy, and will probably drop out. Undergraduate record, third decile.

1—263	
2—263	d-6

No. 42   **Age** 21   **Race** N   **Ht** 68   **Wt** 145   **Somato** 2-5²-3   3—253   g-1.1
                                                       type   4—253   t-3.5
                                                                  5—253

IT 2-6-3   **V** 42   **S** 112   **C** 67   **Health** 6   **Strength C** 5
Strength P 4   **PI** 7   **IQ** 110   **AI** 1   **S** 3   **Gp** 1

Comment: A star basketball forward, and track man (sprint). He has a beautifully balanced body. Plans to study agricultural economics. Academic standing, third decile.

1—262		
2—263	d-16	
3—353	g-1.5	
4—353	t-1.3	
5—263		

No. 43   Age 23   Race N-A   Ht 65   Wt 128   Somato 2^2-5^2-3
type

IT 2-7-2   V 45   S 125   C 41   Health 6   Strength C 5
Strength P 5   PI 4   IQ 114   AI 1   S 2   Gp 1

Comment: This boy was incorrigible in college, leaving after three months. As a high school youth he had once taken part in a holdup with a gun. Now works in a filling station. Recently acquitted of a homicide charge.

1—253		
2—253	d-4	
3—253	g-2.0	
4—353	t-2.8	
5—253		

No. 44   Age 21   Race N   Ht 72   Wt 167   Somato 2-5-3
type

IT 3-4-4   V 59   S 78   C 82   Health 5   Strength C 5
Strength P 5   PI 5   IQ 125   AI 2   S 4   Gp 2

Comment: Average (fifth decile) college record. Doing well in premedical courses. Working his way through college and carrying an unusually heavy load of outside work. Generally trusted and well liked, although he lacks humor. Excellent tennis player.

1—163		
2—253	d-22	
3—254	g-1.8	
4—253	t-1.6	
5—245		

No. 45   Age 22   Race N-A   Ht 68   Wt 137   Somato 2-5-3^2
type

IT 2-5-4   V 51   S 99   C 73   Health 4   Strength C 4
Strength P 5   PI 2   IQ 133   AI 1.5   S 4   Gp 2

Comment: A chronic alcoholic at 22. This youth was a drinker in high school but had a good high school record. He left college as a sophomore at 20, with a bad record, virtually a confirmed alcoholic. Spent five months of the past year in an institution for treatment of alcoholism.

1—172		
2—244	d-28	
3—253	g-2.5	
4—254	t-2.6	
5—263		

No. 46   Age 24   Race N-A   Ht 69   Wt 145   Somato 2-5^2-3^2
type

IT 1-6-4   V 28   S 111   C 77   Health 2   Strength C 4
Strength P 5   PI 3   IQ   AI 3   S 2   Gp 3

Comment: A brilliant graduate student of psychology, now also a medical student. He is aloof and overly suspicious, regarding most of his contemporaries with distrust. He has twice been hospitalized for tuberculosis. Undergraduate record, tenth decile.

                                                            1—253
                                                            2—262   d-8
No. 47   **Age** 28   **Race** N   **Ht** 68   **Wt** 145   **Somato** 2-5-3   3—253   g-2.2
                                                  type   4—253   t-1.5
                                                            5—253

IT 2-6-2   **V** 44   **S** 116   **C** 47   **Health** 7   **Strength C** 5
Strength P 4   **PI** 6   **IQ**   **AI** 1.5   **S** 3   **Gp** 1

Comment: A successful real estate salesman and sales manager. Undergraduate record, fourth decile. Good basketball player in college. Has worked for one firm for the past six years and has been steadily advanced. No intellectual interests except fiction and bridge.

                                                            1—252
                                                            2—253   d-12
No. 48   **Age** 21   **Race** N-A   **Ht** 67   **Wt** 131   **Somato** 2-5-3   3—253   g-2.0
                                                  type   4—253   t-1.5
                                                            5—163

IT 2-6-3   **V** 49   **S** 108   **C** 62   **Health** 5   **Strength C** 5
Strength P 4   **PI** 4   **IQ** 119   **AI** 2   **S** 3   **Gp** 1

Comment: An undergraduate who has repeatedly consulted the college psychiatrist for "nervousness" and sexual perplexities. He is highly aggressive and unpopular. College record is poor. An excessive cigarette smoker. Wants to be a psychiatrist. Academic standing, second decile. Has a duodenal ulcer.

                                                            1—253
                                                            2—253   d-4
No. 49   **Age** 25   **Race** N-M   **Ht** 69   **Wt** 144   **Somato** 2-5-3   3—253   g-2.4
                                                  type   4—253   t-3.2
                                                            5—254

IT 2-5-4   **V** 44   **S** 95   **C** 85   **Health** 5   **Strength C** 5
Strength P 4   **PI** 3   **IQ**   **AI** 2   **S** 4   **Gp** 2

Comment: Law student. Near the top of his class in academic standing. Rather ruthless and coldblooded in outlook. Although a bitter cynic, he is aggressive and alert. Plans to enter business. He is quarrelsome and is generally disliked or feared.

                                                            1—253
                                                            2—253   d-10
No. 50   **Age** 26   **Race** N-A   **Ht** 65   **Wt** 127   **Somato** 2^2-5-3   3—253   g-2.5
                                                  type   4—453   t-1.4
                                                            5—353

IT 3-6-2   **V** 59   **S** 117   **C** 40   **Health** 6   **Strength C** 4
Strength P 4   **PI** 4   **IQ**   **AI** 1   **S** 3   **Gp** 2

Comment: A bustling, aggressive medical student. One of the most successful poker players in his class. He does poorly on academic tests but does well in practical and laboratory work. Although overbearing, he is rather well liked. He is tireless. Undergraduate record, fourth decile.

		1—253	
		2—254	d-4
No. 51 **Age** 24 **Race** N **Ht** 72 **Wt** 160 **Somato** 2-5-4		3—254	g-2.5
type		4—254	t-1.6
		5—254	

IT 2-5-4   **V** 48   **S** 100   **C** 73   **Health** 6   **Strength C** 5
Strength P 6   **PI** 3   **IQ** 121   **AI** 1.5   **S** 4   **Gp** 3
Comment: A theological student with a terrific, bone-breaking handclasp, of which he is proud. Rather poor (third decile) academic record. He has a powerful, resonant voice and great energy. His feeling for his profession is intense but intermittent. He has a duodenal ulcer.

		1—262	
		2—262	d-0
No. 52 **Age** 22 **Race** A-N **Ht** 72 **Wt** 182 **Somato** 2-6-2		3—262	g-2.5
type		4—262	t-2.8
		5—262	

IT 3-5-2   **V** 62   **S** 102   **C** 50   **Health** 6   **Strength C** 7
Strength P 4   **PI** 7   **IQ** 111   **AI** 2   **S** 2   **Gp** 2
Comment: One of the college football heroes. He is ordinarily quiet, well-composed and modest, although capable of extreme pugnacity when aroused. He is a handsome mesomorph and is fairly worshiped by most of the student body. Academic record, fifth decile.

		1—262	
		2—263	d-6
No. 53 **Age** 21 **Race** A-N **Ht** 71 **Wt** 171 **Somato** 2-6-2²		3—262	g-2.0
type		4—262	t-1.8
		5—263	

IT 2-6-2   **V** 42   **S** 114   **C** 51   **Health** 7   **Strength C** 6
Strength P 5   **PI** 5   **IQ** 113   **AI** 1   **S** 3   **Gp** 1
Comment: A rather unsuccessful football player. He is easily injured, particularly in the legs, and has never been a star. He is aggressive and reckless, especially with automobiles. Poor academic record, second decile.

		1—371	
		2—262	d-14
No. 54 **Age** 20 **Race** A-N **Ht** 64 **Wt** 132 **Somato** 2²-6-2		3—262	g-2.2
type		4—262	t-2.2
		5—362	

IT 2-7-1   **V** 51   **S** 130   **C** 32   **Health** 6   **Strength C** 6
Strength P 4   **PI** 6   **IQ**   **AI** 1.5   **S** 3   **Gp** 2
Comment: A case of excessive somatotonia associated with a short, mesomorphic physique. He is one of those small, muscular people in whom extreme aggression is tolerated or approved. He is on the wrestling team. Academic standing, second decile.

```
                                                            1—362
                                                            2—262   d-8
No. 55   Age 23   Race A   Ht 71   Wt 175   Somato 2-6-2    3—262   g-2.8
                                             type           4—252   t-2.6
                                                            5—262
```

IT 3-5-2 V 61 S 99 C 44 Health 5 Strength C 6
Strength P 5 PI 5 IQ 129 AI 3 S 3 Gp 3

Comment: This is a 2-6-2 with too much gynandromorphy for football, but he is one of the best collegiate swimmers in the country. Excellent (ninth decile) academic record. Now a senior and popular. Plans to study for the diplomatic service.

```
                                                            1—262
                                                            2—262   d-10
No. 56   Age 23   Race A-N   Ht 67   Wt 151   Somato 2²-6-2  3—261  g-1.5
                                               type          4—362  t-1.4
                                                            5—362
```

IT 3-6-1 V 66 S 118 C 34 Health 7 Strength C 6
Strength P 5 PI 6 IQ 118 AI 1 S 2 Gp 2

Comment: A chunky mesomorph who in spite of short stature was a star basketball player. Now a medical student of about average standing. This boy is excessively hirsute. Undergraduate record, sixth decile.

```
                                                            1—262
                                                            2—263   d-14
No. 57   Age 24   Race J   Ht 68   Wt 152   Somato 2-6-2    3—262   g-2.6
                                             type           4—261   t-1.7
                                                            5—271
```

IT 2-7-2 V 48 S 124 C 41 Health 7 Strength C 6
Strength P 4 PI 5 IQ 115 AI 1 S 3 Gp 2

Comment: Excessive aggression, especially vocal. Average (fifth decile) academic record. He is an excellent swimmer (sprinter). Now in serious danger of being dropped from the law school.

```
                                                            1—263
                                                            2—263   d-4
No. 58   Age 26   Race N   Ht 72   Wt 174   Somato 2-6-3    3—263   g-3.5
                                             type           4—253   t-2.6
                                                            5—263
```

IT 3-5-3 V 59 S 100 C 65 Health 6 Strength C 5
Strength P 6 PI 3 IQ 140 AI 4 S 5 Gp 4

Comment: A gynandromorphic mesomorph. He never attempted collegiate athletics, always regarding himself as "awkward," although he is a good natural swimmer. He won high scholastic honors as an undergraduate and now gives promise of a brilliant career in biological sciences. He is sometimes considered "queer," but is not homosexual.

```
                                                 1—263
                                                 2—263  d-8
No. 59  Age 23  Race N  Ht 72  Wt 173  Somato 2-6-3  3—262  g-2.0
                                         type    4—263  t-1.7
                                                 5—253
```

IT 2-6-3 V 46 S 117 C 60 Health 6 Strength C 6
Strength P 5 PI 4 IQ 103 AI 1.5 S 3 Gp 2
Comment: A rather unsuccessfully aggressive mesomorph. He is loud and truculent. Now a senior. Has tried hard to play football, but 3's in ectomorphy do not play college football successfully. Academic record, first decile.

```
                                                 1—371
                                                 2—371  d-6
No. 60  Age 22  Race A-M  Ht 71  Wt 205  Somato 2²-7-1  3—271  g-1.6
                                         type    4—271  t-1.3
                                                 5—271
```

IT 3-6-1 V 69 S 117 C 30 Health 6 Strength C 7
Strength P 5 PI 6 IQ 96 AI 1 S 3 Gp 1
Comment: Star football player. Very close to all-American. He is a Polish-Italian. Although still an undergraduate, he has made some money through an association with Chicago racketeering, and drives a $3000 automobile. Plans to be a "businessman." Academic record, second decile.

```
                                                 1—334
                                                 2—424  d-20
No. 61  Age 21  Race M  Ht 68  Wt 125  Somato 3-2²-5  3—335  g-4.0
                                         type    4—326  t-1.8
                                                 5—335
```

IT 4-3-5 V 80 S 62 C 94 Health 6 Strength C 2
Strength P 3 PI 2 IQ 122 AI 2 S 4 Gp 5
Comment: Considered a sissy. An undergraduate with no specific plans. No overt homosexuality. Good intelligence but very poor (second decile) academic record in arts and literature. He is lazy, comfortable, effeminate, slightly arty. In danger of being dropped from college.

```
                                                 1—415
                                                 2—326  d-14
No. 62  Age 20  Race M-N  Ht 66  Wt 114  Somato 3²-2-5  3—325  g-4.0
                                         type    4—425  t-1.6
                                                 5—425
```

IT 4-1-5 V 76 S 33 C 95 Health 2 Strength C 2
Strength P 1 PI 1 IQ AI 3 S 1 Gp 6
Comment: An undergraduate in the school of music. Studying to be an organist. Extremely effeminate. He has underdeveloped genitalia and suggests the Froehlich syndrome. Has had pulmonary tuberculosis. Academic standing, sixth decile.

                                                                    1—325
                                                                    2—325   d-4
No. 63 Age 22 Race M-N Ht 69 Wt 128 Somato 3-2-5 3—326   g-3.2
                                                type   4—325   t-2.6
                                                                    5—325

IT 3-2-6 V 60 S 45 C 112 Health 5 Strength C 2
Strength P 2 PI 1 IQ 156 AI 7 S 7 Gp 4

Comment: A brilliant graduate student of literature who was once expelled from
another college, and has recently been in trouble with the police, because of
"Peeping Tom" activities. Has a passionate love for the French language. Academic
record, tenth decile.

                                                                    1—326
                                                                    2—335   d-10
No. 64 Age 25 Race N-M Ht 72 Wt 144 Somato 3-2-5^2 3—325   g-3.2
                                                type   4—326   t-1.4
                                                                    5—325

IT 3-2-5 V 66 S 46 C 100 Health 6 Strength C 1
Strength P 2 PI 1 IQ AI 5 S 5 Gp 3

Comment: A medical student who is doing very poorly and is bewildered by his
failures. His father is a physician. He had a good undergraduate record (seventh
decile), but did only passing work in the biological sciences. His real love lies in
literature and the arts.

                                                                    1—325
                                                                    2—316   d-12
No. 65 Age 19 Race N-M Ht 67 Wt 120 Somato 3-2-5 3—225   g-3.4
                                                type   4—325   t-1.2
                                                                    5—325

IT 3-2-4 V 61 S 49 C 82 Health 3 Strength C 2
Strength P 1 PI 1 IQ 102 AI 1.5 S 3 Gp 5

Comment: A weak, helpless youth, of very low t, who as a freshman was taken to
the university psychiatrist in a daze, and then for a period of observation in a
mental hospital. Tentative diagnosis: schizoid personality. Academic record, first
decile.

                                                                    1—334
                                                                    2—334   d-8
No. 66 Age 27 Race M-N Ht 69 Wt 133 Somato 3-3-4 3—345   g-2.5
                                                type   4—334   t-4.0
                                                                    5—334

IT 3-3-5 V 61 S 63 C 102 Health 6 Strength C 3
Strength P 3 PI 3 IQ AI 4 S 6 Gp 3

Comment: Graduate student in natural science and assistant in the Department of
Chemistry. Excellent record both as graduate and undergraduate (ninth decile).
Has been married twice.

1—343		
2—444	d-18	
3—335	g-2.0	
4—334	t-2.2	
5—344		

No. 67   Age 23   Race M-N   Ht 70   Wt 144   Somato 3-3²-4
                                        type

IT 2-4-4   **V** 44   **S** 77   **C** 86   **Health** 6   **Strength C** 3
Strength P 3   **PI** 2   **IQ**   **AI** 2   **S** 5   **Gp** 2

Comment: An intent, serious student in social science. First year graduate. He is sharp and harsh in his attitudes, and is considered ruthless. Well regarded in his academic department. Undergraduate record, eighth decile.

1—334	
2—334	d-10
3—334	g-2.8
4—435	t-1.9
5—434	

No. 68   Age 22   Race M-N   Ht 68   Wt 134   Somato 3²-3-4
                                        type

IT 4-3-4   **V** 80   **S** 61   **C** 84   **Health** 5   **Strength C** 3
Strength P 3   **PI** 2   **IQ** 121   **AI** 2   **S** 3   **Gp** 3

Comment: An easygoing, tolerant young man who has been only an ordinary student (fifth decile) and has distinguished himself nowhere. Now a senior. Well liked. No history of trouble of any sort. No plans.

1—345	
2—334	d-16
3—335	g-1.8
4—334	t-1.7
5—245	

No. 69   Age 21   Race N-M   Ht 71   Wt 146   Somato 3-3²-4²
                                        type

IT 2-4-5   **V** 43   **S** 76   **C** 96   **Health** 7   **Strength C** 4
Strength P 4   **PI** 3   **IQ**   **AI** 1.5   **S** 5   **Gp** 1

Comment: Notably tense. General manner suggests cerebrotic hyperattentionality. An undergraduate interested primarily in engineering, but his record in the School of Engineering is mediocre. Has much better grades in the School of Liberal Arts. Academic standing, sixth decile.

1—343	
2—334	d-12
3—335	g-1.8
4—334	t-2.8
5—334	

No. 70   Age 22   Race M   Ht 69   Wt 137   Somato 3-3-4
                                        type

IT 3-4-4   **V** 63   **S** 75   **C** 85   **Health** 7   **Strength C** 3
Strength P 5   **PI** 2   **IQ** 130   **AI** 2   **S** 3   **Gp** 2

Comment: Senior in the undergraduate school. Among the first ten in his class in scholarship. He seems to have no distractions or conflicting interests. All of his activities center around his academic success. Wants to teach, but does not care what.

No. 71   Age 21   Race M-N   Ht 72   Wt 153   Somato 3-3-4² type

1—334	
2—334	d-14
3—245	g-2.5
4—335	t-2.2
5—334	

IT 3-3-4   V 66   S 66   C 78   Health 6   Strength C 2
Strength P 3   PI 3   IQ 127   AI 2   S 4   Gp 3
Comment: Considered unusually handsome and admired by women. He is rather complacent or undisturbed about his future. Now an undergraduate with academic record falling in the third decile. Fraternity boy. Background of wealth. May awaken later.

No. 72   Age 22   Race N   Ht 68   Wt 131   Somato 3-3²-4² type

1—245	
2—345	d-16
3—334	g-2.5
4—334	t-2.0
5—334	

IT 3-3-4   V 59   S 69   C 85   Health 7   Strength C 3
Strength P 5   PI 2   IQ   AI 3   S 5   Gp 2
Comment: A somewhat shy, intent young man who upon closer acquaintance reveals a good deal of humor and insight. He plans to do research in biology. Principal interest just now is sexuality. First year graduate student. Undergraduate record, ninth decile.

No. 73   Age 25   Race M-N   Ht 69   Wt 132   Somato 3-3-4 type

1—334	
2—334	d-20
3—325	g-4.5
4—343	t-1.2
5—434	

IT 3-3-3   V 65   S 56   C 70   Health 5   Strength C 1
Strength P 1   PI 1   IQ 83   AI 1.5   S 2   Gp 7
Comment: Long history of frustration and failure. Almost a female in general behavior, but of the weak, shy, mousy sort. He got through college (standing, second decile) by majoring in art, but has never had a job or a plan. Passive homosexual. He is emotionally very grateful for any kindness.

No. 74   Age 24   Race N-M   Ht 72   Wt 150   Somato 3-3²-5 type

1—335	
2—335	d-14
3—345	g-2.2
4—335	t-2.5
5—244	

IT 2-4-5   V 50   S 79   C 101   Health 7   Strength C 5
Strength P 7   PI 2   IQ   AI 3   S 5   Gp 2
Comment: An intent, resolute person. Graduate student in social science. He has been an ardent communist but is now an equally ardent proponent of the "rights of labor." A brilliant academic record (tenth decile). Note the unusual peripheral strength.

No. 75　Age 21　Race M　Ht 67　Wt 121　Somato 3-3²-5　type

```
1—435
2—345  d-10
3—345  g-3.0
4—335  t-2.5
5—335
```

IT 4-3-5　V 77　S 64　C 96　Health 5　Strength C 2
Strength P 2　PI 2　IQ 139　AI 5　S 4　Gp 4

Comment: A rather well-relaxed, good-natured youth who is yet fragile and sensitive, and has a brilliant college record. He is known as a softie and is teased a good deal by classmates, but he takes it well. Plans to study law. Now very close to the top of the senior class. Academic standing, tenth decile.

No. 76　Age 21　Race M-A　Ht 68　Wt 126　Somato 3-3-5　type

```
1—334
2—335  d-4
3—335  g-2.5
4—335  t-3.5
5—335
```

IT 3-3-5　V 62　S 67　C 94　Health 7　Strength C 3
Strength P 4　PI 3　IQ　AI 6　S 6　Gp 2

Comment: A quiet, well-liked youth does things well but gives little present indication of brilliance. In the seventh decile scholastically. He is an outdoorsman and a naturalist. Seems much younger than he is.

No. 77　Age 20　Race M-N　Ht 67　Wt 122　Somato 3²-3-5　type

```
1—434
2—435  d-10
3—335  g-3.0
4—435  t-1.5
5—335
```

IT 3-2-5　V 69　S 48　C 97　Health 5　Strength C 2
Strength P 3　PI 1　IQ 134　AI 3　S 5　Gp 5

Comment: A weak, affectionate personality. Romantic and idealistic but without much strength in any quarter. Excessively poor physical coordination. Walks with an exaggerated up and down spring. Throws like a girl. Fifth decile in scholastic standing.

No. 78　Age 23　Race N-M　Ht 66　Wt 116　Somato 3-3-5　type

```
1—345
2—235  d-24
3—435  g-2.2
4—334  t-2.0
5—326
```

IT 3-3-4　V 61　S 66　C 80　Health 6　Strength C 3
Strength P 2　PI 2　IQ　AI 2　S 4　Gp 3

Comment: Rather a passive or negative person, although sensitive and shy. Lacks fire. No particular ambition. Has done fairly well scholastically. Now a graduate student in social service administration. Undergraduate record, eighth decile.

No. 79 Age 21 Race N-A Ht 67 Wt 129 Somato 3-4-3²

1—334	
2—443	d-26
3—343	g-1.4
4—254	t-1.3
5—253	

type

IT 3-5-4 V 65 S 95 C 78 Health 5 Strength C 4
Strength P 4 PI 3 IQ 131 AI 1.5 S 3 Gp 2
Comment: An undergraduate in the School of Business. Considered aggressive and alert. Has a supporting scholarship. Seventh decile in academic standing. His dean predicts a good future for him. Liked better by the faculty than by other students.

No. 80 Age 24 Race A-M Ht 66 Wt 125 Somato 3-4-3

1—343	
2—343	d-8
3—253	g-1.6
4—343	t-1.4
5—343	

type

IT 2-5-3 V 49 S 99 C 60 Health 6 Strength C 4
Strength P 4 PI 4 IQ AI 1 S 3 Gp 1
Comment: A rather hard-boiled or tough-minded medical student. Aggressive, unpleasant, hard-working and reliable. He dislikes and is disliked by most of his acquaintances. Academic standing, sixth decile.

No. 81 Age 30 Race M-A Ht 66 Wt 138 Somato 3²-4²-3

1—453	
2—452	d-16
3—353	g-1.6
4—343	t-1.4
5—343	

type

IT 4-5-2 V 76 S 94 C 51 Health 5 Strength C 4
Strength P 3 PI 4 IQ AI 1 S 2 Gp 2
Comment: An aggressive and fairly successful insurance salesman. Noted for his remarkable memory for names and personal data, in which he takes pride. He is agreeable but would be considered tiresome by many. A great bowler. A quick mind, but no intellectual interests. Garrulous.

No. 82 Age 25 Race M-N Ht 69 Wt 143 Somato 3-4-3²

1—344	
2—343	d-6
3—344	g-2.0
4—343	t-1.9
5—343	

type

IT 3-4-4 V 65 S 79 C 82 Health 4 Strength C 5
Strength P 4 PI 3 IQ AI 2 S 4 Gp 2
Comment: An up and coming young journalist. Has a very wide acquaintanceship, is bright and observant, cynical, sophisticated, and on the whole well liked. Father of three children. Undergraduate record, eighth decile.

```
                                                1—344
                                                2—343  d-4
No. 83  Age 25  Race A-M  Ht 68  Wt 135  Somato  3-4-3   3—343  g-1.8
                                          type          4—343  t-2.2
                                                5—343
```

IT 3-4-3 **V** 64 **S** 85 **C** 61 **Health** 5 **Strength C** 4
Strength P 4 **PI** 4 **IQ** 124 **AI** 2 **S** 2 **Gp** 1
Comment: Graduate student in physics, and considered a good one. Unprepossessing in appearance. Weak eyes and receding chin, but well regarded by the faculty. Undergraduate record, seventh decile. His interests are very limited. Morally of the harmless, safe sort.

```
                                                1—343
                                                2—443  d-8
No. 84  Age 24  Race N-A  Ht 67  Wt 131  Somato  3-4-3   3—343  g-1.5
                                          type          4—343  t-2.0
                                                5—353
```

IT 3-5-3 **V** 67 **S** 92 **C** 70 **Health** 6 **Strength C** 3
Strength P 4 **PI** 4 **IQ** 117 **AI** 1 **S** 2 **Gp** 1
Comment: A run-of-the-mill medical student. Slightly below average in academic standing (fourth decile) but above average in industry and in the faithful carrying out of assignments. Considered insensitive and unpleasantly aggressive by some.

```
                                                1—344
                                                2—443  d-10
No. 85  Age 20  Race A-M  Ht 69  Wt 146  Somato  3²-4-3  3—443  g-2.4
                                          type          4—443  t-2.2
                                                5—343
```

IT 4-4-4 **V** 78 **S** 84 **C** 80 **Health** 5 **Strength C** 4
Strength P 4 **PI** 2 **IQ** 139 **AI** 2 **S** 4 **Gp** 2
Comment: A perplexed, somewhat confused undergraduate, who has not yet found himself. Has shown interest and ability in half a dozen directions, but as yet has no vocational orientation. His IQ is high but his academic record is in the fourth decile. A very pleasant youth.

```
                                                1—262
                                                2—343  d-22
No. 86  Age 18  Race J  Ht 66  Wt 127  Somato  3-4²-3   3—453  g-1.7
                                        type          4—343  t-1.3
                                                5—343
```

IT 2-6-3 **V** 42 **S** 109 **C** 59 **Health** 6 **Strength C** 4
Strength P 3 **PI** 5 **IQ** 128 **AI** 1 **S** 2 **Gp** 2
Comment: Well-developed somatorosis. Excessively aggressive, with high energy. Troublesome, noisy, and truculent. Academic standing, second decile. Plans to study law.

1—244
2—344 d-14
No. 87 Age 21 Race N Ht 72 Wt 155 Somato 3-4-4^2 3—344 g-1.9
                                          type   4—345 t-2.5
5—335

IT 2-4-5 **V** 41 **S** 83 **C** 92 **Health** 7 **Strength C** 4
Strength P 6 **PI** 2 **IQ** 148 **AI** 3 **S** 5 **Gp** 1
Comment: A senior, considered one of the influential young men on the campus. Captain of the debating team. Brilliant academic record (tenth decile). Excellent prospects. To enter the field of international relations. Something of an idealist.

1—334
2—344 d-12
No. 88 Age 25 Race N-M Ht 69 Wt 140 Somato 3-4-4 3—245 g-1.8
                                          type   4—344 t-3.5
5—344

IT 3-4-5 **V** 64 **S** 75 **C** 93 **Health** 6 **Strength C** 3
Strength P 5 **PI** 3 **IQ** **AI** 5 **S** 5 **Gp** 2
Comment: A gifted young man, but seems to be a victim of too many gifts. Excellent undergraduate record (ninth decile). One year of graduate work in the philosophy department. Good record there but shifted to physiology and neurology. Good record there also but after eighteen months shifted to chemistry. Unhappy in chemistry.

1—354
2—354 d-14
No. 89 Age 27 Race N-A Ht 71 Wt 158 Somato 3-4^2-4 3—344 g-1.4
                                          type   4—253 t-2.3
5—344

IT 2-5-4 **V** 48 **S** 101 **C** 76 **Health** 7 **Strength C** 5
Strength P 5 **PI** 3 **IQ** **AI** 2 **S** 4 **Gp** 3
Comment: A young lawyer of good achievement and excellent promise. He is of a somewhat idealistic sort, interested chiefly in social legislation and similar uplift. Undergraduate record, eighth decile.

1—344
2—344 d-4
No. 90 Age 24 Race N Ht 69 Wt 141 Somato 3-4-4 3—334 g-1.7
                                          type   4—344 t-2.5
5—344

IT 2-4-4 **V** 51 **S** 81 **C** 77 **Health** 7 **Strength C** 3
Strength P 5 **PI** 2 **IQ** **AI** 3 **S** 4 **Gp** 2
Comment: A very unhappy senior theological student. Much disillusioned about his chosen profession. He likes theology but cannot preach convincingly and lacks the viscerotonia for "pastoral work." Will probably become a sociologist. Undergraduate record, fifth decile.

	1—343	
	2—344	d-10
No. 91 Age 27 Race N-A Ht 73 Wt 174 Somato 3-4²-4	3—344	g-1.8
type	4—354	t-2.0
	5—354	

IT 3-5-4   **V** 63   **S** 93   **C** 79   **Health** 7   **Strength C** 5
Strength P 4   **PI** 5   **IQ AI** 2   **S** 5   **Gp** 2

Comment: A vigorous, energetic, successful young educator. Teaching high school and coaching athletics. Good tennis player. Mediocre (fifth decile) undergraduate record. Ran on the track team, middle distance runner.

	1—244	
	2—344	d-8
No. 92 Age 23 Race N Ht 70 Wt 146 Somato 3-4-4	3—345	g-2.0
type	4—344	t-2.0
	5—344	

IT 3-4-4   **V** 70   **S** 80   **C** 76   **Health** 6   **Strength C** 4
Strength P 5   **PI** 3   **IQ AI** 2   **S** 4   **Gp** 2

Comment: A wealthy youth who after finishing college with only a fair (sixth decile) record, spent a year abroad and now is "tasting" in academic political science. He will probably enter a manufacturing concern owned by his father. An average young man, with no striking characteristics.

	1—444	
	2—434	d-14
No. 93 Age 24 Race N-M Ht 72 Wt 163 Somato 3²-4-4	3—344	g-2.4
type	4—444	t-2.5
	5—345	

IT 3-4-5   **V** 67   **S** 85   **C** 90   **Health** 7   **Strength C** 5
Strength P 5   **PI** 3   **IQ AI** 5   **S** 5   **Gp** 3

Comment: A perplexed, intellectually gifted and ambitious youth who has not yet found himself. He wants to be a writer but does not quite know what he wants to write. Now a graduate student in social psychology. Academic record, ninth decile. He seems youthful, is shy, and has an excellent humorous insight.

	1—354	
	2—344	d-10
No. 94 Age 24 Race M-N Ht 69 Wt 144 Somato 3-4²-4	3—344	g-1.6
type	4—254	t-1.4
	5—354	

IT 2-5-3   **V** 50   **S** 99   **C** 62   **Health** 6   **Strength C** 5
Strength P 3   **PI** 3   **IQ** 102   **AI** 1   **S** 2   **Gp** 1

Comment: A practical young man who has set out to make money. Left college in second year, poor (second decile) record. Now running a small cooperative which markets dairy products. Doing fairly well. He has few distractions, and no intellectual interests.

1—344	
2—344	d-6

No. 95   Age 21   Race N   Ht 67   Wt 132   Somato 3^2-4-4   3—344   g-2.0
                                              type   4—444   t-1.6
                                                                5—444

IT 4-4-3   V 76   S 82   C 61   Health 5   Strength C 3
Strength P 3   PI 3   IQ 107   AI 1.5   S 3   Gp 3

Comment: An undergraduate who is failing badly (first decile) in his courses, although he seems to try sincerely enough. Mediocre high school record. Sociable and extremely well liked. He has been given several "second chances."

1—343	
2—444	d-18

No. 96   Age 24   Race N-M   Ht 68   Wt 141   Somato 3-4^2-4   3—344   g-1.6
                                                type   4—354   t-1.8
                                                                  5—254

IT 3-5-3   V 65   S 95   C 68   Health 6   Strength C 4
Strength P 4   PI 4   IQ   AI 2   S 3   Gp 2

Comment: A promising young graduate student in agricultural engineering. Conspicuously energetic and favorably considered everywhere. Undergraduate record, fifth decile. He gets things done on time, is levelheaded and even-tempered.

1—334	
2—245	d-14

No. 97   Age 26   Race N-M   Ht 71   Wt 150   Somato 3-4-4^2 3—345   g-2.8
                                                type   4—344   t-1.8
                                                                  5—344

IT 3-3-5   V 58   S 68   C 93   Health 7   Strength C 3
Strength P 5   PI 2   IQ   AI 3   S 5   Gp 2

Comment: A weak, emotionally unstable young man who appears immature for his age and has not shown any intellectual promise. Graduate student in the School of Education. He is concerned about his "secret sinfulness." Undergraduate record, third decile.

1—444	
2—344	d-4

No. 98   Age 25   Race N   Ht 74   Wt 175   Somato 3-4-4   3—344   g-2.2
                                              type   4—344   t-2.5
                                                              5—344

IT 4-4-4   V 75   S 84   C 83   Health 5   Strength C 4
Strength P 4   PI 4   IQ 136   AI 2   S 3   Gp 2

Comment: A beau brummell of this academic community. He is tall, smooth, almost sleek, and very genial. Now slender, although he will be heavier later. He ran several undergraduate organizations and now as a graduate in political science is a conspicuous figure. Ambition, diplomatic service. Undergraduate record, eighth decile.

1—344		
2—344	d-14	
3—344	g-2.8	
4—443	t-2.0	
5—434		

No. 99   **Age** 23   **Race** M-N   **Ht** 72   **Wt** 166   **Somato** 3^2-4-4   **type**

IT 4-3-4   **V** 79   **S** 63   **C** 84   **Health** 6   **Strength C** 4
Strength P 5   **PI** 3   **IQ**   **AI** 2   **S** 4   **Gp** 3

Comment: A pleasant, agreeable, but intellectually flabby young graduate student in psychology. There is no temper in his mental steel (trait V-16), although he learns well and has almost an excellent scholastic standing. Undergraduate record, ninth decile.

1—345		
2—345	d-8	
3—345	g-4.2	
4—435	t-2.4	
5—345		

No. 100   **Age** 25   **Race** N   **Ht** 71   **Wt** 146   **Somato** 3-4-5   **type**

IT 3-3-6   **V** 63   **S** 58   **C** 107   **Health** 6   **Strength C** 3
Strength P 4   **PI** 1   **IQ** 149   **AI** 5   **S** 6   **Gp** 4

Comment: Conspicuously cerebrotic (apprehensive, strained, self-conscious), with intermittent spells of viscerosis. Shows flashes of original and brilliant thinking, but is torn between being a scientist and an aesthete. Just now registered as a graduate student in journalism. Has fought homosexuality for years, with intermittent relapses, but is also heterosexual.

1—344		
2—345	d-4	
3—345	g-1.8	
4—345	t-2.4	
5—345		

No. 101   **Age** 26   **Race** N   **Ht** 69   **Wt** 134   **Somato** 3-4-5   **type**

IT 3-4-4   **V** 59   **S** 78   **C** 97   **Health** 7   **Strength C** 3
Strength P 5   **PI** 3   **IQ**   **AI** 3   **S** 4   **Gp** 2

Comment: Regarded as one of the most promising young scientists on the campus. Now a research assistant in physiological chemistry. Sane and secure in his emotional outlook, with excellent, rather cynical humor. Brilliant academic record, tenth decile.

1—352		
2—352	d-10	
3—353	g-1.8	
4—452	t-2.0	
5—452		

No. 102   **Age** 23   **Race** J   **Ht** 67   **Wt** 150   **Somato** 3^2-5-2   **type**

IT 4-5-2   **V** 80   **S** 99   **C** 41   **Health** 6   **Strength C** 6
Strength P 4   **PI** 5   **IQ**   **AI** 1.5   **S** 2   **Gp** 2

Comment: A hard-driving but sociophilic freshman medical student. Good-natured and tolerant. Well liked. Dependable rather than brilliant. Will almost certainly succeed and will grow fat. He seems easygoing but actually works with great energy. Undergraduate record, seventh decile.

                                                        1—261
                                                        2—352 d-14
No. 103   Age 21   Race J   Ht 64   Wt 130   Somato 3-5²-2   3—362 g-1.4
                                             type   4—352 t-1.4
                                                        5—362

IT 2-7-1   V 53   S 126   C 32   Health 7   Strength C 5
Strength P 3   PI 3   IQ 125   AI 1   S 2   Gp 2

Comment: An unusually conspicuous somatorosis. Excessive aggression in all areas of expression. Possibly a case of somatorotic overcompensation for short stature, but it should be noted that such overcompensation seems to occur only when the second component predominates morphologically. An undergraduate majoring in psychology. Academic record, sixth decile.

                                                        1—353
                                                        2—452 d-12
No. 104   Age 22   Race A-N   Ht 68   Wt 153   Somato 3²-5-2²   3—352 g-2.0
                                               type   4—452 t-1.6
                                                        5—353

IT 3-5-3   V 58   S 96   C 67   Health 6   Strength C 5
Strength P 4   PI 5   IQ 109   AI 1.5   S 3   Gp 2

Comment: A graduate student of physical education who is not quite sufficiently mesomorphic or sufficiently somatotonic for this work as it is conventionally taught. He is unhappy, feels inferior, and will probably drop out. Undergraduate record, fifth decile.

                                                        1—353
                                                        2—352 d-14
No. 105   Age 24   Race M-A   Ht 68   Wt 152   Somato 3-5-2²   3—352 g-3.5
                                               type   4—352 t-3.0
                                                        5—443

IT 4-4-3   V 86   S 77   C 61   Health 6   Strength C 7
Strength P 5   PI 3   IQ   AI 3   S 5   Gp 3

Comment: A rather subtle, substantial young man who is now a graduate student in philosophy. He is almost "pretty," with secondary gynandromorphy in his face (long eyelashes, cupid mouth, fine-textured skin, pink complexion). Yet he is physically solid and sturdy. Will probably not stay in philosophy. Undergraduate record, eighth decile.

                                                        1—352
                                                        2—352 d-8
No. 106   Age 25   Race A   Ht 66   Wt 142   Somato 3-5-2   3—352 g-2.4
                                             type   4—452 t-2.5
                                                        5—362

IT 3-6-2   V 84   S 110   C 50   Health 6   Strength C 5
Strength P 4   PI 5   IQ   AI 2   S 3   Gp 1

Comment: A graduate student in psychology who shows a moderate somatorosis. He is aggressive enough to be offensive to many, and suffers from his resulting unpopularity. Undergraduate record, eighth decile. A dependable student. He has a duodenal ulcer.

```
                                                    1—453
                                                    2—453   d-18
No. 107  Age 24  Race A-M  Ht 69  Wt 158  Somato 3²-5-3   3—453   g-2.2
                                          type      4—353   t-1.8
                                                    5—353
```

IT 4-5-3 **V** 80 **S** 91 **C** 66 **Health** 7 **Strength C** 5
Strength P 5 **PI** 5 **IQ** **AI** 2 **S** 3 **Gp** 2
Comment: A happily adjusted student of dairying in the School of Agriculture. He is good-natured, is considered tolerant, and is popular. He loves the smell of the barnyard. Undergraduate record, sixth decile. He has a highly palatable, salty good humor, with a rich barnyard flavor.

```
                                                    1—353
                                                    2—353   d-4
No. 108  Age 25  Race N-A  Ht 71  Wt 167  Somato 3-5-3   3—354   g-1.8
                                          type      4—353   t-2.3
                                                    5—353
```

IT 3-5-4 **V** 61 **S** 98 **C** 78 **Health** 5 **Strength C** 5
Strength P 6 **PI** 4 **IQ** **AI** 2 **S** 4 **Gp** 2
Comment: A handsome, well-liked young man who has already begun to make a mark for himself in forestry. He is a little shy and self-conscious, especially among women, but is not cerebrotic. Undergraduate record, sixth decile.

```
                                                    1—354
                                                    2—353   d-6
No. 109  Age 23  Race N-A  Ht 70  Wt 160  Somato 3-5-3²   3—354   g-1.8
                                          type      4—353   t-2.0
                                                    5—353
```

IT 3-5-4 **V** 41 **S** 103 **C** 72 **Health** 5 **Strength C** 5
Strength P 5 **PI** 5 **IQ** **AI** 1.5 **S** 4 **Gp** 2
Comment: An energetic, big-boned youth who is trying unsuccessfully to be an insurance salesman. He is too self-conscious and conscientious for this work in a city, although he plans to return to his own small town in the Southwest, and hopes to succeed there. Undergraduate record, fourth decile.

```
                                                    1—353
                                                    2—453   d-6
No. 110  Age 26  Race A-N  Ht 67  Wt 146  Somato 3²-5-3   3—353   g-1.9
                                          type      4—453   t-2.1
                                                    5—453
```

IT 4-5-3 **V** 82 **S** 91 **C** 64 **Health** 5 **Strength C** 5
Strength P 4 **PI** 4 **IQ** **AI** 1.5 **S** 2 **Gp** 1
Comment: A well-liked and well-considered young instructor in the School of Engineering. He is a most pleasant and thorough teacher, greatly admired by his students. Undergraduate record, ninth decile. Most conservative in outlook. Slow spoken, deliberate, steady. Humorless as the Sphinx.

1—452
2—353   d-10
No. 111   Age 25   Race J   Ht 65   Wt 135   Somato 3²-5-3   3—353   g-1.8
                                             type   4—453   t-1.8
                                                          5—453

IT 3-6-2   V 59   S 112   C 40   Health 6   Strength C 5
Strength P 4   PI 4   IQ   AI 1   S 3   Gp 2
Comment: A somewhat somatorotic law student. Harsh and intolerant, with an unmellow social philosophy, but he is bright and is well considered by his faculty. Hated by many student contemporaries. Undergraduate record, ninth decile.

1—443
2—453   d-16
No. 112   Age 25   Race N-A   Ht 70   Wt 160   Somato 3²-5-3²   3—453   g-3.0
                                               type   4—354   t-2.3
                                                              5—354

IT 4-4-4   V 75   S 83   C 78   Health 4   Strength C 4
Strength P 4   PI 3   IQ 116   AI 2   S 2   Gp 3
Comment: Graduate student in social science. Singularly soft-spoken and polite. A very proper, conventional person, yet possessing a fairly alert mind and good work habits. A "pet" of one of the influential professors. Academic standing, seventh decile.

1—254
2—344   d-8
No. 113   Age 21   Race N   Ht 68   Wt 144   Somato 3-5-4   3—354   g-2.2
                                             type   4--354   t-2.0
                                                          5—354

IT 4-5-3   V 83   S 94   C 59   Health 5   Strength C 5
Strength P 6   PI 3   IQ 110   AI 2   S 3   Gp 2
Comment: Recently dropped from college in his junior year for low grades. He is somewhat viscerotic (overly sociable in particular), habitually wasting his time in idle social gatherings, beer drinking and the like.

1—354
2—354   d-16
No. 114   Age 21   Race N-A   Ht 73   Wt 176   Somato 3-5-4   3—354   g-1.4
                                               type   4—344   t-2.4
                                                            5—263

IT 2-6-3   V 49   S 114   C 59   Health 6   Strength C 5
Strength P 6   PI 5   IQ   AI 2   S 4   Gp 2
Comment: President of the senior class. Tennis captain. Excellent (tenth decile) academic record. After striving unsuccessfully for two years to make the football team, he turned to tennis, where he achieved great success. His surplus somatotonia thus goes into conventional athletics. He is popular, and is regarded as modest.

```
                                              1—362
                                              2—345  d-22
No. 115  Age 23  Race N  Ht 66  Wt 133  Somato 3-5-4  3—354  g-3.0
                                        type   4—354  t-1.9
                                              5—344
```

IT 3-6-3 V 62 S 108 C 61 Health 4 Strength C 4
Strength P 3 PI 2 IQ 119 AI 1.5 S 2 Gp 2

Comment: An overly aggressive youth who has not yet found an occupational program and is strained, unhappy. He wants to be an aviator, but also is intellectually ambitious. He has made several false starts toward academic enterprises. Graduated from college with a mediocre (fifth decile) record. Now enrolled for graduate work in chemistry.

```
                                              1—353
                                              2—354  d-12
No. 116  Age 23  Race N  Ht 73  Wt 178  Somato 3-5-4  3—354  g-3.0
                                        type   4—354  t-3.5
                                              5—444
```

IT 4-4-4 V 79 S 77 C 85 Health 5 Strength C 5
Strength P 6 PI 3 IQ 143 AI 5 S 5 Gp 4

Comment: Formerly a campus leader but now as a senior he has become something of an aesthete and has also developed into an overt homosexual. Pleasant, sociable, and intelligent, but a sissy. A student of literature. Academic standing, tenth decile.

```
                                              1—271
                                              2—362  d-14
No. 117  Age 21  Race A  Ht 71  Wt 204  Somato 3-6²-1  3—361  g-1.6
                                        type   4—361  t-1.3
                                              5—371
```

IT 3-7-1 V 58 S 129 C 30 Health 6 Strength C 7
Strength P 5 PI 7 IQ 101 AI 1 S 2 Gp 1

Comment: The pride of the university. An All-American football player. He is jovial, hearty, pleasantly aggressive and good-natured. Has not yet begun to grow fat, since he keeps in physical training. Academic standing, second decile. He has a thin, shrill, rather harsh voice (as do many of this general physical pattern).

```
                                              1—362
                                              2—352  d-14
No. 118  Age 24  Race A  Ht 69  Wt 174  Somato 3-6-1²  3—362  g-2.4
                                        type   4—461  t-2.2
                                              5—361
```

IT 4-5-2 V 83 S 101 C 40 Health 6 Strength C 6
Strength P 5 PI 4 IQ AI 1.5 S 2 Gp 2

Comment: An industrious medical student. Very popular, hard-working, and highly regarded by his faculty. Tolerant and complacent in outward expression, but he drives himself constantly. Excellent habits of work. Academic record, eighth decile.

1—461
2—451   d-14
No. 119   Age 24   Race J   Ht 64   Wt 162   Somato 3²-6-1   3—361   g-1.5
type   4—461   t-1.1
5—371

IT 4-7-1   V 74   S 127   C 35   Health 7   Strength C 5
Strength P 3   PI 2   IQ   AI 1   S 2   Gp 1

Comment: An excessively somatotonic medical student. Called "the blight" by some of his fellow students, but well regarded by many of his faculty. He works prodigiously and is invariably in the forefront of what is going on. He is extremely hirsute. Highly sociable in his own group. Academic record, seventh decile.

1—362
2—362   d-0
No. 120   Age 21   Race A-N   Ht 71   Wt 183   Somato 3-6-2   3—362   g-2.2
type   4—362   t-2.5
5—362

IT 4-5-2   V 77   S 94   C 45   Health 6   Strength C 7
Strength P 5   PI 7   IQ 136   AI 2   S 2   Gp 2

Comment: A popular blond youth who is both on the football team and high in academic standing (ninth decile). Jovial, a natural leader, and full of fun. He is considered modest. He does his work faithfully and systematically, rather than in brilliant spurts. Has the happy knack of being aggressive without being manifestly so.

1—362
2—362   d-4
No. 121   Age 22   Race A-N   Ht 66   Wt 147   Somato 3-6-2   3—362   g-1.2
type   4—362   t-1.6
5—361

IT 2-7-1   V 41   S 125   C 36   Health 7   Strength C 6
Strength P 4   PI 7   IQ 115   AI 1   S 2   Gp 1

Comment: An excessively somatotonic undergraduate of short stature, who desires to enter the profession of physical education or athletic coaching. His short stature may be a handicap there. However, he is a star forward on the basketball team. He is a dynamo of energy. Scholastic standing, third decile.

1—453
2—362   d-22
No. 122   Age 22   Race J   Ht 71   Wt 183   Somato 3-6-2   3—352   g-3.5
type   4—371   t-1.6
5—362

IT 2-6-3   V 52   S 110   C 57   Health 5   Strength C 6
Strength P 5   PI 6   IQ 128   AI 2   S 4   Gp 3

Comment: A highly somatotonic but also somewhat cerebrotic youth who suffers from a number of "functional" bodily ailments. Exceedingly aggressive, yet strained, tense and self-conscious. He is a substitute on the swimming team. Greatly confused about his plans and his vocational future. Academic standing, seventh decile.

No. 123 Age 19 Race M Ht 67 Wt 125 Somato 4-2-4²
                                        type

1—415	
2—325	d-14
3—424	g-3.5
4—424	t-1.6
5—424	

IT 3-2-5 V 70 S 42 C 99 Health 6 Strength C 3
Strength P 2 PI 1 IQ 135 AI 4 S 4 Gp 5

Comment: A weak, baffled undergraduate to whom college is like a bad dream. He wants to cry on somebody's shoulder but instead, is required to attend gymnasium classes. He is as shy and fearful as a mouse, and seems younger than he is. He seems too young and immature to be in college. No vocational plans. Academic standing, sixth decile.

No. 124 Age 23 Race M Ht 66 Wt 129 Somato 4-2-4
                                        type

1—424	
2—424	d-4
3—424	g-4.0
4—524	t-1.8
5—424	

IT 5-1-4 V 93 S 32 C 83 Health 5 Strength C 1
Strength P 2 PI 1 IQ 109 AI 3 S 4 Gp 7

Comment: A viscerotic young graduate student in art and literature. Overly sociophilic, effeminate, soft as a jellyfish. Loves small talk. He has a homosexual inclination but is not overtly homosexual. Academic record, second decile.

No. 125 Age 25 Race M-N Ht 69 Wt 144 Somato 4²-2-4²
                                          type

1—425	
2—425	d-12
3—425	g-4.0
4—524	t-2.6
5—524	

IT 4-2-5 V 84 S 50 C 91 Health 6 Strength C 2
Strength P 4 PI 2 IQ AI 5 S 7 Gp 5

Comment: A graduate student and assistant in botany. Always a weak and rather arty person. Undergraduate record, eighth decile. Shy and secretive. Now an overt homosexual but also heterosexual.

No. 126 Age 19 Race M-N Ht 67 Wt 125 Somato 4-2-5
                                          type

1—326	
2—424	d-16
3—415	g-6.0
4—425	t-3.0
5—425	

IT 3-1-5 V 69 S 29 C 100 Health 1 Strength C 1
Strength P 1 PI 1 IQ 94 AI 4 S 1 Gp 7

Comment: An excessively weak, fragile, soft person. Looks and behaves much like a girl. Has never shown any initiative but did passing scholastic work in high school. Became confused during the first months of college. Tentative mental hospital diagnosis: hebephrenic schizophrenia. The arms are singularly delicate and fragile, almost flaccid. He now has pulmonary tuberculosis. He is hypogenital.

1—425
2—425   d-4
No. 127   Age 26   Race N-M   Ht 71   Wt 155   Somato 4-2-5   3—425   g-3.8
type   4—424   t-2.5
5—425

IT 4-2-4   **V** 83   **S** 43   **C** 80   **Health** 6   **Strength C** 2
Strength P 2   **PI** 2   **IQ**   **AI** 5   **S** 4   **Gp** 4

Comment: A promising young biological scientist. Graduated from college with highest honors and has turned out brilliant research work in bacteriology. Now also studying in the medical school. Yet his physical energy is low. Normal sexual outlook. Called a sissy as a boy.

1—444
2—425   d-14
No. 128   Age 25   Race M   Ht 68   Wt 132   Somato 4-2^2-5   3—425   g-2.8
type   4—435   t-1.6
5—425

IT 4-3-4   **V** 75   **S** 66   **C** 79   **Health** 7   **Strength C** 2
Strength P 3   **PI** 3   **IQ**   **AI** 3   **S** 3   **Gp** 4

Comment: A medical student of good promise. The dean of the medical school calls him one of the brightest men in the third year class. He is always aloof, and is considered effeminate. Extremely shy and unhappy as a child, but has made a good adaptation in recent years. Undergraduate record, tenth decile.

1—434
2—433   d-14
No. 129   Age 22   Race M-A   Ht 70   Wt 152   Somato 4-3-3^2 3—424   g-3.5
type   4—533   t-1.6
5—434

IT 5-2-4   **V** 94   **S** 46   **C** 76   **Health** 5   **Strength C** 3
Strength P 2   **PI** 2   **IQ** 118   **AI** 3   **S** 4   **Gp** 5

Comment: Now a senior. Rather lazy, viscerotic, overly dependent on people. Insecure and self-conscious. No formulated plans. Regarded by other students as effeminate and uninteresting. Halfheartedly studying philosophy. Academic standing, fourth decile.

1—433
2—433   d-4
No. 130   Age 23   Race M   Ht 70   Wt 155   Somato 4-3-3   3—433   g-2.6
type   4—433   t-1.9
5—434

IT 3-3-4   **V** 68   **S** 60   **C** 81   **Health** 4   **Strength C** 3
Strength P 2   **PI** 1   **IQ** 114   **AI** 2   **S** 2   **Gp** 3

Comment: An apologetic, self-depreciative graduate student in education. He has a shapeless, fat face with a thin neck, and wears thick glasses. Is called kindhearted by his friends. Academic record, fourth decile.

1—444
2—433 d-12
No. 131 Age 22 **Race** M-N **Ht** 70 **Wt** 153 **Somato** 4-3²-3² 3—444 g-2.2
type 4—433 t-1.8
5—444

IT 4-4-4 **V** 79 **S** 81 **C** 84 **Health** 6 **Strength** C 4
Strength P 3 **PI** 3 **IQ** 138 **AI** 2 **S** 4 **Gp** 2

Comment: An undergraduate who has many interests but no central interest. He goes to everything but is never more than a hanger-on. No vocational plan. Loves to discuss himself. A nuisance to faculty advisers because of his mental fickleness and lack of intellectual anchorage. He seems to learn easily in all fields. Academic standing, seventh decile.

1—434
2—435 d-8
No. 132 Age 22 **Race** M **Ht** 71 **Wt** 156 **Somato** 4-3-4 3—434 g-2.0
type 4—444 t-1.8
5—434

IT 3-4-4 **V** 58 **S** 80 **C** 87 **Health** 5 **Strength** C 3
Strength P 3 **PI** 2 **IQ** 127 **AI** 2 **S** 5 **Gp** 2

Comment: An unhappy senior who is considered tactless and aggressive. Actually insecure and apprehensive. He has a knack of rubbing people the wrong way. He craves friendship but his close associates are recruited only from the tag end. No plans. Academic standing, seventh decile.

1—433
2—434 d-12
No. 133 Age 19 **Race** M-N **Ht** 68 **Wt** 138 **Somato** 4-3-4 3—434 g-3.0
type 4—434 t-2.4
5—524

IT 5-3-3 **V** 94 **S** 65 **C** 67 **Health** 6 **Strength** C 3
Strength P 2 **PI** 3 **IQ** 120 **AI** 2 **S** 1 **Gp** 3

Comment: A good-natured, lazy, viscerotonic undergraduate who cannot be bothered about things. He has a good time, spreads good cheer, and contemplates life complacently. Academic standing, third decile. No plans. He is hypogenital.

1—334
2—434 d-14
No. 134 Age 25 **Race** M **Ht** 68 **Wt** 136 **Somato** 4-3-4² 3—434 g-3.6
type 4—425 t-1.8
5—435

IT 3-2-5 **V** 66 **S** 45 **C** 101 **Health** 2 **Strength** C 2
Strength P 3 **PI** 1 **IQ** **AI** 1.5 **S** 2 **Gp** 4

Comment: A weak young man of mediocre (sixth decile) academic record who has taught school a year and now seeks an M. A. degree in education. Plans to teach history in high school as a profession. He teaches Sunday school. He has had poor health, being peculiarly susceptible to digestive trouble and "food poisoning."

```
                                                          1—353
                                                          2—434  d-24
No. 135   Age 21   Race M   Ht 67   Wt 133   Somato 4-3²-4   3—434  g-1.8
                                               type       4—435  t-1.9
                                                          5—443
```

IT 4-4-3   V 78   S 79   C 62   Health 6   Strength C 4
Strength P 5   PI 4   IQ 116   AI 1   S 3   Gp 2

Comment: This youth has been a nuisance to himself. Rules of any sort are only an irritant to him. He feels constrained to break rules flauntingly. As a high school boy he was once arrested for stealing an automobile. Recently expelled from college for drunkenness. History of alcoholism since adolescence.

```
                                                          1—435
                                                          2—434  d-10
No. 136   Age 22   Race J   Ht 71   Wt 152   Somato 4-3-4²   3—424  g-2.5
                                               type       4—435  t-2.0
                                                          5—435
```

IT 3-3-5   V 67   S 62   C 98   Health 5   Strength C 3
Strength P 3   PI 2   IQ   AI 3   S 2   Gp 2

Comment: An undergraduate Jewish boy who is shy and considers himself an aesthete. He has made something of a religion of "discriminative taste." He is a symphony addict. Will sit for hours in almost a catatonic state listening to music and daydreaming. Academic standing, sixth decile. Now studying in the School of Business.

```
                                                          1—435
                                                          2—435  d-4
No. 137   Age 26   Race M-N   Ht 73   Wt 164   Somato 4-3-5   3—435  g-3.2
                                               type       4—425  t-2.5
                                                          5—435
```

IT 3-2-5   V 71   S 42   C 98   Health 5   Strength C 2
Strength P 3   PI 2   IQ 122   AI 1.5   S 3   Gp 4

Comment: A weak, flaccid sort of individual who yet is in a sense successful. He is polite, conservative, adaptive, and exercises the most thoughtful care never to offend. Now a doctor of philosophy in psychology and holds an assistant professorship. Undergraduate record, seventh decile. He pleases most of his superiors but is considered a bore by his students.

```
                                                          1—344
                                                          2—435  d-12
No. 138   Age 24   Race M-N   Ht 70   Wt 144   Somato 4-3-5   3—435  g-2.6
                                               type       4—435  t-2.8
                                                          5—435
```

IT 3-4-4   V 63   S 77   C 84   Health 7   Strength C 3
Strength P 4   PI 3   IQ   AI 4   S 5   Gp 3

Comment: A rather brilliant young graduate student of social science who regards himself as a misunderstood genius. He is humorous and is usually aggressive at the wrong time. He continually offends people. But his closest acquaintances swear by him. Academic record, tenth decile.

```
                                                1—444
                                                2—435   d-12
No. 139  Age 24  Race J  Ht 69  Wt 136  Somato 4-3-5  3—435   g-2.5
                                          type         4—435   t-3.0
                                                5—335
```

IT 3-4-4 V 62 S 85 C 81 Health 7 Strength C 3
Strength P 4 PI 3 IQ 153 AI 4 S 4 Gp 2
Comment: A personality extraordinarily similar to the last. He is satirical, humorous, and offensive to many people, but this youth is widely recognized as brilliant and is hailed by some as a rising young social scientist. He is somatorotic but is intellectually of the first order. Highest scholarship.

```
                                                1—443
                                                2—442   d-12
No. 140  Age 22  Race J  Ht 66  Wt 141  Somato 4-4-2  3—442   g-1.8
                                          type         4—442   t-1.5
                                                5—352
```

IT 3-5-2 V 66 S 99 C 41 Health 6 Strength C 4
Strength P 3 PI 4 IQ AI 1 S 2 Gp 1
Comment: A senior student in the School of Business. Average (sixth decile) academic standing. Aggressive and shrewdly watchful for the main chance. Well recommended by his faculty. He suffers from no orientational uncertainties. Purpose of life, to make money.

```
                                                1—443
                                                2—443   d-12
No. 141  Age 22  Race A-M  Ht 70  Wt 165  Somato 4-4²-2²  3—443   g-1.6
                                          type            4—452   t-2.5
                                                5—452
```

IT 3-5-3 V 69 S 93 C 58 Health 5 Strength C 4
Strength P 3 PI 4 IQ 132 AI 2 S 3 Gp 2
Comment: Senior student, School of Business. Academic standing, second decile. Poor record. Considered erratic and irregularly aggressive. Usually lazy. Poorly recommended at present. But IQ, 132. He is orientationally confused.

```
                                                1—443
                                                2—442   d-10
No. 142  Age 26  Race A-N  Ht 67  Wt 149  Somato 4-4-2²  3—442   g-2.8
                                          type           4—543   t-2.0
                                                5—443
```

IT 5-4-3 V 97 S 82 C 60 Health 5 Strength C 3
Strength P 4 PI 2 IQ AI 1.5 S 2 Gp 3
Comment: A viscerotic young preacher, two years out of Seminary. He fairly slobbers on people. Universal brotherhood is his message. Overly fond of eating, especially social eating. A personality highly offensive to the scientific temperament. Blandly optimistic. Pacifist. Undergraduate record, fourth decile.

No. 143 Age 26 Race A-M Ht 69 Wt 175 Somato 4²-4-2 type

1—443		
2—442	d-14	
3—442	g-3.0	
4—542	t-3.2	
5—532		

IT 4-4-3 V 83 S 84 C 62 Health 6 Strength C 5
Strength P 4 PI 4 IQ AI 2 S 3 Gp 2

Comment: An airline pilot who has done rather well in his three years of flying service, although now dissatisfied with this work and more intellectually ambitious. He is taking a part-time course in physiology. Academic record, seventh decile.

No. 144 Age 26 Race A-N Ht 68 Wt 166 Somato 4²-4-2 type

1—542	
2—442	d-10
3—442	g-2.5
4—442	t-1.8
5—532	

IT 5-3-2 V 102 S 67 C 43 Health 5 Strength C 3
Strength P 2 PI 2 IQ 116 AI 1.5 S 2 Gp 3

Comment: A weak but buoyant and expansive young man who has now for four years been employed by a publishing house. Well liked and successful in this work, although his advancement has been only nominal. Intellectual outlook, childish and commonplace. Academic record, fifth decile.

No. 145 Age 22 Race A-N Ht 71 Wt 164 Somato 4-4-3 type

1—443	
2—443	d-4
3—443	g-2.0
4—453	t-2.8
5—443	

IT 4-3-4 V 76 S 63 C 86 Health 6 Strength C 4
Strength P 4 PI 2 IQ 123 AI 1.5 S 4 Gp 2

Comment: A college playboy, on the weak and somewhat alcoholic side. Amiable, sociable, pliant and easily influenced. No positive ideas or plans. Loves to spend afternoons drinking and playing bridge. Academic record, second decile. An extreme coward.

No. 146 Age 22 Race N-M Ht 68 Wt 152 Somato 4²-4-3 type

1—533	
2—442	d-14
3—443	g-1.8
4—443	t-1.7
5—543	

IT 3-3-3 V 69 S 68 C 64 Health 2 Strength C 2
Strength P 2 PI 3 IQ 86 AI 1 S 1 Gp 2

Comment: A borderline defective. Flaccid, weak, pleasant, incapable of learning. Son of a wealthy family. Probably $50,000 has been spent trying to "educate" this youth. He has been in four colleges. Temperamentally there appears to be a decrement of all three components. Standing, first decile.

1—452	
2—453	d-10
3—453	g-2.2
4—443	t-1.6
5—443	

No. 147 Age 26 Race A-M Ht 72 Wt 178 Somato 4-4²-3
type

IT 3-5-2 **V** 66 **S** 96 **C** 49 **Health** 7 **Strength C** 5
Strength P 5 **PI** 4 **IQ** **AI** 1.5 **S** 3 **Gp** 2
Comment: A shrewd, mercenary young lawyer. Life is a serious business for him. Purpose, to make money and gain prestige. He tolerates no foolishness. Undergraduate record, seventh decile.

1—444	
2—443	d-14
3—443	g-1.5
4—354	t-1.6
5—444	

No. 148 Age 25 Race M Ht 71 Wt 164 Somato 4-4-3²
type

IT 3-5-4 **V** 63 **S** 95 **C** 81 **Health** 5 **Strength C** 4
Strength P 5 **PI** 3 **IQ** 112 **AI** 2 **S** 3 **Gp** 2
Comment: Dropped out of medical school after one year. Now recently graduated from a School of Chiropractic. Generally regarded as peculiar. Works hard and humorlessly. Undergraduate record, fifth decile.

1—453	
2—453	d-10
3—453	g-1.5
4—443	t-1.5
5—442	

No. 149 Age 24 Race M-A Ht 66 Wt 135 Somato 4-4²-3
type

IT 3-5-2 **V** 68 **S** 101 **C** 48 **Health** 6 **Strength C** 4
Strength P 3 **PI** 4 **IQ** 104 **AI** 1 **S** 2 **Gp** 2
Comment: Finished college in the fourth decile. Now a salesman for a real estate company. Drinks a good deal, although he is no drunkard. Inveterate cigarette smoker. Associates with no other college graduates. No intellectual interests.

1—443	
2—443	d-4
3—443	g-1.6
4—453	t-1.8
5—443	

No. 150 Age 23 Race J Ht 67 Wt 137 Somato 4-4-3
type

IT 4-5-3 **V** 79 **S** 94 **C** 59 **Health** 6 **Strength C** 4
Strength P 3 **PI** 5 **IQ** **AI** 1 **S** 3 **Gp** 2
Comment: Graduated a year ago from the School of Business. Now working as assistant to a buyer in a large department store. Likes the work. Maintains very few college contacts. Thinks his college education was a waste of time. Academic record, third decile. Boasts that he is "hardheaded," realistic.

```
                                                              1—353
                                                              2—444  d-14
No. 151  Age 24  Race M-N  Ht 67  Wt 136  Somato 4-4-3²      3—444  g-2.4
                                               type           4—444  t-1.5
                                                              5—443
```

IT 4-3-3 V 76 S 59 C 63 Health 4 Strength C 3
Strength P 2 PI 2 IQ 126 AI 2 S 3 Gp 3

Comment: Now a clerk in a bookstore, having married the daughter of the proprietor. An effeminate, although not altogether an ineffectual, youth. He does his work efficiently. Great bridge player. Undergraduate record, sixth decile.

```
                                                              1—443
                                                              2—443  d-6
No. 152  Age 24  Race M-A  Ht 71  Wt 165  Somato 4-4-3²      3—443  g-2.0
                                               type           4—444  t-1.8
                                                              5—444
```

IT 4-4-4 V 80 S 85 C 74 Health 4 Strength C 5
Strength P 4 PI 3 IQ 124 AI 1.5 S 3 Gp 2

Comment: Graduate student, School of Education. Mentally soft, conventional, but a faithful student on specific assignments. Well regarded by his faculty. Probably has a good future in educational administration. Undergraduate record, seventh decile.

```
                                                              1—444
                                                              2—453  d-12
No. 153  Age 23  Race N-M  Ht 72  Wt 176  Somato 4-4²-3²    3—444  g-1.6
                                               type           4—453  t-1.8
                                                              5—444
```

IT 3-5-4 V 65 S 94 C 77 Health 5 Strength C 4
Strength P 6 PI 3 IQ 118 AI 1.5 S 4 Gp 1

Comment: A senior in the School of Engineering, with a fair (sixth decile) record. Not brilliant but sound. He regards himself as shy and introverted. Actually he is aggressive and rather well received. Highly regarded by women.

```
                                                              1—444
                                                              2—543  d-12
No. 154  Age 20  Race A-M  Ht 68  Wt 153  Somato 4²-4-3²    3—444  g-3.5
                                               type           4—543  t-1.8
                                                              5—444
```

IT 5-3-4 V 96 S 61 C 83 Health 5 Strength C 3
Strength P 3 PI 2 IQ 110 AI 1.5 S 3 Gp 3

Comment: An overly dependent, somewhat viscerotic youth who makes a nuisance of himself by demanding attention. Sociophilic, anxious, humorless. Undergraduate standing, first decile. No vocational plan.

No. 155　Age 22　Race N-A　Ht 70　Wt 161　Somato 4-4^2-3^2
type

1—354
2—443　d-16
3—444　g-2.0
4—443　t-2.2
5—453

IT 3-5-4　V 68　S 90　C 82　Health 6　Strength C 5
Strength P 4　PI 4　IQ 129　AI 2　S 3　Gp 2

Comment: A highly ambitious undergraduate, but his ambitions are changeable and poorly sustained. Changed from School of Engineering to Chemistry, and lastly to psychology. Feels internally insecure. Undergraduate standing, eighth decile.

No. 156　Age 24　Race N-M　Ht 73　Wt 176　Somato 4-4-4
type

1—344
2—444　d-4
3—444　g-1.5
4—444　t-3.0
5—444

IT 3-4-5　V 59　S 76　C 98　Health 7　Strength C 4
Strength P 5　PI 3　IQ 150　AI 1.5　S 3　Gp 2

Comment: A young man sometimes referred to as the pride of the Law School. Brilliant record there and also as an undergraduate. But he is overly tense and anxious, seeming always to be under a strain. He desires to remain in academic work rather than to enter practice. Highest academic honors. No humorous insight.

No. 157　Age 24　Race M-N　Ht 69　Wt 150　Somato 4-4-4
type

1—444
2—444　d-12
3—444　g-2.5
4—444　t-1.8
5—353

IT 3-5-4　V 69　S 90　C 78　Health 6　Strength C 4
Strength P 5　PI 4　IQ　AI 3　S 3　Gp 2

Comment: A vigorous youth who has pretended to be much tougher than he is. Lives the outdoor life. Likes to rough it. But he cannot fight, and has at last learned this fact. A graduate student in geology. Undergraduate record, eighth decile.

No. 158　Age 23　Race N-M　Ht 70　Wt 155　Somato 444
type

1—444
2—534　d-8
3—444　g-3.5
4—444　t-2.0
5—444

IT 4-4-4　V 72　S 79　C 86　Health 5　Strength C 4
Strength P 4　PI 2　IQ 131　AI 1.5　S 3　Gp 2

Comment: First year graduate student in sociology. A little overpolite and proper in his outlook. Liked especially by nice ladies. Well regarded by his faculty. Undergraduate record, seventh decile. He is a soft, effeminate person who has frequently been accused of homosexuality.

1—444
2—444 d-8
No. 159 **Age** 27 **Race** N **Ht** 74 **Wt** 185 **Somato** 4-4-4 3—444 g-5.0
                                                            type   4—534 t-2.2
5—444

IT 5-4-3 **V** 93 **S** 83 **C** 60 **Health** 7 **Strength C** 2
Strength P 4 **PI** 2 **IQ** 142 **AI** 2 **S** 2 **Gp** 6
Comment: A young instructor in music. Very highly regarded by some of his faculty superiors. He is supreme at an afternoon tea. Has a large collection of symphony records. His speech is effeminate, affected. Tremendous localization of gynandromorphy at the hips. Undergraduate record, seventh decile. No humor.

1—452
2—451 d-10
No. 160 **Age** 25 **Race** J **Ht** 66 **Wt** 152 **Somato** 4-5-1^2 3—451 g-1.4
                                                            type   4—451 t-1.4
5—35^2

IT 3-5-3 **V** 67 **S** 95 **C** 62 **Health** 6 **Strength C** 6
Strength P 4 **PI** 2 **IQ** 147 **AI** 1 **S** 3 **Gp** 1
Comment: Graduate student in chemistry, and a good one. Considered unusually brilliant in one branch of industrial chemistry. Has been made an assistant in his department. Socially harsh, ruthless, intolerant, impatient. Undergraduate record, ninth decile.

1—541
2—451 d-14
No. 161 **Age** 21 **Race** J **Ht** 65 **Wt** 153 **Somato** 4^2-5-1 3—461 g-2.2
                                                            type   4—451 t-1.8
5—551

IT 5-4-2 **V** 89 **S** 87 **C** 40 **Health** 6 **Strength C** 4
Strength P 2 **PI** 2 **IQ** 114 **AI** 1 **S** 2 **Gp** 3
Comment: A student in the School of Business. Considered lazy and shiftless by his dean. Viscerotic. Overly dependent on people. Babyish about his family, especially the mother. Academic standing, third decile.

1—352
2—461 d-14
No. 162 **Age** 22 **Race** A **Ht** 68 **Wt** 161 **Somato** 4-5-1^2 3—452 g-1.6
                                                            type   4—451 t-1.8
5—451

IT 3-6-2 **V** 65 **S** 114 **C** 45 **Health** 7 **Strength C** 5
Strength P 4 **PI** 6 **IQ** **AI** 3 **S** 2 **Gp** 1
Comment: Senior in the School of Agriculture. Doing good work in animal husbandry. On the swimming team. Very well regarded by his dean. Academic standing, eighth decile. He is highly energetic, but is one of the pleasantest persons to interview among the entire group. Always carries the rich fragrance of the cowbarn on his garments. Has a humorous drawl.

                                              1—453
                                              2—453 d-10
No. 163 Age 28 Race A-N Ht 72 Wt 187 Somato 4-5-2² 3—453 g-1.7
                                       type   4—452 t-1.9
                                              5—442

IT 4-4-3 V 80 S 78 C 61 Health 7 Strength C 6
Strength P 5 PI 4 IQ AI 2 S 2 Gp 2

Comment: A high school principal who is well regarded in his profession. Taking a year off to get a higher degree and a salary raise. He is tolerant, even-tempered, good-humored. Secure in his world. No intellectual interests. He was a substitute on the football team in college. Now coaches football. Undergraduate record, seventh decile.

                                              1—452
                                              2—452 d-4
No. 164 Age 27 Race J Ht 66 Wt 153 Somato 4-5-2 3—452 g-2.5
                                       type   4—352 t-3.5
                                              5—452

IT 4-5-3 V 75 S 101 C 67 Health 6 Strength C 5
Strength P 5 PI 3 IQ 162 AI 3 S 2 Gp 3

Comment: A young rabbi studying psychology. Polite, ceremonious, yet watchful and critical. His fine black eyes are disconcertingly observant. He is hyperattentional and overly intent. Excellent scholastic record, tenth decile. Highly ambitious.

                                              1—453
                                              2—453 d-6
No. 165 Age 27 Race A-N Ht 70 Wt 170 Somato 4-5-2² 3—453 g-1.3
                                       type   4—452 t-1.6
                                              5—452

IT 4-4-4 V 74 S 84 C 76 Health 4 Strength C 5
Strength P 3 PI 2 IQ AI 3 S 4 Gp 2

Comment: Graduate student in Education. Fairly good record (seventh decile). Good-natured and amiable. But singularly insecure and apprehensive of his future. He manifests what some psychologists would call a pronounced inferiority complex. Overly apologetic. Overly solicitous to the point of becoming offensive.

                                              1—551
                                              2—452 d-8
No. 166 Age 26 Race J Ht 65 Wt 148 Somato 4-5-2 3—452 g-2.4
                                       type   4—452 t-1.2
                                              5—452

IT 4-6-1 V 77 S 117 C 32 Health 7 Strength C 4
Strength P 3 PI 4 IQ 132 AI 1 S 2 Gp 2

Comment: Senior medical student. Considered unpleasantly aggressive by most of his classmates. A better than average student. Eager and cooperative from the standpoint of most of his instructors. Undergraduate record, eighth decile.

1—352
2—362 d-18
No. 167   Age 23   Race J   Ht 66   Wt 145   Somato 4-5-2   3—452   g-1.5
                                              type   4—452   t-2.0
                                                              5—551

IT 3-6-1   **V** 71   **S** 115   **C** 25   **Health** 5   **Strength C** 5
Strength P 4   **PI** 5   **IQ**   **AI** 1.5   **S** 3   **Gp** 2
Comment: First year law student. Hard-working, aggressive student. Academic standing a little above the middle of the class. Very strong drive for money, status, power. Well regarded by his instructors. Undergraduate record, eighth decile.

1—444
2—452 d-12
No. 168   Age 25   Race A-N   Ht 71   Wt 168   Somato 4-5-3   3—453   g-2.6
                                                type   4—453   t-2.0
                                                                5—453

IT 4-4-4   **V** 75   **S** 80   **C** 77   **Health** 6   **Strength C** 5
Strength P 5   **PI** 3   **IQ** 141   **AI** 1   **S** 1   **Gp** 2
Comment: A graduate student of Social Science. Highly apprehensive about his health. At one time he thinks he has ulcers, at another time there is something the matter with his head. Sociophilic but shy. Works hard and well. Academic standing, tenth decile. No trace of humor. Excessively low sexuality.

1—453
2—453 d-4
No. 169   Age 21   Race A-N   Ht 69   Wt 160   Somato 4-5-3   3—453   g-2.5
                                                type   4—452   t-1.7
                                                                5—453

IT 3-4-4   **V** 62   **S** 80   **C** 76   **Health** 6   **Strength C** 5
Strength P 4   **PI** 2   **IQ** 139   **AI** 3   **S** 3   **Gp** 2
Comment: Has shown apprehensiveness and cerebrotic symptoms throughout most of his life. Now a junior in college. The University psychiatrist calls him a psychopathic personality. Academic standing, second decile.

1—452
2—453 d-8
No. 170   Age 26   Race J   Ht 67   Wt 147   Somato 4-5-3   3—453   g-1.5
                                              type   4—453   t-1.3
                                                              5—353

IT 3-6-2   **V** 70   **S** 116   **C** 41   **Health** 7   **Strength C** 6
Strength P 4   **PI** 5   **IQ**   **AI** 1   **S** 3   **Gp** 1
Comment: Graduate student, School of Business. A most businesslike and practical young man, who entertains little sympathy for "academic theory." He wants to know how to make more money, and is not overly pleased with the School of Business. Undergraduate record, eighth decile.

No. 171 Age 25 Race N-A Ht 72 Wt 181 Somato 4-5-3
type

1—354		
2—453	d-12	
3—453	g-2.8	
4—443	t-2.4	
5—453		

IT 4-4-4 V 73 S 75 C 80 Health 6 Strength C 5
Strength P 6 PI 3 IQ AI 4 S 4 Gp 4
Comment: A Scoutmaster who has made a full-time job of boys' work, summer camps, and the Scout movement. He is a little too easygoing for this job, and perhaps a little too romantic and idealistic. His discipline is poor. Boys take advantage of him. But he does pretty well. Undergraduate record, sixth decile.

No. 172 Age 28 Race J Ht 71 Wt 216 Somato 4-6-1
type

1—461		
2—461	d-8	
3—461	g-1.5	
4—461	t-1.3	
5—551		

IT 5-5-1 V 91 S 99 C 24 Health 7 Strength C 6
Strength P 4 PI 4 IQ 124 AI 1 S 2 Gp 2
Comment: A young psychiatrist who is successfully practicing psychoanalysis. He is both aggressive and singularly relaxed and complacent. There is no trace of doubt or inhibition in him. Undergraduate record, seventh decile. Medical record, average. Markedly hirsute.

No. 173 Age 31 Race J Ht 69 Wt 196 Somato 4-6-1
type

1—271		
2—461	d-20	
3—461	g-2.8	
4—551	t-1.8	
5—461		

IT 3-7-2 V 58 S 134 C 38 Health 6 Strength C 6
Strength P 5 PI 5 IQ 135 AI 1 S 3 Gp 3
Comment: A graduate of Medical School who interned and then "cracked up" mentally. Now institutionalized. Diagnosis: manic-depressive psychosis. Was always overactive and overly aggressive. He suffers much from a duodenal ulcer. Undergraduate record, fifth decile.

No. 174 Age 23 Race J Ht 67 Wt 151 Somato 5-2-2
type

1—523		
2—522	d-8	
3—522	g-3.5	
4—622	t-1.6	
5—522		

IT 6-1-2 V 118 S 30 C 49 Health 3 Strength C 2
Strength P 2 PI 2 IQ 107 AI 1 S 1 Gp 3
Comment: A viscerotic, sociophilic youth who refuses to believe that life is serious. He loves food, company, bridge, the movies, symphonies. Finally dropped out of college as a junior after five years of attendance. He is closely attached to his mother. Academic record, first decile. He is effeminate, with markedly hypoplastic genitalia.

```
                                                        1—524
                                                        2—524  d-12
No. 175  Age 19  Race M-N  Ht 70  Wt 153  Somato  5-2-4  3—415  g-6.5
                                            type         4—524  t-2.2
                                                        5—524
```

IT 4-1-5 V 88 S 27 C 96 Health 2 Strength C 1
Strength P 1 PI 1 IQ 105 AI 5 S 1 Gp 5

Comment: A youth who presents a moderate degree of what is known in medicine as the Froehlich Syndrome (obesity, low mesomorphy and hypogenitalism). He has had extensive endocrine therapy. Entered college, stayed two months, went home. He is highly dependent, especially upon the mother.

```
                                                        1—534
                                                        2—434  d-14
No. 176  Age 27  Race M-N  Ht 69  Wt 153  Somato  5-2²-4  3—523  g-3.0
                                            type          4—524  t-2.5
                                                         5—524
```

IT 4-4-4 V 85 S 72 C 87 Health 6 Strength C 2
Strength P 3 PI 1 IQ 159 AI 4 S 4 Gp 3

Comment: A young instructor in psychology who has given promise of a productive scientific career. Brilliant undergraduate and graduate record (tenth decile). He is slightly effeminate.

```
                                                        1—532
                                                        2—532  d-10
No. 177  Age 19  Race M-A  Ht 67  Wt 154  Somato  5-3-2²  3—533  g-2.8
                                            type          4—632  t-1.8
                                                         5—533
```

IT 6-3-2 V 120 S 56 C 51 Health 6 Strength C 4
Strength P 2 PI 1 IQ AI 1.5 S 1 Gp 2

Comment: A gluttonous youth who lives for his first component. He is a sort of social clearing house. Now a freshman for the second year. Academic standing, second decile. He is a well-liked youngster, who seems to enjoy life.

```
                                                        1—632
                                                        2—532  d-12
No. 178  Age 23  Race A-N  Ht 66  Wt 157  Somato  5-3-2  3—532  g-2.0
                                            type         4—541  t-1.8
                                                        5—532
```

IT 6-4-1 V 107 S 86 C 28 Health 7 Strength C 4
Strength P 3 PI 2 IQ AI 1 S 2 Gp 2

Comment: First year graduate student in the School of Business. Everybody knows him and likes him. He is not only viscerotonic but also energetic. All social affairs center around him. He is called Porky. Academic record, sixth decile.

```
                                                        1—542
                                                        2—532  d-14
No. 179  Age 26  Race N-A  Ht 70  Wt 181  Somato  5-3²-2  3—533  g-2.5
                                            type          4—442  t-2.3
                                                         5—542
```

IT 4-4-3 V 80 S 80 C 58 Health 6 Strength C 4
Strength P 3 PI 3 IQ AI 1.5 S 3 Gp 2

Comment: A graduate pharmacist who has settled into a hospital job happily and satisfactorily. Considered one of the best among the younger members of his profession. There is no ambition to go further. He is married and saving money. Academic record, fourth decile.

```
                                              1—533
                                              2—533   d-14
No. 180  Age 23  Race N-M  Ht 69  Wt 157  Somato  5-3-3²   3—524   g-3.6
                                    type              4—534   t-2.8
                                              5—434
```

IT 5-2-4 V 104 S 39 C 84 Health 5 Strength C 2
Strength P 2 PI 1 IQ AI 6 S 4 Gp 5
Comment: A highly intelligent but delicate-minded, discriminative youth who entered theological seminary but after a year transferred to sociology. He found the "theologues stupid," and now finds the "sociologogues crass." Plans to try philosophy next. He has a homosexual leaning, but no overt homosexuality. Undergraduate record, tenth decile.

```
                                              1—524
                                              2—534   d-10
No. 181  Age 27  Race A-M  Ht 71  Wt 183  Somato  5-3-3²   3—533   g-5.0
                                    type              4—533   t-2.6
                                              5—533
```

IT 6-2-3 V 114 S 45 C 61 Health 5 Strength C 3
Strength P 3 PI 2 IQ AI 4 S 4 Gp 4
Comment: A somewhat effeminate young preacher who is now a graduate student in Sociology. He is interested in boys, and in welfare work. Has organized a troop of Boy Scouts. Academic record, ninth decile. An overt homosexual. Highly viscerotic both to people and to food.

```
                                              1—543
                                              2—532   d-26
No. 182  Age 22  Race M-A  Ht 68  Wt 156  Somato  5-3-3   3—524   g-4.5
                                    type              4—524   t-1.3
                                              5—632
```

IT 5-1-4 V 103 S 26 C 82 Health 4 Strength C 2
Strength P 2 PI 2 IQ 92 AI 2 S 1 Gp 5
Comment: A helpless, apprehensive, weak-minded fat boy who is dependent upon people and affection, but cannot hold any friends. He wants to be a social worker. Usually passes barely enough courses to stay in college. A chronic pest to psychiatrists and "guidance people." Has recently been psychoanalyzed, without visible effect. Academic record, second decile.

```
                                              1—542
                                              2—533   d-18
No. 183  Age 22  Race A-N  Ht 68  Wt 161  Somato  5-3²-3   3—543   g-3.0
                                    type              4—623   t-1.4
                                              5—543
```

IT 6-3-2 V 109 S 60 C 42 Health 6 Strength C 4
Strength P 4 PI 1 IQ AI 1.5 S 2 Gp 3
Comment: A rather lazy and gluttonous but fairly intelligent young graduate student of journalism. He is quite a famous lunch room and beer garden orator. A campus authority on politics, aesthetics, economics, sex, etc. He is suspected of being virginal, but vigorously denies it. Undergraduate record, sixth decile.

1—533
2—533 d-10
No. 184 Age 24 Race N-M Ht 68 Wt 152 Somato 5-3-3^2 3—534 g-4.0
                                              type 4—534 t-2.5
                                                    5—434

IT 4-3-4 V 85 S 58 C 86 Health 7 Strength C 3
Strength P 5 PI 2 IQ 170 AI 3 S 3 Gp 3

Comment: A brilliant medical student who plans a research career. IQ said to be
170. One of the campus geniuses. He graduated from a large university at the
head of his class.

1—543
2—543 d-12
No. 185 Age 24 Race M-N Ht 70 Wt 171 Somato 5-3^2-3^2 3—543 g-2.8
                                              type 4—534 t-1.8
                                                    5—534

IT 4-4-4 V 79 S 80 C 83 Health 5 Strength C 3
Strength P 3 PI 2 IQ AI 1.5 S 3 Gp 3

Comment: A somewhat perplexed young man who has a good mind but cannot
decide what to do with it. Good academic record (ninth decile). One year of
graduate work in social service. Changed "in disgust" to the biological sciences but
he does not measure up in laboratory courses. He writes poetry and is a great
symphony listener. Is becoming sophisticated and cynical.

1—533
2—434 d-8
No. 186 Age 22 Race N-M Ht 66 Wt 137 Somato 5-3-4 3—534 g-4.0
                                              type 4—534 t-1.7
                                                    5—534

IT 4-2-5 V 78 S 44 C 99 Health 6 Strength C 4
Strength P 2 PI 1 IQ AI 2 S 1 Gp 5

Comment: One of the campus "sissies." Excessively effeminate. Known as "Daisy."
He is cerebrotic and overly solicitous. Studying to be a musician. Undergraduate
record, fourth decile. No homosexuality.

1—541
2—541 d-4
No. 187 Age 22 Race N-A Ht 68 Wt 177 Somato 5-4-1 3—541 g-2.6
                                              type 4—551 t-4.0
                                                    5—541

IT 6-4-1 V 121 S 77 C 33 Health 5 Strength C 5
Strength P 4 PI 6 IQ 120 AI 2 S 1 Gp 2

Comment: An undergraduate who is one of the best long-distance swimmers to
have attended the University in many years. He is a fine-looking lad with a high t,
and is popular. Has a good tenor voice. Hopes to become a professional singer.
Academic standing, fourth decile.

1—451
2—541 d-14
No. 188 Age 24 Race J Ht 67 Wt 178 Somato 5-4²-1 3—542 g-2.0
type 4—541 t-1.4
5—55¹

IT 4-5-2 V 86 S 101 C 50 Health 5 Strength C 5
Strength P 4 PI 3 IQ 133 AI 1 S 2 Gp 2
Comment: Graduate student, School of Business. This rather sociable youth is often tactlessly aggressive and is pointedly disliked by some of his associates. The dean considers him "neurotic." He is a good student, however. Undergraduate record, ninth decile.

1—542
2—541 d-4
No. 189 Age 24 Race A-N Ht 66 Wt 161 Somato 5-4-2 3—542 g-4.5
type 4—542 t-2.0
5—542

IT 4-3-3 V 75 S 59 C 62 Health 4 Strength C 2
Strength P 2 PI 2 IQ AI 2 S 4 Gp 5
Comment: A quiet, complacent little pianist who loves his music and is very pleasant to everybody. He is a graduate student in the School of Music. Undergraduate record, seventh decile. His gynandromorphy almost suggests pneumatic inflation posteriorly.

1—542
2—542 d-12
No. 190 Age 27 Race A-N Ht 65 Wt 155 Somato 5-4-2 3—541 g-1.8
type 4—632 t-1.4
5—542

IT 6-3-1 V 110 S 70 C 28 Health 6 Strength C 4
Strength P 2 PI 2 IQ AI 1 S 1 Gp 2
Comment: An expansive, popular, garrulous young man who wasted his time as a medical student, but has since become an oculist with quite a lucrative business building up. Has joined the Masons and one or two other fraternal organizations of the sort. He is married to a gluttonous, gleeful little 6-3-1. They set a fine table.

1—543
2—543 d-12
No. 191 Age 20 Race N-A Ht 67 Wt 152 Somato 5-4-3 3—444 g-3.0
type 4—542 t-1.6
5—543

IT 4-3-4 V 79 S 62 C 82 Health 5 Strength C 3
Strength P 3 PI 2 IQ 134 AI 3 S 2 Gp 3
Comment: An inconspicuous, overly viscerotonic undergraduate who is shy but "heart-hungry," and is most grateful for attention. He plans to be a teacher. Academic standing, fourth decile.

```
                                                    1—543
                                                    2—543  d-8
No. 192  Age 22  Race A-N  Ht 69  Wt 169  Somato  5-4-3  3—543  g-2.5
                                          type          4—533  t-1.9
                                                    5—542
```

IT 5-3-4 **V** 100 **S** 63 **C** 78 **Health** 6 **Strength C** 3
Strength P 3 **PI** 2 **IQ** 122 **AI** 1.5 **S** 2 **Gp** 4

Comment: A senior who plans to enter vocational guidance work and is studying psychology. He is an emotional slobberer, especially with new acquaintances. Is very apprehensive about his health, wears rubbers when it is cloudy, and makes a nuisance of himself by seeking attention from his professors. Needs constant reassurance. Academic standing, fifth decile.

```
                                                    1—623
                                                    2—623  d-14
No. 193  Age 23  Race J  Ht 69  Wt 180  Somato  6-1²-3  3—613  g-4.5
                                          type           4—613  t-2.5
                                                    5—522
```

IT 5-2-4 **V** 97 **S** 45 **C** 86 **Health** 4 **Strength C** 2
Strength P 1 **PI** 1 **IQ** 130 **AI** 3 **S** 1 **Gp** 4

Comment: An unhappily fat youth presenting a rare somatotype. He is hypogenital and has been under endocrine treatment of various sorts. This is a borderline Froehlich case. Senior in the School of Business. Academic record, fifth decile. He loves to swim.

```
                                                    1—532
                                                    2—622  d-8
No. 194  Age 24  Race A-M  Ht 69  Wt 190  Somato  6-2-2  3—622  g-2.8
                                          type           4—622  t-2.0
                                                    5—622
```

IT 6-3-2 **V** 109 **S** 62 **C** 53 **Health** 5 **Strength C** 3
Strength P 2 **PI** 2 **IQ** **AI** 1.5 **S** 2 **Gp** 2

Comment: A heavy but active youth who has entered his father's manufacturing concern and contemplates becoming a professional capitalist and executive. In college he was the fat, good-natured boy in one of the wealthier fraternities. Academic record, "gentleman's standing" (third decile).

```
                                                    1—631
                                                    2—622  d-14
No. 195  Age 26  Race A-M  Ht 71  Wt 210  Somato  6-2²-2  3—622  g-2.4
                                          type            4—532  t-1.8
                                                    5—632
```

IT 5-4-2 **V** 90 **S** 86 **C** 38 **Health** 7 **Strength C** 4
Strength P 3 **PI** 4 **IQ** **AI** 1.5 **S** 1 **Gp** 2

Comment: An aggressive, vigorous, exceedingly active young fat man who is already assistant manager in a chain of grocery stores. In summer sweat pours off him in streams, and he becomes all the more bustling and happy. Like most endomorphs he likes heat and loves to swim. This is the "bustling endomorph" type. Undergraduate record, fifth decile.

1—641
2—631 d-6
No. 196 Age 25 Race A-M Ht 67 Wt 194 Somato 6-3²-1 3—631 g-2.0
type 4—641 t-1.6
5—641

IT 6-4-1 V 107 S 76 C 35 Health 6 Strength C 5
Strength P 3 PI 4 IQ AI 1 S 1 Gp 2

Comment: A medical student with great energy and a fairly good record. He is known among his classmates as "the porpoise," perhaps because of his shape and his bounding, ungainly walk. Perspiration pours off him like water off a porpoise. An excellent swimmer. He is exceedingly good-natured and popular. Aggressive in his work. Undergraduate record, fifth decile.

1—632
2—632 d-0
No. 197 Age 22 Race J Ht 70 Wt 197 Somato 6-3-2 3—632 g-3.5
type 4—632 t-3.0
5—632

IT 5-4-3 V 93 S 88 C 69 Health 6 Strength C 4
Strength P 3 PI 3 IQ 157 AI 3 S 3 Gp 3

Comment: An endomorphic Jewish youth of rather high t. His features and his body as a whole are well molded. This boy is a brilliant student in mathematics and physics. Considered almost a mathematical genius. Highest academic honors.

1—721
2—721 d-10
No. 198 Age 22 Race J Ht 67 Wt 221 Somato 7-1²-1 3—711 g-2.0
type 4—712 t-1.5
5—721

IT 6-1-1 V 114 S 35 C 31 Health 4 Strength C 4
Strength P 2 PI 1 IQ 95 AI 1 S 1 Gp 2

Comment: A viscerotic youth who failed out of college in three months and seems hopelessly bogged in most respects. He is as gluttonous as a suckling, eats uncontrollably, especially sweets, and suggests nothing so much as a huge baby. Promiscuously affectionate, and possibly was graduated from high school because of a certain likableness. Has never learned to study, or to discipline himself in any way.

1—712
2—712 d-12
No. 199 Age 22 Race A-N Ht 68 Wt 213 Somato 7-1²-1² 3—712 g-2.8
type 4—721 t-1.6
5—721

IT 6-2-3 V 110 S 39 C 60 Health 4 Strength C 2
Strength P 1 PI 1 IQ 121 AI 1 S 1 Gp 4

Comment: A somewhat pitifully helpless, soft endomorph who is overly sensitive about his endomorphy, diets intermittently, and also is intermittently pious. Academic standing, fourth decile. Has been offered a scholarship in the theological seminary, and believes he will accept it.

                                                          1—731
                                                          2—731   d-8
No. 200   Age 22   Race J   Ht 71   Wt 256   Somato 7 3-1   3—731   g-1.8
                                              type   4—641   t-2.4
                                                          5—731

IT 6-4-1   V 111   S 85   C 33   Health 7   Strength C 6
Strength P 4   PI 4   IQ 126   AI 2   S 2   Gp 2
Comment: A huge, popular senior who gets about with tremendous vigor and
energy. He plays guard on the football team. Highly sociophilic and conspicuously
present at whatever is going on. Overly fond of eating. Loves alcohol but is never
drunk. Plans to study medicine. Wants to be an obstetrician. Academic standing,
seventh decile.

APPENDIX 2

THE WISCONSIN SCALE OF RADICALISM AND CONSERVATISM

(See p. 30)

This is an inquiry into the nature and measurement of conservative and radical opinion. Its purpose is to provide a rough quantitative measure of these intellectual habits, and to discover if possible some of the environmental and hereditary factors associated with them.

The inquiry contains a graded series of typical opinions relating to a number of controversial social problems. Under each problem five opinions or attitudes are stated, ranging from a definitely reactionary to a definitely radical view. You are requested, after reading each topic through, to put a check mark in the left margin beside that view which corresponds most closely with your own. You will of course find that you are conservative on some problems, reactionary on some, and radical on others.

It is possible that you will find problems stated here, concerning which you have done insufficient thinking to justify an attitude. Or there may be problems here concerning which you have done a great deal of thinking, but none of the views stated even approximately matches your own. These two contingencies are provided for in the Scale.

We have found that the following general procedure appears to offer the most satisfactory method of approaching the Scale: Under each topic, read the number 1 view carefully. If it corresponds exactly with your own opinion, check it and go on to the next topic, omitting the other views. If number 1 fails to match your attitude, read number 2, then number 3 and the others, until you find a view that matches your own. If none does so, then check the one which is closest. Do not resort to number 6 or 7 unless you are sure that not one of the five views stated even approximately corresponds to your own.

491

A. *Limitation of Profit*

1. Every person should be free to buy any article or product at the lowest price he can persuade others to accept, and to sell it at the highest price he can persuade others to pay. If it costs three cents a quart to produce a commodity, and the stuff can be sold at three dollars a quart, this is strictly ethical.
2. In general, the above plan is ethical, but a few restrictions should be placed upon it, to prevent monopoly of necessary commodities, such as foodstuffs and clothing materials.
3. There may be some question concerning the ultimate soundness of the whole principle.
4. This plan of *laissez faire* is probably unsound. It apparently encourages dishonesty, insincerity, and may contribute materially to the general breakdown of human character.
5. Uncontrolled profiting is unqualifiedly one of the worst evils man has developed. It is one of the central causes of human misery. Profit should be rigidly controlled.
6. I have done insufficient thinking on this problem to check any of the opinions stated.
7. I have done a great deal of thinking on this problem, but my attitude is fundamentally different from any of those stated. The following three or four phrases indicate my general opinion:

B. *Wealth Distribution*

1. The traditional capitalistic system provides for the best possible distribution of wealth, human nature being what it is. Under present conditions those who most deserve and can best employ wealth are generally the individuals who gain control of the larger quantities of it.
2. On the whole the present distribution is probably a wise one. Men of great wealth generally make the best use of their money, for the general good, although of course there are exceptions.
3. There may be some question concerning the soundness of the system.
4. The system is probably fundamentally unsound. Generally speaking, wealth is not being used to its best advantage, and those who control it are not on the whole the best fitted to do so.
5. The present arrangement for the distribution of wealth is altogether unsound. There is a crying need for radical and revolutionary revision of it.
6. Insufficient familiarity with the problem.
7. A different attitude, as follows:

C. *Inheritance of Wealth*

1. The idea of maintaining great wealth through succeeding generations of the same family is sound and natural. Unless children were to inherit whatever riches their parents have been able to accumulate, men would lack their main incentive to creative work, and this incentive can never be supplied in any other way.
2. Possibly there should be some restriction of inheritance. Certain social evils do appear to arise from the inheritance of large fortunes. Yet it would be unwise to change the inheritance laws radically.
3. It may be that the transmission of large fortunes from one generation to another within the same family, is based on an unsound economic principle.
4. Apparently the present system of property inheritance is in need of revision. In all probability the inheritance of large fortunes should be discontinued.
5. No individual should under any circumstances inherit or control any considerable amount of private wealth which he himself has not earned.

6. Insufficient familiarity with the problem.
7. A different attitude, as follows:

D. *The Economics of Fashion Change*

1. Rapid change of style in various commodities, such as clothing, is economically a desirable rather than an undesirable condition, since it increases business and the consumption of goods. The waste factor is of little consequence compared to the good derived from increased volume of trade.
2. It is probably well to use the fashion idea in stimulating volume of trade, although certain extreme fashions, such as those of college students for example, are doubtless unduly wasteful.
3. There may be some question concerning the wisdom of exploiting the fashion idea to stimulate trade.
4. Probably this business of style changing has become an abuse, both as a waste of resources, and a destroyer of the virtue of thrift.
5. The style changing racket is a vicious and insidious factor in modern economics. Any person contributing to it is a direct contributor to the breakdown of human character.
6. Insufficient familiarity with the problem.
7. A different attitude, as follows:

E. *Advertising*

1. Modern advertising is a most beneficial institution. It increases human happiness greatly by raising the standard of living. Advertising is without question directly responsible for an enormous share of human happiness and prosperity.
2. Advertising as it is now carried on is probably beneficial and necessary. It is no doubt overdone, but by and large it adds a good deal more than it detracts from human well being.
3. There is some question as to the wisdom of permitting uncurbed advertising.
4. Advertising probably does more harm than good. It is a wasteful device.
5. Modern advertising is a menace to ultimate human happiness and welfare. It establishes altogether false values, creates false appetites and desires, and exerts an immeasurably bad influence on young minds.
6. Insufficient familiarity with the problem.
7. A different attitude, as follows:

II. PROBLEMS OF THE SECOND CONSCIOUS AREA (SOCIO-POLITICAL)

A. *American Democracy*

1. The American practice of democracy is the wisest and most adequate instrument of social control possible.
2. We have what is probably a highly satisfactory form of government on the whole, although there are minor weaknesses.
3. There is some question concerning the wisdom and efficacy of the pattern of government we are trying to follow in this country.
4. The American conception of democracy seems to be a somewhat impractical and unsound method of social control. We seem often to fail to bring our best minds to any effective governmental influence.
5. Democracy in America is a bad failure. The fundamental assumptions upon which it is founded are wholly unsound. Democracy places a premium on mediocrity and aggressiveness, and a penalty on the more highly civilized personality.
6. Insufficient familiarity with the problem.
7. A different attitude, as follows:

B. *Patriotism*

1. Every child should be taught to be first of all a patriot, and to love and to fight for his flag above all things. We cannot have too much patriotism.
2. Americans should be patriotic, of course, and a child should be taught to love his country. Perhaps the present emphasis upon patriotism is enough, however. We ought not to be a warlike nation.
3. There is some question concerning the wisdom of a strong patriotic emphasis in education.
4. The teaching of patriotism is doubtless one cause of war. It certainly ought to be de-emphasized.
5. All forms of patriotism are vicious. It is criminal that our children should be taught to worship soldiers and to become wavers of flags.
6. Insufficient familiarity with the problem.
7. A different attitude, as follows:

C. *The Observance of Law*

1. To break a law voluntarily is never excusable under any circumstances. If a law exists it must always be observed, and any person breaking it should be punished as a criminal.
2. Probably there are extreme cases when the breaking of a law can be justified, although ordinarily even bad laws should be rigidly observed.
3. There is some doubt about the wisdom of building up too strong a respect for law.
4. Perhaps it is a good thing to break some laws deliberately. This is one good way to get rid of bad laws.
5. A man is duty-bound to break certain laws. It is his duty to society to break unfair and useless laws, in order that such laws may become unenforceable and thus disappear.
6. Insufficient familiarity with the problem.
7. A different attitude, as follows:

D. *The Free Speech Question*

1. The public expression of opinion or circulation of propaganda which may be hostile to the government, to morality or to sacred institutions, ought to be strictly prohibited.
2. On the whole the public expression of subversive opinion ought to be controlled, although in a democracy much is to be said for the value of free debate.
3. There is some doubt of the wisdom of trying to curb free speech.
4. On the whole, there should be an entirely free expression of opinion on all sides of public questions, although certain exceptions should be made to this rule, as in wartime, and in matters of moral decency and the like.
5. No exception should be made to the principle of absolute freedom to express publicly any opinion.
6. Insufficient familiarity with the problem.
7. A different attitude, as follows:

E. *Socialism*

1. Socialism as a form of government is the wild impossible dream of radicals and visionaries. There is nothing in the idea worthy of the serious consideration of an intelligent person.
2. Socialism is probably out of the question as a serious form of government for civilized peoples, but it does involve certain interesting and attractive speculations.
3. There is a possibility that socialism may be worth serious consideration.
4. Probably in the end the most practicable form of human government will

prove to be some form of socialism. We ought to move toward it, although there are certain serious difficulties in the idea.

5. Socialism is beyond question the one practical answer. There is no doubt that we ought to go over to a thoroughgoing socialism, as the way out of the present situation.

6. Insufficient familiarity with the problem.

7. A different attitude, as follows:

III. PROBLEMS OF THE THIRD CONSCIOUS AREA (SEXUAL)

A. *Monogamy*

1. A strict monogamy is the only natural and respectable form of human sexual life. Society should under no circumstances tolerate any deviation from it, either in men or in women.

2. Although monogamy is without question sound and desirable, it is possible that certain circumstances do justify some temporary deviation from it.

3. There may be a question as to the psychological soundness of a strict monogamy.

4. There is serious doubt as to the wisdom of a strictly monogamous life. It is possible that more harm than good may have come from the attempt at monogamy.

5. Strict monogamy is altogether contrary to nature. There can be little doubt that a great share of human misery has arisen from our ill-advised and childish attempts to force monogamy upon ourselves.

6. Insufficient familiarity with the problem.

7. A different attitude, as follows:

B. *Birth Control*

1. Birth control is a problem with which man has no business meddling. There is no justification for any human attempt to interfere with the natural reproductive process.

2. It may be that sooner or later some sort of population control will be justified, although on the whole it would be better to let this matter alone.

3. It is possible that a birth control program is worth considering.

4. Probably the matter of birth control is one of the important problems that need straightway to be faced.

5. We urgently need the widespread application of such birth control techniques as are available, and further study and research in this field is one of the most vital needs of the day.

6. Insufficient familiarity with the problem.

7. A different attitude, as follows:

C. *Sacredness of the Family*

1. The family is the sacred and permanent unit upon which our society and our happiness rest. The family must above all things be kept inviolate. To weaken the structure of the family means ruin and social chaos.

2. Although certainly a permanent form of human life, the family like other institutions is doubtless subject to some modification. It may be that the "home," as we think of it, ought to change considerably in the future.

3. There may be some question as to the soundness of the family unit idea.

4. Probably the family exerts a serious restraining influence upon the development of the human personality to its best possibilities. It is likely that the family relationship ought to be considerably changed.

5. The family arrangement of society exerts an appallingly inhibitory and frustrational influence upon ultimate human welfare and happiness. It has been but a poor makeshift, and its replacement should be welcomed.

6. Insufficient familiarity with the problem.
7. A different attitude, as follows:

D. *Premarital Sexual Experimentation for Women*

1. No young woman should ever under any circumstances be permitted an opportunity for sexual experimentation. A woman should above all things maintain absolute virginity until the time of her marriage.
2. On the whole the idea of sexual knowledge or preliminary experimenting for women must be definitely discouraged, although theoretically some wisdom and experience in this area of awareness may be justifiable.
3. It is possible that a limited amount of sexual experimentation may be wise for women.
4. There is little doubt that some wisdom and experience in sexual matters is desirable for women before marriage, although it is dangerous.
5. Sexual wisdom, and a rich background of sexual experience, should be regarded as of paramount importance for young women who contemplate marriage. It is absurd for young women to enter upon marriage without the preparation of a good training and experience in sexual matters.
6. Insufficient familiarity with the problem.
7. A different attitude, as follows:

E. *Elasticity of Sexual Morality*

1. Sexual morality is one thing which is fixed and unchanging in the world. There is only one possible standard in this matter, and that is a fixed code of what is right and what is wrong, a code which applies equally to everybody at all times.
2. On the whole, sexual morality should rest upon an unchanging standard, however intelligence and other factors may vary. Yet there may be some circumstances which might make the picture a little different.
3. It is possible that sexual morality should be regarded as a somewhat more elastic thing than the above statements would imply.
4. Our notions of what is right and wrong in sexual matters are changing rapidly, and it is probable that the moral code in this area needs a general revision.
5. The old suppositions concerning sexual morality are wrong. This is a relative and elastic matter. There can be no fixed right and wrong here, but what is best depends altogether on the persons and the circumstances.
6. Insufficient familiarity with the problem.
7. A different attitude, as follows:

IV. PROBLEMS OF THE FOURTH CONSCIOUS AREA (ORIENTATIONAL, RELIGIOUS)

A. *The Church*

1. The Church is the one sure and infallible foundation of civilized life. Every member of society ought to be educated in it and required to support it.
2. On the whole the Church stands for the best in human life, although certain minor shortcomings and errors are necessarily apparent in it, as in all human institutions.
3. There is a certain doubt concerning the nature of the total influence of the Church. It is possible that the Church may do a good deal of harm.
4. While the intentions of most individual Church members are no doubt good, the total influence of the Church may be on the whole harmful.
5. The Church is a stronghold of much that is unwholesome and dangerous to human welfare. It fosters intolerance, bigotry and ignorance.
6. Insufficient familiarity with the problem.
7. A different attitude, as follows:

B. *The Reality of Divine Inspiration*

1. The eternal religious truths were certainly given to man by divine inspiration, which is the one real and infallible source of truth, so far as human beings are concerned.
2. Divine inspiration is probably a real thing, and truth has probably been revealed to man in that manner, although this may not be the most important source of truth.
3. The reality of divine inspiration is perhaps open to question.
4. Probably there is no such thing as divine inspiration, in the sense that man can in some manner receive knowledge and guidance direct from a higher consciousness.
5. The divine inspiration notion is a delusion, and originates either as a form of wish fulfillment arising from suggestibility, or as a clever lie to dupe the credulous.
6. Insufficient familiarity with the problem.
7. A different attitude, as follows:

C. *The Supernatural Idea*

1. Religion should have to do entirely with man's relation to the supernatural. That is what religion should be, namely a belief, or revelation, or set of practices concerning our relation to the supernatural.
2. While religion is principally concerned with the supernatural, and the supernatural surely embodies the main idea of it, religion should also be concerned with human natural affairs.
3. There is some question as to whether the primary function of religion has to do mainly with the supernatural, or with natural life.
4. The supernatural idea ought to play only a minor part in religious thought and teaching. Religion should be mainly a matter of orientation to life on the earth.
5. Religion, if it is to play a useful role in life, should be entirely a natural human function. It should have nothing whatever to do with supernatural notions.
6. Insufficient familiarity with the problem.
7. A different attitude, as follows:

D. *Individual Immortality*

1. We are as individuals immortal beings, retaining an individual personality through the whole of time. It is necessary to retain this belief, for otherwise human life would be meaningless.
2. We are probably individually immortal, although it may be that this idea is not altogether vital to the general conception of human purpose in the world.
3. Possibly the idea of individual immortality is not necessary to human purposive orientation, and hence to human happiness.
4. In all likelihood the idea of personal immortality is unnecessary to a good orientational outlook. It is probably possible to build a system of religious education in which this idea plays no part.
5. The idea of personal immortality ought never to enter into the picture at all. Not only is it unnecessary and preposterous, but it confuses young minds and leads to later disillusionment and disorientation.
6. Insufficient familiarity with the problem.
7. A different attitude, as follows:

E. *The Idea of God*

1. It is absolutely necessary to retain the belief and the teaching that God exists as a personal Being, conscious of human affairs. Without this as a

    cornerstone there could be no meaning to religion, or to the idea of purpose in the world.

2. Probably the idea of God needs to remain central to the whole plan of human purpose in the world, yet it may be conceivable that God is not especially concerned with human affairs, and that even in the face of this thought men will be able to live purposefully.

3. Perhaps the idea of God is not essential to human purposive orientation.

4. We probably do not need to postulate the existence of God in order to build an orientational point of view which will lead to the development of the best human fulfillment.

5. The assumption of the existence of God ought never to enter into human thought and teaching. This assumption is misleading, dangerous, and confusing to young minds.

6. Insufficient familiarity with the problem.

7. A different attitude, as follows:

COMPOSITE DISTRIBUTION OF RESPONSES. SCALE OF CONSERVATISM AND RADICALISM.
3010 UNIVERSITY OF WISCONSIN STUDENTS, IN 1930

1496 Women   1514 Men

Response No.	1	2	3	4	5	Total[1]
Profit Limitation	461	742	1141	401	144	2889
Wealth Distribution	313	808	909	572	327	2929
Inheritance of Wealth	627	1092	879	206	61	2865
Fashion Change	211	562	1040	907	240	2960
Advertising	483	760	975	507	342	2967
1st Panel Totals—	2095	3954	4844	2596	1114	
American Democracy	126	904	1531	282	52	2895
Patriotism	66	741	872	883	389	2951
Observance of Law	292	758	712	803	411	2976
Free Speech	126	455	922	1097	291	2891
Socialism	532	581	563	920	377	2973
2nd Panel Totals—	1142	3439	4600	3985	1520	
Monogamy	963	704	716	301	112	2796
Birth Control	581	842	519	482	533	2957
Sacredness of the Family	571	724	910	695	58	2958
Premarital Experimentation	782	761	525	479	383	2930
Elasticity of Morality	261	583	1011	636	477	2968
3rd Panel Totals—	3158	3614	3681	2593	1563	
The Church	124	724	1142	421	433	2844
Reality of Divine Inspiration	165	964	1014	592	214	2949
Supernatural Idea	406	1025	613	635	291	2970
Individual Immortality	476	519	724	838	337	2894
Idea of God	990	766	365	342	362	2825
4th Panel Totals—	2161	3998	3858	2828	1637	
Grand Totals—	8556	15005	16983	12001	5834	

[1] The No. 6 and No. 7 responses are not included in these totals.

SEX DIFFERENCES IN CONSERVATISM AND RADICALISM. SCALE OF CONSERVATISM AND
RADICALISM. 3010 UNIVERSITY OF WISCONSIN STUDENTS, IN 1930

1496 Women   1514 Men

Response No.	1		2		3		4		5	
Panel	M	W	M	W	M	W	M	W	M	W
1st	1193	902	2260	1696	2133	2712	1195	1401	535	579
2nd	475	667	1632	1807	2206	2394	2234	1751	816	704
3rd	1799	1359	1821	1793	1761	1920	1255	1348	701	862
4th	683	1478	2054	1944	2131	1727	1566	1262	820	817
Totals	4150	4406	7767	7240	8331	8753	6250	5762	2872	2962

THE CHICAGO SCALE OF MENTAL GROWTH

(See p. 30)

Use the margin for ratings (seven-point scale), and for explanatory justifications of ratings. Rate each of the three primary components under each topic.

First Panel. Gauge the development of the affective, conative and cognitive components of this personality with respect to the following first panel considerations.

F-N, *food and the necessities of life.* How warm is this person's love for and appreciation of food and the basic necessities? Has he compassionate feeling for his food and for the things which give him comfort and shelter? Has he a high feeling component in this first panel?

Has this person been dynamic and vigorous in striving for the food he likes and for other elemental needs of which he is fond? What has been his aggressiveness and push in this area? To what extent does he "go after" the basic things that he wants? How persistent, vigorous and systematic has his effort been? What is the conative component here?

How highly developed is this person's cognitive awareness in the general area of basic economics? Does he systematically and accurately *understand* his own relationship to the basic materials of life? What is the rationale of his eating habits, his attitudes toward clothing and housing and necessary equipment, and toward physical health? How accurate and how extensive is this person's cognition in this first field of human experience?

L-SS, *luxuries and the secondary supports of life.* Is there in this person a marked fondness for and warm appreciation of the "nice things"? Has he great feeling for luxuries and for the "extras" which seem so necessary to viscerotonic people? What is the affective component at this level?

Has there been vigorous effort and dynamic push in getting these secondary supports of life, or in seeing to it that life is lived among surroundings which provide luxuries? What is the conative component at this level?

Is there any considerable cognitive development centering on this area of interest? Does he have well-defined specific knowledge or accurate information with respect to some area of luxury interest? What is the cognitive component at this level?

W-M, *wealth, money.* What is the affective state in this mind concerning wealth? Is there any strong feeling about money? Any great craving for it, or any marked feeling at all concerning money and what it stands for?

How dynamic and vigorous has this person been with respect to money matters? Has there been much drive toward getting money, or possibly toward getting rid of it, or in the direction of most effective investment and the like?

How much does this person know and understand about money? What is the specific knowledge of theoretical economics in this mind? Any cognitive development here? Any critical intellectual maturity?

W-OI, *work, occupational interests.* How much feeling is there here for work or for an occupation? Does this person deeply love his work, or some other work, or does he find warm emotional fulfillment in his occupation? Is there a strong feeling-identification with something which has been accepted as a main job?

How much display of dynamic effort has there been in connection with occupational or work interests? Has this person endeavored with any vigor to make a place and to win a foothold in a line of work?

How much cognitive comprehension has been developed with respect to the main work interests? Has this person become a precisely and accurately informed student of his work field?

Second Panel. Gauge the development of the affective, conative and cognitive components of this personality with respect to the following second panel considerations.

P-ICG, *people, intimate contact group.* What has been the history of this person's emotional and affective relationships with people, in the intimate sense? Is there a strong tendency toward emotional appreciation of people, and much warm feeling in the matter? Have there been many warm attachments?

Has a good deal of dynamic energy been manifested in maintaining close contacts with other people? Has this person been one who spends his energy freely in holding friends? Is he an industrious writer of letters and a frequent visitor and entertainer? Is he actively in touch with a large group of close friends?

How much critical insight has this person developed with respect to his intimate friends? Is there any accurate understanding of what these other people are really like, of what they stand for in life, and of what their true achievements and significances are? Does he really know his friends? Has he intellectually "got the goods" on them?

P-WAG, *people, wider acquaintance group.* Is this a person who is "fond of people," in the general sense? Does he love to know a lot of people? Is there an emotional dependence upon having a large number of acquaintances?

Does this individual actively maintain a large number of superficial friendships and acquaintances? Does he spend much energy in keeping track of a great number of people? Does he send Christmas cards and the like in goodly numbers?

Is there here a good critical insight into people in general? Has this person been a close observer of human character and personality? Does he really know human beings, in any thorough, systematic sense? Does he have discriminative understanding of personality variation?

I-FSO, *institutions, family, state, organized society.* To what extent is there a warm emotional tie-up with his family, with the immediate community, with church or school? Is there a powerful patriotic element here, in the sense of emotional identification with a group or social unit of some kind? Is this a person of "loyalties," and of warm identifications?

Is he dynamically active in an institutional sense? Is he a great joiner of clubs, societies, fraternities and the like? Does he take an active part in drives, family reunions, political campaigns, or civic duty enterprises of one kind or another? Does he get up early and work late to save the family honor, or democracy, or communism, or the Elks Club mortgage? Is he an organizer and a "builder"?

Is there an active and alert critical interest in some of these second panel matters? Has this person a fund of accurate knowledge concerning the family, or concerning his own family, or concerning any of the social matters in which he is interested? Is he critically aware of the meaning and significance of second panel institutions? Is he accurately informed in some special field, such as civics, politics, or political history?

SL-SI, *society at large, sociological interests.* Is there strong feeling for any of the general problems of human social life, such as international destinies, the idea of a world state, population pressures and population control, racial intermixture, war and its control, free speech, forms of government and the like? Are there genuine emotional involvements or only word habits and idea stereotypes?

Is there active participation in some of these idealized second panel interests? Does this person spend much energy in attempting to *do* something in this area? Does he have the "gumption" to get out and discover facts, does he read avidly and systematically on these problems? Is there vigor here—or just "attitudes"?

Is there intellectual maturation in this area? Does he know what he is talking about at this level of thought? Is he accurately posted concerning some special sector of broad sociological interest? Has he information to offer, and is it well assimilated to his point of view?

Third Panel. Gauge the development of the affective, conative and cognitive components of this personality with respect to the following third panel considerations.

BR, *the elemental wish for biological reproduction.* How strong is the simple reproductive wish? Is there a deep emotional desire for progeny, or warm involvement with progeny already produced? Is the parental wish a strongly dominant note in this personality?

Has the reproductive desire given rise to active steps in the direction of its fulfillment? Does a large part of this person's energy go into the business of being a parent, or of getting ready or into position to be a parent? Is there vigorous resolution here in the direction of reproduction?

Is there much critical insight into the meaning and implications of reproduction? Has this person become well informed about children, or about heredity, or about population or education? Is there a large store of specific knowledge of parental problems such as child care, hygiene, feeding, growth, and so on?

ISE, *individual sexual expression.* Apart from reproduction and its problems, how warm an interest does he reveal in his personal sexual life and sexual expression? How much affect is there in connection with the problems and interests directly associated with his individual sexual fulfillment?

Has this person tended to take active steps toward sexual fulfillment and experience? How vigorously and perseveringly has he carried out his own sexual consummation? (This does not necessarily raise the question of promiscuity, or even of an extensity of sexual interest. A high conative sexuality may be intensive, or monogamous.)

How keenly does this person think about his individual sex life, and how accurately and widely has his mind ranged in third panel areas? Has he specific information, or does he, like most people, bluff a knowledge of the third panel? How intensively and how extensively does he think about sexual matters?

PP, *population problems.* How warmly does this individual feel the significance and portent of the general population problem? Is he vitally concerned about the perplexities which confront the race in this matter? Is he feelingly involved in the pathos of the human breeding muddle?

How active has he been concerning these problems? Has there been any vigorous identification with a legal attack, or research attack, or propaganda attack, or some other attack on the problem? Has there been any effort to do something in this area?

How much critical inquiry has there been and how much knowledge has been accumulated in this area of thought? Does he have facts at his command concerning population changes, concerning the sociology of reproduction at various levels of culture, concerning differential fecundities or heredity, or concerning eugenics and techniques for the discouragement of reproduction? Does he have any views or ideas or theories in this sector?

PISP, *problems of individual sex philosophy.* Is there here a strong feeling about the significance or importance of the sexual life in general? Does this individual have much feeling concerning the general question of love and the sexual relationship? Does he perhaps feelingly deplore sexual perplexity, and yearn for a world of happier sexuality? Does he *feel* the sexual problem?

Has there been vigorous activity of any kind in connection with these problems? Has there been evidence of the crusading impulse with reference to some problem of sexuality? Has this person shown signs of bending some of his energy upon any general problem associated with sexuality?

What is the state of his intellectual grasp in the general field of knowledge of sexuality? Is there any sharp mental focus here? Is he critically alert and intellectually alive in this area?

Fourth Panel. *Gauge the development of the affective, conative and cognitive, components of this personality with respect to the following fourth panel considerations.*

I-IPG, *ideals, immediate personal goals.* Is he one who warmly feels personal goals, so that they seem to be an important and integral part of his personality? Are there immediate goals of life and ideals of conduct which seem warmly real and vital to him? Such as personal ideals in business, social and sexual relationships, integrity of reputation, etc.?

Is there an active carrying out of such fourth panel objectives? Does this individual exert himself to live up to his elemental ethical propositions? Is he industrious and persevering in these matters?

How much insight and cognitive content is there in his set of ideals? Has he understanding and critical maturity in these matters, or has he just a sorry little bundle of moral platitudes that he carries around? Is there cogency and discrimination here? Or is this merely a righteous and moral person?

I-DPG, *ideals, distant personal goals.* How warmly does he feel distant or ultimate goals? What is the affective content of this mind with respect to the final purposes of life? Is there a rich emotional realization of his life objective, whether it be personal salvation, immortality, entrance to heaven, maturity of understanding, or something else? Is there enough warmth in this personality to carry clear through to the final reaches of fourth panel consciousness?

How vigorous and dynamic is this person in his effort to live up to his conception of his ultimate life purposes? Does he strive consistently toward his main life objectives, or is his conation intermittent and spotty?

How intellectually mature is the formulation of his life purposes? Does he reveal knowledge of life, a reading acquaintance with the wisest writers, awareness of the drift of the maturest human thinking, and does he show any insight into his own individual nature in relation to his life purposes? Or has he perhaps only bought a ready-made theology in somebody's shop?

I-HSO, *ideals, human social objectives.* How much warmth is there for ideals and goals of human society at large, and for wider objectives of life which lie beyond individual salvation? Is there any emotional identification with the general enterprise of human civilization? Does this person feel warmly involved in matters of social destiny?

Has there been much evidence of dynamic effort growing out of such a sense of wider social responsibility? Has this person shown the resolution to enter into any specific educational or ameliorative enterprise having its center in such an identification?

How much critical understanding and insight has been developed in this area? How far has this individual thought through the wider implications of biological and sociological science? What intellectual grasp has he upon problems of social amelioration? Is there any true extension of cognition into the fourth panel?

O-HPT, *orientation—history, philosophy, time.* How much warm feeling is there with respect to what may be called the time dimension of consciousness? Is there emotional identification with the past and the future? Has this mind affectively entered into the implications of the idea of time in human life?

Has there been any vigorous prosecution of a plan of investigation or of study and research, or of teaching or some other pursuit which is essentially orientational, philosophical or religious in nature?

What intellectual acuity is there in this area? Has this mind penetrated through to mature insight in some of these sectors of thought? Is there systematized knowledge here, and habits of clear thinking, or has the individual sold out to some convenient word formula?

Fifth Panel. Gauge the development of the affective, conative and cognitive components of this personality with respect to the following fifth panel considerations.

SNAA, *sensitivities to nonanimate things and artifacts.* What are the feeling sensitivities and empathies of this consciousness with respect to the nonanimate environment? How warmly and vividly does this person *feel* the surroundings in which he lives? To what extent does he emotionally enter into an awareness of the earth, trees, weather, shapes, smells, textures, sounds and colors in his immediate world? How affectively sensitive is he to simple beauty in nature? What about artifacts of human creation, such as architecture, art work of various kinds, sculpture, paintings, children's toys and the like? How much feeling warmth is there in this person with respect to his environment?

Does he exert himself particularly to get into closer touch with nature, or with the kind of physical environment he loves? Does he make vigorous attempts to keep or renew contact with his favorite places or favorite scenery and surroundings? Does he actively try to keep in touch with some artifactual field, or does he do something artifactually himself, such as paint or draw or make ships, or does he take some especial artistic pride in a manufacture?

How extensively and accurately is this person informed on matters of art or natural history (apart from animal and bird study, which we place in the next group of interests, with personality study)? Is he a connoisseur in some field, or has he intellectual hobbies touching on these areas? Has he a close and accurate acquaintanceship with stars, flowers, leaf variations, smells and perfumes, music, painting, the flora of an area, architectural styles?

SPLT, *sensitivities to people and living things.* What are the affective sensitivities and empathies with respect to other living personalities? Is this person warmly aware of the differences in personality among people, among animals, birds, insects, or other animate creatures? Does he feel the pathos, the humor in the incompatibilities, and the affection in the people who are about him? Is he *feelingly* sensitive to the resemblances between animals and people, between birds and people, between insects and human personalities? How warm and how extensive is the feeling for personality?

Has this person taken active steps and shown perseverance in the direction of seeking out, encouraging and associating with personalities which have especially aroused his own sympathies? Has he vigorously "cultivated" and lent moral and material support to the sort of people whom his affective taste favors? Or is his discrimination only a passive one which does not translate itself into overt action? Similarly with respect to his favorite birds or animals—does he actively protect and succor them, or is his interest only passive?

What is this person's specific knowledge of the variations of personality and how much critical, systematic or scientific observation has he made in this field? Is he accurately aware of the qualities and peculiarities of other personalities? Has he learned how to think objectively and comparatively about human beings? Can he cut through compensational masks and superficial attitudes and verbal habits, and pick up the true thread of a personality pattern?

FSC, *fineness of sexual consciousness.* What are the feeling sensitivities and empathies of this personality with respect to sexuality? Is there warm, sensitive appreciation of the potential beauty and delicacy which lie in the third panel? To what extent is this mind warm and earthy, while remaining sensitively discriminating in the area of sexual consciousness?

Is there a fine sexual *humor?* (Note: Humor is, possibly, a manifestation of affective response to the cognition, or re-cognition, of an incompatibility. Humor then is one kind of marriage between the first and third components at the conscious level. Sometimes it also involves the second component, which then breaks out into such overt action as laughing. Epigrammatically, humor is a uniting in consciousness of the first and third components in response to recognition of conflict. The third panel is the focus of much of our best humor because of the great effort made to suppress this panel from consciousness.) Humor may be the saving grace of human life. The fifth panel is in one sense the panel of the quality of humor.

What has been the fineness or quality of this person's own behavior in the third panel? Has he shown energetic address in the discovery and cultivation of sexual companionship of the finest nature available to him? Or has he been satisfied with ordinary, coarse, or mediocre personalities as sexual companions?

How much cognitive apprehension of sexual quality does this person possess? Has he first-rate intellectual assessment of the sexual quality and fineness of another personality? Has he accurate insight as to the sexual quality of his own physical personality? Is this a delicate, thoroughbred mind or an indelicate one in the third panel?

SPTC, *sensitivity to the problem of toleration of conflict; the humor principle.* What is the feeling state of this mind with reference to the central philosophical problem of toleration of conflict and of uncertainty? Has this mind developed the warm humor support necessary to the toleration of doubt, and hence necessary to mental maturity? Does the affective warmth of this nature reach through to and support the toleration of conflict, even at fourth panel levels? Or does humor fail this mind, and does the mind fall back on some theology which pretends to "resolve" conflict and doubt?

How extensively and how energetically has this person searched human philosophies, theologies, and history, and how widely has he explored human experience itself, in quest of the wisdom and facts upon which to build a philosophy? Has he had the courage to strive hard to become discriminating and thoroughbred in the fourth panel (which is the realm of philosophies and theologies and also of mind traps), or has he fallen short?

What is the intellectual *quality* of this mind at the philosophic level? As this consciousness plays on questions of a philosophical or theological nature, is there fineness of insight, humor, personal reserve, tentativeness of statement, toleration and awareness of alternatives and objections? Is this mind sensitively responsive to the implications of the conflict principle in human life? Has this person (for his age) achieved humorous toleration of doubt at a level of intellectual maturity?

INTERCORRELATIONS AMONG THE SIXTY TRAITS

(See p. 18)

In these correlation tables, N = 100 throughout. The decimal points have been omitted for convenience in printing. All of the correlations included in Tables A, B, and C are positive; all of those in Tables D, E, and F are negative.

A. Intracorrelations Among The Twenty Traits Defining Viscerotonia

(Positive Correlations)

Trait	V-2	V-3	V-4	V-5	V-6	V-7	V-8	V-9	V-10	V-11	V-12	V-13	V-14	V-15	V-16	V-17	V-18	V-19	V-20
V- 1	82	76	68	63	69	67	61	67	73	64	66	76	70	81	85	68	62	74	76
V- 2		79	70	65	75	72	65	64	69	64	67	76	78	79	80	66	71	76	77
V- 3			75	66	68	66	69	72	67	69	74	78	75	83	81	75	77	79	68
V- 4				68	86	74	70	75	67	67	69	75	76	73	66	74	74	75	70
V- 5					72	84	85	82	79	80	74	77	80	76	74	79	78	80	78
V- 6						75	76	74	76	71	66	78	74	78	65	72	76	76	75
V- 7							77	73	84	78	69	73	77	76	67	75	76	72	70
V- 8								79	82	78	74	78	75	68	76	83	84	82	80
V- 9									79	78	80	81	76	74	75	80	77	78	75
V-10										81	76	82	81	75	76	73	76	79	73
V-11											72	75	77	76	66	76	70	78	75
V-12												73	78	76	65	76	73	75	76
V-13													80	79	84	69	68	70	65
V-14														82	77	77	74	76	77
V-15															75	65	77	64	66
V-16																63	71	76	81
V-17																	81	78	73
V-18																		76	74
V-19																			77

B. Intracorrelations Among The Twenty Traits Defining Somatotonia
(Positive Correlations)

Trait	S-2	S-3	S-4	S-5	S-6	S-7	S-8	S-9	S-10	S-11	S-12	S-13	S-14	S-15	S-16	S-17	S-18	S-19	S-20
S- 1	81	80	82	73	69	76	66	67	71	77	76	72	78	75	79	76	82	80	75
S- 2		83	80	72	78	79	81	71	69	73	72	70	80	73	82	79	76	76	80
S- 3			82	74	81	79	79	81	75	78	74	76	77	81	76	76	75	79	79
S- 4				69	73	75	78	75	67	79	70	73	76	79	76	74	76	75	78
S- 5					85	76	72	81	78	78	87	75	64	66	70	72	69	78	68
S- 6						78	81	81	82	76	82	73	85	77	67	75	78	75	66
S- 7							76	78	77	75	79	80	71	81	75	76	79	76	77
S- 8								72	76	80	81	73	84	76	80	82	74	74	78
S- 9									76	75	83	81	67	77	73	75	82	80	79
S-10										79	85	79	70	76	76	82	81	78	75
S-11											76	77	75	79	76	81	80	78	77
S-12												73	67	78	69	70	75	73	72
S-13													67	85	80	83	81	81	82
S-14														65	81	78	64	72	72
S-15															67	86	82	81	79
S-16																77	71	73	70
S-17																	82	81	81
S-18																		80	83
S-19																			79

C. Intracorrelations Among The Twenty Traits Defining Cerebrotonia
(Positive Correlations)

Trait	C-2	C-3	C-4	C-5	C-6	C-7	C-8	C-9	C-10	C-11	C-12	C-13	C-14	C-15	C-16	C-17	C-18	C-19	C-20
C-1	81	79	76	82	79	75	77	78	74	80	72	79	81	82	76	75	79	79	75
C-2		82	77	81	78	78	80	81	83	76	74	70	79	85	76	75	84	76	77
C-3			75	83	77	83	74	81	77	75	85	69	76	79	80	79	77	75	68
C-4				74	83	78	86	83	66	83	65	84	81	67	75	84	85	85	86
C-5					82	84	79	84	78	81	81	82	79	79	83	78	80	75	76
C-6						66	84	82	78	86	68	85	83	77	79	85	84	86	78
C-7							74	76	74	79	85	76	82	83	82	81	80	78	76
C-8								84	80	85	76	82	81	78	78	83	80	85	77
C-9									75	84	76	83	80	74	77	80	75	78	77
C-10										66	83	76	81	86	64	67	70	75	74
C-11											78	82	79	75	78	79	75	83	79
C-12												75	74	83	74	77	75	75	72
C-13													81	72	73	79	81	80	78
C-14														79	76	80	81	75	76
C-15															78	77	86	76	71
C-16																75	77	71	79
C-17																	79	78	73
C-18																		76	75
C-19																			78

D. Intercorrelations Between Viscerotonic and Somatotonic Traits
(Negative Correlations)

Trait	S-1	S-2	S-3	S-4	S-5	S-6	S-7	S-8	S-9	S-10	S-11	S-12	S-13	S-14	S-15	S-16	S-17	S-18	S-19	S-20
V- 1	40	33	42	37	39	40	32	35	32	30	33	33	36	31	35	37	31	37	32	32
V- 2	31	30	36	34	33	37	32	38	40	31	35	33	36	34	32	37	33	38	35	32
V- 3	33	35	32	36	35	30	30	32	35	34	33	34	39	31	33	31	31	30	34	35
V- 4	36	34	33	31	37	33	38	34	33	41	39	32	30	32	33	38	36	33	36	37
V- 5	30	32	33	31	35	32	34	35	37	33	36	34	38	43	30	32	31	33	31	33
V- 6	34	44	42	39	31	41	33	45	35	32	32	30	38	46	33	31	31	34	37	30
V- 7	31	40	36	41	30	39	46	32	31	31	40	42	32	39	33	33	32	35	32	33
V- 8	33	33	30	31	37	41	35	40	38	38	31	39	30	32	31	35	34	32	36	31
V- 9	37	41	40	37	36	37	34	40	32	32	34	35	30	36	31	34	33	32	39	30
V-10	33	36	39	35	33	38	34	34	35	31	32	35	37	41	32	31	30	32	35	33
V-11	35	40	36	37	30	31	33	38	32	32	31	33	42	35	34	32	31	38	33	32
V-12	32	38	41	36	40	34	30	31	37	35	33	32	31	32	32	31	30	35	34	34
V-13	41	34	34	34	37	33	32	33	36	34	35	39	31	37	37	32	39	34	32	40
V-14	43	39	42	34	36	35	31	35	34	33	32	35	31	31	32	33	30	40	41	35
V-15	39	32	34	31	30	39	33	37	36	33	34	37	32	39	40	38	31	35	33	30
V-16	34	37	38	41	36	32	39	42	33	31	34	32	40	38	40	33	38	38	38	36
V-17	32	35	32	34	30	33	30	36	31	31	33	31	33	41	32	32	30	34	33	33
V-18	37	32	33	35	31	31	34	34	32	32	33	31	30	37	31	41	32	38	39	35
V-19	35	39	37	39	31	34	33	38	35	36	41	35	34	40	30	38	31	34	40	36
V-20	41	36	37	36	42	40	36	37	32	43	33	42	37	44	31	33	32	38	36	35

E. Intercorrelations Between Viscerotonic and Cerebrotonic Traits
(Negative Correlations)

Trait	C-1	C-2	C-3	C-4	C-5	C-6	C-7	C-8	C-9	C-10	C-11	C-12	C-13	C-14	C-15	C-16	C-17	C-18	C-19	C-20
V- 1	43	39	42	38	47	44	46	40	36	34	42	37	36	32	43	39	34	39	37	35
V- 2	44	37	38	37	41	41	39	36	38	35	40	39	37	34	41	36	37	38	39	34
V- 3	46	42	51	36	42	38	45	36	31	34	33	35	37	40	43	39	42	35	32	32
V- 4	38	40	41	44	38	38	36	41	40	36	39	38	35	37	36	34	36	41	36	37
V- 5	43	37	37	47	35	43	34	46	44	39	44	42	40	33	37	33	33	42	43	42
V- 6	40	44	41	39	45	42	38	43	39	42	36	38	37	41	36	34	32	37	39	38
V- 7	36	37	35	41	38	40	37	37	34	41	37	42	30	31	33	41	35	35	40	35
V- 8	44	35	34	47	37	35	36	52	47	34	39	37	46	41	37	42	44	45	45	46
V- 9	39	38	37	41	35	45	32	44	42	37	34	42	35	37	46	34	39	39	43	43
V-10	35	39	37	47	36	40	34	45	39	38	42	37	41	33	37	39	36	40	42	39
V-11	37	37	36	39	37	39	35	40	41	39	32	35	35	33	34	32	35	35	38	33
V-12	42	40	39	40	43	40	41	44	48	45	36	46	38	34	42	42	37	41	39	37
V-13	39	43	44	38	41	37	42	31	39	32	34	34	37	36	39	36	35	36	35	34
V-14	44	42	46	40	45	41	39	38	43	36	37	37	38	36	42	43	43	40	37	42
V-15	47	44	45	39	46	36	46	35	33	33	32	41	34	32	49	43	39	37	38	36
V-16	38	37	43	31	45	34	42	33	32	33	31	34	33	30	33	34	32	32	34	35
V-17	45	40	38	42	43	44	46	46	48	38	39	41	37	32	38	33	36	37	38	36
V-18	39	41	39	43	44	38	37	40	35	35	34	33	35	33	42	35	42	45	39	37
V-19	40	36	35	40	38	40	38	45	37	39	33	39	34	31	33	32	35	38	43	39
V-20	43	35	39	37	36	41	35	39	35	36	33	37	33	30	39	36	34	36	37	43

F. Intercorrelations Between Somatotonic and Cerebrotonic Traits

(Negative Correlations)

Trait	C-1	C-2	C-3	C-4	C-5	C-6	C-7	C-8	C-9	C-10	C-11	C-12	C-13	C-14	C-15	C-16	C-17	C-18	C-19	C-20
S- 1	68	66	60	51	55	59	61	66	58	67	60	65	67	70	56	65	64	57	54	67
S- 2	65	58	56	55	57	54	52	56	50	68	65	62	60	71	59	69	57	55	49	71
S- 3	71	61	57	62	59	60	55	49	52	62	72	66	67	65	63	68	56	60	53	67
S- 4	62	56	59	64	61	65	58	59	60	61	59	57	56	69	65	66	58	57	55	57
S- 5	58	56	53	71	56	67	62	67	66	60	71	66	67	57	54	63	63	55	65	56
S- 6	69	61	59	73	59	59	58	68	67	65	70	62	66	69	61	67	68	63	66	71
S- 7	70	60	66	64	61	62	73	56	74	60	62	67	71	64	60	65	67	61	61	62
S- 8	63	58	68	61	69	60	72	57	59	68	59	70	56	72	70	72	62	64	56	60
S- 9	66	58	62	69	65	68	61	65	74	64	63	65	60	61	67	67	64	66	67	62
S-10	63	68	66	62	69	60	66	67	65	69	59	68	58	71	69	70	72	62	70	66
S-11	65	61	59	71	58	68	59	57	60	61	66	59	56	69	58	64	57	58	54	56
S-12	59	62	61	57	60	63	55	57	55	67	53	55	58	57	69	60	67	70	59	67
S-13	72	63	57	65	59	66	58	65	62	64	66	61	67	64	59	55	60	58	58	62
S-14	60	72	70	61	71	57	69	55	57	61	59	64	52	71	66	70	55	56	55	59
S-15	71	61	56	64	58	62	60	67	69	54	56	63	64	64	62	68	62	65	63	61
S-16	62	59	61	57	55	60	64	57	54	61	56	60	52	62	57	73	57	56	53	66
S-17	63	60	55	69	59	66	57	64	65	62	66	56	67	59	57	61	69	61	64	66
S-18	53	57	56	58	55	53	60	68	67	57	64	54	70	53	51	53	56	66	53	54
S-19	58	61	56	59	62	63	58	55	59	54	68	61	54	67	57	66	59	63	65	61
S-20	62	58	56	63	56	64	55	57	59	56	64	61	67	65	59	69	64	59	60	67

INDEX